A MARRIAGE OUT WEST

A Marriage Out West

Theresa and Frank Russell's Explorations in Arizona, 1900–1903

THERESA RUSSELL, NANCY J. PAREZO,
AND DON D. FOWLER

THE UNIVERSITY OF
ARIZONA PRESS
TUCSON

The University of Arizona Press
www.uapress.arizona.edu

ISBN-13: 978-0-8165-4209-3 (hardcover)
ISBN-13: 978-0-8165-4071-6 (paperback)

Cover design by Leigh McDonald
Interior design and typesetting by Sara Thaxton
Typeset in 9.7/13 Warnock Pro (text), Elbie WF, and Cutright WF (display)

Publication of this book is made possible in part by the proceeds of a permanent endowment created with the assistance of a Challenge Grant from the National Endowment for the Humanities, a federal agency.

Library of Congress Cataloging-in-Publication Data
Names: Parezo, Nancy J., author. | Fowler, Don D., 1936– author. | Russell, Frances Theresa, 1873–1936. In pursuit of a graveyard.
Title: A marriage out West : Theresa and Frank Russell's explorations in Arizona, 1900–1903 / Theresa Russell, Nancy J. Parezo, and Don D. Fowler.
Description: Tucson : University of Arizona Press, 2020. | Includes bibliographical references and index.
Identifiers: LCCN 2020011875 | ISBN 9780816542093 (hardcover) | ISBN 9780816540716 (paperback)
Subjects: LCSH: Russell, Frank, 1868–1903. | Russell, Frances Theresa, 1873–1936. | Archaeologists—Biography. | Archaeology—Arizona—History—20th century.
Classification: LCC F811 .P24 2020 | DDC 979.1/0530922 [B]—dc23
LC record available at https://lccn.loc.gov/2020011875

Printed in the United States of America
♾ This paper meets the requirements of ANSI/NISO Z39.48-1992 (Permanence of Paper).

In honor of

Raymond H. and Molly Thompson,

Natalie and Richard Woodbury,

and our other friends

who had lifelong archaeological marriages

Contents

Illustrations

Figures

Tables

Maps

A MARRIAGE OUT WEST

Introduction

In 1928 the novelist Agatha Christie traveled to Istanbul and Baghdad. Visiting Ur, she met a young archaeologist, Max Mallowan, whom she married in 1930. She accompanied Max on many research trips to Syria, Iraq, and Egypt, working at famous sites like Nineveh and Nimrud. Christie supervised excavations; cleaned, repaired, and catalogueed artifacts; and restored pottery. She also developed photographs, wrote field notes, and sketched in situ artifacts. Back in England, she helped manage collections and produce exhibits. Christie used the skills taught to bourgeoise British women, turning their supposedly decorative activities into scientific assets. Independently wealthy, she anonymously underwrote Max's field expenses. She never, however, wrote site descriptions, summary articles, theoretical monographs, or popular accounts recounting her experiences at the end of a field season.

Christie did discuss her archaeological excursions in her autobiography, *Come Tell Me How You Live*, which chronicled her Syrian trips. The travel narrative consisted of episodes in a life journey, reconstructed from memories and journals. She included impressions about places and Indigenous peoples, colonial settlers, and travelers. At first, she conveyed her observations using explicit comparisons to British culture with its stratified social norms, but she gradually wrote more culturally nuanced accounts as she learned to overcome ethnocentrism. Her narratives revealed her travels were also periods spent learning skills to undertake British-style archaeology. She never, however, focused on daily tasks, the tedium of working in heat and dust, or the joy of uncovering artifacts. Christie gave no indication she wanted to answer research questions, claim a scientific persona, or provide proof of scholarly authority. She did not want to be an archaeologist. Instead, her travels became fodder for her novels, contributing to the settings, characterizations, and plots of mysteries like *Murder in Mesopotamia*.[1]

After World War I, other archaeologists' wives used field experiences as the basis for memoirs demonstrating they had lived lives of value and adventure. Most experiential accounts were reflective, written late in life by women who aspired to be scholars. Their stories told of important archaeological discoveries and how society had benefited from their work. Authors described a wealth of purposeful investigation and focused travel; of difficult-to-reach, isolated places little known to their audiences; of travel in Model Ts along perilous routes or blazing new trails. Authors told of caring for children and a research team in field camps; of sifting soil; of sketching, photographing, and reconstructing pottery. Writers conveyed the essences of exotic or unusual places through word depictions of physical and cultural geography showing how the new was distinctive from the author's home locale. The goal was to enable the reader to see through the author's refined eye, to vicariously experience glorious sunsets and plants with thorns. Authors wrote of overcoming dangers stemming from inclement weather and inhospitable lands, and of meeting captivating people; their thoughts and feelings enlivened the accounts. Beyond documenting scientific activities, these women demonstrated their lives mattered for they contributed to the evidential record. They had undertaken challenging work and done it well. Splendid storytellers, they wrote explicitly for the public so readers could understand archaeology and its societal value, emphasizing how information was acquired and what it was like to bring artifacts to light.[2]

More rarely a wife wrote engaging travel stories at the end of a field season. Published by popular journals, museums, and research institutions, these stories were designed to explain the archaeological enterprise and create images of the wonders seen. Secondarily they served to impress scholarly audiences, gain recognition, and establish authoritative reputations for the author. In addition, they garnered new financial research support and furthered husbands' careers by broadcasting each man's scientific acumen. The best articles were turned into books, which sold well; the royalties helped support families. It was a conscious socioeconomic strategy for a two-person, single-career household.[3]

The most famous American authorial wife was Ann Axtell Morris. She worked with her husband, Earl, in northern New Mexico and Colorado, sponsored by the American Museum of Natural History (AMNH). Today Morris is famous for *Digging in the Southwest*, a book that has been in print for 80 years. We both read this travelogue during our undergraduate days. It stimulated our interest in archaeology, entertaining us with activities we dreamed of emulating. Like Morris's companion book, *Digging in Yucatan*, *Digging in the Southwest* differentiated professional archaeology from looting, telling how systematic methods enabled scholars to gain data about past ways of life. The books were effective disciplinary recruiting tools; Morris spoke of *being* an archaeologist, looking forward to each field season. She also conveyed how wives had access to sites when it was difficult for women to obtain anthropological employment—a strategy especially important to women who wanted an unconventional life that included enjoyable, purposeful travel.[4] Morris proved such a life was possible, if not easy. But then if it had been easy, it would not have been an adventure. And archaeology was always an adventure.

But what about earlier generations, when American anthropology was a natural history endeavor, just beginning its quest for professional status? Several women accompanied their husbands on geographical expeditions. For example, during the 1860s–70s, Matilda Coxe Stevenson accompanied her husband, James, on several of Frederick Hayden's surveys, serving as an unpaid botanist. She used her artistic skills to produce watercolors of specimen samples. The pair began systematically to search for archaeological sites in the Southwest when James was hired by John Wesley Powell for the new Bureau of Ethnology (BAE). Yearly, until her death in 1915, Matilda sent data to the BAE's director, who distributed the information to staff members Jesse Walter Fewkes and Walter Hough. Matilda did not write popular articles about this work, although she and James were the subject of frequent newspaper stories. Her lack of popular and scholarly publications was one reason she has not been remembered for her archaeological research.[5]

After the railroads came to the American Southwest, wives without small children accompanied their archaeologist husbands. In the 1880s, Cosmos Mindeleff and his wife, Marion, worked at Casa Grande and along the Verde River, where they mapped more than 50 sites. She "lived for six months to a year on those expeditions, traveling most of the time in the saddle." Fewkes's wife, Harriet Cutler, participated in restoration activities at Mesa Verde in the 1890s–early 1900s and at Casa Grande in 1906–7. Unfortunately, neither woman published a travel account so there is little to document their activities. This was the norm. Also normative was lack of participation in formal reports or summary research accounts by the archaeologist husband. This lack has affected how we understand the history of archaeology. It has been mainly in letters or diaries that historians have seen the range and depth of wives' natural science and anthropological activities. We can wish wives had been publicly acknowledged for their hard work as well as their loyal companionship and ability to make coffee and wash clothes. As Emil Haury reflected, "The life partners of distinguished scientists are often the unsung contributors to the unfolding drama of learning." Many a helpmate was an "archaeologist in her own right."[6]

The finding of experiential accounts is significant for our understanding of women's attempts to gain recognition, credibility, and professional status in academic disciplines. A specialized travel narrative is also important as an example of gendered regional writing about the exploration of frontier zones, especially American attempts to gain understanding of a region's history, society, and culture as it was integrated into the nation. Such an account provides information on cross-cultural interactions with Indigenous peoples and colonial settlers. We can learn what it was like to be a female explorer-archaeologist, someone who would not become a permanent resident of a region but who undertook a specialized form of travel and soon thereafter told her account to the world.

Frances Theresa Peet Russell was an archaeological wife who was not going to be left sitting alone impatiently in Iowa while her new husband explored the Colorado Plateau. Theresa had married Harvard anthropologist Frank Russell in June 1900, and they left immediately on a busman's honeymoon. Their goals were twofold: (1) to travel to an arid environment to quiet Frank's tuberculosis and (2) to search for archaeological sites containing human remains to further his anthropometric research on ethnic diversity within racialized categories. They conducted a focused survey of Western Ancestral Puebloan sites on the Hopi and Navajo reservations—a purposeful and highly specialized research project, unusual for the time. It also marked the beginning of a four-year marriage exploring Arizona Territory for archaeological sites, identifying settlement patterns and site types, and deciding which should be excavated, for they were in danger from vandalism and pot-hunting. The Russells undertook one of the territory's first multiyear surveys to assess cultural preservation needs. Unfortunately, their activities are little known today because Frank never published summary accounts after each field season nor a final report. He died in November 1903 while writing the final chapters of *The Pima Indians*, the major work for which he is remembered. Theresa finished the ethnography but never tackled the archaeological survey report, nor did Fewkes or Hough, although they used Frank's data in their work.

In 1906 Theresa Russell published "In Pursuit of a Graveyard: Being the Trail of an Archaeological Wedding Journey," a twelve-part serial in *Out West*, a magazine published by Charles Lummis in California. Her articles constituted an experiential narrative based on field journals and remembrances. The work had features of both a biography and a seasonal field narrative, but one that emphasized personal experiences rather than discussing the materials uncovered. Theresa chose not to simply produce an observational documentary account. Although ironically these articles would become the expedition's only public research record, they were not written as professional informational notes like those found in the *American Anthropologist*, *Science*, or *The American Naturalist*. Theresa did not record field work to acquaint Frank's colleagues with their activities, noting where they went and what they found. Nor did she write to promote a specific theory about Puebloan origins or attempt to argue that Frank had solved his archaeological research problem.[7]

Instead, Theresa provided a participant's perspective of 1900 archaeology. She consciously selected what was most important to her on their journey. This included describing aspects critical to understanding the generation of archaeological information and how methodology established or undercut credibility. Her texts were a primer on early survey methods as a small group activity. She conveyed how a single researcher with a spouse and local assistants sought to find appropriate sites. She also told of methodological problems, of the hasty errors Frank made in his attempt to gather data before he ran out of time, and how they rationalized decisions. Given that Frank's goal was to acquire human remains, Theresa surprisingly raised critical moral and legal concerns about collecting data (that is, exhumation without community or governmental permission). Most archaeological summaries mentioned little of the questionable aspects of anthropological knowledge production, concentrating instead on field season successes. Theresa provided an early account of Native peoples' criticisms of archaeological methods and how they resisted scientific encroachment. The Russells' activities were ones encountered many times in anthropology's history: privileging the acquisition of information at the expense of all other considerations. This included the requests of Indigenous peoples and the sacrifices obsessive scientists and their families made in pursuit of knowledge.

Structurally, the serial was composed of overlapping topical stories designed to entertain readers. Each installment had a central theme. This was sometimes professional (how a woman learned to be an archaeological assistant, an integral participant in her husband's career) and sometimes mundane (how one ate new foods like condensed milk and tortillas or drove a wagon through an arroyo). As a record of her honeymoon, "In Pursuit of a Graveyard" was a humorous, self-reflexive account of Theresa's feelings, thought processes, and reflections on enculturated class values as she became an archaeological explorer. Humor was a rhetorical technique she used to portray her personality, an important feature since Theresa had studied psychology at Radcliffe College. The reader meets a mature, strong, secure woman, who found herself on a new personal growth cycle. Unlike some women who wrote travel narratives, Theresa was not searching for freedom, solitude, or dangerous adventure to make her feel alive. She was not arguing to initiate reform for Indigenous peoples or women or escaping stultifying gender norms. She showed she was thinking thoughtfully about her own scholarship and what were critical philosophical questions for the humanities.

Wittiness and satire were the dominant features by which Theresa discussed issues of identity and nationality as well as her own cultural expectations and culture shock. Her enculturated biases infused her discussions of gender issues; critiques of Boston, midwestern, frontier, and American Indian societies; as well as cultural diversity as she realized taken-for-granted norms were not natural and all-powerful. Understated humor also provided a mechanism to demonstrate how Theresa strove to philosophically understand personal and social issues through intellectual debates with herself, her husband, her mentor William James (one of the most respected scholars in the United States), and the reader. She also documented her psychological journey through numerous literary references that at times seem to overwhelm the reader; they certainly dazed us.[8] She produced a journey of the spirit, a search for philosophical understanding as much as human remains in archaeological sites.

Theresa conveyed her experiences in a strange land with aplomb, for she was well versed in what constituted multicultural travelogue writing. She told of personal quests, concerns about gendered scientific travel, and her own foibles as a coming-of-age tale, where she was the heroine of her own adventures. She used a wealth of scholarship and popular culture to frame her experiences and convey how she reacted to and interpreted situations and novelty. For example, she transformed descending safely down a steep mesa, with the horses and mules pushed to their limit, into a "triumphant touchdown," with all participants wanting to punt everything in sight. The mesa was the vanquished football opponent, while the expedition participants, the winners. "In Pursuit of a Graveyard" contained many analogized incidents in which Theresa poked fun at herself as she overcame hubris while mastering new skills, including how to travel in an arid land without water. Her storytelling contained ample evidence of her central thematic interest: people, especially women. Her quest was to find an educated, articulate individual who could verbally joust with her as previous companions had in Boston salons. As a result, Theresa's articles constituted a synchronic glimpse of northern Arizona life and how one traveler interpreted its ethnic diversity and class composition and how it compared to the rest of American society. Theresa's culture shock as she interacted with people unlike herself was on full display, as were her attempts to understand peoples as Frank understood them, moving from the ethnocentric standpoint of "why are they not like us?" to seeing peoples as the products of their environment. Particularly fascinating was how Theresa categorized social groups to fit her worldview and understand human behavior using the new tools of psychology.[9]

From her position as a widow, Theresa wrote the series as a tribute to Frank to enhance his reputation as an outstanding anthropologist. "In Pursuit of a Graveyard" memorialized her husband as a healthy scientific explorer with a future. Ignoring his chronic disease and tragic death, except in the initial dedication, allowed her to portray their journey as a hopeful time, appropriate for a bride on her honeymoon. More critically it enabled her to pave the way for the new life she greatly desired. Theresa wrote her archaeological travelogue to help secure an academic position teaching English literature, as a credentialing device to claim authority as a literary scholar, psychologist, and philosopher. The *Out West* publications verified that Theresa was an erudite, witty scholar who could effortlessly use literary allusions that challenged the reader while documenting the breadth and depth of her classical knowledge. After reading her stories, we can imagine her in the classroom teaching any text, from the Bible to contemporary Broadway plays. Unlike Anne Morris, Theresa did not use her travel narrative to tell the world she was an archaeologist. Instead, she used archaeology to tell the world she was a literary scholar, foreshadowing her future focus on nineteenth-century British poetry, novels, and satire. She also demonstrated why she was philosopher

William James's protégée. Theresa furthered James's groundbreaking philosophy and psychological insights while demonstrating she could take them to another level, influencing the development of literary scholarship into the 1930s. Archaeology was her literary hook. Writing an archaeological account helped establish Theresa's reputation in literature and philosophy but not anthropology.

Telling the Russells' Stories

In *A Marriage Out West: Theresa and Frank Russell's Explorations in Arizona, 1900–1903*, we tell the story of the Russells' four-year marriage, focusing on their archaeological, ethnographic, and physical anthropological research during territorial times. It is a grounded case study of early anthropology in the American Southwest. The book is divided into three parts. Part I, "Scholarly Lives and Explorations," is our reconstruction of Frank and Theresa's lives and careers, focusing on their work as Arizona anthropologists, especially archaeologists. It begins in chapter 1, "Frank Russell and Theresa Peet," with biographies and intellectual portraits of the couple prior to 1900. Full biographies have never been written about these two captivating individuals, and we believe such accounts are important. Family backgrounds, personal experiences, educational attainment, and youthful goals are vital to understanding any scholar's professional choices and subsequent experiences. Most American Southwesternists think of Frank Russell as the ethnographer who wrote *The Pima Indians* but did nothing else of import in his short life. We contend that there was more to his anthropological contributions while acquainting readers with how his work fit into anthropology's turn-of-the-century agenda. We also introduce readers to Theresa as a young scholar to presage how her classics training influenced her anthropological endeavors and how she would write about her archaeological experiences. We know more about Frank than we do about Theresa, but both accounts are incomplete. We hope that other scholars will uncover more of their life histories in the future.

Chapter 2, "An Archaeological Survey, 1900-Style," centers on Russell's style of archaeology and physical anthropology, contextualized within the history of Arizona archaeology, the needs of osteological research, and the development of anthropology as a profession. Many histories of archaeology focus on the development of grand paradigms, interpretive frameworks, and theories, as well as the personalities of those considered the field's great practitioners. There is no need to repeat this impressive body of historiography, and we use existing knowledge to frame our study of the development of methodology to produce evidence needed for the production of disciplinary esoteric knowledge.

Frank Russell was an empiricist and worked to answer specific hypotheses. We discuss his 1900 reconnaissance methods, the what and how of identifying specific kinds of sites (large settlements with burial grounds not previously studied by archaeologists or extensively pot-hunted), and how a small research expedition was organized and executed. We emphasize the distinctiveness of his undertaking as a problem-oriented endeavor to lead to the amassing of information on a specific topic. It was similar in intent to the 1880s Bureau of Ethnology (BAE) surveys designed to map and then model the architecture of aboveground sites. Such problem-oriented research surveys would continue in later time periods, when institutions such as the Museum of Northern Arizona would search for and excavate sites containing specific types of ceramics. The 1900 Tusayan survey located sites containing human burials so Russell could collect skeletons, crania, and associated grave goods; it would differ from Frank and Theresa's 1901–2 general reconnaissance surveys of Arizona Territory, where they searched for sites of any kind, plotted their location on a topographical map, and assessed damage from vandalism.

The Russells' 1900 explorations are distinct in another way. They were done in haste and at first glance appear to be random wanderings to locate a Holy Grail. They often appear this way because the party rode back and forth across the mesas, conducting what was essentially a referential snowball survey to locate a specific kind of site. Frank was not interested in discovering where Ancestral Pueblo peoples lived (a reconnaissance survey goal that was systematized once there were statewide databases and permitting requirements under the 1906 Antiquities Act). Russell sought only large communities with cemeteries, assuming they would contain the data he needed. Unfortunately, due to this focus, Frank did not record information on the sites visited, a loss for archaeology's database. But then, few practitioners at the time kept these types of records.

Chapter 3, "Travels through Tusayan, 1900," is a detailed historical reconstruction of Frank and Theresa's 1900 trip, a quasi-pilgrimage quest without a fixed destination. Our account is based on their journals (see appendix A) housed at the Stanford University Library Special Collections, as well as Frank's correspondence and reports found in the Peabody Museum and Harvard University Archives (HUA) and the National Anthropological Archives (NAA) of the Smithsonian Institution. We detail their journey, identify whom they met, and discuss how these social interactions affected where they went and where they searched for potential sites. We recount how Frank decided when to trench and when to leave sites untouched. This chapter can be read with the journals in appendix A, which convey what Frank and Theresa thought about specific places and memorable individuals and what these individuals knew about what are now categorized as Western Ancestral Pueblo sites—or, in the case of Navajo and Hopi men and women—what they were willing to share with the Russells.[10]

The next two chapters, "Arizona Archaeology, 1901" and "Ethnography, 1901–1903," are historical reconstructions of the Russells' archaeological and ethnographic work in central and southern Arizona. The chapters reflect Frank's quest for meaningful work and intellectual fulfillment while gravely ill. It is a tenacious but sad tale of trying to teach on the East Coast, only to have his tuberculosis flare. It is also a tale of Theresa caring for Frank for better or for worse. Russell's story tells of being a professional in an era before the growth of American colleges in the West—events that would not occur for 20 to 30 years. Staying in the arid Southwest was a life-or-death proposition, as important as securing an anthropological position that would not require him to live in a damp, cold city—the location of most academic institutions in 1900. A chronic condition caused by a bacterium that hemorrhaged the lungs, tuberculosis killed many people in the late nineteenth and early twentieth centuries. As Nancy Owen Lewis recounts in *Chasing the Cure in New Mexico*, 70–90 percent of urban residents in the eastern United States and Europe were infected.[11] Temporarily seeking relief in a pollution-free, dry climate was the only known treatment. New Mexico and Arizona were considered among the healthiest locales. The climate cure—living outdoors with plenty of strenuous exercise—offered a chance for Frank to live. But securing anthropological employment in these locales was all but impossible, for the educational infrastructure did not yet exist.

"Arizona Archaeology, 1901" discusses Frank's options for finding alternative employment at Harvard and how he partially succeeded in obtaining research funds and a temporary position with the federal government by offering to expand the BAE's archaeological agenda. As a result, the pair extensively surveyed a huge swatch of Arizona in 1901, concentrating on the southern parts of the territory and going into Sonora, Mexico. This survey is documented for the first time, based on Frank's reports to and correspondence with the BAE director. We also describe the paper-work problems Russell faced in a federal government that was fighting corruption and nepotism by extending the reach of the Civil Service Commission and fiscal oversight over the Smithsonian Institution and the Bureau of American Ethnology.

"Ethnography, 1901–1903" concentrates on the Russells' ethnographic activities among the Akimel O'odham in 1902, undertaken as a way to avoid the rugged surveys that were sapping Frank's strength. While they continued to look for archaeological sites and assess vandalism, they concentrated on learning about the culture and culture history of what W J McGee called a Desert Group. We briefly describe how the pair worked with Native anthropologist José Lewis and how Theresa concentrated on women's lives and activities. This was a research strategy that the other husband and wife team of the BAE, James and Matilda Coxe Stevenson, had successfully used at Zuni. The result was what is today considered an early classic ethnography and ethnohistory. We build in this chapter on the excellent historical analyses of Bernard Fontana and other scholars who have worked with the Akimel O'odham. The final section of this chapter brings us back to the problem of having a chronic illness. We recount the events of 1903, when the Russells permanently moved to Arizona without the benefit of anthropological employment. They purchased a ranch in northern Arizona and began raising goats. It was strenuous, outdoor work, and it proved too much for Frank. He died in November, leaving his magnum opus for Theresa to finish as well as several articles on folklore and numerous unpublished field notes, including those on archaeological sites along the Gila River.

Theresa was left to build a new life. How she did this, including the decision to publish "In Pursuit of a Graveyard," are the foci of chapter 6, "Life without Frank, 1904–1905." We discuss how Theresa decided to establish her own intellectual career in the humanities, and the choices she made to accomplish this, including returning to her intellectual mentor, philosopher and psychologist William James, and continuing her studies. Following James to Stanford University in 1906 as a teaching assistant, Theresa decided to stay and transformed her 1900 journal into a witty, serialized travel narrative that would impress Stanford University administrators enough to hire her as a member of the English faculty. It was a remarkable feat, one that few women accomplished. And it produced a unique archaeological narrative.

The writing choices Theresa made about which parts of her archaeological experiences to include in her first foray into semi-scholarly publishing, and whether she would portray herself as a neophyte anthropologist or a bride on a honeymoon, are discussed in chapter 7, "Writing a Travel Narrative." We introduce Theresa's publication with a brief discussion of exploratory archaeological travel narratives and their rhetorical strategies to situate her account and show how it was both typical and singular. We summarize and assess Theresa's decisions about what to include and exclude in order to guide readers on their journeys with her. This includes discussions of what she chose to share and who she decided to name as individuals or turn into psychological and social archetypes. The resulting essays were as much an early exploration into the new field of psychology as they were archaeology, and how understanding American personality types helped a scholar understand literature as well as popular culture.

Part II, "'In Pursuit of a Graveyard' by Theresa Russell," republishes unaltered Theresa's 1906 serial of their honeymoon as it appeared in *Out West* magazine over a period of twelve months. The centrality of Theresa's texts to our story is why we have honored Russell as the senior author of this monograph. We consider Theresa's series a quasi-pilgrimage narrative: while Frank searched for specific types of Ancestral Pueblo sites, Theresa searched for women like herself to engage in the witty conversations she treasured.[12] Like Agatha Christie's accounts, Theresa's stories are autobiographical snapshots of selective parts of her journey and how she wanted her contemporary readers to see her. What she omitted were Frank's memories, for Frank was no longer available to help Theresa reconstruct and order her reminiscences as she transformed them into entertaining stories. Nor do the texts contain the elder wisdom that would have filtered her assessment of episodes from the perspective of a lifetime. Theresa's chronological distance as a writer composing her accounts placed her temporarily between field season summaries and an autobiography written later in life. But this level of distance makes her retelling valuable, for it fills a gap in our understanding of how science is remembered by participants. The trip had not faded, but there was enough distance—and grief—so Theresa could romanticize when she wanted. At the same time, she was demonstrating that she was still—by choice and intellectual preference—a classical scholar who would teach philosophy and literature, and do it better than any male scholar her age.

Theresa Russell was successful in her credentialing publications and was hired by Stanford University in 1906. Part III returns to our biographical account. Unfortunately, this section is brief because our information is scanty. Chapter 20, "An English Professor at Stanford," focuses on her career, or what little we know of it. From what we have learned, Theresa's life centered on the university, her teaching, and her research. This assessment may reflect, however, the lack of correspondence that would illuminate her personal life or journals to provide clues to her intellectual and emotional reflections. The only journal from this period that has survived is about the San Francisco earthquake of 1906, which Theresa experienced. We do document what we have learned of her research for her doctorate from Columbia University during World War I and her trips to England to read British literature and learn about the lives of her favorite authors. This was but the first of her many subsequent philosophical and literary analyses and numerous publications that were well received by literary critics. The studies of satire, especially, elaborate the many topics she presented in her *Out West* articles. One can think of our account as honoring Theresa's distinguished life after her excursions in Arizona archaeology and as a Southwestern anthropologist. She was a remarkable woman and we hope that historians of the humanities, with better backgrounds in literature than we, will delve more fully into her oeuvre.

In closing the volume, we present Theresa's and Frank's final words on the Southwest. We trust giving the Russells the last word will convey how they felt about their time in Arizona.

Our text and analyses are supplemented by two appendices intended for readers who would like additional detail of Frank and Theresa's activities and thoughts. They are also included to help readers understand the operation of archaeologists on specialized and reconnaissance surveys in the early 1900s. We include the 1900 field journals in appendix A so readers can see how Theresa transformed her remembrance into a travelogue and to provide Frank a voice.[13] Like all scientific exploration narratives, Theresa's archaeological account was authenticated by these journals, then interpreted through a variety of lenses, as discussed in chapter 7. Keeping systematic records in the field was an important step in claiming authentic observations used in the production and verification of esoteric knowledge. The scientist logged chronological observations of people, places, flora, and fauna, and unexpected or interesting incidents without emotionalism, using understatement to avoid hyperbole. Some journals included information scientists would later place in field logs or field notes, distinguishing personal emotional reflections from direct observations. Journals might contain expressions of frustration or excitement as well as philosophical speculation about life. When transformed into a publication, however, the material that personalized the trip for the reader made its way only into popular accounts. Subjective perspectives were excluded from field reports. Theresa, however, decided to make interpretive observations the centerpiece of her account, but these were not necessarily observations about archaeological locales. For archaeologists who want an account of the sites visited, the journals contain some information.

Contextualizing the Russells' Lives

We have long studied how women overcame economic and social barriers as they strove to be successful anthropologists. We have emphasized the hard work, perseverance, and resilience this required, given the asymmetrical reality in what was always considered the most welcoming of the sciences. Anthropology had its limits to the welcome, of course.[14] Interested in the rise of professorships as a form of professional occupation in America, elsewhere we have looked at how anthropological careers compared to those of women who became professionals in the hard sciences, the natural sciences, sociology, and history, but we have never studied someone who pursued a career in English and philosophy, intentionally leaving anthropology behind. This is one reason Theresa Russell's story is important.

Like several of our colleagues, we have focused primarily on the careers of women with a passion for anthropology who succeeded. We have used grounded methods to identify their strategies to overcome societal and professional obstacles, generate resources, and find interesting problems to tackle. This is one reason why we have both been fascinated with how women have thrived at disciplinary boundaries and margins, often espousing theories and writing programs that would take years for men to discover and exploit. From these biographies we have discovered patterns that reflect access and participation in American professions as a form of specialized work based on esoteric knowledge. One was that women gained initial recognition by writing popular accounts of their adventures in the field—that is, travelogues—and getting paid well for these works. Theresa employed this option to establish a new scholarly path, but it was not a path to an archaeological career. It is one where anthropological exploratory research was used as the entry into English, philosophy, and psychology. We welcome other scholars to look for similar instances. We are sure they exist.[15]

The Russells' experiences are important on another level. They are snapshots of life in northern Arizona in 1900 and in central and southern Arizona in the next years. For many in the United States, Arizona Territory was an unknown and foreign land. We have sought to understand how the American Southwest was studied in the late nineteenth and early twentieth centuries, how it became a field laboratory where anthropology defined itself and honed its methods and techniques, and gained Indigenous perspectives that informed theories and interpretive frameworks.[16] We especially analyzed how Frank Russell learned from and about the region's Native peoples, and how he implemented methods of data acquisition and analysis for archaeology and previously unanalyzed intentional physical anthropology research. For example, by examining Frank's experiences both before and during his and Theresa's marriage, we saw changes in Frank's approaches to Native peoples. He went from incidental observations about the Hopi and Navajo while engaged in opportunistic and referential interviews about ancestral places of residence to more intensive and systematic inquiry about standard topics of culture and history, beginning with language foundation and a population-household survey among the Akimel O'odham. He utilized standardized survey forms and kept separate notes by category of information. These later methods were typical of formalized ethnological techniques: a paid, seated key informant (hopefully an elder) answered questions and dictated texts to a Native translator at the researcher's instigation. These changes reflected the difference between superficial ethnic tourism, where Natives were part of the setting, to be queried about where to travel, and intense, long-term observation with focused interviewing needed to produce a standardized descriptive ethnography. It was not participant observation. The Russells remained distanced from the community and their specialized activities. The fact that Frank did not conduct such interviews in 1900 was one reason he did not consider his research ethnological and never published anything from his memories; it was not systematic. This was an unusual stance, for it was common for anthropologists to publish brief articles on noteworthy information gleaned from their travels, often customs and activities considered unusual from the anthropologists' home culture that had not been previously published. For Russell, simply noting random occurrences was not science but amateur tourism.

Our reconstruction of a focused reconnaissance survey should be considered more than a grounded chronicle of idiosyncratic archaeological practice. The Russells did not work in a void, and the themes on which we focus resonate with what we have learned over the last decades studying the history of anthropology from a regional perspective. The period's main characteristics have been extensively researched. Archaeologists were interested in utilitarian documentation of antiquities, settlement patterns (establishing which ancient people lived where), how people built structures that had remained through time, and how ancient villages were parts of larger social and cultural units. These taxonomic and classification issues were pursued as part of a search for answers to compelling continental and global problems: where ancient peoples came from and who were their descendants. Concomitantly, all were interested in collecting artifacts to form collections useful for research and exhibits.[17]

The Russells' work took place within the context of multiple research activities on the Colorado Plateau, especially those underwritten by anthropological institutions (the Peabody Museum of Archaeology and Ethnology at Harvard University, the federal government's BAE, and Chicago's Field Museum). These organizations' quests for intellectual authority as holders of esoteric disciplinary knowledge, the setting of disciplinary goals, evidential control, and resultant territorial fights, combined with the emerging use of government bureaucracies to enforce control, affected Frank. We witness this in the controversy over Frank's lack of formal permission to conduct an archaeological survey and exhume human remains and how this altered his research design and activities. This instance of change in how archaeology was conducted is part of a broader story for control over federal lands in the West. It is also a story of how politics entered into archaeological practice. It is the background that helps explain Frank's interactions with other foundational anthropologists, who all wanted to control anthropology. Our contextualization demonstrates how Frank's life was influenced by the activities of institution builders such as Frederic Ward Putnam, John Wesley Powell, W J McGee, Aleš Hrdlička, and George Dorsey. Their decisions and quests for intellectual supremacy influenced Frank's ability to conduct research, as well as his ultimate inability to obtain a job or pursue his lifelong goal to be a lauded research scientist.

Also critical for understanding the Russells' fieldwork were the development of anthropology as a national discipline and the growth of physical anthropology/anthropometry as a distinct subdivision of the multifaceted endeavor to understand humanity's development and variability. This involved more than expounding interpretations and developing framing theories. Striving for professional status included demonstrating that anthropology was a natural science, with original data that could be standardized and measured. Frank was concerned with improving anthropometric and osteological techniques, inventing precise measuring tools, and standardizing methodologies as well as with how anthropology would be taught in universities.[18]

When they made their first trip, the Russells had intended to return to Harvard University, where Frank would pursue the institutionalized academic year of teaching and a summer fieldwork schedule. Theresa could continue to study philosophy and have stimulating conversations with her peers. They did not think they would spend the next two years surveying Arizona and participating in ethnographic field work full time. They covered a phenomenal area. Frank estimated that by October 1902, they had traveled 4,000 miles exclusive of train travel each year. The undertaking was comparable to the areas covered by European scholar explorers Adolph Bandelier, who looked for sites in Arizona between 1880 and 1885; and Alphonse Pinart, who searched for sites in 1876, traveling from San Diego to Tucson and around central and southern Arizona. As J. Jefferson Reid and Stephanie Whittlesey discuss in their excellent history of Arizona archaeology, archaeologists in the 1880s and 1890s did not attempt to survey the entire state as they searched for suitable sites. Most men and women worked in a single region each season.[19] This in itself makes Theresa and Frank's stories memorable.

Part I

Scholarly Lives and Explorations

Chapter 1
Frank Russell and Theresa Peet

How Theresa felt about her husband was apparent from her references to him throughout her *Out West* publications. He was the Anthropologist, the Man of Science, the Wandering Boy. All references to his occupational role were capitalized as Frank became an archetype as well as a healthy, capable, and unflappable scientific explorer. Theresa depicted Frank as larger than life: the Man Himself and her Knight. How proud she was of the intelligent gentleman she had married after a multiyear courtship. She imbued Frank with all the virile talents a romantic heroine could ask of an American male: reliability, steadfastness, practicality, diligence, fierce independence, bravery, tenaciousness, intelligence, graciousness. He had the ability to transverse the wilderness with style and wit, joking as if they were at afternoon tea with colleagues in Cambridge, while ensuring their safety. Theresa never mentioned characteristics that could irk, although there were hints that the Hunter of Sites was impatient, especially when unable to locate the longed-for major discovery that would enhance his reputation. He was always the meticulous, unsentimental scientist who rarely saw the romance in beautiful landscapes. That concern for beauty Theresa left to herself as his classically trained poet.

Theresa referred to herself as the Tenderfoot whom the Man of Science educated, a neophyte who had never been in a wilderness without the comforts of civilization and did not know how to cook over a campfire. Her attempts to make edible biscuits were a running joke throughout her journals. Theresa never portrayed herself as a pioneer woman destined to bring civilization to the frontier. She was a displaced scholar who belonged at a college. But there was playfulness in the newlywed's relationship. Frank was the Jack to her Jill, Hare to her Tortoise, Fair Heart to her Faint Lady. After working with a Spanish speaker for a month, Frank became a man of stature who had earned the title, the Señor, and she, by marital association, the Señora.

Together they were the Pursuers of Knowledge, Instigators of the Expedition, and, as the journey progressed, Intellectual Conspirators. After Theresa learned to systematically observe like a natural historian, the husband and wife became colleagues, a detail-oriented pair who recognized important information and accumulated data that Frank would analyze and transform into knowledge. In

Theresa's publications, Frank had legitimacy and authority as a recognized and experienced field scientist, just as he did in the anthropological community. Who better to guide Theresa through her purposeful travel adventure?

Theresa presented herself as writing a genteel adventure memoir, speaking directly to the reader. She was a poetic turn-of-the-century writer who created vivid images and sought parallels to characters in novels. Her articles and her future life as a scholar of nineteenth-century British literature at Stanford University demonstrated where her heart and intellect lay. She wanted the world of her imagination and the world of reality to co-exist, if only through her words. In this way a honeymoon, essentially Frank's data gathering exercise, became Theresa's journey to observe and reflect on diverse people and places.

These portrayals, however, were partially Theresa's imagination. Who were the real Frank and Theresa? What were their lives like before their marriage? What had they accomplished? What did they aspire to do? How did their 1900 expedition fit within their career plans? We have only one brief newspaper obituary for Theresa, essentially a death notice, so we only know that she was recognized as an authority on Victorian literature. We have found no professional obituary. This lack of critical assessment for female scholars was unfortunately common and was one reason most have been more invisible than male scholars.

We know more about Frank but even that is incomplete. His peers considered him one of the best of the initial group of professionally trained anthropologists. Frank was a man who should have had a long, fruitful career. Alexander F. Chamberlain described him as "a devoted student and an enthusiastic investigator, whose zeal recalled that of the lamented [Frank Hamilton] Cushing."[1] Both men, who had died in their prime, were good scholars and had assumed the image of explorer-adventurer to help establish their reputations as scientific culture heroes. Both men had been full of promise, but their contributions were crippled by ill health. Chamberlain wondered what might have been had their journeys continued. Both Franks in death were adorned with the mantle of tragic hero, lost to the new profession.

Frank Russell

Frank Russell was born in Fort Dodge, Iowa, on August 26, 1868. He was the younger son of farmers and teachers David Chandler Russell (from Pennsylvania, 1825–1900) and Elizabeth Carleton (from New Hampshire, 1825–1906). The Russells came from Wisconsin near the end of the Civil War, hiding from Union conscription officials. They purchased land on Lizard Creek, 15 miles west of Fort Dodge. Frank had two older brothers (James, who served with Union forces, and Carleton) and three sisters (Mary Ellen, Sarah, and Flora). Neither brother was listed in the Russell household in the 1880 Iowa Census, so they had probably left home.[2]

Fort Dodge was in Webster County's prairies. It was founded in 1850 when U.S. Army soldiers built a fort at the confluence of the Des Moines River and Lizard Creek and incorporated in 1869. Located amid farm and ranch country, the town served as the commercial center for north central Iowa. In the 1870 Census, the town had a population of 3,000 individuals of Irish, German, Norwegian, or English heritage, and a few Native Americans.

According to one State University of Iowa professor, Russell had a typical childhood of physical labor but with an unusual emphasis on education. The Russells were a bookish family. With a house full of books, they read nightly. The family wrote poetry and debated history. Frank "was wont to say but little concerning his early life, and that little was likely to be in reference to his mother, for whom he felt even more than the usual affection and honor."[3] He earned his way through high school doing odd jobs, caring for cows and delivering milk, and spent most summers with brother James's family on their farm outside Gilmore City. According to his nephew, Roland, Frank went abroad one summer, working on a cattle ship and bicycling for three months in Germany and France.

From the age of 10, Frank painted, hoping to eventually find employment as a scientific illustrator. Family tradition recounted that he made crayon drawings, sitting for hours at the kitchen table. Frank also learned to take and develop photographs. After completing secondary school, he worked as a grammar school principal in Gilmore City, Iowa (1889 to 1890). This position meant the twenty-one-year-old and a second individual taught all the children in the area.[4] Russell would have been county certified. We found no evidence that he earned a state teaching certificate, which required three years of successful teaching experience and passing an examination. Teaching for a short period was generally a temporary occupation for young Iowa men, but fewer than 20 percent of primary and secondary school teachers were male, due to exceedingly low wages. Also, Frank desired to see more of the world beyond central Iowa, and to combine travel with an intellectual career. He does not seem to have been enamored with any particular discipline at the time. Russell went to college to explore his options but was quickly drawn to natural history, one of nine basic courses of study at colleges at the time.

In retrospect, it was somewhat risky for Frank to relinquish his low-paying teaching job. His family did not have the funds to support his college education. Caught in the middle of a multiyear drought, few farmers were solvent in Iowa, Kansas, or Nebraska. Prices for agricultural products were low, and the wheat market had crashed. Simultaneously, railroad fees to transport products rose. Everyone was in debt and land values fell. America was in an economic depression, precipitated by the collapse of the Philadelphia and Reading Railroad and the National Cordage Company. Eventually more than 15,000 businesses went bankrupt, following a series of banking and Wall Street failures and a run on the U.S. gold supply. Numerous farms ceased operation, and many families became homeless. Unemployment soared to 18 percent.[5]

Russell did what generations of young men and women have done during depressions: work their way through college to obtain new knowledge and skills. He decided to attend the closest public university, the State University of Iowa, in Iowa City, west of Davenport. Iowa City had a population of 7,000 in 1890; it had been founded in 1847 right after Iowa became a state. The college was the first public university to admit men and women equally. Since 1858 it had supported a natural history museum, the second oldest west of the Mississippi River. Frank matriculated and funded his entire education drawing scientific specimens for the museum's faculty. He also earned more than $1,200 painting portraits. Many Iowa City and Gilmore residents ordered portraits and paid Frank $20 for each rendition. The literary society had him paint its members.[6]

Russell was a focused, no-nonsense student who had "a pride that allowed no financial indebtedness." He was "unusually modest and retiring in disposition

FIGURE 1.1. Frank Russell, Sacaton, Arizona, 1902. Photograph by Theresa Russell. Courtesy Stanford University Library, Frances Theresa and Frank B. Russell (SC0166), Department of Special Collections and University Archives, Stanford University Libraries, Neg. No. BP-3617.

and having neither the means nor inclination to enter largely into the social life of the University, he confined himself strictly to the business of getting an education, the value of which he never underestimated."[7] Still, he played clarinet in the college band, joined the Zethagathian Society, and attained the rank of captain in the equivalent of ROTC. Significantly, Frank became the assistant of famed naturalist Charles Cleveland Nutting, the museum's curator and head of the Department of Systematic Zoology, who was interested in the geographic distribution of mammals.

Frank declared a zoology major. His goal was to be a university researcher-explorer like Nutting, not simply an all-purpose natural historian. Combining travel, adventure, and science was alluring. Russell was uninterested in being confined to a classroom or library. He certainly had his own ideas of how his education should proceed. Although he worked with several instructors in laboratory settings, Frank was really interested in *doing* activities rather than listening to a lecture. Luckily, Nutting and the natural history faculty were willing to allow him to learn through active experiences in the form of apprenticeships, a type of education that would later be labeled work study, internships, or engaged learning.

Arctic Adventures

In 1891 Frank accompanied Nutting and his mathematics professor, A. G. Smith, on a trip to the Saskatchewan River and Cedar Lake in the Canadian Northwest to create a collection of waterfowl specimens. His first field trip to the Subarctic enabled Frank to graduate from the university in June 1892 with a double major in geology and zoology based in large part on his original research, an unusual accomplishment at the time.[8] Frank wrote an undergraduate thesis titled "Variation of Animals in a State of Nature."

Frank immediately enrolled in the university's master's program in systematic zoology, based on an agreement with Nutting that he could continue experiential education. On the 1891 trip, Russell had been inspired to pursue further exploration after meeting longtime Hudson's Bay Company employee Roderick MacFarlane. The noted explorer, who had made significant ornithological collections across the Arctic North for the Smithsonian Institution and Canadian museums, taught Russell how to survive in the Arctic. Frank later wrote of MacFarlane, "His enthusiastic description of the field, as yet almost unexplored, roused in me a strong desire to visit the far North."[9] Frank would be a scientific explorer.

Nutting received approval from the State University of Iowa regents for Russell to use the proposed two-year solo expedition as the core of his graduate studies in lieu of formal classroom instruction and laboratory work. His journey was recognized as an official university trip to collect large mammals, especially musk-ox, which were becoming rare. Like other naturalists, Nutting felt it essential to collect specimens for posterity as quickly as possible. Frank said he was also instructed to "pick up everything else that I could lay my hands on," which meant birds, insects, fossils, smaller mammals, plants, and cultural artifacts. He was to map his route and collect meteorological data.[10] Russell would start at the mouth of the Saskatchewan River and proceed north through the Subarctic into the Arctic. Unfortunately, the regents did not obligate travel, per diem, or collecting funds, but the university's president, Charles A. Schaeffer, gave the young explorer more than the expected "to whom it may concern" letter (dated June 21, 1892) requesting assistance. Schaeffer underwrote Russell for one year, using his personal money. The second year was covered by public donations from faculty, students, and Iowa City citizens. These monies provided Russell with his second adventure and the opportunity to make a name for himself. He established a reputation as a naturalist and culture hero explorer.

FIGURE 1.2. Illustration from "Hunting Musk-Ox with the Dog Rib." Drawing by Frank Russell, *Scribner's Magazine*, 1896.

The Arctic trip made Frank a seasoned traveler able to use multiple transportation modes to reach inaccessible areas, a skill greatly admired by Theresa during their Arizona travels. He crossed hundreds of miles of tundra on foot and snowshoes, drove a dogsled, rode on a skiff, and even experienced the luxury of an occasional steamboat. Frank estimated he traveled more than 5,000 miles! He was not shy in claiming American explorer "firsts," which garnered prestige and celebrity, or in lauding his tenaciousness. As Frank told one professor after returning home, he was "the first man to descend the Mackenzie [River through its valley] and reach civilization by passing through the Arctic Sea and around Alaska."[11]

The journey's arduousness gave Frank explorer notoriety,

but he had much to learn. He gained practical suggestions on how to survive harsh environments from Hudson's Bay Company employees, whale hunters, and the Cree, with whom he spent his first fall and winter. Opportunistic and haphazard at first, Frank became increasingly systematic, mapping geographic and geological features and recording animal behaviors and habitats. He spent solitary weeks "body-snatching," as he called his collecting activities. And he began his journey to anthropology. He took advantage of opportunities to interact with the First Nations peoples around Great Slave Lake and Herschel Island: the Slavey, Dogrib, Yellow Knife, Inuit, Cree, and Chippewa.

The trip was not easy. Like all tundra explorers, Russell withstood voracious mosquitos and intense cold.[12] It was a hard way to earn a master's degree, but such trials were expected of a nineteenth-century explorer-scientist. There would have been no honor if the trip had been comfortable and easy. Nor would Russell have earned a new identity, one that sustained his self-image later: a smart, vigorous, detail-oriented man, dedicated to science above all else, who had conquered a wilderness and could claim the right to name landscape features or animal species. He had the focused perseverance in the face of extreme adversity needed to advance his scientific agenda, to be a discoverer. Through hard work he felt he had earned the credentials, recognition, and rewards of an explorer-scientist. Frank was now a robust man who could conquer a wilderness.

Unfortunately, this unswerving resolve to conduct science included ignoring the views of Indian communities, the region's stewards. To Frank's mentors, such Native beliefs and desires were obstacles to be overcome. The needs of science came first, and Frank recognized this. He had proven himself by outwitting them. As Nutting proudly reported to his *American Naturalist* readers:

> The difficulties overcome at this time [during March and April] were such as to demonstrate the fact that Mr. Russell must take rank among the very foremost of plucky and persevering explorers in the far north. The musk-ox were four hundred miles from Fort Rae and two hundred miles from the edge of the woods. The Indians were unwilling to aid the explorer, having a firm belief that if a musk-ox were taken from the Barren Ground, and mounted in some distant country, all the others would go to join it. Those who have had to deal with Indian superstitions know the hopelessness of arguments, bribes or threats in such cases. Undismayed by this unforeseen and seemingly fatal obstacle, Mr. Russell allowed the Indians to depart without him, well knowing that it is their custom to camp on the edge of the Barren Ground for some time for the purpose of killing caribou before going on the long musk-ox hunt, and knowing also they would get out of ammunition and have to send a man two hundred miles back to the Fort for a new supply. When this messenger made his appearance as expected, Mr. Russell

> announced his determination to accompany him to the Barren Ground, *nolens volens*. He persuaded him to make the best of the inevitable and accept pay for the enforced service.[13]

The pay was food, tea, and one dollar per day.

Such was the power of scientific exploration in colonial settings and the unquestioned intellectual and social assumptions of American civilization's superiority over Indigenous forms of knowledge combined with fierce personal zeal. In order to acquire type specimens for a "doomed" species, Russell helped speed its endangerment. He apparently did not think this ironic.[14] Scientific need was always foremost in Frank's life and influenced all his work. He would endure almost anything for new information, including imposing his will on others, breaking rules, or proceeding despite Indigenous disapproval.

Russell had to recognize and respect some Native hunting rules, however, if he was to be successful. Frank and a Cree ("Andrew") traveled together during the second year for 22 days, and were soon joined by Andrew's relatives. On the 10th day, the Cree hunting group saw a herd of musk ox. They raced ahead and left Russell to struggle with his sled and supplies. By the time Frank arrived, the hunters had killed the animals and claimed them. There was no museum specimen. Russell was better prepared when they came across a second herd six days later. This time, leaving his sled and bulkiest clothing, Frank ran with the men and shot three musk oxen, whose skins and skulls he claimed. His companions distributed the meat. Three days later, they spotted another herd, but Frank's sled was bogged down in soft snow on a steep hillside. He recorded that when he saw the hunters over a quarter mile ahead, he felt his chances of collecting the desired specimens had vanished. Extremely frustrated, Frank briefly imagined shooting the Cree men. Then his luck changed. Unexpectedly, a group of four large bulls broke from the herd and ran in Frank's direction. He killed them all and claimed the skeletons for a museum display.

The Cree men allowed Frank to keep five musk ox skins and skulls and enough bones to erect a complete specimen in the museum, even though he had personally killed at least a dozen animals. The load exceeded 700 pounds, and his top-heavy sled often tipped over. Russell never seriously considered abandoning his specimens, which would have meant scientific defeat. But the sheer bulk presented a challenge. Frank walked alongside the sled, holding onto a dog to keep from being separated in blizzards. His feet were often stuck in mud during the miserable spring. The group's firewood ran out and they burned tent poles; the dwindling food supply was given to the dogs. Russell lost weight and was often ill but persevered. The Cree men were also heavily burdened with the meat, skins, and bones needed by their community. To abandon these hard-earned resources would have meant starvation. Luckily, they did not have as far to go as Russell.

On May 10, Frank gave his dogs and dog sled to his hunting companions and left Fort Rae. He traveled by canoe to Fort McPherson, down the Mackenzie through the ice floes to the Arctic Sea. He spent two months on Herschel Island collecting ornithological and ethnographic materials. On August 30, Russell stowed his large scientific collection in the hold of a whaler and traveled to Siberia. Here he secured a polar bear skin and Yupik ivory carvings, before heading south. Russell arrived in San Francisco on October 27, 1894. He soon boarded a train heading east.

Frank arrived in Iowa City on November 2. He was met enthusiastically "by the faculty, students, and citizens, to the number of several hundred."[15] The rugged explorer was lauded.

> As the train pulled in bearing Mr. Russell, a glorious display of fireworks was set off. The university's band played its most stirring airs which with the shouts of all present made the occasion a grand affair. Prof. Nutting who had gone as far as Des Moines to meet the explorer, ushered him into the depot where a general hand shaking with the adventurer was indulged in, after which he was placed in a three seated carriage and driven to the Post Office corner, closely followed by the band and battalion and a large number of friends all shouting in their loudest strains: Russell, Russell, who is Russell? The man who went to the Arctic sea—hi-wa, hi-wa—back to Iowa.[16]

The recognition went beyond the university and local community. Nutting reported to other scientists that Russell had secured specimens of the larger mammals (from moose to Arctic hare), birds, and plants. He had also gained geographic skills, accurately describing the land and constructing maps of his route.[17] He estimated the ornithological and ethnological specimens were worth $100,000 exclusive of the nine Barren Ground caribou and musk-ox skeletons.

This trip served as the basis for Russell's 1895 master of science degree in zoology. The solo expedition through terra incognita established Frank as a naturalist with a thirst for discovery and wanderlust. Equally important, he soon honed skills required to gain public recognition for his feats and become a celebrity. He became an explorer-storyteller, following the example of John Wesley Powell and his rousing accounts of trips down the Colorado River through the Grand Canyon.[18] Powell's lectures and narratives helped him build support for future explorations as well as established him as a scientific authority. Despite a disability, Powell demonstrated he was committed to pursuing knowledge and desired to help America understand its land, natural resources, and people. His self-depictions bordered on the quasi-mythological: a man fulfilling the nation's Manifest Destiny through rugged individualism in the face of adversity, leading to bountiful accomplishments.

Frank used Powell's rhetorical techniques and themes when he told of his trip. He began presenting public lectures in March 1895. His first publication, "A Naturalist's Voyage Down the Mackenzie," appeared in *Midland Monthly*. This regional Des Moines magazine was wide-ranging in content but always included a lively educational adventure. Frank interspersed his story of how he reached inaccessible places and his collecting activities with episodes about interesting people and hair-raising escapades. He composed a rousing Horatio Alger–style story of a determined young man with the character to successfully pursue field science, despite his limited wealth and social status. It was a coming-of-age account based on attained merit. Frank became a scientist by surviving an unforgiving wilderness. In the conclusion, Frank wrote he was rewarded when his accomplishments were praised by scientists and the general public. He also gained membership in a sought-after social group. Russell's individuality and pioneering spirit were highlighted, as was his tenacity. Yet he told of his contradictory feelings of despair, anxiety, and elation as he pursued his unusual career. Like Alger's many young male protagonists (especially the impoverished Ragged Dick), who each rose from a humble background to middle-class security and respectability through hard work, courage, and resolution, the scientific culture hero became a man who used his talents to decisively seize opportunities and overcome challenges that would stop a less tenacious man. Unlike Alger's protagonists, there was no luck or wealthy patron to help with social ascent. Frank had to rely only on himself. Overcoming obstacles through an overzealous Protestant work ethic earned Russell an authoritative voice. One newspaper described the article as his "thrilling adventures in the heart of British America."[19] It was even read by a young State University of Iowa undergraduate, Frances Peet, who was, we can guess, impressed.

Russell took advantage of his celebrity. His nephew Roland Russell remembered Frank spending most of his time traveling around Iowa giving lectures.[20] These, like his book, *Explorations in the Far North*, published two years later, were engaging travel narratives. Over time, Frank increasingly infused them with information about the lives of Native peoples. *Explorations in the Far North* had as many ethnographic sketches as personal travel adventures. It also contained information on how Frank's interactions with Natives affected them; his travelogue can be considered a "new ethnography," written 80 years before anthropologists coined the term.

Frank developed a second lecture series that was pure masculine adventure. His second publication in *Scribner's Magazine*, for which he was paid, focused on the musk-ox hunting story. The editor took the rousing tale and republished it twice, in the American and British editions of *Hunting* and *Big Game Shooting*. Scientific exploration and ethnography were minimized in these accounts. Male adventures and individualism in the outdoors were expounded.

Writing his thesis and travel narratives as well as lecturing helped Frank decide where his true passions lay. Simply hunting large game to place carcasses in museums and be recognized as an outdoorsman was no longer enough. Nor was a career as a natural historian. Frank wanted to be an anthropologist.

Off to Harvard

There was only one place to obtain credentials in the new field: Harvard University, studying with Frederic Ward Putnam. Putnam (1839–1915) was an ichthyologist who immersed himself in all aspects of anthropology, including the study of comparative human and cultural variation. He was especially interested in North America, where he felt scholars "must study the art of [its] races to find out about their migrations and distributions."[21] In 1875 Putnam was appointed curator of the Peabody Museum of American Archaeology and Ethnology, funded by philanthropist George Peabody. Putnam became a critical figure in anthropology, writing well over 400 publications. He helped identify the questions that distinguished anthropology from other natural sciences. A firm evolutionist, he strove to collect material culture and human remains as scientific evidence for groups he thought would either disappear or assimilate under the government policies he supported.

Putnam was one of anthropology's great institution-builders. He co-founded *The American Naturalist*, played a critical role in ensuring that anthropological knowledge was found in the pages of *Science*, and was the permanent Secretary of the American Association for the Advancement of Science (AAAS) for many years. He helped found the Archaeological Institute of America (AIA) and the American Anthropological Association (AAA). Putnam was instrumental in creating anthropology programs at the American Museum of Natural History (AMNH), Columbia University, the University of California at Berkeley, the Field Museum, and Harvard. Putnam developed the educational program neophytes would study, including insisting on the prerequisite that students be "properly equipped [high school] graduates."[22] His pedagogy was firmly based in immersion in museum and field experience. Like Russell, he thought men should learn by doing.

Putnam was equally concerned with defining how anthropology should be taught. In 1894 he developed an introductory undergraduate course that included physical anthropology, archaeology, and theoretical ethnology. If advanced undergraduate students did well in Anthropology 1 and demonstrated knowledge of "elementary chemistry, geology, botany, zoology, drawing and surveying," they were admitted to Anthropology 20, a three-year research course in archaeology and ethnology. This in turn led to independent work for a doctorate. Participation required laboratory and collections management work, attendance at periodic public lectures, fieldwork, and production of new knowledge leading to a publication. For physical anthropology, learning was almost completely experiential, concentrating on describing and measuring human skeletons and comparing different races using anthropometric techniques. Student training relied heavily on mentorship, tutorials, and apprentices. Putnam gave Chautauqua-style public lectures and gallery tours, emphasizing actual artifact analysis rather than formal classroom instruction with assessment tests. Between 1894 and 1904, Frank Russell, George Dorsey, John Owens, Roland B. Dixon, William C. Farabee, George B. Gordon, Charles Peabody, Charles Willoughby, John R. Swanson, and Alfred M. Tozzer followed this plan of study.[23]

Frank left the State University of Iowa for Harvard soon after receiving his master's degree. Unexpectedly, either Putnam or the university did not give him credit for his education since he was changing fields. He started over on an expedited schedule. Russell worked hard, earning a second BA in 1896 and a second MA in 1897. He had come at an opportune time, for Putnam's older students had graduated. Putnam wanted to free his time to continue his excavations, and Russell was happy to help by teaching and overseeing collections.[24]

Putnam obtained funds from Elizabeth Ware and Clarence Moore to support Russell to prepare a descriptive catalogue of the osteological collections. He began a basic inventory by constructing a card catalogue; he numbered each bone and placed identification and contextual information on the card. He organized the osteological collections using natural history museum collection principles and the categorization schemes Putnam had learned from Louis Agassiz at the Museum of Comparative Zoology. They included historic context and geographical region.[25]

The collections were extensive. Putnam, like Jeffrey Wyman earlier, had collected human remains from archaeological excavations (his own and those of his colleagues and students) as well as independent researchers and individuals trafficking in Native American skeletons. These were seen as necessary to study American Indian origins, migration patterns, and population diversity as well as develop a basic taxonomic classification. There were also specialized studies of cranial deformation, cannibalism, demographic profiles, the effects of diet on the body, growth, and disease. The collections were not without order. Cordelia Adelaide Studley, a medical doctor who had trained at Boston University and the University of Michigan, had worked on them extensively. Falling ill in 1881, she had taken a medical leave to volunteer at the Peabody Museum. Her task had been to organize the Coahuila, Mexico, materials Edward Palmer had excavated. Putnam hired her the next year to analyze the remains from the Turner Mound group. She also assisted Putnam excavating shell mounds and curating resulting materials. Remarkably, given all these duties, she still published her analyses. In 1886 she resigned because her pay was so low.[26] The osteological collections had grown extensively after Studley left; Putnam and his associates, Ernest Volk and Charles Willoughby, excavated in Ohio, New Jersey, and Maine. In addition, in 1895 the Hemenway Southwestern Archaeological Expedition materials from northern Arizona had been received and placed on display. There was much for Russell to do.

When George Dorsey left for the Field Museum, Putnam assigned Frank to teach the introductory courses. Frank was given the title assistant in anthropology. The next year, 1897, he was promoted to instructor in anthropology, which conferred faculty status. Harvard's faculty consisted of Putnam, Dixon, and now Russell. Putnam cobbled together monies to pay his salary and doctoral expenses using undergraduate tuition fees, private subscriptions, and the prestigious Hemenway Fellowship with a stipend of $500. This provided Russell with $1,000. Putnam required him to do more than teach, however; he was instructed to make the Peabody Museum a place where budding scholars could conduct research. Russell prepared ethnographic and archaeological specimens for student use and established the student anthropology library. By 1906 the library had the largest anthropological collection in North American, in excess of 6,000 works. Putnam developed an eclectic course of study for Russell. He studied geology and mapping so that he could conduct archaeological surveys. Putnam also had Frank work on his professional skills. Frank was required to give several lectures on his Arctic research to local scientific and literary groups in order to raise funds for the museum and hone his public speaking skills.

Developing Somatology and Osteology

Physical anthropology was just in its infancy in 1896 and researchers attempted to follow scientific protocols with mixed results. It concentrated on the human body, its functioning and its evolutionary development, and issues of race. Practitioners utilized several methodologies, including anthropometry, or somatology as the subdiscipline was called in Europe. This was a system of measurement of living human bodies. Osteology analyzed skeletal remains. Craniology concentrated on the skull. The measures were designed to help anatomists research human growth patterns and define "racial" categories.[27] Frank focused on the osteology collections, moving through the entire assemblage thinking about how they could be used for research. He also thought about the pedagogy of early physical anthropology and quickly developed a new laboratory course. This focus and his training in the next two years would determine Frank's 1900 research.

To advance his skills in physical anthropology, Putnam had Russell enroll in anatomy classes at Harvard Medical School, where he learned dissection. To gain specialized instruction not available at Harvard, Putnam sent Frank to work with Austrian doctor and anthropological explorer Professor Felix von Luschan in

Berlin for six weeks in the late summer of 1897. Here he learned state-of-the-art anthropometry techniques as well as Paul Broca's craniometric standards, the Bastian system of anthropological taxonomy, and the particulars of the Frankfort Craniometric Agreement. He was introduced to the debates concerning statistical problems, especially sample size, and as a result began to think critically about methodological issues. Russell began to question what it was somatologists and osteologists were actually measuring and whether the variation in measurement techniques undermined scientific reliability and validity.[28]

Putnam encouraged Russell to continue Arctic fieldwork in order to expand the regional diversity of the osteological collections. With museum and university support, Frank headed north in early summer 1897, traveling to Labrador. He was a member of G. H. Perkins's University of Pennsylvania natural history expedition, composed of 10 scientists, including Baron Adolf Nordenskjöld. As they explored Elsmore Island, Russell conducted ethnographic and environmental research as well as collected ancient and historic skeletal material for his dissertation.[29]

These activities earned Russell a doctorate in 1898. His dissertation was titled "A Study of a Collection of Eskimo Crania from Labrador with Observations on the Prevailing System of Craniometry." Frank basically described shared and ethnically distinct physical characteristics among Inuit groups. Importantly, he assessed interpopulation variability and change over time. As an exercise in standardizing taxonomy, he chose type specimens, that is, "the most typical" skulls that would be used as the "standards" for any future racial and sexual identification of human remains found in the Arctic. In terms of understanding North American Indigenous population diversity, Russell used discrete trait analysis. While he did not publish his dissertation at this time, planning on gathering more data from other parts of the Arctic, he published a smaller study with his student Henry Huxley comparing crania and long bones from New England and Labrador Natives. It was one of the first studies that demonstrated that "Native Americans" were not a single group but composed of diverse populations that existed over time.[30]

Russell strove to improve craniology methods in his dissertation analysis. He challenged the efficacy of skull measurements, calling for researchers to standardize their measures. This was a critical technical issue that affected replicability, precision, and reliability. Researchers were introducing what is today called investigator error, invalidating their conclusions. He did not challenge the validity of somatology or craniology, however. Russell felt increasing precision was the only way to ensure that somatology could be an "exact" science based on believable data. He called on other practitioners to refine techniques at the 1899 AAAS meeting during his presentation, "A Comparative Study of the Physical Structure of the Labrador." Russell's research still rested on the contention that skull and body shape could be used to indicate race as broad social groupings, an idea developed by German anatomist Johanna Friedrich Blumenbach in the 1770s.[31] Importantly, Frank insisted that these racial groups had to account for, and the researcher control, internal variation before they were useful. He presented similar papers in the coming years, striving to help make somatology, with its emphasis on categorization, accurate.

One sees skepticism in Russell's anthropometric publications as well as belief in the enterprise as a way to organize and understand human body types. But to test his refined techniques, Russell needed more skeletons and skulls from different North American human populations so he could construct a grounded, evidence-based study using a large data set. Rather than propose or reinforce grand typologies that relied on anthropometric measures to reify races, Frank looked for variation and similarity *within* populations across space and over time. He felt one had to thoroughly establish actual ranges of variation within North American subgroups before universal associations could be proposed or theoretically extended back to suggest commonalities about human evolution. While Russell did not write grand abstract theoretical or summarizing papers, we gained the impression that at this stage of his career, he felt small, controlled research projects on specific groups were more important for understanding human mobility and history than associating a supposed body type to humanity's development in terms of psychological, social, or cultural commensurability.

These were critical scientific and social issues that could affect a budding career. Russell had taken a chance by not producing an ethnographic narrative or an archaeological report, which would make him more marketable at any place except Harvard. Franz Boas, who was also working in anthropometry at the AMNH and Columbia University, thought there was no need for another researcher who was interested in the questions that the human body could answer. Nor did he distinguish that Russell was actually an osteology expert, an archaeologist in emphasis. Similarly, Dorsey, who was now at the Field Museum, began teaching forensic anthropology using human remains at the University of Chicago. No other institutions appeared interested. As early as 1881, Powell felt that classifying tribes based on body characteristics was flawed and called for categorization based on language. It was self-evident that Powell would not support somatology through the BAE.[32] By 1898 anthropometry was viewed as a questionable method in anthropology that provided an apology for, and a challenge to, theories about human personality, intelligence, and racial or ethnic potential. It had become a method widely used in criminology, psychology, sports science, sociology, anatomy, physiology, and the nascent eugenics movement. Popularized anthropometric and craniometric data were used to support social policies relating to immigration, education, citizenship, social welfare, and even popular notions on the choice of a "proper" mate based on the shape of women's noses or ears. Russell was disdainful of these uses and how most practitioners were not challenging misuse. He needed more data to make anthropometry and osteology a core part of anthropology. He intended to acquire this by staying at Harvard.

A Turning Point

Russell was on track for a productive career. He was recognized as an Arctic expert, and normally he would have returned there to claim the region as his research territory. Unfortunately, Russell contracted tuberculosis during his 1897 trip. He showed symptoms by autumn: weight loss, coughing with blood-tinged sputum, fever, throat irritation, and chest pain. He probably consulted a doctor, but there was little medicine could do. There was no known cure. The only treatment was climatological: go to a dry climate, live outdoors in a tent if possible, and engage in strenuous exercise. While the disease did not stop Frank from pursuing his career, it soon came to define its direction, especially with regard to fieldwork locales. He needed to "chase the cure."[33] The Arctic was absolutely the wrong climate for someone with chronic lung problems. Frank needed a new field area in a salubrious climate, like New Mexico or Arizona. This was a hard choice. It meant leaving his dissertation project behind and looking for new regional populations to test his revised anthropometric measures.

And what about Boston, where Frank was teaching in the fall of 1897 and the winter of 1898? What about that intended career at Harvard? Doctors told lungers to leave New England and indeed to leave the East Coast and any industrialized areas with air pollution. What Russell needed was a permanent position at a museum or university in a drier climate. But there were none. Anthropology was seen as an adjunct to well-established disciplines like philosophy, history, geology, and the natural sciences; it was not yet considered an essential subject in higher education. In addition, it was competing with other social science disciplines (geography, sociology, and psychology) for places in science curricula.[34] The few institutions interested in anthropology (Clark University, Columbia University, the University of Chicago, and the University of Wisconsin) already had their anthropologists, generally one per institution. There were no offers for a young man eager to teach at some new institution where he did not have social and professional connections. And the midwestern institution where Frank had his connections was not interested. The State University of Iowa had no burning desire to train future anthropologists; it did not establish an independent department until 1963. Nor did it hire a physical anthropologist until 1986. The national academic situation left the federal government and those museums with research programs as an alternative to Harvard. Again the few positions were already filled.

Putnam wanted Russell to remain at Harvard. He named Frank a permanent instructor, making him part of the Arts and Sciences faculty in January 1898, but still only paid him $1,000 per year. Frank taught as a generalist. He was still considered the best instructor for Anthropology 1. But this does not mean he was not recognized for his expertise as a North Americanist and a physical anthropologist. As a postdoctoral instructor, he was expected to engage in important theoretical and methodological debates. For Russell, this required gaining more experience in archaeology while continuing to hone his osteological skills. Now Russell needed a new culture area as well. Putnam agreed Frank could not specialize in the Arctic. Luckily, Putnam was fascinated by questions of North American antiquity, especially possible chronological associations among Paleoindian, Mound Builders, Puebloans, and historic groups. Putnam hoped Russell's osteological studies would provide conclusive data about early time periods in North America.[35]

Putnam approached these issues through the study of diversity among contemporary Native societies. He assigned Frank to analyze the human remains and associated artifacts found at the Delaware Valley's Trenton gravel pits originally excavated by C. C. Abbott and Ernest Volk. Russell thought the human remains had been understudied. He analyzed the crania found at the site to see if the population was related to the Lenni Lenapé, who occupied the area until 1737. He concluded that all the precontact human remains were definitively ancestral Lenni Lenapé. This was Frank's first—and, it turned out, only—contribution to one of the major questions of the time period: the identity and antiquity of precontact groups.[36]

As a permanent Harvard faculty member, Russell contributed to anthropology's professional growth. This meant building on Putnam's immense network and activities. Between 1873 and 1898, he served as AAAS's permanent secretary, and in 1898 he was elected the association's president. Russell assisted with AAAS's Anthropology Section activities, first as Putnam's unnamed assistant and later as an elected council member and secretary. From this base, Frank built his own professional network.[37] He would spend the rest of his life developing anthropology's professional identity in college educational curricula.

Russell argued for anthropological majors as the foundation for specialized courses of study. He claimed anthropology's intellectual centrality was the basis for other disciplines, including natural history. Anthropology's "very comprehensiveness is a virtue; for thereby it is rendered suitable to serve as a framework for all other knowledge, a symmetrical framework lacking which the student but too often builds a series of mental watertight compartments that give no unity or harmony to the intellectual edifice."[38]

Frank's tuberculosis worsened. His colleagues urged him to leave Cambridge. If Frank continued on his present course, he would die. Still, he refused to take a rest cure in a dry, hot climate or even rest. A resilient man who never gave up, Russell was determined to finish the academic year. He was a man of work, not someone defined by a medical condition. Frank's decision was also pragmatic. He did not have the wealth to follow a recuperative course in this era before paid disability or sick leave. He had to work or he would be destitute. But what about calling on his family? Could he go and live with them? Could they lend him money?

Frank's family had sold their Iowa farm during the Panic of 1896, which followed several years of a depressed economy. Historians have said that this time period was as bad as the Great Depression of the 1930s and hit farmers especially hard. The Russells moved to Galveston, Texas, a place that environmentally would not have been an improvement on the Northeast for Frank. We have no indication that Frank asked any of his siblings, his parents, or other relatives for assistance. Putnam called on his colleagues to help find the young scholar a new summer field site, and a more suitable place of employment than cold, damp New England. The problem, of course, was that donors and other institutions did not want to employ someone who was ill with a disease assumed to be fatal.

Putnam offered to raise money for a position for Russell at the American Museum of Natural History, but that would mean spending days with collections in dark, damp storage areas. New York City was no better than Boston, and its air pollution was worse. Franz Boas already held the one available position in cultural anthropology and anthropometry. Frank's services would have been considered duplicative by the museum board. Putnam and Russell explored other options, especially European museums, but again the climates were not conducive to relieving his hemorrhaging lungs. Few other options in an amiable climate came to mind. The universities in Texas, Arizona, New Mexico, and Utah were not yet supporting anthropology, and Putnam had few institutional ties in these areas. Nor were there museums with research programs in the territories. One possibility could have been the University of California at Berkeley, which Putnam would help found with Phoebe Apperson Hearst, but that would not happen until 1901. At that time, the goal of the department was to document California languages and cultures, not physical anthropology. We have no indication that Russell was ever interested in linguistics. If Russell considered returning to a natural history position, we again have no indication.

No one wanted Frank to quit his secure Harvard position to lead an itinerant life. This would not help his health; the stress would make it worse. Putnam also wanted Russell to continue to work within his sphere of influence and the institutions he controlled if possible. The best option seemed to be to have Frank remain at Harvard during the academic year but spend the summer outdoors in an arid environment. Putnam and Russell now concentrated on finding a new field locale. They turned their attention to the American Southwest.

One anthropologist who answered Putnam's call was William John McGee, who signed all his publications *W J* and was nicknamed "No Period" McGee. A powerhouse in anthropology, geology, and later water conservation policy, the self-trained Iowa native was one of Powell's protégées. After 1894, when Powell was forced to resign as director of the United States Geological Survey (USGS), McGee became the BAE's de facto chief executive. He gave himself the title "Ethnologist-in-charge" when Powell became ill, without seeking approval from the Secretary of the Smithsonian Institution, who had oversight for the BAE. Theoretically, this allowed McGee to make personnel decisions. He had met Frank, a fellow Iowan, and been impressed, viewing him as a future star who should be working for the BAE. An ambitious man, McGee shared Powell's goal of leading a coordinated North American anthropology corps. Putnam's call to help Russell was a way to consolidate Washington-Boston anthropology under his guidance.[39] To have Frank in his camp would greatly advance McGee's dream.

Initially, Russell saw the federal government as a temporary employer. He did not contemplate leaving Harvard permanently but hoped the BAE could expand his field possibilities. The BAE was noted for its work in the American Southwest. In addition to the climate, working there would provide Frank with the opportunity to encounter new populations and help him think through issues of whether behavior was racially innate or environmentally conditioned. He wrote to McGee in February 1898, without mentioning his real reason for the proposed switch in research area.

> Will you kindly inform me if there will be any opportunity for me to join one of the field parties sent out by the Bureau this summer? I am not particularly interested in the region where the exploration funds of this museum are to be spent. I had thought of going to the east coast of Hudson Bay but the time seemed rather short for such a trip. I expect to be through my work here on the first of June and should be back about the 25th of September. I hope to secure my Ph.D. this spring so that I would have time next winter to work up the summer collection if it should be desired.[40]

McGee replied that the BAE did not have funds to hire anyone on such short notice. All moneys had already been obligated.

Russell decided to leave Cambridge anyway and use his own limited funds. He tried McGee again, this time by looking him in the eye when he made his request. Frank stopped in Washington, D.C., and called on McGee as he began his trip to New Mexico and Arizona. He told McGee he intended a "get acquainted" project: to focus on the Hopi and Rio Grande Pueblos and attend summer ceremonies to understand their philosophies and religious systems. McGee told him that this research emphasis duplicated the work BAE ethnologists had been conducting since the late 1870s. He strongly suggested that Russell change his plans and conduct basic ethnographic interviews with the Jicarilla Apache, since they had only been studied briefly by James Mooney in 1892. McGee also said it would be useful for Russell to look for archaeological sites. Frank could do this on his way to the Hopi villages to see the famous Snake Dances and Niman ceremonies. McGee found he could not turn down the young man. The Ethnologist-in-charge would pay him $100 for his summer's work on receipt of a report or publication. Russell agreed.

McGee's proposal was a common promissory method by which individuals, called Smithsonian collaborators, could be reimbursed. It had been used extensively to support Franz Boas over the years. McGee had no other option. At the time there were no procedures with Treasury Department oversight that allowed non-employees to receive advances. Nor was there a means by which fieldwork could be contracted to an independent scholar. Technically, the payment was only available for a completed service and product, that is, a field report or scholarly manuscript. McGee could also make agreements for raw data.[41] McGee could supply Frank with government vouchers to be signed when he purchased something, and he convinced a merchant that they were legitimate. These were needed for any reimbursement if McGee somehow located funds over the summer. McGee also gave Frank maps from the USGS office. He promised Russell other equipment and supplies, like film, but these did not arrive until after Russell had completed his trip. After Russell agreed to visit the Jicarilla Apache reservation, he talked briefly with Mooney, who gave him advice about the community.

The 1898 Southwest Journey

Assured he would eventually receive reimbursement, Russell spent July 1 to September 16, 1898, conducting ethnographic research with the Jicarilla Apache in Dulce, New Mexico, while keeping his eyes peeled for possible archaeological sites.[42] McGee expected him to do a great deal for $100. He requested Frank collect basic cultural information, vocabulary (using survey forms developed by Powell), origin stories, and trickster myths. The goal was to compare the Southern Athabascans to the Northern Athabascans Russell had met in the Subarctic. McGee gave Frank the how-to guide and data forms that the Smithsonian sent to their citizen collaborators.

Russell was also expected to participate in Jicarilla Apache daily life and attend religious rituals and curing ceremonies. Hopefully, he could sketch a drypainting, if any were made, so they could be compared to Navajo ritual designs. McGee instructed Frank to conduct a census and plot settlements on a USGS map. For these geographic efforts, McGee offered to send him USGS survey forms and General Land Office (GLO) maps, but these did not arrive until Russell was almost done.[43] Preparations for government research projects were not speedy, even when couriers hand-delivered memos. Then again, we do not know how swiftly an often-ill McGee forwarded the requests, nor how long his requests languished on someone's desk.

Russell proceeded to Dulce, New Mexico. After introducing himself to the community and finding a place to sleep, his first task was to hire two Jicarilla Apache men to interpret. Unfortunately, Edward Ladd, who had worked for James Mooney in 1893 for $2.25 per day, now charged what Frank considered "high rates," which he could not afford. The lack of sufficient research funds hindered all the proposed research activities McGee had requested, especially Frank's ability to compile a dictionary.[44] Nevertheless, in November and December he sent McGee a large amount of language information: 143 pages of vocabulary and linguistic notes interpreted by Gun'-si Vigil, who had been educated at the Santa Fe and Fort Lewis Indian schools.

Russell had used Powell's printed outlines to collect basic linguistic information. Completed forms were intended to be given to the BAE linguists to assist detailed comparative analysis. Frank had had little linguistic training and did not appear to have been interested in language analysis. He chose to study folklore, storytelling as a social activity, and basic ethnography. Russell sent McGee copies of his ethnographic field notes on technology, social organization, kinship, food, basket making, tools, games, and religion. The information was later used by Frederick W. Hodge for the entry on the Jicarilla Apache in the *Handbook of American Indians North of Mexico*.[45]

Frank conducted the first ethnobotanical research in the region, identifying about 50 species of plants used by the Jicarilla Apache. He followed Stanley Coulter's procedures in his identification manual and was assisted by the missionary teacher, Miss Sarah E. Moore, and an unnamed individual from the Department of Agriculture.[46] Information was provided by elder Juan Quintana, who was considered a local authority on plant names. Quintana also narrated the animal tales Russell later published; the interpreter was Juan Reuben. Harkening back to his earlier Arctic collecting trip, Frank told McGee the following winter that if he returned, he would take Ridgway's 1887 *Manual of North American Birds* with him and produce a Native ornithology. He felt his 1898 information was not yet systematic enough but another field season would produce data worthy of publication. Frank also gathered data on the local geography and settlement patterns McGee desired. He noted historic Jicarilla Apache camp sites and three cliff dwellings warranting further investigation.

Russell must have eventually received some money from Putnam; the ethnographic items he purchased came to be housed in the Peabody Museum. What he gathered constituted a basic type collection, including examples of what the Jicarilla Apache made and used. Collecting was expected of all fieldworkers. McGee gave Frank a copy of Otis T. Mason's guide on how to record information on artifacts, hoping he would gather for the United States National Museum

(USNM), but apparently gave him no money.[47] Demonstrating one could gather documented artifacts was often seen to lead to funding for future research projects. It was certainly a requirement for anyone who wanted to find permanent employment in a museum but it was a gamble for a poor, ill man.

Russell purchased 70 items with his own money with the expectation he would be reimbursed by McGee. While McGee would have liked to reimburse Russell and place the artifacts in the USNM, there was evidently no money nor the hope of reimbursement in the next fiscal year, as he learned when he returned at the end of the summer.[48] Luckily, Putnam found funds to purchase the artifacts for the Peabody Museum. They were contemporary items. Most were what the Jicarilla Apache were producing for sale. The largest category of material culture consisted of hunting equipment and weapons, followed by baskets of various kinds. Table 1.2 shows that Russell also bought musical instruments, a few pieces of clothing, bags, and horse equipment: a whip and beaded halter. He also collected one Hopi wicker basket from an undesignated cliff ruin. Russell did not purchase any souvenirs or ethnic art for himself. This was a pattern he would replicate during his 1900 honeymoon journey; all his funds were expended conducting research. Russell was never a collector of ethnographic art or antiquities. Unlike other anthropologists, he did not purchase many personal ethnic items during his trips. While this could have been personal preference, he certainly did not have discretionary money.

Working in Dulce was not easy. Russell descended on the Jicarilla Apache settlement of 830 individuals at the Office of Indian Affairs' subagency without any prior notice. No one asked the community—which had recently experienced an allotment fiasco, had been increasingly confined due to unchecked settler encroachment, and whose crops had recently failed—if they wanted to be studied, especially by anyone associated with the federal government. Russell also had not informed the Office of Indian Affairs central office in Washington, D.C., or the reservation agent, N. S. Walpole, of his intentions.[49] He therefore failed to obtain permission to work on the reservation, as was required of all individuals. It was also a professional discourtesy. Many agents were opposed to anthropologists studying traditional culture because they felt such research ran counter to federal policies of assimilation by encouraging traditionalism.

Nevertheless, Russell expected both the reservation agent in Santa Fe and local Euro-Americans to open doors for him. Evidently, he was not summarily barred from the reservation as he could have been. It was unclear how much assistance the agent offered; there was no evidence that Frank stopped in Santa Fe to formally introduce himself, but it is possible. Walpole apparently did not impede him. According to Frank's notes, the Methodist missionaries, especially Sarah Moore, were his main support.

Russell did not meet any formalized community opposition but rather what we might term *polite passive aggressiveness*, a studied Native response of silence to colonial intrusion. The Jicarilla Apache community did not stop him from working among them but initially offered no help. Frank's lack of prior contact to gain a respectful verbal consent to participate in a research project meant he did not immediately obtain the information he wanted. This frustrated him, for he felt he had little time to accomplish the research. Additionally, Russell was disheartened by the reservation's economic situation and the resulting despondency. Like other Indigenous peoples, the Jicarilla Apache had suffered terribly from the impact of wars and military constraints on their freedom of movement, epidemics, settler incursions, and government policies designed to eradicate their cultures. Now here was a government official who wanted their knowledge; they questioned his motives. Frank blamed what was to him unreasonable Native skepticism toward a Euro-American stranger who asked all kinds of questions, as well as their current heightened poverty and lack of resources, on their recent experiences with their neighbors, the New Mexico Hispanics: "If some means could be found for removing the Mexicans who have occupied the best lands of the Jicarillas, they would stand some chance of advancement."[50] This view of "Mexicans" (Russell's ethnic label for anyone whose primary language was Spanish) as exploitative colonial settlers who stole land and resources from an Indigenous community mirrored his views of the group in his 1900 journal.

Russell never questioned whether his data collection methods or his attitude that science and its immediate research needs mattered more than anyone else's desires could be factors in a community's reception. Nor did he recognize or even question that federal policies that undermined Native economies, curtailed individual freedoms, and opened hunting and gathering lands to non-Jicarilla could lead to suspicion of a government official. The fact that promised rations from treaty obligations failed to reach the community also underscored suspicion.

There was a second issue Frank would have failed to recognize: the need for commitment to a community. Russell made it apparent he would have no long-term ties to the Jicarilla Apache; he would only be there for a short time. He would have no investment in the community's future. The residents recognized this and acted accordingly. Russell also conveniently forgot, as the limited time pressed heavily on him, that it took a long time to establish trust. He seems to have forgotten the lessons he learned in the Arctic in his fervor to complete his assigned tasks and earn the promised BAE reimbursement.[51]

Russell stayed at Dulce for longer than he had planned. He discovered a research truism: any basic ethnographic fieldwork takes three times longer than originally envisioned. The basic Apache research differed from the thematic research on hunting and survival techniques he had conducted in the Subarctic and Arctic. No Harvard graduate student received any training in conducting ethnographic research. BAE instructions for collecting ethnographic and linguistic information were geared for what we today term *salvage ethnography* (the rapid collection of information on Indigenous ways of life and language before the people were inevitably changed by Euro-American contact). This required inclusiveness, interviewing more than one individual to ensure memory culture was not lost.[52] The BAE desired information on what traditional Jicarilla Apache life was like before they were confined to a reservation, not what reservation life was like in 1898. The aim was to produce a picture of life as it was lived about 1850, and then write about it as if it were still occurring. This remembered, reconstructed, traditional culture became a baseline from which change due to European contact could be measured. It was an attempt to reconstruct "pure" cultures as if they existed in isolation and to identify distinctions among cultures and societies. Russell thus had to consult with key respondents—aged individuals with experiential knowledge and good memories who might remember their childhoods and could strip away Euro-American and Spanish borrowings. He also had to ignore much of what he saw around him, for he was not recording daily life in 1898.

Convincing people to participate required diplomacy and cross-cultural translation to a greater degree than Frank anticipated. Again, this was a common ethnographic research occurrence. An ethnographer rarely, if ever, immediately identified and convinced a knowledgeable individual to talk at length about a topic the researcher wanted. The elder required respectful persuasion over a period of time in order to assess the ethnographer's trustworthiness. In addition, no single individual held all the desired information. The same process had to be repeated with each new individual approached. And this was after the ethnographer had some idea of what was being said in the Indigenous language. Another problem was explaining why the information was sought. Frank had to translate nineteenth-century anthropological categories into meaningful Jicarilla Apache categories; this took time and could not have been accomplished in two months. Frank was never completely successful, even though he told McGee, "The people interested me very much and toward the last seemed to realize that I was not trying to work some little game at their expense."[53] Russell had had a valuable lesson for his later work with the Akimel O'odham, but he was still frustrated.

Simultaneously, Russell collected anthropometrical data for his real research project: to understand physical similarity and difference among the Athabascan peoples. This required convincing as many individuals as possible to be measured.[54] His goal was to obtain images of the body and head shapes of most of the people and from there establish averages based on age and sex. He needed standardized body measurements and two photographic "mug shots," an unsmiling profile and an open-eyed frontal face, for each research participant.

We have found no raw data for body measurements in Russell's scattered archival documents, so it is difficult to know what he measured. Generally, researchers recorded external characteristics of height, weight, age, sex, skin color, hair color, and eye color. The standardized body and facial photographs would allow him to later assess head form, facial angles, nasal angles, and what was called eye attitude (placement and shape) to produce a somatic profile. The photographs, if they were generated and developed by a competent photographer, were considered good evidence, as long as the poses were standardized. This proved to be more a problem for full-body poses, unlike the basic head shots Russell took.[55]

Russell's intention was to add Jicarilla Apache records to the Peabody Museum's large collection of human subject photos that had been started by Louis Agassiz. Agassiz wanted to document basic and mixed racial and ethnic types around the world as evidence for his evolutionary theories of biological determinism.[56] Putnam had continued supporting the effort, insisting his researchers amass otherwise uncollectable information that could be used to hopefully answer a wealth of research questions. Russell believed in this intellectual agenda.

Russell shot more than 100 facial and profile head portraits, paying each individual 10 cents per photograph. He apparently did not try to have the men or women disrobe, as other scientists had their subjects do, which would have violated Athabascan modesty norms. He sent the film to Harvard, but unfortunately the film processer could not develop the photos. There are three possibilities why: (1) the film processor was incompetent; (2) the film was flawed, damaged in transit; or (3) Russell had not tested his equipment. If the latter is correct, it was a neophyte field researcher mistake and indicated that this was the first time Frank had used a camera during a field trip.[57] Given the questionable quality of some of Frank's photographs and his haste to leave Boston, we can well imagine he was not yet proficient with the new lightweight Eastman Kodak box camera. But then few researchers were. Powell encouraged the BAE staff to use photography as a research tool to produce permanent documents of the land, architecture, and people, and take compelling images to be used for public dissemination. But no one had the competency of a John Hillers, the BAE's and USGS's professional field photographer.

Russell may have obtained the camera from McGee. Copies of the Jicarilla Apache photographs are housed in the NAA, not the Peabody Museum or its archives. This would explain why Frank did not practice before the trip. He probably obtained film from McGee for his general ethnographic shots and used his own or Putnam's money for the anthropometric photos, which went to the Peabody to be developed. There was apparently not enough film for Russell to take pictures of daily activities and special events like Stevenson was doing at Zuni. Frank evidentially figured out how to use the camera and took acceptable field shots of one special event (the Feast of San Antonio, foot races during the feast, and the race preparation area). The local missionary Moore gave Frank her negatives, which are of better quality. The photographs that have survived are listed in table 1.1.[58]

It was an adequate research trip despite the loss of the anthropometric data. Frank had material for several articles. McGee and Powell were satisfied with his effort. Importantly, Russell liked the region; the climate suited his health needs. He felt better. He felt productive. He now believed the Southwest had great potential for him professionally and physically.

Russell had been unsuccessful in one central reason for coming to the Southwest, however: witnessing the famous Hopi summer Niman ceremonies and Snake-Antelope Society rituals, events that quickly came to be required of all American anthropologists. As he told McGee, "I had expected to go to the Moki [Hopi] Reservation, with an Apache and horses, to witness the Snake Dance and flute ceremony but the Apaches [approached to serve as guides] thought they could not be gone for ten days." The trip, he continued, would mean any guide would miss an important Apache medicine ceremony and feast. Should Frank be

FIGURE 1.3. San Antonio Festival march before race to Boulder Lake, showing ritual attire and spectators. September 15, 1898. Photograph by Frank Russell. National Anthropological Archives, Smithsonian Institution, INV 02020100, Neg. 88-16,166, NAA MS 4086.

a heritage tourist at Hopi or an ethnographer at Dulce? "This branch of the tribe holds but one regular feast each year and I do not wish to let the opportunity escape."[59] Frank chose research; he would go to Hopi after the Jicarilla Apache ritual and hope to see one village's Snake-Antelope rituals. He would attend the summer Niman ceremonies another year.

Unfortunately, Russell did not have enough money for the train fare to Winslow, Arizona, nor the funds to hire a teamster, wagon, and team to take him to the Hopi mesas. No Jicarilla Apache man agreed to guide him and no one would steer him to a straight cross-country route. However, he was not deterred. A firm believer in outdoor life and physical fitness, Frank had brought his bicycle to Dulce. He had ridden it to visit informants and attend Jicarilla Apache communal activities. He decided to ride his bicycle across northern New Mexico and Arizona to the Hopi mesas and back, about 700 miles in total. He would find his own route, asking for directions along the way. It would be no more difficult than his Arctic travels.

FIGURE 1.4. San Antonio Festival march before race to Boulder Lake, showing ritual attire and spectators. September 15, 1898. Photograph by Frank Russell. National Anthropological Archives, Smithsonian Institution, INV 02020300, NEG 88-16,162, NAA MS 4086.

Frank left Dulce on August 10 with his camera, a blanket, a change of clothing, rain gear, and enough supplies "to be independent of everything but wood and water." As he told Putnam, he rode through the San Juan River valley before turning southwest to Gallup, New Mexico. From there he cycled to Fort Defiance, Ganado, and Keams Canyon on a long-established trail. He saw Snake Dances at Walpi and Oraibi. He wrote, "I rode the entire distance on my wheel over blind trails, sand, two mountain ranges, and forded the San Juan [River] five times and 'astonished the natives,' both white and red, with the appearance of a bicycle in the back country."[60]

It was a hard trip. Frank's descriptions of the unrelenting heat after hours of pedaling over rocks and sand, resting in boulder shadows at noon, or listening to ravens and thinking they would later pick his corpse clean showed he could complete an adventure as challenging as his Arctic trips. He acknowledged he had often wondered whether he was on the correct trail. In her 1900 journal, Theresa remarked about another worrisome feature of the 1898 trip: the lack of water. For Theresa, Frank's trek to Hopi came to serve as "a glimpse of real hardship, beside which our present outing seems conducted on lines of affect and enervating luxury."[61]

Russell turned his Hopi excursion into a reconnaissance journey, hoping it would lead to future employment with the BAE. He quickly tried to entice McGee with his archaeological potential: "I found some unexplored ruins in the Chuska [Mountains] country and of course saw those at Pueblo Colorado [Kin Tiel], Awatobi, and Moki [Hopi]."[62] This report provided hints about where the Russells would go on their honeymoon.

What Frank did not see on his journey also offered an indication that his and Putnam's relationship may have become strained. Frank passed within 25 miles of the Chaco Canyon excavations (under the direction of George Pepper, an AMNH staff member), where Putnam was working with the Hyde Exploring Company. Work in this area had begun in 1896, under Putnam's oversight and AMNH sponsorship. Apparently, Frank did not stop on his way to or from Hopi. One can think that on the route west he was in a hurry, but there were no such constraints on his return trip. Russell did meet many other individuals, especially Indian traders John Lorenzo Hubbell, Thomas Keam, and George Manning, who would prove to be extremely helpful on his 1900 trip.

Frank returned to the Jicarilla Apache reservation on August 30. Completing his formal research and "rest cure," he boarded a train but went south to Phoenix instead of heading east. His goal was to see if he could set up a field site with the Akimel O'odham (Pima) near Sacaton. McGee was trying to steer Frank to the region to record information on O'odham traditions prior to Spanish contact. Russell proposed a salvage ethnography project to begin in 1899 after he had visited Hopi to see the Niman ceremonies and finished his Jicarilla

Apache research. Hopefully, the BAE would provide field support for two or three months, payable on completion of a manuscript for the *American Anthropologist*. Russell assumed that McGee would be amenable to the scheme, for it was the one McGee had used for the 1898 fieldwork as a way around government hiring rules. And it was one that would have consequences for the rest of Frank's life.

Boston, Fall 1898–Spring 1889

Frank returned to Cambridge, wrote reports, and taught throughout the fall. He was not particularly pleased with his situation. As he told McGee in November, his salary was still the same as it had been as a second-year graduate student. Putnam gave Frank little hope that it would ever be raised significantly, despite his heightened professional worth. His degree and the completion of fieldwork in a new region should have warranted an increase. Russell had an additional grievance. He carried a heavier teaching load than other faculty members; 47 students were enrolled in his introductory anthropology class, while Dixon had only 5. Yet they were both paid the same. The salary was enough for Russell to pay his rent and eat, but he did not feel it was enough for him to consider marrying. And Frank had someone he was interested in.

The lack of discretionary funds also affected Frank's ability to raise money for future research. He was unable to meet McGee at a professional meeting, where he planned to seek a new and larger subvention for 1899 research. He had wanted to hand McGee his 1898 research results and then discuss employment opportunities. Russell knew McGee was more apt to help him following a face-to-face encounter. But Frank was periodically sick as well as poor. He mailed his research photographs on December 10, 1898. Field notes and other records were mailed to Washington, D.C., soon thereafter. His $100 article, "An Apache Medicine Dance," was duly submitted. Frank considered it a "semi-scientific account of about 2,000 words," somewhat akin to his *Scribner's* article, although it had nothing of a daring young hunter's adventures.[63] An article on Jicarilla Apache mythology was slated for the *Journal of American Folk-lore*. Russell hoped that with each submission, whether it was requested or not, McGee would feel compelled to provide him with additional funds. He needed to return to the Southwest if he were to complete any of his research projects.

Russell and McGee continued to think of schemes to obtain BAE support and, hopefully, a permanent job with the federal government. A BAE research job would be ideal; it would allow Frank to spend most of his time in the Southwest. During his times in Washington, D.C., he could teach for a semester each year at Columbian University (George Washington University). Other Smithsonian scholars were following this employment pattern.

But there was a problem. Both Secretary of the Smithsonian, Spencer Baird, and Director Powell were thinking the BAE needed ethnographic coverage in other parts of the country, someone to focus on the Plains, Northwest Coast, or Southeast. These were not climates for a tuberculosis sufferer. In addition, the BAE already had two individuals classified as Southwestern ethnographers, Stevenson and McGee. McGee had no discretionary funds, nor could he assume Powell or Baird would simply approve adding more personnel to the permanent payroll. Baird refused to use his yearly $5,000 reserve from the BAE budget to hire Russell. McGee was not defeated, however. He had thought of a scheme; it would take a year or two to implement, a fact he neglected to tell Frank.

If there was no permanent position, then another period of temporary Southwestern research was in order. McGee decided to pay Russell $100 for an *American Anthropologist* article. McGee had used this approach repeatedly since the late 1890s, primarily to support Franz Boas and his associates. But this time the personnel method would come back to haunt him. As we will discuss later, during a 1903 Smithsonian investigation of the BAE administration, McGee was accused of using federal funds, without proper authorization, to support a private journal.[64] At the moment, Russell welcomed the funds.

Frank was left to his own devices and meager savings again, for he needed to leave Boston for the summer. Putnam, again, did not take him to Chaco Canyon when he returned.[65] We have no indication that Putnam had any funding for him and he did not collect any artifacts this year. Nor are there any photographs in the Peabody Museum. But Frank returned to the Jicarilla Apache reservation and continued his research from the previous year. As a returning outsider, he received a better reception than he had the previous year. He obtained more Jicarilla Apache vocabulary from Grover Cleveland, a student at the Ramona boarding school in Santa Fe. As before, his sent his notes to the BAE for use by their linguists.[66] Apparently he conducted more ethnographic research and collected more folklore. But did he search for sites? Did he try to reconstruct his anthropometric research? Did he even have a camera and film? Unfortunately, we have no more information about this trip or other activities during the year. If Frank kept a journal or sent reports, we have not located them. We do know that on February 7, 1900, Frank gave a lecture on the Hopi Snake Dance at the State University of Iowa. Since he illustrated this with slides, we assume he finally made it to the Hopi mesas, probably seeing the rituals at Oraibi, or he borrowed slides from the Peabody Museum.

By early 1900, Russell knew he had to return to the Southwest, for he was often ill during the fall and winter semester of 1899. This time he would not concentrate solely on the Jicarilla Apache. He did not think additional fieldwork would lead to significant information from the community. At the beginning of his eastern and midwestern lecture tour, Frank went to Washington, D.C. On February 2, he presented "Explorations around the Arctic Circle" for the National Geographic Society. He tried again to talk to McGee, but we do not know if he was successful. In mid-February, Frank wrote McGee requesting money to survey for archaeological sites around Navajo Mountain. This region had been described to him by one of his Harvard undergraduate students, who had journeyed there during the previous fall.[67] No survey had been previously attempted for the area located near the San Juan River and the Arizona-Utah border on the Navajo Reservation. It was accessible by rail, horse, and bicycle. McGee responded that he had no funds but hoped the BAE could eventually be able to employ him.

Frank was not defeated. He was gaining professional prestige. He had just received an invitation from the U.S. Exposition Commission to attend the International Congress of Ethnography, to be held at the 1900 Paris International Exposition, as its official delegate. This was an honor, demonstrating Russell was gaining a well-deserved reputation. He did not go because he did not have the personal funds for the trip and apparently Harvard would not sponsor him.

Frank decided to present a paper on human diversity in North America. But before he could write a good paper, he needed osteological data from the western Puebloan Southwest. There were too few examples from the area in the Peabody's collection of over 2,000 crania to reach statistically valid conclusions using Daniel Brinton's classification system. In addition, Russell wanted new skulls to test his new measurement techniques. He hoped these refinements would increase reliability and decrease sampling error.[68] He had to return to the field and this time concentrate on the archaeological excavation of specific burials. His research in the Southwest would not simply be a rationale for being in a dry climate.

Russell's plan was now to locate large, undisturbed ancestral settlements that had intact burial grounds from which he could collect skeletal materials and associated artifacts. This included places he had heard rumors about in 1898 and probably 1899. He had vague ideas of where the possible sites might be, but knew it would take a month or so of exploration in geographically uncharted areas to locate potentially rich ones. If this failed, Frank could follow in the Mindeleffs' and Fewkes's footsteps and see what they might have missed. He would have to be frugal again. At the last moment, Putnam provided Russell with some money from the Warren Fund for research expenses to obtain human remains and any other artifacts that could be used as a basic research reference collection for the museum.[69] It was thus a Harvard-sponsored collection project.

Putnam's funding would not cover all expenses. Luckily, Frank had saved some money. All he now needed was federal permission. Prior to the passage of the Antiquities Act of 1906, the Indian Service provided permits to researchers who wanted to conduct ethnographic or archaeological research on Indian reservations. Since the Jefferson administration, the commissioner of Indian Affairs had required trappers, traders, miners, and other explorers to fill out questionnaires and report on Indian customs, languages, and prehistoric monuments. The information was often sent to the Smithsonian Institution. Besides collecting basic information, the permitting served another purpose. The Indian Service strove to isolate Natives from Euro-American men of ill-repute who might lead naïve or gullible Indigenous peoples astray from government assimilation policies. At this time, the U.S. government attempted to control all areas of Native life, including whether they were allowed off reservation and with whom they could interact.[70]

Access to Indian reservation sites through permits was thus a long-standing procedure but not one required for access to public lands under other agencies' control. On the day he left Cambridge, through Putnam, Frank sent Commissioner of Indian Affairs William Arthur Jones a request for a permit to excavate archaeological sites on the Hopi and Navajo reservations. Since Russell was a credentialed professional, working under the auspices of a respected institution, he assumed the request was pro forma. He did not feel he needed to wait for an official response or an approval letter. Nor apparently did Putnam, who was on his way back to Chaco Canyon. Neither man checked on the status of their requests.

Frank left Cambridge but did not go directly to the Southwest. He stopped in Iowa to marry his twenty-seven-year-old sweetheart. She was a woman he had known for almost nine years. She must have finally convinced him they could lead an intellectual life together and live frugally on his salary. This meant a new adventure for Theresa, who had never been on an archaeological reconnaissance survey, excavated a site, or camped out. Nor had she ever been to Arizona or anywhere in the West.

Frances Theresa Peet

Compared to Frank, we know little about Theresa Peet's early life but more about her family's background. Frances Theresa Peet was born on May 18, 1873, in Greenfield Springs, Iowa, the eldest child of Adelbert Carlton Peet (1848–1917) and Emma Jane Perkins (1849–1913). Her father, Adelbert, was the son of Gideon N. Peet (d. 1861), an early pioneer of the Fairview, Iowa, area, who homesteaded in 1839. Her grandmother, Cordelia Olivia Wilcox (1816–96), migrated from upstate New York at about the same time and married Gideon in 1840. Theresa's father had two brothers, Collis and Eber, and a sister, Theresa Vernette (later Mrs. Charles T. Myrick). Adelbert's early years were spent on a farm near Fairview and a Greenfield Township homestead of more than 500 acres. Their homes served as the local schools. All these siblings settled in Anamosa as a tight family group.[71]

Theresa's mother, Emma, was the daughter of George and Elizabeth Perkins, who arrived in Anamosa, Iowa, in 1839. We do not know from where the Perkins migrated, but the family was originally from Connecticut. We assume her family homesteaded and farmed. Emma had at least four sisters, two of whom lived in Anamosa as adults, and another in nearby Cedar Rapids. We have not unearthed any information about the fourth.

Emma and Adelbert married on April 4, 1872, and lived on the Peets' farm in Martelle, a rural community in Greenfield Township. Martelle had just been founded in 1872, when the Chicago, Milwaukee, St. Paul, and Pacific Railroad laid tracks through the region. The town had a population of 150 people in 1900, mainly of German, Scottish, and English heritage. Theresa and her siblings would have had little opportunity to encounter Mexicans, Native Americans, or individuals of other ethnic groups during her formative years.[72]

Theresa and her siblings—Delbert Clinton (1875–1932), Ava (1878–82), and Grace Olivia (1883–1948)—would have followed Iowa's typical education path, studying at home and in whatever schools were available in their rural community. Aiming to train future American citizens so that the nation would be stable and prosperous, Iowa communities practiced localism, with school boards setting curricula. Studies varied in quality, for there was a good deal of teacher turnover, in part because wages were so low. Of 28,934 teachers employed in Iowa county schools in 1889, 3,944 had no previous teaching experience and 4,043 had taught for less than one year. While some educators were good and others adequate, most were inexperienced and poorly prepared. How far a student could advance varied by community. There was no high school in Martelle in the 1880s and 1890s; one was not built until 1914. Students would sometimes attend secondary-level classes held in the opera house/saloon sited next to the general store.[73]

This situation was not acceptable to Theresa's parents, who highly valued education. In 1883 they moved to Anamosa, a town with a population of 2,891. Anamosa was home to the Iowa State Penitentiary, a number of limestone quarries, and a regional market. It also had schools, so the Peet children could receive a formal education and there was a good probability they could participate in the community's cultural life. Literacy, music, and understanding the world were particularly important in the Peet household, and all the Peet children graduated from Anamosa's high school with honors.

The Peets were considered a quiet, well-respected family. Adelbert was deemed a man of "highest integrity and upright Christian character."[74] A Republican, he served on the city council for several years. The family attended the Baptist church, and everyone participated in civic events. Emma made sure they took advantage of Chautauqua courses and the Fortnightly Literary Club. As teenagers, Theresa and her siblings gave recitations at holiday events, which were often recorded in the local newspaper's society page. Theresa sang in a girl's quartet and played the piano, serving as the musician for weddings by 1887.

Travel was also appreciated, although not much was undertaken in the early years. Adelbert's mother, who came to live with them in 1890, attended the 1893 World Columbian Exposition with her daughter, Theresa, in Chicago. They brought back many stories to tell Adelbert and Emma's children. What Aunt Theresa told the young Frances Theresa must have sent her dreaming.

Given Theresa's later love of fiction and nonfiction books, and her parents' evident love of learning, we feel assured in concluding they valued advanced education for women as well as men. Emma insisted all her children attend college, and they did. All were supported through college, so they did not have to work.

On to College

When Frank returned to the State University of Iowa for the 1891 fall term, he met entering freshman Frances Theresa Peet. We have no letters or other records to indicate when or how they met. Nor do we know if they developed a passing acquaintanceship or began a growing friendship at this time, but we think the latter is possible. We know that Theresa considered this the beginning of their relationship and that it extended into a long courtship. In her 1900 journal (which can be seen in appendix A), Theresa noted that a July day in 1891 was their "Ninth Anniversary."

There is little record of Theresa's academic activities during her undergraduate years. She took a humanities and classics course of study and majored in English. This meant she took composition courses that focused on expressive correctness more than creative writing. There would have been classes in journalism, debate, pedagogy, rhetoric, oration, and drama. We can guess Theresa would have focused on philosophy and literature, including historical studies and the cultivation of critical skills and good taste.

We know much more about Theresa's social activities. She joined Kappa Kappa Gamma, a national sorority, and remained a member for her entire life.[75] She was also a member of the Daughters of the American Revolution chapter, as she had been in Anamosa. During her senior year, she was student president of the YWCA in Iowa City. She played Ophelia in 1893 as a member of the theater club, and *The Daily Citizen* reviewer said, "it was a very pleasing part."[76] She often attended dances and her presence was noted in dozens of newspaper accounts. For example, at an art opening and ball at the Amory Hall in 1892 she wore a cream China silk dress. She must have been pleased that her good taste was noted; she certainly was interested in proper attire in her 1900 journal. She also served as the mail carrier at a fundraiser the following Valentine's Day, delivering "precious messages" to would-be lovers. She was a frequent guest at Phi Delta Theta events.[77]

FIGURE 1.5. Frances Theresa Peet Russell, ca. 1920. Photographer unknown. Courtesy Stanford University Library, Frances Theresa and Frank B. Russell (SC0166). Department of Special Collections and University Archives, Stanford University Libraries, Neg. No. BP-3616.

Theresa was smart and quickly recognized as a budding scholar. As early as her freshman year, she won a declamation contest. She composed a blank verse poem, "The Senior," for their graduation ceremony that *The Iowa City Daily Republican* reporter said was "another evidence of her brilliant mastery of the power of words." Two days earlier at Campus Day literary program, she "recited an original poem of remarkable artistic beauty and polish."[78] She graduated with an honors degree, earning a bachelor of philosophy on June 13, 1895, the same day Frank was awarded his master of science degree. Theresa was elected to Phi Beta Kappa, an honor Frank had not accomplished. Her program of study required research and a thesis and was considered a pre-doctoral degree. Since she had taken several graduate courses, her degree was considered a graduate degree, the equivalent of earning a BA and MA simultaneously.

We can assume Theresa was beginning to aspire to a life of scholarship, although she might not have articulated her ultimate aspirations to be an employed professor at the time. And if there were no jobs for men, there were also none for women. Only independently wealthy people could spend their time in a life of leisured scholarship and intellectual debate in the late 1890s. Theresa and her family were not rich. If she wanted to study and write full time, she needed to marry into a wealthy family. We have no indication this was ever a possibility. There were no accounts in any local or regional newspapers in this period announcing her engagement or even who she was accompanying to dances if she were officially courting. One newspaper account said she returned to Anamosa with her parents the day after graduation, just as Frank left for Cambridge.[79] Theresa needed a job. As is the case for many English and philosophy majors today, her degree had not trained her for practical employment. What was open to her was secretarial work, manual labor, life with a relative serving as a nanny, or teaching. We know that Theresa had not taken any course in specialized educational training for a teaching certificate even though a few courses were offered at the university. But this was not critical.

Theresa did what many other educated women have done: she taught school. As Frank pursued his graduate work and traveled to Greenland, Theresa served as principal of Villisca High School, located in eastern Iowa, near Omaha, from the fall of 1895 to the summer of 1898. The job title meant she was the main teacher for the institution and also performed administrative duties. She received county certification. We have no evidence she took the state certification examination, although she would most certainly have easily passed, for the tests were designed to be taken by someone without a college education. The position provided a monthly salary of $31 per month for women (as opposed to the $39 men earned).[80] According to historian Keach Johnson, the average grade school teacher taught no longer than four years due to the low pay. Theresa's three years was typical.

At Radcliffe

Given the low wages, it is doubtful Theresa saw teaching secondary school as a life choice. And Theresa wanted something more intellectually demanding than life in Anamosa. She saved her money and this opened up a new opportunity. In the academic year of 1898–99, she took graduate courses in English literature, psychology, and philosophy at Radcliffe College, a women's liberal arts college affiliated with Harvard. Radcliffe began hosting classes taught by Harvard faculty in the 1880s as the Harvard Annex; its first degree was awarded in 1894, when the institution was formally chartered.[81] It was not cheap. Tuition was $200 per year and there were living expenses. Luckily, Theresa had been exceedingly frugal for the previous three years. It was an exceedingly wise decision.

Radcliffe accepted Theresa's degree, probably because she remained in the same field. She did not have to redo her senior year, as Putnam required of Frank. She took four lecture and seminar classes per semester. There was a wealth to choose from in classics, contemporary literature, economics, history, and the sciences. We know from her 1900 journal that Theresa did not take Spanish or Italian but began to study psychology. According to Radcliffe's annual report for 1898–1900, Theresa would have taken courses with famous scholars, including George Kittredge (Shakespeare), George Baker (nineteenth-century drama), George Santayana (ethical thought), William Schofield (comparative literature), and William James (philosophy of nature and psychology). The association with James was especially important for Theresa, influencing how she came to see the world. In fact, Theresa came to be considered one of James's most faithful students. We can imagine that she spent evenings with him and his family, engaging in the witty intellectual discourse she loved. The relationship between James and his wife and Theresa grew over the years and was especially important after Frank's death.[82]

We assume Theresa chose Radcliffe to be with Frank as well as for the education she would receive. We cannot know for sure because no correspondence between Frank and Theresa has survived. Boston was more intellectually and socially stimulating than Iowa and offered a life unavailable for the budding scholar in her home. They probably courted during the academic year and attended concerts, lectures, and plays. They visited museums and went to James's or Putnam's houses together for salons and special dinners. Unfortunately, Frank was laid low by bouts of tuberculosis, and Theresa would have spent many hours nursing him when his fever raged. This does not mean that Theresa did little but nurse Frank. Their daily lives were distinct, for Radcliffe had separate dormitories and dining facilities from Harvard. They also moved in discrete intellectual worlds. A review of the membership lists of Frank's scholarly associations did not reveal Theresa's name. She was not apparently interested in anthropology, natural history, folklore, or ethnic studies.

Return to Iowa

After completing her studies, Theresa returned to Iowa and resumed teaching for the 1899–1900 school year. She did not have the funds to remain a second year and pursue a thesis for a formal second master's degree. We assume that this would have been her desire if she had had the money. This would also have allowed her to stay near Frank. Theresa's increase in credentials seems to not have led to a more prestigious job; she became the assistant principal of Anamosa's high school. She lived in her parents' home, as was considered appropriate for an unmarried woman. This would have saved Theresa money, although she contributed to the household economy. She was apparently respected as "a lady of many accomplishments," who was "an exceptionally talented and refined young lady and a great favorite with all who know her."[83]

Theresa did not apparently decide to pursue a career as a professional writer, poet, essayist, or journalist. We have found no early articles written under her name, although this does not preclude a pen name. She did not intend to follow the path of public education service. She had decided to marry Frank. We think that Frank was the only person she had ever considered marrying, based on comments in her 1900 journal. But again we have no collaborating correspondence from the period so we cannot be sure. The same appears true of Frank. To the best of our knowledge, Theresa was the only woman and intellectual partner with whom he ever considered spending his life. Their union was a marriage that allowed Theresa to pursue one of her life goals—to live in a university community and be a scholar. Marriage was a feasible option to independent employment in a low-paying profession that had little opportunity for advancement, even if her new husband was not wealthy. But it also meant that Frank's career and health took center stage.

Chapter 2

An Archaeological Survey, 1900-Style

Frank and Theresa had been married two days when they arrived in Gallup, New Mexico. They had wed at Theresa's Anamosa home, which had been "prettily decorated with ferns, vines, palms and smilax, the drawing room in green and white, the library in yellow and white, the dining room in pink and white."[1] The service began at 4:00 p.m.; Reverend W. E. Glanville presided under a bridal arch. Seventy friends and relatives attended the ceremony. State University of Iowa professors and Theresa's sorority sisters attended, but none of Frank's siblings, parents, or relatives were there. The local newspaper reported, "At 7:10 the bridal couple took the west-bound train en route for Arizona, where the honeymoon will be spent in investigations of ancient Indian life." The newlyweds were accompanied to the station by friends who "showered them with rice and tossed in a few old shoes for good luck."[2]

Now it was 3:00 a.m. on July 3, 1900, and their busman's honeymoon had officially begun. It was the first day of what would be a three-and-a half-year camping adventure in Arizona, interspersed with brief periods of academic residence on the East Coast, where Frank had his permanent, if low-paying, job. Their time in Cambridge constituted periods of intense scholarly work—teaching, writing, data preparation, and scientific analysis—as well as the activities undertaken by a middle-class urban couple. The trips to Arizona were times of convalescence and strenuous outdoor climatic therapy combined with difficult travel to explore uncharted areas. These would constitute a series of archaeological reconnaissance surveys. The 1900 survey was a different kind of endeavor, one designed to answer a suite of research questions.

Research Questions to Pursue in Tusayan

Descending from an Atchison, Topeka and Santa Fe Railway car, the newlyweds stepped into the world of the scientist-explorer searching for new information. For Frank, it was a continuation of his bicycle trip to Hopi. For Theresa, it was an entry into a new world. They would locate the human remains of the ancient Pueblo people, who are today referred to as the Ancestral Puebloans, Western

Pueblos, or the Kayenta Pueblos. The research would advance Frank's study of physical diversity in North American human populations.

There was much to learn. Were all the region's Puebloans and Cliff Dwellers members of the same population or were there differences based on locale? Were the ancestors of each contemporary Pueblo members of one or several demographic groups? Did physical differences indicate social diversity? Did social units correlate with the cultural distinctions indicated by pottery styles? Were Puebloans like other Native peoples in North America or could regional distinctiveness be seen in human remains? Specifically, what about those who had lived in the Province of Tusayan?

By 1900 the Province of Tusayan—a name for the Hopi villages and their surrounding traditional use areas—had been established in historical literature for nearly 350 years. In 1540 the governor of Mexico sent Francisco Vásquez de Coronado and a large entourage to seek out the rumored Province of Cibola, thought to be one of the legendary "golden cities" that so fascinated Spanish imaginations from the 1490s until the late 1500s. Cibola turned out to be several Zuni pueblos. The Zuni told Coronado about the Province of Tusayan to the northwest, and Coronado sent Captain Don Pedro de Tovar to investigate. He found Hopi villages on and around the southern fingers of Black Mesa but no signs of gold. Subsequently, Cibola and Tusayan became firmly established names in histories of Spanish and Indian relations and later Euro-American and Indian relations in the American Southwest.[3]

In 1870 Powell spent three weeks studying the Hopi. He published "The Ancient Province of Tusayan" in *Scribner's Monthly*. Thereafter, he was fascinated by the Tusayan region and ensured that his staff worked there. In 1881, after becoming USGS director, he sent his cartographer, A. L. Webster, to map the Hopi mesas and surrounding area. The published "Map of the Province of Tusayan" showed the Hopi mesas but presented no boundaries for the region since none had ever been drawn historically. The subsequent legal boundary between the Hopi and surrounding Navajo lands was not firmly established by the Office of Indian Affairs or the General Land Office for many years. When these were, they did not correspond with the scientific concept of where Cibola sites ended and Tusayan sites began. In the 1880s, Powell ordered Victor and Cosmos Mindeleff to make detailed studies of the architecture of Zuni ("Cibola") and Hopi ("Tusayan") architecture; their classic report was Russell's main guide for seeking potential burial sites. Powell hired Jesse Walter Fewkes to continue the BAE's Southwestern archaeology program in 1895. Fewkes concentrated on Tusayan, aided by the talented amateur ethnographer Alexander Stephen, who lived on First Mesa, combining ethnographic and archaeological work. In 1896 Fewkes published a summary of his work to date, "The Prehistoric Culture of Tusayan."[4]

Thus, by the time Russell was planning his 1900 archaeological survey, the term *Province of Tusayan* as a label for Hopi Country was well established in the historical, geological, and anthropological literature. This enabled Frank to ask specific questions. Were the Hopi the Ancestral Pueblo's in situ descendants? Could physical distinctions reveal specific clans and possibly their migrations within the region? Did the osteological evidence support the oral history and legends Fewkes and Stephen had collected? Where were the most likely sites that could provide additional information?

These questions were similar to the ones Russell had addressed when analyzing the Trenton Gravel human remains: Was there evidence of a direct association between ancient skeletons and historic Delaware tribes? There was. Based on this result, Frank hypothesized he would find a similar direct association in Arizona between ancient Tusayan and contemporary Hopi. He did not believe popular speculations that the Hopi were Aztec descendants, a Lost Tribe of Israel, or any other far-fetched origin story constructed by settlers. Russell hoped his research would help lay those conjectures to rest, just as Fewkes was aiming to do.[5]

The relationship between archaeological sites and historic Native Americans had been at the forefront of North American archaeological and historical scholarship since the late 1790s.[6] The USNM's Cyrus Thomas had been assigned by Powell from 1880 to 1900 to investigate the Mound Builder regions. He wrote that several dedicated men were working on these issues.

> The investigative spirit of the age will not brook delay; wherever there is an unbroken field some scientific plow is sure to enter, though but poorly equipped for the work. However, of late years more strict methods of approaching the many problems involved have been introduced, and now, instead of attempting by imagination or theorizing to reach conclusions at once, slow and patient investigation is the process pursued. The spade has to a large extent replaced the pen, and instead of building theories chiefly by imagination, there is a careful sifting of all the evidence which appears to have any bearing on the subject. The fragments of data are fitted together and tentative theories deduced simply as a plan of further progress, often however to be cast aside or modified, as new material, which will not readily drop into place, is discovered.[7]

Powell and Putnam considered discovering Puebloan origins crucial.[8] Both men felt that Frank could provide information to solve two taxonomic issues: (1) identifying and delineating precontact societies before hypothesizing which were ancestral to specific contemporary tribes and (2) understanding intraregional and interregional variation. Once these were established, regional and specific culture histories could be reconstructed without speculation. The classificatory information about populations would be used for discussions of cultural and social development, to correlate with variables, such as environmental constraints and opportunities, and provide evidence for cultural continuity, change, diffusion, and settlement patterns.

Thomas's quest for evidence meant learning all researchers could from archaeological sites and creating a narrative of what life was like in a localized area. Russell, however, had a narrower goal. He wanted to learn about the people themselves, their physical natures. To do this, he needed anthropometric measurements from each of the historic, pottery-producing Pueblo societies he had visited in 1898 and 1899. Every community refused to be measured and was opposed to disturbing their deceased ancestors. Russell had no intention of being a grave robber, sneaking into villages and churchyards at night, unlike army physician and physical anthropologist Robert Shufeldt.[9] This meant he had to discretely seek archaeological burials at sites that he considered to be distinct from the graveyards of contemporary communities. He asked knowledgeable Hopi, like Fewkes's collaborator, Tom Polacca, for assistance.

Focusing on late precontact and Spanish-contact period sites had additional benefits besides identifying and delineating distinct human populations. Russell hoped to place new sites on the Tusayan map. He aimed to categorize these, as he identified the ones needing to be excavated more fully. He would collect whole ceramic vessels and sherds associated with burials. The ceramics would later be used in seriation studies, to determine the relative ages of pottery types for use as chronological indicators.[10] The pottery the Russells collected would, ultimately, contribute to future studies as part of a growing cumulative database used for pattern recognition analyses.

Scholars in 1900 classified ceramics based on design. They named types using background and decoration color, followed by design placement. In addition, the motifs and design elements—and, to a lesser extent, materials, form, manufacturing technique, hypothesized use, and surface finish—were considered diagnostic. To the basic designation they affixed a place-name. Researchers used stylistic variation as a basis for establishing—and hopefully actually identifying—cultural and social units. They asked two questions of their ceramic typologies: (1) did each social group produce culturally distinctive styles and (2) were these styles population identity markers?

This exercise required many examples from multiple places and contextual information about where each sherd was obtained. The protocol was straightforward. A field researcher collected pieces of all pottery types found at a site. Often researchers did not record where within a site the sherds had been found. What was considered important in terms of provenience was the geographical location of the site. Hopefully, each specimen was labeled by site for future reference, but this was not always done. Even Russell gave sherds to the Peabody Museum with no location information, just the general area.

The artifacts were arranged in groups based on stylistic similarities and compared to sherds in existing collections to determine if the design style had been previously defined. If not, the researcher named the ceramic style and published a research note describing it and its geographical location. Pottery types were assigned to time periods: *prehistoric, transition* or *contact era*, and *historic*.[11] Researchers had begun to sort these types in sequences, but this exercise was still in its infancy in 1900. Southwestern researchers who created catalogues of ceramic collections used W. H. Holmes's model as an organizing framework. This included the method of production as well as style.[12]

As pottery types were defined and culture areas based on environment and geographic area established, questions about spatial occurrence became more refined. By 1900 researchers could ask basic distributional questions, for example, where did the makers of black-on-white pottery decorated with style *x* live? Russell took this inquiry another step. He was hopeful he would be able to correlate human remains with pottery styles to help identify specific populations. This meant that the human remains he would find would vary with changes in pottery types through time. Frank just had to ensure he collected pottery sherds at each site where he exhumed burials, and hope that there was only one time period represented at a site.

Where was the best place to look for these human remains? Could Frank locate sites that had not been excavated or looted, the skeletons destroyed and the bones scattered? And how should he and Theresa proceed with such limited funds and so little time? They could not waste it aimlessly wandering. They had only two months and a few days before they had to be back in Cambridge.

Where to Survey in Tusayan

Frank followed a plan that reflected the type of information he needed to address his research problem. His key need was for human skeletons and skulls from multiple sites in different places (and hopefully from both prehistoric and historic time periods). This required looking in more than one place. Russell had to guess where he was likely to find remains, at what type of site, and where these sites were located. These guesses were influenced by what predecessors had found, what they had published, and what they were willing to tell him about what they had not yet published. It also was based on what locals knew and were willing to tell and Frank's analytical abilities to make educated guesses.

Russell had two basic choices for his research exploration plan: (1) he could conduct a survey to see what he could find on the surface of untouched sites or (2) he could excavate a few sites known to have well-preserved burials. By 1900 several Tusayan sites had been excavated by Jesse Walter Fewkes and Walter

Hough. Others had been recorded by Victor and Cosmos Mindeleff, James and Matilda Coxe Stevenson, and John Wesley Powell. Caves and shrines had also been explored.[13] The archaeologists from the Field Museum were excavating and surveying as well. There had been and still was a lot of activity. Much had already been done. Ideally, Russell needed sites where nothing had been disturbed. Almost all known sites, however, appeared to have been looted for artifacts for sale in the growing antiquities market. Maybe he should look in more isolated areas?

The survey approach had the advantage of finding unknown sites but the disadvantage of requiring weeks of constant travel without the promise of any results. The second approach had the advantage that Frank and Theresa could travel relatively quickly to known ruins, even though it was likely they would have been picked over and skeletons destroyed. In this case, they had to hope there were undisturbed sections at the known sites. There was another disadvantage to this approach. To reuse the leftovers of other researchers was not something Russell would have found desirable. It would not enhance his reputation. Scientist-explorers were expected to uncover something new. He needed the scientific newness he had encountered in the Subarctic and Arctic to make a name for himself in the new region.

Frank would not have considered spending an entire summer excavating a single site, worried about provenience control, or meticulously searching for everything one could learn from a single site.[14] Concentrating on a single site would not provide evidence for his research problem, nor was he equipped to undertake such a project with only his wife and three assistants. He needed both entire skeletons and skulls from multiple sites located in several Tusayan subregions for his comparison study.[15] This required a reconnaissance survey that ideally searched areas no archaeologist had explored—Navajo Mountain, Shonto, northern Black Mesa, Cedar Mesa, the Chuska Mountains—in the hopes of finding pristine sites. These he would quickly trench, extracting the burials and type ceramics. He would return to work intensively in 1901. It was a strategy aimed at job security and meant to establish Frank as a regional authority.

Frank's second option was to search areas known to contain aboveground pueblos where burials had been exhumed (for example, Antelope Mesa). No area had been completely surveyed. Under either option, Russell would only search for a certain kind of site. He reasoned it would be in large, multiroomed communities he would find burials rather than in small communities of fewer than 100 rooms. And he thought that cliff dwellings were not as likely to have easy-to-uncover burials. He searched for sites built on level ground in valleys or on mesas.

If these two search schemes failed, Frank had a third option: visit selected places (such as Awatovi or Fire House) where the Mindeleffs had sketched multiunit structures or Fewkes and Hough had excavated and hope some intact burials still remained.

Russell was not starting from terra incognita, and what others had done was of great help. Sites had been identified by Euro-American explorers since 1846, beginning with the reports of the U.S. Army Corps of Topographical Engineers as they surveyed the newly acquired American Southwest. When Congress established the Bureau of Ethnology in 1879, Powell launched an ethnographic and archaeological survey program in the Puebloan areas. As mentioned earlier, he specifically sent Victor and Cosmos Mindeleff to locate and map ruins inhabited by Hopi and Zuni ancestors. These were the types of sites that should contain the burials Russell desired to search.[16]

Others had already been to Tusayan and were moving into other areas of Arizona. The most important for Russell was that conducted under the privately funded Hemenway Southwestern Archaeological Expedition (1886–94). Frank Hamilton Cushing led a major excavation and survey program in the Salt River Basin in south and central Arizona—in the same general area Frank and Theresa would survey in 1901 and 1902. For the last couple of years of the initiative, Fewkes took over for an ill Cushing and concentrated on ethnographic collecting on the Hopi Reservation. The archaeological and ethnographic collections went to Harvard University in 1895 after being shown at the Madrid and Chicago international expositions.[17] Since they were never unpacked but only placed in storage, Russell probably did not consult the artifacts. There were reports he could have read.

Simultaneously, with the help of Alexander Stephen and Walter Hough, Fewkes launched a Tusayan excavation program that continued for decades. It began in 1894, when the Smithsonian's George Brown Goode convinced Powell to hire Fewkes, at first on a contract basis and later as a permanent staff member. Fewkes aimed to understand Hopi clan migrations and associations with places identified in legends. A prolific writer, he had published several reports by 1900, which Frank read. Russell asked Fewkes where he should go before he left for Arizona. Fewkes gave him a starting point: the northern part of the Hopi Mesas as well as along the Little Colorado River (called Colorado Chiquito in Theresa's texts). He needed to head for Black Mesa and from there to Navajo Mountain.[18]

Russell had a general field plan to ensure that he would not haphazardly ride around before stumbling on a potential site—if they were lucky. He could not structure their route before arriving at Hubbell Trading Post, however. He needed to talk to local residents and travelers. Local knowledge and residents' willingness to share information were critical to Frank's search strategy. It was needed not only to identify possible site locations but to find routes for a heavily laden wagon to approach them. Frank also had to learn where to find water and animal forage. He initially received a fair amount of information, some of it useful, some not. Much was conflicting, as both Frank and Theresa would record repeatedly in their journals.[19]

Collecting Human Remains in Tusayan

As can be seen throughout his journal entries, Russell thought collecting human remains a questionable activity but one necessary for the study of demography and mortuary practices. Exhumation was an activity Native people generally opposed but neither looters nor archaeologists really considered yet alone privileged Indigenous cultural rules about desecration.[20] Frank's journal entries and letters show he knew that his excavation activities were questionable. Yet he always acted with the belief that science's need for evidence to solve questions of human origins, race, and human variability overrode other ethical concerns.

Scientific privilege was a common assertion in 1900. It served as a rationalization when people questioned the morality and appropriateness of research acts. Few practitioners acknowledged that Indigenous peoples had claims that superseded Caucasian-generated scientific interests, as historian Ann Fabian has shown in her seminal study *The Skull Collectors: Race, Science, and America's Unburied Dead*. It was recognized that to simply take remains was as dangerous, if not illegal, as it was to disinter bodies in Christian settler graveyards. Native people actively fought to save their ancestors. For example, according to Franz Boas, who worked on the U.S. Northwest Coast and adjacent Canada, "It is a rather perilous business to procure Indians' skulls. . . . The Natives are so jealous of you that they watch you very closely while you are wandering near their mausoleums & instant & sanguinary vengeance would fall upon the luckless, who would presume to interfere with the sacred relics. . . . [It is] most unpleasant work to steal bones from a grave, but what is the use, someone has to do it."[21] Boas further noted opportunities due to the decimation of Indian populations: "There is an epidemic raging among them which carries them off so fast that the cemeteries will soon lack watchers. I don't rejoice in the prospects of death of the poor creatures, certainly, but then you know it will be very convenient for my purposes." Boas collected more than 100 complete skeletons and 200 skulls. He sold them to the Field Museum and to Berlin anthropologists; he also used the anthropometric data for his Columbia University classes in statistical analysis.

Whatever Russell thought about the wishes, cultural norms, or "feelings" of his Indigenous research subjects, he likely assumed American Indians would soon be either assimilated into American society or cease to exist as distinctive societies. As a result, they could be ignored collectively and individually. Euro-American culture's needs took precedence. Russell assumed "primitive" peoples around the world did not have the same sensibilities toward burials as "civilized" peoples. They did not bury the deceased in recognizable cemeteries, where families owned the land. Their burials were not cared for by the community but allowed to decompose organically. Therefore, he reasoned, Indigenous human remains could be conceptualized as abandoned, just like the materials left in shrines. The collecting logic at the time then argued that since Native peoples had treated bodies and sacred materials as abandoned, Euro-Americans should "rescue" them. It was collectors' duty to take remains and artifacts to museums where they could be cared for properly and "saved" for future generations.

This was not the case, of course. Native families knew where their ancestors were buried and respected them according to their own cultural norms.[22] They avoided the power of the places in order to let them return to the earth naturally. Frank knew this, just as he knew he would face opposition because he was stopping an organic process. His attitudes lay firmly with science as a noble quest, one needed by American society so it could continue to develop. And it was a quest to which everyone, including Indigenous peoples, should yield.

Theresa seems to have had no prior feelings about these issues but followed Frank's assessment of the scientific need for a complete evidentiary database located at the Peabody Museum in order for him to discuss human physical diversity. Indeed, she calls her *Out West* series "In Pursuit of a Graveyard." Her only indication that what they were undertaking was questionable was that it was strange to sleep on a cot atop boxes of bones. It was something she had never envisioned happening, just as she had never thought that all burials were not the same. Who knew that every culture did not use six-foot-long wooden coffins?[23]

Frank was not the only individual collecting human remains on the Colorado Plateau or the Rio Grande Valley. Collections of human remains had been made throughout the Ancestral Pueblo homelands by several institutions. Noting where his Peabody Museum or AMNH contemporaries had recently gone helped Frank determine where he should search. The most important was avoiding Ales Hrdlička, then working for the AMNH, under Putnam's direction.

Hrdlička had excavated skeletal remains from the Mancos area near Mesa Verde and the Animas River valley in September 1899.[24] He also spent eight days at Kin-bi-iola—a great house 12 miles from Pueblo Bonito in Chaco Canyon—and uncovered at least 50 graves. He gathered associated burial goods and made an extensive photographic collection of petroglyphs. Gathering these skeletons, as well as obtaining body measurements on living populations, was a goal for Putnam, as he told his colleague Washington Matthews.

> Dr. Hrdlička and his party have been very successful in their anthropometric work among the different tribes of New Mexico taking in the different groups of Apache, the various Pueblo tribes, the Navajo and now the Utes. They have also made a hundred or more casts of different individuals and many hundred photographs. Hrdlička has made full measurements of two or three hundred individuals in each tribe; so, we are getting pretty good data for comparing the present people with those who lived in the past. For this purpose, we have also obtained several hundred skeletons from the various regions: cliff houses, caves,

> ruined pueblos so you see we are making a very thorough and exhaustive study of the whole region past and present.[25]

Hrdlička thought the overall collections were "quite fair" but "not what I should wish them to be." There were few skulls: rats had caused extensive damage to the crania, which physical anthropologists thought were the most diagnostic part of the body. Hrdlička explained, "Notwithstanding all this I think I will be able from what I got and from what was obtained before to be able to reach some definite conclusion as to the physical character of the ancient Pueblos."[26]

Since the Peabody Museum had few human remains from Tusayan, Russell intended to add to its two reference collections of skulls and skeletons needed for craniological and anthropometric research. With this geographical focus, he would not duplicate Hrdlička's AMNH work. However, Hrdlička's incredibly productive 1899 field season created expectations. The manner and speed with which he worked became an all but impossible model for Russell to emulate. Hrdlička had created a high benchmark in terms of the number of human remains Russell should exhume if he wanted his field research to be considered a success. That meant excavating as many burials as possible in numerous sites, gently removing them from the ground so they would not disintegrate, carefully brushing the soil from each bone, cataloguing and inventorying each skeleton, and boxing the remains as a set with any grave goods so they would not be mixed in when they reached the Peabody Museum. And Russell had to do this without the assistants Hrdlička had on his well-funded expedition.

Another major problem Frank encountered by concentrating on burials was pot-hunting. As mentioned earlier, large sites had been extensively looted by Euro-Americans, Mexican Americans, Navajos, Hopis, Utes, and Southern Paiutes seeking intact pottery to sell to traders. The traders, in turn, sold the pottery, as well as ethnographic artifacts, to collectors and museums in both North America and Europe. The business had been booming for two decades.[27] When looters took pots, they scattered the fragile human remains. Frank needed whole specimens, hence his search for undisturbed graves. Several entries in his journal mention that when he, Theresa, and their companions came upon a possible site, they found scattered bones that frequently crumbled when touched. There was nothing to take back to the Peabody Museum.

Trenching Sites, 1900-Style

Theresa had no idea how one found a burial or trenched a site. They were certainly not marked with headstones as in a Boston or Amarosa graveyard, and one did not simply use a shovel to dig up a coffin. As Willey and Sabloff note in their history of Americanist archaeology, there were few standardized ways to excavate a site in 1900. The techniques used at Harvard, however, were state of the art for the time. In the interest of thoroughness, Putnam used the systematic "Peabody Museum method" to excavate Ohio Hopewell mounds. He first mapped the site, then laid out trenches with straight side walls, beginning at the base of the mound and moving inward. He took photographs and measured as he progressed. He noted in situ provenance of artifactual materials. He followed a similar method when he worked in the American Southwest at Chaco Canyon, using masonry walls as orientation features.[28]

Russell knew Putnam's techniques and how they varied for different kinds of sites. In his Harvard Anthro 4: Prehistoric Archaeology-European Ethnology course lecture on November 5, 1902, Frank presented the proper methodology for cave excavations. The deposits should be divided into blocks one foot deep and three feet square. Materials should be removed in layers. For open sites, one first walked around the entire settlement and made an orientation map. Next one sketched and measured the room blocks and buildings, starting with the exterior structures, plotting them in relation to each other. As with a mound, one worked toward the site's center. Surface artifacts were plotted on the maps as well.[29]

Table 3.1 illustrates that abstract theory and practical application were not always the same.[30] For most objects he removed, Russell noted the name of the site and, if the site was complex, whether items were taken from within a structure, outside a structure, or near a structure. He noted if material came from a cemetery, by which he meant a readily apparent burial area. In many cases, he simply noted that a ceramic sherd came from "a site near Hopi." In a few cases, he provided no provenance at all. While we have not found Frank's complete orientation maps, we know that he made basic site plans for his important or named sites. Some still remain in the Peabody Museum collection files. Whether he plotted more than room blocks and noted the location of the human remains is not known.

When a site looked as if it had potential, Russell probed with poles. If he found artifacts or bones, he quickly dug holes or trenches, extracted what was found, and moved on.[31] Again, we have located no in situ drawings, but this does not mean they did not exist at one time. We expect Frank did not take excavation photographs, saving his precious film for contextual landscapes. Given his artistic skills in scientific illustration, we expect he made drawings of at least part of the excavation areas. If he did, they have not survived nor have any written site notes.

Russell knew how to do a careful job. He just did not follow his own instructions on his frantic busman's honeymoon. We think we know why. He sought numerous intact skeletal remains, and he collected as quickly as possible. He rushed. He probably assumed he would fill in the contextual aspect of his data later—but never did. As a result, he reverted to exploration archaeology techniques—simply taking what one could find and ignoring everything else. Thinking one would have time to "fix" or "complete" notes later was risky. Life often got in the way. In this case it would be Frank's tuberculosis.

We obtained a basic idea of how Russell worked from his description of how he approached a large site in 1901. The locale was "Old San Rafael," located in the San Rafael River valley, about five miles north of the Arizona-Sonora border. Searching for ceramic sherds, Russell created a series of test pits up to five feet deep in the middle of a mound. If he found a wall or other feature, he continued. If not, he started another small pit seeking something interesting. In 1900 that would have been human remains or pottery.[32] This technique left a series of holes across the site's surface. He did not take the time to backfill.

Archaeological excavation techniques were reflected in the way resulting collections were organized once placed in a museum. Ideally each artifact was given a separate inventory number. These were recorded on a master list. Preferably these identifying numbers were assigned to an artifact or set of skeletal remains while in the field, hopefully at the end of each day. Frank and Theresa sometimes did this, sometimes not. We do not know why Frank did not rigorously follow the advice he gave students because to not follow protocol led to confusion when unlabeled artifacts were analyzed in the laboratory. We think he was tired and sicker than his or Theresa's journals indicated, and that living and travel tasks required much of his precious energy. Also, leaving one site in an afternoon to move to the next before dark meant that Frank never caught up with his record keeping. And unfortunately, whatever inventories were produced in Arizona have not been retained with the collections.

The result was that the artifacts and human remains Frank and Theresa collected are poorly labeled. There is little indication of where in each site specimens came from. The number of potsherds used for establishing ceramic types does indicate one of the participants looked at each shovelful of dirt. His equipment purchases do not indicate he had a screen or sieve, tools Putnam was using by the mid-1880s. Again, haste is indicated. Once the group reached a site, they worked as quickly as possible because they had spent so much time searching. One can see this documented in how Theresa describes her experiences. Living and traveling are her major topics in her journal rather than archaeological activities like digging or record keeping.

The Neophyte Archaeologist and Camper

As noted earlier, Frank had learned to be an archaeologist through guided learning, advice from mentors, and actual practice. Theresa had no archaeological or travel experience. Now it was her turn to learn how to be a wilderness explorer and camper as well as an archaeological spouse. Moving from neophyte to experienced professional involved a four-stage process. One had to learn to: (1) travel in a wilderness, travel over land without roads, and see it with new eyes; (2) plot a survey and recognize potential sites; (3) test sites, exhume bodies, catalogue and transport artifacts; and (4) analyze and interpret using a new paradigm, one often at odds with Theresa's beliefs. Her training was essentially an experiential apprenticeship with Frank as her teacher and guide. In her journal, Theresa concentrated on the activities in the first stage. She described how she learned to cope without the taken-for-granted comforts of home. The most important of her new skills was how to search for water and coax a mule up a steep grade. The second was how to live without daily baths. This required Theresa to rethink her standards of cleanliness. Another skill was how not to become lost, but if one did, how not to panic. Theresa wrote of her survival education slowly eliminating initial helplessness. When she had no chores to perform on her first day, she explored with a curious child and found new animals.

Theresa also had to learn to "see archaeologically," what Frank called "keen watchfulness."[33] Through discussions with Frank as they traveled, Theresa learned about landscape features and their names but needed repetitive experience to efficiently read the land to distinguish camouflaged sites from rock outcrops. These were not skills Theresa could acquire from the prized books she had brought. Early in the trip, Frank would explore while Theresa remained with the wagon and read. Soon bored, she began to care for the horses and mules, and then took short walks to possible sites as her body adjusted to the heat. Frank was hesitant about Theresa's forays at first. He had to learn that Euro-American women were not frail. This gender competence would be a theme in Theresa's writings, one she highlighted when she watched Mormon women free a wagon stuck in the sand. Theresa never complained, even when acquiring skills constituted a hard lesson. By the end of the trip, she saw herself as competent, able to traverse an arid land, but never an autonomous archaeologist. She was always the competent assistant.

Crucial lessons in archaeological practice were poking a pole in likely places, then exhuming and finally caring for what been extracted. Rather than learn excavation techniques, Theresa learned photography using the smaller of their two cameras. One can generally identify her pictures, because they are of people rather than generic landscapes or site walls. Theresa also became enamored with pictographs late on the trip and recorded many panels. Unlike other archaeological, geographical, or naturalist wives on survey expeditions, she did not collect plants, animals, or birds. Theresa was not interested in becoming a botanist, ornithologist, or zoologist. Nor did she eventually care for the camp, another common activity assigned to scientists' spouses, even after Frank fired some of his Navajo and Mexican assistants. As she jokingly wrote in her journal, she could never cook and apparently never would have passed that archaeological field school rite of passage, learning how to make edible biscuits in a Dutch oven.

If she ignored actual excavation initially, Theresa did convey lessons about survey methods and their consequences in her writing. First, despite systematic planning, researchers were opportunistic travelers who stumbled onto finds as well as individuals who carefully chose locales based on extant research reports. Second, perseverance paid off. Third, her archaeologist had little patience for slow, methodical work when he had limited time and resources and an ambitious goal. Like his contemporaries, Frank felt compelled to demonstrate success in the form of collected treasures.

Theresa was not often called on to undertake digging or probing. Until she showed interest in these activities, Frank seemed to have assumed she was too weak to throw shovelfuls of sand or move rocks.[34] Alternatively he had never seen her express interest in physical activities over the years. He did not force her to undertake any activity. But she changed. About halfway through their trip, Theresa started to participate more fully. By the time they reached the Little Colorado River, she was pursuing every type of archaeological activity, having shed her required gloves and slowly losing the hairpins needed to keep her plaits properly in place, as was expected of a married woman of her age. Theresa constantly laughed at herself in her *Out West* articles as she transitioned from a well-clothed tenderfoot to a seasoned scientific explorer who could get dirty. As she learned new forms of work, she overcame her preconceptions about proper dress and ladylike behavior. Frank was especially helpful in this regard; he convinced her that spending the day without donning her white gloves or dressing for dinner did not mean she had lost her dignity. The definition and implications of *proper* for the middle-class scholar had expanded to include flexibility and situation dependency. It was certainly not an expectation based on conspicuous consumption that required a fashionable but modest woman to dress distinctively for certain times of day and to use accessories to make fashion statements.

The post-digging tasks also required practice. They were activities that many archaeologists' wives have described. Theresa learned that artifacts and human remains must be cleaned, labeled, and inventoried in the field. Her journal describes spending time undertaking these tasks, preparing materials for transport. To accomplish this, she acquired skills using a new tool: a typewriter. A typewriter was a rarity for field parties, especially surveys constantly on the move. They soon became basic equipment, as important as a plane table, shovel, trowel, sieve, and hand broom. And typing would have been a skill needed for any writer in the first decade of the 1900s.

Such pre-laboratory tasks were the housekeeping activities wives, and later female students, were assigned. Theresa learned how to pack artifacts for transport but never built crates. In addition, she learned the rudiments of reconstructing pottery, appropriate work for women assumed to be detail-oriented and good at repetitive hand work. Learning and honing these skills was never the focus of Theresa's journal. She did mention the fun part of archaeology—finding something unusual—but she generally did not dwell on the tediousness of rapid reconnaissance. She was not enamored with archaeology—nor increasingly, as their trip continued, was Frank.

Chapter 3
Travels through Tusayan, 1900

Traveling across northern Arizona was not easy, and the practical problems the Russells encountered were often mentioned in their journals. They had to search for potential sites in places without roads and often without trails. Theresa frequently described the labor of the poor draft animals as they pulled the overloaded prairie schooner, and how the group daily shed unnecessary weight to make it through the rugged terrain. They rarely knew what they would find as they proceeded, nor did anyone they tried to hire. There was no willing tour guide, for no Navajo intimately knew all the areas Frank wanted to go. This made planning difficult. They constantly needed local assistance with geographic knowledge as they tried to wind their way across plateaus with deep canyons, climb rocky talus slopes, and avoid sandy foothills where a heavy wagon would quickly became stuck. Where was the best way up from a river bed? Could they move west without having to travel extra miles around a mesa? One did not gain the necessary knowledge to answer such questions easily. One learned from years of living in an area. This was especially important when searching for water and fodder, the major challenges of the summer. Frank knew what he was getting into. Theresa did not. Thus, learning about the land and how to survive were major topics in her journal.

Theresa's first venture was to step off the train in darkness, a common travel narrative trope for an unknown wilderness. She jokingly referred to the Atchison, Topeka and Santa Fe Railway station in Gallup, New Mexico, as a civilized metropolis. Here the hungry newlyweds got their bearings. Next Theresa showed she was not above taking literary license with her journal entries to become a bold heroine in her imagination. Her northwestern trek onto the Navajo Reservation in her serial was a flight of fantasy, the only imaginative journey that she would publish in her *Out West* essays. Rather than discuss Hubbell's wagon, in which they spent most of their time according to her journal, Theresa had them make a hilarious 27-mile bicycle journey, an unexpected mode of transportation and a tribute to her husband's vigor. Bicycling was much more engaging than submissively riding in a wagon. It helped Theresa establish an association to Frank's 1898 journey. Theresa saw herself as a fearless traveler, who described new things, places, and modes of transport. The bicycles made them unique and adventurous.

Gallup to Ganado

The couple traveled northwest to the Hubbell Trading Post at Ganado, Arizona, to outfit their trip. They stopped at St. Michael's Mission, where a Catholic religious order was building a school. St. Michael's (Ts'ihootso, Mountainside Meadow, or "area that extends out in yellow and green") is located in a wooded meadow on the western slope of Black Creek Valley. It was a Franciscan mission officially founded in 1898 on the site of a convent, donated by the order of Mother Superior Katharine Dexel, head of the Sisters of the Blessed Sacrament of Philadelphia. Building at the site, which remains important in Navajo history, had begun in 1896, continuing in 1897 under the direction of Father Anselm Weber. The sisters ran the boarding school, which focused on elementary education as well as industrial labor. The school buildings would be officially opened in October 1902. In 1900 Weber had been named mission superior, and two young priests, who arrived on October 12, Fathers Leopold Ostermann and Berard Haile, served as his assistants. All three spent the rest of their lives at the mission, learning Diné and much about Navajo culture and religion. The monk Theresa and Frank met was Father Juvenal Schnorbus, who left for Cincinnati in late October.[1]

Frank relied on an important local resident, whom he had met in 1898. John Lorenzo Hubbell, the savvy proprietor of the famous trading post at Ganado that bears his name, had agreed to provide Frank with the resources and supplies needed for a scientific expedition: horses and a wagon, a Navajo guide and translator, food, water, equipment, and two assistants. Hubbell and his family loom large in Theresa's journal. She saw Don Lorenzo as a courteous Spanish gentleman who provided hospitality but ate strange food. Many other popular writers had written widely read articles about Hubbell, depicting him as a fascinating frontier man bridging three worlds: Euro-American, New Mexican Hispanic, and Native. Always highlighted was the sense of welcome visitors received at a safe oasis. Hubbell provided Elbridge Ayer Burbank (1858–1949), who painted some 1,200 portraits of Native Americans during his career, with a studio and meals. Burbank repaid his hospitality with portraits of Navajo and Hopi people and copies of Navajo rug designs.[2] Theresa photographed one 1897 painting, which she included as the first illustration in the second *Out West* installment (figure 9.1). She, however, did not transform Don Lorenzo into a friend but indicated he was a potential ally of science because he helped her husband reach his goal. One does not obtain the impression from their journals that Theresa or Frank would ever consider Hubbell a lifelong friend, unlike numerous writers, artists, and anthropologists. But Frank knew he needed Hubbell if his fieldwork was to be successful.

Hubbell (1853–1930) was born in Pajarito, New Mexico. He was a prominent trader, instrumental in promoting Navajo weaving. After serving in the U.S. Army as a Spanish interpreter and working at a Fort Wingate trading post, Hubbell homesteaded near Ganado Lake and the Pueblo Colorado Wash in 1878. He chose Lu-ka'nit-quel (Place of Water Reeds); Spanish travelers called the locale Pueblo Colorado, or Red Village, which referred to the Ancestral Pueblo of Kin Lichee, about 10 miles northeast. Hubbell was remarkably successful and eventually owned more than 30 trading posts and retail establishments in Arizona, New Mexico, and California. He was Apache Country sheriff, a member of the Arizona Territorial Legislature, and, after statehood, a state senator. A prominent Republican, Hubbell had just returned from the Republican National Convention when he met the Russells in Gallup and offered them a ride to Ganado. To Frank this was a mixed blessing, for it meant they had to wait an extra day in Gallup when he was impatient to start his search. Centered on his own needs, Frank in his journal entries complained that Hubbell would not alter his plans.[3] This was an important lesson for conducting archaeology that practitioners will recognize. The needs of the archaeologist rarely coincide in importance with the activities of those being asked to help equip or guide a field team. Second, it points out the importance of planning and that planning takes longer than hoped. It also introduced other themes found throughout the journals: Frank's impatience and annoyance with any delay.

By 1900 Hubbell's store had been the staging site for many anthropological research trips. His support was critical to their success. The Stevensons, Cushing, Mindeleffs, Powell, Hough, and Fewkes of the Smithsonian Institution, as well as Dorsey and Charles Owen of the Field Museum, and many independent researchers had begun and ended their trips at the post, enjoying Hubbell's hospitality, expertise, and friendship. Botanists, zoologists, geologists, geographers, writers, and artists exploring the Colorado Plateau did so as well. Like Russell, these men and women bought tents, supplies, and trade goods for exchange with Natives, hired guides and teamsters, and rented wagons and teams. Hubbell's store served as a network node, the place where scholars came to figure out where to look and to find out where other researchers were going. They met Navajo and Hopi men who took their measure (based in part on Hubbell's recommendation) and decided whether to help them or not. Hubbell's assessment of character was critical to the success of a field season.[4]

Frank spent July 7–8 interviewing potential assistants. He relied on Hubbell to identify and persuade individuals to sign on for the extended journey. Two Hispanic teamsters became the group's backbone: experienced Erminio Pena, who acted as driver for the wagon; and young neophyte Nosifor Garcia, who rode in the rented wagon and acted as brakeman (figures 3.1 and 5.3). Both men searched for sites, trenched, and dug. Pena quickly became a jack-of-all-trades who could identify sites and trench as well as Frank. Sliver—a dignified Navajo who had worked for Hubbell for more than 20 years—served as guide, interpreter, and cook but refused to exhume bodies. Each man was paid $30 per month and a little

FIGURE 3.1. Erminio and Nosifor near Oraibi Wash. Erminio "is a thick-set fellow with a pock-marked face and clear blue eyes and he minds his own business" and Nosifor "a cheerful young thing with a glib tongue and a beautiful voice." Theresa Russell, journal, July 9, 1900. Photograph by Frank or Theresa Russell, late July 1900. Identification written on board with photograph attached. Frank Russell photographic collection. Courtesy of the Peabody Museum of Archaeology and Ethnology, No. 2004.29.4425.

extra for the use of their animals. They were joined briefly by Lorevio, a Navajo who supposedly knew where springs were to be found, but Frank soon found him unreliable. He was only involved for a few days. Theresa described these men in her July 9 journal entry and referred to them repeatedly on later dates. They constituted her main companions and she had great respect for them, even when she did not completely understand their cultural behaviors. Such instances served as opportunities for Frank to explain the fundamentals of culture from an anthropological perspective to her.

These men knew little to no English, and Frank knew no Navajo and little Spanish. Theresa spoke only English. Her training in German, French, and Latin were not of great use. At first, communication was a major problem. Theresa spent many hours practicing Spanish with Pena and Garcia. She was never as proficient as Frank, however, so pantomime and visual cues were used. They all made it work, although translation problems with Navajos occurred often, as Theresa noted extensively in her journal. One of the most frequent issues was what constituted a small versus a big site. This set the stage for adventures, adaptation, creativity, frustration, and humor. A second issue was whether there was water in a spring. Theresa wrote that these different referents had amusing consequences as well as presented logistical problems. The worst were dead ends, no water for the hardworking animals, and becoming stuck in a wash for several days.

Outfitting a scientific expedition was expensive. Frank made his meager funds go as far as possible. Almost every service cost money, however, including acquiring information and presenting gifts for reciprocity. After the Russells paid Hubbell's freight company transport fees for their trunks and equipment, Hubbell charged them $1.40 to store their large trunks filled with their city clothes in his warehouse for the summer. Similarly, supplies were costly. Hubbell supplied the necessities: basic utensils (coffee pot, pot, frying pan, cups, buckets, canteens, bedding, water kegs, a wash basin, and gunny sacks). He also sold the Russells, at cost, a tent ($7.00), half a dozen shovels ($6.26), an axe ($1.00), a coffee mill (75 cents), a box of matches (15 cents), 15 feet of rope (13 cents), 6 bars of soap, cutlery and plates for six people, and a dish pan. These initial purchases totaled $84.40. Hubbell loaned the couple two picks and a Dutch oven but charged them $3.25 for a memorable breakfast. The idea that Hubbell never charged anyone for food at his home was exaggerated storytelling. Nevertheless, Theresa certainly enjoyed it.

The Russells and their companions did not live off the land, nor could they count on obtaining a sheep. They relied on trading posts—most importantly, Thomas Keam's—once they left Hubbell's to replenish food (flour, sugar, salt bacon and beef, lard, coffee, prunes, potatoes, canned ham, corn meal, canned corn, and condensed milk) as well as replace items (a pocket knife and a pair of shoes) and obtain extra shovels.[5] The couple and their coworkers generally ate a typical settler diet of coffee, beans, rice, salt, baking powder, crackers, tomatoes, canned peaches, dried fruit, preserves, and corned beef. Candy was reserved as gifts for Navajo and Hopi children.

Northern Arizona was experiencing a dry spell, so the Russells took hay, grain, and water for the animals. Frank packed for his wife's comfort and in expectation of finding his ideal site quickly where they could settle in. This meant their wagon carried about one ton, too heavy for one team of mules to drag over the rough terrain. As a result, Frank hired a second team, which he planned to return to Hubbell once they established the summer's camp. He soon realized the heavy load made travel unfeasible, and they were not going to find the ideal site quickly. Weight had to go, starting with their comfort items, which were returned to Hubbell's for storage. The extra water and the second team were returned to Hubbell. As a result, the Russells never had enough water for overworked animals. And it was these beleaguered animals that Theresa remembered most at the end of her journey.[6]

Theresa had never experienced a drought in a high desert. It meant no bathing and little face or hand washing after a dusty day, challenging her ideas of cleanliness. She was hot and tired, and slightly depressed by the monotonous landscape. Other travelers had felt the same way. As Victor Mindeleff reported, "There are large areas that do not support a blade of grass, where barren rocks outcrop through drifts of sand or lie piled in confusion at the bases of the cliffs." Tusayan, with its "scattered growth of stunted pinon and cedar, interspersed with occasional stretches of dull-gray sage, imparts an effect of extreme monotony to the landscape. The effect is in marked contrast to the warmth and play of color frequently seen elsewhere in the plateau country." The area, Mindeleff continued, had a "remarkable similarity of appearance, and the consequent monotony is extremely embarrassing to the traveler, the absence of running water and clearly defined drainage confusing his sense of direction."[7] Luckily, miles of neutral tones were punctuated by red sandstone. Still, Theresa yearned for green. She was determined not to be a depressed burden to her husband, however. Frank rarely mentioned landscape characteristics in his field log. But then he knew what to expect and he did not become depressed by the land dullness. He was depressed by their lack of progress, frustrated by not finding his ideal sites quickly.

The lack of water meant the Russells had to think constantly about where to camp. Theresa and Frank frequently referenced "dry camps," describing them as failures. Camps with access to water became a desired luxury as well as a necessity if the animals were to assuage their thirst. There were long distances between watering holes. The group moved slowly; the heavy wagon tired the mules and horses. The slopes up the talus were steep. As Theresa recorded in her July 11 journal entry, the animals were always exhausted. By the time they reached the Little Colorado River, they required several days of rest.

The Russells made many false turns or reached dead ends. They found that a promised site was nonexistent, too small to have the hoped-for graveyard, or a promising well was dry. After the first week, they changed their exploration plan, for the wagon limited possible routes. Now one or two of the group went ahead on horseback. This new strategy added a new dimension to our reconstructing where the Russells went, but it made logistical sense.

Sites and Areas Visited

The Russells visited many sites. Unfortunately, we have found no definitive list, and it has proven difficult to identify many based on journal entries. (See table 3.1 for those we have identified from Peabody Museum artifact records.) Neither Frank nor Theresa listed exact locations.[8] Nevertheless, we have been able to trace their basic route, even if we have not definitively identified a specific valley or wash. A basic summary map indicates important places visited. However, we have not produced a map of their route because their backtracking was so confusing. Nor have we included all the side trips on the map; it was simply too jumbled. Our endnotes accompanying journal entries provide what specifics we have.

Frank's survey route was an opportunistic mishmash, reflecting hearsay about where potential sites were located and how they could be reached. This strategy relied on local knowledge, which was often contested or incomplete. Sometimes Navajos conveyed misinformation intentionally, possibly as a way to keep strangers from easily traversing the land. Russell decided not to search region by region sequentially but to wander back and forth across Black Mesa. The team often took what seemed like the hardest path, crossing deep arroyos, steep hills, and mesa cliffs, because Frank heard it was the most direct way. These routes might have been possible for a man on horseback but not a one-ton wagon. The wagon required much backtracking, but Frank felt it was necessary for Theresa's comfort. It was a testament to Frank's and Erminio's ability to read a landscape that they did not have more disasters reaching specific locations and locating water. In all instances, Frank's travel choices reflected his research goals and data needs.[9]

We know from Russell's correspondence with Putnam that he searched during July for large, impressive sites. When this proved futile, Frank "settled down upon some smaller ones to collect for a few weeks lest the summer slip away and I get left without any material results to show for the long days spent in 'strenuous' effort to further the interests of the Museum." Mindful that it was in his best interest to emphasize success, Frank stressed the quality of what he had collected. "I have some mountable skeletons and about twenty that are in very fair condition. I have not found any 'cream-colored' ware but have a good series of other kinds including some of the finest pieces of red ware that I have ever seen."[10]

This reference to a specific pottery style meant Putnam had alerted Russell to look for it. The "cream-colored" ware was the exquisite style later named Sikyatki, associated especially with sites on and around Antelope Mesa. After 1895 it was replicated by the famed Hopi potter Nampeyo and her relatives. Fewkes had called attention to the pottery style and Nampeyo's efforts in the 1890s.[11] The Peabody Museum needed examples.

Ganado and a False Start

Russell's search for the right kind of site officially began with a visit to an unnamed site near Ganado. This was most likely Wide Reed Ruin, near Hubbell's store. Fewkes had surveyed the Pueblo Colorado Valley in 1897 but recorded only small ruins without burial areas. He had told Russell the region did not have the type of preferred sites. Hubbell, however, encouraged Frank and Theresa to visit the site, thinking it might still yield human remains, but Theresa recorded, "We found nothing except a number of little circles, squares, etc., made of sharp, flat stones stuck in the sand."[12] Brief trenching revealed firepits. Frank had no interest in pit structures, so he did not record the brief excursion in his field log. This was a pattern he continued throughout the trip. Table 3.1 (appendix B) lists the major sites the Russells visited and trenched. These were not all the sites they saw or even briefly walked over but only those we can confidently identify. Our list probably constitutes about half of the sites Frank or Erminio checked.

In the late afternoon of July 9, the Russells, with an inflated staff of eight employees, finally left Ganado in their rented prairie schooner. With them were two teams of mules, a couple of horses, and a small dog. Erminio directed the team from Billy, his saddle horse. Nosifor steered the heavily laden wagon with Frank and Theresa sitting at his side. Sliver rode his pony. They headed west on a trail that would become Arizona State Route 264, then turned north into the Chinle Valley following a trail that would become Arizona State Route 191 (see figure 10.1). Theresa remembered they rode 12 bumpy miles over deteriorating sheep paths before heading cross-country, crossing dry spring beds and other obstacles, then camped and watched a glorious sunset. They had taken this route because Lorevio had told Frank there were "very large ruins that have never been explored by a white man."[13] Frank hoped to go to Blue Canyon after visiting them.

Thus began a linguistic impasse that plagued the Russells throughout their field season. What Frank considered "big" was not the same as the Navajo concept, and all the Navajo sites did not meet Frank's definition. Such miscommunication was often accompanied by vague directions to reach an ancient pueblo. Head into the wrong arroyo and one soon became lost. It accounted for many needless miles and numerous detours. This was the downside of relying on local knowledge and referential informant selection—all ancestral sites were "undeniably chiquito" or in a different place than originally thought. Innumerable translation problems occurred in Russell's requests for local information.

Frank informally studied Navajo local knowledge of the land and how Navajos thought about landscape features. He had many occasions to make a great contribution to Navajo ethnography if he had been interested and systematic. Provided with an opportunity for a linguistic study of core Navajo concepts, Frank did not appear to have had any desire to learn. Apparently, he took no notes about what he learned. It was a missed opportunity for Diné studies. Frank focused exclusively on finding his ideal large sites.

Theresa described their first day in detail: north through the Chinle Valley, intending to survey sites before heading west. They were flanked by the Defiance Plateau to the east and Black Mesa to the west. They stopped at Cottonwood Wash across the valley from the entrance to Canyon de Chelly, where the town of Chinle is located today.

Here they encountered Navajo conceptual and temporal differences, resulting in a hard lesson for Frank. Rather than simply wait for Lorevio, who was following

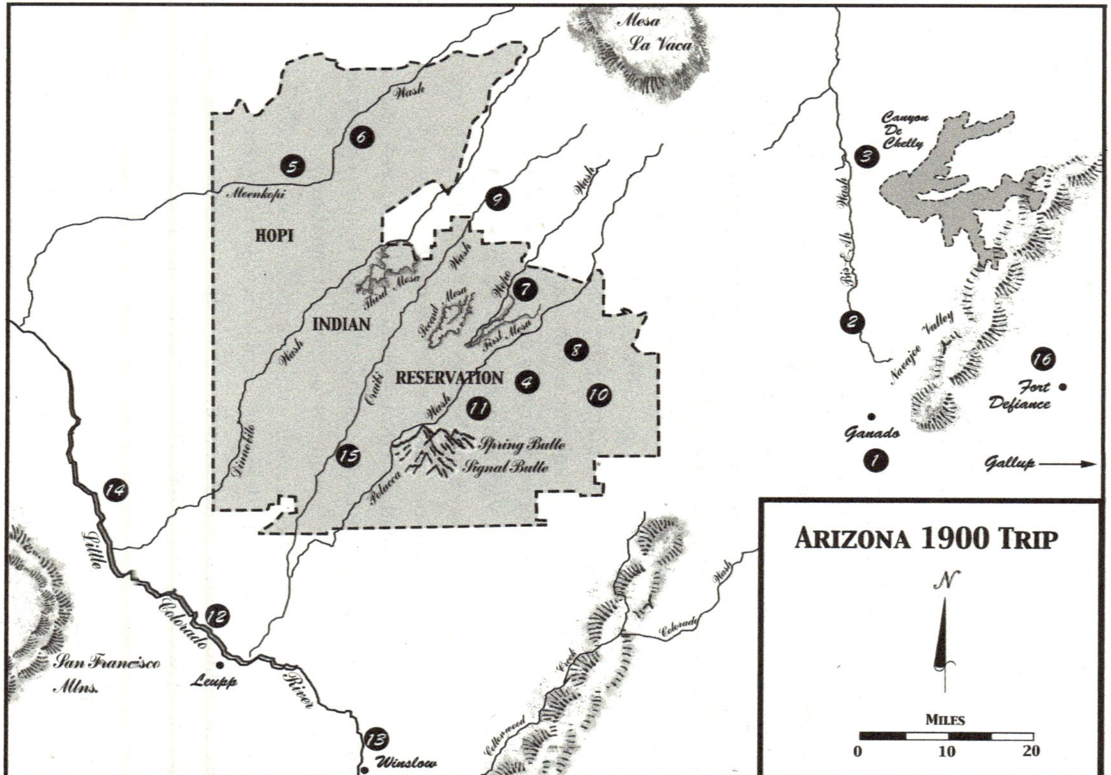

MAP 3.1. Important locales on the 1900 trip. Numbers reflect the order in which places were visited. 1. Ganado–Hubbell Trading Post; 2. Chinle Valley; 3. Chinle–Cornfields; 4. Keams Canyon; 5. Togoholtazze–White Corn Spring; 6. Blue Canyon; 7. Wepo; 8. North of Keams Canyon; 9. Kwaituki; 10. Awatovi; 11. Hopi villages; 12. Leupp; 13. Homolovi–Winslow; 14. Black Falls; 15. sand dunes west of Oraibi Wash where stuck; 16. Fort Defiance. Map by Patricia DeBunch.

from Ganado, they headed west. Leaving Theresa with the wagon, Frank and Erminio visited the small site of Has-tin-tì-sal, next to Navajo cornfields.[14] They found a pair of single-room structures. A disillusioned Frank did not bother testing. It met none of his criteria. When Lorevio arrived, he was happy they had already found the site. As Theresa said in her journal on July 11, Frank decided Lorevio's "imagination was large and active, the ruins themselves hopelessly chicito [*sic*]."

More disappointment surfaced as Frank, Sliver, and Erminio talked to residents. Now Theresa learned about Navajo's extended community discussions and consensus decision-making. There was no way, they were told, the wagon could make it to Blue Canyon. The terrain was too rugged and broken. Despite their comments, Frank still tried a few miles of what he thought was the correct trail, but climbing a steep slope required incredible labor. Theresa learned that her honeymoon travel meant unloading and reloading the wagon and carrying the heavy load uphill. Frank admitted defeat. They turned around and headed back down the Chinle Valley toward Ganado.

They camped near 15-Mile Spring, about seven miles west of Hubbell's, at the junction of the wagon road to the Hopi Mesas. They lightened the wagon, eliminating comfort items. Frank returned the second team, restocked, and had another lesson in idiosyncratic Navajo behavior. Hubbell informed Frank that Lorevio knew about the Blue Canyon trail; he had simply not shown it to him. Frank decided not to rely on Lorevio again. Theresa was indignant when the young man Frank had just fired asked for gifts.

The Road to Keams Canyon

Starting again on July 13, they headed toward Keams Canyon, hopefully to obtain advice on a new route to Blue Canyon. Frank served as guide since he had traveled the route in 1898 and 1899. On the way, they walked up a steep trail to Tebugkihu (Fire House), located about 14 miles from Keams Canyon. It was a small, compact settlement built by the Hopi's Fire Clan, with a distinctive layout. Victor Mindeleff thought it resembled the building style of Chaco Canyon residents.[15] Russell was impressed with the large stones in the outer wall and took documentary photographs but decided not to excavate. He had seen no clear indication of burials.

The party reached Keams Canyon, a three-mile-long canyon, 13 miles east of First Mesa, the next morning. The Hopi called the area Pongsikya after a local plant, Masiptanaga, or Moth Canyon; the Navajo called it Lók'a'deeshjin, "reeds extend along black." Today the canyon is home to about 260 individuals. In 1900 the number was much lower. Russell looked unsuccessfully for the agency superintendent, Charles E. Burton, to see if his permit had been approved. Burton was not there. Instead, he talked to Mr. Rausch, the Indian Service's general factotum.

Russell told Rausch about his intentions to excavate unspecified sites. Rausch gave his tentative approval but reminded Russell he still needed formal written consent from Washington. Frank was still waiting to hear from Putnam but assured Rausch he was "working in the interests of an accredited public institution." He found it inconceivable that the permit had not been approved.

The Russells went to the trading post, located five miles from the school. Keam had homesteaded the area under the Desert Lands Act before it became part of the Navajo and Hopi reservations. His improvements were impressive. There was a dressed stone and adobe house with four plastered and whitewashed rooms, a trading post, warehouse, blacksmith and carpentry shops, stables, and wagon shed. Employees and tenants lived in a series of small buildings. Theresa was as enthralled as she had been at Ganado, captivated with the hard-working, unpretentious man with the lovely English accent. Thomas V. Keam (1842–1904), an immigrant from Truro, England, had served as a merchant marine, Union soldier, metallurgist, prospector, cattle rancher, and Spanish interpreter at the Fort Defiance Agency before turning to trading. He lobbied for American Indian rights and fought dishonest Indian Service personnel. He was known as a sophisticated and well-educated gentleman who assisted anthropologists. John Bourke, who visited in 1881, recalled that Keam's house was filled with English literature, magazines, newspapers, assaying chemicals, Smithsonian photographs, bric-a-brac, and plants. What struck Theresa most was Keam's gigantic collection of ethnographic art and his staff, especially Jim, an elderly man who cooked them delicious food: real coffee, fresh meat, and creamy butter. Theresa recalled the repast philosophically as a call to appreciate taken-for-granted aspects of her normal life. Enjoying food made her reflect on what was important about her other life. Her travels were becoming a journey of self-discovery, much as learning psychology was a journey of self-appraisal.[16]

Keam was a good individual for Frank to consult, more knowledgeable than Hubbell about potential Tusayan sites. Keam had explored nearby ruins, including those on Antelope Mesa. John Bourke had been impressed when Keam took him to Awatovi and obtained a skull. Frank, however, decided not to go where Keam and his companions had pot-hunted so extensively. Other travelers and Hopi and Navajo residents had told him about large sites to the north and west as well as brought him artifacts. He would look there.

On to Blue Canyon and Kwaituki

Russell still thought about Blue Canyon, a lengthy, cliff-bound section of the Moenkopi Wash, which included Coal Mine Canyon, Ha Ho No Geh Canyon, and Bat Canyon. In 1898 or 1899, he had heard it contained many ruins and petroglyphs. Furthermore, Frank was told by U.S. census taker and the head teacher at the Navajo boarding school Milton Needham that he had recently visited a ruin two and a half miles in length and brought back a pottery olla. Frank's July 14 journal entry made a case for searching for the supposedly gigantic site: a trader, William Williams, who had grown up in the area, had heard of a "big city."[17] Hubbell had been skeptical; he thought Williams was thinking of the multistory Ancestral Zuni home of the Le'atakwe Clan at Kin Tiel (Wide Ruins), which the Mindeleffs had recorded. Kin Tiel was 23 miles north of Navajo Springs but in the wrong direction from the theoretical gigantic site. One Navajo gentleman thought Kin Tiel was small. Indian Service employee Rausch encouraged Frank to go to Blue Canyon to look for Needham's large site. Keam was skeptical it would be a worthwhile trip. An area of uninhabited badlands and hoodoos, Blue Canyon's drainage was accessible from the Red Lake Trading Post via a sandy and deeply rutted track. Russell debated whether it was worth the difficult journey. Navajos at Keams Canyon said there was nothing in Blue Canyon or for 50 miles around it. Frank decided not to believe them, rationalizing that the men were mining the sites themselves to sell pottery to Keam and other traders. They did not want him to take pots away, undermining their income source.[18]

The Russells left Keams Canyon on the morning of July 15. To be sure of their route, Frank rode to Hano to consult one of Fewkes's Hopi excavators, a man named Percy. Percy did not know of any Blue Canyon sites. Theresa had stayed with the wagon at Wepo Wash and greeted Hopi who stopped to visit. That night they made a dry camp just north of Donkey Spring.

The party continued north the next morning. They headed up the east side of First Mesa onto what today is the joint-use partition area of the Hopi and Navajo reservations. They passed Little Black Spot Mountain, going as far north as Water on the Rock Spring (To-da-hal-ta-sa), northwest of contemporary Pinon. Here were three small springs, but they were almost dry. Frank talked to Pel-a-si-shazzy, whom he said had water use rights. Pel-a-si-shazzy could not think of any Blue Canyon sites nor any feasible route for the wagon. While he and his compatriots were not sanguine, they were welcoming. Other Navajo came and set up camps; Theresa distributed candy sticks to the children and immediately took informal snapshots with her small camera. As she received her first lesson in making fry bread, Erminio and Nosifor trenched four medium-sized sites but found no burials. Frank and Sliver explored northeast, covering more than 20 miles without success. Frank decided he needed to find the Blue Canyon's boarding school teacher. He had supposedly seen large ruins.

On July 17, the group traveled approximately 30 miles across Black Mesa west toward the Moenkopi Wash, north of Third Mesa. Frank aimed for a place with water and hopefully feed for the animals: Togoholtazze Spring (Wild Horse Spring) and Bokodokleesh Cañon.[19] After a very strenuous day traveling without trails, they camped just before reaching White Cave Spring, about 16 miles directly north of Oraibi. The next morning, Frank sent Sliver with a note for the teacher requesting a meeting, a journey approximately 36 miles round trip. But Sliver never made it. Meanwhile, Nosifor searched for water, while Erminio hunted for the horses and mules, which had traveled more than 10 miles as they foraged, before exploring the locale area. Theresa stayed with the wagon and played (as she called her practice sessions) with the typewriter. Frank did not record his activities but he was probably searching for sites.

Theresa had a new experience the next day. She rode on horseback with Sliver and Frank as they again searched for the boarding school. This time they located it, but only a Navajo caretaker was in residence. This unnamed gentleman, who had accompanied Needham on his census tour, told them there were no large ruins in Blue Canyon, only small sites. The trip was an excellent example of wishful thinking and the enhancement of site size in secondhand retellings. All was not lost, however, for to their immense pleasure, they found clear running water. Theresa could wash.

It was time to reevaluate. On July 20, the group headed south toward Hopi. Frank decided to return to Wepo Wash via one of Keam's trails. The next day was spent with the Polacca family, and an impressed Theresa wrote extensively about them in her journal. Frank wanted to entice Polacca to take them to a site, but Tom refused; he had religious duties.[20] He did have the information Frank sought. Instead Tom told them about another location. They followed his directions for approximately 10 miles but found nothing. After Frank and Erminio searched in several directions, Sliver returned to Polacca for further information. July 22 was a repeat of the previous day: Frank and Sliver fruitlessly searching. But then Frank saw a medium-sized site with an aboveground structure near the Oraibi Wash. They broke camp. It was not the hoped-for large site, but Frank thought it had potential.

Around the Oraibi Wash

The Russells were still in Mindeleff country. Where the wagon road from Keams Canyon to Tuba City crossed Oraibi Wash, about seven miles north of Oraibi, Russell revisited several sites the brothers had mapped. The one that drew Frank's attention was 7-Mile Ruin (Hoyapi), a 150-room pueblo on a knoll, covered by extensive debris.[21] They spent an entire day tracing the masonry walls in the main pueblo and side buildings and used the site as a base for exploring nearby sites and performing domestic chores. After Erminio and Frank trenched for two days but found no human remains, Frank decided it was not worth further effort.

Frank wrote yet again to Williams on July 24, this time sending the letter to Winslow, where people thought the trader was. When Sliver returned with the mail, he had news of a ruin 35 miles east, back where they had been. Leaving Pena and Garcia to trench an unnamed site, Frank, Sliver, and Theresa headed over a sheep path. Theresa noted they passed large Hopi corn fields. Greatly impressed, she decided Hopi men had much to teach Iowa farmers.[22]

After spending the next morning tracking their wandering horses, they found the unnamed ruin atop a mesa. It looked like a contemporary Hopi village.[23] It was near a spring, but Frank felt it too small to warrant moving the wagon. They turned around and rode west, making it halfway back to their camp, a welcome wash, and rest. Theresa laundered their clothes. Frank and the men dug at another unnamed Oraibi Wash site and found a burial area, but all the bones crumbled when exhumed. Since the site had been extensively looted, Frank sent Sliver to find a guide to look for another Kin-Tiel, this one 20 miles northward on Black Mesa toward Shonto.

On July 31 and August 1, they headed toward the Moencopi Wash at House Spring or Sweetwater Spring to search for Big Mountain Ruin. Sliver and a local Navajo went north each day, approaching Blue Canyon from the east. Erminio stayed in the Oraibi Wash and trenched at an unnamed site. Frank and Theresa rode to Kwaituki. Not having heard from Williams, they packed up on August 2. It was a fortuitous decision. They had found their graveyard.

Kwaituki, located on the west side of Oraibi Wash, 14 miles north of Oraibi, had approximately 200 rooms around a plaza. Mindeleff had thought it looked like a citadel, built in the same style as 7-Mile Ruin.[24] Kwaituki sat atop a rocky knoll; Theresa thought it was a beautiful location and was fascinated with its rock art, considering it the best she had seen. While Kwaituki was not the pristine site Russell longed for, it had surface debris, including several in situ grinding stones and a cave used for storage. Frank saw Kwaituki as a series of distinct areas and labeled the 85 artifacts uncovered accordingly (see table 3.1). Unfortunately, his journal provided little information about where he decided to dig or his results.

Everyone was tired. Sliver decided to leave on August 4 to return temporarily to Ganado to care for his seriously fatigued horses; he returned on the 11th. Frank and Theresa welcomed him back. Nosifor, who claimed he had a back injury, decided to leave permanently. Frank and Theresa were not adverse, for they felt he was lazy. Frank sent the team of mules with him. He did not return.

On August 8, Russell sent Putnam a brief report, presenting his revised plans while proclaiming acceptable work had been accomplished.

> Having spent nearly all of July to reach my big ruins I have at last settled down upon some smaller ones to collect for a few weeks lest the summer slip away and I get left without any material results to show for the long days spent in "strenuous" efforts to further the interests of the Museum. We are up at half past four and work while daylight lasts so I use the term "strenuous" advisedly!

> I have some mountable skeletons and about twenty that are in very fair condition. I have not found any "cream-colored" ware but have a good series of other kinds including some of the finest pieces of red ware that I have ever seen.
>
> Having spent so much money in travelling with a four-horse team I am now economizing by working alone with one man. This seems "small" to you probably, but I do not think the Museum need be ashamed of the results.
>
> I send by this mail the skull of what may be a coyote (I have no means of determining here) but which I hope is a dog that I hope may be of interest to you. It was found in the ashes and sand at the bottom of a room in which there were our human skeletons in about the same condition that the skull presents. So far as could be seen it had lain there since the time the skeletons were deposited. It was about four feet from the surface, most of the material above being ashes and sand mixed together.[25]

The smaller crew did not deter Frank at Kwaituki. He and Erminio had found a burial area and exhumed several skeletons and associated burial items. Theresa felt each day yielded better material, including the remains of more than one family and several infants (see table 3.1). Now they had so many riches, as Theresa called the human remains, they "threatened to turn us out of house and home."[26] Frank and Theresa alternated among excavation and cataloguing and packing items for shipment to Harvard. Theresa felt she had become a real archaeological assistant. As her journal entries for August 4 and 5 illustrated, she now recognized pottery types, spent hours collecting different kinds of sherds, and knew how to exhume and clean a body. Her special assignment was to look for small objects, like beads. She also knew how to reconstruct a broken pottery bowl.

Trouble at Awatovi

It was now August 10. Erminio and Sliver rode east to Antelope Mesa. They had seen Awatovi, a huge site of more than 5,000 rooms, located at the mesa's southern tip, and told Frank they should head there next. Even though they were finding good materials and human remains at Kwaituki, Russell decided to move on. He still needed materials from multiple sites. They broke camp the next morning and stopped to see Tom Polacca, who had a house at the base of First Mesa. Polacca seconded the idea of visiting sites on Antelope Mesa and in the Jeddito Valley. As the two men talked, Mrs. Polacca entertained Theresa, who took a photograph of their unexpected iron bed. It was a symbol of the family's advancement toward civilization.

Camping overnight about four miles from Keams Canyon, Frank and Theresa rode ahead of Sliver and Erminio, who drove the wagon on the morning of August 13. Following a "short cut" that proved to be more taxing than anticipated, they reached Keams Canyon by midmorning. After restocking and obtaining their mail, they had dinner with Keam and Thompson. They would have learned about other archaeologists who used the trading post for supplies and their intended activities, that is, where they intended to excavate. They had to hurry. They reached Awatovi at sunset, just before another group of archaeologists.

Archaeologists in northern Arizona generally tried to avoid each other while working at sites. Fewkes was in the upper Little Colorado drainage, searching for sites mentioned in Hopi and Zuni migration stories. Walter Hough, Peter and Gertrude Gates, photographer A. C. Vroman, and Juan Baca, "the most assiduous pottery digger of the region," had already visited 55 ruins located in a 270-mile region bordered by Forestdale, the Little Colorado River and Petrified Forest, the Hopi Mesas, and the Jeddito Wash.[27] Fewkes, Gates, and Hough apparently had no territorial problems with Frank working in the same area; in fact, Hough decided not to return to Awatovi during the 1900 field season assuming Frank would excavate its graveyards. But what if two groups who were rivals reached a site at the same time? Then archaeologists acted like European countries claiming the Americas under the Doctrine of Discovery. Articulating arguments to justify imperialism and colonialism, the person who reached a site first claimed prior rights to excavate and own resulting treasures. Those who came next could excavate leftovers, but only after the first group was done. As Theresa argued, ethical researchers did not work in a scientifically claimed area, and one only claimed an area upon arrival. And of course no one bothered to ask the region's Natives.

If Frank was no threat to Fewkes or Hough, he was to Dorsey. When the Russells reached Awatovi, they knew Dorsey had told colleagues the site had been "claimed" a priori by the Field Museum for the 1900 field season. Awatovi, called Talla Hogan by the Navajo, was a well-known location. The Mindeleffs had mapped its complex sections, emphasizing architecture. Bandelier had visited to study mission history. Fewkes and Hough had collected objects and established basic pottery typologies during their three years of research between 1893 and 1895.[28] Keam took many visitors there, and Navajo, Hopi, and Euro-American residents supplemented their incomes by selling pottery to Keam. Still, its long history and size meant Russell might find skeletons of individuals from before and after European contact. Awatovi could provide useful data for his research project.

Theresa thought Awatovi looked like a real archaeological site. It met her preconceptions and expectations. She could see why people had been drawn there, even though sand and masonry debris obscured room-block outlines. The Russells camped near the mission. Theresa used its walls to dry their clothes and watch magnificent sunsets. Frank planned to stay at Awatovi for several days, but excavating quickly proved unproductive. Theresa noted extensive vandalism in the lower cemetery. Numerous human remains were "decayed and useless."[29] As a result, Frank and Sliver searched for other sites on Antelope Mesa, leaving

Theresa and Erminio to test near the church. They uncovered pot sherds (including the desired cream-colored ware), stone tools, and a few toys, but no burials.

Awatovi was not viable for another reason: institutional territorialism. The Russells met Charles L. Owen, who had come to work the site but was "unnerved" because the Russells reached it first. In 1897 the Field Museum had had only three small cases of Hopi materials, all obtained from Keam. George Dorsey, the museum's curator of anthropology and Frank's Harvard classmate, found this unacceptable. He wanted a multiroom exhibit.[30] He visited Mennonite missionary Henry Voth at Oraibi and persuaded him to sell his collection. Dorsey erected two halls of Hopi religious and secular items. Wanting an assortment of precontact pottery to represent a single tribe from the distant past to the present, he convinced Stanley McCormick to fund collecting trips. At first Dorsey decided not to work where Fewkes was excavating near Hopi. Later, he changed his mind, and Owen headed to the heart of Tusayan country to preempt the USNM and the BAE.

For their fourth field season, Dorsey obtained a government permit, signed by the Commissioner of the General Land Office, Binger Hermann, rather than an Indian Service employee. This allowed Field Museum archaeologists to excavate prehistoric ruins on Hopi and Navajo reservation lands.[31] Dorsey interpreted the federal permit to be like a homesteading deed—a exclusive claim to every Tusayan site, all research activities, and excavated materials for the year. Like Russell, Owen worked rapidly and moved around extensively looking for large sites, digging for artifacts rather than seeking to acquire cultural history information. After finishing on Antelope Mesa, he intended to turn "his attention to ruins of the North, many of which had never been previously visited by any scientist." Dorsey bragged that Owen discovered "ruins which we have reason to believe had never been seen by any white man." Owen collected over 3,000 artifacts, including the yellow ware bowls Putnam asked Russell to find. Dorsey was pleased. He wrote Voth, "I am glad to tell you that in my estimation we have left Washington in the rear so far as prehistoric Hopi pottery is concerned."[32] This quest for territorial resource exclusivity now was extended to prevent Harvard gaining any foothold as well. Russell was an institutional threat, just as the Field Museum was an impediment to Russell. To find Owen established at a site meant Frank had to ignore it. This would have eliminated graveyard possibilities since Owen and Russell were looking for the same site type. According to Frank's logic, if this had happened, he would have simply moved on, for it was the "ethical" thing to do. Not Dorsey. He, and by extension Owen, had decided to use new bureaucratic permitting protocols to advance territorial aspirations, and this included making sure Frank was simply not allowed on the reservations to excavate and even survey. From Frank's standpoint, Dorsey was changing the rules of the archaeological game, but the rules had already changed. Dorsey wanted Russell evicted from Tusayan. He asked the OIA central office and the Hopi agent Burton to ensure his monopoly. Unfortunately for Russell, he had left himself and Harvard vulnerable by not thinking about the politics of archaeology and how they were now included in Washington, D.C., political favoritism.

Russell knew about Dorsey's ambitions, his competitiveness, and his quest to claim areas as Field Museum exclusive domain. Frank had not been deterred but underestimated Dorsey's ability to work the federal government for his own ends. Frank thought he could excavate based on his reputation, even if the permit were slow in arriving. He also argued that permits had never been intended to grant institutional exclusivity, limiting the scientific activities of others in the noble quest of science. He still held that the researcher group that established a camp first and sunk the first hole had the right to excavate. This discovery stance gave a research team the "rights" to a site like Awatovi until they moved on.

We can note, of course, that none of the archaeologists included the Hopi or Navajo in their discussions, for their rights were not even considered in territorial research claims. Nor did either Russell or Owen discuss their stewardship in their journals or field notes. Instead, the two men and Theresa postulated arguments for their two points of view and their ethical rights. In his field notes, Owen mentioned meeting the Russells at Awatovi just hours after they arrived. He further recorded he had sent a Hopi assistant to establish their camp. He presented no opinion about the Russells, nor does he say that he informed Russell he had prior, federally approved rights to work at the site, but we can infer this from what Theresa wrote. She journaled disparagingly about Owen as she constructed a Socratic apology for Frank and his rights to Awatovi. Unfortunately, her stance relies on an ad hominem argument. Theresa sarcastically said in her August 14 journal entry that Owen had sent the unnamed Hopi employee to "spy" and "size them up": "We were suspicious that he would precede us here, . . . and were much relieved to find ourselves the first arrivals last night." Theresa felt Owen knew they had reached Awatovi, for he had stopped at Keam's store. He therefore should have moved on, for archaeology's "code of ethics does not allow him to intrude onto another man's preserve."[33] In fact, Theresa thought he had gone after their initial meeting, for he said he planned to visit the Niman ceremonies at Second Mesa. He did not return the following day for a long conversation with Frank. Russell was disappointed, for the two men had not previously met. Owen returned after the Russells had left, avoiding an awkward confrontation.

Had Frank made his point to his right to excavate at Awatovi? Did Owen's absence mean he agreed? How sorry were Frank and Theresa that they had no conversation with Owen? Frank likely valued talking with a "like-minded individual" besides Theresa. When Theresa used this phrase, she meant educated, white, and middle class, as well as a person who understood archaeology. Intelligent conversation seemed especially important to Theresa after so many days of talking with only Frank and her quest to interact with witty people while in

Arizona. She had lost a rare opportunity. Theresa recounted their disappointment at not having company. At the same time, she distanced herself from her regret. She hinted that any chat with Owen would probably have been unedifying, for he was not a scholar and therefore not a true peer of Frank and, by extension, herself. She belittled Owen, calling him simply "a plain scientist," one who had not attained Frank's intellectual level or credentials. Theresa expressed little respect for Owen. Instead, she stated humorously that Frank drowned his disappointment at not entertaining his fellow professional by drinking an extra cup of tea and eating pickles for dinner, food normally reserved for special occasions.

But there was still the basic issue, a silent elephant in the room. Frank had made an error, but Theresa was not ready to acknowledge that her Man of Science was not perfect. This affected her Socratic apology though more flawed logic. First, Theresa attacked the validity of a premise by accepting Frank as the ultimate authority even though he was not a federal policy maker. She dismissed the contention that archaeological work on reservation lands required a valid permit before Frank could start fieldwork. Frank had done his due diligence. He had applied to the Office of Indian Affairs for permission to excavate and appropriately, if vaguely, identified his focal areas. But he had left this task until the last minute. That should not have mattered. It was the federal government that had not done its job.

Since he was in a hurry to leave Boston, Frank did not wait for the permit as he should have. He assumed that since he was a credentialed anthropologist, approval was pro forma. It turned out he was wrong. On August 17, 1900, Putnam wrote Frank that an unnamed GLO bureaucrat had denied him permission to excavate anywhere on the Hopi or Navajo reservations. In a case of bureaucratic overextension, the bureaucrat noted that Putnam also did not have a valid permit. He extended the denial to all Harvard archaeologists and then included all federal off-reservation lands such as those in Chaco Canyon. This denial had been forwarded to the OIA, which apparently simply rubber-stamped the denial based on the additional approval of the Secretary of the Interior, a political ally of the director of the GLO. This second unnamed bureaucrat sent the denial to Putnam at Harvard, and since Putnam was at Chaco Canyon, it took a while to reach him. Russell and Putnam had an enemy who knew how to manipulate Republicans, the party in power.

Frank was apparently not surprised by Putnam's letter. He had been running into problems, and the lack of a valid permit was curtailing his research. "I am told the agent here is on my trail. Notices [have been] posted at the stores, schools, etc. about the reservations," Russell told Putnam.[34] Agent Burton had labeled him a vandal. Frank was a wanted man.

Russell assumed Owen had alerted Burton, who deemed his discussion with Rausch insufficient. But how did Owen know that Frank did not have a permit? Russell hypothesized Dorsey was to blame and had used his political influence as well as that of his sponsor, the wealthy Stanley McCormick. Theresa was incensed. In her opinion, hindering Frank and his research was a mortal sin. Owen was the most immediate scapegoat.

The Indian Service often asked the General Land Office to oversee permitting, and this was where Russell and Putnam's request had been sent. The GLO was under the direction of Hermann, the commissioner who had awarded Dorsey and the Field Museum their permits. There were many instances of GLO corruption and cronyism during the period; staff responded to political pressure, especially when it came to the control of national resources. The Indian Service was also known to yield to political pressure. James Snead has uncovered evidence that Stanley McCormick asked Secretary of Interior Ethan A. Hitchcock for a favor. Dorsey alerted McCormick that Russell and Harvard would undermine his sponsored expedition, resulting in fewer treasures for the Field Museum.[35]

This situation was compounded by Frank's impatience. But no matter if Russell had waited; it probably would not have mattered. Fixing the situation required Putnam to activate his Massachusetts political and professional allies. Explaining to the GLO officials, Putnam emphasized Russell's credentials and the fact that he was already excavating. Putnam was told to have Frank cease. He was to also stop digging at Chaco Canyon, for he had no permit.[36] Since Putnam had never needed a permit to work in off-reservation lands, he was surprised. Putnam was now worried about his own future research activities, including those not on reservation lands.

Russell knew he had no good response except impatience and his urgency for data for his scholarly presentations. Burton, an autocratic bureaucrat, would not have accepted this argument, especially since Dorsey had written him to be on the lookout for Russell. Frank also did not want to be curtailed and lose more of his precious time. He had already tried to rectify the situation once, and according to his reasoning, that should have been enough. He would not lose the rest of the summer.

Russell decided on a new strategy: they would leave Awatovi to Owen and become tourists at the Hopi Snake Dances—but only after seeing what else was available on Antelope Mesa.

Moving Up Antelope Mesa

The morning after Owen's visit, Frank and Nosifor began to search for a new site, one where the human remains were less vandalized.[37] Between August 15 and 19, the Russells excavated at five Antelope Mesa sites. As table 3.1 summarizes, they uncovered more than 46 usable skeletons, several crania, and what Russell calls in his inventory "miscellaneous bones: femerae, humeri, jaws, radia, ulna and tibia." Knowing they had to move quickly before Burton returned, they hastily amassed grave goods, ceramics, and stone tools. In his notes housed at the

Peabody Museum, Russell referred to all these sites as Awatovi 2 through 6, but archaeologists recognize them as distinctive communities with different names.

The first site explored was Mishiptonga, the southernmost and largest of the ancient Antelope Mesa communities and the closest to Jeddito Springs. It had been occupied in the fourteenth and fifteenth centuries. Mindeleff stated the site was irregular in arrangement, with a number of plazas enclosed by large and small room clusters. Russell trenched in several areas and found his longed-for graveyard. He exhumed more than 40 "usable" skeletons in two and a half days. The group collected associated funerary materials and pottery, photographed wall etchings, and made notes on boards, which are now housed in the Peabody Museum's collections.[38]

Moving north, the Russells worked even faster, although it barely seems possible they could have beat their excavation speed at Mishiptonga. They dug at Chakpahu, situated halfway between Mishiptonga and the Jeddito Trading Post, on August 17. Contemporaneous with Awatovi's early occupation, Chakpahu was a large mason pueblo, like Mishiptonga, with a defensive wall. It was approximately the same size as Kookopngyama (Horn House) but not as elongated. Most rooms were concentrated in the northern portion, and it was there Frank trenched. In their haste, they missed much. The next year, Hough would demonstrate how much had been overlooked in Russell's focus on human remains. Hough thought the pottery was the finest in Tusayan, and the village its manufacturing center. Frank did collect several pieces, including a clay figurine and a bird vase, both of which now reside in the Peabody Museum.[39]

Pink Arrow was visited on August 17 during a rainstorm. It was located at the head of a small side canyon between Chakpahu and Nesheptanga, about one mile downstream from the Jeddito Trading Post. Erminio and Theresa dug while Frank and Sliver explored other sites (three small and two large). Pink Arrow was a small Pueblo III–IV masonry site (50 rooms and 1 kiva) occupied in the second half of the fourteenth century. Not described by Mindeleff, Fewkes, or Hough, Russell's artifacts were possibly the first to be placed in a museum. The Russells quickly moved on, searching for an "undefiled, undiscovered cemetery."[40]

The next day, the research team descended on Nesuftangu, a Pueblo IV site with one large enclosed plaza. They exhumed portions of two skeletons and moved on to Kookopngyama. The pueblo was ancestral to the Horn Clan and had a large enclosed quadrangular plaza and a good water supply. It was located two miles east of Keams Canyon on the western flank of the Jeddito Valley. Mindeleff stated the village was almost demolished, its walls now low ridges of masonry covered by drifted sand. The site was strewn with sherds from Navajos excavating for pots. The Mindeleffs earlier had seen two partially excavated rooms, "the work of some earlier visitors who hoped to discover ethnologic or other treasure."[41] The Russells spent only enough time to poke a few holes but did uncover a few disarticulated bones.

FIGURE 3.2. Russell, Erminio, and Nosifor digging at Kawaika-a, with Sliver walking away when a burial is seen. August 14, 1900. Photograph by Theresa Russell. Courtesy of the Peabody Museum of Archaeology and Ethnology, No. 2004.29.4394.

On to Hopi

Without a legal foundation for possessing the objects that were taking up every inch of spare room in their small canvas tent, Frank decided to cease excavating and pack the collections for transport to Cambridge. On August 20, they traveled to Keam's Trading Post, only two or three miles to the west. After a good dinner and meeting Keam's famous guests who had come for the Snake Dance, they boxed up and stored 300 pounds of human remains and associated burial goods. They also learned that Burton was due back at Hopi in a few days. Frank decided it was time to leave his jurisdiction and head to the Little Colorado River.

But first it was time to take a day off from archaeological exploration and go to Second Mesa. As Theresa remembered, the "day of grace was short, and since the Moki [Hopi] Snake Dance was to take place at Shungopavi," they would stop there. It was a whirlwind excursion into ethnic tourism or very rapid ethnographic observation. On the way, they stopped at First Mesa and entered the middle village, Sichomovi. Both Frank and Theresa had a camera. They each spent their time watching, interacting with the Hopi, and taking pictures. In her journal entries, Theresa wrote with wide-eyed detail. She painted word pictures of activities: a woman sweeping with a new store-bought broom, a shy naked child, young boys playing, and women talking. There were also people exchanging poses for a piece of candy—reciprocity in action. Underneath these descriptions were indications of how the Hopi felt about the photographic intrusions, the consequences of which Theresa and Frank, like everyone else, ignored to some extent. At other times, they honored Hopi delays, especially when women whisked their children away to don their best attire, before the image was snapped. She might still call herself a Tenderfoot, but Theresa was now a photographer with an eye for composition and what was visually and culturally interesting. She had mastered one of the main skills of an archaeological wife. She could see with an anthropological eye and now gather data.

Unexpectedly, Theresa condemned touristic visitors like herself, including any professional and amateur ethnographer, whose "intruding body hops and skips about with tripod and note-book . . . mars the wonderful site" and "Prayer" of the rituals. There were a large number of tourists in 1900, for earlier in the year the Atchison, Topeka and Santa Fe Railway had published Walter Hough's popular pamphlet on the Hopi Snake Dance to attract visitors to the area.[42] Hough emphasized that the Hopi were not dangerous but living examples of humanity's childhood. The Snake Dance, Theresa realized, was not a touristic spectacle or an entertainment performance but an active prayer. The tourists were intrusive, and the villagers watched their antics from rooftops with mixed humor and unspoken annoyance. She was distancing herself and providing another apology for questionable behavior she felt helped Frank complete his work. Again, Frank and his professional needs took precedence before any other consideration.

While at Second Mesa, Russell received a summons from Burton, who had returned early from his trip. He requested that Frank present the official permit to him at Shipaulovi on Thursday, August 23. Frank sent his regrets, broke camp, and quickly headed west on the road below Third Mesa. He quickly reached off-reservation lands where Burton had no jurisdiction.

The Little Colorado River Valley

Frank, Theresa, and Erminio turned south on the Oraibi Wash, traveling toward Leupp and the Little Colorado River. They were now leaving the Mindeleffs' survey area and heading toward regions visited by Dorsey, Fewkes, Hough, Gates, and Owen. According to Frank, the Indian Service denial said nothing about working on the Navajo Reservation. Technically he still needed a work or excavation permit, but again he rationalized he did not need one. When meeting the Navajo agent, the gentleman had not explicitly told Frank he could not survey or excavate. Burton's rulings, Frank now held, had no standing on Navajo reservation land. Therefore, they could search the new Navajo lands west of Hopi. He informed Putnam of his decision and reasoning. President William McKinley had signed an executive order on January 8, 1900, extending the Navajo reservation's western boundary to the Little Colorado River, an area of approximately 1.5 million acres. Most of this land had not been scientifically explored. However, to ensure he did not run into further Indian Service troubles, Frank decided he would concentrate on the off-reservation area near Winslow.

The next weeks were spent searching for more elusive large, pristine sites and now what Frank was willing to try—smaller medium-sized ruins. On August 22, they trekked cross-country toward Burro Spring. The next day, they followed a trail paralleling the Oraibi Wash and reached Red Lake Trading Post. They were off-reservation by evening. It had been a demanding journey. Even though the animals were completely spent, they still pushed on, heading straight south. Their goal was McAdam's store near present-day Leupp, about 20 miles distant.

Theresa made no record of having seen any sites on their way south. At Sunrise, Arizona, they switched to brief excursions on horses borrowed from McAdams. (Their horses needed several days of rest.) Theresa stayed at the trading post while McAdams, Frank, and Erminio explored. Frank and McAdams had made a deal: any pottery would belong to McAdams, while Frank would take all human remains. The only site Theresa mentioned the men visited was on private property 10 miles west of the trading post. They did nothing there because the owner, a Mr. Diamond, wanted to dig it himself to enhance his personal collection. Finding that the Field Museum crew had preceded them along this route, Frank, Erminio, and McAdams searched away from the river for three days but without positive results.

On August 28, Erminio retrieved their horses and they continued to Winslow. As Theresa drove the wagon, Frank, McAdams, and Erminio explored on horseback. They saw a few ruins but after cursory trenching moved on. The next two days followed the same pattern. They came upon unnamed sites that the Field Museum or Hough had "all worked out."[43] Other sites, also unnamed, Frank considered too small to even bother testing. Theresa concentrated on the abundant pictographs.

The group reached the Homolovi ruins and decided to explore for several days. They dug first at what was probably Homolovi I followed by Homolovi II but uncovered no human remains. They did excavate one kiva; Frank was quite impressed with its construction. What Theresa remembered of the experience was the wind and the continuing "disappointed expectations."[44]

Heading Back to Ganado

It was time to head home. They would go back to Ganado, stopping at Keams Canyon on the way to ship their collections. Hopefully, they would have time for a side trip to Canyon de Chelly. Inexplicably, rather than take the direct route to Winslow and go northeast on an established wagon road, they headed back up the Little Colorado River. Frank thought a "short cut" would save a day and a half. As it turned out, it was a bad decision.

Russell's route was to head up the Dinnebito Wash and cross country to Burro Springs. When they neared the Dinnebito branch, Frank left to take McAdams's mule back to the trading post. He also took their tent and excess food, which he wanted to barter. His aim was to lighten the wagon. This plan required a solo 25-mile hike. In the meantime, Theresa and Erminio drove the wagon through a rainstorm until sunset. To Theresa, the trying day was a great success, for she found potable water, a triumph in her abilities to succeed in the inhospitable environment. She had finally learned to read the land.

Journal entries are unclear about what happened next. Theresa and Erminio took a wrong turn, heading back into the Little Colorado River drainage, west of Ward Terrace. They were in the Painted Desert, which was slick with mud during and following the monsoon. By the time Frank located them, he had walked all night. His trek had been much more than 25 miles. He decided they should keep going north. However, as Frank slept, Erminio made another wrong turn over "the roughest, bumpiest, and most horrible piece of country, driving around in a circle."[45] The horses were exhausted. To make matters worse, they saw no sites.

The trio continued north, climbing mesas and buttes to look for sites as they worked their way up the wash. They went as far as Black Falls, just north of what would become Wupatki National Monument. Here Frank and Erminio dug pot holes briefly but only collected odd artifacts, probably ceramic sherds. They did not exhume human remains or find grave goods. Theresa had a more productive day. She took photographs of petroglyphs. As table 3.2 shows, while there was only one shot of petroglyphs at earlier sites, Theresa took 16 at Black Falls. She was more confident with her camera; her focus was sharper.[46] She also recorded encounters with the "Red Mesa" men and made notations about Navajo activities and behaviors along with her interpretations.

Turning east on September 4, they aimed cross-country. As Theresa and Frank explored a mesa top, Erminio drove the wagon into sand dunes west of the Oraibi Wash. He became stuck. It was clear that Erminio had no experience in the area or with local conditions; he could not read the land. Luckily, the error occurred near fresh water and there was grass for the tired horses. The dunes were probably near Garces Mesa. Frank went for help when they could not extricate the wagon. Frank walked south about 10 miles to Enderly's post at Red Lake to rent a team. There were no horses available, however; he walked back disheartened. The next day, he sent Erminio to Oraibi to rent two teams. Frank and Theresa sat with the marooned wagon until an unnamed Navajo arrived, sent by the Oraibi trader Scholy, to pull them out and guide them to Keam's Trading Post. They set out on September 7 and found Erminio at Burro Springs. They rode as far as Second Mesa that evening.

September 8 was an easy trip to Keams Canyon. Theresa and Frank spent the afternoon and the next day preparing their specimens for shipment. They filled "seven coffin boxes and one smaller box."[47] Unexpectedly, they met the Gates, who were continuing their travels. Frank was excited. He wanted to see if he could cultivate Gates for a research venture in 1901, a joint Harvard–Gates research project. They agreed to meet at Hubbell Trading Post for a long discussion.

Bill and Bob were harnessed for the last leg of the journey, a walk along the good wagon road for 22 miles. The Russells and Erminio explored one more set of ruins, Steamboat Springs, even though they were on the reservation. They secured a good deal of pottery but no human remains. As Frank and Erminio trenched, Theresa carried a note to Gates at Keams Canyon, telling him where to find them. Frank thought this would be a good site for a joint venture. While waiting for the Gates, Frank, Theresa, and an unnamed local Navajo explored. Erminio went ahead to Ganado and returned on the 12th with four fresh mules to take the wagon to the Hubbell Trading Post.

Going Home

The Russells reached Ganado on September 13 and had a welcome bath and dinner. They spent a day packing specimens. The specifics of what they shipped are listed in table 3.1, but unfortunately the listing is not complete. From the skeletal ID numbers on Frank's inventory list, he recorded and shipped 221 sets of human remains. These included full skeletons, crania, or postcranial fragments from adults, juveniles, children, and babies. Of these groupings, only 76 were retained in Frank's laboratory and inventoried in the Peabody's collections. We think that many bones were destroyed in transit or Frank found them unusable later and discarded them. Others were removed from the museum at some later time, but we do not know by whom. Only seven sets remained during a 1990 inventory conducted by osteology curators.

More of the objects survived transport and still remain in the collections today. Some are associated with enough contextual information to be treated as useful research specimens. Again, complete information is lacking. We have made our best assessment, using all available sources, but we deferred to the Peabody Museum collection's inventories and accession records. In some cases, Russell kept the burial goods associated with a skeleton together with the bones, for this was important for his research design. In other cases, the artifacts are listed separately, indicating they were probably not found with human remains. Depending on how one counts catalogue entries with multiple pieces, we have noted 375 objects, pieces of raw materials, and fragments. When picking up materials not associated with a specific burial, Russell concentrated on pottery, per

Putnam's request. But he did not neglect other items that could be diagnostic and serve as a Tusayan type collection. These were not integrated into other Ancestral Pueblo collections at the time.

Frank settled their accounts and gave Sliver $37 in wages, Nosifor $23, and Erminio Pena $63. Pena had obviously been given a raise or a bonus since the amount was greater than their agreed-upon compensation rate. The Russells bought a blanket for $25 and silver spoons for $2.90.[48] These were their only souvenirs of their adventure. They were ready to leave but were quickly tempted by a new opportunity. As Theresa's September 14 journal entry recorded, Hubbell offered to supply them with a fresh team if they wanted to accompany the Gates to Canyon de Chelly. Hubbell also offered Frank and Theresa free transportation from Ganado to Gallup; he was taking his family to winter in Albuquerque. The Russells were torn but knew they had to return to Cambridge for the fall semester. In fact, Frank was already late.

As a substitution for his actual presence, Frank gave Gates his camera to photograph Casa Blanca and Canyon del Muerto sites. These photographs are now in the Peabody Museum, listed under Frank Russell as the donor and collector, along with documentary photographs of Navajo activities. Gates took them all but provided no accompanying written descriptions or provenance. It is possible that Russell did not ask for such information, for he rarely documented Navajo activities in his journal. Frank did record they attended the final night of a Navajo Enemyway, calling the ceremony by its popular name, "Squaw Dance." This designation reflected the fact that women chose partners during a social dance. Frank does not give the location, but it would have been on the road they took to visit his old friend, Fort Defiance trader George Manning. Unfortunately, Theresa's journal entries had become increasingly cryptic by this time, as though she had little time for reflection. As a result, we know less and less about the Russells' final days in Arizona.[49]

Theresa and Frank boarded the train at Gallup on September 16. They were so behind schedule that they did not stop in Iowa to visit Theresa's relatives or inquire about Frank's parents and their situation in Texas. Their telegrams apparently did not reach Theresa's family, and they stood at the 10-minute whistle stops alone. In Kansas City, they had time for a hot meal but not in Chicago. Then it was across Canada to Montreal, where they had two hours for a real meal. The Russells reached Boston, with its "little dose of domestication," on September 20. Theresa was glad to return to her civilized land with its physical comforts. At the same time, she looked forward to going west again.

Chapter 4
Arizona Archaeology, 1901

The Russells returned to Harvard University. During the fall semester of 1900, Frank pursued his usual professorial activities: teaching, professional service, research analysis, and publishing. As usual, his classes had more students than any other professor. He now advised graduate students as well; he served on John Swanton's PhD examination committee, along with Frederic Ward Putnam, Franz Boas, and Charles Bowditch. While Putnam questioned Swanton on his archaeological experience, Boas his linguistic competency, and Bowditch his knowledge of Mayan archaeology, Russell had Swanton discuss pedagogy, specifically what questions should be on a professional examination. In his memoirs, Swanton remembered that Frank stated, "It is foolish to hold an examination of this character and we shall not give anthropology a respectable status until we specify a major and minor as in other departments." Russell was quick to state that his remarks had nothing to do with Swanton's knowledge base or abilities; he wanted a discussion with a future colleague.[1] Given later events, this was an ironic situation but demonstrated Frank was thinking seriously about anthropology's place in academia and what it must do to move beyond its laissez-faire approach to credentialing. Such issues of educational reform loomed large in Frank's professional agenda during the next two years, just as they would during Theresa's tenure at Stanford University.

Frank was immersed in professional service; he was president-elect of the American Folklore Society and had spent part of the summer addressing his leadership duties. One can imagine him writing letters sitting in the back of their wagon. He was now secretary of Section H, AAAS, and in charge of the meeting at Johns Hopkins University in December; on the board of the American Folklore Society; and the secretary of the American Society of Naturalists. Frank had several papers and book reviews to write on a variety of subjects. At the annual meeting of the American Folklore Society, held in association with the American Society of Naturalists on December 27 and 28, he presented a paper on the Native peoples of the Southwest. This required a good deal of preparation, for it consisted of colored stereopticon slides of his fieldwork photographs. He prepared a second general ethnographic paper for the American Society of Naturalists and demonstrated his new apparatus for measuring long bones.[2]

Theresa met with her Radcliffe literary acquaintances, including William James, and read extensively. She tidied up her journal, producing the version that appears in appendix A. She assisted Frank with the museum work stemming from their summer activities: more than 500 artifacts to be identified and inventoried. Putnam expected Frank would catalogue them, although there was no funding for this stage of his research, an all-too-common situation that still plagues anthropology today. As the Peabody Museum catalogue files show, Russell never completed the task. Then there were the human remains to analyze and integrate into the Peabody Museum's extensive osteological collection. Once Frank had completed this work, he was to place the new information into his personal research database (if we may call it that) and write his conference paper on the human remains. There is no evidence Theresa assisted with this analysis or what progress Russell made in terms of collection management or ultimately analysis.

Frank was doing work he loved, but he was disappointed with his employment situation. His salary was still $1,000 (just as it had been as a second-year graduate student), even though Frank had asked for and expected a raise. It was the old problem many young scholars have faced: there were no merit increases or rewards for stronger credentials, greater experience, or productivity through well-received publications. Why should a university offer higher pay for someone who had worked for a low rate? And wasn't Harvard the place people dreamed of working? There was no incentive for the employer to recognize theoretical market value, especially when the researcher had no alternative job offers. From Putnam's standpoint, employing Russell was actually a problem. Putnam had to find new funding, for Frank was no longer eligible for fellowships. Putnam wanted Russell to stay. Frank was valuable, for he freed Putnam to concentrate on professional service and institutional development, but there were real costs to retaining him as well as the uncertainty about his health. With his limited budget, Putnam had little extra cash or incentive to pay Russell more than a minimum wage. The argument that Frank was now married evidently carried no or little weight. Frank was in a buyer's market—one that existed for all disciplines but was especially bad for anthropology, which was not yet well established in academia.

Remaining at Harvard had an additional cost for Russell besides having to reside in an inhospitable climate and live in near poverty. As a former student, Frank continued to be seen by other anthropologists as Putnam's valued assistant, not as an independent scholar. This was a problem encountered by all the young men Putnam hired permanently and one that later scholars who were hired by their alma mater have encountered. Even years after their graduation, employed alumni were often not viewed as autonomous scholars with their own research or teaching agendas. Frank needed other possibilities.

Searching for Employment Options

Russell thought about the national employment situation often, and the need for institutional development to include anthropology. In his 1902 American Folklore Society presidential address, he would note that only about 30 colleges offered anthropology courses. There were more than 30 experienced men waiting to fill those positions. Anthropology was a major in even fewer institutions. For the discipline to succeed, it had to socially reproduce itself, and that required expectations for well-remunerated careers, reputational rewards, and recognition of labor and esoteric knowledge, the hallmarks of late nineteenth-century American professions. The number of anthropology courses offered and the number of students taking them was rising, however, but had not reached the critical mass where Russell could easily locate a position, especially one in a suitable climate. It would be 12 and 25 years, respectively, before the University of Arizona and the University of New Mexico established anthropology departments.[3] It was either Harvard or unemployment in the fall of 1900 and the spring of 1901, even if Frank's salary would barely support the newlyweds.

It was time to think about the future, and that meant the 1901–2 academic year. Where could Frank try? One option was museums, but like the colleges and universities, they all had their anthropologists. Frank did not apply to the Field Museum after their summer experiences. We have no indication that he approached anyone in other museums. This left one alternative: the Smithsonian Institution. The USNM had seven full-time employees, and the BAE a slightly larger number. Both units were supplemented by collaborators and correspondents.[4] The USNM was focused on preparing a major exhibition for the Pan American Exposition in Buffalo, New York, and Hough was helping Mason prepare a series of technological comparative exhibits. Holmes was directing the construction of architectural models, including a cliff dwelling and a Tohono O'odham grass and adobe house. Russell had never built exhibits and had no interest in learning. He wanted to conduct research, not perform general museum activities to enhance mass education. Research and then curation management were his areas.

The most appropriate USNM possibility was an osteology curatorship. Since 1898 Powell had worked to have the cranial and somatic materials in the Army Medical Museum transferred to the USNM. The first honorary curator was Washington Matthews, with the U.S. Army paying his salary. Russell had trained for this position, but Holmes had someone else in mind. As early as 1898, he had been impressed with Aleš Hrdlička, who carried impressive European credentials. McGee thought Holmes "will make efforts to put him in the way of further researches whensoever conditions permit."[5] Unfortunately, there was no funding for other anthropometric or osteological research in 1900. This left the BAE.

If Russell was going to make a case to Powell, he needed to broaden his ethnographic and archaeological portfolio.

The BAE's concentration on the Southwest continued in fiscal 1900–1901 as it would in 1901–2. McGee worked in southern Arizona and Sonora during October and November 1900, searching without success for Seri, before turning to the Cocopa. Stevenson worked on her Puebloan materials near San Ildefonso. Fewkes furthered his archaeological explorations in southern Colorado and northern New Mexico, and then explored southwestern New Mexico, western Texas, and northern Chihuahua, Mexico. Hough returned to his 1900 activities, spending April 1901 collecting among the Western Apache and excavating in Socorro County, New Mexico, before rejoining Gates in Tusayan territory.[6] Russell needed to work around these initiatives and propose a research plan that would entice Powell and McGee. Should he suggest additional archaeological survey or ethnography? He decided to pursue archaeology.

Russell recognized that ethnography was still more prominent at the BAE, but the researcher needed to concentrate in areas outside the arid region. Pressured to concentrate on non-Southwestern areas, Powell had hired Harvard's newest PhD, John Swanton, to concentrate on the Southeast.[7] It was an excellent choice. Swanton had begun as an archaeologist working with Putnam, Volk, and Willoughby on eastern mounds, then excavated at Pueblo Bonito with Pepper. Swanton had studied comparative linguistics with Dixon and ethnography with Boas, participating in the Jesup North Pacific Expedition. Apparently, he had no interest in physical anthropology or spending his life immersed in museum collections. A versatile ethnographer, his work has stood the test of time. For Russell, however, Swanton's hiring meant Powell would not need another ethnographer.

Frank felt he had a persuasive archaeological argument. He would work in unexplored areas, concentrating on the Upper Gila River drainage, and resurvey previously charted regions looking in the unmapped areas. Another advantage to this plan, he felt, was that he was already associated with the BAE. McGee had claimed his 1900 research in the 1901–2 annual report. He was a known scholar who had successfully proven he could fulfill the BAE's mission. From Russell's viewpoint, it should have been enough to obtain a permanent position. In addition, it appeared another Southwestern ethnographer-archaeologist would be welcome. Where previously McGee had told Frank there were no permanent funds, the "Ethnologist-in-charge" now seriously courted Russell to see if he was still interested in permanent employment: "Will you kindly tell me what you would now think of transferring your affiliation from Harvard to the Bureau? A contingency is arising which makes it desirable to contemplate an addition to the corps, and you are naturally prominent in my mind in this connection. I note no details, because the general question of scientific opportunity stands paramount in your estimation as well as my own."[8]

While we have not located Russell's response, we expect he was skeptical about a "contingency." Frank also wanted to know where his current reimbursement was. The next day McGee sent another letter, stating that Frank's salary for the fall was late due to his absence from the office. He was now sending some of the funds and dangled a carrot: "I have in mind for action, should conditions permit, your desire to excavate the ruin west of Sacaton."[9]

Frank responded a few days later. He was gratified to know which way the wind was blowing. He must have expressed hesitation at McGee's lack of detail, however, for McGee responded quickly: "I have considered your inquires with some care, and appreciate their importance; but the questions raised in my mind thereby are so numerous as hardly to be dealt with adequately in correspondence."[10] A face-to-face meeting was necessary.

To hire "a rising star on the Harvard faculty" would be a coupe for McGee and help the BAE retain its Southwestern dominance.[11] Russell traveled to Washington, D.C., at the BAE's expense, to work out employment details. This included a summer assignment with regular orders. Frank would start after the semester ended in June or sooner if possible.

Unfortunately, McGee did not tell Frank the specifics of the personnel plan but simply insisted there was money. Unbeknownst to Frank, the BAE's annual budget had not been increased. Someone on staff would have to be furloughed or fired to hire him. McGee planned to fire Matilda Coxe Stevenson, claiming she had failed to finish her Zuni manuscript in a reasonable period. McGee formally offered Frank a permanent position with an annual salary of $1,800, substantially higher than his Harvard pay. They agreed Frank would survey central and southern Arizona and conduct ethnographic research with a Desert group. This time, McGee did not mention digging the site near Sacaton, but that was always possible in the future.

The offer came at a most propitious time. Frank had not been well; he had made it through the fall semester but had made less progress than anticipated on his research projects. The spring semester had already begun. Could he teach successfully during the winter? Russell was still hesitant, for he and Theresa did not really trust McGee, given that his past promises had been very, very slowly fulfilled. Frank still had not been reimbursed for all the previous summer's expenses. After agonizing the evening following their January meeting, Frank declined McGee's offer. He cited his hope that Harvard's administration would soon value anthropology more highly and expand their department (that is, he hoped President Eliot would match the salary offer).[12] He was also loath to leave the collections he had built as well as his anthropometric research just when it was starting to produce results. Frank did not mention his current teaching obligations to McGee, but one did not leave in the middle of a semester as McGee hoped he would. Could they believe McGee when he insisted, *Trust me, all will be well soon*? It would mean severing ties with Harvard and would cause problems for Putnam.

The situation soon changed and their hesitation vanished, however. Frank deteriorated rapidly with a tuberculosis flare a few days later. His doctor feared he would not survive the semester unless he resumed the climate cure. After Russell suffered a severe throat hemorrhage, he contacted McGee and agreed to McGee's proposal with an official start date of March 1. On February 3, Frank resigned his Harvard position. The Russells would live on their meager savings, calling on her family for help if necessary. McGee immediately revised his agency budget, but he was still just making promises. He did not have actual funds for Russell's salary. To make matters more tenuous, McGee had intentionally not sought approval from Smithsonian secretary Samuel Langley, to whom the BAE director reported. McGee wanted to make the need to fire Stevenson an accomplished fact so Langley would not argue. Frank and Theresa did not know this.[13]

Russell's resignation from Harvard was not unexpected but still unwelcome. Putnam reassigned his classes to J. D. Wood, Roland B. Dixon, Henry Miner Huxley, and William C. Farabee, a division of labor that indicated just how crucial Russell was to the Harvard anthropology program.[14] Putnam changed Russell's hastily written notification to an unpaid leave of absence request due to unexpected illness. He hoped Russell would return for the fall semester. Putnam wanted Frank to have some options should his health improve, and he did not trust McGee. This was wise. McGee was playing a shell game.

Before the Survey

The Russells left immediately. There was no time to arrange advance funding from McGee, and the Peabody Museum was not able to provide any support. The goal was to be in Tucson on March 1, 1901, to "officially" begin BAE work. Before starting, Frank and Theresa would visit old friends on the Colorado Plateau and search areas not visited in 1900. Frank's preliminary orders were twofold. First, he would conduct an archaeological reconnaissance of southern and central Arizona. He would then combine the preliminary surveys undertaken in 1898, 1899, and 1900 with the results of the new surveys to produce a comprehensive report prioritizing future archaeological activity and assessing the extent of pothunting and preservation needs.[15] Second, he would arrange fieldwork with the Akimel O'odham (Pima) to produce an ethnography about a "typical" tribe living in an arid region, a category of Indigenous people McGee called Desert People. McGee found $200 to cover expenses for the survey near Tucson between March and June. He insisted once again Frank's position would improve when the new annual appropriation began in July—or at least theoretically, because political wrangling often meant the funds were not available until the end of summer or even the fall. The Russells had to be very, very frugal, but as evident from their honeymoon, they had practice. Significantly, McGee did not mention salary in his correspondence at this time.

Whatever work Frank and Theresa accomplished in northern Arizona before they headed to Tucson would be considered part of Frank's official assignment. Surveying Arizona during 1901 would later include a transect across northern Arizona to the flanks of the Kaibito Plateau, northeastward across Monument Valley, and along the San Juan River to Bluff, Utah. Most of this journey was undertaken after they had finished their southern Arizona explorations. We have not located either Frank's or Theresa's journals for the February and March 1901 survey, so we do not know where they went. Again, Frank did not have Indian Service permission to excavate in Tusayan, and there is no indication that he even tried. What information we have is found in terse monthly reports that began soon thereafter and a few letters to McGee in which Frank detailed his needs (that is, money and transportation) rather than documented research results. It seems that Frank and Theresa might have been assessing pot-hunting damage to known sites. Russell noted he based his route on the Mindeleff surveys of the Colorado Plateau and would do the same when he visited the Verde Valley as well as consult Fewkes's reports for the Little Colorado River and central Arizona.[16] The Russells' 1901 survey was thus the beginnings of a systematic effort to assess the extent of antiquities' looting. They would also look in new areas, for the BAE was branching out in response to McGee's interest in desert adaptation. McGee wanted to claim central and southern Arizona as the BAE's research territory. He was particularly concerned with ensuring that the Field Museum did not move south.

Dorsey was on the move again. He had sent his research assistant, Stephen C. Simms, to collect ethnographic art and locate archaeological sites in central and southwestern Arizona. He clearly wanted Simms to assess the potential of the regions Hough had visited in 1900 and where he had heard McGee was steering Frank. From January to March, Simms visited the Akimel O'odham, Maricopa, Walapai, Tohono O'odham, and Colorado River tribes near Yuma. He hoped to work extensively with Mr. Ewing, the Pima's agent, but Ewing was busy. Dorsey also told Simms to search for human remains; Simms responded he would "land" him "a few skulls at Laguna or Isleta" due to the dispersed burial practices. In other words, he would steal them. Simms's letters from Phoenix did not mention any similar opportunities for grave robbing or sites worth excavating. He noticed only one possibility near Gila Bend.[17]

Simms spent weeks where the Russells would work later in the year. We have gained the impression Dorsey wanted to ensure there was nothing left for the BAE to collect, rivaling the Awatovi situation. Simms collected only a few baskets, for he was traveling behind two curio dealers, who eliminated all opportunities in the O'odham and Maricopa communities. Simms was frustrated and had many tales of woe. He encountered countless transportation delays, errors loading the film in his camera, and inclement weather. Unlike Frank, he intensely disliked the region: "dust, dust, dust everywhere and on everything." After the first rains for a year it was "good mud, nice mud, black mud, clinging mud and more mud." He considered the region to be "the most God forsaken place." Numerous letters recorded Simms's unhappiness as well as why he was not amassing collections. Dorsey's chiding responses ordered him to continue, reach all the inaccessible communities he had missed, and then proceed to Southern California before the University of California at Berkeley and Alfred Kroeber tied up the area for themselves. It was a tiring trip, and Simms was not sanguine about future research in central Arizona, but he did relay gossip to Dorsey.[18] The Russells had left northern Arizona and taken a train to Phoenix and from there a stagecoach to Tucson. Who knew what they would find, he speculated.

Reconnaissance Trip 1

Frank's official orders were to conduct a survey for archaeological sites in southern Arizona and compare "lowland antiquities with those of the highland."[19] Fewkes and Hough had explored sites around Tucson in 1897 and sent 1,300 specimens of pottery and "relics" to the USNM. They thought there were more sites that could be profitably excavated in the Tucson Basin and its surrounding mountains. Russell was to locate possible ruins for excavation the next fall. When the Tucson Basin survey was completed, Russell was to search southern Arizona before it became too hot. Then he would undertake a second survey of central Arizona before heading to the Colorado Plateau to avoid the summer heat and blowing dust. The first survey would concentrate on the upper Gila River valley and extend south to the international boundary before turning west to search the Papaguería, where McGee had visited in 1894. He would not officially excavate on any Indian reservation where Indian Service permission was required but would simply trench to see what was in a site. Then Frank would return to Tucson. Their official southern Arizona survey would begin in the Tucson Basin in March 1901, even though Frank had not yet been officially hired. Frank was eager to start. He wanted to take advantage of a remission in his tuberculosis and not simply wait idly in Tucson, spending $1.50 a day on a hotel room because McGee was slow obtaining his credentials and funds. Besides, McGee had promised. To Frank, this written commitment was as binding as a formal contract.

The Russells visited Tucson residents familiar with the area's antiquities and saw the artifacts University of Arizona Spanish instructor Mrs. M. B. Aguirre had collected from local mountain caves. She gave them directions. They used their trusty bicycles, then rode on horseback or walked but found little. Since the mountains were daunting, they reconsidered their transportation needs. Frank concluded that a team and wagon were necessary for longer excursions. But how to secure one when he had no letter authorizing vouchers and no indication that he was an official federal employee? How could he assure owners they would be paid eventually?

Russell's reports and letters reported difficulties securing transportation, for this required owners to trust him. Frank insisted that McGee fulfill his promises, for he had used up the few voucher blanks McGee had given him by the end of March. In desperation, Russell made his own vouchers based on McGee's model, but these were obviously unofficial, in essence as worthless officially as personal promissory notes. Frank could give merchants and citizens no proof he really worked for the government. People were naturally skeptical that his handmade IOUs would be honored. McGee was sympathetic but responded as always: "Soon, be patient, keep working." Frank received no money and no letters to officially declare his status. Frank felt he and Theresa were missing their window of opportunity—the good weather would only last so long.

The Russells' odyssey for suitable transportation continued without the help of their landlord, Mr. Berger, one of the oldest inhabitants of Pima County. Berger knew of no available team that could withstand their intended journey or find an owner willing to loan animals on Frank's promises of future payment. After five weeks, Frank and Theresa stopped waiting. Frank purchased a team of mules, harnesses, and a wagon for $400, using a good portion of their remaining savings. He wrote McGee that the equipment and team were his "personal contribution" to the project, to be treated as personal property. The teamster he hired on April 6, 1901, for $1.50 a day, however, was to be placed on the government payroll. Russell would pay him until vouchers arrived but expected to be reimbursed. It is unclear how long Frank employed the unnamed teamster, but we imagine it must have been for most of the spring and possibly the summer. McGee did not officially respond to Frank's scheme.[20]

On April 7, Frank, Theresa, and their teamster-guide began their first trip. The USGS surveying equipment McGee had promised, however, was sitting somewhere in a railroad car in the Midwest. The trio proceeded around the north end of the Santa Catalina Mountains and "up" the San Pedro River (that is, north), where they made camp. From this unspecified location, they took side trips on foot to see three caves where Mrs. Aguirre had obtained pots. They found no new artifacts, and Frank assumed Mexican or Euro-American settlers had picked up other pieces. They also searched for pictographs in the mountains but took no photographs of what they saw.

The Russells proceeded along the San Pedro River and made side trips to see cave sites and pictograph panels, which they sketched and photographed.

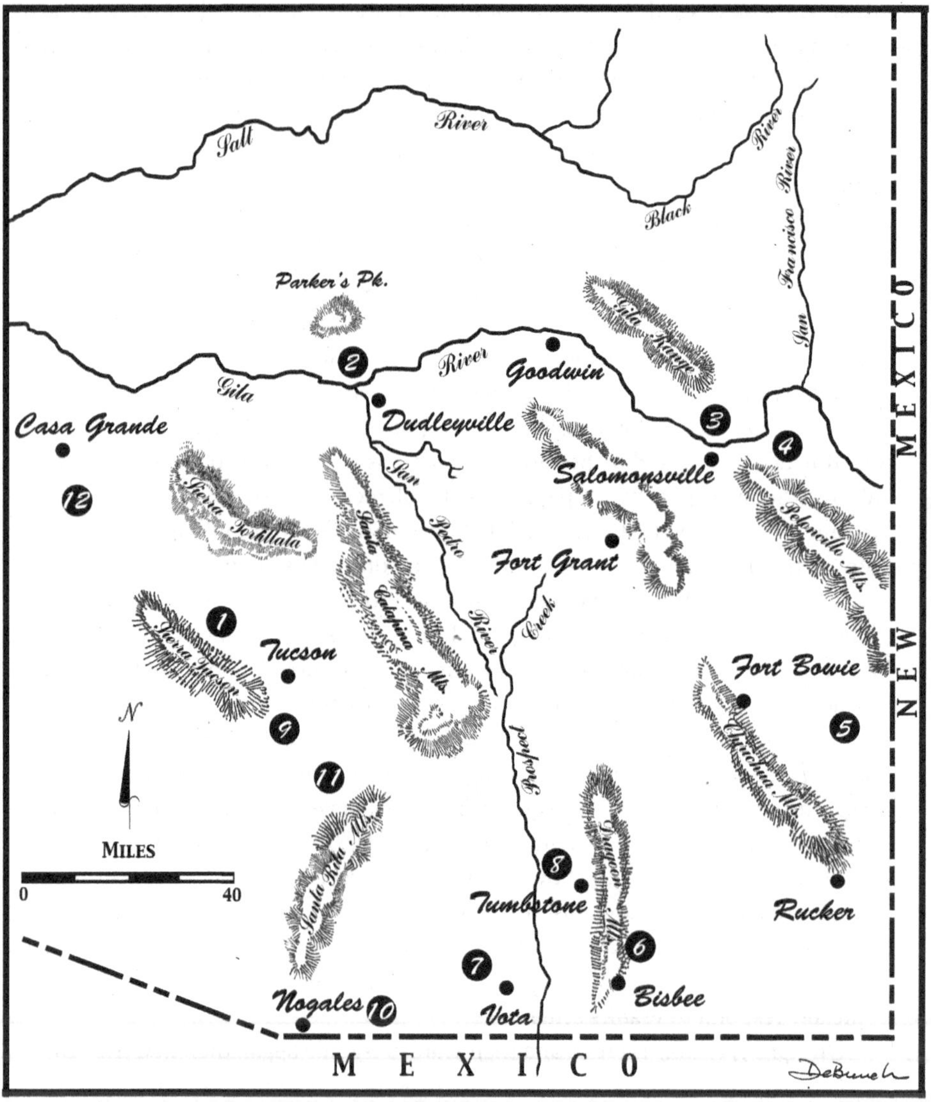

MAP 4.1. Russell Reconnaissance Survey 1, 1901, southern Arizona. 1. Tucson basin; 2. Santa Catalina Mountains; 3. Dudleyville; 4. Solomonville; 5. Old San Rafael; 6. east of Chiricahua Mountains; 7. Bisbee; 8. Vota; 9. Tombstone; 10. Tucson; 11. Nogales; 12. Pantano-Tanque Verde; 13. Casa Grande. The two circuits begin and end in Tucson. Map by Patricia DeBunch.

Proceeding 15 miles north of the mining and agricultural settlement of Mammoth, the Russells spent three days examining the architectural sequence at a platform site, most likely Dudleyville. Frank concluded that "the extensive wall (which seemed very old and built by the aboriginal inhabitants) was erected shortly before the abandonment of the pueblo, that the walls were of rounded boulders covered with plaster within and without, etc."[21] Russell next mapped two nearby sites using the plane table that had finally arrived. He rarely used it later because the sites they visited required considerable excavation to define basic features. Moving a few miles north toward Winkelman, the Russells found what Frank considered a puzzling archaeological feature: a stone wall connecting two conical buttes, which the Mexican American inhabitants considered prehistoric.

Turning southeast, they visited the Galiuro Mountain and saw what Russell termed "cliff-houses" before returning to the Gila River drainage in what is now the Coronado National Forest. From there they rode through Nugent Pass and entered the Aravaipa Valley heading to the Graham Country line; they visited a small group of "cliff-houses" Frank considered "most-interesting."[22] What they found raised as many questions as answers, however, for the sites were different from what the Russells had seen near the Hopi mesas six months earlier. One ruin near Bryce, located about seven miles north of Safford on the Gila River in a town today called Pima, he found especially perplexing.

> On a barren mesa, a hundred feet above the river bottom are three large areas and several smaller ones over which the rounded lava boulders have been piled in rows forming rectangular areas about fifteen feet across. One of the two largest of these fields measured 2600 by 880 feet. There seemed to be not the slightest sign that human beings had ever been there except for the piles of stones. Where the water-worn boulders had laid thickest the walls were highest, where they were few the walls became thin attenuated lines; rarely, the larger stones bore pictographs [*sic*: petroglyphs]—coils, lizards, etc. In a few places, the stones were piled in long parallel lines, but these places might easily be overlooked in an extensive examination of the place. At a few other points the stones were piled in round heaps and I am forced to conclude that the ground was cleared for some crop. . . . The place excites considerable local interest and is really impressive by its magnitude.[23]

After recording the site, the Russells and a local guide journeyed north over Eagle Pass in the Graham Mountains before taking the established trail to Fort Thomas on the Gila River.[24] Here Frank and Theresa visited an Akimel O'odham community to discuss research opportunities. This may have been a southern village on the Gila River Indian reservation or some village not on the reservation; we are not sure. Frank had learned his lesson about simply showing up in a

Native community. He also asked about local sites. Since Russell did not recount the residents' responses to his queries, it was probably negative. The explorers quickly moved on.

Continuing along the Gila River, Frank made two side trips into the Graham Mountains to record abandoned Apache camps and supposedly "ancient Pueblo settlements" while Theresa stayed with the wagon. They stopped briefly in the mining community of Solomonsville, five miles east of Safford, and noted destroyed ruins. One unnamed site's walls had been transformed into adobe brick and mounds leveled to enable irrigation. Despite this, the site and others nearby had potential. Frank noted numerous funerary urns and recorded that residents often uncovered them while plowing. He himself saw eight urns in a row in one level field but did not collect them. He had no money to purchase any antiquities he found there or in settlers' homes.

The Russells likely visited Epley's Ruin, the largest site near Solomonsville, located on the road to San Jose. Fewkes and Hough had visited it in 1897 and excavated a small area.[25] Fewkes had had one of his crew, a Mr. Adams, excavate the largest behind the farmhouse; he uncovered some thick walls and the outlines of house walls that extended down to the Gila River floodplain. Mr. Epley let Russell record how much had changed in four years.

Russell looked to see how other sites had fared since Fewkes's and Hough's visit. The second major ruin Frank mentioned in his report, "San Jose de Pueblo Viejo" (Buena Vista), had been largely demolished. Located eight miles northeast of Solomonsville on a high bluff above the Gila River, the site had been cut through by a new canal, 25 feet wide, since 1897.[26] While many local residents had dug in the ruin for many years, they had not yet completely destroyed the "Repressa" or "Sun Temple." Russell described this feature as one of the largest of a dozen ball courts they had seen. Ever the scientist, Frank began to analyze what he had seen. He tried to figure out how the ball courts were situated. His initial hypothesis had been that they were oriented toward water supplies, but after seeing numerous examples, he felt the ball courts were slanted in every conceivable direction. More research was needed to understand the ancient religion and its rituals. This topic, he felt, could be a fruitful research project.

After resting in San Jose village, Russell concluded so much had been destroyed by the region's burgeoning agricultural development, there was little worth excavating. He decided to try a new direction. Heading south, the couple visited what Frank decided were three promising sites, what he called "Old San Rafael," located five miles north of Sonora, and two ruins a couple of miles south of the international border. At all three, the Russells dug pits to a depth of five feet and found what Frank called "tastefully decorated" pottery. He sent sherds to Fewkes for identification. We have found no response with type names and do not know what happened to the sherds.

The Russells needed supplies but rather than go to Tombstone, Arizona, where they had no credit line established, they returned to Tucson. Somehow Frank convinced a merchant to sell them food and fodder. Resupplied, they headed east along the railroad past Wilcox and Benson and turned south, searching along San Simon Creek near the New Mexico border. Frank technically had no orders to survey this far east or south of Tucson, but a lack of orders never deterred him: "As I had not yet received my appointment as temporary assistant and feeling somewhat at liberty to take advantage of the favorable circumstances, I decided to extend the survey south to include the entire southeastern portion of the Territory."[27] They then passed Bowie Station before walking along the Chiricahua Mountains' eastern slopes. Somewhere in this area, Frank secured the trip's only "artifacts" (four Apache skulls), which he sent to Tucson for shipment to the Smithsonian Institution. His reports provided no other information about these human remains, nor where he found them. Hrdlička later included them in his craniology collection.

Turning southwest, the trio crossed Apache Pass, then flanked the eastern slopes of the Swisshelm or Huachuca Mountains, examining canyons for cave sites. They drove their wagon down the road to Bisbee and Naco, stopping at the Mexican border. Beginning their return trip to Tucson, they stopped at a site near Vota, then investigated the eastern canyons of the Huachuca Mountains, but Frank recorded no sites. After traveling to Fairbank, located about halfway between Tombstone and Fort Huachuca, Frank left the team and Theresa to rest and walked 25 miles to Benson, surveying as he went. Russell hitched a ride back to where he had left Theresa and their guide. They drove the wagon east to Bowie, along the stagecoach route. Here they received news from McGee; Russell had a formalized, approved, permanent BAE position as an ethnologist beginning on April 15, 1901. It was only six weeks later than McGee originally promised. Frank immediately wired his acceptance, requesting money and vouchers.[28]

The welcome news was soon followed by a second letter: the official appointment would now start on May 1. No money was authorized and there were no vouchers. Russell now wrote to Powell, not McGee; he was angry. He had not received a contract he could sign, nor a letter authorizing him to use official vouchers. He reminded Powell in his monthly report that the formal government appointment, his "definite standing," was "to be desired because of my relations with the people there."[29] More than the weather and Frank's resentment was heating up. Frank knew that legal consequences were imminent if McGee failed to honor his promises. Frank had pushed his and Theresa's credit to its limit, and the Territory had laws against not paying outstanding debts and committing fraud. Their transportation and living expenses continued to mount. Funds had to be in Tucson when Frank returned for supplies. Otherwise he could go to jail. Russell could be a wanted man again as he pursued archaeology.

Not inclined to simply sit waiting for McGee yet again, the Russells continued their survey. Frank somehow convinced someone to extend more credit for supplies. They headed southeast to Patagonia, Babacomari, and Sonoita. Then it was on to Harshaw and the San Rafael Valley before crossing into Mexico east of Nogales, possibly at Lochiel.[30] Returning to Arizona, they began the journey to Tucson, passing the Santa Rita Mountains' eastern flank. Frank did not mention any sites on this circuit in his next monthly report. Cave sites were seen near Greaterville. Little was viewed in the Pantano Wash east of Tucson, and nothing on the Tanque Verde wash near Vail. Before returning to Tucson, the Russells looked for sites in Sabino Canyon and took several side trips into the Rincon and Santa Catalina Mountains.

In three months, the Russells had traveled 927 miles by wagon. Frank walked an additional 75 miles. They recorded about 100 large and small ruins. They excavated little but recorded where others had dug previously. They reported that "here and there a wall was laid bare or a cliff-house cleaned out." They had spent the longest time (three days) at one ruin 15 miles above Mammoth on the San Pedro to assess the age of the extensive wall ("very old").[31] Several sites merited intensive investigation, but once again, Frank failed to report which ones. Russell recommended an additional survey, which he would conduct. McGee agreed but still failed to send the official appointment letter or money. There were new problems.

Civil Service Problems

On reaching Tucson, Frank thought his financial troubles would finally be solved, but he was in for another surprise. There was no contract to sign. No money had been wired. Bureaucratic complications had arisen. Frank was informed he had not been properly sworn in as a federal employee, and as a result, his voucher submissions for reimbursement had been denied. The letter from one Mr. J. Julius Lund, a Treasury Department personnel officer, raised questions about the duties of a government ethnologist since there was no title on the approved civil service list and no approved job description. Lund specifically stated he had no evidence Frank was qualified to use horses. Lund refused to approve Frank's reimbursement vouchers for the wagon team because Frank had only been authorized to use a bicycle. This meant the civil service rating and job title Lund assigned Russell was "urban memo courier." It was the lowest one possible. According to Lund, Dr. Russell did not have a high enough job rating—or apparently the intelligence—to travel using mules and horses.

Frank was understandably frustrated. As he wrote Lund: "Your note has just reached me. No. I was not aware that a plain 'ethnologist' was expected to swear before beginning to drive mules in this benighted country. However, having driven them seven weeks, I am ready to swear to anything if you will explain what."[32]

Lund assigned a new rating, one allowing Frank to use horses and mules in addition to his bicycle and walking. Still, no funds came with the new ranking although he was assured his vouchers would now be covered. Frank began planning the next reconnaissance trip, but his troubles with the civil service bureaucrat were not over.

Now, the research scientist, with a degree from one of the country's finest colleges, could not be an "official government employee" until he had taken the civil service exam, had it graded, then taken and signed an oath of office before a public notary. This meant no funds would be forthcoming to repay his debts or enable him to extend his credit. Frank was now informed that the Pendleton Civil Service Reform Act of 1883 required him to demonstrate he could read (his ability to read letters did not count) and that an exam had to be given to access his writing ability and general intelligence. Credentials like a doctorate were not acceptable proof, for they had not been approved by the Civil Service Commission. Lund held he had no authority to make an exception to the rule.

What was the real problem? Was Russell a scapegoat who had bad luck? The test was a regulatory step required for any federal appointive position, but the federal employment system was only now being implemented within the Smithsonian Institution, the USGS, and the BAE. These federal units had ignored the rules for professionals whose work required specialized knowledge, individuals above the level of clerks. And they had done this for 18 years. Previously, past research experience, publications, and educational credentials were considered adequate evidence of reading and writing ability as well as content knowledge. Lund refused to approve employment or payments for new professionals until all civil service requirements and paperwork were complete. Frank was the first BAE employee to encounter the implemented rules. With creditors looming, Frank agreed to do anything to obtain his reimbursement and obtain his salary.

Russell said and then signed the oath of office after searching for an appropriate official for several days. The properly notarized paper was sent to McGee, who sent it to Lund at the Treasury Department. But Lund again ruled it insufficient documentation of competency. Dr. Russell still needed to take a civil service examination that assessed his writing prowess and ability to think at the level for which McGee was hiring him. No such test existed, however. McGee had Putnam send a copy of Russell's Harvard PhD diploma as evidence for his education but Lund ruled it inconclusive. While there were standard examination questions for clerks (to see if they knew how to spell correctly) or entry-level accountants (to see if they could add and subtract), there were none for any PhD scientist in any government agency. A test had to be created. Lund, the consummate bureaucrat, also again stated that since all civil service examination results had to be correlated with a job description's requirements, McGee had to submit a job description. This then had to be approved and classified to a civil service level before a test could be written and taken. Once this was completed and approved, McGee had to compose a special test and submit a copy, the results, and the grade to Lund. McGee continued to argue with Lund, who remained firm on the need for a job description and a rigorous examination. McGee appealed to Lund's supervisor, and with each rejection, tried administrators up the political chain, but to no avail. The Treasury Department personnel officers had been charged by the new McKinley administration to control political patronage and nepotism.

McGee should not have been surprised that ignoring federal law would catch up with him and hurt whomever he tried to hire.[33] Nor should Russell, given his interaction with the Indian Service and the GLO the previous summer. McGee finally wrote a job description and exam. He sent a copy to Lund and another to the postmaster in Tucson, explaining Russell had to take the timed examination under the supervision of a federal employee. Then more bad news arrived as McGee tried to manipulate the bureaucracy. Russell "may be subjected to inconvenience by reason of non-arrival of funds." The Treasury Department made McGee take Frank off the May payroll. McGee informed Russell he still hoped to reinstate him in June. In the meantime, it would take time to pay Frank because McGee was now under scrutiny from Smithsonian Institution accountants as well as Treasury Department officials. More approvals had to be obtained. McGee was no longer free to simply move funds where he wanted. His past practices ("irregularities") were catching up with him. Russell was an unfortunate victim of McGee's administrative gamesmanship and the guinea pig for the new procedures.[34]

Since the exam took so long to schedule, the Russells stayed in Tucson. Bored, they took another short unauthorized side trip. They traveled onto the Papago (Tohono O'odham) reservation and visited Baboquivari Peak. Traveling west, they crossed the international border at Sonoyta, Sonora, and then followed the San Rafael Valley east, traveling just south of the boundary. They recrossed the border somewhere near Sasabe, then headed north to Tucson, working their way around the Sierrita Mountains.

Russell learned that the timed test had been postponed again because no government official was available. The only qualified person authorized to administer the examination was a postal employee who was out of town. Frank and Theresa decided to visit more Tucson Basin sites, walking, riding their bicycles, and using their now authorized mules and wagon. Finally, Frank and the post office official were in Tucson at the same time. As he later wrote Powell, "It [the examination] was finally held in the back part of the post office." The "Commissioner," as Frank called the postal clerk, "began sweeping out the post office as I began the examination and it was also hot. I hope you will not read the papers!"[35] The dust for a tuberculosis sufferer must have made the task excruciating.

The exam was essentially the equivalent of a PhD qualifying examination. It consisted of five sections. The first was a 20-point essay of no fewer than 1,000 words, defining the science of ethnology and archaeology and indicating their chief applications. McGee instructed Russell to avoid all allusions to the author's political or religious opinions. The second section consisted of curriculum vitae–style listings of Russell's ethnological experience, focusing on fieldwork and teaching. This section was also worth 20 points. The third, 30-point section required Frank to list all his publications in ethnology and archaeology, including full citations. The examination also requested that if convenient, copies should be furnished with this statement. Since Russell's papers were in Boston, we can assume he submitted a basic listing. The fourth section, worth 20 points, evaluated Russell's knowledge of the geographic, ethnologic, and archaeological features of Arizona and New Mexico. The fifth section, a review of the ethnology and archaeology literature on the U.S. Southwest, counted for 10 points. Theoretically, the last two topics were to be an oral examination between McGee and Russell. Since McGee gave Dr. Russell a score of 100, we conclude their previous meetings and discussions fulfilled this requirement. Finally, Frank was to provide the names of five individuals who could speak to his expertise, experience, and capacity to perform the position's duties. We presume Putnam was one of the named references but doubt one was Dorsey.

It is ironic that the civil service system required McGee, a geologist without a college education, to assess a Harvard professor with an anthropology doctorate. The questions were general enough that Russell's answers were similar in scope to articles he had written for *The American Naturalist.* We suppose that Russell used his reflections assessing regional scholarship later for his magnum opus, *The Pima Indians.* We know from correspondence that McGee was embarrassed having to write and grade a test. Russell was embarrassed by his essays, for he had no reference materials to ensure proper citations. And he recognized a more sensitive problem: could he really say how he felt about the quality of past research produced by BAE scholars, especially McGee? Responding to a letter in which McGee praised Russell's efforts, Frank stated his concerns. These were ones that are well known to anyone who has had firsthand experience with credentialing situations where honesty could anger assessors: "I had found the greater part of the literature worthless so far as I could judge and needed some assurance that because my observations did not tally with the literature it was not necessarily the fault of the former."[36]

Once McGee graded the examination, Lund certified the results. McGee was allowed to send Russell an approval letter, co-signed by Lund. Lund now recertified that Dr. Russell was sufficiently educated to use a horse or mule and drive as wagon. He could read and write at a level to serve as a government ethnologist. Lund required no further evidence of Russell's suitability. However, he had one more hurdle. A second oath was required, administered by a public notary or a justice of the peace, for another small fee. It took Russell several days to find an appropriate official in Tucson.

With all the paperwork theoretically completed, McGee wired funds he called "salary" but not funds to reimburse what the Russells had expended in March to May research. The couple paid some of their creditors but not all. McGee assumed Frank had enough presigned vouchers for a couple of months, but he did not.[37] McGee had neglected to send any. Still, the Russells hoped to survey without fear of a debt collector, now assured of a more permanent flow of money.

Russell was technically official according to the Treasury Department, for he had met all civil service requirements. Unbeknownst to him, Frank had still not been officially hired, however. There was another administrative barrier that had to be broken and Frank had not been informed of its existence. Powell and McGee needed permission from the Smithsonian Institution administration to hire any research scientist. Again there were delays. It took time for the request and resulting negotiation correspondence to wind their way back and forth across the Washington Mall. Powell did not receive a notification from the Smithsonian's acting secretary, Richard Rathbun, of an employment start date of July 15 for Russell until July 9. When he learned this, Frank was surprised, for he had thought he had already had a job with an agreed-on salary. Again, he had worked for free, now since May 1. There would be no back pay. McGee's "salary" had actually come from the research expenses category. Further, McGee and Powell had failed to inform Frank that Rathbun had final approval since Frank's salary would come from the Secretary's Reserve, part of the $5,000 the Smithsonian secretary controlled of the BAE's $40,000 budget. Unfortunately for the Russells, the salary Rathbun approved was only $1,500, not the $1,800 McGee had promised.[38] There was no recourse, Frank now discovered. He could take it or leave it. He needed whatever funds he could get immediately, for he was again in debt. Frank signed the final employment documents. He and Theresa were not pleased.

We think the decreased salary reflected the fact that Rathbun directed McGee to reinstate Stevenson and pay her during July 1901, after which McGee could place her on furlough due to ill health. Rathbun approved McGee's scheme to pay Stevenson "a suitable sum" for any ethnological manuscripts she prepared.[39] Her freed-up salary could be used for Russell in August. But it was only a temporary solution, not the permanent employment Russell thought he had earned and been promised. His contract was for nine months—until the end of March 1902. Russell did not have the permanent job McGee had guaranteed him.

Reconnaissance Trip 2

Still living on promises and credit, the Russells left Tucson on June 12. Frank reported to Powell later that they had decided to visit sites east of Tucson after the summer heat had dissipated. Now they were headed north, looking for what Frank would later call Hohokam settlements. They visited an extensive fortification site at the north end of the Tortolita Mountains: "It is in an out of the way spot and seems to have escaped the shovel thus far." The next day they traveled to an adobe site located on a slope about 10 miles south of Florence. The small mound (the Tom Mix Site) was about nine feet high and in pristine condition, but Russell reported it was not worth excavating, for there was no pottery. Florence would be their first major base. He would "excavate there for a week or two [and] learn much of the Casa Grande type of ruin and possibly learn something new of the ancient people since this ruin is in the southern border of the Gila-Salt River group." They reached Casa Grande, the first archaeological site to be set aside by the U.S. government. Russell was glad Mindeleff and Cushing had recommended its preservation but noted "the place needs a custodian. The warning against defacing the building seems to act as an incentive to some persons to do that which is forbidden."[40] Assessing looting and the defacing of sites would be a major theme of this survey.

Russell decided to proceed to the Superstition Mountains, where he hoped to hire pack animals. On seeing the range and talking with residents, however, he decided it would be a waste of time to explore them. This would be a scientific loss, he stated in his monthly report, for "thanks to a 'lost mine,' they are perhaps the best-known range in Arizona."[41] Theresa and Frank turned toward Phoenix and camped on Baseline Road. Frank interviewed members of an unidentified geographical survey and learned that the Pima and Maricopa made religious pilgrimages to the area and Apaches used to camp nearby. The surveyors had found more than 800 projectile points and many beads in a cache on South Mountain's summit. Frank decided not to visit. The next morning, the Russells visited one small cliff house in the Phoenix Mountains, and then rode among the base of the foothills visiting several ancient village sites. Unfortunately these were not named in his report. Frank was quite impressed with one located on Queen Creek, however. This was probably the San Tan Ruin. Frank reported it should be investigated further since it was extensive and untouched.

The Phoenix Basin was as sweltering as Tucson. The dust was also affecting Frank's breathing. He realized he needed to head to a higher altitude, curtailing their immediate assignment. He and Theresa headed along the Salt River toward the Tonto Basin and recorded numerous (but again unnamed) archaeological sites that would later be associated with Mogollon and Salado cultures. An unexpected number were undisturbed but had not been previously recorded by government geologists, geographers, or anthropologists. Russell told Powell he was uncomfortable trenching, for he was treading into Fewkes's territory. It was apparent, however, that Fewkes had missed a great deal during his earlier survey of the area.

The distance from the Superstition Mountains to Globe was about 80 miles over what Frank described as all-but-impassable trails. Crossing between Apache Junction and Florence Junction, the pair skirted the Superstition Mountains, looking briefly at small defensive ruins and a few cliff dwellings. They rode near the Silver King Mine and south to Riverside on the Gila River before turning north to Globe. Russell wrote McGee of his revised plans: "Not being detained at the Superstition Mountains and only wishing to make a survey in the Tonto complete enough to show Dr. Fewkes what is in here, I find myself with time enough to undertake the original plan of a reconnaissance down the lower Little Colorado. I am equipped for that kind of work and had better continue I think until after the Denver meeting when I can settle down to the business of excavation."[42] Frank aimed to finish the 1900 survey.

Not waiting for McGee's reply, which this time came quickly agreeing to the plan, the Russells turned toward the Verde Valley. During July, they surveyed north of Globe, near the Salt River, in an area occupied by Salado peoples between AD 1225 and 1400. Frank found an interesting site about 15 miles north of Globe. This was probably the site at Wheatfields that Bandelier had visited on his survey.[43] It was an extensive fortified camp that Frank felt should be excavated. Proceeding up the Salado (Salt) River Valley, east of what is now Lake Roosevelt, Frank left the wagon at a small settlement; he and Theresa walked north across rolling hills to Coon Creek and Cherry Creek. Heading still further north, they viewed Sierra Anchas cliff houses, each with half a dozen rooms. Next, they superficially examined three ruins and a medium-sized pueblo at the pine-covered summit of the Sierra Anchas, probably on Aztec Peak. They returned to Globe, having traveled 75 miles on this short loop.

Leaving Globe again, they proceeded along what is today Arizona State Route 188 to two cliff houses near the mouth of Tonto Creek and the Salt River. Frank decided these were important, undisturbed sites. He estimated one had 30 rooms, the other 45. Figures 4.1 and 4.2 are Russell's sketches of these ruins he attached to his June report.[44] He also reported that a man securing a bee swarm had burned the larger ruin. Nevertheless, Russell felt the floors and roofs were in almost perfect condition in many rooms. He recommended a major excavation.

Theresa and Frank proceeded northwest through Tonto Creek valley. Russell reported few ranchers lived in the area, which meant several ruins lay undisturbed. He located a dozen sites, four of them large, in the first 15 miles. The most impressive was Cline Terrace.[45] Frank measured the wall: 225 × 375 feet,

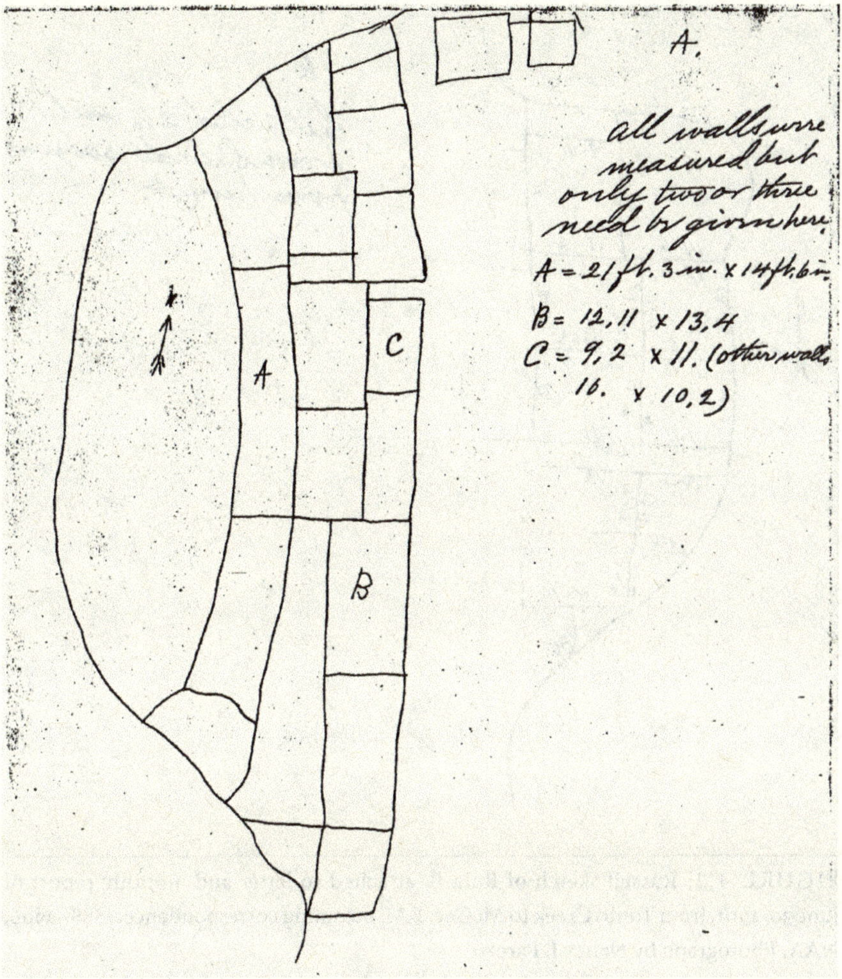

FIGURE 4.1. Russell sketch of Ruin A, Salado (Salt) River area, attached to letter and monthly report of June 30, 1901, from Tonto Creek to McGee. BAE incoming correspondence, 1888–1906, NAA. Photograph by Nancy J. Parezo.

most parts 9 feet high. Inside were only three potholes, one of which had human remains lying beside it. Russell reburied the skeleton.

Frank and Theresa excavated Cline Terrace for a week to learn how the main building was constructed and how the people lived. Russell wanted to conduct these excavations because he found the existing literature on the site did not tally with his observations. He intended to write a major paper as well as a field account after the summer field season, so he sent his notes to McGee for

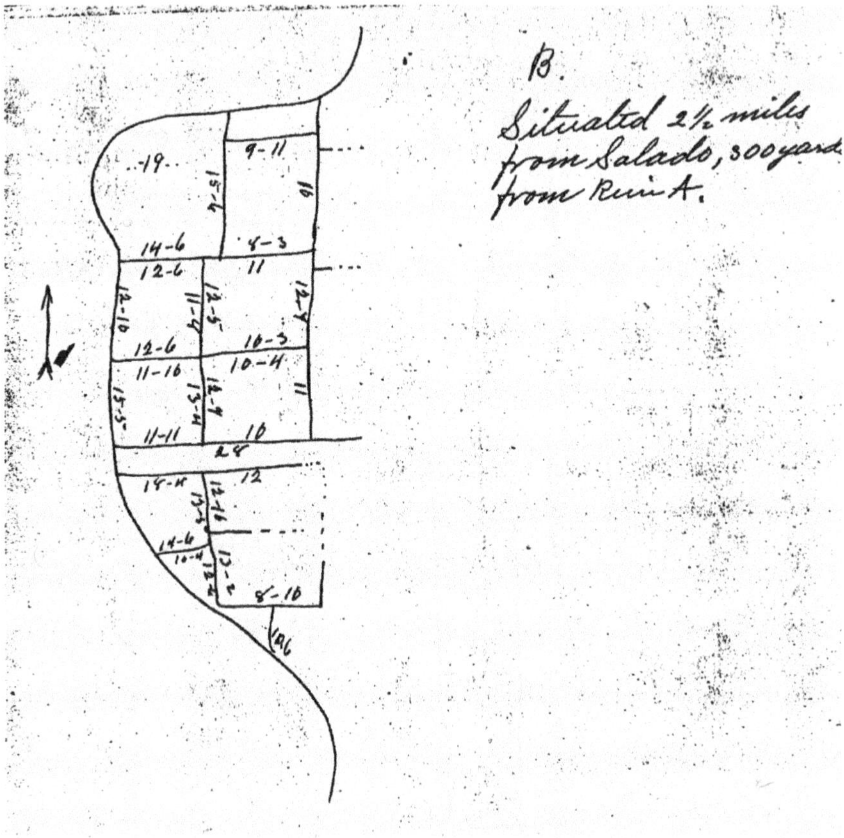

FIGURE 4.2. Russell sketch of Ruin B, attached to letter and monthly report of June 30, 1901, from Tonto Creek to McGee. BAE incoming correspondence, 1888–1906, NAA. Photograph by Nancy J. Parezo.

safekeeping. He intended to work on it in the fall in Washington, D.C. Frank's summary was apparently never published, and we found no manuscript. We do not know what McGee did with Russell's field notes. They probably went to Fewkes.

On June 27, the Russells rode three miles toward the Mazatzal Mountains, located to the west of State Routes 88 and 188. Here, in a broad dry wash, they mapped a medium-sized site with a mound and wall. Considering the mountains impassable, the Russells turned east, driving their team 13 miles into the Sierra Anchas Mountains over "the worst road in America."[46] Along the way, Frank recorded six small ruins on hill summits, a large number given the lack of

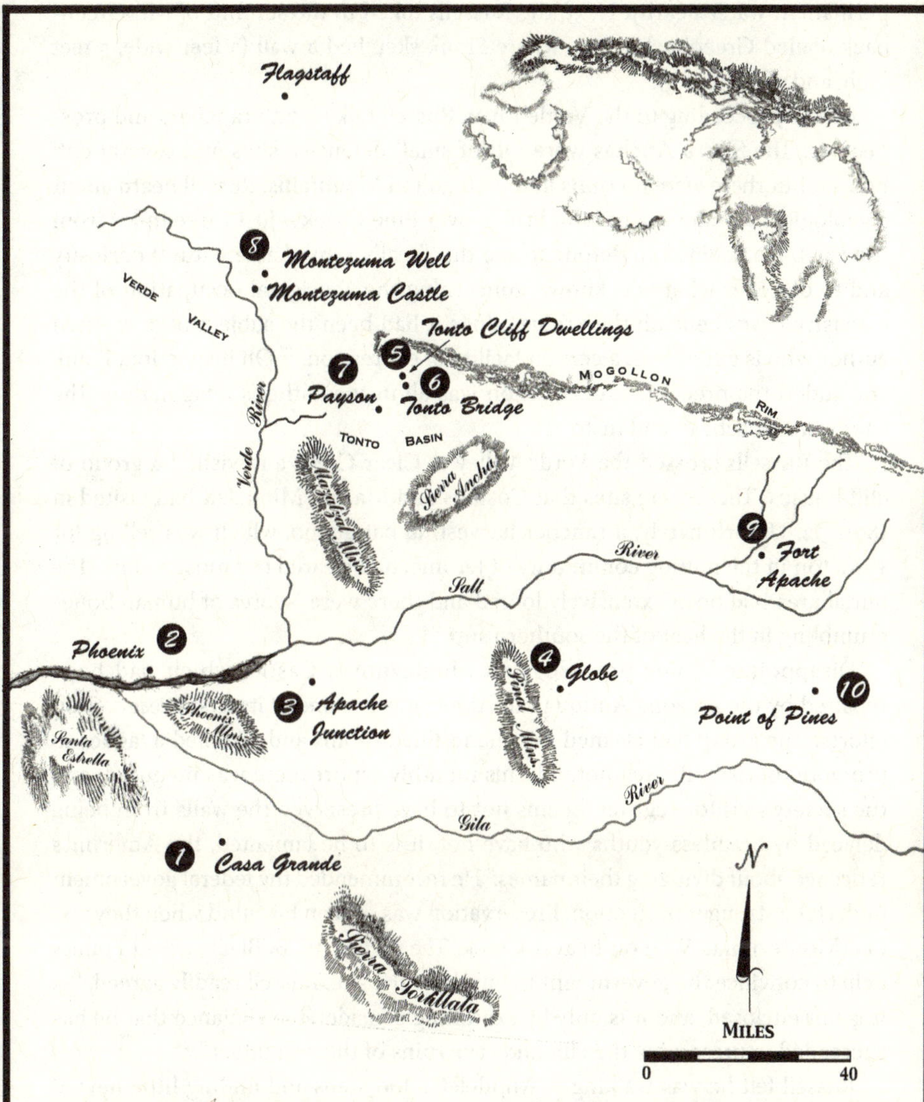

MAP 4.2. Russell Reconnaissance Survey 2, part 1, 1901, continuation of journey north from Casa Grande to Camp Verde area. 1. Casa Grande; 2. Phoenix; 3. Apache Junction; 4. Globe; 5. Tonto Cliff Dwellings; 6. Tonto Bridge; 7. Payson; 8. Montezuma Castle and Montezuma Well; 9. Fort Apache; and 10. Point of Pines were visited on the return trip to Tucson. Map by Patricia DeBunch.

permanent water nearby. Next, the Russells hiked to the summit of Mt. Greenback (called Greenback Peak), where Frank sketched a wall (3 feet wide, 5 feet high, and 75 feet long).

Before proceeding to the Verde River, Russell talked with ranchers and prospectors. The Sierra Anchas were full of small defensive sites and several cliff houses, but there were no ruins in the Mogollon Mountains. Russell heard about a geological wonder—a natural bridge over Pine Creek—just three miles from the road. He decided to detour to see this "really remarkable natural curiosity and to discover what was known concerning the aboriginal occupation of the extensive caves beneath the bridge" since it had been the subject of "a western author who is gifted with a certain facility of expression."[47] On inspection, Frank concluded the precontact occupation was all in the author's imagination. The sites were Apachean and historic.

The Russells crossed the Verde Valley at Clear Creek and visited a group of cliff houses. These were sites that Cosmos and Marion Mindeleff had visited in 1891–92. Unfortunately, a rancher harvesting bat guano, which was selling for $25 a ton in the mining community of Jerome, had cleared out most rooms. The burial area had been extensively looted and there were "scores of human bones crumbling in the heat of the southern sun."[48]

Disappointed, they proceeded to Montezuma's Castle, which had been repaired by the Arizona Antiquarian Association as one of its first preservation efforts. The group had cleaned the guano-filled rooms and installed a ladder to promote tourism. Russell noted in his monthly report there was no guard, and the society's visitor register "seems not to have preserved the walls from being defaced by brainless youths who have not, it is to be lamented, the Amerind's reticence about divulging their names." He recommended the federal government undertake stronger protection. Preservation was also on his mind when they visited Montezuma's Well on Beaver Creek. The owner, W. B. Black, asked Frank's help to convince the government to purchase the site. Russell readily agreed, "as it is not enclosed, and it is only by exercising considerable vigilance that he has succeeded in preserving the cliff and cave ruins of the well intact."[49]

Russell felt he was walking in Mindeleff's footsteps and finding little new of importance. Nevertheless, he recognized that much more could be learned about the ancestral and historic peoples who lived in the Verde Valley. Still, his goal was to locate new, promising sites for Fewkes and his team to consider. What Russell did not fully realize was that his observations of site pot-hunting and vandalism meant his reports constituted the first state- or territory-wide archaeological damage assessment. They were later used by William Henry Holmes and Edgar Lee Hewett when they argued for the passage of the federal Antiquities Act in 1906.

Returning to the Colorado Plateau

It was still ridiculously hot. The Russells headed for higher ground in Flagstaff. After resting a few days, they traveled to Willow Spring, a few miles west of Tuba City on the Navajo reservation. Russell still wanted to survey around Navajo Mountain, an objective of their 1900 honeymoon itinerary. They were back on reservation land, however, without formal permission. There was no indication that Russell or McGee informed the Indian Service of Russell's intentions. It was a repeat of old patterns; Russell did not like asking for permission. We can imagine he was sick of government paperwork after the civil service debacle and rationalized he did not need permission as a federal employee. Also, he was not intending to excavate. Officially, he was looking for rock art this time. Surely no permit or permission was needed to sketch or take photographs.

The Russells found rock art immediately. Near Willow Spring were several very large boulders of red Wingate sandstone covered with Hopi Clan symbols left by travelers on the legendary Salt Trail, which extended from the Hopi mesas into Marble Canyon at the confluence of the Little Colorado and Colorado Rivers.[50] Frank had heard reports of archaeological sites in Marble Canyon and the lower end of Glen Canyon. He planned to move in that direction. However, an unnamed Southern Paiute man told him the tinajas (natural water tanks in bedrock) on which they would depend were dry. There had been no winter rains, and the summer monsoons had yet to make their appearance. Frank wisely abandoned his plan. The couple turned northeast to the Kaibito Plateau canyons and adjacent areas near Navajo Mountain, the Navajo's sacred mountain of the north. It was a scientifically unexplored area south of the San Juan River.

At Red Lake Trading Post (24 miles northeast of Tuba City), Russell hired trader Eugene Powell as their guide and an unnamed Navajo interpreter.[51] Local Natives were not happy with Frank's plans and told him so. Russell had not asked the Navajo and Southern Paiute residents for permission and was upset when these men informed him they would protect the region from strangers. They did not want dangerous archaeologists, who planned to defile the homes of the people they called the Anasazi, to roam freely and take what they wanted.

Russell decided to ignore the local council and proceed, but word had spread about the new strangers. They were met at the mouth of Nĕt-sĭ^{n}-be-ko Canyon (Navajo Canyon) by

> a small deputation of well-armed Navajo who announced that this was the end of our journey. Mr. Powell explained and re-explained that the Great Captain at Washington had sent me to see and to photograph the ruins. They wanted the

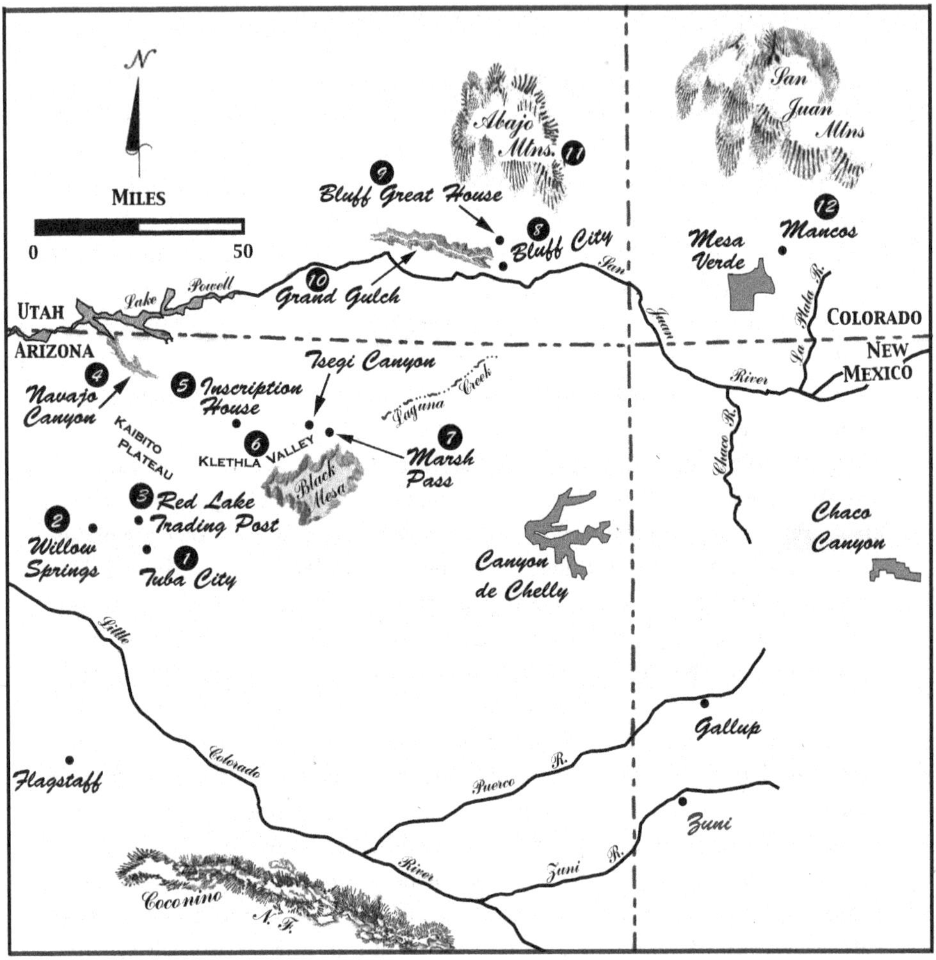

MAP 4.3. Russell, Reconnaissance Survey 2, part 2, 1901, from Flagstaff to Mancos. 1. Tuba City; 2. Willow Springs; 3. Red Lake Trading Post; 4. Navajo Canyon; 5. Inscription House; 6. Klethla Valley; 7. Marsh Pass; 8. Bluff City; 9. Bluff Great House; 10. Grand Gulch; 11. Abajo Mountains; 12. Mancos. Map by Patricia DeBunch.

"chalchiwite" and they did not want a white man in the maze of canyons that had sheltered every Navajo criminal for half a century. They cited the case of the Field Columbian Museum parties that worked the Little Colorado ruins last year. The party they said (and they spoke truly for I saw them myself) had dug about the ruins of the ancient people and left their bones lying about on the grounds. "If any of our women who are with child see those bones while herding the sheep it will be bad for them."[52]

The Russells should have remembered what they already knew about Navajo culture: the dead could bring illness to innocent people. As he had before, Frank was not particularly interested. He ignored the residents' concerns and arguments. He focused on what he felt Euro-American science needed, asserting this trumped Diné philosophies and concerns as well as their observation that archaeologists like Owen and Burt did as much damage as pot-hunters.

The Diné contingent took the opportunity to express other concerns about the federal government since Russell presented himself as its representative. One man asked Frank to tell Washington to stop driving iron stakes in their land. This gentleman was referring to the USGS and GLO surveyors who had conducted topographic, mineral, transportation, and allotment surveys. Russell recorded these concerns and might have begun to recognize that other government employees' activities affected him and his plans. He tried to disassociate himself from geographical practices, arguing that his science was distinct. He also tried to distance himself from the Field Museum. To the best of our knowledge, Russell never wrote to the Office of Indian Affairs, the GLO, or the USGS about the discussion. Perhaps he felt placing the encounter in his monthly report was enough. The complaints then became Powell's and McGee's responsibility.

Eventually, the frustrated Navajo contingent stopped arguing. They agreed the group could proceed, but only after Frank and Theresa fed them, as Diné hospitality required. This significantly depleted their rations. They left the next morning. They soon found, as they had been told repeatedly, that there was little grass for the animals due to the drought. As a result, the quartet only visited 20 sites, 2 of which were relatively large. One, built in the bottom of a narrow canyon, had an intact burial area the wind was slowly eroding. This was possibly Inscription House in Nitsie Canyon, a large community with 85 rooms. Russell did not gather any human remains or collect any artifacts. He did not want to gain Indian Service notice via the gossip grapevine.[53] And he apparently had all but abandoned his 1900 osteological project, at least for the moment while he worked for the BAE.

The Russells never reached Navajo Mountain. Instead, they returned to the Red Lake Trading Post and rested a few days. After replenishing their fodder, provisions, and water, they sallied forth in a new direction with a Southern Paiute guide. They proceeded uneventfully over the difficult terrain until the second evening, when the guide attended a ceremonial "sing" and elders instructed him to conduct the group no further. With tired horses and no guide, Russell abandoned his plan once again and returned to Red Lake.

It was time to go to Denver without more side trips. Theresa and Frank headed northeast through the Kletha Valley toward Marsh Pass by themselves. With Black Mesa to the south, they searched for sites along Laguna Creek, at the base of Coombs Ridge. Russell made no mention of Betatakin in his monthly report but might have entered Tsegi Canyon. Russell knew of the work of John and Richard Wetherill but seemed to have avoided the men. Frank and Theresa must have visited at least one site the Wetherills had dug because Frank wrote Powell and McGee about how little the brothers had left for real scientists. They had taken "five hundred boxes of pottery and the like out of the district." Russell did not say exactly where the pottery was from, but it was probably Kiet Seel.[54]

The Russells aimed to cross the San Juan River at Bluff City. Frank found their route difficult. All my "time and energy were needed to get my team through alive. There was no grass in the country," he recounted in his monthly report. Searching for ruins thought to be hidden in deep canyons was a luxury they could not afford. Not wanting Powell or McGee to think him a failure, Russell told of other prospective sites: "A citizen of Bluff informed me that he knew the whereabouts of several ruins, as yet unworked, in the Blue Mountains north of Bluff, Utah. It occurs to me that an investigation of these so called 'Basket-makers' may yield valuable information bearing on general problems of relationship and migration."[55] Other sites farther north of Blanding in the Abajo Mountain region were probably the famous Alkali Ridge sites. Russell learned of theoretically important sites to the west. He did not say where these ancient communities were located, but some may have been in Grand Gulch. Throughout the 1890s the Wetherills had found rich troves of burials and baskets but no pottery beneath "Cliff Dweller" materials. They designated these peoples Basket Makers. The Russells visited one site just north of Bluff that local Mormons intended to preserve as an example of "Hebrew architecture." This was probably the Chacoan outlier known as the Bluff Great House.

Frank and Theresa headed east toward Cortez, Colorado, visiting sites in the Hovenweep area previously described by Jackson and Holmes. The Russells' route took them through the McElmo Valley, where they briefly examined several small pueblos. They stopped at Ruin Canyon and Cannonball Ruin, places that would later be recorded by Alfred V. Kidder, Sylvester Morley, and J. G. Fletcher as part of the legendary Hewett's 1907 "field school."[56]

A Professional Meeting in Denver

It was now the last half of August 1901. Arriving in Mancos, Colorado, the Russells left their horses at a livery stable and boarded a narrow-gauge Denver and Rio Grande (D&RG) train. At Alamosa, Colorado, they changed to the regular line headed to Denver to attend the AAAS meeting from August 27 to 31, "a notable gathering of savants, among them men high in American education and research" and several affiliated societies.[57] Frank met McGee. We have no record of their discussions, but they probably included an assessment of Frank's work, his plans, and future expectations. They worked on their AAAS leadership duties, including the progress of the anthropometric measurement committee charged with increasing methodological rigor and improving techniques. Another topic was their report for the committee on teaching anthropology, which they presented to the AAAS board.

Russell's main AAAS presentation summarized the 1901 survey, and according to the *Denver Post*, it was a success. He announced he had discovered 150 new sites that "had not been previously trodden by the feet of modern investigators." Emphasizing the extent and physical difficulty of the reconnaissance trip, the reporter further noted that Frank said "he located them in almost inaccessible places, which required unusual efforts of brain and physical endurance. To reach one of the most valuable it was necessary to lower his wife and wagon down the side of a precipice for 250 feet by means of block and tackle, and slide the mules down the side of the mountain."[58] The image was vivid and belied any rumors that Frank was ill. It was a heroic, though almost impossible, account worthy of any archaeological culture hero.

Equally important to the reporter were Russell's conclusions about the origins of the cliff dwellers: "Dr. Russell believes that the cliff dwellers were natives, that their evolution was from the south to the north, and that they were separate tribes with constant tendencies toward civilization instead of retrogression, similar to the evolution of the Algonquin and other Eastern Indian tribes." Russell argued that the cliff dwellers were not recent Asian immigrants: "They had no Asiatic customs. That idea is a revival of antiquated theories based on dead data."[59]

Another Busman's Holiday

After a week of scholarship, association politics, collegiality, and real food, the Russells returned to southwestern Colorado. Frank was technically on leave, so he decided to extend his "vacation" to look at Mesa Verde sites. Frank and Theresa joined a junket arranged by Virginia McClurg into Soda Canyon on September 5 and from there traveled to Cliff Palace. With them were other AAAS attendees: Jesse Walter Fewkes and his wife, Harriet; George Grant McCurdy; Lucy Peabody; Jesse Nusbaum; professors H. B. Ward and A. B. Lewis of the University of Nebraska; Frank's undergraduate mentor, Charles Nutting; and several Colorado women interested in archaeological preservation: Miss Putnam, Miss Helen M. Ring, Mrs. Sutherland, Mrs. J. D. Whitmore, and Mrs. J. L. McNeil. They stayed at "Camp Science." Fewkes showed them a small two-house structure in a rock shelter named Hemenway House after his benefactress, Mary Hemenway. The trip was arranged by the Colorado Cliff Dwellers Association, headed by McClurg. It was a philanthropic organization incorporated to preserve Mesa

Verde archaeological sites by having the federal government designate the region as a national park.[60] The excursion included a trip into Mancos Canyon, where the group saw dozens of sites.

It was time to head back to Tucson, but there was one more outing. On September 8, the Russells rode the D&RG from Mancos, Colorado, to Antonito. There they transferred to the Texas, Santa Fe and Northern Railroad (known locally as the Chili Line) and traveled to Santa Fe. During the next week, the couple visited the Rio Grande Pueblo communities of Santa Clara and San Ildefonso, which captivated Theresa. They also visited sites on the Pajarito Plateau, including Puyé. They took at least three dozen photographs, which Frank intended to use for slide lectures in the coming winter. It was evident from his correspondence that he liked these ruins more than most they had visited. He recommended that the BAE work in this area, which it eventually did in the 1910s.[61]

Returning to Mancos, the Russells retrieved their animals and wagon. They headed south to Bloomfield, New Mexico, to undertake a new professional duty: a review of vandalism at Chaco Canyon, taking photographs of any damage. Frank's assignment was to evaluate how sites had fared since Jackson's 1887 survey as well as how much "damage" had been done by the Wetherill-Hyde excavations, even though they had been under Putnam's direction. Russell was also to assess whether the federal government should preserve the sites and control future excavations. Theresa and Frank spent September 19 and 20 camped at Pueblo Bonito and worked in a seven-mile radius. Theresa felt this was a highlight of their 1901 trip; the Chaco Canyon sites were wonderful.[62]

According to his monthly report, Frank found less evidence of vandalism than expected; the Wetherills had done a good job of protecting Pueblo Bonito, he concluded. However, based on what he had seen, he felt the federal government should take over care of all sites in the area. Future excavations by the Hyde Exploring Company and the Wetherills, who had not worked there that summer, should be contained: "The company controls fourteen trading stores and owns considerable coal and oil lands. I should say without hesitation that the stories of vandalism that have been circulated concerning that region are utterly false. The party of students sent out from the Peabody Museum to work about ten miles below Bonito this summer accomplished practically nothing."[63] Russell was no longer impressed with Harvard archaeology.

It was evident whom Russell thought should control the Chaco sites as important archaeological resources on public land. His loyalties had shifted to his new employer. The contest was like that between Russell and Dorsey over the "right" to excavate Awatovi. This time the fight was staged by Hewett against the Wetherills and, by extension, Putnam, the AMNH, and Harvard, all Eastern institutions that Hewett did not want poaching on the West as he built an archaeological infrastructure in New Mexico.[64] Frank agreed with Mindeleff that Chaco

Canyon was an area of intense scientific potential. McGee, Holmes, and Powell felt the BAE and the USNM should lead any scientific studies there. Despite Russell's assurance that the region was not in imminent danger and the Wetherills' excavations had not done irrevocable damage, he agreed the area required more protection. The question was who would do the protecting, and which archaeologists were the most qualified to oversee it. According to the Smithsonian archaeologists, it was not Richard Wetherill, George Pepper, or Putnam. Pueblo Bonito should not "belong" to Wetherill, the Hyde Company, the AMNH, or Harvard. Like a good government employee, Russell felt future excavation should be done by the Smithsonian, and he would be happy to take on the job.[65]

Returning to Tucson

The Russells now turned west and south, enlarging their reconnaissance area. It appears they stopped again at a mission (probably Church Rock) before reaching Gallup, New Mexico, to replenish their supplies. Then it was on to Zuni, where they stayed on September 23 and 24. Frank felt Theresa needed to see the famous village, the site of so much systematic research by the Stevensons and Cushing. Russell reported to Powell that the Zuni had had a prosperous year.

Theresa and Frank headed south along the New Mexico–Arizona border into mining country. Proceeding along the San Francisco River, they traversed 200 miles of waterless volcanic land. Luckily, there were few small ruins so they did not feel compelled to linger.[66] Leaving Theresa and their team at Clifton, Arizona, Frank went by himself on a four-day reconnaissance of the eastern border of the San Carlos Reservation, probably along Eagle Creek. Again, he did not have Indian Service permission to excavate. However, on the 150-mile side trip, Frank saw and mapped several large masonry ruins, all, he thought, previously unknown. The most important was Point of Pines.

Frank appears to have been the first archaeologist to report on the Point of Pines complex on Nantack Ridge, an area that later would become home to the University of Arizona's field school and a great deal of research. Frank visited six stone ruins in the Prieto Region, the area Emil Haury referred to as Circle Prairie. The largest, Point of Pines, was 1,210 feet long and 225 feet wide, with two large ruins within 200 yards of each other. Russell thought it was the most promising locale for archaeological investigation he had seen on his more than 4,000-mile journey: "I should like very much to work at that ruin next spring. It is very high, and the winter is too severe for me to have any digging done now even if money were available."[67]

Moving 20 miles east, Frank visited another Prieto Creek ruin with several outliers. He reported it lay near the junction of Eagle and Willow Creeks. He wrote to McGee, "Frozen ground would probably prevent digging there this winter but I should like very much to work that large ruin next May if the money can be provided."[68] He could accomplish a great deal with $2,000 to $3,000. Thinking that ethnographic work might also be possible with a Western Apache group, the Russells met with Indian Service personnel, traders, and tribal leaders to assess whether he could work with the San Carlos community. If this proved feasible, he considered staying in Globe and finding a place to live on the reservation. If unsuccessful, he planned to return to Tucson and then proceed to the Gila River reservation to see if the Akimel O'odham would be open to ethnographic fieldwork.

Since the Russells returned to Tucson on October 10, 1901, we believe Frank was either unsuccessful in his overtures to San Carlos communities, realized he had infringed on Hough's plans, or found McGee unresponsive. Frank and Theresa were tired, with good cause. Frank estimated that since June they had traveled on official business over 1,535 miles in their wagon and 200 miles in other people's wagons, ridden on trains for 220 miles (not including their excursion to Denver), 50 miles by horseback, and 100 miles on foot—more than 3,000 miles total. Russell told Harvard president Charles Eliot that from March, "We sometimes drove our wagon where vehicles had never gone before. . . . Sometimes we walked all day in burning sand with the temperatures ranging as high as one hundred and twenty in the shade."[69]

Assessing what they had seen, Frank reported that between June 12 and October 10, he had "determined the value of the Tonto region; the existence of untouched and extensive cliff-dwellings in the Navaho Mountains country, examined the Mesa Verde ruins and those of the McElmo River and San Juan canyons, studied the Pajarito, Chaco and Prieto ruins: the last being an entirely new locality." To further entice McGee, Frank sent him a box of potsherds "that exhibit the highest skill in decoration and a combination of colors that I have not encountered elsewhere." Next, Frank proposed work for the 1902–3 fiscal year and the rest of 1901.

> All this work becomes available to me the moment I undertake the exploration of a large ruin for the purpose of making a report and I do not see how I can make much immediate use of such knowledge in any other manner. I shall remain in Tucson until the holidays engaged in the preparation of a presidential address [to the American Folklore Society] to be delivered at Chicago and in such other literary work as I can do here. I shall pay my own expenses as the amount at my disposal (now about $300) will be spent before the end of the fiscal year if I carry out my present plan of working among the Pima during the winter.[70]

The entire reconnaissance effort was never equaled again. Russell was still able to master harsh environmental conditions and accomplish Herculean goals. One could expect another travelogue-scientific adventure was in his future, but only if he could remain in Arizona, with its dry climate. Financially, they were fine until March 1902—or at least they hoped so—but could they trust McGee? Now they awaited McGee's next orders. Russell had certainly given him enough research options. He would have to like one of them.

Chapter 8

Ethnography, 1901–1903

Normally after the close of a field season, the teamsters and support staff would have been released to look for other jobs, the team and camping equipment sold, and the scientific equipment stored for the next field season. The scientists and their companions would have returned to their homes to show relatives they had survived their journeys. Then the scientist would go to his sponsoring institution's office or laboratory. Months of hard work followed, putting field notes in order, mapping, analyzing data, and writing a report.

But Frank was again extremely sick; his tuberculosis flared. Where could he go? Boston? Washington, D.C.? Iowa? He was better off in Tucson. The city would soon become a mecca for health seekers.[1] Many well-to-do respiratory sufferers came to the new sanatoriums, but Frank was not interested. He wanted to live productively, not simply exist, awaiting death. He would remain with Theresa, who was caring for him for better or for worse. And it was definitely worse.

The Russells resided in a boarding house for six weeks, costing them about $12. Lying in bed, Frank made progress on his reports. Unfortunately, Tucson was not a good location for a scholar, for at the university he "found nothing but a set of BAE Reports and a standard dictionary."[2] Added to these problems was uncertainty about their future. Would they have the promised money? Would McGee come through for them? He had not written for a while. Should they return to Harvard? While Harvard was a secure salary source, it was ill-advised given his health. They had to let Putnam know soon. He hoped Frank would come home but had to find a replacement to teach Frank's courses if they remained in Arizona. Frank did not let him know how ill he was, nor did he tell McGee that future archaeological excavation or surveys would be taxing.

In Washington, McGee had been thinking about Frank's plight. He encouraged the couple to stay "in the field" and trust him. The BAE would employ Frank. McGee proposed Frank focus on one culture rather than continue strenuously traversing the state. Russell should build on the initial contacts he had made with the Akimel O'odham and study them as an example of a Desert people. He could demonstrate how their way of life was adapted to their environment, focusing on how housing and technology were influenced by location and climate. McGee also wanted Russell to accumulate evidence to document community continuity and change. This meant continuing his archaeological survey but in a limited area. Frank's charge, as a BAE ethnologist, would be to collect a full series of artifacts representative of traditional O'odham arts and industries for the USNM and to concentrate on tools. In addition, McGee desired Frank to find evidence to support his theories of cultural evolution, environmentalism, and psychological development.[3] Russell would in this way become part of the Powell-McGee brand of anthropology and contribute to their theories.

The Russells had been thinking along the same lines, but could they trust McGee? Russell never really considered proving or even supporting unquestionably McGee's theoretical positions, but he was open to exploring cultural adaptation to the desert. After visits to the area in previous years, Frank thought the Gila River Pima would be an excellent example of an agricultural group. He agreed to address McGee's data needs but informed him that he would spend time on social organization, mythology, and religious beliefs, and how the O'odham thought about their history. Of course, like any other BAE employee, he would conduct linguistic research as the foundation for all the other work. And he would send copies of his data to the BAE's linguists for comparative analysis.

Finding an Akimel O'odham Community

Frank and Theresa were unsure which Pima community should serve as their home base. Foremost in their minds was that Frank should be near a doctor. He suggested Sacaton, Arizona, where he could have access to an agency physician. McGee was skeptical that it would be a good place for research; the residents were too assimilated to remember the old ways. They might be too corrupted by Western culture.

> I am in some doubt as to whether Sacaton will be the best place for work among the Pimas, though it will doubtless be best for you to go there at the initiation of the work. When I was at Sacaton in 1895, the aged chief of all the Pima and Papago [Tohono O'odham] peoples was located there and conditions seemed to be favorable for the study of the tribes with his aid, save that I had other engagements; but it is my impression that this chief is now deceased. I think it probable that the western part of the reservation (i.e., the settlements in the Gila Canyon southwest of Phoenix, which I have not visited) may be a better location for deliberate study, since these settlements are away from lines of travel, and so located as to encourage hunting, etc., in accordance with aboriginal customs. Of course,

> though, you will remember that the final judgment should be your own. When at Sacaton in 1895, I found the Agent most courteous, but I understand that the personnel of the Agency was changed not long afterward.[4]

McGee was not thinking about Frank's physical needs but basing his assessment on the assumption that contact with Euro-Americans and Mexicans inevitably corrupted Native cultures. When this happened, old ways were quickly forgotten, as if people had lost their memories. This, of course, was not the case.

Frank and Theresa visited Sacaton and were encouraged. Sacaton (Ge'e Ki:) was the Gila River Indian Reservation's main settlement and home to both Akimel O'odham and Pee-Posh (Maricopa).[5] The reservation had been established in 1859, and Sacaton housed the Indian Service headquarters, a school, and a Presbyterian mission. Both the agent and missionary welcomed them. They could settle in for an extended field season and continue Frank's survey for Hohokam settlements, this time focusing on the Gila River south of Phoenix.

Russell still yearned to return to Massachusetts or Washington, D.C. Remaining in Arizona would hopefully curtail his tuberculosis. It had negative professional consequences, however. Frank did not have money to make trips back East and increase his professional network. He missed the AAAS meeting in Baltimore and the inauguration of Henry Smith Pritchett as MIT's president. More missed meetings would occur in the future, including a key summit to organize the American Anthropological Association in early 1902. Russell was one of the official delegates from AAAS's Section H but had to relinquish the position as he stayed in the West.[6] But at the moment, McGee's proposal was their best option. Now to negotiate which community on the Gila River Indian Reservation would be their home base.

José Lewis

The next negotiations occurred before the plan was actualized. McGee encouraged Frank to hire a Tohono O'odham assistant, José Lewis. McGee had employed Lewis during his 1894 ethnographic and geographic expedition in the Papaguería. Lewis had much to commend him. He was literate, perceptive, experienced, and interested. He spoke passable English and Spanish as well as two relevant dialects of O'odham.[7]

Equally critical was that Lewis knew how to be an interpreter, could locate Native specialists and convince them to participate, help take household censuses, and work independently, thereby doubling data collection efforts. McGee had given Lewis basic instruction in recording observations in detail and phonetically recording oral texts. McGee had brought him to Washington, D.C., several times. Here he partnered with linguist John N. B. Hewitt and was recognized for his intellectual expertise. Lewis was listed as an independent Smithsonian collaborator in annual reports under the name José Lewis Brennan. He was obviously a good choice for a Native coworker. But McGee had another reason to advocate for his employment. As he told Russell, "Jose is indebted to me in the sum of $150, expended in defending him at Tucson, and it would be well for you to help him manage his affairs in such a way that this obligation can be repaid, preferably in part out of his first checks."[8]

McGee repeated his request to hire Lewis in October 1901, this time providing an explanation. After reiterating Lewis's value, and stressing he knew how to use government vouchers, McGee described the problem. Lewis had been charged with selling liquor to Indians.

> I found him by all odds the most trustworthy Indian assistant I have ever employed, and have had much confidence in his integrity; yet, through an unfortunate combination, he has gained the antagonism of Captain J. M. Berger, the Indian Farmer at San Xavier, in whom I have otherwise great confidence. Now Jose protests his innocence to me, and explains that the charge was trumped up against him for the purpose of keeping him away from the reservation, and he has indicated his ability to prove an alibi provided opportunity were offered. Accordingly, after correspondence with Professor Forbes, I placed the case in the hands of Charles Blenman, Esq. of Tucson, who seems confident of his ability to secure acquittal.[9]
>
> Now, in the event of acquittal it is important that Jose get away from Tucson and from the San Xavier reservation as soon and as far as practicable; and it occurs to me that you may be able to help him, with the expectation of utilizing his services in your work among the Pima. He is competent to write traditions, under instructions, both in the original and in the literal translations, and it is my impression that he can speak Pima well enough to serve as an interpreter in that language. If you will employ him for two or three months at a living rate, the cost thereof may be borne outside of your allotment. The chief difficulty in the way of doing so will of course lie in relations with the Indian Office through Captain Berger; and it is this aspect of the matter which would especially require discretion on your part.[10]

Lewis had been acquitted, McGee continued, but he urged Lewis to leave Tucson as soon as possible. McGee told him to go with the Russells to Sacaton.[11] For some unknown reason, McGee paid a second bond to the courts and assured the judge Lewis would work under Russell's supervision. McGee insisted Frank would garner part of Lewis's wages. It was a questionable procedure legally but effective from McGee's perspective. Not unexpectedly, given prejudice against

FIGURE 5.1. José Lewis, 1902. Photograph by Frank Russell. National Anthropological Archives, Smithsonian Institution, INV 06414900, Neg. 02738 A.

American Indians and assumptions about their trustworthiness to pay off debts, the court agreed.

Frank was pleased that Lewis's salary would not come from his allocation. The next consideration was how much Lewis should be paid. Frank thought $25 to $30 per month, less than McGee had suggested. McGee told Russell the going rate for Indian federal employees who were research assistants was $25 with room and board or $50 without living expenses. Frank could use his discretion with the following stipulation:

> You will of course find it needful to avoid such overpayment to any Indian as may prove an embarrassing precedent. . . . On the other hand, Jose should be paid an adequate compensation for his services, which it may be hoped will suffice to enable him to meet the obligations he incurred in connection with his trial. This I am sure he will want to do. I should not hesitate to pay him a rate of $2.00 per day or $60 per month for the winter.[12]

The Russells met Lewis and agreed on a salary of $40 per month with living expenses. Lewis would work independently. Every Saturday he would submit a written report of what he had done and with whom he had talked. Lewis seemed pleased to have employment and leave Tucson behind.

Among the Akimel O'odham

Lewis arrived in Sacaton two weeks before the Russells and immediately began to work. Things went well from the start. As he told McGee, "All of these few days I have been very bussy [*sic*] in writing the Pima language. I may probably next week have a talk with the chief [Antonio Azul] and see what I can find from him about the Pima history. All the Pimas are glad to see me and seemed to be all contented."[13]

The Russells arrived on November 16 and rented a room from the local Presbyterian minister, Charles H. Cook. Cook had lived with the Pima and Maricopa since 1871 and had established the reservation's first school. He helped Lewis and Russell find individuals who would discuss O'odham history and customs. Frank felt Lewis spent his first weeks well. His basic linguistic and ethnographic activities jump-started Frank's work: "I find him disposed to aid me materially. Mr. Hadley, the agent, is also friendly and helpful."[14]

There was a reason for the good relationship. Russell had learned his lesson from the 1900 incident. He and McGee sought Indian Service approval before Frank began, and Frank this time waited until it arrived. Following bureaucratic mandates made everything easier. As a federal employee, it now seemed to go without saying that Russell could conduct any kind of research under BAE oversight. The Russells were befriended by Indian Service employees and given access to the agency wagons and animals, enabling José to use theirs. Frank could view records. Hadley helped them find knowledgeable individuals to ask for interviews and went with them on excursions.

Conducting Ethnographic Research

Frank, Theresa, and José conducted a demographic and household survey during the winter months. They traveled throughout the reservation and to several off-reservation communities but focused only on the O'odham. They also visited nearby reservations to see if dialects were developing. As Russell reported, the "house-to-house canvass of the villages, week after week, month after month, led to personal contact with nearly every household on the reservation."[15] From this base, they located individuals with good memories willing to talk about O'odham culture. Elders and noted speakers were willing to have their speeches and stories recorded.

By January 1902, Russell had a small research team. Lewis found interpreters, Melissa Jones and Jacob Roberts, whom he paid $10 per month each. Lewis worked steadily on O'odham vocabulary and grammar, completing two-thirds of Powell's vocabulary list. Frank worked with a man writing myths in English and four elders who related oral history. Concentrating on technology, Frank spent January learning how the Pima lived in a desert. He was disappointed with the results of this endeavor, however, for his informant did not know much—or at least did not want to convey the information Russell sought.

Frank and José concentrated on men while Theresa interviewed women. Due to O'odham rules about who owns and can use knowledge, Frank admitted she could obtain information to which he had no access as a man. Frank asked her to acquire historical remembrances about warfare and women's work. Theresa had practiced close observation and semi-focused and informal interviewing techniques and talked to many women. Frank integrated her data with his own. Then Theresa went in a new direction. One interviewee proved especially intriguing. After passing the unspoken O'odham tests for trustworthiness, Theresa obtained the life story of an elderly woman, Sikachu, whose name was translated as "Dry." Euro-Americans referred to her as "Old Mary." She was one of Frank's official respondents, Antonio Azul's half sister, and a respected healer and midwife.[16] She was also the mother of Melissa Jones, the Indian Service agency's official interpreter. Over several months, Sikachu told Theresa of her past experiences, children being born and dying, daily events, and the strength of a woman overcoming violence, abandonment, and marginalization. Constructing Sikachu's life history was Theresa's own research project, and she produced a manuscript quite different from Frank's presentation of O'odham history and culture in *The Pima Indian*. It was a compelling, personalized account situated in a 1901 O'odham household, without generalization, and with Theresa an integral part of the telling.

By February, Frank had several hundred pages of typed notes on art, daily life, and technology, as well as speeches, songs, texts of stories, and individual histories. He was especially interested when Lewis introduced him to Too'kŭt Nak, who could recite history with the aid of a mnemonic calendar stick, extending historical recollection back to the 1830s.[17] This marked the beginning of Frank's ethnohistorical research. Russell was excited about compiling a full Akimel

FIGURE 5.2. Portrait of Sikachu (aka "Old Mary") in Native attire with *kiaha* burden basket loaded with wood on her back outside adobe house, 1901 or 1902. National Anthropological Archives, Smithsonian Institution, INV 10045800, Neg. 2686 B.

O'odham history, for it would help him achieve his goal to record for posterity O'odham culture as lived by the grandparents of his oldest key respondents. This picture would become the baseline against which subsequent historical and cultural changes could be measured for accuracy, consensus, and purity (that is, lack of Western contamination in terms of core values, beliefs, and social practices). As Joshua Roffler notes in his excellent article "Frank Russell at Gila River," Russell wanted to uncover what it was like to be O'odham and to think like an O'odham, unadulterated by Christianity.[18] His focus was on the 1830s and 1840s. While Frank noted some contemporary problems, especially issues that dealt with colonialism and the actions of Euro-American settlers, he did not discuss life in 1900.

Russell worked under the paradigm of salvage ethnography.[19] Unfortunately, as Bernard Fontana notes, this produced an ethnographic description that disassociated Native people from their contemporary setting, making them seem as if they were caught in the past. It produced an "as if" portrayal—as if the Akimel O'odham had never interacted with the outside world, including the Pee-Posh. Russell concentrated on memory culture, not what he saw on a daily basis. As a cultural evolutionist, he described a "primitive" culture adapted to the desert by using irrigation agriculture, but one that had not yet reached civilization's level of technology. McGee would have liked what he uncovered.

Archaeological Reconnaissance in the Desert

Russell continued his archaeological reconnaissance but no longer simply sought to locate sites that could be excavated by others. He now looked for places he could excavate to understand O'odham prehistory. Every time he visited a new household, he searched for sites. On weekends, he and Theresa took longer jaunts. On November 27–28, for example, they traveled from Sacaton to Phoenix. Frank was most impressed with a site near Tempe he felt resembled Tonto Basin sites. Pueblo Grande, as the site is now called, "is about 200 by 300 feet and is perhaps 18 feet high. There are at least two in the Tonto Valley that are as large."[20] In December the Russells explored south of the Gila River and sketched Sweetwater Ruin with its platform. They also recorded smaller sites west of Maricopa. They mapped three sites between the Gila and Salt Rivers in mid-January. On January 22, they returned to Florence because Frank wanted an overview of the entire valley. They revisited Casa Grande and found that the keeper had discovered a valuable piece of pottery. This provided suggestions for the origin of the O'odham basketry symbol that Euro-Americans called the swastika. Frank photographed clay pits used by Akimel O'odham potters and later placed the photographs in the BAE archive.

The Russells also roamed the countryside looking for historic sacred places. Frank felt he had "found some that are yet in use and much surprised the local authorities who thought they knew of everything of that character hereabouts."[21] To reach these places, they used their trusty bicycles or borrowed Hadley's team and buggy. In exchange, Frank gave Hadley McGee's old saddle that McGee had left at San Xavier the previous year.

These weekend forays, as well as their 1901 survey, led Russell to conceptualize ethnography as a historical enterprise despite the concentration on the ethnographic present. Russell posed an appropriate series of questions as he surveyed: What was the nature of the relationship between the Akimel O'odham and southern Arizona's monumental prehistoric remains? How did the irrigation canals, decorated pottery, sites located near water sources, and large living structures correlate with contemporary cultural features?[22] These were questions similar to what he had asked in 1900 about the Hopi and Ancestral Pueblos, but now he did not rely on anthropometry or human remains. In fact, there is no record that he conducted any anthropometric research after 1900. He certainly did not publish anything on O'odham bodies and took no series of physical anthropology "mug" shots of people's heads.

Russell chose to address research questions through excavation. McGee wrote he had Indian Service permission to excavate ruins west of Sacaton if he wished. The one that most interested him was Casa Blanca, a platform mound site located 12 miles downriver from Sacaton. The Russells visited the site on January 17, 1902, and mapped the main building, which measured 60 × 100 feet, with walls

FIGURE 5.3. Frank taking a picture of Theresa in buggy on a Sunday jaunt in Gila River riverbed. Photograph by Frank Russell, winter of 1901. National Anthropological Archives, Smithsonian Institution, INV 10047800, Neg. 2695 C.

FIGURE 5.4. Lower platform mound below San Tan, Gila River reservation looking toward the west. The canal in the foreground is P-MIP and it was excavated by GRIC under the direction of Chris Loendorf in 2005–6. Russell taking photo, Theresa on mound, fall of 1901. National Anthropological Archives, Smithsonian Institution, INV 10047100, Neg. 2694 E.

extending from a mound about 12 feet above the foundation. Russell told McGee that Cushing had tried to excavate the site during the Hemenway Southwestern Archaeological Expedition but been unsuccessful due to local opposition. Always thinking about future employment, Russell predicted that with his good relationship with the residents, he could gain their permission and secure artifacts for the BAE. He requested Powell extend his appropriation, due to end in March, to excavate in April and May. This "would round out the season here very nicely."[23] He did not hear from Powell, who was very ill, nor did he hear from McGee.

Collecting O'odham Material Culture

All BAE employees were expected to collect ethnographic objects for the USNM. In November, Frank began acquiring objects, hoping to be reimbursed. It was a risky undertaking, for his BAE allocation did not include money to buy objects. Holmes, seconded by Powell and McGee, requested that part of the Smithsonian secretary's 1901–2 and 1902–3 appropriations be allocated to Russell. Frank heard nothing in January but decided to continue and hope for the best. Holmes eventually convinced Secretary Langley to provide reimbursement for the objects Russell had purchased as well as support for his two months at Sacaton (February and March). Holmes considered what Frank collected acceptable because the USNM already had Pima artifacts obtained by Edward Palmer in the 1870s and Jesse Walter Fewkes in 1887.[24]

It was the second time Frank made an ethnographic museum collection. This time he did a far better job recording information than he had for the 1898 and 1900 Jicarilla Apache artifacts for the Peabody Museum. We think Russell now considered material culture items as data to help his research—a large section of his final Pima manuscript dealt with material culture and technology—and took more care in collecting such items. Frank, Theresa, and José obtained 359 objects: pottery, basketry, medical and religious equipment, old weapons, stone and wooden tools, clothing, raw materials, and even a fourteen-pound loaf of bread (see table 4.1). They intentionally did not try to obtain the full series of O'odham arts and industries that McGee had requested. They realized that the objects they were gathering came from people whom poverty had induced to dispose of so many of their old belongings, that for a month or two after going into their midst there seemed but little opportunity of securing anything approaching a representative series. Several specimens that were finally collected are believed to be the very last of their kind among the Akimel O'odham, although such a statement must be made with reserve.[25]

Russell had ethical objections to collecting such items, feeling he was taking advantage of people impoverished by Euro-American settlers appropriating their water and undermining their economy: "These people are starving so that I am getting specimens and information that would not otherwise be obtainable." And he had opportunity after his household survey was complete: "The Pimas all know what I am after and all are friendly and are bringing the specimens to me."[26] Frank overcame some qualms about cultural alienation of artifacts. As when questionable research ethics had arisen in 1900 and Theresa used scientific necessity as a justification, Frank deemed rare Akimel O'odham artifacts essential to understand Akimel O'odham culture. He would take these pieces to Washington to preserve them. His reasoning was similar to obtaining the last musk ox hide to preserve it but in the process furthering the species' extinction.

There was a difference, however. Not everything went to the USNM; some items needed to stay in the community. Russell felt the most important historic artifact was an old calendar stick, which he had found in the Salt River. He returned it to its owner, who, in appreciation, made him a duplicate and then read it. Russell also recorded the history of a second calendar stick, one that included the 1832 meteor shower and calibrated the events with Euro-American historic records. These sticks were important from a theoretical standpoint but not as a benchmark for theories of cultural evolution as McGee contended. Recording Pima history from their standpoint presented the Native point of view about historic events and conveyed what the O'odham considered important. Frank was excited about the possibility of compiling a full O'odham history based on additional memory devices in the future and requested another year of funding.[27]

Russell's collection did contain a series of both historic baskets and modern forms designed to sell to Euro-Americans. He also collected information on production techniques and raw materials. When USNM anthropology curator Otis T. Mason heard Russell was working in southern Arizona, he wrote McGee to request that Frank secure baskets and answer questions about O'odham basket making. McGee earlier had informed Holmes that Russell could obtain O'odham baskets for Mason, but Holmes would need to obtain funding. He assured Holmes, "I am confident the expenditure would be judiciously made."[28] Holmes did obtain some funds from Secretary Langley as an aide to Mason, but it was not available until July, long after the Russells had left Sacaton.

The Russells' research went well. But as the end of their field season neared, they were unclear about future BAE employment. Federal funds were more precarious than McGee had led them to believe. In letter after letter, Frank asked when he would know if his appointment would be renewed. He received only statements stating "soon." McGee was focused on Powell's health and worried about whether he would take over the BAE administration when Powell retired or died. His responses to Russell stopped. None had come by June when Frank and Theresa left Sacaton. Luckily, they began to make new plans and had enough saved to support themselves for several months. Now Frank had to convince Harvard to give him another chance.

Thinking about the Future

While Frank had been working in Arizona, he became a founder of the American Anthropological Association but did not become embroiled in the debates about membership. He was also elected president of the American Folklore Society in 1901. Much of the fall semester was spent dealing with disciplinary matters. On January 1, 1902, he gave his presidential address in Chicago, arguing that anthropological discourse differed from traveler's accounts: "Modern anthropology does not formulate theories from travelers' tales nor indulge in metaphysical speculations. It proceeds to its conclusions by the scientific method of direct observation and experiment, a method that is obtaining so much popularity that most students desire some acquaintance with it."[29] This assertion was based on the idea that an enlightened civilization was a product of science. The "Science of Man," as Frank referred to anthropology, was "the crown and completion of the sciences" due to its comprehensiveness. He held that a well-trained anthropological corps—which taught at "the leading universities of most civilized countries" and was supported by national societies, well-equipped laboratories, and rigorous journals—would enable humanity to understand itself and advance further. To Frank, anthropology imparted vital information for any educated individual. It constituted a way of life, providing disciplined thought. Frank saw himself as a young professional—the model for anthropology's and society's future.

By February 1902, Frank's tuberculosis seemed to be in remission. In fact, he felt so well that he began to think he had been misdiagnosed. This was a common fantasy for individuals with chronic, episodic illnesses. Frank felt Theresa's ministrations and the climate treatment had cured him, even though doctors told him he still had the disease. Maybe they could return to Cambridge? With no definitive offer from McGee, Frank lobbied Harvard University president Charles Eliot for reinstatement, arguing that his tuberculosis bouts were no longer an issue. He also argued that Eliot should consider what he had done with his time after leaving Sacaton.

> My wife and I traveled one thousand miles in a mountain wagon; visiting ruins and traces of the pre-Columbian inhabitants of the country. Early in June we started northward in the same wagon upon a journey that extended over fifteen hundred miles with side trips on horseback aggregating five hundred more. We sometimes drove our wagon where vehicles had never gone before; in one case, I lowered it over a cliff, three hundred feet in height. Sometimes we walked all day in burning sand with the temperature ranging as high as one hundred and twenty in the shade.
>
> I think the results show that the work was not done by an invalid. On the contrary, I have not had a day's illness nor any return of the symptoms that drove me from Cambridge. I am regarded as tough by tough men. I feel ready for my life work again.[30]

To further support his argument, Frank had doctors testify to his good health and stamina.

Russell had resurrected his old image as the indefatigable scientist who could not be laid low. He painted himself in almost superhuman terms, one who could overcome extreme hardship without undue repercussions. He could undertake Atlassian feats of strength. His field environment was harsh; the average man could not tolerate it. But he had overcome the heat and dust in his dedication to science. He had succeeded, just as he had in the Arctic. He was still the tireless explorer who brought honor to his sponsoring institution. Why should the federal government, rather than Harvard, reap the rewards of his research and enhanced reputation?

Eliot and Putnam were convinced. Russell should return to Cambridge in the fall. He accepted the offer in late February and informed McGee he could only work through the end of June. He could, however, work the first two months of the next fiscal year, July and August. He outlined work from April 1 to September 1, continuing his BAE relationship as a summer employee or special consultant. He would stay at Sacaton until the end of June. Beginning July 1, he proposed, they would tour southern Mexico to gain an understanding of Mesoamerican sites for comparison to the Hohokam before coming to Washington, D.C., to work on the Pima manuscript. There was a downside, however. Frank did not stop to think that with this plan, he could lose his civil service status and lay himself open to furlough.[31]

Frank received no response from McGee about the grand busman's holiday. He submitted a new plan. He would finish outstanding projects. He and Theresa would then go into Sonora, Mexico, and survey along the U.S.-Mexico border. He would excavate "Old San Rafael," located about five miles north of the international border, and two ruins directly south. As Frank reminded McGee, this would complete their Tucson survey: "We dug a pit at San Rafael five feet deep and found much broken pottery tastefully decorated. I sent a few pieces to Dr. Fewkes. This ruin figures in a land claim now before the Supreme Court I am told." Russell also asked permission to clear out two chambers of the cave near Greaterville he had been "compelled to pass by with only a superficial examination on account of not having appliances for working in suffocating dust."[32] Finally, he would explore a rock shelter and cave near Vail, and three medium-sized pueblo sites in the Tanque Verde and Rincon Valleys on the east side of the Tucson Basin.

McGee made no promises. Frank was worried. This was wise, for unbeknownst to Frank, his position no longer existed. Secretary Langley had made it clear to Powell and McGee that they should concentrate on the *Handbook of North American Languages* and only obligate discretionary funds to Boas for editorial assistance and to William Jones, H. H. St. Clair, Montgomery Schuyler, and Livingston Farrand for linguistic research. McGee was to curtail new ethnographic and archaeological fieldwork, and Russell was new. Furthermore, Frank's 1901–2 salary had come from funds previously obligated to Matilda Coxe Stevenson before she had been furloughed. She had not taken dismissal passively but pursued and won reinstatement after rallying her and her brother's formidable political allies. As a result, McGee no longer had money for Russell: no permanent or temporary salary, no field resources, no reimbursement for what Frank had undertaken without written authorization. Having to compensate Stevenson for lost wages, McGee was in arrears for the new fiscal year as well. And there were fewer possibilities that McGee could play personnel and fiscal roulette. Secretary Langley distrusted and disliked McGee; he refused to use any reserves to fix the BAE's fiscal situation. Fortunately for Frank, the monies to purchase completed manuscripts remained. McGee could eventually give him some compensation for his final report to the BAE—the book-length manuscript based on the Pima ethnographic and linguistic research.[33] Regrettably for the Russells, this could be done only after completion, so there were no funds for summer fieldwork, analysis, or writing. They would also need to find the money to travel back to Cambridge.

Russell had made the correct assessment in terms of employment for the academic year. It was Harvard or nothing. He intended to work on the first draft of the Akimel O'odham manuscript during the summer. The Russells stayed in Sacaton for May to conduct more ethnographic interviews to obtain information to fill holes, paying interpreters with their own money. It was cheaper than coming back later. We have no information about whether Lewis stayed with them or how he was paid, or about how McGee was doing on the repayment of his loan. McGee's letters are mum on the subject. Given the friendship and deep respect Frank and José had for each other, we can speculate Frank gave him some money, at least for living expenses. McGee did find some money for film from some unknown source. Russell took a series of profile and full-face photographs of many Pima adults on McGee's orders for use in future anthropometric studies. And there was one final collection made that was eventually used by Hrdlička in later years. In collaboration with J. J. Thornber of the University of Arizona, he collected 50 botanical specimens along a 40-mile stretch of the Gila River.[34]

Summer 1902

The Russells left Sacaton in early June 1902. Rather than head east, they conducted one more survey at their own expense. They rode north to Flagstaff, then turned west, exploring Hualapai territory north of Kingman. Next they became ethnographic tourists and traveled to the Grand Canyon to visit the Havasupai. The three-day trip into Havasupai Falls proved memorable because Frank persuaded a large Havasupai party to stage a dance. At the time, he thought a description would be an important contribution to the literature, for which he could earn $100. Proceeding across the Navajo reservation, they stayed with Hubbell for a few days and actually bought a Navajo rug, the only souvenir of their trip. Thinking about settling in the Territory, Frank conferred with Hubbell about sheep and goat ranching. Before they left, Hubbell gave Frank a list of items to purchase for him in Chicago and Washington, D.C.[35]

Frank could not resist one final archaeological excursion. He and Theresa explored sites near Fort Defiance, recommending to McGee that he excavate two groups, including the ruins at Cienega, nine miles south of Fort Defiance. This site contained a cliff house and surface room blocks. Frank reiterated his value to advancing the BAE's goals: "I also learned of a cliff house in a side canyon west of Defiance which must fairly rival those of the Mesa Verde. I did not have time or money to visit the place."[36] The lure of supposedly big sites still dominated Russell's research plans, for he thought only large sites would entice McGee.

The Russells caught the train at Gallup. They stayed with Theresa's relatives in Iowa for a couple of weeks, and Frank worked on his field notes. He also spent several days in Tama, Iowa, helping Frank's former student, William Jones, conduct ethnographic interviews with the Muskwaki (Fox/Meskwaki) for his dissertation in linguistic anthropology under Boas at Columbia University. Russell had taught Jones for two years while he earned his BA. As they proceeded, Russell became intrigued with Muskwaki culture and began to consider future fieldwork among them.[37] McGee found a few dollars to pay Frank's travel expenses since he was helping Jones.

The Russells reached Washington, D.C., on July 3, 1902, and Frank wrote with Theresa's help. Somehow McGee found money for housing but not salary. Frank organized the rest of his data and edited Lewis's 150 pages of notes on philosophy, religious belief, and language. He placed a copy in the BAE files.

The couple arrived in Cambridge in early September. Throughout the following months, Frank spent his days teaching and working on the Pima manuscript. We think Theresa helped him, kept their apartment, and visited friends. Lewis, whom McGee somehow continued to pay, wrote that he was working to acquire the remaining artifacts and botanical specimens Russell requested. He went to Tohono O'odham country to obtain *Rsu-kai wutea brofu* and some seeds, which he sent to Harvard. Russell still needed *vi-ipam* but would have to wait until it matured in the spring.[38] It was clear that the Akimel O'odham project would drag on. Frank would work without remuneration, a situation every archaeologist and ethnographer understands.

Powell died on September 23, 1902, and soon thereafter an institutional investigation into McGee's administrative practices began, including his manipulations to terminate Stevenson.[39] Frank's formal association as a permanent BAE employee ended on October 30, when he was furloughed. BAE employment had always been more precarious than Russell realized. Now he was suspected of malfeasance and not told about or given an opportunity to respond to the accusations and innuendos. McGee's questionable accounting practices to pay Frank were noted extensively by Stevenson and other employees during the winter of 1902 through the spring of 1903 interviews. Stevenson labeled McGee's administrative practices "dishonest." Prominent in her testimony was how McGee had hired and supported Russell at her expense.

> Then Mr. Hewitt goes on: "Barnett told me that the accounts of Russell, who visited the Pimas, collecting vocabulary, tales and so forth, were doctored in all sorts of ways, calling them by wrong names." Those are the exact words of Mr. Hewitt.

> Then he goes on "This man, referring to Russell, spent a thousand dollars over his allotment and it was all paid; his manuscript is in the safe, nothing has been done with it."[40]

Stevenson and Hewitt did not have their details correct, but it no longer mattered. Russell was an easy target, for he had been hired using Stevenson's salary. McGee wanted to replace her with Frank, and he paid for Russell's research expenses with the funds that were usually reserved for Stevenson's fieldwork. Stevenson felt she had been robbed. She argued that Russell had been extravagant, and her research suffered as a result. Whether this was actually the case or not was immaterial. Stevenson implied a misuse of taxpayer money; in her opinion, Russell, like McGee, was guilty of embezzlement and fraud, not to mention sloppy scholarship. In this instance, she concluded Russell was as poor a scholar as McGee. It was guilt by association.

Russell had never been extravagant, but he had sent bills for expenses never approved and also did not fill vouchers in correctly. He had been desperate, creating debts for McGee to recompense. He had gambled, come out satisfactorily in 1901, but lost in 1902. He would never be reimbursed for all his current research expenses, especially those not officially approved but promised by McGee or imagined by Russell. It was wishful thinking as well as an attempt to push McGee into a corner where he was somewhat coerced to support Frank in order to preserve his reputation as the government official who made things happen. Frank continued to act as if McGee would pay because his work was so valuable. We are unsure if Frank fully realized that due to the scandal and Stevenson's and Langley's enmity, there was no hope for an increased BAE appropriation to cover his salary and research expenses in fiscal year 1902–3 or 1903–4. Stevenson was the Southwestern ethnologist, not Russell or McGee, and her Congressional friends supported her contention. Langley agreed with her. Stevenson's position was now secure, and her Washington political supporters in Congress would not threaten the Smithsonian's or the BAE's appropriation by revisiting the matter. The BAE would not reactivate Russell. The political situation was now whether the BAE needed McGee or whether McGee's pride and diminished position meant he would leave. McGee lost his administrative position. Holmes was now head of the BAE as well as the Department of Anthropology at the USNM.

Nevertheless, Russell felt he had to keep trying. Working at Harvard in the fall of 1902 was not satisfying. Frank felt underappreciated and underpaid. Putnam had not increased his $1,000 annual salary to match the BAE's $1,500 as he thought he had been promised. (Russell had asked for $1,800.) As Russell told colleagues and complained to President Eliot, he had not had a pay raise for the last seven years, even though he was more experienced and credentialed. His pay was the same given to a second-year graduate student. It was not enough to support himself and his wife. The Russells were increasingly in debt since the BAE monies were not forthcoming. Frank was embarrassed: "My butcher, my baker, et al., refuse to be content with the information that they will be paid when in the grace of the Lord and the fulness [*sic*] of time the Smithsonian 'gets around' to settling my accounts."[41] Life in Cambridge in 1902 was no different than it had been in Tucson in 1901.

This was not an unusual situation. The BAE correspondence files contain numerous complaints from scholars who failed to be reimbursed in a timely manner, despite McGee's promises. Correspondence files of the Department of Anthropology in the USNM and the Smithsonian Institution Archives similarly are replete with complaints regarding red tape, requests sitting on bureaucrats' desks, and a lack of policy to provide pre-service per diem for staff and special correspondents. To this we may add McGee's preoccupation with other matters, as well as the serious illnesses that kept him from the office, providing the opportunity for a clerk to steal funds, including those designated for Russell. We were not surprised at Frank's skepticism, fatalism, and humiliation. The wonder is that he continued to believe McGee would honor his promises. We can interpret this in two ways: (1) Frank knew he had to ask several times before McGee acted or (2) Frank and Theresa felt they had no other options. They worked diligently on the Pima manuscript so Frank would be paid.

Unfortunately, this strategy did not pay the butcher or baker in a timely manner. So, the Russells tried a second option—submitting shorter papers for recompense. Frank finished a paper on Akimel O'odham technology but sent it to Holmes. He also wrote a paper on Pima history for the *American Anthropologist* and one on Pima government and leadership for the *Journal of American Folklore*. Holmes, using USNM funds, sent Frank a check for $100 on February 5, 1903, even though McGee had promised Frank $300. Holmes could only use the standard Smithsonian Institution rate. Frank and Theresa also completed an artifact catalogue for the USNM, expecting to be paid. Frank received no compensation for this effort; the BAE and the USNM both held that the other was the responsible fiduciary agent.[42]

Unfortunately, Frank's illness flared. His symptoms were worse than in previous years. He must have accepted finally that he had not been misdiagnosed. He barely completed the fall term. Then he worsened over the winter break. He taught for six weeks in the spring until he could no longer stand to lecture. Confined to his bed, he wrote even as he lost weight, grew more fatigued, and coughed up blood. In March, he filed for a medical leave, realizing he could no longer teach. He and Theresa had to go to Arizona if he had any chance of living. Leaving Harvard meant no income, for there were no alternative employment opportunities for a critically ill individual at this time, and no disability financial net.

Ignoring the institutional politics and severity of the BAE situation, Frank again requested the agency immediately fund another research trip to the Pima. He argued that he needed to "pick up a number of loose threads" and secure drawings and photographs for his monograph.[43] He never mentioned his tuberculosis had flared. To admit illness would have jeopardized his proposal. McGee must have known, however. While sympathetic, McGee could no longer allocate research funds, let alone reinstate anyone. Secretary Langley decided enough had been spent on Russell's research. It was time to conduct new research in other culture areas. In addition, to restore Russell to active employment would have weakened the Smithsonian administration's case against McGee, and Langley wanted to ensure that McGee had no credible institutional standing or administrative BAE post.

For the first time, McGee bluntly told Frank to rely on Harvard. Remarkably, Frank tried McGee again, this time asking only for transportation so he could use the federal government's reduced railroad rate. He would work without salary and pay his and Theresa's living expenses. Frank offered to pay Lewis's salary as an interpreter, thinking this would entice McGee, who had not yet been completely repaid for Lewis's legal fees. It must have been a tempting offer, but McGee reluctantly declined. To have accepted would have given extra ammunition to the investigation, for Lewis's salary, with part of it going back to McGee, was being interpreted as a bribe.

McGee was forbidden to make any administrative decision when the official Smithsonian investigation found him guilty of unsystematic financial methods, careless and probable corruption in purchasing manuscripts, misuse of taxpayer funds to support independent professional associations, and hostility toward Smithsonian administrators. Langley refused to name him BAE director as he had expected after Powell's death. Instead, Langley appointed Holmes as director.[44] Holmes could not reinstate Russell, for Langley would not approve. He did, however, honor some of McGee's promises by combining BAE and USNM funds. There was a hierarchy of need, however. Boas's and his field assistants' appropriations to work on the linguistic project for the *Handbook of North American Languages* came first. Completing the Pima manuscript was a lower priority. None of Russell's new suggestions were even considered. Holmes liked Russell and thought he was an excellent anthropologist. He knew Russell needed assistance but would not circumvent Secretary Langley's orders or play fiscal Russian roulette. This was a wise decision, for Langley now had oversight over all aspects of the BAE. Russell had to think of new options.

Theresa and Frank knew they had to leave Cambridge or Frank would die. There would be no recompense from Harvard. Frank had used up his social capital with Putnam and Eliot since he could not finish another semester. He officially resigned his position, and this time his resignation was accepted. There were no more leaves of absence. Frank was extremely ill, but he could still walk and board the train for his and Theresa's new home.[45]

Becoming Arizona Ranchers

It was April 1903 when the Russells arrived in Kingman, Arizona. They were starting the last phase of their Arizona adventure. Frank had finally accepted that he must live in an arid climate permanently. The question was where. They did not want to return to the hot deserts near Sacaton or Tucson. With the help of Theresa's brother and A. G. Smith, Frank's old mathematics professor, they had purchased a ranch near Chloride, Arizona, in Hualapai territory, in June 1902, before traveling to Cambridge for the last time.[46]

Why Chloride? They had visited the town on their way to the Grand Canyon. Prospectors had been coming to the region since the 1840s, searching for silver, gold, lead, zinc, and turquoise. Chloride had been founded in 1863, named for another mineral—the silver chloride used in photographic emulsions. Settler growth occurred following a Hualapai band's removal in 1870. As the Mohave County seat, Chloride was prosperous, seemingly stable after the railway laid the Kingman spur in 1899. More than 75 mines operated, and the town had a population of a bit over 2,000 in 1900. The Russells arrived during the area's economic peak, with land marketed for ranches. And, importantly, there was a doctor in Kingman.[47]

Chloride was in dry uplands, and Frank and Theresa had contemplated moving there for some time. Their ranch was at 4,000 feet, suitable for raising sheep and goats. They had decided to go into business with José Lewis before they left Sacaton, but we have no indication whether Lewis ever joined them. In April 1902, Frank had written to Hubbell asking how to acquire Navajo goats, planning a small herd of 400 or 500 adult animals.[48] After building a corral and pens, and planting corn and fall crops, Frank purchased some goats, with Hubbell brokering the deal. Life in Arizona was better for Frank, even with all the hard work. He temporarily improved, but it was another strenuous climate cure.

During the spring and summer, Frank somehow found the strength to write. He needed to fulfil his professional and BAE obligations. He mailed the bulk of the Pima ethnography to the BAE for copyediting. In addition, he wrote two short articles on Akimel O'odham history. Assuming the same compensation system existed, Frank asked Holmes to pay him $100 for each manuscript. Holmes did not send $200 but began new negotiations. He offered to give Russell $100 in total if he would come to Washington, D.C., and finish *The Pima Indians*.[49] This would not have covered Frank's professional or personal expenses but left the Russells further in debt and ruined his health further. It would also have meant abandoning his and Theresa's investment in fall crops and livestock. Furthermore, Holmes made no response to his suggestions for future work, especially excavating the Arizona and Mexican sites. He responded, "I regret that I cannot comply with your request. Just as I am installing an engine and straining every atom of energy to get ready in time for a fall crop on my as yet raw land you will see that one hundred dollars a day would not reimburse me for my time if I went to Washington."[50] Russell was angry.

In the End

Russell was disillusioned with how the quest to control anthropology was ruining researchers' lives, leaving them marginalized and pauperized. Despairingly, he had decided, those in power had not shown loyalty to him. Putnam and Holmes, in turn, felt Frank was asking the impossible; he could not work reliably. They had a fiduciary responsibility to only spend money on actual work, and it was clear Frank was physically now unreliable and always would be. Frank was humiliated and weary. He no longer wanted to waste his precious energy by constantly begging for research funds and salary. He and Theresa needed some control over their future. But Frank still felt he had a duty to fulfill obligations—writing book reviews and an article on anthropological pedagogy. He ceased his professional service as soon as he completed his term as the American Folklore Society's president. We do not know if he dropped his professional associations, but he was less active, reducing committee obligations and not attending meetings.[51]

Whether Russell was permanently turning his back on anthropology and academia or whether he was taking a leave of absence, we will never know. He was still interested in the subject matter, just not in the gamesmanship required to earn a living. And he had run out of time. His condition deteriorated. Theresa's parents came to help in September and stayed on. Frank died on November 7, 1903, in Kingman, Arizona. He was thirty-five years old. His body was shipped to the Peet family in Los Angeles, cremated, and the ashes scattered.[52]

If Russell was done with anthropology, anthropology was not done with him. Putnam mourned the death of a "strong man" who had departed "but not without leaving a heritage" of which all could be proud. While the rising star of anthropology is relatively unknown today, his peers mourned his loss and celebrated his short career.[53] At the 1903 American Folklore Society's annual meeting, Roland B. Dixon sponsored a resolution, stating that with Russell's death the association had "lost a zealous and earnest member and officer, whose studies in the folk-lore of several American Indian tribes are of lasting value and importance, and whose services in arousing the interest of students in the study of folk-lore and related subjects will always be recognized."[54]

Frank was portrayed as a resolute and honorable scientist. His obituary in the *Iowa City Daily Republican* stated he was "one of Iowa's greatest graduates and a leading light in the world of science . . . a brilliant scholar and an upright man whose friends were legion."[55] A. G. Smith recalled that Frank

> was a quiet, reserved man, with hatred of bombast and hypocrisy that was unique; a man who held his friends with hooks of steel. He loved his fellow man and hated not the man but the evil the man did. He was a man of the strongest convictions who paraded them but little. He acknowledged no such thing as the impossible; he overcame difficulties that other men would have refused to try.[56]

Similarly, George Pepper told AAAS members, "In the death of Dr. Russell the association had lost one of its most efficient and faithful workers in the field of anthropology, and one whose industry and patience, through years of physical suffering, will remain a noble example to his co-workers and all who knew him."[57] It was a nice way of saying that Frank had worked himself to death. C.C. Nutting echoed these sentiments when he wrote a brief statement in *The Iowa Alumnus* in December 1903. Interestingly, while he remembered Frank, he concentrated on the other alumna, Theresa, who had been Frank's "constant companion during his explorations in Arizona and other parts of the West, sharing with him the vicissitudes and hardships of camp life. . . . The deep sympathy of the great body of Alumni, of the Faculty, and of the men identified with the sciences to which Dr. Russell devoted his life, is with the brave woman who was the wife of our dear and honored friend."[58]

Pepper's words painted a different picture from the portrayal of Frank that Theresa would paint in her *Out West* essays. There he would be a decisive man of action and health, working hard to fulfill his scientific duty and potential. It was how Theresa wanted herself and others to remember her late husband as she worked through her grief and began a new life.

Chapter 6

Life without Frank, 1904–1905

Theresa was officially named Frank's estate and literary executor by an Arizona probate court clerk on November 25, 1903. Since Arizona was a community property territory, she was already his heir. His death left Theresa with a ranch in Arizona, a large mortgage, hundreds of goats, crops to harvest, and few savings. Before she could begin a new life, the old one had to be put in order. Although long prepared for Frank's passing, Theresa grieved. Luckily, she was not alone. Theresa's parents stayed through the winter.[1]

Theresa felt it necessary to finish Frank's scientific papers, her duty as his intellectual partner. It was also an activity that would generate $100 reimbursements. She spent November finishing the writing and editing of the 660-page Pima manuscript. She seems never to have considered inserting her name as co-author, even though she had done much of the work. The same standard applied to José Lewis, who had contributed extensively to the text if not the summary writing. Frank mentioned Lewis as his "principal interpreter," excluding his roles as facilitator, data collector, and analysist. As Bernard Fontana has insightfully stated, Lewis should have been credited as a co-author in Frank's Pima writings.[2] He had essentially compiled the data on linguistics, myths, stories, and songs, the basic cultural texts of O'odham culture. Lewis also wrote substantial portions of the final report. Often, Russell served as the compiler, sitting at his typewriter, transcribing Lewis's notes. But collaborative authorship was rare at that time.

Theresa sent the completed manuscript to Holmes. He remitted a check for $500 as final payment. This brought official financial but not intellectual closure to their southern Arizona work. Preparing the manuscript for publication required Theresa's periodic attention throughout 1904 and 1905. After she had finished with Hodges's editing suggestions, Theresa sent the illustrations Frank had completed. She also remitted the remaining photographs as well as the field notes to Holmes, who put them in the BAE's "record repository"; that is, they were stored in someone's office. Since there was no one assigned to work in southern Arizona, we do not know on whose desk the materials came to rest. We think Hodge, who was charged with ensuring that BAE publications were ready for the printer, used the data for several topical articles and the Pima entry in the encyclopedic *Handbook of North American Indians*.[3]

No research program materialized from Russell's archaeological reconnaissance of the Hohokam region, in part because he insisted his work was preliminary and limited in scope. He had kept calling for more research as his employment lure, but this strategy had consequences for how his work was remembered. While the BAE annual report for 1900–1901 mentioned Frank had discovered some sites and identified new types of housing and possibly settlement patterns, McGee hedged that to really assess the region's potential, a dedicated archaeologist needed to cover more area and extensively excavate. Russell agreed. Throughout his correspondence, Frank noted repeatedly that he had conducted little excavation, only "here and there a wall was laid bare or a cliff-house cleaned out," and had seen nothing along the Gila River he cared to investigate more fully.[4] As a result, there were almost no artifactual records on archaeological materials in the USNM, but there were some photographs. We think it likely that he left some site and context photographs taken in 1901–2 and survey field notes not needed for the Pima book in Washington, D.C., when he and Theresa stopped there in 1902. In 1904 Theresa sent Holmes the remaining archaeological survey notes and site photographs taken on the Gila River reservation and in the Phoenix-Mesa area. Theoretically, a separate report was to have been written on southern and central Arizona's archaeological potential and vandalism threats combining the 1901, 1902, and Pima reservation surveys. If Frank or Theresa ever produced such a report, we have not seen it. We assume that the Russell materials probably found their way into Fewkes's or Hough's materials. Both men used the Russells' data for their own work in the Safford Basin.

Apparently, Theresa had no interest in becoming a professional anthropologist. After four years with Frank, she probably found the entire endeavor too precarious. From her 1900 journal, we received the impression she was not enamored with archaeology, and we can guess she did not want to continue its pursuit. In her records at Stanford University, we found no indication that Theresa did anything with her and Frank's ethnographic data beyond editing the Pima manuscript. Similarly, she had no interest in Frank's physical anthropology and anthropometric data; she never finished the paper he was writing on Syrian somatology. There was no indication she ever looked at their 1900 osteological materials. The specimens remained in storage at the Peabody Museum, awaiting a future scholar. Archaeologist Earnest Hooton, who became curator of somatology in 1913, revived interest in anthropometric studies. By 1915 he was teaching the introductory somatology course as well as an upper-division course titled "Criminal Anthropology and Race Mixture." Hooton became known for his work on evolution and racial classification systems based on comparative anatomy using morphological characteristics.[5] The materials from the Russells' 1900 honeymoon survey could have been reused as part of Hooton's corpus of works, but they are not specifically referenced in any publication.

The one part of anthropology that did interest Theresa was folklore. She finished Frank's intended articles, including a five-part series on Pima myths, published in *Out West* in 1909.[6] This coincided with a reemergence of Theresa's own intellectual interests in English literature. Interestingly, she did not make herself a co-author, even though she and Lewis had helped collect the material and did the editing. It was her last service to Frank. But that was in the future. In the meantime, she revitalized her interest in another kind of literature.

Changing Direction

Theresa was ready to move on, literally and figuratively. Her duties as a literary executor, ghost writer, and editor no longer sustained her intellectually. With Frank gone, she had no need to remain in Arizona. She had never expressed a desire to be a pioneer woman, living in an isolated area without engaging female companionship. She, her brother, and Smith sold the ranch. Theresa went briefly to Los Angeles before returning to Iowa to help her siblings relocate to Goraldine, Montana.[7] She secured a position at Anamosa's high school, where she taught one of its favorite sons, painter Grant Wood, but was no more enamored with teaching high school in 1904–5 than she had been in 1897–98. Knowing she wanted an academic life, Theresa returned to Cambridge during the summer to talk to William James. It was another turning point.

Theresa had met the pragmatist philosopher and psychologist in 1898–99, during her Radcliffe year. They had continued meeting while she was a faculty spouse. James must have been as impressed with Theresa's vibrant mind and wit as he had been earlier, for he hired her as his research assistant–secretary. Theresa held this position during the fall and winter of 1905, as she studied advanced psychology. She was not enrolled in a graduate degree program, for they were closed to women. This, however, did not stop her from reengaging with the literature and philosophy that fascinated her, now combining them with theology and psychology.

James was invited to present a series of lectures at Stanford University, the equivalent of a semester as a visiting professor today. James, his wife, Alice, and Theresa left Cambridge on January 1, 1906. Theresa guided them on a side trip to the Grand Canyon in the snow with the temperature just two degrees Fahrenheit. The visit was the trip's highlight, as they made their way to Los Angeles and up the coast to Palo Alto. They arrived on January 7. Theresa traveled in an official capacity; Stanford gave her the title assistant in philosophy, while James was in residence, and paid her salary. Theresa worked hard. James had an introductory philosophy class of 450 students that met three times a week, and Theresa helped with the examinations. James found the atmosphere at Stanford utopian: "Classic landscape, exquisite climate, about 1500 students of both sexes, very earnest, every one comparatively poor, almost no domestic servants obtainable except students who come in for an hour or so a day to sweep and dust, while in most cases the wives do the cooking, and yet all the essential higher needs of man, like music, are provided for by the University."[8] James thought it a simple life compared to Boston, and he and his wife wished that they had not come. Theresa thought Palo Alto was better, even after they experienced the famous San Francisco earthquake on April 18. Stanford was five miles from the fault line, and according to Stanford president David Starr Jordan, "Tall structures, as chimneys and spires, were snapped off as by a lash of a whip."[9] Luckily, campus buildings were steel-reinforced, so the damage was not as devastating as in San Francisco. The earthquake unsettled James's wife. They decided to return home when Stanford ended the semester early. Theresa decided to stay. She had become enamored with the locale, the university, and its welcoming intellectual community. She recorded in her diary that at Stanford, she experienced less prejudice against women scholars than at Harvard.

Theresa now had a new goal: to become a permanent faculty member. Stanford president Jordan offered her a temporary position in the English Department, with the possibility of a permanent position. She had to prove she was an independent scholar, however, not just James's highly competent assistant.[10] Jordan had seen that Theresa could lecture and grade papers for the introductory philosophy course. Now she had to prove she could conduct research, interpret texts, and publish. And she had to do this quickly. This meant choosing a topic uniquely her own that addressed contemporary English literature issues. What did she have that would demonstrate originality in thought as well as her ability to write engagingly? Regrettably, Theresa had no manuscript dealing with literary criticism or a philosophical topic. What she had was the Sikachu manuscript and her 1900 journal. She chose to transform the journal into an archaeological travelogue but one that could only be written by a well-educated, erudite Classics scholar.

Theresa needed a respected outlet that would publish her articles quickly. A new acquaintance had just the magazine. The editor, Charles Lummis, must have been impressed with Theresa and her knowledge of Arizona when they met at Stanford. He suggested his *Out West* magazine for a series of essays, for which Theresa would be paid, and James seconded the idea. President Jordan, a member of the magazine advisory board, approved. *Out West* was a monthly magazine composed of "concise, interesting, expert, and accurate articles" of interest to both Western and Eastern audiences, highlighting cultural and intellectual content. The West was defined as anything "which is far enough away from the East to be Out from Under."[11] Lummis aspired for *Out West* to be a periodical that all educated individuals read, along with *The Nation* and *The Atlantic*. The audience was decidedly middle class and affluent. Buying the magazine was not cheap. A mailed subscription cost $2 a year; single issues sold for 20 cents.

Lummis designed *Out West* to provide a national platform for his political philosophies and progressive social views and encouraged the work of creative writers, poets, scientists, artists, musicians, political and social essayists, historians, and ethnologists. He was a fan of adventurous, insightful, and entertaining travel narratives. He had written famous examples while he "tramped across America" in 1884–85, traveling 3,507 miles in 143 days. During his audacious trek, Lummis wrote two sets of serialized travelogues, published weekly by the *Los Angeles Times* and the *Scioto Gazette*. Writing about later travels in Peru, Lummis advocated the study of archaeological sites as a travel goal as well as the need for site preservation to benefit humanity.

From their initial discussions, Lummis envisioned the complex personal travel narrative Theresa could tell. There would be natural science objectivity and purpose: a geographic and multicultural regional portrait, based on specialized work that benefited the West by uncovering its prehistory. This would not be travel for the sake of travel. The themes would be integrated into a personalized professional chronicle. Theresa Russell was an unexpected explorer, a woman pursuing archaeology who knew how Hopi and Navajo cultures should be valued and understood. Lummis was particularly interested in how her tales could help him promote the rights of American Indians and curtail federal efforts at forced acculturation and assimilation. He contended that the more American citizens knew about specific Native peoples and where they lived, the better it would be for Native peoples. In association with the other essays in each issue, Theresa would help paint a portrait of Lummis's West.

Importantly for Theresa's purposes, Lummis encouraged women writers. He was one of the first editors to publish female authors under their own names rather than pen names or a husband's moniker. Thus, Theresa was Theresa P. Russell, not Mrs. Frank Russell. While she was promoted at first as an independent scholar, after the first two essays, Theresa's scholarly affiliation with Stanford University was prominently acknowledged. In this manner, Lummis recognized credibility and authority as well as her intellect and experience.[12] This acknowledgment accomplished one of Theresa's goals with her series—to have the public recognize she was a scholar who intimately knew the American West. Now she had to make choices about who else she wanted to be and how the essays could help her accomplish her goals.

Theresa needed to be an anthropologist, a wife, a bride, an archaeologist, an explorer, a traveler, an observer, a philosopher, a connoisseur and literary critic, and a published scholar. It was a large, complex undertaking, one never tried before.

Chapter 7

Writing a Travel Narrative

Theresa had many decisions to make as she reviewed her 1900 journal. What type of travel did she want to present? Would she be a neophyte scientific explorer or a mature woman on her honeymoon? How could she demonstrate her extensive knowledge of philosophy, literature, and psychology? Should she be starkly objective and literal in her account? How dull would the prose be if she simply reworded her journal records? How much literary license could she take to generate engaging stories? Could she exaggerate or use satire à la Mark Twain to entertain? Should she be enthusiastically touristic, or would that undermine her or Frank's credibility? The reader's acknowledgment of authority was critical if Theresa were to use the articles to secure a faculty position. She could not be seen as an amateur. Natural history anthropologists tried to distance themselves from tourists, whom they contended wrote superficial, unanalytical, romanticized accounts of exoticized people and places. Theresa's narrative had to be factual, based on actual experiences, but more than a simple recounting of impressions. She had to analyze what she observed, just as an archaeologist had to interpret excavated artifacts before publishing field season results. She had to use paradigms meaningful to anthropology, literary criticism, and philosophy as well as travelogue themes, rhetoric, and formats. It was an ambitious undertaking to blend such seemingly disparate agendas into a seamless, witty narrative.

Theresa recognized one aspect of anthropological travelogues that would interest *Out West* readers. Anthropologists sought out cultural newness. Frank believed all anthropologists had common personality traits—they were curious, loved to travel, and wanted to experience novelty: "Field research enables the student to travel, and thus add to his resources for happiness throughout life. For it is not alone the viewing of new scenes and new peoples that gives him pleasure, but there is the more lasting enjoyment resulting from the addition of new territory to his literary domain."[1] Purposeful wanderlust made one a better scholar, observer of life, and cultural critic. Theresa could show that she was more refined and self-aware after her adventures. Following Frank's logic could demonstrate she was a better scholar for having traversed Tusayan as a thoughtful observer.

Being directly factual did not mean writing dry prose. Archaeological sites in exploration accounts were generally described as part of a region's natural wonders, using language designed to convey an author's impression of place. Theresa certainly did not want to be bureaucratic in her portrayal, simply recording the coordinates of routes traversed, the number of skeletal remains exhumed, or tallies of pot sherds collected. This left two alternatives. She could try to trigger the reader's imagination of what life might have been like in an ancient settlement or what life was like for the scientific traveler. Theresa's literary background and fascination with evocative language was especially suited for the latter approach. The result, however, was that the reader would learn little about Ancestral Pueblo life. She would not produce an archaeological synopsis.

Second, how should Theresa portray herself and Frank? Should she be the center of the work, or should that honor go to Frank? She chose herself, transforming Frank into an intentionally unnamed, healthy, culture hero-teacher-mentor and companion. This choice eliminated presentation of herself as a nurse or helpmate. It freed her to concentrate on topics of interest to a university English faculty, specifically how Theresa as a woman would handle a man's job yet remain an upstanding widow. Especially important were considerations stemming from expectations of Gentile, middle-class American women and their proper behavior while traveling, as well as Theresa's attempts to learn the basic domestic survival skills needed to survive in a wilderness. These had been central concerns of her journal. She had been unable to follow stereotypical bourgeois norms and was deeply concerned how people would judge her. She would discuss this conflict via symbols that demonstrated increased competence and independence; she chose to purposefully ignore clothing conventions that hindered her work. Clothing became a potent symbol for each stage of Theresa's journey, as she progressed farther outside her comfort zone. This decision also allowed her to comment on gendered expectations of propriety, a strategy that would require a delicate balance, acknowledging some sartorial alterations were necessary for desert survival. And how celebratory should she be? Was the male explorer's courage, as Frank had glorified himself in his Arctic adventures, appropriate for a woman? Suspenseful travel stories stressed boldness, tenaciousness, quick thinking, and often brute strength. But these were characteristics assigned to healthy men in America, not women, especially in the many guides for ladies' proper behavior.[2]

Theresa's subtle anxieties about propriety during scientific travel were similar to concerns authors expressed in travel narratives when they explored a foreign land and were unsure of local customs.[3] This included recognizing appropriate hospitality protocols while retaining social conventions expected at home. Could one discard confining social behaviors and still be considered an upstanding faculty member? It was this inability to practice expected daily rituals that triggered Theresa's reflections. She decided to discuss taken-for-granted activities relevant to female travelers in colonial situations, where one felt ambivalent about imperialism and emerging settler cultures with new class structures. In the process, she could convey as much about Cambridge and Iowa as the multicultural frontier. She could demonstrate she had mastered a new normal and reflect on what parts of the old normal could be altered without damaging a reputation.

Another decision Theresa needed to make dealt with her marital status. How important was it to her narrative? Scientific explorations were not leisure trips like honeymoons. Since the early nineteenth century, upper- and increasingly middle-class couples took a "bridal tour" to visit friends and relatives who had been unable to attend their weddings. During the Belle Époque, the honeymoon became a special vacation during the first month of marriage so the couple could celebrate their nuptials and become accustomed to each other. The journey constituted a period in which love and harmony were cemented. While the Russells' 1900 trip was intended to facilitate their adjustment to married life, Theresa decided to rarely mention it. When she did, she wrote humorously about learning to cope with Frank's field behaviors or learning to camp rather than dealing with a new husband. More significant was the internal intellectual growth that overshadowed her change in social status. Who would Theresa be after her journey? How would her personality change? How would marriage to an anthropologist influence her life? Would it affect her scholarly interests or how she interpreted the world? Living out of a wagon in northern Arizona was not a romantic vacation to Niagara Falls. It was a journey about who Theresa would be at the end of her honeymoon and, by extension, who she had become by the end of her marriage, and who she would be if she remained at Stanford University.[4]

This decision allowed Theresa to employ a key feature of travel narratives: the author's journey toward more astute understandings of oneself while mastering new skills and problem-solving abilities (that is, gaining independence). A journey of personal discovery dovetailed nicely with a journey of scientific discovery and understanding a new region. The reader would see how far Theresa had come since stepping off the train in Gallup, New Mexico. In the process, she could educate her readers. Without pontificating, Theresa would offer instruction on a range of travel and professional topics to women, encouraging them to travel for science.[5]

Looking back over her journals, Theresa must have realized that she had learned more than she could convey in 12 installments. She chose to discuss her new skills in two arenas: (1) being an archaeologist and (2) surviving in the desert. The latter was symbolized as mastering activities like walking by herself without becoming lost, understanding how to navigate a landscape through geographical features, learning to ride a horse, and recognizing when not to ride a horse. Theresa was not always successful, allowing her to introduce narrative unpredictability. She was never the defenseless damsel in distress, although she did need to be rescued from her own hubris. She chose to acknowledge she would not survive in this environment without her husband. The archaeological survey was never going to be something Theresa felt competent to undertake by herself. Scientific fieldwork was a team activity.

How Theresa should balance her descriptions of guided archaeological instruction and survival skills became a main concern, for they were not usually activities that were used for philosophical reflection. How could she convey that her intellectual growth was a reinforcement of her Classics scholarly worldview? She chose a number of mechanisms: self-reflections, internal discussions, conversations with strangers, and intellectual debates with Frank. These conversations would be how Theresa introduced her literary knowledge and intellectualism to her readers. The topics she chose to debate with herself and Frank would demonstrate that the archaeological journey had not stultified her nor threatened the loss of who she was—a sophisticated, highly educated literary scholar. In fact, Theresa could use reconstructed conversations to demonstrate how she had reified many of her existing interpretations as well as inscribed those parts of her civilized life she did not want to alter. She portrayed a desire for a life engaged in witty conversation in congenial settings where friends and colleagues discussed new novels or debated ideas and philosophical theories. She was not able to follow her preferred life in Arizona, but she could in California in a university community.

Theresa had to document that she had been changed by her journey. She chose to do this through her reactions to new places. She had been aesthetically affected by new vistas, which triggered novel understandings; Theresa was fascinated with the land even as she found it challenging. Northern Arizona contained vast panoramas that required rethinking ideas of landscape. Wide vistas and incomparable sunsets called for perspectives not evident from inside a windowless library. Theresa developed this new facility as she traveled. She decided not to write as effusively as travel writers, who articulated their emotive responses to what they saw, usually using poetic language. Instead she chose cautious understatement, verbal decisions more in keeping with Frank's rhetorical style. When the land captured her imagination, she used literary quotes to summarize qualities of light or feelings sunsets drew forth. Theresa was a person who lived through books, but now she encountered minute details of a physical environment not found in publications. She overcame this problem by reinterpreting the new region's land, people, and past. Most travel writers used the reality of a new land to question their own ideas and preconceptions. Theresa, however, decided to do the reverse: she incorporated scientific travel into her established worldview rather than modifying her fundamental beliefs and philosophical understandings. New interpretations would be found in the last few installments, as she included Jamesian psychology to explain her encounters and reactions. Theresa would write an early psychoanalysis of the traveler.

Other new scholarly interpretations were left to Frank. Theresa gave him the voice of modern rationality as her intellectual sparring partner during playful but serious argumentative debates. Her character of the professional scientist, "The Archaeologist," demonstrated how an anthropologist theorized and interpreted old and new worlds as a foil for her humanistic, Enlightenment, and philosophical stances. The debates would also provide Theresa a forum to reconcile Frank's nineteenth-century evolutionary paradigm, conceived as a more encompassing type of thought under which religious belief and action are but one subset, and her foundational Protestant theological beliefs. Frank became the mouthpiece for the new integrative holism that caused Theresa to question what she had been taught in her Classics education and with which she was comfortable.[6] The *Out West* articles thus constituted a basic lesson in anthropological interpretation as well as how one undertook archaeological research. Theresa served as a popularizer of anthropological thought, even though it was an interpretative framework she would ultimately discard. Since Frank never wrote basic theoretical articles or a textbook, their debates posit his ethnological views, how he understood universalized human culture, and specific cultural distinctiveness. Anthropology opened minds to more fruitful ways of thinking, Frank believed, and Theresa showed how this worldview was actualized, even when she disagreed with him.

Theresa's presentation of self thus had a twist that we do not see in narratives of other archaeological travelers, who were more concerned with conveying facts about a region's past and what this information could tell readers about humanity's development. She was the erudite, humanist scholar in an uncultivated territory. On her journey, she became capable of processing excavated artifacts but not interpreting them. She was a data collector who brought raw materials back to civilization for others to interpret, to ready them for new uses as scientific data. Simultaneously, Theresa portrayed herself as the bringer of sophisticated, elite culture to the wilderness after serving as a critic of Arizona's society. The bearer of civilization was a common role for Euro-American women and literary heroines. Arizona existed as a frontier zone, located between the wilderness and the advanced culture of home that was thought of as civilized. The western region was definitely not yet seen on a par with Boston. In this sense, Theresa's travelogue constituted an assessment of the current state of the explored area using academic society as a benchmark. Northern Arizona was a land to which Frank would bring interpreted history, incorporating the region into America's heritage through archaeological investigation. This was one of the purposes by which archaeology claimed its disciplinary authority from American society. In some cases of nineteenth-century exploration, such a message was blatantly colonial; in Theresa's account, the colonialism was subtle but still would be only peripherally questioned.

Part II

"In Pursuit of a Graveyard"

BY THERESA RUSSELL

Chapter 8
Over the Hills

Establishing herself as an adventurous heroine, an excited Theresa took her first footsteps on a dusty street in the middle of the night. Fatigue made her long for a bed. She intentionally omitted the four-day train journey, a tedious time after the excitement of her wedding from her narrative introduction. It was not a crossing she felt would interest readers: it was too boring. As in *The Wizard of Oz*, the Midwest was prelude and postscript, black and white to the colors of the strange new land. Nebraska, Kansas, and Colorado were knowable and therefore not part of the transformative journey.

Theresa used an unpretentious style, as if she were sitting in a parlor talking directly to the reader. She began on a solemn note with a stanza by Rudyard Kipling to emphasize hers and Frank's distinct perspectives on their journey, companionship, respect, and love.

"But each, for the joy of the working,
And each in his separate star
Shall draw the Thing as he sees It,
For the God of Things, as They are."[1]

Next, Theresa dedicated her narrative to an unnamed man whom she mourns. She was a grieving storyteller, overcoming an interrupted life journey by telling of time spent together. Her first sentence was reminiscent of a headstone epitaph. If Theresa relied on quotes taken from other authors to start each installment to establish an intended mood, here she wrote her own poem. The poignant statement conveyed her desire for the one lost to know he was remembered, and his strengths appreciated. Like a Greek tragedy, Theresa's words bridged the chasm between life and the hereafter, requesting that Frank's spirit join her one more time to remember their best journey. In the process, she begins to elevate Frank's personality and character to a scholar hero.

IN MEMORIAM
TO THE ONE WHO WENT ON
Somewhere, dear heart, thy buoyant spirit is still a-questing.

And if there be, beyond the Veil, any shadows, thou art smiling up at them blithely.[2] *If there be any obstacles, thou art making thy way through them patiently. If there be companions, thou art to them an inspiration for thy tenderness, thy merriment, thy dauntless resolution. And if there be remembrance—thy thought turns often, as does mine always, to that illumined path we trod together in the summertime of joy.*

Then quaff with me this silver Cup of Memory, in the tremulous hope that it may be an earnest of the golden Cup of Fulfilment.[3]

Beginning her first vignette, Theresa called on Alfred Lord Tennyson to set the mood.

"The path by which we twain did go
Which led by tracts that pleased us well."[4]

"LIVE in Gallup?" inquired the porter.

"Oh no. Our home is in the East."

"Lawd! Must have a grudge agin yerselves, then, stoppin' here!"

But he consented to put us off at the forlorn little station, in the darkness of three AM, and volunteered solicitous instructions to the heavy-eyed deputy from the only hotel in town to "give us the very best they had."

The "very best" held no hint of enervating luxury, nor yet did its simplicity spell discomfort. The chief distinction was a front exposure. The first thing exposed was a landscape of freight cars, with the squat, white Harvey eating-house of plastered adobe enlivening the foreground, a stretch of Santa Fe track defining the middle distance, and a row of mountains standing aloof in remote perspective.

En route to breakfast—for our highly differentiated accommodations supplied bed only, under the caption of "Lodging," and required the "transient" to browse for board—we discovered the remainder of the metropolis. It was seen to be no radical, this town, but a strict conformist to the accepted plan of frontier architecture. The Plan flanks its one Main Street with the paraphernalia of transportation on one side and a line of saloons, punctuated by an "Emporium" or two, on the other. Celestial restaurants will be tucked in here and there, and the post office shoved around the corner. For we must drink first and must, if you please, consider grub next, acquire raiment of what remains, and relinquish foreign correspondence to the Tenderfoot.

A view from the hilltop revealed our city in relation and proportion, a small plebeian intruder into a vast patrician domain, tolerated of necessity, but with inflexible reserve and hauteur. Let vulgar engines scream, if they must, machine-

FIGURE 8.1. "The Accepted Type." Photograph by Frank Russell, 1900.

devils snort and throb and whirr, pistols crack and raucous voices shout. Let the deafening sum of the man-made tumult hurl itself into the Infinite Silence.[5] It is as impotent as the ancient slingshot of the child Crusader against the Holy Walls.[6] The projectile recoils feebly, and the Immense Thing remains.

"I am a little afraid of that wheel of yours," said the Anthropologist. "It is too wobbly to put confidence in for so long a trip. Perhaps you'd better wait in town for the wagon, and let me go on."[7]

A glance forward at the trail winding on forever over the ridges and up the ridges and up the gradual but inexorable slope caused my intentions to waver. A glance backward toward the one populated spot in sight took cowering hesitation by the neck and shot it into erect determination.

"I'll ride as long as the wheel will stand up. Then I can walk."

We pedaled on vigorously, eyes shining back into the pure light of the morning sun, pulses bounding with the wine [*sic*] in the air. Coasting down the first grade, my left pedal, righteously endeavoring to live up to its reputation, fell off, and my heart to the ground with it. But the Man of Science put them both in repair, and the procession made an assault on the next hill.

At the summit, after having pushed our wheels a good part of the six-mile ascent, we were rewarded with a breath-taking panorama, and a dislocated joint. The former was open to the public, but the latter was held in monopoly, not by my own impaired but persevering little steed, but by the trusted pet of the Man Himself—his own reliable, safe-and-sane chainless.

We decided to sit down and eat awhile.

FIGURE 8.2. "Just Put Down Anywhere." Photograph by Frank Russell, 1900.

What a joyful companion is a canteen, and what an incomparable flavor its presence imparts to ham sandwiches and ginger cakes! From it, indeed, one may imbibe a fresh endowment of resource and enthusiasm, may even transfer a portion thereof to a disabled wheel and thereby persuade it to continue in service, if only to carry passenger on down grades and levels smooth.

Most of the levels ahead were not smooth, but the descent came first, and gayly away started Jack and Jill. Only it was Jill this time who fell down and scraped her crown and rolled over and just managed to pull her spinning merry-go-round out of the way before Jack came, not tumbling after, but gliding imperturbably by, leaving her ruefully to shake her head at the Manes of Virgil and mutter as she dug the sand out of her feathers, "*Descensus Averni non semper facile est*—it depends on the method of locomotion!"[8]

Thence down by less violent stages to the sand-floored valley, and we found ourselves on a plain that came near being without any boundaries at all, and yet could not quite escape them, those ever-circling, never-approaching hills. In its spacious midst were the hugest of rocks, boulders, and cliffs, just put down anywhere; the playground of Titans, where human pigmies had no business to go.[9]

And yet, there they were. For at last, ten hours and thirty miles from morning, we saw some houses and hailed the sight as kin in a far country. The haven we had gained was an embryonic mission school for the Indians.[10] Three Catholic monks, it seems, had spent many years here in lonely labors, and were now become the nucleus of a rapidly developing enterprise, founded by the Church.

FIGURE 8.3. "The Playground of Titans." Photograph by Frank Russell, 1900.

FIGURE 8.4. "A Land of Ancient Ruins." Photograph by Frank Russell, 1900.

So now the placid surface of their cloistered life was being churned into a gentle froth of excitement. Stone-masons, freighters, cooks, and carpenters were pouring a rushing stream of activity into their whilom peace-locked tranquil bay. We had come to a land of ancient ruins, but the first incomplete walls and empty belfries we encountered spoke not mournfully of the past, but hopefully of the future. And to a scenery-sated Jill, there was also a cheerful note for the present.

FIGURE 8.5 "Mournfully of the Past." Awatovi mission. Photograph by Frank Russell, 1900.

"Come right in," said the landlady. "You don't mean to say you've came all the way from Gallup today. Mercy on us! Ain't you awful tired? Here," whisking a pile of fashion plates and some sewing out of a chair, "sit down."

Jill sat down, without stopping to argue about it, and enjoyed, by something nearer her own size. The restfully minute room—it was a ten-by-twelve tent, with floor, frame and wainscoting of pine—was as small as its dooryard was great, as crowded as that was bare. Nearly half of its space was occupied by the bed, a double-decked, curtained arrangement, like a Pullman section, officiating as a reduced synthesis of four sleeping apartments for the landlady and her three daughters.

"No, we don't live here," they explained; "we've just taken this boarding contract while the school is being built. No, we don't get lonesome. Too busy, feeding such a huge crowd. Then we go over to Fort Defiance, every once in a while to a party or picnic. Ever been there? No? Better stay and drive over with us next Sunday. Mighty nice people at the Fort."

It was our privilege, later in the summer, to verify this kindly saying, but now we were obliged to hold it in indefinite anticipation.

After supper, Father John, of the Brotherhood, solved the problem of a place for the wayfarers to sleep. One of the old buildings, just then used as a storeroom for the accumulating invoice of new furniture, was unlocked; a vacant nook found in the midst of ceiling-high stacks of desks and washstands, cots and Navajo blankets were brought in, and the bicyclers slept like a top—at least I should suppose a top slept by ceasing from a rotary motion and cultivating an attitude of repose, shouldn't you?

FIGURE 8.6. "Sprained Its Ankle in the Same Place." Photograph by Frank Russell, 1900.

FIGURE 8.7. "Promoted to Pines." Photograph by Frank Russell, 1900.

FIGURE 8.8. "'Where You Goin'?' He Demanded." Photograph by Frank Russell, 1900

Then in the morn, what doth our cassocked friend, Captain of Emergency? He trotteth out a wheel of his own and proclaimeth himself delighted to have it used in place of the one now laid up for repairs. So, with this welcome fresh relay, the Pursuers once more fare forth.

In length and landscape, the day's journey was a duplicate of yesterday. It proved a duplicate also in accidents. For again at the end of a six-mile climb, the borrowed "bike," with weak conservatism, followed the established precedent and sprained its ankle in the same place. In her sleeve of sleeves must Jill confess to a wee smile at the not uncompensated trick, for the crippled steed could yet nearly equal her own in speed, as she was spared from playing tortoise and trundling along twenty minutes behind.[11]

Yesterday we ascended from creosote and sagebrush to mesquite, cedar and scrub-oak. Today we are promoted to pines.

Pines! The aromatic breath of them, the noble park-like sweep of them, the alluring vistas through their sun-flecked aisles, the soft, yielding, lovable brown beneath, the hard, immaculate, Pharisaical blue above. And the sharp silhouette of pointed green tops against the brilliant azure, so insistent, so assertive, so uncompromising. Yet in those very tops trembles an appeal from the too illuminating glare, a requiem to perished illusions, a sign for the merciful sweetness of shadows, a plea for the vague winsomeness of dreams, a Mnemonic refrain.

Out of the Hills of Enchantment we rode reluctantly, and over the ups and downs of foothills to another valley.[12] Once more we encounter a drop of humanity in the great gulping ocean of wilderness—a freighting outfit, bound for the trading post that was also our destination. The black eyes of the Mexican bulged with incredulous amazement at the unwonted spectacle of a petticoat-ridden bicycle in those forbidden regions.

"Where you goin'?" he demanded.

"All same place as you," we reply.

"Oh, no, you never make it. Too mucho arena!" with an emphatic, disapproving shake of sombreroed head.

As we rode out of the hills the overlook widened and the horizon was far away when darkness fell. But near at hand the little light in the window, that winked indulgently at a naughty world, and twinkled a merry welcome to its home in the desert.

Chapter 9
The Trading Post

Joseph A. Munk, in *Southwest Sketches*, wrote, "A stop at Hubbell's is alone worth the trip. Anybody who has the good fortune to receive the hospitality of this home will not be disappointed, as the host knows how to entertain friends and takes the very best care of his guests."[1] Theresa also clearly welcomed the man's hospitality but appreciated his family more, conveying how they made Ganado unique. Theresa depicted them as Spanish–heritage landed gentry, the last outpost of female sanctuary she would experience for two months.[2] Theresa distinguished the women's domain from the drawing rooms she used as her standard for comparison and evaluation. Hubbell's was like nothing she had seen, with its melding of styles and cultures. The home became an oasis after the visitor's long, dusty ride, one that more romantic writers had depicted as exotic as the Middle East. To Theresa, it was an enigma. The Hubbell home was American but Spanish, stylishly modern yet traditional. Theresa emphasized both the commonalities with and differences from her readers' worlds. This perspective made her chapter different from anything that had been previously written about Hubbell while fulfilling the travel narrative requirement of portraying her impressions of interesting people. Her chapter was full of the Hubbell women as she began her quest to find women she could engage in witty conversation.

Theresa treated her time at Hubbell's trading post as a transition, the beginning of her real adventure into the male world of 1900 Southwestern archaeology. If the previous installment was about experiencing an unknown land, orienting the reader to a distinctive landscape, this chapter was about meeting its inhabitants. Stopping at the store gave Theresa time to anticipate the desert, to gather strength and courage. The Robert Browning epigram made this point and subtly hinted how Theresa saw herself and would like readers to regard her story.

"And I shall thereupon
Take rest ere I be gone
Once more on my adventure strange and new."[3]

The floor of our room was carpeted in Brussels, so that even in the desert we trod upon roses, with tacks for thorns, each strip being thus fastened to the bare, uneven boards, for a saving of needle-and-thread labor. The low ceiling was canopied in muslin, spiked on by the same forcible method. Between them, near the middle of the apartment, flourished a supporting pillar, festooned full length in prismatic bunting.

An expansive square table was loaded to the groaning (never mind whose groaning) with a collection of objects. Sainted images were satellites to the central sun—a marvelous pincushion containing no pins, eloquent testimony of the thrifty state of the family aesthetics with its corresponding disregard for the trifling points of utility.

Back of the toilet stand the whitewashed wall was protected by a pinned-up newspaper, whereon you might peruse words of editorial wisdom as you washed. These, however, were not of so engaging a nature as to defer your appearance at the breakfast table.

Here you find assembled the family *in toto*—the first time, indeed, that it has been in such complete toto for many moons. The four children are just home for a vacation from their various schools: an aunt from Albuquerque is a newly arrived guest, and the Señor himself has recently returned from a trip East. A picturesque assortment of nephews and cousins completes the family circle, or rectangle, to be accurate, for you discover them arranged in rollicking rows along the festive board—why, yes, I should think "festive" a fitting term to apply to a red tablecloth decorated with newspaper doilies in black and white, shouldn't you?

At the head of this happy arrangement sat the Señor, a man of some fifty interesting and prosperous years, whose seasons had brought portliness to his form, just verging comfortably towards corpulence, and shrewd benignity to his face. From his Saxon father came the gift commercial; from his Spanish mother, the inimitable Latin courtesy. The one faculty had enabled him to accumulate a fortune; the other, with its twin trait of generosity, had prevented him from keeping it. One had made him successful in business; the other has won him the reward of many friends.

"May I have the pleasure, Madam?" is his gracious inquiry as he fills my plate with a substantial breakfast and goes on without pause to address in their respective languages his Spanish relatives and Navajo servants. Equally fluent in all three tongues, his utterances flow as smooth and swift as cream from the jug.

It wasn't a jug, however, that held our coffee trimmings that morning. The evaporated fluid was brought on in the original package, and as it was my first set-to with this ubiquitous denizen of the desert, I looked askance at the little round tin with the two little round holes punched in the top. As I now view in retrospective vision the multitude of these cans punctured and emptied by my own had, memory wades through a veritable Milky Way, unstintedly strewn with shining tin stars. But every intimate familiarity was once an untried novelty, and at the sight of this one I was fain to whisper surreptitiously to the Man of Science, "How do you get it out?" but that Mine Host anticipated and explained, "Just tip it almost upside down and shake it. No, don't wiggle it that way! Shake it in strokes."

But this accomplishment was no sooner mine than another problem was passed up for solution. It consisted of a large platter heaped with tortillas. I was as embarrassed as I knew how to be. I did crave a sample—but a whole tortilla! Again, our host to the rescue. "Why, you just hold the top one down with your knife, so, and tear off with your finger as big a piece as you want."

A favorite dish was the capacious tureen of chili—not capacious enough, however, for it was soon emptied and sent kitchenward for replenishment. The Anthropologist fell in love at first taste, but as for me, I still prefer ice cream.

After breakfast we all went over to the store. I found the term demanded a liberal interpretation. The "store" proper, occupying the middle of the long stone building, was flanked on one side by a big ware-room, and on the other by a sleeping room and a room-of-all-work.

In this last, ranged along the walls at a respectful distance from the center table, stood furniture of infinite variety. An Æolian was there, a sewing machine, a grate and chimney, guarded on either side by shelves of unbound magazines. Opposite, a wooden bench supported a bucket of water, and the cup that stood by it. Nearby, a wash stand lifted up its little bowl, and lived on neighborly terms with the wide bed in the corner. The next corner was inhabited by the Post Office and Place of Business, where the typewriter clicked busily.

In the well-filled book case one came upon autographed copies of the stories of a distinguished writer who had been a guest, and on the wall hung a painting presented by another guest, a well-known artist.[4] The picture enjoyed the mural companionship of a Swiss clock, a portrait of the family, grouped with painful but praiseworthy precision, an ornately framed diploma or two, and a genuine priceless Correggio, heirloom brought, generations before, from the land of religion, warfare, and romance.[5]

After a morning spent in reveling over the treasure trove of the Navajo silversmith and blanket-weaver, until we were ashamed to look another spoon or rug in the face without adopting it by purchase, I was committed to the merry mercies of the Señorita, and we went off to play. She conducted me straightway to a room full of old trunks, opened up one after another, and displayed, to my delight, her own pride, and our mutual entertainment, all her pretty possessions, inherited and acquired. The former were more interesting, particularly the quaintly beautiful gowns with accessories, which her mother had worn in a day gone by.

"Let's dress up and be kodaked," I suggested.

"Bueno!" she agreed.

FIGURE 9.1. "On the Wall Hung a Painting." *The Weaver* by Elbridge Ayer Burbank. Photograph by Theresa Russell, 1900.

After a delightful, but not too brief, session of prinking, charming Miss Butterfly was ushered into her father's presence and presented as "Señorita Rubelino," the maternal name.[6] He threw a quick, quizzical glance at the demurely resplendent figure, decked out in pink-and-white silk of a much beflowered and beruffled fashion, of a dainty lace and gleaming jet trimming, adorned with jewels

FIGURE 9.2. "A Genuine Priceless Correggio." Photograph by Theresa Russell, 1900.

and provided, as behooved a maiden of Castile, with coquettish fan and teasing mantilla.

"Humph!" was the paternal verdict. "She's not half so handsome as her mother was at her age."

La Señora herself blinked affectionately at the bright vision of her vanished youth, but preserved her accustomed jellified silence—all plump and shiny and quivery, prone upon being gently shaken by enjoyment to cleave into slow, sweet fissures of smiles. Presently she asked a question in her husky, difficult utterance. On hearing the reply, she aspirated another remark, the evidently joyful nature of which sent her frolicsome auditors into spasms of mirth. One observed these anti-lugubrious attacks to be of a cheerful frequency in the household. The kettle of fun seemed to be perpetually simmering over a fire of good-natured raillery, ready to boil over if stirred up by the flimsiest splinter of a joke.

As soon as she was able, the Señorita hastened to interpret to us, for her mother's knowledge of English was about as limited as our own of Spanish.

"She says, 'How much you weigh, child?' I tell her. Then she counts up and says, 'I weigh seventeen pounds more than twice as much as you!'"

"Santa Maria!" the girl went on, "and must I some time be as fat as you?"

FIGURE 9.3. "Señorita Rubelino." Photograph by Theresa Russell, 1900.

"Si, si, querida mia," breathed the buxom dame, with complacent confidence.

"But never!" in vehement denial. "I shall be a slim saint, a poor Sister of Charity, and walk leagues every day to give away alms and lose flesh."[7]

Whereupon she pirouetted out of the room, whistling the tune of a very worldly and unsanctified waltz.

Back of the Post, across the arroyo, rises a large butte. To ascend this, what time the evening shadows are also climbing wearily up its ragged slope and from its cactus-crowned summit, to watch for that "certain moment" that "cuts the deed off, calls the glory from the grey," is to exult in the blessing of eyesight as heaven's choicest gift to man.[8]

"Well, what do you think of it?" asked the Man of Science.

"What the Amæba doubtless thought of the Megatherium.[9] How can there be so much of anything?"

"Already? Well, you'll just carry that little problem of Immensity around with you as long as you run about in the desert. You'll never be able to leave it behind. You may shut your eyes, but you cannot help knowing—"

"That the miles are long and your thirst is growing?"

"Amen. And your spirits are bluer than the sky"—

"When there's never the ghost of a trail hard by."

"And a trustworthy guide is ever more rare than a day in June. The truth do you never get for the asking, and knowledge you buy with a whole soul's tasking."[10]

FIGURE 9.4. "That Little Problem of Immensity." Photograph by Frank Russell, 1900.

"And it please you, kind sir, I am thirsting for information right now. Could you be persuaded to hand out a cold fact or two?"

"Gladly, if I could first be persuaded that that is what you really want. But it's been my observation that cold facts are so many wet blankets to you, tolerated for medicinal purposes only. I'll wager you an Indian bracelet that what you have in mind is that I shall contribute some opinion or theory or postulate or hypothesis for you to work over in that syllogistic gymnasium you keep up there under your chapeau—now isn't it?"

"I never did like bracelets, anyhow! They're barbaric. And besides, there really is a fact connected with it. Even if the Admonition of Science be to 'touch not, taste not, handle not a theory,' I thought perhaps it might be allowable for you just to look at one, being properly chaperoned by a dignified Datum."[11]

"Bring on your plunder, then, and we can pool our ideas, anyway."

"Well, then, there are two regions in which to live seems to reduce a man to his lowest terms."

"Necessity being the Greatest Common Divisor?"[12]

"Precisely. And those, of course, are the extremities of heat and cold, the Arctic and the Desert. Now you have an intimate, personal knowledge of both of them, while my acquaintance is second hand. And by this hand-me-down method, at least you get one uniform impression."

"And that is?"

"And that is that while in the very last extremity the effect is the same, ultimately benumbing, the antepenultimate cry, so to speak rings different."

"In what way?"

"The freezing man flings a last robust curse in the teeth of the raging Enemy that is beating, pounding, buffeting the life out of him. But the heat-smothered, thirst-tortured victim clutches waveringly at the remnants of the reason sucked remorselessly from him by a serene, smiling Siren, and whispers for mercy.[13] Is that true? And why should it be so?"

"Your first question I shall be obliged to answer in the words of the meritorious Mr. Wiggs, "Land sakes, Nancy, how c'n I tell? I ain't never died yet!"—although there were times when it was no one's fault but my own that I did not—but there is a measure of truth in the distinction, and perhaps you have hit upon the explanation in the word 'siren.' If we must personify them, the North, of course, typifies the masculine in nature, and the South the feminine."[14]

"Sure. I see. The Snow King is rough, frantic, frankly cruel. The Sun Queen is suave, alluring, treacherously cruel."

"Neither is cruel at all. The trouble with this whole interpretation is that we insist upon reading ourselves into these places, when we do not belong there. If we could only take them impersonally, without projecting our own alien needs into them and entering complaints, besides, if our environment—which did not choose us, but we it—does not happen to be able to supply what we want and failed to bring along. If we could learn to consider dispassionately, we should be better able to grasp the real meaning and beauty of both."

"But even so, in this difference between them, does the balance fall in favor of the North? Is it true, as the books, unconsciously perhaps, lead us to believe, that the Arctic clarifies the vision, hardens the muscles, stimulates the nerves? And that the Desert deludes the sight, exhausts the system, and makes morbid the senses? Is it fascination only that the passionate Desert arouses, while our glowing admiration is reserved for the virile Arctic?"

"Can't prove it by me. I am neither advocate nor judge. Because I have suffered in them both, I love them both, and love does not analyze."

"Well, if the Desert is '*das weige Weiblich*,' it is with excuse that she '*zieht uns hinan*.' It is her right to be beautiful, her prerogative to be mysterious, her privilege to beguile."

"Granted. And she has oases."

"Mirages, too."

"Both are feminine."

From far below came through the dusk sounds of a violin and liquid Spanish melodies, bursting into ebullient bubbles of laughter.

"If appears," I remark, "that we are missing either some of the fun all the time, or all of the fun some of the time. Let's go down and see what's up."

Stanford University

Chapter 10
The Caravan

Theresa moved into her wilderness. The reader was immediately reminded of a Middle Eastern trip with mules instead of camels. Theresa could have begun by describing Frank's plan to locate ruins and burial grounds. Instead she painted a picture of companions working together in a dangerous world. When compared to the seemingly haphazardness of the search acquired from reading the journals, this approach focused on what it was like to be on an elusive search. The reward was a beautiful sunset.

Theresa introduced her readers to Mexican laborers—teamsters Nosifor and Erminio—and a Navajo *hatatli*, Ned Sliver, who acted as guide, cook, and interpreter. Theresa found these men upstanding yet mysterious. She was pleasantly surprised with the Mexicans but unsure about the Navajo. The common stereotypic tropes for American Indians as stoic Noble Savages emerged clearly. The Native inhabitants became analogous to Arabian nomads with the extra dignity saved for Romans. Sliver carried a cognomen, a Roman male citizen's third name, which served as a distinguishing epithet.

"Our four-horse team
Shall soon be seen."[1]

The first day out we kept going along until we came to no place in particular. Then we stopped.

"Dry camp tonight," remarked Nosifor, genially.

It was noted that if anyone did remark anything, it was liable to be Nosifor. When not engaged in making remarks, he zealously occupied himself in rendering Mexican ballads—rending the atmosphere in the process. His repertoire was inexhaustible. Much of it was unmentionable. We knew enough of the language to be thankful we knew no more. As an avocation Nosifor sat on a box in the front of the huge, canvas-covered prairie schooner and administered the brake.

Erminio's talents, useful and ornamental, lay in another direction. He sat astride of Macho, the brown mule (who had to perform double shift as night-wheeler

FIGURE 10.1. "Our Four-Horse Team." Leaving Ganado to head up the Chinle Valley, July 9. Erminio sits on Billy, Nosifor sits on the wagon, and an unidentified Navajo man stands to the right. Photograph by Frank Russell, 1900.

and saddle-steed for the driver) and flung his writhing black-snake about with a practiced hand. He was a thick set fellow, with a pock marked face that made him repellently ugly at first; but he had clear blue eyes, and the habit of minding his own business. This reticence appeared to be due partly to shyness and partly to ignorance of our language, but before the summer had waned we learned it to be the reserve of a worthy nature and a faithful heart.

On an elevated spring seat, amid a mighty conglomeration of supplies and effects, sat the Instigators of the Expedition in lofty state and looked far down upon the little dog below.

Alongside, or perhaps to the front or the rear, paced Sliver's pinto pony, plus Sliver. What was the real Navajo name of this dignitary, we of course, could never discover. No possession of the Indian is to him more inviolable than his name. But it should have been Daniel, or words to that effect, for he wore a perpetual come-to-judgment aspect. He was a medicine man of the old school, and had the detached, esoteric air provided for those of his high calling, be they labelled swami, rabbit, priest, prophet, or shaman. His to approach the sacred Shekinah, his to converse with the oracle, his to impart to the people in cautious segments the words and the will of Those Above.[2]

It was not for this purpose, however, that he had been enlisted as a member of the Expedition. Being of versatile accomplishments, at least by reputation, he had been engaged as guide, interpreter, and cook. The meager fact that he proved pretty much a failure in all these capacities did not prevent him from being worth the price of admission, just to look at and listen to. Not that he ever voluntarily looked at or spoke to us—but perhaps that only enhanced his charm. He would ride along, bareheaded in the sunshine, forever chanting in subdued monotone the rhythmic cadences of the Indian song. Unlike the roundelays of Nosifor, Sliver's music awakened the keenest interest in its meaning. If one might only know the significance of those subtle, eerie strains! Breathed out into the Desert, the Desert seemed to absorb them as her own—akin to her in barbarism, in mystery, in appeal at once yearning and resigned.

And even more, one longed to know what mental processes were going on behind that impassive shield of features, the tropic-browned skin, the meditative brow, the experienced wrinkles radiating around the kind, dreamy eyes with the light in them, the thin lips and good, square chin. His slender form was still as erect as though it were youthful. Its slenderness was, indeed, the *raison d'etre* for his current cognomen. The Señor from whom we had acquired him, believed in the fitness of names. His own cook, being epileptic, was called "Crazy."

The one analyzable attribute about Sliver was his costume, and that, save when he dressed up *a la Melicano*, was a simple solution.[3] His shirt and trousers of figured calico, different in pattern, but alike in magnificence, made a fine dash of color on the landscape. His moccasins were fastened under the ankle by silver

FIGURE 10.2. "Dressed up a la Melicano." Sliver, their Navajo guide and cook, with mule Bill. "A dignified Indian of the old school . . . he has the physiognomy of a statesman, reserved and meditative" (Theresa Russell, journal, July 9, 1900). Photograph by Theresa Russell, 1900.

quarters made into clasps. His black hair was bunched up into a wad and tied with a white string, escaping locks being confined by a bandana fillet bound around the forehead.

If Sliver had been of the aristocracy of wealth, instead of mere culture, he would have been clad in corduroy. He would have worn a heavy, splendid, silver necklace with many pendants. He would have gloried in fine earrings of turquoise, tied on with a bit of twine or an old rag. He might even have had a handkerchief of silk knotted around his neck, and he would certainly have had an impressive cartridge belt buckled around his waist.

But he had none of these things. And probably being a theologian, he desired them not. In any case, his garb was suitable and satisfactory, and that, as we all know, is a millennium difficult to attain. He was also, being a desert Indian, possessed of a spontaneous cleanliness, and thus formed a happy combination of the gaudy and the neat.

"What are we stopping here for?" I inquire. In one's tenderfoot days one will ask questions.

FIGURE 10.3. "Clad in Corduroy." Unnamed Navajo guide and Nosifor. Frank's shadow is in the lower right as he takes the picture. Photograph by Frank Russell, 1900.

FIGURE 10.4. "What Are We Stopping Here For?" Photograph by Frank Russell, 1900.

"Cause."

"What kind of Cause? Final or Efficient?"

"Both. Final, because we're hungry, and efficient, because it's time to eat."

"I fear me the dread Professor would have decorated your answer with a nice, plump zero, in the good old Phil. IV Days."[4]

"But even he would admit it to be a sufficient reason."

"Especially if he were here. What shall I be doing?"

"Oh, hunt around in the sage brush and find a funny little horned toad to play with."

Instead, I discovered an Arizona ants' nest. It was of a size proportionate to the space surrounding it. No ignoble saucer could cover its curving dome. Indeed, it could scarcely have hidden itself under a bushel. It was no cheap adobe shack, either, but a palace of marble halls. Through its white and shining corridors hurried the black-costumed inhabitants, hurrying ever silently.

Not far away, a swift little lizard, all dressed for some social function, his grey livery gemmed with iridescent sapphire and emerald, issued from underneath a greasewood bush, and glided away, gliding silently.

Yonder a busy jack rabbit, having all at once recollected an overdue engagement in the next county, rushed from his covert of *cholla* and bounded away, bounding silently.

Away over there, a watchful coyote sneaked from an arroyo, covering his alertness under an affectation of indifference, and paced rapidly along, pacing silently.

But later on, when night is fairly come, he, of all these mute citizens, will find a voice, and that a voice that cuts the silence sharply. A series of short, staccato notes, a long drawn, quivering breath, rising into a cry of anguish, the wail of a lost soul.

"Lost soul, indeed!" sniffed the Man of Science, in a parenthesis between changing the camera plates and unrolling the bed. "The soul of the coyote is a multiple personality, and every one of him is irreclaimably lost and consigned to perdition."

After that I sat down on a roll of blankets and watched the boys make camp. No, there is no cause for alarm. I shall neither describe to you how they did it, nor explain to you how it should not be done. "For on this subject," as his Double Who Undid Him was instructed to say, "so much has been said, and so well said, that I feel I can add nothing of interest."[5] But of that first camp in the open, with the sand for a mattress, the sky for a ceiling, and stars for midnight tapers, two impressions can never be effaced.

One is of sound—the contended crunching of the equine quintette, the audible, artless, enjoyment of the well-earned supper. What positive, if reflected, comfort there is in it!

The other is of sight—the withdrawing sunset, yielding its vivid splendor to the calm, white radiance of the rising moon. Somehow you feel yourself in the presence of a Great Change that makes you hold your breath. It is as though some one dear to you had flaunted herself all day, and flouted you; as though she had dazzled and jeered and broken your heart with her flippant garishness and hollow pretense; as though she had finally seemed about to depart with a

FIGURE 10.5. "The Withdrawing Sunset." Photograph by Frank Russell, 1900.

riotous, Bacchanalian adieu—and then—quite suddenly, quite unexpectedly—had turned back to you with a rush of penitence and apology and given you a glimpse of the tender sweetness that had dwelt in the heart of her all the while. A cool touch caresses your cheek. A soft illumination trembles against your tired, strained eyes.

"Why, my beautiful Desert," you hear yourself saying, "I did not suppose you had it in you!"

Chapter 11

Up and Down the Chinle Valley

Each day brought new experiences. What had previously been new became routine. Theresa habituated to required exploration activities and soon took them for granted. When this happened, she no longer mentioned them. Her next installment concentrated on the hardships of expedition travel, learning Navajo culture, translation issues, and disappointment.

Theresa intellectualized the newness of language barriers and contextualized them with her first accounts of Navajos as individuals. She made analogies to Euro-American culture as a way to understand what she saw. She used the same technique to distract Frank from his dissatisfaction over the lost days and effort: witty repartee, wordplay appropriate to an Oscar Wilde play, a playful discussion of wildernesses. She made herself a romantic heroine but not in a mundane way. She became a costumed frau in her own play, "The Good Frau in Flour," based on the popular novel and play *When Knighthood Was in Flower*. The story told of a woman who wanted to be removed from her daily life and developed a fantasy world to keep her sanity. In the process, the heroine defied bourgeoise convention. Theresa effectively used self-deprecating humor as her mechanism for adaptation. She emphasized her neophyte status, symbolized by trying to make biscuits, and the romantic transformation of her new husband into a knight sent to rescue her from ridicule by their camp crew. Theresa was traveling in her imagination.

Nothing to do but ride, all day, except when you climbed out and walked. In the beginning you saw far to the north the southern slope of the Black Mesa, and your attention became riveted to one distant spot, where, thrown into distinct relief against surrounding somberness, shone in the morning light a Temple of Ivory. Entrance to a transfigured Parthenon you thought it must be and half expected to glimpse a clear-eyed Athene—you recognized her ægis hanging by the door—attended, perchance, by a silver-footed Thetis.[1] The white, fluted pillars, the Doric

FIGURE 11.1. "A Temple of Ivory." Photograph by Frank Russell, 1900.

FIGURE 11.2. "A Real Wet Spring." Photograph by Frank Russell, 1900.

columns, with mystic blue shadows lurking among—It all looked so clear and so near.

At noon, when you halted for a wayside luncheon, it looked just the same—so clear and so near.

At night, when you camped opposite, it still looked just the same—so clear and so near.

One thing, however, was nearer—a real, wet spring of water. It dispensed its moisture graciously but charily, like the entertainment of a reduced gentlewoman; its poor-but-proud offering was partaken of in a corresponding spirit of gallant appreciation.

And one thing was clearer—the intimation that the hitherto smoothness of our way was about to become distressingly rude and rough. No one seemed to welcome the rebuff, at least, not with a Browningesque enthusiasm, so we made a cisalpine camp.[2] It's also good philosophy, you know, to keep something to look forward to. It wards off ennui. Wherefore, we were obliged to initiate activities next morning by the precipitous descent of a hill, not long but steep, and the deliberate ascent of another, not steep, but long, and very soft with sand.

FIGURE 11.3. "So Clear and So Near." Photograph by Frank Russell, 1900.

FIGURE 11.4. "The Deliberate Ascent." Photograph by Theresa Russell, 1900.

FIGURE 11.5. "Navajos—For Dinner Guests." Chinle Valley camp, July 9, 1900 Photograph by Frank Russell.

FIGURE 11.6. "By the Family." Photograph by Theresa Russell.

FIGURE 11.7. "Finished Up the Cherries." Photograph by Theresa Russell.

But by and by, in the hot by-and-by, we arrived at a place that had some sense. There were scrubby cedars for shade, there were cliffs and ravines for artistic effect, and there were Navajos by the family for dinner guests.

The old squaw finished up the cherries out of the can and discoursed volubly with many gestures.

"What is she talking about?" I ask.

"She say," replied the ready Nosifor, "she plant these cherry seeds in the ground, sometime tree grows high, she sit in heap big shade and eat 'um plenty."

"Good for you, Auntie," commended the Anthropologist. "We'll put you down for a speech at our next Arbor Day celebration."[3]

Auntie did not manifest any flutter of excitement over the proposition, but consented to have and to hold the sack of sugar we gave her as barter for using the water from her spring.

After that she and I had to be quiet while the men talked. For the assemblage had resolved itself into a Committee on Ways. We had come hither by and with the advice and recommendation of one of the oldest inhabitants, who had spoken magnificently of large ruins, "heaps big casas, plenty wesos, ollas, mucho everything." Now it seems to be true that a great blaze of imagination may be kindled from a few insignificant chips of facts. And it appeared to be due to this interesting phenomenon—interesting, if you are a psychologist and not a mere archaeologist—that our grand potentialities had shrunken, under the light of investigation, to actualities that were undeniably chiquito. Moreover, this place was to be directly en route to the real objective point we had in mind. Now, it developed that the road across was impassible. There was plainly nothing to be done but to sound a retreat to the end of the mesa, round that point, and head northward on the west side of it instead of on the east.

That sounds easy, but, bless you, what a pow-wow it involved to corral all the scattered evidence and brand it as conclusive! What a prolonged session of the contemplative crescent under the cedars! What a drawing of maps on the sand! What a meditative rolling and puffing of cigarettes! What queries and arguments bandied like tennis balls from speakers to interpreters! What free handed gesticulations to all points of the cosmos! What slow and conclusive shaking of heads!

It was finally agreed, however, that we had better do the only thing to be done, and right-about-face orders were given. To the stoical Sliver, the volatile Nosifor, the non-committal Erminio, one kind of order was as good as another, being all in the day's work. But the Instigators had hard work to look happy. It was evidently desirable to make up some joyful conversation.

"Which do you think is the hottest?" I asked, by way of beginning, "the sun or the sand?"

"We'll excuse your use of the superlative degree," equivocated the Man of Science, "for in this case there is no comparison. But you are not getting your money's worth of experience. Just feel of the sand with your hand."

We were trudging on in the van of the retreat, and I stooped down obediently and patted the pathway.

"Oh, but you are shirking yet! Take your gloves off. There is that hot en——"

"Beware! That question is ruled out in the Etiquette Book, even in Hades."[4] "Indeed? And why must the poor firebrands be so punctilious?"

"I'll not vouch for it, but I've heard it reported that it is due to an amendment put through by the Delegation from the Hub, declaring it to be 'a violation of the canons to mention meteorological conditions, particularly with interrogatory reference to their effect upon the temperature of the questionee.'"[5]

"Can't blame the Bostonians. While the atmosphere of their native environment is admittedly of precious quality, the climate they've been brought up in is not a suitable subject for polite discussion. For my part, I should rather be toasted in a nice, clean oven than put to soak on a moldy, old rain-barrel."

"Even rain-barrels have their mission. If I should happen to meet one right now, I know where there would be an awful splash. There is vast superfluity," I continued reflectively, "in Some Definitions I Have Known."

"Apropos of what?"

"What you tried to ask me a while ago. Someone has cleverly described this country as 'Hell with the fires burnt out.'"[6] It's correct enough up to the end of the first word. But it's a judgment by sense of sight only, and that left the deluded judge under a hallucination. If someone had made him take his glove off, he would have left the phrase off, of his own accord."

Thus discoursing, Fair Heart and Faint Lady came anew to the hilltop of painful memory.[7] Over it rolled the wagon with the easy unconcern of one anticipating an unbroken career of down-grades. But having reached the nethermost point, Easy Unconcern butted right into Trouble. It never means to, but it always does, someway. And Trouble has such an unfortunate penchant for requiring attention and entertainment. In this case, the demand was that we rid the load of all human freight and some other, and do battle with an unpardonable hill.

Crack of whip, yells and cries of drivers—the hoarse Erminio on one side, the shrill Nosifor on the other. To this vocal stimulus the faithful beasts respond with all that is in them, the mules stolidly, the horses sensitively. Every muscle is strained, tense. Utmost effort is exerted without apparent effect. Crack, scream, a desperate plunge, white Bill [the horse] fairly leaping from the ground in his frantic endeavor, breathless pull, and gain of five yards. Down, and a rush to block the wheels and apply the brake. A pause for the hard, quick taking of breath, and the lines are reformed for another rush. Two downs, and a yard to gain! But the

FIGURE 11.8. "Two Downs, and a Yard to Gain." Erminio and Nosifor push the horses and mules to drag the unloaded wagon up a steep rise. Photograph by Theresa Russell, 1900.

goal is creeping nearer, and at last the visiting eleven (counting the dog) score a triumphant touchdown, and kick everything in sight in order to finish the game with a good punting effect.[8]

Retiring from the scene, however, did not mean leaving the gridiron. The entire field of operations was raised to the boiling point. But we went on far enough to get out of sight of our vanquished opponent and made a dry camp for the night. (A Dry Camp is the kind where it is superfluous to ring for either hot or cold water, unless your own kegs or canteens can supply the demand.)

By the next afternoon we had completed our detour and were again headed north, and this time on an up-to-date thoroughfare. Not to advance at once, however, for this camp proved to be another of the dry variety, and the regiment was obliged to mark time of the rest of the day while a detachment was sent back to the [Hubbell's] Post for water. After the detail had departed, it was discovered to have included everybody but the Instigators, who were thus left to keep house by themselves.

To the Tenderfoot, the weather seemed hot, really hot, even intensely hot. The sun bent down close to the earth in order to shrivel it with his fiendish breath. The earth was a wilderness of wind-blown, drifting impertinent sand. Between the two conspirators, poor humanity was caught and flayed to a frizzle.

"Wouldn't you like to go to the matinee this afternoon?" I inquired.

"Where shall we go?" replied the Anthropologist, in the soothing tone one uses toward the demented.

"Let's try 'When Knighthood Was in Flower.'[9] Anything in flower would look good."

"Just my thought. How would 'The Good Frau in the Flour' do, for a substitute? We need some biscuits for supper."

"I fear the Frau wouldn't know how to act, never having made any biscuits in her present incarnation."

"Oh well, she might make a bluff at it. We'll call it a dress rehearsal."

So, the Frau made herself up for the part, puttered about on her sanded stage, accumulated a number of ingredients, mixed them together, and tucked them up in the Dutch oven. Although in the time to come she was to be on familiar and affectionate terms with this indispensable adjunct to camp cookery, and to coax it to turn out for her many a delectable loaf, her initial acquaintance with it cannot be truthfully designated as auspicious. It was consoling to reflect, however, that it was unquestionably by the grace of Providence—that enigmatical Lady who so loves to interfere in our affairs, but reciprocates by permitting us to put on her the responsibility of our blunders—that the greasy, gritty mess was saved from consumption by being burned to a crisp beneath while it was yet in a raw state of nature above.[10]

The Instigators tried to conceal their terrible secret before the boys should return, but Sliver came in time to catch them at it. He comprehended, and gravely explained in his eight-by-ten vocabulary about the use of concave lids and baking powder and coals of fire and things. And the Man of Science, who had somehow contrived to have this disquisition directed to himself, as gravely listened and promised to remember, hypocritically insinuating that he, and he alone, had been the perpetrator of the culinary joke.

"Well, it was quite a dramatic play," concluded the Leading Lady, "and one is very proud to discover that knighthood is still in flower."

Chapter 12
The Writer Lady and the Mormons

Theresa missed green trees and running water. She needed an oasis to escape the sun and dust and someone to cook her a "real" meal. She anticipated reaching Keams Canyon but not to meet another famous man. Tired of men, Theresa yearned for stimulating conversation with a woman who could verbally joust as she did with Frank. Instead, she met two women, whom she deemed tiresome, an instance of "be careful what you wish for."

The first was the gregarious Mrs. Rausch, who had lived at Keams Canyon for several years and was lonely and starved for intelligent female companionship. After spending just a few minutes with her, Theresa longed to flee, and poked fun at her pretentions, incessant advice, and nonstop monologue. The second woman was Mrs. Allen, a young Mormon woman who had settled in the trading post only the day before. Theresa's first interaction with a Mormon was portrayed as an opportunity to gently interrogate and hopefully educate one whom she felt was burdened with nonsensical belief. The two women discussed religious tolerance, blind faith, and skepticism based on Protestant logic. Theresa concluded Mrs. Allen had unshakable convictions, which Theresa equated with a lack of intellect and critical thinking. Her assessment was similar to how she assumed Navajo and Hopi beliefs were interesting yet flawed.[1]

In the process of learning about others, Theresa intellectualized the absence of the commonplace, beginning by defining the phenomenon explored and followed by clever wordplay. She realized she preferred Frank's company to that of others; he could talk in allegories. Theresa and Frank could have a discourse on Greek Stoicism using strawberry jam, butter, and a bread crust as illustrations. She could not converse in this manner with Jim, Keam, Rausch, or Allen. Contemplating female loneliness and ignorance, Theresa realized that only Frank was her intellectual equal in Arizona. The western settlements and wilderness were not sophisticated Boston.

"There's as much human nature in some folks as there is in others, if not more."[2]

It was ours the next night to enjoy a sylvan camp again, with spring water, and shade of cedar and piñon—a place to leave with regret, modified, as is the usual way with regret, by anticipation. For were we about to see people today—real, white people?

Sure enough, about ten o'clock of the morning, we perceived evidence of them, distant and enchanting—the waving, beckoning branches of cottonwood trees, all in a nice row, and casting real, green shade. A nearer view disclosed the vista of which they formed one side to the outline on the other by a corresponding row of whitewashed adobe buildings—the housing of the Government Indian School.[3]

We arrived, and the first thing I knew I had been whisked out of the wagon and was sitting in a large chair surrounded by a small room. It was a cool room, and well ordered—in spite of its overdose of furniture. The lady of the room was rapidly sewing up a diminutive muslin bag on the machine. It would, perhaps, have been interesting to those philosophers who believe that we spin our surroundings out of ourselves, to have noted that the mind of the mistress did seem to be a counterpart, in a way, of the apartment. "Psychical archetype?"[4] Yes, thank you, Plato! Anyway, the psychical furniture appeared to be of a comfortable, commonplace, of a more or less useful sort, methodically arranged. When the little bag was finished, it was filled with dry starch and presented to me for my complexion's sake. As a matter of veracity, one feels impelled to mention that its usefulness remained entirely potential until, one day, the Man of Science was making a big map and wanted some smooth paste to stick the sections together. Thus, you see, little children, we should never despair if we are not allowed at once to enter the service for which we think we are fitted. It is merely that we are being preserved for a more noble purpose—perhaps, even for a high, sacrificial career—when the time comes.

Meanwhile, my hostess was instructing me how to construct a chamois-skin mask as a freckle-preventing apparatus. It was on another day, also, that I met her riding to the Flute Dance at Walpi, manifestly a practitioner of her own precepts. She was so completely encased in her color-protective armor that I should undoubtedly have been moved to greet her with a "Speak, speak, thou fearful guest!" had not her proportions been so far from sepulchral.[5]

Now, however, as I drank her delicious lemonade and let her talk to me, the burden of her confession was not of Viking-bold propensities but of aspiring literary inclinations. She was, in fact, almost an authoress.

"And so, you have just sent on your manuscript to be published?" I inquired, respectfully.

FIGURE 12.1. "A Place to Leave with Regret." Entrance to Keams Canyon. Photograph by Frank Russell, 1900.

FIGURE 12.2. "The Beckoning Branches of Cottonwood Trees." Settlers planted cottonwood trees as windbreaks. Photograph by Frank Russell, 1900.

"Yes, I've been working on it for nearly a year. Then when the ethnologist from Washington was here, he helped me to get some pictures, and it was all ready.[6] The pictures turned out splendid."

"It is an Indian story, you say?"

"Partly, and partly Spanish. It's very romantic."

"You certainly have had a good opportunity to draw your characters from real life."

"Oh, yes, of course I see enough of the natives, but I did not take any of the characters from life. I made it all up out of my own head."

"Western stories are very popular just now. I suppose you have read some of the recent ones?"

"No. I haven't had much of anything to read since we've been out here; and besides, I think it is better not to. I do not want to be in danger of imitating anyone else. That is why I believe my story will be such a great success—it is so original."

"There's nothing like originality," I agreed. "And the plot is your own invention?"

"Yes. It goes something like this"—

But here the narrative was brought to its dramatic close, the narrator's audience was obliged to move on, in order to reach the trading post, two or three miles beyond, in time for luncheon.

"I'll just get in and ride down with you," volunteered the writer-lady, not to be interrupted by a mere exodus, "and I can finish telling you about it as we go along."

"Dear Dame Loquacious!" I sighed when no one but the Anthropologist was around. "How she did love a listener!"

"No more than you would, probably, if you had been kept as long on short rations of companionship. She was simply, as someone expressed it, ridding her system of a lot of accumulated conversation."

"It accumulates pretty fast, I fancy, in her system, but it does not harm, so long as she finds it so easy to dispose of. And I doubt if she really minds the loneliness so much as a more repressed nature would. She has more need of telling it out, to be sure; but on the other hand, she is saved by her broad views respecting auditors. She has the faculty, useful if not happy, of making the most of what is, where to be fastidious is often to go without."

"Like the Apache on the warpath, who can find abundant living on the very trail where his pale-faced pursuers would starve."

"And what does one gain by being in the midst of the crowd, if the grocer's boy or the ice man can furnish as stimulating companionship as a college president? Hath not each and every one a pair of ears!"[7]

"According to Scripture, the possessor of ears is in duty bound to bear, and the possible advantage of a population is that this duty can be divided up among the several and sundry ears, thus diminishing the individual tax."[8]

This communistic conclusion was reached over our tête-à-tête spread in the Post dining room, where we had been made as kindly welcome as though we had arrived at the appointed eating-hour. We were served by a faded, elderly Anglo-Saxon called Jim. Jim had a twinkle in his eye, and a way of making a McKinley pie that was simply captivating.[9] I haven't time, now, to tell you what a McKinley pie is like, but if you will ask him, he will doubtless give you the recipe.

"What a beautiful menu!" I exclaimed.

"Good in itself, and made better by a contrasting experience. It's an illustration of what the poet says about the prerequisite 'to appreciate Heaven well.'"[10]

"'Tis true. But even the Other Place has its compensations. For one thing, you don't have to associate with saints. Our tinned and salted camp fare, washed down by crude coffee, may be purgatorial, but brightened by Sliver's pagan smile and enlivened by Nosifor's naughty songs, it becomes quite palatable. However, as you say, this is not only good but good for a change, and I'll take another potato, please."

"You have never before regarded a plain boiled potato as a luxury, have you?"

"Forsooth, dear sir, what is a luxury?"

"In this case, it's a sort of reincarnation—the unconsidered commonplace idealized by absence. But, in general, I should say it is the butter on your bread."

"The lubricant of life?"

"Yes, and more. As a matter of fact, it is what makes the bread worth eating. Of course, a hungry man relishes a dry crust, a starving man feasts on it, but a steady diet of dry crust will in time cause the appetite to fail.[11] The struggle for the bread is an instinct, knowing neither judgment nor desire. It's winning the butter that calls judgment and desire into play and adds a zest to the fight as well as the reward."

"And when you add marmalade?"

"The strife degenerates into a hunt. A little is good, but more is bad. When it comes to be a feverish scramble to see who can find the most expensive kinds of jam, spread it on the thickest, and swallow the stickiest mixtures, it were better to chew a crust."

"And eschew sweets?"

"Oh, not altogether. Just pass me the strawberry preserves, will you? But plain bread and butter represents the temperate zone—well enough to leave for brief excursions to torrid opulence or frigid poverty, but most desirable as a dwelling place for generations."

"How comforting for those who lack the equatorial purse! But really, you can't pin the word down to a hard-and-fast definition. It's like impaling a butterfly. By the time you get it where you can focus your scientific eye upon it, it's a dead specimen."

"A dead specimen is a good specimen. But, in this case, your butterfly is a chameleon."

"Every fellow's luxury takes its color from himself?"

"Even so. And that implies another thing—that every fellow does have his luxury, or his idea of it. The dry-crust diet is not so common as we suppose. The most pinched and frugal of us manage to get hold of some oleomargarine or molasses once in a while."

"And, our taste being in harmony, we banquet."

"At least, we think we do, and that's sufficient. Every life has some share of color and music and fragrance. Judged by an alien standard, the hues may be tawdry, the strains discordant, the odors unrefined. But his own is every man's treasure."

"And existence unadorned"—

"May be existence, but is not life."

Our host [Keam] is not a Westerner. He was not even an Easterner. He was an Englander, and he had brought his accent with him. It was as striking a feature as his modern frame cottage within its woven-wire enclosure that contrasted so refreshingly with the all-prevailing adobe. The two together imparted a civilized flavor to the place that not even the groups of loafing Indians without, nor the superb collection of strange curios within, could render wholly heathenish. In manner, too, one felt the change from the address of the former host. There was no less of chivalry, nor yet of hospitality, neither any more shrewdness. But kindness and calculation alike merged their currents under a more placid surface, a more polished calm, touched with native cynicism and tempered by frontier-trained humor.

FIGURE 12.3. "Down at the Store." Keam's Trading Post with Navajo and Hopi customers. Photograph by Frank Russell, 1900.

FIGURE 12.4. "His Modern Frame Cottage." Keam's house near his trading post. Photograph by Frank Russell, 1900.

There were bachelor quarters; but down at the store, in a room at the end of the long building, I found Another Woman. She was the wife of the new clerk, and they had just arrived. Their household was in as great a confusion as could be caused by not much of anything, and their minds also seemed to be of a corresponding type. Yet there was a certain winsomeness about the young woman,

FIGURE 12.5. "Superb Collection of Strange Curios." Thomas Keam's curio room. Photograph possibly by Theresa Russell, 1900.

with her wistful eyes, spiritual brow and sweetly-shy manner. Her husband, poor boy, hadn't any brow at all, to speak of; his eyes were pale, and his manner merely diffident. But he was well-meaning, my dear, and he surely had a kind heart, the eternal compensation of the incompetent.

So, the little lady and I, we spent the afternoon together, and talked a good deal. She, too, loved a listener, but wisely, and not too well. The lotion of sympathy was necessary to draw out her confidence, but it seemed the better for the relief of expression.

"It is not often," she said, "that anyone who is not a Mormon will listen to our side, or believe there is any good in it."

"That may be because they don't understand it."

"Oh, yes, I'm sure that's the reason. Anyone who understood it could not help believing it!" she responded fervently.

"'To know all is to pardon all,' I thought within me, "but to believe little."[12] Aloud I queried, "The Book of Mormon is your Scripture, isn't it?"

"Yes, but we believe the Bible, too, and we accept all of it, and not just the parts we like, as some of the Gentiles do. And the same with the Book of Mormon. The best thing about that is that you know every word in it is true. You can be sure of that."

"It's from that, isn't it," I hazarded, "that you learn about the Indians being descended from the Ten Lost Tribes of Israel?"[13]

"Yes, and isn't it foolish for these scientists" (she was unaware of treading on any scientific toes) "to waste so much time trying to find out where the Indians came from and all, when it is right there, and proved so plain?"

"How proved?"

"Why, they are a fulfilment of prophecy. It says, 'They shall eat with their fingers and be filthy still,'—meaning those descendants, you know. Well doesn't that fit the Indians exactly, and prove they are the very ones meant?"

In the face of this blinding glare of evidence I could only blink helplessly, and endeavor to turn the searchlight on another point.

"But you don't get your authority for polygamy from the Bible, do you?"

"Sure we do, though the special revelation came later. But Solomon had many wives, you know, and the Bible says, 'The Lord is the same yesterday, today, and forever.'[14] So, of course, what was right then must be right now."

"And you women really like that sort of life?"

"Well," with a visible but reluctant shrinking of enthusiasm, "of course, we are naturally selfish and jealous, and some of us feel that we cannot endure it. But that is because we are not as we should be ourselves. If we would take it right, we might not be any happier, but it would surely make us better. For we know that if we are patient and brave, our reward will be all the greater. Our happiness will come in the future life."

"Oh, Future Life," said my thought to me, "what crimes are committed in thy name! What insults offered to the bounteous Present, what blindness to her beauty, what trifling with her opportunity, what stupid rejection of her gifts. Oh, baffling Life, what folks these martyrs be!"

To the Lady of Zeal, I remarked, "But polygamy is not practiced among your people now, is it?"

"No. We are law-abiding citizens, and although we still think polygamy is right, we do not believe it is right to disobey the law."

"Well now, since it is not your fault that you cannot be as unselfish and sacrificing as you would like, you can live happily here on earth and get your reward in Heaven just the same, can't you?"

"Why, yes, I suppose so."

"And you don't mind having it that way, do you?"

"Not very much, I guess."

The arch, tender smile that illuminated this Confession of Selfishness would have been puzzling, remembering its adored but unadorable object, had it not been for the reflection that, after all, Love, more than Man, is precious in the sight of Woman; and Love, one of life's luxuries, is an obliging chameleon.

Stanford University, Cal.

Chapter 13
Togoholtazze Spring and Bokodokleesh Cañon

Theresa turned to the Navajo. She expressed the views of a stranger, assuming cultural and racial superiority tempered by historical circumstance. Both Frank and Theresa were abstractly aware of how racialized colonialism was affecting Indigenous peoples globally. While they knew that Native Americans were no longer free to follow their own ways of life, they failed to observe consequences right before their eyes. Theresa for the first time acknowledged that some effects of imperialism, colonialism, and assimilation attempts surprised her.

What dominated Theresa's descriptions of the Navajo-Russell interactions was Sliver's "unexpected" behavior; her quiet Navajo companion had become loquacious now that he could talk to someone who spoke Diné and cared about the same topics. Frank saw this simply as a communication issue while Theresa turned the occurrence into an abstract exegesis on rough versus well-formed individuals and the importance of formal education in the transformation of "primitive" into "civilized." It was another philosophical-psychological ramble into evolutionary psychology. Theresa used one of William James's theories about social and spiritual selves. This dealt with who individuals were at their cores and how this core was expressed in different social situations. For James, people changed how they acted depending on who they were with and the nature of their interactions. This became Theresa's explanation for Sliver's new personality.[1]

This installment took the group to Moenkopi Wash. As in all travel narratives, Theresa focused on the rigors of the long journeys, the terrain's harsh beauty, and their search for water. She provided readers with the exploits of hobbled animals that searched to assuage their thirst. And again, there was disappointment, for despite all their efforts, they had not found the perfect site. They once again turned back, returning to their wagon at Togoholtazze Spring by retracing their route down Bokodokleesh Cañon.[2]

"Little drops of water
Little grains of sand."[3]

Next morning the Expedition embarked once more in its white-sailed prairie schooner and continued its cruise over the billows of sand. But it was the evening of the second day ere it arrived at a place. The place was a sort of Rip Van Winkle dell—without the flagons. The intruders were not invited to partake of a cup, inebriating or otherwise, but they were quite welcome to help themselves and furnish their own cup. By holding it high up, close against the rock cliff, one might in time accumulate a sizable, clean drink of the water that oozed out, drop by drop, and was taken up as fast as issued, like popular Government bonds. Otherwise, one might dip it up out of the shallow, muddy pool, and be comforted with what had been left by the Navajos, their babies, their dogs, their sheep, and their goats.

The proprietor of Togoholtazze Spring and patriarch of this flock, biped and quadruped, we called Belshazzar.[4] His name sounded as much like that as anything, and moreover, there was a feast. We dined on one of his kids (quadruped) while he regaled himself on our canned peaches and deviled ham.

Belshazzar lived in a very good imitation of a house; that is, he had one. It seemed to exist for the same reason that the rural parlor of our grandfathers had its being—just to show that it could have a being if it wanted to. The adjoining courtyard, bounded by a stone wall, was the real living room. It boasted some imported chairs, but they, too, were in the nature of ornaments, or reserved seats, perhaps, for those who liked that sort of thing. The Indian prefers to squat on the ground; then he is in no danger of falling off.

Leaning thus at ease against the outer wall, Belshazzar and Sliver were enjoying an animated conversation; that is, Belshazzar was animated. Evidently, he was relating a dramatic and detailed account of the wanderings of his Aeneas, harkened to by his auditor with an interest now serious, now amused, as indicated by the varying tone of his responsive grunts.[5] As I watched them, wishing I could understand the recital, I was filled with amazement that this could be Sliver, our speechless, distant, inscrutable Sliver.

"Did you dream that such vivacity lay under the impassive mask?" I inquired.

"It wasn't so much a mask," amended the Anthropologist, "as the side he chose to turn toward us, strangers and aliens as we are. This is the side kept for his tribal brother and friend. Humans are hexagonal, you know."

"All humans?"

"Well, from that point of view, we might say, speaking geometrically, that primitive man is something of a rhomboid: an unsymmetrical figure, with angles both acute and obtuse, difficult to fit in anywhere. As he is whacked into shape by the processes of civilization, he assumes more regular proportions, but still presents many angles to view. It is only after the file of education and the hammer of experience have done their work upon him, that these sharp, insistent points are worn and pointed down, and your 'well-rounded man' emerges from the stress of life. For a sphere is simply a body of infinite sides and invisible angles."

"And capable of touching another sphere only at an infinitesimal point?"

"I believe it has been so alleged. But, granting that, we must consider that even solid bodies are capable of radiation and absorption, that the influences are interpenetrating and permeating, and that the impact of even a slight contact is communicable to the whole inner substance."

"Clear to the center?"

"Sometimes; but always the center is protected and concealed. It is the perimeter that has to bear the brunt of the blow."

"Only, in some cases, there isn't much space between circumference and center."

"To be sure. That's the advantage of being big. All vital instruction is reducible to this, 'Lengthen your diameter.' The more surface you present to life, the more impression you can receive from it, and at the same time, the more invulnerable rests the Core of the Self."[6]

"And what is it the blessed old Autocrat says about the arc a man subtends?"

"That a very small one will show his size."

Meanwhile the [Navajo] women were getting supper. A fire was built on the ground in an angle of the stone enclosure, meat roasted, and bread baked. The preparation of the meal seemed to be more by way of being a social function than was its consumption. Each dusky sister, curled up comfortably on the ground, reclining languidly against the wall, reaching around the babe in arms, tossed and passed the dough into shape with a leisure and aplomb that would have scandalized the scurrying Saxon housewife.[7] The tortillas may have been seasoned with sand, but they were certainly flavored with mirth and garnished with the gossip of the hour. As each morsel was cooked, it was handed or flung to one of the numerous members of the family, loafing or running about, and thus all managed to dine before the last shred of daylight was gone.

Thereupon, darkness having fallen, naught remained but to roll up in warm blankets and dream and dream into another day.

When we weight anchor next morning, we knew it would be thirty miles between drinks, for the next water island in our ocean of sand was to be a certain White Cave Spring, a long day's journey beyond.

Now to toll along a wearisome trail all day toward an essential goal may have the incentive of anticipation. But to arrive painfully and late and not find any goal there after all is somewhat dispiriting. There were some sounds by night, but they were not of revelry, and we made a very dry camp indeed.

By early morning light, however, that shy, retiring White Cave Spring, that had played hide-and-seek with us the night before and won the game, had to give up and be found—away up the cañon, so coyly disposed behind barriers of rocks, reached by such a wavering, half-hearted trail than it was something to win out even with daylight playing on your side.

But when we went joyously to round up our thirsty beasts and give them the glad tidings, one was not present at roll call. Brown Bob, in his disgust and despair, had decided that a tavern without a bar was indescribably blanker than a Hamletless Hamlet, so he, while his companions slept, went backward, toiling through the night. His unspeakable scorn at being trailed and made to retrace his truant miles was as measureless as his thirst. But when the one was assuaged, the other was softened, and he concluded to forgive Bill and Erminio for the chase and capture; to forgive them, as we also, of our magnanimity, forgive those against whom we have trespassed and upon whom has fallen the retribution for our misdeeds.[8]

From that point it was decided to make a hasty horseback trip to Bokodokleesh Cañon. Wherefore, leaving the mules and the Mexicans to keep camp, Sliver and the Instigators sally forth.[9]

Now equestrianism is a jaunty exercise, when properly performed. Otherwise it is a jolty one. It hoists your temper up and your philosophy down—that is, if you are a novice, and are perched aloft on ponderous old Bill. Like some of your friends, Bill has never acquired the light touch. Consequently, he bears down hard on whatever happens to be in the way, nerves or anything else. But he is good, oh so good, and uncomplaining, and earnest, and capable of grinding out such quantities of hard work!

Therefore, you pound along, and in your imagination the score of miles waxes to three score and ten, and their increase is indeed trouble and sorrow. Yet will the utmost flight of fancy not make of Bill a Pegasus, nor equip you with the wings of a dove—no, not even a buzzard, although you see the black piñons circling above you, silent, darkling, ominous.[10] But the stubborn miles are worn out at last, as is the way with things, and you find that, after all, they were leading you to something worthwhile. For you are standing on the brink of a cañon.

Much is said about mountains; and the most that can be said is not enough. In their sublime presence, fluency turns into faltering. But before the cañon we stammer yet more. The cañon is the complement of the mountain. It is the mountain reversed—as though Nature had used it as a seal to stamp some mighty state secret, and left forever imprinted there the wonderful intaglio.

Man looks up at the mountain, and feels his own puny stature and limited view. He looks down into the cañon, and exults in his own vantage ground. It has his truer comprehension, because of his juster point of view. It arouses his keener joy for its beauty of contour and color. It wakens his deeper reverence for the majesty of its vastness. It quickens his more solemn awe for the mystery of its depth. And always it claims his whole hearted affection; for, with all its beauty and vastness and depth, it casts no frowning shadow over him. He is still dominant; and the hush that falls upon him is for the wonder of himself as much as of that other wonderful thing.

Then you go down into the cañon. And as you go, you wish that the deep-sighted old Scot, who was so sensitive to the marvels of the universe, might have seen this surpassing marvel. More than ever would he have exclaimed, "He who cannot wonder, who does not habitually wonder and worship, is but a Pair of Spectacles, behind which there are no eyes."[11]

This thought flits about in your mind, albeit your own eyes are well night blinded by mere weariness of the flesh. So that when Men of Science make remarks to you about the loveliness of the place you are approaching, you murmur to yourself, "Gott sei dank, *approaching*!" and mumble incoherently aloud, "Yes, indeed, it's almost picturesque, isn't it?"

Then you part company with Bill so suddenly that they run to pick you up and carry you inside. For the place has an Inside. It is another Uncle Sam Indian School. The school is closed for the summer, and the youthful *discipuli* are returned to their Native hearth and preferred costume, though the scenery is on duty the year round. Closed with the back door open, fortunately, so the Expedition goes in, a la Little Goldenhair [*sic*], and sits on all sizes of chairs and eats an aristocratic luncheon from a sure-enough table. It has to make its own porridge, though, and the bears never came home at all.[12] Nobody comes but a cat, and later, a few Navajos, all of whom seem equally well-disposed and uncommunicative.

There is something that babbles, however—a stream of running water. It wouldn't know what you meant if you called it a "brook," but it has all the symptoms of one, and in addition, a spring bubbling up out of the sandy bottom right in the midst of it. Altogether, it is a dear; and you tell the Expedition that it may go on and leave you to stay on, forever. When you see, however, how forlorn and dejected your devoted Bill looks at this announcement, you repent, and are again hoisted to his ample but uneasy back.

It is too far, of course, to make the entire return trip today, but it is necessary for the unprovisioned excursion to reach supplies as soon as convenient. So, it travels till dark, sups on rations of coffee and biscuits, and goes to bed.

Going to bed is so easy when you journey without impedimenta. You hang your hat and shoes on a cedar tree, roll up in your saddle blanket with the saddle itself for a pillow, and shut your eyes.

Going to sleep is another matter.

Next morning a ride of three hours brings you to camp in time for a seven o'clock breakfast. You are glad the boys have spied you coming and have the bacon curling up over the coals when you arrive.

This happy episode over, the entire caravan puts itself into motion, and covers the distance to another spring before noon. It is not thirty miles away, though. But since that be chronicled, the fact that yet another spring is our portion for supper should receive honorable mention.[13] This one is called Weepo, but not for the same reason that Eve named the Dodo.[14] At least, it does not look lachrymal to the wayfarers. To complete the liquid extravagance, a shower comes up, and we are well moistened inside and out.

This was to last through two more dry days, and then, behold, the Ship of the Desert swings into port, and all hands are ordered to disembark.[15]

Stanford University

Chapter 14
A Local Habitation

Finally, a potential site: Kwaituki. It was time to stick holes in the ground, shovel quickly, and extract artifacts. Theresa presented a brief exposition on performing these tasks, but it was not her missive's focus. The archaeological activities gave her something to do, eliminating her idleness and assuaging Protestant guilt. They also presented dilemmas, including living in a small space overflowing with artifacts and having to sit on boxes filled with bones. She thought it ghoulish but tried to convince herself otherwise using Jamesian theories; her "social self" guided her "spiritual self," overcoming the confines of her "material self."[1] She pragmatically suppressed a belief that exhuming and cleaning bones was disrespectful and repugnant, inappropriate for a Gentile woman. It would not be done in Boston but was necessary in Arizona.

Theresa contrasted her justifications about scientific need with Sliver's cultural decisions not to touch the dead: was the archaeological exhumation of bodies a morally questionable or dangerous activity as the Navajo held? She was not sure, but she called on the Greek goddess of retributive justice, Nemesis, to pardon her just in case. She did not call on the Holy People as Sliver would have, for she had no conception of Navajo philosophy, and if she had, she would have labeled the theology superstitious paganism. Theresa never attempted to explain how the Navajo felt about death, for she had no understanding of central Diné concepts and values.[2] Thus, the reader had no opportunity to understand why Sliver saw their tent as an "unholy scene" and found some archaeological tasks unacceptable. Theresa reasoned Sliver's behavior regarding actual excavation with the possibility of finding a skeleton was unreasonable; she did not distinguish digging a fire pit and exhuming human remains. What one might uncover was irrelevant to the act of digging. For the Navajo, what one might find was critical, especially if one was not to be near ghosts and the negative supernatural power that any remains contained. As a result, her explanations of Navajo belief and behavior sunk to the realm of ethnocentric stereotypes; not even James's theories of spiritualism, grounded in Judaism and Christianity, could serve as the basis for understanding Diné belief.

Theresa further argued that Sliver's "sophisticated commercialism," which allowed him to excavate for remuneration, demonstrated he was not maximizing profit. Again, James's theory of pragmatism, where truth was measured by measurable consequences (such as amassing material wealth), led Theresa astray. Since the crew earned bonuses for discovering and uncovering burials, Sliver was not showing "intellectual fitness" or economic rationality. Pragmatic individuals were able to thrive in precarious environments because they considered economic concerns fundamental.[3] Further, Sliver made decisions that did not help her husband. According to Theresa's premises and valuation of logical action, anyone who did not assist Frank was making irrational personal affronts. Her rationality held that science, that is, Frank's needs, took precedence over all conflicting considerations. She fell back on the conceit that Sliver had an unenlightened mind since he had different criteria for moral acts. Such uninformed reasoning was a common technique for travelers trying to understand cultural norms.

"The bed was made, the room was fit.
But punctual eve the stars were lit."[4]

The reason for the dismemberment was that we had found the thing we long had sought—a ruin that looked suspicious of harboring graveyards.

Out came the shovel and the pick, the measuring rod, and the camera. Up went the tents, and presto, there on the unblossoming desert had sprung forth a full-grown Home. It was immediately as much at home as though its advent had been awaited from the beginning. As though the cedars had been growing, all these years but to shade the little tents, whose new whiteness now shone so entrancingly against their encircling browns and greens. As though tawny sands and somber sage and rocks of ecru and cream had been blending their harmony for its approving delight. As though over these neutral shades had bent the brilliant blue to brighten its monotony. As though the sunsets, practicing for centuries, had perfected their splendor to bring to a triumphant close its every day.

As for the day, one might not say which part of it were best—whether the morning with its tonic air, the essence of wine inhaled; whether the glittering noon, when this same air at once quivers with heat and trembles with the errant breeze, unfailing, cool and sweet, as if it came from grottos and dripping, dim retreats; or yet the twilight time, with its deep hush on earth and mystery on high; or even yet the night, with stars shining so close you reach out for them, for no smoke nor dust nor grime floats like a veil between you and their light. Each yielded up its charm to us, and each in its own speech said, "Welcome home."

There was the thought, too, that it had been home in unknown years gone by to this long-buried people. But though the Archaeologist may wear the flower

FIGURE 14.1. "That Looked Suspicious of Harboring Graveyards." Frank Russell tests a potential site for a burial. Photograph by Theresa Russell, 1900.

FIGURE 14.2. "A Full-Grown Home." View of a dry camp. Photograph by Theresa Russell, 1900.

of sentiment, its fragrance dissipates into the atmosphere of sense, and Science holds full sway.

When we had first set up our tiny habitation and furnished it with its bed of cedar boughs and Navajo blankets, its boxes of provisions, trunks, tables, and chairs (i.e., things to sit on), we thought its little space was pretty well utilized. But we discovered its capacity to be an elastic property. For, as the excavations progressed and the ancient trophies were exhumed, it had to officiate as museum also, until our valued specimens were like to turn us out of house and home.

No longer could we use empty boxes as chairs, but were obliged disrespectfully to sit above the bones of the departed. Skulls grinned at us from every corner, and the floor was paved with pottery. True, as a Nature lover says, "A family which lives in a tent never can have a skeleton in the closet," but this family had one in the table.[5] It did not disturb the family any, but caused gaping consternation in Sliver, who stumbled upon it while hunting for the bean bag, and occasioned his precipitate, retrogressive retirement from the unholy scene. For, you must know, to his yet unenlightened mind, anything dead is very bad medicine.

This cast to his religious views of course prevented Sliver from delving with a scientific spade, although his broad tolerance and sophisticated commercialism permitted him to associate amiably with those who did. The avenging gods would

FIGURE 14.3. "Consideration of Their Cuisine." Photograph by Frank Russell, 1900.

FIGURE 14.4. "Mutton on the Hoof." Photograph by Theresa Russell, 1900.

FIGURE 14.5. "Conventional Representations of Birds and Animals." Pottery vessel Theresa glued together. Photograph by Theresa Russell, 1900.

doubtless visit wrath upon them, but anticipation of their Nemesis was the least of his troubles. It was the consideration of their cuisine that chiefly engaged his attention at this time. He had no objection to digging a little pit in the ground for an oven to bake frijoles in. He enjoyed negotiating with the passing shepherd for mutton on the hoof, that the household might dine on the fat of the lamb. He boiled rice and made many biscuits. He hauled water from an arroyo six miles away.

For, with all its preparation, our Promising Land had overlooked the trifling matter of a centrally located, well-filled reservoir. But even the most thoughtful foresight cannot be expected to include every little detail; and for herself, the Desert doesn't think much of water, anyway. The fluid we secured with such effort was of a rich tan shade, and had, as to taste, a soft, warm effect—very pleasing, regarded as a bit of pastel.

But my religion was not like Sliver's, and I was glad to be given a share in the archaeological gold mine; to be allowed to sift sepulchral dirt for turquoise arrowheads, and various relics; to clean up the vertebrae; to glue together the fragments of pottery; to pack and catalogue the collection as it grew apace, and was boxed up for the journey to its University home. The bowls and ollas, particularly, were a joy forever, with their quaint shapes and geometrical designs, or perhaps, conventional representations of birds and animals. Two color schemes seemed to prevail, black and white, and all shadows of red, from terra cotta and maroon up to a dull pink. Occasionally one would find a combination of red and black; still more rarely, red and white.

And these, my small vocations, are just urgent enough to give zest to dreaming while they wait. For in this remote, self-sufficient world you come to grasp at the *dolce far niente* which must ever be fruitage forbidden to the intimate, interdependent world you have hitherto known.[6] You may even postpone the making up of your rolling bed by reason of your absorption in the morning tablecloth, dwelling avidly on news you scorned to give time for perusal when it really was news, months before—and nobody whispers that you are a delinquent housekeeper.

Then, if you do have any troubles you want to forget, you can become oblivious to them also by climbing the round knob of a hill that forms a part of your front lawn, clambering on up to the top of Nature's feudal, surrounding fortress, and looking around you, you see illimitable plains, all chaotic with chasms and *cañadas*, all wrinkled up into ridges and ravines, strewn with disorderly boulders, and patched here and there by a vivid bid of Navajo corn. Splashed, too, with shadows of clouds, wavering, shifting, vanishing here, appearing there, as restless and as constant as the shadow of the heart.[7]

This, far and away. Then the delicate, evanescent outline of Mount Ziltagini, tinted peaks and domes and terraces that can be naught else but castles of Fairyland.[8] It was from this little butte of ours that we loved best to watch the sunsets.

Sometimes the last light of the day was simply clear; more often, a boasting fantasy, flashing its glories east, north, and south.

"Isn't it gorgeous?" I explained, on one of these pyrotechnic evenings.

"Sure," agreed the Anthropologist, "and the gorge goes all the way round."

Twice during our three weeks at home did we go visiting. Once on a morning the Instigators enjoyed a twelve-mile tramp to call on a neighboring ruin. And once the Bokodokleesh Cañon party took another horseback trip. What we went forth to see was an ancient pueblo of good archaeological report. It was thirty-five miles away, and that seemed plenty long enough for a summer-day's journey.

When the spring—which always means the goal of endeavor—was reached at five o'clock, never did the water taste so good. Though, in fact, it was alkaline and not good at all. And never did the ground—just plain old ground—feel so good. To lie stretched full length on a bed of sand, with our heads hanging over the root of a piñon, and watch Sliver get supper—that was luxury in the concrete.

We had intended to see the sights and be gone early in the morning. Intentions are superfluous and might as well be mostly discarded in the first place. To see the sights was easy, as they consisted chiefly of landscape. It would have been an ideal site for an archaeological camp—approved by everything except the facts. But to be gone was not so easy, owing to the discovery that the White Rat had

FIGURE 14.6. "Approved by Everything Except the Facts." On route to Bokodokleesh Cañon. Photograph by Frank Russell, 1900.

taken it into his mulish pate to be gone himself and do a little nocturnal exploring all his own. Although his hobbled progress had been conservative and slow, he had nevertheless covered ten bountiful miles before Sliver and Bill—always poor, vicariously punished Bill—could overtake him and persuade him of the error of his ways.

Meanwhile, the Instigators, having nothing to do but wait, sat in the shade of the trees and speculated about Determination and Free Will.[9] "Trees" in the plural advisedly, for, although you could get under one only at a time, owing to their unsocial distribution, it was necessary to take their skimpy shade in rotation, if you would avoid solar impertinence. Owing to her capers with Bill the day before, the Tenderfoot was not able to accomplish these peregrinations with that sweet, attractive grace supposedly bequeathed by Mother Eve. Instead, she illustrated the evolutionary rather than the theological theory, by reaching the erect posture through a slow unfolding of humps. But let us be an example, if not exemplary.

Starting late, therefore, we camped on the trail that night and reached home next day in time for a bath before dinner. No, indeed, this was no oh-don't-mention-it occurrence. It was an Event. During our "pleasant exertion" (with thanks to Samantha), our ablutions had been perforce mainly of the Christian Science description—there wasn't any such thing.[10]

Soon after this, two more events occurred. Secondly, we pulled up stakes, folded our tents, and migrated to the next scientific station [Awatovi]. And thirdly, our household suffered a subtraction. Nosifor and the mules went home.

By reason of his self-saving disposition, this lad had not proven an ardent archaeologist. Erminio, the awkward, hadn't a lazy bone in his body. Nosifor, the debonair hadn't any other kind. It was entertaining, though, that pathetic way of wiping hypothetical sweat from his brow. We missed a few little tricks like that, but were consoled by the fact that his companion, left alone, did as much work in a day as the two of them had ever done together.

But be thou not offended, thou useless little Nosifor. There are yet other factors of the human problem which may be eliminated and still leave the sum total the same, or even greater than before. For some there be who can be attached only by the minus sign, and inevitably lessen the value of any proposition of which they form a part. While some have the property of a plus prefix, and their addition means increase, wherever they are placed.

And if both kinds were not necessary to make the equation work out right, we may fairly take it that both would not be found in the Great Arithmetic.

Chapter 15
The Next Station

In Theresa's journal entries about their Awatovi activities, the institutional rivalry to control archaeological excavations and artifacts was highlighted. In her *Out West* article, however, it received only two cryptic paragraphs, which must have left readers wondering. The participants were institutionalized: Frank was "Harvard" and Charles Owen "F. C.," standing for Field Columbian Museum. Only archaeologists would have understood the abbreviations. Was Theresa trying to avoid embarrassment or raising questions about her husband's reputation? Frank had been in a weak position legally, but Theresa clearly believed him and accepted his rationalizations. She gave him the moral high ground by invoking disciplinary ethics of not-poaching on an area.

More important to Theresa was her other guest: an older Navajo woman who had come to see what the strangers were doing. She was a unique and unexpected individualist, one who surprised Theresa by not merely exhibiting stereotypes. Theresa had found one of the intellectually curious and fascinating women she had sought, a woman not bound by cultural expectations or religious beliefs that circumscribed her behavior. After a nonverbal conversation, a brief nap, and a cup of tea, the two women proceeded to the excavation site. The elder certainly knew her way around; she possessed a small shovel and worked alongside Theresa, uncovering artifacts, with what Theresa described as an enthusiasm that outweighed her superstition about being near the dead. She had excavated this before. She was probably one of the Navajo who unearthed pottery for the ethnic art and antiquity market. We unfortunately know little about them. Theresa's August 15, 1900, journal entry and this article extend our knowledge.

"With me along some Strip of Herbage strewn
That just divides the desert from the sown,
Where name of Slave and Sultan scarce is known,
And pity Sultan Mahmud on his Throne."[1]

When we awoke next morning, after a night spent in the open, we found a lonesome-looking camp. The horses had both deserted us this time, so Sliver explained, and Erminio had gone to hunt them.

"Good for Bill!" I could not but exclaim. "He has at last discovered that he might as well go along in the first place and have some fun out of it himself. Miles are so much shorter when you travel them in freedom and gay vagabondage."

"Bill is just catching on," rejoined my breakfast companion vis-à-vis, "that martyrdom is out of date. But this belated discernment, in its reflex action on us, leaves us the choice of waiting on time, or going on ahead—and afoot. Which shall it be?"

"The standing-and-waiting sort of service never appealed to me. Let's vamoose."

"By taking a straight line over the mesa, we can shorten the distance. It can't be more than eight or ten miles across, though of course much farther around the point by the wagon road."

So, leaving Sliver to welcome the wanderers home, and appointing a rendezvous on the other side, we vamoosed.

"Seems to me even the Man-in-the-Boat would enjoy this," I said as we swung out into the long-distance stride, breathing deep with the exhilaration of six A.M.

"Why shouldn't he?"

"Well, he has a prejudice against this time of day, you know. Don't you remember his complaint about early risers, that they are conceited all the forenoon and stupid all the afternoon?"

"He'd have a glorious time travelling with our outfit, wouldn't he? By the time he would get around to his toast and English breakfast tea, the place that had known us at coffee and flapjack time would know us no more."

"Worse yet. He never could have his toast and tea at all."

"Pourquoi?"

"A Britisher to breakfast before he has tubbed! And how much of a plunge could he extract out of a canteen?"

"Oh well, people sometimes learn new tricks. I've known a young woman, for instance, whose natural devotion to water leads one to suspect an amphibious ancestor, to scrub her shining morning face with the damp corner of a towel, and feel dressed up."

"Maybe so. But she wasn't born on an island. In any case, though, the sunbath you get out here without extra charge does help to keep your cuticle clean and your temper sweet."

"Although one observes that the remaining part sometimes proves a sprightly corpse. Still, when I write an epic I shall sing of suns and the morn."

"Good enough. But don't begin on it now, please. One should never construct poetry as long as he can enjoy himself in any other way."

"Might one quote a little piece then?"

"If one can't help it."

"Oh, that line just came into my mind—'The soul partakes of the season's youth.'"[2]

"If it were only of the season's youth, and the poor soul had to wait for an annual freshening up, along with the spring house-cleaning, we would be an even more jaded set of mortals than we are. But thanks to the system that gives the sad old earth a twelve-hour shift of ageing day and rejuvenating night, the soul is enabled to partake of the dayspring's youth. And if it would make the most of its chances, it might learn to laugh in the face of Time."

"So, you wouldn't regard the 'sulphurous rifts of passion and woe' as 'burnt-out craters healed with snow?'"[3]

"Snow melts; and its cold comfort besides. I should prefer to have mine healed with sunshine."

"Well, if you happen to have any along with you, they ought to meet with speedy repair under the present dispensation."

For our morning had by now become a full-grown day, rioting with insolent abandon over our path. It was a strenuous as well as a shining way, for it led either uphill or downhill, or it was filled with plenteous, soft sand, or it forgot to have a trail entirely. But time and perseverance wore it out, and the descending sun looked down upon a re-united family building its rag-house upon the sands of old Awatobi.[4]

FIGURE 15.1. "Down to the Diggings." Erminio searching for places to dig at Awatovi. August 14, 1900. Photograph by Theresa Russell, 1900.

The discovery next morning was not of loss but of increase. We had a neighbor. He [Charles Owen] had come, as do angels and thieves, in the night, and his white tents now shown with startling glare against the unscreened sand.[5] For the First Arrivals [the Russells] had coolly (meaning, in an attempt to be cool) appropriated all the shade there was. From preceding rumors, however, we knew our neighbor, who he was—neither an angel nor a thief, but just a plain scientist, like ourselves, and on the same business bent.

Wherefore, Fair Harvard, as became the oldest inhabitant, made a fraternal call upon Field Columbian and invited him to dinner. F. C. [Charles Owen] would have been pleased to accept, but he had already planned to go to a festival over at Mishongnovi.[6] So, F. H. [Frank Russell] had to drown his disappointment in the extra cup of tea and mitigate his regret by having pickles for dinner just the same.

Yet our camp was not without company. Early in the afternoon, a calico-clad old dame, bare as to head and feet, sauntered complacently into my tent, seated herself with deliberate composure, and watched with passive interest the white squaw at her sewing and writing. Being presented with a paper of pins and some coveted scraps of cloth, she wrinkled up her withered face into

FIGURE 15.2. "Roofless Bits of Walls." Frank looking at Awatovi wall. August 14, 1900. Photograph by Theresa Russell, 1900.

a somewhat grudging smile and toyed with them until they seemed to have a hypnotic effect, for presently she ejaculated in plain but astonishing English, "Me sleepy!" put her grey mop of a head down on my table and took a nap. When she awoke she accepted a cup of coffee and an invitation to go with me down to the "diggings."

When I took up my little trowel and went to work, she gazed intently for a while, then took a silent and somewhat speedy departure. Knowing the abhorrence of her race for "los muertos," I supposed she was fleeing from the devil and all his works; but in a moment here she came marching back, armed with a shovel and an air of determination. Then she proceeded to assist. She would uncover the buried treasures and point them out to us, being very careful not to touch the evil thing. But as she warmed to the work, enthusiasm must have unconsciously outweighed superstition, for she did actually pick up some of the bones with her own fingers. If, as a Wise Man says, we are convicted of sin by our religious training rather than by our judgment, this woman was a terrible transgressor and probably paid the utmost penalty.[7] But now, having once yielded to temptation she seemed bent on making an orgy of it and seeing to it that the crime should fit the punishment, which, of course, is a good economy.[8]

When Erminio explained to her that she must not break up the bones and pottery, she went off again and this time returned with the fire-stick, with which mild implement she punched industriously. The Mexican "jollied" her, she talked to him like a grandmother, and I enjoyed the nimble repartee as well as though it had been intelligible. Altogether it was quite a successful social function, inasmuch as everybody stayed late and nobody was bored.

Our new ruin had more of the picturesque effect above ground than any we had yet encountered. But this part was not aboriginal. The roofless bits of walls, with yawning holes where once were doors and windows, were pathetic monuments to the Jesuits, those pioneer missionaries, who threw into their pious work among these remote heathens a full measure of that unreflecting ardor that most of us reserve for our secular affairs. The end of their years of faithful labor came one night, when the Indians, in a sudden revolt against the half-accepted but totally unassimilated religion, did away with it by the simple, direct expedient of pitching the priests over the cliff and tearing down the church.[9]

And now, two centuries later, on these ancient parapets flutters the family wash, and around them cluster the fancies of these Anglo-Saxon visitors, who, alien to Indian and Spaniard alike, can give to each an equal share of pity and of justice.

And yet, with all our open-mindedness, it is perhaps easier, in these days of laissez-faire, to comprehend the motive of the murderers than to realize the incentive of the martyrs. The beauty of freedom appeals to us more poignantly than the holiness of crusades. And with all reverence for its high purpose, we

FIGURE 15.3. "Where Once Were Doors and Windows" on Antelope Mesa. Photograph by Frank Russell, 1900.

find ourselves saying to the mission-fevered soul, "How is it possible that you can suppose that what another man believes is of such consequence that to induce him to discard his own interpretation of life in favor of yours is worth the sacrifice of your own life?"

"You haven't touched bottom yet," said the Man of Science, as he reloaded the kodak. "The real undercurrent is not a matter of belief or unbelief. It is the principle of conquest, the joy of wielding influence and dominating another's thought. And, moreover, it touches the innate human passion for accumulating. Some choose to collect dollars; others have a fancy for wreaths of laurel; still others prefer souls. And may not a man have what he wants, if he is willing to pay for it?"

"He is prone to take it, anyhow. And is he thereby justified in any kind of choice?"

"Justification of others is not a human prerogative any more than condemnation. But the wise man will pray for an honest ambition and the grace to use it independently and unselfishly."

"Supper all leady!" sings out Sliver, and in a trice, all our philosophy is plumb forgot.

Stanford University, Cal.

Chapter 16
In Hopi-Land

Rather than describe more archaeological duties, Theresa turned to a new topic—the Hopi Snake Dance. The series of Hopi ceremonies had become an ethnic tourism event all but required of any Euro-American visiting the Southwest. Anthropologists abandoned their activities at a moment's notice to see the famous rituals. Many hired Navajo or Hopi men to periodically visit villages and trading posts to learn when each community was ready to begin. Putnam insisted Russell attend and capture the events photographically.[1] Theresa was also ready to help with the task.

Theresa portrayed herself as more than a typical tourist taking intrusive photographs. She strove to demonstrate she transcended the mistakes made by insensitive people who swarmed over other cultures during their public rituals. She was now a knowledgeable anthropological traveler, an active and purposeful scientific seeker with a duty to humanity to record, even if her recording was invasive and unwelcome by Native participants. Theresa's identity was shifting with regard to Frank; she was no longer the student but a colleague who worked as an independent recorder and conveyor of sophisticated knowledge.[2]

Theresa's word pictures, however, reflected her vivid imagination and joy at being in a venerable and thriving world, full of life and tradition. Her portrayals were not ethnographic facts. She equated unidentified Hopi individuals with figures from the Bible, Greek mythology, and Shakespeare's plays. They became personality types of both the non-mechanized and industrialized world of turn-of-the-century America, laden with her interpretations and fantasies. Theresa apparently never asked the Hopi any questions. As depicted, quiet Hopi were almost people of Theresa's imagination, and her travelogue rhetoric emphasized the exoticism.

Theresa spoke of watching the Antelope priests perform their musical rituals as though she were in a dream. Futilely struggling to understand what she saw, Theresa fell back on theoretical evolutionary anthropology, racial superiority, and James's intellectual fitness argument. She labeled the Hopi, like other Indigenous people who had not accepted Christianity, *Barbarians*. Barbarians were more advanced than *Primitives* but were still stuck in a lower social and cultural stage than Americans who were classified as an example of *Enlightened Civilization*.

When she talked about Polacca and his wife as sophisticated and curious individuals who understood American as well as Hopi etiquette, she did not equate Mrs. Polacca's interest in her and her apparel as equivalent to a tourist's gaze. This asymmetrical bias meant Theresa did not further explore the logical flaws in American worldview nor how certain Native individuals were crosscultural mediators. This, unfortunately, was a common distancing mechanism, negating the need to understand Hopi religion and philosophy as an advanced sociocultural system with its own logic. Theresa thus missed that Mrs. Polacca was one of the sophisticated women she sought. It was sad they did not have a lingua franca by which to communicate or that Theresa did not try to learn a few words of Hopi.

"Shine on our gardens and fields,
Shine on our working and weaving;
Shine on the whole race of man.
Believing and unbelieving;
Shine on us now through the night,
Shine on us now in Thy might,
The flame of our holy love,
And the song of our worship receiving."[3]

The Indian bucolic is an interesting phenomenon, not to say instructive. You will come upon him in his field of corn, melons, squash or what-not—an irregular patch of most any size. Perhaps it will be distinguished by a fence. If so, your preconceived ideas of fences will experience sudden change. This fence will be wireless, boardless, nailless. It seems to hang together by affinity and to stand up through disregard of Newton's Law—never having heard about it, probably. As to cultivation, the Brown Man drills not, neither does he plow, and yet his cornstalks are arrayed and flourishing. The desert farmer digs ditches and irrigates. He places a shade over each individual hill in its infancy. He hangs out scarecrows so like himself that it is hardly fair to the marauders. He builds a little shelter for himself, where he may sit and watch things grow. Thus, is he assiduous and not neglectful.

The Navajos, as you know, live in hogans, distributed country fashion, with fields to match, while the Moquis [Hopi] reside in pueblos, up on the narrow mesas, whence they scatter forth by day to their fields below, and whither they return at night, like reversed suburbanites.

Thus Mr. Thomas Palaki [Polacca] a Moqui of prestige and distinction, had a country estate, with a whole house just for his own family, where he could be right at home with his growing crops, and where his children might run about without being in constant peril of rolling over the edge. Tom had real bedsteads, too, with sheepskins and Navajo blankets strewn about over the bare springs and trailing off to the ground. For, of course, the beds were out of doors, where beds should be. For himself, Tom was of pleasing aspect, with his clean white suit neatly encasing his short stocky form, and his abundant black hair trimmed off squarely across his brow and around his neck. Also, he was of facile speech, with his handy vocabulary in three or four languages.[4]

Mrs. Palaki was not so accomplished as a linguist, but you could understand her very well, even if she was not able to "speak your talk," as Kipling's little story-boy says.[5]

The haven of her home I had sighted from afar, for it stood conspicuously on a side hill, attracting your eye to the bright picture of red chilis [*sic*] festooned over the adobe walls and green corn waving against a setting of sand dunes. What appeared to be the front of the house, as you approached, had only a port-hole between the windows where the door should have been; but when you got there you found the back door to be the front also, and to stand hospitably open.

In easy English we were asked to "come in and have a chair." We complied for sweet ceremony's sake, until we had become well enough acquainted to feel comfortable with each other. Then we all went outside where we could be comfortable with ourselves and our surroundings.

My hostess had also been viewing me at long range as I trudged up the sandy slope, walking on ahead of the team, and now expressed her motherly commiseration by pointing down the hot, heavy, sunburnt road, then at me, shaking her head, and sighing dolorously. Like all sympathy, hers was as cheering as though it had been deserved, although its object was so far from the point of exhaustion that it was not so well appreciated as was the cup of cold water (only it was a good, practical two-quart pail) which she also offered.

Along with her condolences, her undisguised interest in her guest was quite flattering, it was so un-Indian. She plucked at my sleeve, with delicious feminine curiosity as to the fabric. She denoted admiration in the bunch of scarlet flowers I had found on the way—blossoming amid sand and rocks in the hard dessert fashion. She fondled my braids—worn à la schoolgirl because I had lost all my hairpins but one, and was preserving that to remember them by—murmuring over and over, "Lolomai, Lolomai." The Man of Science, being called upon for a translation, rendered it as "good to look at, beautiful," but how could I know but what that was to be taken as Politeness of Interpreter?

However, I adopted the charming word on faith, and translated it to a dear urchin of tender years, who mused pensively by the bedpost, finger in mouth, a genuine brown study, until the surcharge of his brooding—there seemed to be no other cause—welled up into a fervent wail, and he must flee to the maternal lap for consolation—that queer thing, Consolation.

"Isn't it strange," I mused in turn. "Our need of it and our instinct to seek it outside of ourselves and [to believe] in something larger than we are?"

"Larger and wiser," added the Anthropologist. "What we really want is the assurance that it is all right somehow, and that can come convincingly only from Those Who Know."[6]

"Stranger yet, that in its mighty comfort we should take it to be one of the real joys of life instead of the make-shift that it is; as though it were a true gladness 'to be glad that for a little while we were so sad.'"[7]

"Be that as it may, we go on just the same, and going on seems to be the program immediately ahead of us just now."

For the expedition was en route to the Snake Dance at Sichomovi. Reaching at eventide the outskirts of our destination, that is to say, the foot of the First Mesa, we camped upon the hem. We found it bordered with a fringe of civilization, under whose gentle influence the strolling gypsy band ate fresh eggs for supper and slept, for once, under a carpentered roof. Yet one could hardly wait for day to dawn, the day that held so much in store. Morning came, however, as mornings have a way of doing whether you are ready for them or not, and with it, the visit to the villages.

Armed each with a camera, according to size, the Instigators climb the trail that seems so long and steep to foreign feet. To the inhabitants it is merely a running upstairs, where one does not even lose one's breath.

FIGURE 16.1. "Lifted Sheer Above the Outstretched Plains." First Mesa villages taken from Walpi facing Hano, August 21, 1900. Photograph by Frank Russell, 1900.

FIGURE 16.2. "Flocks of Children Frolic About." August 22, 1900. Photograph by Theresa Russell.

But once over the edge, behold, you are in another world. A very old world, it seems, and yet by no means senile; basking in sunshine, filled with repose, yet holding no faintest suggestion of stagnation. Here, on this narrow tongue of land lifted sheer above the outstretched plains that lie silent and shimmering below, this strip of earth uplifted into the arching sky that swims silent and shimmering above, here in this row of little communities stretching tit-tat-toe to the very edge of the cliff, is to be found a compact epitome of life. A life which displays frankly its comedy, which guards jealously its tragedy, and which is even now in the throes of a very Passion Play, the last, persistent survival of a deeply, rooted ancient faith.[8]

Under the flooding sunlight, then, we walk along, emptying our bags of candy and filling our dry-plates and films. Here is a cluster of women chattering idly in the doorway, while one, in a spasm of industry, sweeps the courtyard with her new "store" broom. Flocks of children frolic about. One mother discovers that her own toddling son is in danger of being caught in the clicking machine of the visitors and hustles him into the house, not for the prevention of the deed —oh no! but for the adornment of a clean apron, that he may make a proud and pretty picture.

Here is another cherub, entirely unaproned and more over off his guard by reason of undivided attention to a huge crescent of melon, the juice trickling through the pudgy brown fingers. He spies us and suspects our intentions—but too late. He flees, but after the event. And his elders are loudly jubilant over his discomfitures.

Further up the street a dark-haired Absalom sun-dries his shampooed locks, sitting on the sloping ladder that forms the stairway to the upper rooms. Hecuba patiently weaves a basket, holding it close to her dimming eyes. Nestor slumbers on the housetop, dreaming of days gone by.[9] Over a balcony leans a smooth-cheeked Juliet, her glossy hair freshly wound into the projecting whorls that are the pride of her maiden heart. Because she still wears them, young Romeo may linger there below and gaze into her lustrous eyes. When she becomes Mrs. Montague, the assertive coils will have to subside into meek braids hanging down her back.[10]

The rest of the lads and lassies are out on the plaza playing a game that looks like Tag or Blind Man's Bluff. There is much running and shouting and brave fluttering of the shawls or capes of bright-hued print worn by the girls.

Thus, through the narrow, populous streets, garrisoned by ruminating burros, with an assisting corps of chickens to sound taps and reveille—one notices with a degree of astonishment that they cluck and cackle just like anybody's hens—then down the trail again, to snatch a hurried luncheon and hasten by wagon on to the Middle Mesa. For the last, and only public, scene of the nine days' [Snake Dance] ceremony is to take place there in the afternoon.

FIGURE 16.3. "The Assertive Coils Will Have to Subside." Two unmarried Hopi women, one with baby on back. August 22, 1900. Photograph by Frank Russell.

Up this ascent the Tenderfoot has her first, last and only-desired burro ride. To one accustomed to the noble proportions of the lofty Bill, the allegation that the burro is "too short to climb up on and too tall to sit down on" appears to be the simple truth, intensified by one's own discovery that it takes a peso's work of exhortation to procure two-bits' worth of action. But by dint of eternal encouragement, vocal and otherwise, we reach the plaza where everybody gets off and walks, or scrambles up, to the top of the mesa.

Half way up this precipitous stairway is a modest spring of water tucked away in a sequestered cave in the rock cliff. We all—for we number quite a party now—stop and scoop up what drink we can in hands and hats, and go rejoicing on our refreshed way. On our return trip we pass this same place just in time to see a young Moqui [Hopi], clothed in born skin, emerge from our erstwhile water-pitcher, which he has been using as a bath tub. He is completing his toilet by squirting water out of his mouth into his hands and thus washing his face. The capacity of his water-bowl is amazing.

Up in the village [Shungopavi] the Tenderfoot is taken in charge by the field matron [Miss Collins] and the school mistress and makes a calling tour with them on some of their Moqui friends. We are, in fact, upstairs enjoying native hospitality, when one comes running with the message that the procession is on the way. We fly down the steps with our slices of pale pink melon in our hands—for the Indian never allows his fruit to ripen if he can manage to eat it all while green—rush across the plaza just ahead of the on-coming actors, and try to behave ourselves during the rest of the performance.

In general, though, it seems to be as much of a performance on the part of the spectators as the official participants, that is, the visiting spectators. The home people, for the most part, view the scene from the upper windows and flat roofs and behold it in quiet absorption, interrupted only when the women, at the proper times, fling handfuls of the sacred [corn] meal into the sacred circle; the feminine part, offering of encouragement and reward. But the foreign delegation, to whom the whole scene is of such utterly different import, viewed it as a Spectacle, and not as a Prayer, as it really is. This intruding body hops and skips about with tripod and note-book and does its condemned best to mar the wonderful sight—a sight, which is in itself so weird, so haunting, so symbolical, that it seems a vision of sleep.[11]

Was it not in a dream, you afterwards ask yourself, that you saw the line of painted Antelope Priests, ranked in order of age from grey haired Priam to lisping Cupid, watching his elders out of the corner of his eye and performing his part with ready imitation? Was it not in a dream that you heard the rattle click unceasingly, the rhythmic stamp of moccasined feet, the plaintive monotone of the chant, now rising into shrill, sharp cries, broken by abrupt, breathless pauses during which the dancers too pause with upraised motionless foot, now falling

FIGURE 16.4. "They Have Not Yet Ceased to Worship." Note Euro-American men intruding on the plaza space near the altar. Russell also was intruding in the sacred area as he took this and other pictures. August 22, 1900. Photograph by Frank Russell, 1900. Our special thanks to the Hopi Preservation Office for allowing us to include this photograph to make this point.

again to the pleading minor cadence? And it surely must have been in a dream that you looked upon the reptiles themselves, the coiling mass of them, writhing, darting, sinuous, now suspended from the mouths of the priests marching in sinistral circuit, now dropped to the ground, now recaptured and carried in hands like so many innocent strands of ribbon.

But it was not a dream.

To the uncomprehending observer it was a show, worth coming out for to see, even if coming did mean traveling to the edge of the accounted universe, and then adding a hundred-mile trip from that Sign of Holy Civilization, the Railroad.

To the participants and their sympathetic, understanding countrymen, who can say just what it was, what it signified, what twined and tangled strands of their lives were woven into it?

But whatever it may have meant to them out from its fantastic, mysterious wrappings came at least one smiting message from the heart of the thing—these people are Barbarians, and they have not yet ceased to worship.

Stanford University

Chapter 17
Colorado Chiquito

Moving off the reservations, Theresa presented her thoughts on traveling toward places of hope. While she described new landscapes using poetic phrases, her real focus was the underappreciated animals that had pulled their heavy wagon over countless miles. Theresa now took the search for sites for granted. As archaeological work had become that-which-was-not-worth-commenting-on, she returned to her first interest: people. She described traders who were less loquacious then her previous examples. She also met Mennonite missionaries, watched a Mormon family returning to Utah, and learned more about Navajo economic behaviors during trading interactions. Theresa emphasized regional values, notions of hospitality, and identity. Who was a *true* Arizonian? Can one tell based on behaviors? How did place affect personality? This became an internal intellectual debate worthy of her mentor, William James.

"Where the sun never slept,
But unwinking, unblinking, from his quiver of ire
Like a desolate besom the wilderness swept
With his arrows of fire."[1]

The next thing on the schedule was an item to go West, Young Man, and reconnoiter the country along the Little Colorado by way of finishing up the summer's work and play.[2] For this voyage, the ship was lightened as much as possible. The Collection was left at the nearest Post for eastern shipment.[3] Sliver and the pony were turned loose, headed for home. Erminio made a present of the dog to the Hopi who entertained us at Burro Spring, the first night out from the pueblos. And thus light-armored we made ready to plunge into the deepest desert yet.

The second night brought us to the second habitation on the road. It was a trading post, dumped down, apparently without excuse, in the midst of the wilderness.[4] Even the fact that it was a human dwelling-place, always of itself an omen of good cheer to the famished traveler, could not throw much of a halo over its desolation. It was so small, and the encompassing waste so outrageously big. It was so unsheltered, and the sun beat down so relentlessly. It stood so alone, and was so far from being complete in itself. Yet it was infinitely better than nothing, even as the tiniest drop of protoplasm is infinitely beyond non-existence, so potent is that little line between what is and what is not.

We were not astonished to find the inhabitant of this dreary abode a grumpy and laconic host. But this should not look discouraging to those who believe that the desert holds forever the potential rose, and that the most arid nature will show signs of sprouting, under sufficient inducement. It came true. Beneath our blandishments a smile responsive to his grim lips sprang, and luster to his eyes.

The Señora was politely shown into the parlor.[5] The parlor ran the entire length and breadth of a building eight feet square. It was carpeted, papered, and painted in Navajo blankets. In addition to the blankets were some snap-shots and the kodak that bagged them, and a guitar. But the apartment did not look as though it were accustomed to occupation, and so, to give it relaxation from the unwonted strain, the Señora, after a brief season of solitary stuffiness, took to the woods—that is, to the cottonwoods, out by the spring. Of course, there was no other Señora about the place,—nobody but the Store-man, and a couple of Japs to cook his meals and save him from death by lonesomeness.

The discovery next morning was neither of increase nor of decrease, but of illness in camp, and that was a real novelty. The novelty was Bill. He lay on the ground, and over him in affectionate guard stood Bob—Bob, the grouchy and distrustful, the rascal with whom you never could tell how much was "can't" and how much "won't," but from whom obedience and balkiness came alike ungraciously. Yet all the time, hidden away in the depths of his evil disposition, lurked this love for his comrade, and he now so far removed his surly mask as to give us a hint of it. Suspiciously and yet anxiously he watched our ministrations to the invalid, and through it all sturdily maintained his station close to his afflicted friend.

"If you can furnish us some ponies," said the Anthropologist to the Trader, "we will take a horseback jaunt down to the river, and give both these fellows a little vacation, on full pay."

Yes, he could let us take a couple of his, and the Mexican might get one from the Navajos. So presently the trio were on again, off again, on for el Rio.

We had not descended the trail from the plateau down to the lower lava-strewn plain before two things were made manifest. One was that we were to have something novel and distinct in the way of scenery. For all desert does not look alike, not by any means, though it may all sound alike to those who have had only the green-field-and-running-brook sort of experience. The other was that we were to have something new and delightful in the way of equestrianism.

This little love of a buckskin pony, beautiful in his silver-mounted bridle and crimson saddle blanket, easy as a cradle in his swinging, soothing motion, swift

FIGURE 17.1. "Does Not Look Alike." Frank standing in Little Colorado River bed. Photograph by Theresa Russell, 1900.

and sure and so full of his own happy life! No, no, my big, white Bill, this is not in disloyalty to you. We need, and we appreciate your patient, plodding feet, your broad back, your dutiful heart. But we are just so saucy, dear old Bill, that we sometimes care more for the beauty than for duty. We fall in love with the lightness of life. We would skim and not plod. We would reach out for an intoxicating cup and disdain plain food. Just for a time, old Bill. Then we come gratefully back to you and your slow, strong ways. Only, not on a morning like this! I fear we should never come back as long as the sweet draught lasted, the buoyancy of motion, the elixir of ozone. At least we must stay until all morbid imaginings, miasmic fancies, moldering in dark corners of the brain, are brushed sky-high, sailing away into the clouds like a witch on a broomstick, and their place is air-swept and clean.

So, we ride on. The rainbow hues of the cliffs behind us grow fainter. The gleaming green line that marks the tree-bordered river grows clearer. The crystal-spread plain, reminder of ancient volcanic fury, grows blacker. Far away, over the translucent obsidian, beneath the flowing azure, quivers the mirage, that mocking sprite of the desert, that lures and laughs and eludes. Then at last, we discern separate trees waving. We perceive water running. We distinguish houses and people over on the other side.

We cross the river and bring up at the Indian Mission. The missionary is not at home, but the missionary's wife sits on the porch. It looks so inviting, as we ride up, to see a lady in a blue gown sewing on a pink shirt. It looked less inviting as we rode on, having been briefly directed by the lady in blue to the trading post, three miles on up the river. She had not found us so interesting to look at as the pink shirt.

We learned afterwards, however, that it was not through lack of a cordial soul, but of a sound mind: and that her mental unbalancing had been brought about by bereavement, a Rachel mourning for her children.[6] We are usually ashamed of ourselves, I notice, when we make lightning calculations about people of whom we know nothing.

But a chain-lightning calculation was enough to size up the missionary and to do his qualities full justice.[7] He was discovered loafing around at the store and eyed you attentively as you flung yourself from your pony, thereby showing that he was no true Arizonian. Besides, he was too fat for the desert, too complacent and communicative. He had worked in a pork-packing establishment for years until the Lord called him to the Navajo vineyard. One observed that grape-picking seemed to agree with him. It was quite certain, too, that no Indian would ever pitch him over a cliff, for with all his drowsy sleekness, he was not of the sort to be caught napping.

I have been told that I should find a Señora at the Tienda on the Rio, and had allowed my anticipations to rise accordingly.[8] But they had to subside in an ebb of disappointment. The Señora was away on a visit, and again we had a preponderance of host, but no hostess.

FIGURE 17.2. "The Tienda on the Rio." McAdams' trading post at Sunrise, Arizona. Photograph by Theresa Russell, 1900.

The Preponderance did its masculine best, however; and for the next two days I took turns staying at home with one of them, while the other went with our two boys to "buscar" around the country. The first day it was the young man, nephew to the Trader himself. He was plainly a little scared of a woman; but he was possessed of information and ideas, back of the tongue that had to be oiled before it would run. Wherefore I sat on a wooden bench in the kitchen while he was making corn bread and peeling potatoes, and swapped observations with him, until he reached the point where he would talk right alone by himself. Then I learned things.

How the Navajos rub sand into their blankets, for instance, to make them heavy-weights, being sold by the pound. How they spread their money out and calculate how far it will go before plunging into investments. Your Indian takes no stock in frenzied finance, but he is bent on coming out even—there must not be any money left over. How fond they are of stick candy, prizing it almost as highly as Star Plug.[9] How they insist on the store having a fresh supply of calico every season, even if there is plenty on hand; for no squaw [woman] is going to buy a new dress off the same piece as her old one. How liberal they are with sugar, how indifferent to cream. How they love to buy a box of crackers and a can of fruit, preferably pears, and eat it then and there, over the counter. And a number of other things.

The next day it was the Uncle. He was young also, a lusty Texan and athletic, and would have made a perfectly splendid center-rush if he had only worn his hair longer.[10] His manner was affable enough, but not, so to speak, ingratiating, and his acquaintance also must be willfully cultivated. But as you sat on the wooden bench, your admiration grew and grew for the deftness of his loose-jointed movements, for his beautiful common-sense and his saving sense of humor.

The event of the day was a procession that passed through our premises and forded the river. There were three or four wagons of the prairie-schooner style, filled with a rattling big crowd of furnishings and folks. They halted only long enough to barter a second-hand wash-tub for some provisions and without dalliance took up their creaking line of march again. But before they reached the opposite bank, they became mired in the quicksand, "all bogged down" indeed, and then how promptly the women (there seemed to be a lively squad of them) slid out from under the white covers, how skillfully they assisted with shovel and crowbar, how successfully they shouted at the teams, until the wheels consented to go round again.

"Looks like a moving village," I remarked.

"Jes' one little family," commented Mine Host, "but it's a Mormon family. They're hittin' the trail back to Utah."

"How can you tell a Mormon outfit from any other?"

"That's a cinch. If the women wear slat sunbonnets, that-a-way, and the wagons have a hole punched in the cover for the stove-pipe to stick through, it's shore Mormon."[11]

In the evening of the third day, Erminio returned from the other store, whither he had gone to exchange our borrowed ponies for the now recuperated team, and we knew that on the morrow it would be ours to ford the stream and disappear into the sunlit, all-swallowing distance.

"Now I shall have to get all undomesticated again!" I bemoaned. "Just when I have established these habits of washing the dishes and blacking the stove."

"Habits are dangerous," said the Man of Science, "particularly that of work. It is apt to develop into an acute case of Americanitis."

"Reckon we-all've got the best prescription for that, out here," drawled the Trader, leisurely tipping his chair back against the wall at that perilous angle achieved only by the accomplished, and deliberately rolling a cigarette. "Jes' take a handful of Mañanas an' dissolve 'em in a glass of Poco Tiempo, an', by gum, you'll think that exertion is a fable an' business a bad dream."

Stanford University

Chapter 18
The Desert at Night

Travel narratives into unknown lands emphasized physical danger, especially situations where travelers were without their normal companions. So, it was time for Theresa to relate a small, potentially perilous adventure, enhanced by her strong imagination. The group split up, proper directions were not given or ignored, and a rendezvous was missed. In her haste to be reunited with Frank, Theresa struck out alone, overconfident in her ability to transverse a trail-less expanse. She became disoriented and lost. She did not yet understand the local environment or recognize its markers. She was not as independent as she had believed.

When Theresa described her unsettling experiences, she framed it as a response to apprehension for Frank, who was "wandering" in the wilderness. Dealing with loneliness and being utterly alone was quite intolerable to a social being with a vivid imagination. Theresa downplayed the fact that Frank had traveled alone numerous times, faced challenges, and solved problems, signs of an expert in American society and one who could successfully traverse trail-less wildernesses. Frank had shown Theresa how to recognize real danger and not unleash her fantasies. As a woman immersed in literature, she could conjure a dragon out of a horned toad. Despite being a good pupil, Theresa still had little sense of direction, so the incident she chose to write about stuck in her mind, allowing her to overcome her hubris and express humility. The humble traveler who makes mistakes is a common figure in travelogues, but only when the errors are so life-threatening so that the author can continue the journey unscathed. Interestingly, Theresa barely mentioned their most dangerous situations—being stuck in the sand for several days, surviving a monsoon, or the lack of water and its effect on the animals. There was value in experience and understanding when to worry. In this case, the danger had limits for a proper woman.

"The Angels of Wind and of Fire
Chant only one hymn, and expire."[1]

When we left the Post that morning we were accompanied by the Trader, or, rather, he and the Anthropologist rode on ahead, leaving "me an' the Mexican" to follow in the wagon. About noon we met a Navajo driving along with a load of melon. We would have passed by as do Ships in the Night, but that we were held up by our highwayman, who impressively called a halt and delivered over a goodly quantity of his rolling stock—at least it seemed disposed to roll when you tried to pick it up—into our wagon. We were at a loss to know whether this was in the nature of a forced sale or a "free gift," but when all was done, Uncle Remus condescended to explain: "Melicano, up the *camino*, he buy 'um plenty. You savey?"[2]

Presently, we caught up with the "Melicanos," who had selected a good camping-ground, and were eating their own melons while they waited.

"Reckon we'd better put this here cumbersome chap in cold storage, that-a-way," suggested the Store-man.[3]

Now there was no refrigerator visible, and no ice-man in sight; but many a Superfluity of life gets itself labeled as a Necessity. The essentials in this case were merely a piece of wet gunnysack to wrap the big, smooth melon in, and a shady, breezy place under the wagon where it might hang until called for.[4] And wasn't it chilly, and red, and sweet!

The feasting over, the column continued to advance in the same order until late in the afternoon. Then the second division met half of the first, homeward bound.

"You-all will meet up with you' man a little ways on," he informed us, "right near the Crossing."

Now, I did not know The Crossing from Adam; but I had had some experience with "little ways" in the Territory, and consequently took no note of the fact that we were really going a good long ways without meeting up with anybody. But when I awoke to the realization that the shadows were long, the remaining shift of daylight short, and no Anthropologist in sight, I began to sit up and pay attention.

Nothing in sight. Only spaces and spaces in every direction; miles and miles stretching on ahead—endless, empty miles. Even the one hogan in sight was an abandoned desolation. With terror catching at my heart, I sprang out and hurried on up the road. It was like projecting myself into a dead world—a more fearful thing than the world of the dead.

"Even Marley's Ghost would look good to old Scrooge, if he were here," I thought, strangling a sob with the foolish fancy. Around me spread an infinite Sea of Silence, a Dead Sea, undisturbed by a ripple, bereft of sound, deserted by motion, abandoned now even by light, for the last ghastly rays were smothering under a pall of darkness.[5]

With them my hope flickered out, and I turned back to the wagon, intending to tell Erminio we would have to stop and spend the night right there. But I found the team turned around and ready to start back. For explanation the Mexican pointed to a banner of light flaring up into the blackness.

FIGURE 18.1. "The One Hogan Was Abandoned." September 7, 1900. Photograph by Theresa Russell.

"El Señor!" he exclaimed. "He make 'em big camp fire."

It was a big fire truly, and a thrice welcome sight, but it looked very far away.

Afterwards we learned that it was about five miles away. Our Man had been waiting for us some distance from the main road, supposing, of course, the driver would know where to turn off. (Our guide, in his directions, had omitted to mention a little thing like that.) He had seen us pass by, keeping idiotically on where we should have branched off, but was too far away to be seen or heard by us, though he made strenuous signals. The Trader had taken his pony home, you see, so he was alone and on foot.

But all this exposition was to come later. Now it was ours not to reason why, but to get there. In my impatience I could not endure the wagon and continued to forge on alone, not minding the ghoulish way now there was a goal ahead. But, the next thing I knew, the goal had vanished; my beacon light had sunk down and died away. I stopped and listened. Even the reassuring rumble of the wheels had ceased. Darkness and silence ahead. Darkness and silence behind. I was alone. It is not often in our intricate, intimate human lives that we are privileged to be absolutely and utterly alone. When we are, we do not seem greatly to appreciate the privilege. To be alone is bad, but to be alone and quiet is intolerable. I started on again. Then, after an aeon or two of aimless, distracted, desperate stumbling along, I suddenly ran right into a pair of Anthropological arms. And out of the "deep and dark abysmal night" I heard a Voice.[6]

"Why, you poor child," said the Voice, "whatever are you promenading around here for? This isn't Commonwealth Avenue. And no wrap over that thin waist?"[7]

"Oh—oh—nothing!" I gasped, unable to think of anything but the breathless little speech of Sarah Maud Ruggles when she arrived bareheaded at the Christmas party. "It's—such a pleasant hat—I thought I'd leave my—short walk home!"[8]

But the next time we were not let off so easily.

The Expedition had now reached the turning point in its career and was headed for home. The road back to Burro Spring, if one followed its safe and orthodox leading, would take one approximately around three sides of a square and cover a distance of some sixty miles. But if one would venture to take a straight line across only one-third of those miles would be one's portion. One would try it.

But here looms up another circumstance. If it were not for Circumstances, how easy would existence be. "Weary, flat and stale also?"[9] Well, maybe so, and unprofitable into the bargain. So, we might as well put up with them. With this one we thought we might make shift to get along by a temporary division of our party.

"If we make this short-cut," said the Man of Science, "we'll miss that place seven miles south of here that I want to see. But it's too much out of the way to take the team. You just go on with the wagon, follow the Nebito [Dinnebito] Wash straight east toward the Red Mesa, and I'll cut across and meet you, about the time that the cows come home."

"Think you can do the base and the hypotenuse on foot while we do the side by wagon, do you?"

"Ought to. There's two of you for your one side and one of me for my two sides, and that makes a good average."

"It will not be necessary in this case, I think."

But it was nearly dusk again when Erminio and I ceased from going along. This time we were late because we had found no water. I had been walking for miles along the banks of the dry ravine, looking for a pool, if perchance I might discover one, and was at last rewarded, just before it would have been too dark to see it if it had been Lake Superior.

"Oh Erminio," I cried out gleefully, "Agua!"

"No," he replied in tones of profound disbelief (the less we know about a thing, the more profound we must be about it), "no agua, no nada, aqui!"

"But come and see," I insisted.

He came and saw. His first chiding explanation "Piedras!!" changed to the dawning conviction of "Quien sabe?" as he ran down the bank of the arroyo. Then I heard, "Oh, mucho agua!" in accents of joyful surprise. This heartened him up wonderfully, for with "agua" the "caballos no vamoose" in the night.

But we might have spared ourselves the worry about water, and saved up the rejoicing over its discovery for some more needful occasion; for we were destined soon to have abundant showers of blessing—in which, for once, we did not feel blest.

Already the thunder was muttering and clouds lowering. Supper was scarcely ready when the storm was upon us. Not that it hurt us any. Erminio made the wagon-cover tight and snug, brought our somewhat waterlogged tortillas and steaming pot of tea inside, and by the light of our little candle we swallowed what we could and smiled grimly at each other over our plight.

But the plight of the absent member of the party was no smiling matter, though it was grim enough. He had, I remembered, not even the protection of his coat, and the trail over which he must now be coming was of the most unaccommodating sort—not a tree, not a cliff, not even a boulder, for shelter. And in the darkness he could not find us even if we were near.

"We must build a fire, Erminio," I said, "for a signal light."

Erminio shook his head disconsolately.

"No burn. Too mucho agua."

"Try it, anyway."

So, the deluge having partially exhausted itself and slackened up a bit, he clambered out, and after some struggles with the damp wood, managed to create a sputtering, cheery blaze. But alas, it was soon quenched by a renewed downpour. This operation was repeated several times and then a steady drizzle put an end to our efforts.

The Mexican made his bed on a hillock where the water would drain off, wrapped himself up on his tarpaulin like a bulky chrysalis, and doubtless dreamed that he was being rocked in the cradle of the deep. As for me, I had no time for dreams. I crouched in the driest corner of the wagon, while my mind buzzed a refrain to the patter on the canvas roof. "Oh, Where Is My Wandering Boy Tonight?"[10]

"If you were in my place," I muttered invidiously to a hypothetical, revivalistic congregation, "would you have something to sing for!"

But at daybreak I head a real sound, more joyful than a Hallelujah Chorus.[11] Just a whistle, clear and sweet, vibrating through the drenched, grey air. Then a familiar, hortatory ejaculation hurled at a recalcitrant Bob, clinched the whistler's identity.

"Erminio," I called, "el Señor is coming!"

The cocoon, by now scarcely distinguishable from the sodden ground, quickly burst its bonds, and the "dull chrysalis cracked" not "into shining wings," but into round, startled eyes and rumpled hair.[12]

Then came the belated member, driving up the horses as cheerfully as though he had been to breakfast. He hadn't, though, and that was the first thing he asked for.

FIGURE 18.2. "Turrets and Towers." Photograph by Theresa Russell, 1900.

"But how did you keep so dry?" I inquired.

"Dug a hole in a sand bank, warmed it up with a sage-brush bonfire, and crawled in."

"Comfortable quarters you must have had."

"Not half bad, if you curled up enough. I christened my hostelry "Squirrel Inn."

"If you had been a tenderfoot," I opined, "it would probably have been baptized as The Last Lay of the Minstrel."[13]

We camped at night under the shadow of Red Mesa. All day, for two days, indeed, it had stood up before us, straight and tall and smooth. But now it resolved itself into a place of many mansions, with turrets and towers and lofty halls, with huge stone stairways winding up, with pillars and vaulted roofs. The deep, rich mahogany of the rock was banded with strata of white birch and maple hues, suggesting a mighty pipe organ.

You thought you were in some Cathedral of the Gods—until you spoke. Then the echoes answering, not shout for shout, but many shouts for one, repeated with clear, beautiful diminuendo, retreating into fainter, dimmer, ever more mysterious distances, told you that you had chanced upon the home of Die Walküre.[14]

Stanford University.

Chapter 19
Omega

As Theresa's journal recorded, there were many more days of exploring, camping, and excavating. These were topics Theresa could have written about: days of travel, horses and mules at work, the area around Black Falls, petroglyphs, Erminio's steadfastness, the wagon stuck in the sand for days, or Erminio and Frank venturing into the desert to secure help. She could have also written about the trip to Keam's and Hubbell's trading posts, packing the cartons and boxes for transport to the railroad, or their interactions with new sets of memorable people.

Theresa, however, was running out of space to recount new activities. It was time for her to tie the entries together and end her travelogue. There was no completion of the journey in a chronological sense or a definitive movement from wilderness to middle-class life. Whole topics commonly included in travelogues did not appear. She eliminated the final days of their journey to the railroad and travel to Albuquerque and their trip across country. Her travelogue ended with the railroad in Gallup, just as it had begun. This brought the narrative full circle. Nor was there a future-oriented epilogue or a discourse on dangerous or scientific travel. She did not reflect on pursuing graveyards. There was little anticipation about starting her new life as a college professor's wife, but there was evidence of the symbolic transition back into her old world: donning a white gown and putting on her gloves as a visualization of her return to civilized women's society with its expectations of proper dress and, by extension, behavior. While Theresa had her "face set toward civilization again," she was not quite ready to relinquish her honeymoon in her last *Out West* installment.[1]

Theresa reflected on her honeymoon journey, what she had learned, and how it had changed both her and Frank. This was phrased in terms of a discussion of the evolutionary theory of the survival of the fittest. The desert had been good for Frank. He was fit, as was Theresa. They had both been able to adapt. They had a future. And with a discussion of successful adaptation, Theresa provided Frank with a lectern from which to educate her audience about the importance of anthropology and archaeology. And Theresa showed she had a psychological mechanism by which to do this: memory.

Theresa's intellectual topic for this essay was the nature of memory and how memory affected the writing of a travelogue. How did what one remembered from a journey full of impressions and activities lead to an understanding of what was important in life? Frank discussed adaptational remembering as critical for survival in a harsh environment, themes he foregrounded in his American Folklore Society presidential address. Theresa treated memory as a philosophical topic worthy of William James. Memory as an intellectual undertaking affected spiritual and social self, part of the process of how Theresa would remember their honeymoon as she wrote these articles after Frank's death.

The wounded storyteller finished on a somber note, reflecting about creation, death, and what happens to the soul. With these thoughts, Theresa came full circle remembering Frank. Her multiple good-byes were as much a farewell to Frank in good health and intellectual vigor as it was a leave-taking of Arizona and its peoples.

"The swallows are making them ready to fly.
Goodby, Summer. Goodby! Goodby!"[2]

Thus, the days drifted into yesterdays. Each Tomorrow was silently swallowed up by the devouring jaws of Today, until not one more Mañana was left to us. Ah, no, it was not the Mañanas that were going away! Each pregnant cloud-wraith of a Day-to-Come would in the fulness of time be delivered of its crystalline Hours; and these in turn, held in poise for one exquisite breath, would be drawn irresistibly into the soundless deeps of the Days That Are Gone, even as the "dewdrop slips into the shining sea."[3]

And as they go, one almost hears them say, "For mortals their Valhallas, their Elysiums, their noisy crowded Paradise. For us the sweet Nirvana, the Eternity of Time."[4]

So shall the eternal process of creation and swift death of days keep its serene, unceasing course, though we are gone. But so long as other days shall be given us, born under howsoever gloomy skies, bearing whatsoever different gifts, they shall at least yield up the Incense of Remembrance, the wistful recurrent memory of these, their sun-kissed, warm-breathed elder brothers.

"What day of the summer are you going to forget last?" queried the Anthropologist, as, reaching the last hilltop, we looked down upon the Town.

"Don't know about days; but that night at Oraibi, when we were favored with a cloud-burst, and the wagon-roof sprang a leak and we had to stand up through the dreary midnight watches, hugging our bedclothes to our bosoms to keep

FIGURE 19.1. "That Night at Oraibi." August 22, 1900. Photograph by Frank Russell.

them out of the wet, that night has a flavor of permanence, me thinks. What event is going to be your Bohemian Girl?"[5]

"When other things and other times their tale of woe shall tell? Well, speaking of flavors, there's a strong taste in my mouth yet of that camp by the muddy waters, when we had a 'strawberry roan' festival three times per diem."[6]

"We did have an effective color scheme for those spreads, didn't we? You did not appreciate it so much in the coffee"—

"At least, not in the top half of the cup."

"But when you shaded it into the canned cream, its beauty burst upon you."

"It was the gravy that always looked particularly giddy to me, coming in that crushed-orange effect."

"And yet, there are few days that have as happy been. And in the future, when the whirlwind of fate scatters our plans to the four corners, I fancy there will some recollection be of those distressing occasions when these same pink-tea repasts were interrupted by the dancing sand-dervishes that swept down upon us like—"[7]

"A batch of unexpected company at meal time?"

"Well, since you put it that way, perhaps our sportive desert visitor was the less devastating. We could flee to our tent of refuge, you know, and save as much food as we could carry in our hands."

"And his call was always of the ultra fashionable limit."

"Another item to his credit. Speedy transit redeems the unwelcome."

"Most everything has its redeeming feature, for that matter."

"That is its leaven, nicht wahr, for the working out of its own salvation?"

"'Work out your own salvation,' translated from Theology into Science, becomes simply, 'Survive if you are fit'; and you probably see a clearer example of that operation here than anywhere, not only in the self-reliant life of the desert itself, but in the lesson it forces us all to learn, when we attempt to partake of its life."[8]

"Is it that, I wonder, that gives most people the shudders at the thought of the desert? That sense of its indifference, inability to help, unresponsiveness?"

"Perhaps. But the desert is not unresponsive. Like everything else, it is waiting for you to strike the vibrant chord."[9]

"It seems, though, always to be associated with two ideas—that of cruelty, a place of punishment for all and mercy toward none, and of isolation. The latter is instanced in a letter from a friend, who writes: 'It seems to me there must be a heartbreak in its very loneliness, an infinite sadness in its vast spaces.'"

"The sadness is there. The question is forever on your lips. 'How can you be so smiling and so sad?' As to the loneliness, that comes from a painful realization of proportion, and is the beginning of wisdom. When we once get a perception of our own speck of existence as it shows up against a background of some size, we are ready to begin growing."[10]

"And by and by we'll be big enough to make up our silly quarrel with our environment?"

FIGURE 19.2. "Guarded Places of Silence." Photograph by Frank Russell, 1900.

FIGURE 19.3. "Mute, Undecipherable Message." Petroglyph on Little Colorado River near Black Falls. September 1 or 2, 1900. Photograph by Theresa Russell.

FIGURE 19.4. "By an Impassive, Ruminating Rider." Navajo on pinto horse. Photograph by Theresa Russell, 1900.

"At least, we might give over sulking because it doesn't appear to be directly concerned with us."

"And yet it does have something to give us, after all."

"Decidedly. But to make the gift effectual we must get out of the desert with it. We are gregarious, and on the whole, do best with the herd."

"But after a sojourn in a world apart, such as this, you are not the same to yourself, nor others to you."

"No; and the difference, I should say, is the result of the acquisition of elasticity."

"A protecting envelope, as it were?"

"Something like that. Then when you take this newly sheathed sphere of self back to the crowd, and punch it into the current, you will find it more sharply defined from the other spheres, and yet more sensitive to their impact. It will yield more easily, rebound more quickly, and hear fewer traces of the blows."

We were now so near civilization that we could hear engines puffing and a bell ringing. The sounds smote sharply upon our unaccustomed ears.

And now we swing into the street, the same old street, as sordid, as trifling, as important, as magnetic as ever. We meet people, the same old people, as busy, as selfish, as clever, as lovable, as ever. We talk and bargain and laugh and fare sumptuously and wear fine clothes in the same old way. Why, the old life gets its old grip on us at the very first touch. Already our dream summer shrinks

FIGURE 19.5. "Adios." Train heading from Winslow, Arizona, to Gallup, New Mexico. September 15, 1900. Photograph by Frank Russell.

back among the Unrealities. Yet with a timid persistence she flings her memory-pictures upon the background of a canvas whose main area is already crowded with things of a different order. Kaleidoscopic in distinctness and in transientness we see them—the merry youth of Moki [Hopi] land, and their homes, ancient of days, but loved even as are our own; the bunches of crimson chilis [*sic*] flashing against white plaster or grey adobe; the heathen more absorbed in their devotions than we know how to be; the ubiquitous burro, idling in doorway or ridden abroad by an impassive, ruminating rider; the guarded places of Silence offering here and there mute, undecipherable messages transcribed in a shrouded past to untranslating rock. Remote but inviolate they are coming—and going. The heat that was not hot, the dirt that was not dirty, the "agua" that was always "muy lejos," the pungent smell of sagebrush after rain, all were vanishing, covered up by the clamorous present, locked away—ah, well, we have the key.

Now we are looking out of the car window. Erminio is the last to bid us bon voyage, and he adds a kind hope for return.

"Adios, Señor. You bring la Señora next summer, is it not? She learn speak Spanish pretty pronto, if she come."

"All right, Erminio. Goodby, Bill."

"Oh, tell Bob goodby, too!"

"All aboard!"

"Adios! Adios!"

"Adios!"

Part III

A Scholar's Life

Chapter 20
An English Professor at Stanford

Theresa had said good-bye to Frank as well as archaeology. In the series' final installment, she had envisioned a bright future with her cherished Anthropologist, anticipating returning to the field the next summer. The bright future was an intentional illusion, a projection of how Theresa had thought her life would continue. She did not return to her initial memorial dedication, bringing her story full circle. That would have been too tragic for the reader and herself. Nor did she want pity. As an exercise in selective memory, Theresa downplayed the times Frank struggled and ignored why they came West. What was important was that he thrived in Arizona. This was the memory that mattered.

Theresa's portrayal of their 1900 journey had presented Frank's focused determination as a virtue. Exploration was a race for the Man of Science. But by starting with the memorial, Theresa set the stage for the reader to see his archaeological survey was an obsessive quest to secure information before he literally ran out of time. While Theresa downplayed Frank's anxiety in her articles when compared to their journal entries, this presented a conundrum. She never conceded that since Frank's data were never used, the 1900 survey did not advance knowledge. This was the first time Frank had not completed a publication. The scientific aspects ended with data collection; there was no hint of an analysis.[1] This lack of completion undermined one of the core reasons for a spouse to write a scientific travelogue: to advance the husband's career and reputation, thereby supporting the economy of their two-person, one career household. Theresa could not transform her valiant Knight into a scientific culture hero, but she could make him a good teacher and loving spouse who helped prepare her for her own career.

The *Out West* magazine series was an exercise in grief resolution as well as a coming-of-age tale for a refined intellectual and a credentialing device. Theresa had altered her scholarly trajectory when she chose to assist Frank with his research, learning the basics of anthropology. She had done what was expected of any woman during this period. She supported her husband and his career. She had chosen a two-person, one-career life, not an unreasonable decision given the lack of satisfying employment she had encountered. The 1906 articles brought closure to Theresa's tenure as an archaeological wife while setting the stage for a one-person, one-career future as an American humanist and English professor.

An Americanist Scholar

Travel authors aimed to transform the new, especially foreign cultures (that is, not the author's social group), into the known. Some contemporary scholars label the groups anthropologists studied at this time "the Other," that is, Indigenous peoples and "peasants." Generally, these people were objects of curiosity and wonder, but they also served as foils by which an author could assess American society, especially industrialization and modernity.[2] For Theresa, Indigenous peoples were simultaneously interesting in themselves and schema to reflect on American society. But unlike most anthropological analyses of the period, Theresa did not stop with "the Other" as she reflected about her society and the peoples in the new land she toured. Her gaze was on everyone in Arizona as part of a complex, plural society. She was not limited to studying supposedly simple societies.

Theresa had created word portraits of northern Arizona's multicultural population: traders, Mormon families, Euro-American school teachers, Mexican workers, Hispanic royalty, travelers, other anthropologists, Hopis, and Navajos. She compared each to her chosen referent groups: Boston's intellectual community and small-town Protestant Iowa. Theresa had come to Arizona with preconceptions that influenced her selection of the social behaviors and customs she used as proxies for socially diagnostic psychological characteristics and the creation of types. For traders and Mexican workers, it was work ethic and time management; for Euro-American school teachers, dealing with loneliness and isolation. Theresa wrote about members of each category by eliminating individuality; that is, she rarely named anyone. It was as if she decided that uniqueness would undermine her goal of defining idealized frontier types based on the roles people assumed. This was partly unexpected because as a student of Jamesian psychology, Theresa knew her encounters demonstrated the importance of idiosyncrasy. Essentializing enabled her to reinforce America's superiority myth and demonstrate that she understood and adhered to many middle-class, Protestant American values. Theresa personified American enlightened culture as a civilizing catalyst while Frank represented science and mental acuity, the peak of rational culture. The frontier and its diverse population became the unformed inferior, waiting to be integrated into a progressive world through Frank's work melding the region's Indigenous past into America's history.

This trope could be best seen during Theresa's personal quest to find erudite and witty women like herself. The search gave her travel a purpose distinct from

Frank's as well as highlighted how unique an individual she was. She was both more and less than a supportive archaeological spouse; she was not domestic and failed to perform many female tasks during the journey. Instead, she was a great thinker. As Theresa searched for home in the wilderness, a feature common to touristic travelogues, she was continually disappointed. Except for the Hubbell family, whom she portrayed as the best of the Southwest, looking for elite "High Culture" proved a fruitless undertaking.[3] The Southwest was not yet a place where well-educated women could thrive. Stanford's president and faculty could see that Theresa belonged at a university, not in Flagstaff or Tucson. The thoughtful scholar needed academia as her home.

But what kind of scholar would she be? Did she become an archaeologist and embrace Frank's evolutionary anthropology? The answer is primarily no. The new discipline influenced her, however, especially with regard to how one viewed the land. She became more observant. Theresa also listened to Frank, who periodically attempted to teach her fundamental anthropological concepts. For example, he held that cultural adaptation, not Caucasian racial superiority, explained human differences. As a result, all cultures should be respected.

> The inherited proclivity of the Anglo-Saxon to despise all non-Caucasians becomes in the anthropologist a passion for studying them. He knows that his self-assured superiority has its limitations, that his own ancestors in times geologically recent were tattooed cannibals as primitive in habit as the Digger Indians of the Sierras.[4] He knows that his culture is in a measure due to environment, to the chance that led those early immigrants to a continent whose vast extent of shore-line rendered it immeasurably superior to all others as the home of commerce. His people were surrounded by animals capable of domestication, while the American race, for example, was handicapped by their absence.[5]

Theresa was not convinced it was only circumstance and environment that separated American Indians from the ancestors of enlightened Americans. She still thought social and cultural differences as well as level of cultural development were genetic, and that Caucasians were culturally superior. It was natural in her mind. But she did not lump all Native Americans as a single undifferentiated unit, where one group could stand for all Indians. Native societies were not fundamentally alike. Nor did she feel that colonized peoples, like Native Americans, were without agency when dealing with Euro-Americans. She agreed with Frank that Indigenous peoples around the world were evaluating travelers in their homelands as much as anthropologists were evaluating them. After years in Arizona, she was not sure Native cultures were laudable and she was unsure if she ultimately agreed with Frank to take a perspective that would become cultural relativity 20 years later. As Frank stated:

> Not only does the anthropologist take a more modest view of the virtues of the Caucasian, but he also learns to credit the savage and barbarian with many praiseworthy qualities. He finds that our aborigines are more devout than we, their happy family life most exemplary, their patience and courage under the wrongs of border "civilization" most admirable. This knowledge induces forbearance and respect. Brought into contact with these and other alien races through field research, the anthropologic student discovers that they can estimate his worth with surprising quickness; they may not have heard of the nebular hypothesis, they may be unacquainted with the units of the metric system, but they can take the measure of a man with a glance.[6]

As Theresa discussed throughout her texts, the Navajo and Hopi took their measure, and the expedition party was often found wanting. Native perusal, using the standards of Hopi, Navajo, or Akimel O'odham cultures, affected Frank's research plans based on their values and cultural assumptions of appropriate behavior. These were challenging assessments for Theresa, given her preconceptions, but she openly acknowledged her discomfort and frustration.

In journal entry after entry, Theresa had struggled to understand American Indians as members of functioning cultures with their own beliefs, values, and acceptable behaviors as did Frank. By the time she wrote her articles, however, she had reengaged with an ethnocentric psychology and Boston academic society. As a result, Hopi and Navajos generally appeared as culturally deficit stereotypes. Natives were stubborn, natural liars, ignorant men and women who ignored "correct priorities" (that is, did not readily help Frank with geographical information or simply told them what they thought Frank wanted to hear). Speech patterns reflected improper English sentence structure. Natives were stupid since they did not immediately understand jokes and allusions to American cultural activities. Theresa never understood that intentional silence and inactivity were purposeful behaviors designed to not embarrass impolite outsiders when they proposed something reckless or stupid. She witnessed a common response by Navajos and Hopi to government officials, and settlers who wanted their water, game, and land. They now encountered a stranger who stated that he intended to excavate sites without gaining their permission. The men and women with whom Frank and Theresa interacted asserted their independence and cultural sovereignty, protecting their families and social homelands from intruders. Writing about such encounters was a rarity for an archaeological travelogue and made Theresa's texts valuable, even if she did not understand what she was witnessing.[7]

Theresa did decide to follow one anthropological goal: to set the record straight without romanticizing or unthinkingly creating stereotyped images of Native peoples. She wrote in her journal that popular accounts were wrong because they held that the Navajo were smart and articulate.[8] She would provide a "more accurate" portrait, based on her own observations during cross-cultural encounters. As a result, she conveyed little basic ethnographic information about the Navajo. It was as if she assumed her readers knew Navajos herded sheep and were semi-nomadic. Continuing to place herself at the center of her narrative, Theresa conveyed her thoughts and feelings about Navajo behaviors, without acknowledging that her background and Americanist framework biased her interpretations. The result was an observational, ethnocentric, but valuable account.

Theresa recounted some information about Navajo culture not found in earlier anthropological and non-anthropological monographs, articles, and newspapers. From reading the extant literature, readers must have been surprised that a Navajo woman freely and eagerly helped Theresa excavate and exhume a burial. A few of her interpreted observations were even astute when seen from a contemporary perspective. For example, Navajo cooking and food consumption were as much about social interaction as nourishing the body. Theresa recorded intertribal differences based on region, community, family, and gender as well as unexpected personality quirks. These later became entertaining stories that kept the journey fresh and eliminated deadening repetition. One clearly sees how regional leaders defended their land, how hospitality worked, and how the Russells were expected to follow Navajo rules of propriety. And one heard Navajo philosophy expounded, which was confusing for Theresa because she did not understand its basic premises. Indeed, she was never comfortable with the Navajos' gentle teasing and humor, nor did she think a Navajo employee should dictate the work he performed. Navajos did not understand the social hierarchy between employers and employees. Theresa basically criticized Navajos undermining colonial power and ignoring the Russells' social status as privileged outsiders. This frustration led to the selective use of her evidence as hosts refusing to cater to unexpected and unwanted travelers.

Theresa was not convinced by anthropological arguments as explanatory tools to understand human behavior. As the series progressed, she intentionally distanced herself from cultural interpretations in favor of psychology, using more and more of the Jamesian theories and humanistic perspectives she had studied in 1905. She identified with scholars in philosophy, Christian theology, and psychology, and with notable writers and thinkers. Their insights were the foundation for her explanations to understand the world and its inhabitants. Theresa rarely quoted scientists, social philosophers, or anthropologists. But this was not unexpected. She was not asking to become part of a social science or science faculty.

An Entertaining Travel Writer

Theresa juxtaposed the unknown with the known, an established technique of travel writing and ethnography, but did so without making her readers uncomfortable. Her series was a popular success because it was complex, engaging, novel, and entertaining. Her portrayal of her coming-of-age quest through scientific pilgrimage met the standards of the best of the genre. Mark Twain, in the introduction to his account of pilgrimage to the Holy Land with a group of American travelers, set the model for Theresa's distinction between a scientific exploration account and a personal, entertaining journey: "[My] book [*The Innocents Abroad*] is a record of a pleasure-trip. If it were a record of a solemn scientific expedition, it would have about it that gravity, that profundity, and that impressive incomprehensibility which are so proper to works of that kind, and withal so attractive."[9] Satire and not taking oneself too seriously had given Theresa license to use wit via literary propensity to both conceal and reveal profound topics without undue pomposity. Like Jerome K. Jerome, she made fun of herself and the people whom she met without resorting to buffoonery.

Theresa had made readers feel welcome on their journey. They did not have to endure an author's whining, sentimentality, or preaching as she proclaimed her curiosity, intelligence, problem-solving abilities, and stamina. She worked much of this magic through self-referential wit combined with humility at her own ambitious nonconventionality. This technique created sympathy and trust as well as set the stage for celebrating accomplishment, while showing foibles and neophyte errors encouraged readers' feeling of superiority and empathy. Theresa was a woman who was never pitied. Like all great exploration culture heroes, she was calm in the face of adversity. She demonstrated she was a good companion, one who did not hide behind the mirage of women's supposed frailty. She did have one overriding character flaw or asset, however, depending on one's perspective. She insisted on uncritical loyalty to Frank and his archaeological quest, one of the few topics not open to humor, except to ridicule his enemies. Theresa was a supportive wife, just as she would be a supportive colleague. And if they could untangle and recognize her allusions and wordplay, readers could assume Theresa would want to know them. They were the companions she had sought.

An Educator and a Scholar

"In Pursuit of a Graveyard" is not easy for contemporary individuals to read for a number of reasons. First, there is a time difference in writing styles and in English conventions. Hyphenation of words in 1900 and today are different. Second, there is Theresa's intentional capitalization of words and concepts to make philosophical and literary points. This can be offsetting to individuals who think they are errors. But each capitalization or italicized phrase is intentional. Third, the text requires readers have at their fingertips a vast knowledge of historic and contemporary literature. Without this, readers could not necessarily understand Theresa's allusions and miss her wit, irony, satire, and serious intellectual points.

Theresa decided to cram each chapter with the literary references she felt were required reading for a sophisticated American who claimed intellectual connoisseurship. She judiciously used these allusions, however, to enliven descriptions, create impressions, convey her thoughts and emotions, and make readers think. None were random, and many were signaled by capitalization of a noun. Quotes also served to articulate explanatory variables and introduce philosophical debates.[10] Their totality verified and demonstrated the breadth of Theresa's knowledge and her ability to use literary resources effectively as an educational tool. They demonstrated she could recognize quality and choose an appropriate text from a wealth of possibilities. She confirmed she could illuminate a large range of topics with this technique and effectively mix and analyze many types of texts—from popular songs to nursery rhymes, hymns to Broadway plays, British poetry to American fiction, Shakespeare to the Bible. The quotes that began each installment reminded readers of poets' insights and how they were applicable to understanding the essence of new lands, new peoples, new experiences, and even new archaeological sites. Theresa's scholarship was ever present.

Debating ideas during their wanderings around northern Arizona helped keep Theresa's texts from becoming repetitively boring. It seems as if she felt there was only so much she could say about the landscape and the seeming monotony of going back and forth across mesas and valleys. From our contemporary perspective, Theresa's credentialing mechanism is overwhelming. If one quote was good, many were better. The technique hits the reader over the head with evidence that Theresa was current on the newest philosophical and psychological theories. And the denseness of Theresa's writing has had a downside for her long-term reputation-building efforts—it meant that her achievement was never analyzed by historians of science, feminist, or humanist scholars. This was not her concern at the time, however. For Theresa, it gained her an immediate reputation as one who could publish, write effectively, analyze critically, and teach with challenging gamesmanship.

Theresa required that readers be familiar with more than the canonical literature. She would win in the competitive discourse of salon culture, where participants played stump-your-conversational-partner for prestige points. Who had the more extensive knowledge of all literature and who had seen a popular play or read a dime-store novel purchased at railway stations? Theresa's intentional lack of attribution required readers to work to identify the source of covert allusions and why they were applicable and clarifying. While in Arizona, the game played with Frank alleviated Theresa's boredom and kept her font of civilized knowledge fresh as they walked in the wilderness. Now the reader played along with her. By extension, it was evident how she would be a challenging teacher.

A Successful Career

By the time the sixty-four-year-old William James and his wife returned east, Theresa had taught her first classes and written her travelogue. Stanford hired her permanently as an instructor in English. After about eight or nine years, however, it became evident she would not be promoted to higher professorial ranks or granted tenure without a doctorate. Theresa decided on nineteenth-century English literature and began to conduct archival research. She obtained a passport and went to England during the summer recess of 1915 to consult documents on Victorian literature, focusing on how authors use satire. It was the first of many research trips to England. Next, she had to find a doctoral program that would accept her Radcliffe studies, Stanford experience, and past research activities, and allow her to complete her dissertation in a year. Taking a leave of absence for the 1916–17 academic year, and with enough original data to write a book, Theresa matriculated at Columbia University as a graduate student of Ashley H. Thorndike, an expert on English literature. To Theresa, he was a severe critique from whom a thick-skinned but discerning student could profit. Thorndike valued her as a mature woman, and they often discussed the finer points of good taste and the art of connoisseurship and how these skills could apply to literature. He awarded her a degree with high honors.[11]

Theresa's doctoral dissertation, "Satire in the Victorian Novel," was published in 1920. She had finished, submitted it to the Columbia faculty, and defended it without revisions in 1917. As a result, she was promoted to assistant professor as soon as she passed her defense.[12] Theresa's degree, in English and philosophy, was officially awarded by Columbia University in 1920 after the manuscript was published. During this period, scholars were not officially awarded their degrees until their dissertations were published by a prominent publishing house.

Satire in the Victorian Novel, published by the distinguished Macmillan Company, sold for $2.50. It became Theresa's best-known book, but it was not easy to read. *Satire in the Victorian Novel* was a dense work, not written for the faint of heart looking to be amused. It was an intellectual appraisal of the concept of satire in British novels from 1850 to 1900. Theresa followed the same allegorical and allusion-laden writing style used in her *Out West* articles. The sentences, however, were longer and more convoluted, conforming to the accepted academic writing style. For example, defining the Victorian novelist, she wrote:

> To our modern authorities, especially such dictators as Shaw and Wells, contemplating him from the vantage ground of a higher rung in the ladder of civilization, the Victorian looks as Wordsworth did to Lady Blandish, like "a very superior donkey," protected by the side-blinders of conventionality, saddled and bridled by authority and ridden around in a circle by sentiment (most tyrannical of drivers), with much cracking of whip and raising of dust, but no real change of intellectual or spiritual locality. Nor can all the cavorting fun of Dickens, all the pungent playfulness of Thackeray, all the sardonic jibes of Carlyle, all the grotesque gesturing of Browning, all the winged irony of George Eliot and Matthew Arnold, not even all the quips and cranks in Punch itself, avail to quash the indictment. The Victorian may be defended, appreciated, exonerated even; he may in time succeed in living it down. But to live it down is not quite the same as to have had nothing that had to be lived down.[13]

Theresa had been exhaustive in her research on twelve novelists and reached conclusions that are still salient today. Where she shone, however, was in her discussions of how novelists used satire as a mechanism to instigate reform and observe life's amenities. This emphasis on life commentaries harkened back to her *Out West* writing on behavior and how it might correlate with gender, ethnicity, heritage, and place. The same was true of her attempts to interpret character using Jamesian psychology and notions of the self. Theresa continued to play with words, phrases, and concepts conceptualized as meaningfully layered thought that could be probed deeply to generate understanding. She had her educated readers join her on an intellectual journey, just as she had asked readers to join her in a reflexive travelogue. *Satire in the Victorian Novel* was full of sophisticated references that required in-depth canonical literary knowledge. Theresa expected everyone to be well read and rarely provided clues to metaphors. This was a dominant feature of a humanistic approach, considered a key tool of a sophisticated modernist essayist to create associations between the known and the unknown without talking down to the reader. Theresa demanded that her readers pay attention to both broad issues and minute detail—and, above all, think as they read—for there was generally more than one meaning to be pondered.

Satire in the Victorian Novel was extensively reviewed in national newspapers and scholarly journals. The reviewer for *The Brooklyn Daily Eagle* wrote, "Satire travels a long road and the author goes all the way with it, from Falstaff and Malvolio to Uriah Heep and Pecksniff." Another reviewer noted that Theresa "is evidently a painstaking student of literature in general and of its aims and tendencies in particular. She is a writer of force, clearness and charm as well as an independent thinker who makes readers think." The reviewer for the *San Francisco Chronicle* said Theresa united "sound learning and pleasant writing." A Sioux Falls reviewer said the book demonstrated that the author had "a rare discriminating spirit and a finely trained mind." *Satire in the Victorian Novel* was an impressive if exhausting work, where "similes and allusions flow freely from her pen."[14]

During the 1920s, Theresa returned to England frequently to conduct research on new topics. She published well-received essays on English poets Robert Browning and Elizabeth Barrett Browning, later compiled into *One Word More on Browning* (1927). The book was not intended for neophytes. It required close reading by all professionals due to its dense arguments. According to reviewers, it was serious, conscientious, and painstakingly critical. Theresa did not only want to write exclusively for her colleagues. Different goals and audiences emerged in the 1930s with *Two Poets, a Dog, and a Boy* (1933). Now Theresa aimed for an easy-to-read account, emphasizing the Brownings' narrative stories and poetry to make them accessible. Seeking to introduce a wider readership to their extensive oeuvre, Theresa even tried her hand at playwriting, adapting and directing some of the Brownings' work in 1935.[15]

The Brownings were not the only authors or topics Theresa addressed in the 1920s. She is still considered one of the foremost authorities on British tragedy. She also branched into analyses of American novelists, writing extensively on Edith Wharton and the nature of melodrama. She continued to publish poetry, and annotated, compiled, and edited several books by well-known authors, writing an extensive introduction to *The Complicated Bernard Shaw* (1930) and essays on Henrik Ibsen and Sinclair Lewis.[16]

Theresa stayed at Stanford for her entire career, advancing to associate professor with tenure in 1925 and full professor by 1930. She seems to have had a typical career. She was recognized as an outstanding educator, one of an innovative breed of English professors who had a "new spirit" and were able to "make literature alive to the student."[17] Like all professors, Theresa wrote book reviews and forewords for other scholars' works, evidence she was valued for her professional acumen. She presented lectures to community organizations in California and Iowa, papers full of theory and critique at national professional conferences, and served on the executive committees of professional organizations. She made popular speaking tours after each of her major publications, talking in locales such as Great Falls, Detroit, Chicago, and, of course, Iowa. Her pithy statements were quoted in newspapers as wise or witty maxims. She was annually listed in *Who's Who among North American Authors* from 1921 to 1936 as well as in later compendia. In 1933 Colonial House in Washington, D.C., listed Theresa, along with several other women such as Eleanor Roosevelt, Jane Addams, and Frances Perkins, as a prominent leader in her field.[18] She was well known and respected, achieving in her own field the scholarly and social reputation Frank had sought in anthropology.

As she aged, Theresa became interested in human rights and justice. *The Case of David Lamson* (co-authored with David Yvors), commissioned by the Lamson

Defense Committee, constituted Theresa's first attempt at investigative journalism. Lamson was a sales manager for Stanford University Press convicted of killing his wife, Allene, in 1933. It was a sensational trial, covered nationally like a tabloid event. Lamson was sentenced to die in San Quentin Prison. Lamson was one of Theresa's former students and Allene the executive secretary of the campus YWCA. Theresa worked with several Stanford professors to convince an appeals court to overturn the original verdict. They argued that Lamson was framed and had been convicted in part because he was the brother of Dr. Margaret Lamson, a lesbian professor; it was guilt by association rather than through a properly documented motive. Margaret lived with fellow Stanford professor Margery Bailey, who later taught John Steinbeck and founded the Shakespeare festival in Ashland, Oregon.[19] The appeals court agreed with their arguments that kinship and anti-lesbian bias were not grounds for convicting someone of murder. Two new trials were held. The juries in each deadlocked, and Lamson was released in 1936. He wrote a best-selling book on his death-row experiences. People still argue about the case today.

Theresa analyzed utopianism as the culmination of her scholarship. One of her final works was the delightful *Touring Utopia: The Realm of Constructive Humanism*. It was here that she re-addressed concepts of mobility, returning to her 1906 travel narrative and her search for engaging individuals. She strove to understand how people effectively wrote about personal experience through wit. Now a mature author, Theresa added a new dimension to her reflections; she reviewed social problems and politics, issues she had ignored in her earlier travelogue. She thought critically about environmentalism, H. G. Wells's worldview, notions of what constituted progressive change, government policies, and the need for free education. Other older themes remained constant: the humanistic search for beauty and truth in all things, her fondness for playing with figures of speech, a lively writing style, and her sense of humor. She never abandoned her love of writers of humorous travel narratives. Her reviewers enjoyed the book immensely and did not comment that it was dense.[20]

Theresa also wrote about contemporary America, particularly with regard to pedagogy, in journals such as *The Sewanee Review*. This journal saw itself as a literary magazine for cultivated people, with articles written by authoritative men and women who wrote in an attractive style. Russell used *The Sewanee Review* to explore new topics. She published a simultaneously scathing critique of, and apology for, American college fraternities and sororities, "Our Victorian Greek: A Diagnosis of the College Fraternity," demonstrating how it was an anachronism, jolly but exclusionary.[21] This assessment stemmed from serving as the faculty advisor for Kappa Kappa Gamma sorority for more than 25 years. Unlike Frank's concern with proper training in anthropology, however, Theresa did not write articles on what constituted proper training in the humanities, philosophy, or English literature. If she did, we have not located them. She was more concerned with the social life on campus and how this affected individual intellectual development. This did not mean she was not concerned with her subject matter. Throughout the 1920s and 1930s, she taught introductory courses as well as lecture courses and seminars on literary criticism, satire, classical literature, Victorian literature, and utopianism. As was normal for professors, the other aspects of teaching—grading, evaluating, and advising—took up much of her time.

Theresa was still interested in new intellectual projects. Late in life, she began a major new research endeavor, returning to the philosophy and theology interests of her youth. In her papers at the Stanford University Archives is an incomplete manuscript on the Bible as a literary text. It would have been a major accomplishment of a mature scholar. Other innovative projects were more manageable. Just before she was diagnosed with cancer, Theresa wrote an essay harkening back to her time spent among the Hopi, Navajo, and Akimel O'odham, "Indians as They Are," for *The English Journal*, the publication of the National Council of Teachers of English.[22] The review essay was an overview of innovative publications for children on the Hopi and Navajo and Theresa's assessment of whether the works could be used to educate American children about Native Americans. She chose works by noted regional Euro-American authors George Philip Krapp, Dama Margaret Smith, Laura Armer, Dane and Mary Coolidge, Frank Applegate, and Oliver La Farge. Her criteria were their realism and accuracy of the works rather than their picturesqueness or imaginary romanticism of Native peoples.

The review began, like her *Out West* publications, with a statement that oriented the reader in time and space.

> On the western side of the northeastern corner of Arizona three long narrow plateaus rise like a trio of thick fingers pointing south, a landmark to the traveler and a diversion from the monotony of wide spreading plains. The plains are the spacious roaming hunting grounds of the seminomadic Navahos with their herds of ponies and flocks of sheep and goats. The mesas are the lofty but restricted perch of the Hopis, clustered so compactly in their snug adobe quarters that they have quite an urban effect of living in apartment houses.[23]

Theresa appreciated Frank Applegate's whimsy and witticisms. She commended all the authors for exposing the folly of government educational impositions and the harm they had done to both Navajo and Hopi individuals who became caught between two worlds. Charles Lummis would have approved of the accuracy of the critique. Evident in her writing was how much Theresa had matured in outlook about the Navajo and the Hopi, and how she no longer saw them as barbarians but as people still mistakenly referred to as "savages," a word she now placed in quotes. Her main measure for the worth of each book was whether the author understood that Natives were "people of a strict code of conduct" who had a "quick response to all the loveliness" evident in their homelands.[24] This maturity of finally seeing people for who they were was an extension of Theresa's story of Sikachu. Unfortunately, she did not return to this text and further demonstrate her argument. It remained in her office.

Theresa never remarried. We do not know if she was ever tempted to find anyone who could replace Frank. She co-owned a house with her Stanford coworker Elizabeth Buckingham. They were obviously good friends as well as housemates and colleagues. They went to New York every few years to see plays, and to Iowa and Montana to visit Theresa's relatives. We can assume they also traveled to see Buckingham's relatives. Theresa returned periodically to the State University of Iowa for alumni events. In June 1920, for example, she was the keynote speaker for the class of 1895 reunion. Unfortunately, what we uncovered were but glimpses of her life for, unlike her honeymoon, Theresa kept her later life private, and if there were any diaries or journals, they have not survived.[25]

Theresa died of cancer on February 5, 1936, after a long, painful illness that lasted two or three years. She was still a member of the Stanford faculty, sixty-three years of age, and had continued to work until a few months before her death.[26] One obituary stated she had no surviving relatives, and by this the reporter probably meant her parents, brothers, and sisters had all passed on. She had no children. She left her estate to Buckingham, her closest friend. This included all of her and Frank's papers, which Buckingham kept until her own death. Buckingham's heirs included the Russell papers in Buckingham's papers when they were given to the Stanford University Archives upon her death. There the Russell papers remained for many years, never noted as a distinctive set of files. Luckily, an observant archivist realized that Theresa and Frank's papers should be separated into their own record group. This act enabled Theresa Russell to no longer remain invisible. It was an archival decision we have argued for in many archives over years when we find the work of a female scholar hidden and not even acknowledged in finding aides. Too often the integrity of a record group—how it came to an archive—has taken precedence to the exclusion of all other concerns, unintentionally but definitely marginalizing some scholars. By making Theresa's remaining papers that were kept by Buckingham visible, it enabled us to locate her. From there we could begin to reconstruct a small part of her and Frank's fascinating lives, especially their unknown archaeological work in Arizona Territory.

Frank's and Theresa's Final Words

Places and regions become distinctive as one learns to see with a critical eye and a nuanced perspective while on an archaeological and ethnographic journey. These places take on special meanings as that which is experienced, interpreted, and known. Places become associated with events, activities, and situations. Theresa knew that traveling through northern Arizona in search of sites and prehistoric graveyards was a personal endeavor, a voyage of personal discovery as well as her husband's archaeological and physical anthropological activity. But the Hopi and Navajo reservations—probably like the rest of Arizona Territory between 1900 and 1903—were also areas about which she was ambivalent. Theresa knew she would never completely understand or embrace Tusayan or Arizona, especially after it was transformed from the land where Frank might regain and keep his health to the place of his death.

Frank was ambivalent as well. He never was a sightseeing traveler who sought escape from a confining East Coast culture. He wanted to stay at Harvard, the place of his professional activities, but knew he needed to be in Arizona. He remained an enthusiastic scientist and a reluctant health seeker in the Southwest until the end. And he found the land and peoples of Arizona fascinating. He found pleasure in learning all he could about the anthropology of the region. He liked the activities of knowledge production, gathering data through archaeological survey, somatology, folklore, and ethnographic research. Near the end of his professional life, however, Frank began to see the region differently; he reflected on being a professional traveler in the region and how Theresa's classical perspectives had influenced how he thought about the desert. Frank told members of the American Folklore Society in 1902 that one continued to

> find the keenest pleasure in reading of the experiences of others in that region of infinite vastness. After a lapse of ten years [from his Arctic journeys] I feel as deep an interest in that "Land of Desolation and Death" as when I left it. Again, those who know the great arid Southwest find in its tragic history and in the writings of its pioneer anthropologists a source of perennial pleasure. He who has felt the spell of the desert has added a priceless treasure to his experience. He can sympa-

> thize with the belief of the desert dwellers that the wraith-like *remolinos* sending their columns of sand toward the bluest of heavens are not miniature whirlwinds, but spirits of air; that the pillars and other strangely eroded forms of sandstone are the figures of men transfixed there in the early twilight of time; he himself has felt the clutch of the demon of thirst that camps ever close upon the trail.[1]

To the best of our knowledge, Frank never wrote poetry, unlike many of his colleagues. It would have been a good medium to express his melancholy, optimism, and ambivalence near the end of his life. But Theresa did. She included one poem amid her *Out West* essays. We include it here to give her the final word in our recounting of her and Frank's archaeological honeymoon and marriage.

The untitled poem summarizes well Theresa's feelings about the high aridity and landscape of the Colorado Plateau as well as her feelings about southern and central Arizona. One sees her memories as she began her new life in California and a return to her first intellectual loves. Note the basic philosophical question as the grieving storyteller rhetorically asks: How could an all-loving God create such a difficult landscape, so harsh and full of silence, danger, and loneliness? One can see that she wonders what her own life will be. Will it too be full of loneliness and silence without Frank? Will it have danger? Will she return to this land? What does this God have in store for her?

"God must have made thee in His anger, and forgot."
Not in His anger, no, but in a mood
Of pure creative power, by any need
Or law, unfettered, uncompelled to heed
Necessity, by Beauty wholly woo'd.
In other portions of His earth he placed
Fair gardens, teeming fields, abounding streams,
Deep somber forests lit with mellow gleams,
Song-filled and fragrant, panoplied and graced.
In wisdom and in sympathy He made
These things for men, His children, that they should
Be clothed and nourished, dowered with every good,
And never feel their lives mocked or betrayed.
This gracious deed accomplished He was free
To fashion what He would for His own joy,
To wield Infinite power without alloy,
To please Himself—then, Desert, He made thee.
He made thy sands and flooded them with light—
Thy sun's hot-hearted passion never faints;
With brush of fine and jeweled hues He paints

Thy skies and rocks and blossoms—e'en thy night.
So dost thou glow and quiver; yet the spell
Of Silence is upon thee, for He willed
The voice of pain and anguish to be stilled
And mirth hushed. Smites His ear nor chime nor knell
Thus, all thy life is silent. Here the snake
And lizard glide; slow circle birds of prey;
The scorpion crawls; wolf and coyote grey
Move stealthily—and none that silence break.
In silence and in mystery thou'rt made,
But thy God loves thee; in thy spaces shrined
He has His dwelling where who seek may find,
Though thy still vastness makes the heart afraid.[2]

Acknowledgments

We wish to thank the staff members of following institutions, who over the past 20 years have graciously helped us: the National Anthropological Archives; at the Smithsonian Institution, the National Museum of Natural History Archives and Registration Office; the Department of Anthropology Collection Records; the Smithsonian Institution Archives; Stanford University Library Special Collections; the Field Museum of Natural History's Anthropology Department, Library, Special Collections, and Photographic Archives; the University of Arizona Library Special Collections; and the American Philosophical Society. In addition to materials from special collections and archives we have amassed slowly over the past 20 years, we have consulted catalogue cards and accession papers at the institutions for which Frank Russell collected. Many thanks to the collections staffs and curators at the Peabody Museum of Archaeology and Ethnology, Harvard University, and the Smithsonian Institution Museum Support Center, National Museum of Natural History. A special thanks to several students who have helped us over the years. We owe many thanks to valued colleagues and friends, including Rebecca Allen, Candace Greene, John Homiak, Jenny Johnson, Robert Leopold, Curtis Hinsley, Kelley Hays-Gilpin, Dennis Gilpin, Steven Nash, the late Willow Powers, Lisa Pasos, Mary Elizabeth Ruwell, and Thomas Sheridan. Special thanks also to John Welsh for his assistance as we organized and reorganized our story, and to Curtis Hinsley for incisive comments on how to improve the manuscript. We would also like to thank all the students at the Smithsonian Summer Institute in Material Anthropology, and colleagues Regna Darnell, Kelley Gilpin-Hays, Christine Szuter, and others who listened to stories about the project and the history of collecting in Arizona for 10 years—and remained our friends. A special thanks also to our friends and colleagues David Wilcox and John Welsh for helping us identify many of the archaeological sites the Russells visited and remaining interested over all these years. We also thank our colleagues at the Hopi Preservation Office who reviewed the Russells' photographs and helped us eliminate those that were inappropriate for republication and also choose those that would convey important points about Hopi culture, intellectual property, and sovereignty rights; our special thanks to Stewart Koyiyumptewa.

Needless to say, we appreciate the hard work of the many individuals at the University of Arizona Press who helped with the editing and production of this book, especially our editors Allyson Carter and Amanda Krause. And thanks to our spouses, Catherine Fowler and Richard Ahlstrom, for their insights and tolerance while listening to us talk about the fascinating Russells for all these years.

Documentary Sources

Our reconstruction of Frank and Theresa's archaeological journeys was based on documentary evidence as well as Theresa's *Out West* articles. The main archival materials for the 1900 research trip were Theresa's journal and Frank's field log. These are housed at the Stanford University Special Collections, along with the data for Theresa's later projects, her reviews, teaching materials, a 1908 "Book of Incidents," correspondence from 1921 to 1936, and some odds and ends. The reconstruction for the 1901 and 1902 archaeological surveys is based on Frank's monthly reports to John Wesley Powell and W J McGee at the Bureau of American Ethnology. They are in the National Anthropological Archives as separate record groups for Frank and as part of the incoming and outgoing Bureau of American Ethnology correspondence record groups. Artifactual information was found in the Anthropology Department's collection files and accompanying documents at the Museum Support Center. Frank's 1898 solo journey was reconstructed from correspondence with Putnam and from files at the Peabody Museum of American Archaeology and Ethnology. The artifactual materials and the records of human remains in the Peabody Museum for the 1900 trip were consulted several times during the mid 2010s; for the 1901 to 1903 trips the collections, held at the National Museum of Natural History, Smithsonian Institution, were reviewed by Parezo over a period of several years while participating in the Smithsonian Institution's Summer Institute in Museum Anthropology during the 2010s. Several students helped to review these materials as class exercises. Artifactual materials were supplemented by letters by John Wesley Powell, William John McGee, William Henry Holmes, Frederic Ward Putnam, and Franz Boas found in the National Anthropological Archives (NAA); the records of the Anthropology Department and the National Museum of Natural History; the Smithsonian Institution Archives; the Harvard University Archives, the Peabody Museum archives, accession records, and Anthropology Department catalogue records at Harvard University; and anthropological documents and correspondence files at the Chicago Field Museum, the American Philosophical Society, the University of Iowa, and the University of Arizona Special Collections.

We have also used newspaper accounts from the Library of Congress's Chronicling America project and Newspapers.com. Ancestry.com was used to develop information on Frank's and Theresa's families, but this information is still spotty. We have checked many other archives and historical societies for information, but generally without success. Most glaring was the lack of personal correspondence between Frank and Theresa, and each of them and their families and friends. If these letters exist, we have not located them, and we think that Theresa and/or Frank probably destroyed them. We should also note that we have only come across a few letters to other colleagues so it is possible neither of them had an extensive professional correspondence. We have not found Frank's field notes, except for the ethnographic materials in the NAA and at Stanford. We think that whatever materials went to Washington were dispersed to BAE employees and integrated in their own field notes. All other field trips have extremely spotty documentation.

A word about illustrations. The *Out West* articles were heavily illustrated, but unfortunately most of the other photographs taken by Frank or Theresa are of poor quality. Generally, photos were indistinguishable landscape reference shots, most so blurry as to be unrecognizable. Think of a person standing at a site and saying, "This is what we saw when we looked in this direction." While we strove for completeness in terms of the texts, we eliminated those photographs that did not enhance Theresa's story. Most were of such poor quality that they could not be reproduced.

We likewise eliminated photographs that Hopi, Navajo, or Akimel O'odham peoples do not want published (e.g., pictures of human remains, Hopi rituals) and those we deemed demeaning, in part because of how they were shot, and again the poor quality, which, frankly, made the individuals therein look stupid. Most of these shots were of Navajo people met during the Russells' journey, often Theresa's attempts at learning composition and focus. The chapter that was most affected by this decision was chapter 16. Eight photos of the Snake Dance and Antelope Dance were published in Theresa's *Out West* entry. We have intentionally excluded those that do not meet Hopi Cultural Preservation Office criteria for reproduction, eliminating those that depict religious ceremonies.[1] We assume that Theresa did not think about Hopi or Navajo sensitivities when she published her articles. But we live in a different time and have different considerations.

We scanned the best photographs from hard copies of the original essays and chose only those with good enough resolution to add to the story.[2] Unfortunately, the original negatives have not been found in the Russell Papers at Stanford or, with a few exceptions, in Frank Russell's materials at the Peabody Museum of Archaeology and Ethnology. Photographs by Frank or Theresa held at the National Anthropological Archives were from their 1901 to 1903 Arizona trips.

Appendix A. Journals Kept during the Summer of 1900 by Theresa and Frank Russell

During the summer of 1900, both Theresa and Frank kept separate chronological records of their trip. To avoid repetition and make the entries easier to read, we have interspersed them. This will allow readers to compare the events Frank and Theresa thought noteworthy. The basic journal entries are Theresa's and as such are unmarked. Frank's entries are marked *FR* and printed in italics. Readers should please remember that these entries were not copyedited and contain some punctuation that will appear questionable. In addition, punctuation and spellings have changed since 1900. Please note that Theresa's Spanish spellings were not necessarily conventional.

Theresa's journal constitutes a chronicle, written in the field and edited in the fall of 1900 in Cambridge, Massachusetts. It later served as a memory aid, receptacle of observations of the strange and unique, and a diary in which Theresa ruminated about her experiences. She used these as her memory devices when she wrote her *Out West* articles; readers who are interested in issues of memory and topic choice for travel narratives can compare the published and private accounts. In contrast, Frank's entries were a field log and concentrated on his increasingly frustrated quest to find promising sites. When he mentioned people, he documented the activities of men, not women. As a result, he provided little reflection or speculation about his activities. He did not use his log as a record of his feelings about what he saw, nor did he conduct reflexive philosophical and theoretical debates like Theresa. His field log was not a reflexive document.

We have minimally edited entries. We occasionally inserted a word in brackets for clarity. Any words or phrases in parentheses were written by Theresa or Frank. The notation [?] indicates an illegible word and [text blank] indicates Theresa or Frank had a word, often a place-name, needing to be filled eventually. We have not changed adjectives and nouns that today will appear offensive. For example, Theresa referred to their Navajo and Mexican employees as "boys." This can be read as a racialized designation for colored men not given adult status. However, Theresa usually included Frank in her designation "the boys," so it may simply be the equivalent of "guys." Theresa used the outdated term *Moki* to refer to Hopi. Since the people were changing to Hopi by 1900, we are not sure why she used the outdated term. We annotated the journals, as we did the *Out West* articles.

Endnotes refer to knowledge, events, and quotations common to highly educated readers in 1900 but often little known today. We have not duplicated a referent annotated earlier in the book.

Frank's entries end on July 31. We do not know if he continued the journal for August or ceased logging his activities. Theresa's July 30 journal entry noted Frank's growing depression at not finding his large, impressive site. We speculate he ceased his field log, feeling it was not worth the effort. He told Theresa he merely had to say, "Ditto, ditto, ditto" about what he had written previously. There was nothing new to document since they had not found his ideal site. We regret his decision, for not finding things conveyed useful information. It is equally possible that Frank's August and September journal entries have been lost.

Theresa's journal is housed in SC0166, Box 1, Folder 7, of the Theresa Russell Papers, Special Collections, Stanford University. Frank's field log is in Box 3, Folder 7. We transcribed these documents from the original handwritten formats, made typed manuscripts, and gave a copy of the annotated transcriptions to Stanford University to become part of the Russell record group. Readers will note that several place-names that derive from Diné are written using more than one spelling in the text. This was a common occurrence for a language that anthropologists recorded phonetically before there was a standard orthography. We have not altered or standardized these words or phrases. Nor have we altered the spellings or punctuation, and readers should note that the use of hyphens in words has changed in contemporary usage. Writing style and publishing conventions for 1900 are different from those used today, and we have not forced contemporary standards on Theresa's writing. Also, we have left Theresa's capitalization, italicization, word choice order, and other personal idiosyncrasies to preserve her meanings and stylistic conventions. These idiosyncrasies and period conventions also demonstrate how she played with language. These are important data for anyone who wants to delve into her works further.

July

Sunday, the First of July

Immediately after the wedding ceremony and supper last evening, my husband and myself took the (7:40) train for the West. After an hour's wait at Marion we took the night train for Kansas City, reaching there about nine in the morning. Here we found a wait of several hours before us, so we took a car that carried us some four miles out to a very pleasant park where we spent the rest of the forenoon. Returning, we had a nice little café dinner, and then went over to the station in time to write a home letter before our train was due.

Such a cursory view of Kansas City does not give one a very happy impression. The situation of the town is rough without being picturesque; little houses stuck in *time* up the steep banks, like galleries in a second-rate theater; cable tracks shooting up and down at an incline that makes traveling there-on seem precarious; a shoddy population, whose idea of a good dinner is one that can be procured for ten cents; and a general air of cheapness succeed to characterize those patrons that came under our view. Decorations were rampant in honor of the Democratic National Convention to be held on the fourth; and the location struck one as very appropriate for the glorification of the party of the populace.

But our brief sojourn ended. We found ourselves about five o'clock established comfortably in our section of the train that was to carry us still further westward.

Monday, the Second of July

For comfort as well as economy, let me recommend the tourist car, for summer travel at least; for cool rattan is certainly preferable to hot plush, abundance of room so that you can shift about to enjoy varied scenery and perpetual shade to crowded apartments, and a cheerful young porter with leisure and interest to bestow upon your own particular needs to a grouchy old porter such as fell to our lot on the Pullman, who being obliged to be all things to all men, was not able to be much of anything to any man.

Passing across Kansas during the night we woke this morning in another world. We had come into that region where man finds nature in too mighty a mood to be trifled with, so he admires her from a respectful distance and saves his parlor tricks for those places amenable to his measuring rod. As we crossed the south-eastern corner of Colorado, we caught a glimpse of Pike's Peak, 150 miles away and of Spanish peaks, somewhat nearer. Viewing these and the infinite stretch of plains between them [the traveler] takes his first lesson in *Immensity*; a problem that never leaves him so long as he dwells in the enchanted land. A constant query: How can there be so much of anything? Like insignificant intruders into this vastness appear here and there (mostly *there*): the adobe huts which houses some ranchman whose herds are seen away yonder, miles from anywhere; or perhaps a shelter for some redskins, living without the pale of their government-assigned localities. Here we see also a new color scheme. Those fields of waving gold do not wave with grain, but sunflowers, looking more like daisies from the car-window. We were fortunate in viewing it at a time when the sunflower was ripe and the cactus in the bloom, for they together with the purples and blues of other blossoms, made a gorgeous carpet with its wide, wide border of green fading into the quieter hues of the horizon.

On we went up grades behind two puffing monsters, downgrades where the engines played at toboggan slides, around grades in serpentine trail, over into New Mexico, with the view growing wilder and wilder.

Not to omit mention of the mundane—we were exceedingly well fed throughout our journey. Meals were served at stations where the Harvey [House Co.] dining rooms were located and so efficient was the service that the "twenty-minutes-for dinner" (we were really allowed 25–30 minutes) gave us ample time. Orders were taken on the train so they were ready for us when we arrived. Menus there were but no time wasted in taking orders on the plans of "meal, cooked *while you wait*." Trim maiden waiters circulated around to tables offering each course in turn and doing it "with neatness and dispatch." Then when you had absorbed enough hot and appetizing *viands* for a Thanksgiving dinner your *Hebe* would sweetly inquire if you would have "anything more?" Three of these *collations* in succession caused us to be weary in well-being so at Albuquerque, having an extra allotment of time, we went up town on a soda fountain hunt and to a raspberry ice cream order for supper.[1]

Thursday, the Third of July

The porter had waxed quite friendly with us. Perhaps it was because he had discovered our relationship to the boot-and-shoe-decorated trunks in the baggage car. Then, too, he owned up to being an Iowa boy, when he learned that fair state had been my home. He was therefore somewhat solicitous over our destination:

"Live in Gallup?"

"Oh, no, our home is in the East."

"Well, must have a grudge against yourselves to go there!"

But he put us off, according to orders at 2:50 AM, giving heartfelt and pious instructions to the man from the hotel to give us "the best room in the house!"

"The very best" at the Page House was not half bad, though not what would be termed luxurious.[2] We were shown two front rooms looking out upon the station, railroad track, and freight switches and yards. But it boasted of a couch besides the usual furniture and that made the situation easier. The place furnished lodging only (excepting the refreshment handed over the bar) so we were obliged to find a restaurant to get our breakfast. This was an easy matter, for a promenade up the one business street of the town (and that built up only on one side) showed that we were not to be perplexed by a wide margin of choice. The "one and only" however (save a Harvey House in the depot) was clean and attractive, and the young sissy in masculine raiment who attended us was alone worth the price of admission.

Across the track at right angles with Main Street is the Indian trading store where I had my first sight of the Navajo, perpetually loafing around outside, and of their blankets displayed within. Here we met Mr. Cotton who said that

Mr. Hubbell had not yet returned from Philadelphia (where he had been attending the Republican convention), nor had his freight train arrived from Ganado. There was nothing to do but wait, so we consumed some time in buying me a light weight felt hat with a ribbon of Harvard crimson for a band. This accomplished we strolled up toward the coal mine and took our first installment of sunshine and sound of the Southwest. In the afternoon I wrote more home letters and helped my husband a little in preparing his report of the section of Anthropology of the A.A.A.S., from the annual meeting of which (in New York) he had come en route to Iowa and Arizona.[3]

After a cozy little fruit supper in our rooms we enjoyed a walk up the hill back of the train, beyond the churches and the stand-pipe, to the mosquito-covered slope whence we could get an expansive view, beautiful in the evening light.

FR: July 3rd: Reached Gallup, New Mexico, at three AM. I had expected to find Mr. J. L. Hubbell or a team from this ranch awaiting me at Gallup but learned that he was in Albuquerque and would not arrive until the next day. Could do nothing but wait.

Wednesday, the Fourth of July

The morning of the ever-glorious Fourth was celebrated by a call from Mr. Hubbell who had arrived 24 hours behind us. But as the team had not yet come he thought [it] best to wait till the next day before starting out, to which we acquiesced as graciously as we could. I had become very much interested in this gentleman through Frank's account of him and his kind hospitality to a wayfaring wheelman two summers ago, and I had looked forward to this meeting.[4] I was presented to a gentleman about fifty years of age; of average height and verging comfortably toward corpulence; by no means fastidious in dress and grooming but wearing an easy courtesy of manner that wins you at once. His alert, businesslike way of settling matters comes, one infers, from his English father; while his ready gallantry and unreserved family pride and affection must be an inheritance through his mother [who comes] from a race of Cavaliers. He is a man well entrenched in his own customs and opinions yet having the breadth of vision to see those of others. He speaks English, Spanish and Navajo with equal fluency and is a well-read man and an interesting conversationalist.

Promising to call later with the members of his family who were with him, he left us, and we amused ourselves during the afternoon by going to the Fourth of July dance, held in a bowery up the street. The participants were Mexicans; the spectators mostly Indians. Both were interesting to this foreigner and the scene was "good as a play" for me. The dances were much like ours, except one, a sort of hybrid between a quadrille and a Virginia Reel. Costumes were gaudy but not neat; music by a violin and guitar.

In the evening we had callers. While Frank and Mr. Hubbell went for a walk and private chat, I played hostess to Señorita Hubbell, a maiden lady, sister of the Señor, on her way from Albuquerque to Ganado for a visit, the first one she has made, though the distance can be covered in 24 hours. She is a peculiar individual; speaks English with some difficulty, is very plain in dress and appearance, but reveals an unexpected fund of playfulness upon acquaintance. With her were the son and daughter of the house of Hubbell; Don Lorenzo, on his way home from Notre Dame, Indiana, where he has been at school for several years, and Señorita Adela, coming from her school in Prescott.

The boy is a handsome lad of athletic build and rich color who attracts you by his boyish frankness and native gallantry; young America toned down by the quaint Spanish courtesy. His education is to be completed at Harvard, but his present interest is to help his father in the store. "He has done so much for me I am anxious to do something for him," he says with a sincerity that has no stamp of the goody-goody about it.

His sister is also brunette, of trim figure and vivacious manner. She is a happy child with a nature kind and affectionate as far as it goes, though there is a certain hardness about her face that warns of selfishness if probed too far. The older sister, Barbara, is ill at Albuquerque and could not come with the rest.

FR: July 4th: Mr. Hubbell arrived on the morning train. I could not go out to his ranch, Ganado, today because Mr. Hubbell has business to attend to and I would gain nothing by pushing on ahead of him for the freight team has not yet come to take out the trunks.

Thursday, the Fifth of July

The day is occupied with the drive to Ganado, between 50 and 60 miles northwest from Gallup, and that far, of course, from the railroad.

The Russell family were loaded up in a brand-new road-wagon, with seats and cushions thrown in. Frank remarked that it was a pity we hadn't given friend Hubbell a little longer notice of our arrival so that he might have built a railway and constructed a private car for our especial use! But the vehicle did very well! Another member of the Hubbell family was in evidence this morning; little Roman, aged about ten, also returning from school, a pretty, clever boy and a spoiled baby. These five tucked their selves away in a two-seated vehicle and we were off.

At first our way lay through rather rough country where you have the feeling of being continuously enclosed by hills though they are so far away you never reach them. Then there were some lively miles of park-effect where the road wound over the mountain top; trees of cedar, mesquite and pine and there is a shrubby little oak, all growing straight out of the sand and rocks without any visible signs of sustenance. Vistas, dales, winding paths, green branches with the azure shining through. It was all beautiful if you could forget about the cool green velvet carpets nature spread out in the Eastern woodlands.

Then the outlook widened and the horizon was far away when darkness fell; far away too the little light that twinkled a welcome forward not long before we reached it.

I must not forget the picturesque bit of scenery on the way called the Haystacks—high rocks rising up in fantastic forms from the sandy plain.[5] These were on the morning's route. We stopped for dinner at the Cienega, a little settlement of some half-dozen buildings, including a church. We drove up to one of the adobe houses and were very cordially welcomed by a host and hostess who seemed to be friends of our companions.

[At Hubbell's,] it was very refreshing to be shown into the little bedroom of neat though primitive furniture and find the blessing of soap and water at your disposal. And it was certainly interesting to loll and loaf in the rocker in the other room, (two apartments are a great plenty for pioneers) and watch the buxom mistress prepare lunch [dinner]. She was good to look upon in her cool blue calico gown that fitted her rounded figure snugly; pleasant to listen to as her words came volubly and in the Queen's English. Perhaps, too, the information that she was an Iowa woman was an added attraction. They have been here six years, but the hardships of life in the desert seem to cause her very little worry. She gave us sandwiches of two varieties, cake, fruit, milk and lemonade. And all as free as water (air would be more appropriate in Arizona!) a very cheerful example of Western hospitality.

FR: July 5. Rode 80 miles to Ganado today in Mr. Hubbell's new buggy. Reached Ganado at 8 o'clock PM. Passed the freight team on the road.

Friday, the Sixth of July

When I awoke this morning [at Hubbell's house], I felt like one at home in a strange land. We had been shown the guest room, distinguished by a Brussels carpet, tacked (not sewed) on the floor; and by a rather large square table, loaded with bric-a-brac, conspicuous being medallions and images of the Virgin and the saints showing the family faith; and a gorgeous pincushion with no pins in it, evincing a sublime disregard of the trifling points in life. In every corner was a recess with shelves, concealed by a curtain, and the bulky pillars that supported the ceiling were twined with gay-hued threads. The ceiling itself was very low and covered with white muslin roughly tacked on, in Spanish-American colors, red, white, and yellow. Behind the washstand a newspaper officiated as [a backstop for] splashes on which you could peruse graphic partisan editorials while you washed. At the foot of the bed stood a heavy upholstered rocker and on the other side of that was the deep, square window, opening in like a door, and hung with white muslin curtains. This window and our door opened onto the wide porch running along the front of the house. On our left was another sleeping room, on our right the door leading into a sitting room where the family assembled before meals as the dining room adjoined it on the rear. The kitchen was to the rear of our bedroom. The sitting room was simply furnished with Navajo rugs, a table and couch with a few gaudy ornaments, while the dining room was strictly utilitarian, only containing a hive-like screened safe [used] for cupboard purposes, and the table and chairs. The table was quite extensive to accommodate a large family; Señora Hubbell and her nephews [were] present beside the seven arrivals of the evening before. The tablecloth was red, newspapers, ever useful, served as doilies and the condensed milk was brought on in the "original package" with two holes punched in the top. But the food was abundant and excellent, of the sort that makes a man thank the Lord for the room there is inside of him. The favorite dish was chili sauce served in a large tureen which was invariably emptied. My husband fell in love at first taste but I could not turn Spanish so easily. Another treat was "tortillas," bread dough made into flat cakes and fried in lard, served hot.

Conversation was in Spanish except when addressed to us and was apparently of a joyful nature. They remind one of a family of frolicsome kittens. After breakfast we went over to the store which is a long rectangular stone building with the end at right angles to the adobe house and joined [on the] north by an irregular fence. There are two high double doors in this end, each one opening into a large living room. The one on the right as you approach seems to be the family sleeping room; it contains two beds, a dresser, table, a grate and a couple of trunks, but no ornaments except a few old paintings, one of which [Correggio's *Madonna and Child*] is valued at $50,000. The adjoining apartment is a room-of-all-work. On the right side of the entrance is a bed and in the opposite corner an office desk, chair and the General Post Office. Beyond the bed is a primitive washstand with tin tub of water on the level and a bookcase nearby, containing among others a set of Hamlin Garland's works presented by the author who has been a guest in this house. Across from this is a fire grate and mantle, flanked on each side by corner shelves loaded with back numbers (untouched) of *Harper's* and other magazines. A sewing machine and a trunk occupy the fourth corner of this side. Across the end is an Aeolian, usually covered with a gray shroud. Nearby is the door leading into the store proper. The usual counter-table, a Swiss clock and the children's diplomas hanging [on] each side [of] a family group [painting] complete the furnishings save for the most beautiful thing in it, a painting by Burbank representing a Navajo woman weaving a blanket.[6]

The store runs across the width of the building with a large door in the end and windows in the other by a capacious wareroom. The curios for us of course were the Indian products. Señor Hubbell has some 120 squaws weaving blankets for him and has a collection unexcelled anywhere.[7] Two beauties had just been brought in, one worth $35 and the other $50. The patterns are simple but artistic showing always an effective color-scheme, dark blue and scarlet bayeta being a favorite combination.

Besides this market, Mr. Hubbell holds many articles in pawn, charging them [Navajo owners] ten percent for the favor. Here you see bridles and belts of silver, the latter set with turquoise stones, a decoration in high favor among the Indians, being used in many ways, most commonly as earrings. Besides, they wear necklaces of silver, coral, and shell beads.

During the morning Señorita Adela entertained me by overhauling the contents of some old trunks to show me her pretty possessions, inherited and acquired. The former were more interesting, especially the quaintly beautiful gown with accessories to match which her mother had worn in ye olden time. At my suggestion she arrayed herself in a typical Spanish costume of a generation ago. Gown of daintily figured print silk much beruffled, puffed, draped and trimmed in Spanish lace, fitted collarette, heavy earrings, watch chain and ring, and a black silk shawl with fringed edges, made the little lady a creature of romance. But when I presented her to her father as Señorita Rubelino (her mother's name) he merely remarked that she was "not so handsome as her mother at the age." The Señora has truly outgrown her beauty by this time, however. She excels her husband in the matter of avoirdupois, her weight being as she expressed, seventeen pounds more than twice as much as mine, and I had just tipped the scales at nearly a hundred. But she is a comfortable old mother with a slow, sweet smile that speaks volumes. It was necessary that it showed in our case for she does not "speak our talk" so that our exchanges of amiabilities had been confined to facial expression. She herself did not talk much (perhaps because the others did not give her time!) and her utterance seemed thick and a trifle difficult. But she leads a happy, contented existence and what more can anyone desire?

Saturday, the Seventh of July

I should soon get tired, I fancy, of having these Navajos forever hanging about, but as a temporary study they are interesting. They take their curiosity as a matter of course and you find them calmly peering in at you from door and windows with quite as much industry as we employ staring at them. At the end of the house is a sort of camp where a group of them is always to be seen, while their ponies are clustered under every tree in the yard. Their owners, with wives and children, stand around in the store or the doorway, sit in a stupid row along the side of the stone house or squat in cozy bunches in the sand directly under the scorching sun. An umbrella would be an unnecessary and degenerate luxury for them.

In the morning Mr. Hubbell guided us to a place some distance from the Post which looked suspicious of harboring graveyards and other things, but we found nothing except a number of little circles, squares, etc. made of sharp, flat stones stuck in the sand. Excavation revealed ashes, so they were probably fire-places. There was also a charming little retreat up there among the trees and rocks, but that's not scientific.

Sunday, the Eighth of July

Rising directly back of the Post, beyond the arroyo, is a large butte and a number of smaller ones. To climb up one of these in the twilight and look around, above and below, is to be convinced that eyesight is Heaven's choicest gift especially when complimented by such an objective gratification of the visual sense. As space and time are indefinable, so this marvelous outlook of distance and color indescribable. One can only repeat the biblical invitation to "Come and See."

As darkness shuts down we descend to earth again and find the family enjoying the amenities thereof. There is music in the air, due to the efforts of the two nephews, one of whom plays the *Aeolian* while they both sing a whole repertoire of Spanish melodies. By and by we have some of our own English songs; "Way Down Upon the Suwanee River" and other free-for-alls, to the delight of the performers if not the audience.

FR: One entry for July 6, 7, and 8, written on July 8: Waiting for the freight tram which came in late this evening. Occupied a part of the day in getting outfit together for the trip. Mr. Hubbell has been very busy since my arrival: the Navajos had been awaiting his return from the East where he has been attending the Republican National Convention for the past month. They have kept him busy from 5 o'clock in the morning until late at night. They have brought in blankets, chiefly, with some sheep and goat skins. Mr. Hubbell has about 185 weavers at work whom he supplies with yarn and also gives or preserves for them the old patterns used for blankets before the whites came to the Navajo country. He has one blanket or rug that is 18 ½ x 22 feet and is double faced.

Monday, the Ninth of July

"Joy to the world!" The wagon returned last night with our trunks; and this morning Suleiman in all his glory was not arrayed like the explorer's wife.[8] The beauty of the raiment, however, was utilitarian rather than aesthetic. First (to begin at Alpha) a union under suit of gauze; next brown hose held up by elastic fastened to girdle waist tape. That comprised the first layer. Second, a divided skirt (with extra fold in front to deceive the uninitiated), supplied with two pockets, and supported by shoulder straps; then a loose blouse with rubber band at the waist and fastening over a collar (sailor style) decorated with an embroidered H on a firmament of Harvard Crimson. Brown bicycle boots, the soft felt hat and thick riding gloves completed the second layer and finished a successful costume for rough and ready wear.

We were delayed in the start, so that it was half past three in the afternoon before the driver cracked his whip and we said adios! Our vehicle consisted of a prairie schooner carrying over a ton in load and drawn by two teams, horses in front and mules hitched to the wagon. One of the Mexicans, Erminio, used Macho, the brown mule as a saddle horse while he acted as driver; and the other, Nosifor, sat on a bench in the front of our private car and officiated as brakeman. Further back, amid a mighty conglomeration that was to meet all our physical needs for the next two or three months sat we, in elevated state and looked far down upon the little dog trotting cheerfully alongside. Alongside also, but more sedately paced, the little cream-colored pony bearing his master, the grave and revered Sliver; a dignified Indian of the old school, who had worked for Mr. Hubbell for 22 years and had been engaged to spend the summer with us in the triple capacity of guide, interpreter, and cook. He is a fascinating old fellow, somehow; you have an increasing longing to get behind that imperturbable reserve and make some psychological explorations. But it is a hopeless wish. Sliver is a closed book. He can speak a few Spanish words and fewer English but he seems sparing even of those few. His native costume consists of shirt and trousers of figured calico of different patterns; soft cowhide moccasins fastened under the ankle by a silver clasp; and a handkerchief or band wound around his head. His black hair is rolled up in a curious wad on his neck and tied in the middle with white string. He has the physiognomy of a statesman; reserved and meditative, with high forehead, wrinkles radiating from dark, kind eyes, thin lips and good square chin. His slender erect figure has given him his name. Mr. Hubbell evidently believes in the fitness of cognomens. He calls his own cook Crazy, because he has [epileptic seizures] fits.

There isn't so much to be said about the boys. Erminio is a thick-set fellow with pock-marked face. That makes him repellently ugly at first; but he has clear blue eyes and he minds his own business; partly from shyness and partly from ignorance of the English language. Nosifor is more accomplished. He is a cheerful young thing with a glib tongue and a beautiful voice.

We halted at about 7:30 in the evening, having journeyed some twelve miles from Ganado; and reached the open, boundless plains. While the boys got supper, I sat on a roll of blankets and watched the sunset. Any number of such marvelous sights hereafter cannot efface the memory of that first one. Huge rolls of clouds massed in the west, underneath which shown the unspeakable glory of Apollo's farewell and up to which he flung a radiant adieu, like the royal shower of gold from departing majesty, causing them to be wreathed in purple and crimson and gold, fold upon fold of this divine drapery, illuminated from beneath and retaining its own soft gray above, outlined against a canopy of blue.[9] This illumination is not only in the West, in the direct path of the king. Far to the North and the South do the remote regions catch and reflect some of the royal magnificence. But by and by that "certain moment" came which "culled the glory of from the gray" and night and silence fell. But even as we unrolled our blankets and made our beds on the sand alongside the sage-brush, another radiance, soft, quiet, restful in its splendor, arose upon us and fair Luna declared that there should be no darkness over us that night.

FR: July 9. Started this afternoon for the Chinle Valley to the westward of which the Indians say there are a number of very large ruins that have never been explored by a white man. Including hay and grain for the horses we have about a ton on the wagon which is too heavy for one team to haul over the rough trails. We have, therefore, taken two teams which are to be returned as soon as we can establish a camp. I have engaged two Mexicans for the summer at $30.00 a month each, and a Navajo with his pony also at $30.00—it being understood that I am to use the pony as much as I wish. One of the men, Nosifor Garcia understands a little English; the other, Erminio, speaks "Mexican" only. "Sliver," the Navajo, knows about 30 words of English and perhaps 50 of Spanish.

We start with two 10- and two 5-gallon kegs for water. The large casks hold nearly enough water for the horses for one night so we are making a "dry camp" tonight in the Chinle Valley about 10 miles from Ganado.

Tuesday, the Tenth of July

As we took up our line of march this morning we saw far north to the left the rugged outlines of Black Mesa's southern end, and at the northern limit of our vision we discerned a beautiful phenomenon—a stretch of white cliffs, so indented that they suggested the pillars of a Grecian portico. One thought it must be the entrance to the temple of the Gods as it glowed in the brilliant morning sunlight. All day we journeyed toward that ever-fleeing temple and finally halted late in the afternoon at some distance beyond it. What we had reached was something more useful than beautiful; the goal of all travelers in Arizona, a spring.

From this point we did not know the way, and as the Indian who had been the instigator of this route had not yet come on from Ganado, we were forced to camp and wait his arrival.

Our way-station was the dreariest place imaginable. A wilderness of wind-blown, drifting, impertinent sand, unrelieved except by some poor little frizzled up growths that weren't big enough to name. This on top of a hill, whose steep descent and steeper ascent must be compassed to bring water from the spring. This center of existence appeared on a hillside and was enclosed by a circular fence, which made a convenient loafing ground for ubiquitous Navajo. On the top of this hill was perched a hogan while others were scattered here and there. Running up the hills were deep precipitous gorges that were almost picturesque. But I fear that I may write in some bitterness of spirit about this place for I became well-nigh swallowed up in sand and misery and had my first attack of longing for the fleshpots of Egypt. The most desirable to my mind being a woman, anybody white and feminine, to tell my troubles to, for I had not yet adapted myself gracefully to an exclusively masculine society. We made a bed out of our wagon and slept some "knit up the raveled sleeve of care" and tarnished crankiness.[10]

FR: July 10. We reached the spring called Ch'íntlj by the Navajos which is on the west side of the Chinle Valley opposite the mouth of Canyon de Chelly.[11] *The spring is in the sand at the side of the arroyo and is situated about five miles out from the margin of the Black Mesa whose cliffs limit the Chinle on the west [and one mile from Canyon de Chelly]. There is one stone house, an earth hogan, and two or three summer shelters at the spring which are occupied by three or four families of Navajos who own quite a number of sheep and goats. The ruins are said to be near but no one seems to know where they are and the Navajo, Lorevio, who is to guide us has not yet fulfilled his promise to come to the spring.*

Wednesday, the Eleventh of July

Our informant and guide appeared upon the scene this morning to conduct the expedition to his archaeological gold-mine. The way lay still farther to the West. Down that hill of sand and up another, just as a starter. [Then] over the turning yellow hills for miles, passing one of those peculiar little oases, an Indian corn field, and landing sometime during the forenoon amid tower-like rocks and groves of stunted cedar.

There we halted, and I waited in the wagon while expeditions on horseback were made to various points in the surrounding hills. Their excursions soon convinced my husband that while our friend's imagination was large and active, the ruins themselves were hopelessly "chicito" (small). No keeper of the corner grocery was ever more eager to ply his wares; there were "casa" (houses) nearby in abundance, but when sight thereof was discovered the admission was made that there were none larger than these and "these" were mere toy-houses.[12]

No one seemed to be living there, no hogan in sight, but a small retinue of Navajo were soon clustered around our camp-fire, a portion of them being self-invited guests to dinner. An old squaw and her daughter took their station under one branch of our cedar-tree and enjoyed the cherries left in the bottom of our can. The far-sighted old dame gesticulated her desire to plant the seeds and have big trees grow therefrom but was not encouraged in the undertaking. She was allowed, however, to take charge of the sugar given our host at the spring in payment for water, and thereafter became a silent but interested spectator of the scene. For the company had resolved itself into a serious-minded committee on ways. They sat in a contemplative crescent before the tree. Communication was carried on in three languages, the mutual ignorance of the speakers requiring numerous repetitions and interpretations, beside the assistance of maps drawn on the sand and free-handed gestures in all directions.

An exhaustive (not to say exhausting) treatment of the subject at length reached the ultimatum that neither was the present location desirable nor was there a way out of it except to retrace our steps; the alleged "camino" (road) to Kin Tiel also failed to materialize. If we had been seeking a place of beauty, merely, for our camp, this would have been ideal. A short climb from the sunny little woodland brought one suddenly upon a panorama that held one fascinated; for you were looking down upon a canyon and your first view of this mighty feature of nature's handiwork is very impressive, even though this in itself is but a small sample. The mountain is called Nature's grandest effort; and the canyon is the mountain reversed, as though it had been used as a seal to close the record of some mighty state secret. This impression was in a hurried glance and then our caravan began its weary backward march.

How hot the sand was where you climbed out to walk in it awhile to spare the poor beasts and relieve the monotony! Frank insisted on my feeling of it with my gloves off. This country has been dubbed "Hell with its fires burnt out." That is only the visual impression. The tactile sense convinces you that they are still unquenched and active in summer perhaps, but more or less effective.

The trial of the day came when we reached the spring and had to make the ascent of that unpardonable hill with loaded wagon and wearied horses. All human freight was of course unloaded and I was foolish enough to run on ahead and from the summit watch the equine struggle. I shall never forget it. Crack of the whip, hoarse, frantic cries of the drivers, intended as a stimulant to which the poor animals responded with all that was in them, the mules stolidly, the horses sensitively; every muscle strained, tense, exerted with no apparent effort; crack, scream, a desperate plunge, the white horse leaping in his utmost endeavor, breathless pull and gain of five yards. Down and a rush to place stones behind the wheels. A little pause for hard, quick catching of breath and the operation is repeated for another short gain. It had all the excitement of a football game without the exhilaration of success for the victory was dearly bought and defeat loses its savor when your opponents are only senseless elements. We traveled on some few miles out onto the open plain and made a dry camp that night.

FR: Wednesday, the 11th. One of the old men having volunteered this morning to guide us we started westward toward the Black Mesa where at 10 o'clock we found a small ruin beside a very pretty valley leading down from the mesa. Two corn fields indicated that the locality was probably capable of supporting a small population at least in the old days. The ruin is very near the edge of the Black Mesa on a projecting spur that has the valley mentioned on one side and on the other a stretch of broken country the appearance of which is suggestive of the Grand Canyon of the Colorado. Close to the first ruin is a second situated upon the top of a butte that may be seen for a distance of twenty miles or more down the Chinle Valley. Both ruins are small, perhaps a hundred feet in length, and a third in the same neighborhood is said to be still smaller. There were no traces of walls to be seen and no indication of the position of the burying places. The Indian, Lorevio, who we had engaged to guide us came along after we had visited the sites of the two ruins: he was very desirous that we should camp there (there is a small spring in the vicinity) and make short excursions about the surrounding country which he declared was full of ruins. After a talk of two hours he admitted upon being pressed that none of the ruins were as large as the small ones before us at the time, that all the ruins in the locality were small because in former times as now the water supply was scanty. This notwithstanding the fact that he had said that on the preceding day at Ganado, that the ruins were large and well worth visiting.

While at the ranch he had also stated that there was a road to the ruins in the Blue Canyon some 80 miles beyond that I intended visiting if these [sites] proved to be too small. Now, however, he declares that the road to the Blue Canyon is impracticable and there is nothing to be done but to turn back nearly to Ganado and go to the Blue Canyon by way of Keams Canyon which lies 48 miles west of Ganado.

We have camped early in the afternoon within 7 miles of Hubbell's ranch on the road to Keams Canyon. The horses have been taken in for water. At about 9 o'clock two Navajo boys arrived which Mr. Hubbell had sent out with a barrel of water. Soon afterward the Mexicans returned with the horses and we are now ready to push on to Keams Canyon. A note from Mr. Hubbell states that he knows that there is a road through to our destination past the ruins left yesterday but that the Indian, Lorevio, did not wish to show them to us. At any rate he had the impudence to camp with us last night and to beg for small gifts. He is one of the most intelligent of the Navajos, Mr. Hubbell tells me, and speaks Spanish fairly well.

Thursday, the Twelfth of July

Renewing our journey this morning we reached the vicinity of the junction of the road with the one from Keams Canyon (now our goal) and cut across the plains, thereby saving a few miles, arriving at our new highway early in the afternoon. From this point the men were sent back to Ganado (about eight miles) with the horses for water, while the Russells camped with the wagon.

It was intensely hot. The sun's rays beat down fiendishly upon the fervent sand and poor humanity was caught helplessly, mercilessly, between them. We made ourselves as much at home, however, as we could, our reception was undoubtedly warm enough. [We] unlocked the trunks, got out the typewriter and played around a while. But my environment was clearly getting the better of my stoicism. It dwindled alarmingly and my poor husband found his "frau" "peevish and disagreeable to live with." The situation was becoming critical! Some antidote clearly was needed with an earnest desire to afford relief and a masculine ignorance of the needful remedy my beloved proposed that I get out and make some biscuits for supper. (It was then about four o'clock.) Biscuits! A suggestion to make a bonfire of myself would have been more acceptable!

However, I took leave of the little shelter afforded by the wagon canvas and puttered about among pots and pans getting together a mixture which contained too large a preparation of lard and sand to be palatable, but which were providentially saved from our palates by being burned to a crisp in the Dutch oven. But meantime the afternoon had waned; the sun had the grace to sink away, seeing it wasn't wanted, and the cool breezes of evening freshened up our "too, too tired flesh" and revived our faint hearts.

FR: Thursday, July 12. We left the ruins which the Navajos call Has-tin̲tì-sai at two o'clock and made a dry camp in the Chinle Valley. As there is very little grass in the country owing to an unusually dry season we are carrying nearly all the feed required by our two teams and the loss of two days' time is a serious matter.

I sent Sliver on to Keam's [trading post] this morning with a note asking Mr. Keam to send a messenger out to the First Mesa to bring in a Moki [Hopi] who might give me information concerning the whereabouts of the ruin I am seeking. As I went over this trail two years ago when on my way to the Oraibi Snake Dance I think I can act as guide for the team.

When near the "Fifteen-mile Spring" this afternoon a Navajo came to meet us. He had evidently been informed of our purpose by Sliver for he intimated that he could show me a "big" ruin near at hand. This proved to be the semicircular pueblo described by Mindeleff and known as Kwaituki. It stands just above the spring. Within the last two years the spring has been enclosed and is now used by a large group of Navajos with their herds, so many in fact that it was almost impossible for us to get sufficient water for our horses so we pushed on a short distance before camping for the night.

Friday, the Thirteenth of July

Our doves returned to the ark last night, bearing an olive branch in the form of permission from friend-Hubbell to keep the team as long as we wished, and bringing likewise a new member of the equine family, a substitute for one of the mules which had grown weary in much pulling. This waif, Mulita Blanco, as the Mexicans call her, we at once named The White Rat for the poor little pigmy looked just about big enough to carry her own harness. She evidently realizes that she is out of her sphere for she wears a chronic air of protest and moreover heaps gratuitous troubles upon herself by a general attitude of unamiability to discipline. If she would only imitate her mate, Macho, in his good natured indifference to circumstances and willingness to work when sufficiently urged she would find her condition improved, for the men are kind enough to their beasts, unless provoked. So, with these two, and Bob ("Pahup"), the brown, we fared forth. All day we ambled along and toward evening reached the one mercy of the Arizona traveler, a spring.

Frank had visited this place two years before so knew where to find it but we were further directed by a self-constituted guide who came galloping up & met us and then turned around and paced alongside. He was a middle-aged swell, dressed in the height of Navajo fashion and elegance with corduroy trousers and calico shirt, a dollar's worth of quarters made into clasps for his moccasins, with the usual adornment of silver and turquoise about his person. After a period of silence, he suddenly inquired of my husband, "Where you goin,' John?" That seemed the extent of his English vocabulary, so further exchange of interrogatories was made difficult. We found a swarm of his companions about the spring, with a hogan or two thrown in. These were built underneath a precipitous cliff, on the top of which was a ruin [Tebugkihu, or Fire House]. With the redskins as guide we ascended a very picturesque natural stairway of rock, completed by an outer railing of man's invention and found the walls still standing of a very large "casa." Not worth excavating, however, so we moved on just far enough to get away from the settlement and camped in a cedar grove, the appearance of which was a "sight for sore eyes" after our sojourn on the plains.

[FR: No entry for July 13.]

Saturday, the Fourteenth of July

About ten o'clock this morning we reached Keams Canyon. The first thing that dawns upon your vision are the various buildings of the government school located here. Down the road we saw a beautiful vista, a row of cottonwood trees casting real shade across the street to the low white washed house in an opposite row. Underneath these trees sat some gentlemen, one of whom came to greet us as we approached. He spoke to Frank as an old friend and received me as such also. He was introduced as Mr. Rausch, one of the friends Frank had made during his visit to the Snake Dance two years before.

Mr. Rausch is in government employ, an engineer or something [general mechanic]. He is a German, betrayed by a decided accent, large, loose-jointed and smiling in cheerful cordiality. We were at once taken into his house, where his wife did not wait for a formal introduction, but encased us in her quaint chairs and gave us good cold lemonade—a veritable nectar—before any explanation of our descent upon them was in order. Mrs. Rausch just escapes being petite, and is a lady of snug, trim proportions, light brown hair, rather prominent round light eyes and a peculiar pallor of countenance. Her teeth are much in evidence through her frequent smile, but though rather large, they are white and even. Neither was a search-light required to detect characteristics of her disposition. Her husband was requested to go and get some water with the cheerful assurance of the strong-willed, self-opinionated woman with a knack of arriving at quick, cheerful conclusions and expectancy to have them sanctioned by others. Her confidence regarding this husband and his work in his absence indicated her to be a proud and loyal wife, ambitious both for her sake and his own, not satisfied with their present situation but cherishing an optimistic belief in immediate improvement. Optimism, indeed, carries her along buoyantly, I should judge, except when downed by a quick, impatient petulance at being thwarted in little things. She was interested in our expedition and anxious to make us a visit when we should have established our camp. Meanwhile she lost no time in making a little bag of starch-powder for my complexion, and showing me how to make a chamois-skin face-mask like hers.

After a call, somewhat exceeding fashionable limits, we loaded up to finish that part of our journey, having in the meantime found our mail waiting for us in the P.O. nearby. As we rode on to the store, about five miles and a half farther, I devoured my first letter from home, telling of all that had happened since we left.

We reached Mr. Keam's establishment about noon and were welcomed with the kind of hospitality that pervades the region. Mr. Keam's house looks more like an Eastern cottage than anything I have seen in Arizona, perhaps because it is a frame building, white with red trimmings, with a neat little walk leading up from the woven wire fence and gate, through an attempt at a flower-bed to the shaded little porch. We were ushered directly into a curiosity shop; for here was Indian pottery galore, Moki [Hopi] baskets of every size and pattern, while one wall was covered by a high panel of dolls and idols, framed in ears of corn, no two of which were alike in color. Otherwise this apartment serves as office and living room and bespeaks in its disorderly convenience, the well contented bachelor.

Mr. Keam is an English gentleman whose accent is the more noticeable so far from home; clean shaven and fastidious in dress, though permitting himself the easy attire of a man of fifty, located in the torrid zone. His keen blue eyes, square jaw and suave utterance bespeak the shrewd man of the world who makes his fortune in the desert and spends it in the metropolis. At dinner, which we had alone as the others had finished, we were served by a faded old Anglo-Saxon who had been a soldier, store-keeper and Heaven knows what before he attained his present position as chef in chief: Tea and chicken and mince pie seemed delicious luxuries after our traveling diet of strong coffee, bacon and hard-tack, or something like that anyhow! [He also] served canned fruit and vegetables.

In the afternoon we went down to the store, a much smaller traveling post than that at Ganado, in one end of which were the apartments of Mr. and Mrs. Allen, the assistants. They are a young couple, just arrived at Keams [Canyon] the day before, and of course in a state of domestic confusion as yet, that is as much confusion as could be caused by not much of anything in the way of furnishings. The lady received us kindly but not effusively, a manner due wholly to shyness and not to any coldness on her part. She was a depressed looking young thing, but neat in appearance and with a certain winsomeness about her clear eyes and spiritual brow. But her husband, poor lad, had no brow at all to speak of with accompanying physiognomy to match. But he looked innocent and well-disposed so perhaps the lack of intelligence was harmless. His wife waxed confidential before the end of my two hour call, and when Frank came for me we had finished her past career, social, domestic and ethical, and were upon politics as a safe general theme, personalities being exhausted. She was a rich find to me because of her religion, a devout Mormon and fervent in her faith. Her people had come from Utah, her oldest brother was a traveling missionary in the South; and her own ideal of blissful existence was to live on a nice little farm about a mile from some town up in her native state [Utah].

She was eager to explain her doctrine to a sympathetic listener, for it "was very much misunderstood." They believe in the Bible and accepted every word of it literally; and not in sections as some of the Christians do. In addition, they believe in the Book of Mormon, spoken of by one of the Old Testament prophets and revealed to Joseph Smith. Revelation, they also believe, comes to anyone who is worthy and in need of it.

As to Polygamy, she said that although they of course did not practice it now, as they were law abiding citizens, they still believed it was the right way to live if only people could be made to see it. It was practiced by the old Hebrews and the Bible says, "The Lord is the same yesterday, today, and tomorrow." Her conclusion does not recognize that though the Lord may be unchanged, the world is not, but one must not look for logic in dogma. She also admitted that it would be more perfect and successful method of living if people were more as they should be. "Yet we are all selfish and jealous," she said, "and some feel that they cannot endure it." That appeal was unconsciously not mine. "But if we do endure and do all we can and live as we should, our reward will be all the greater." I asked her if it was not her belief that now since government had interfered and they had no choice but to obey the law, thus making polygamy not a duty but a crime, that this freed her from the call of conscience. Wouldn't her life be happier here on earth and her reward just as great [in the] hereafter? She agreed with me in this and I think her heart of hearts was saying "Hurrah for Uncle Sam."

We employed the hour just before supper in walking back to the school for a little farewell call on the Rausches. Her pleasant little sitting room, primitive though it was, appealed to me after a session in Mrs. Allen's bare, cheerless room. Here was a large table with papers and magazines, a sewing machine, bed, bureau with photographs and knick-knacks, and an old-fashioned rocker. This time my new friend confided to me her literary secret. She was almost an authoress! She had written a novel and was now waiting to hear its fate from the publishing house. It was a story of Moki [Hopi] life, *The Two Kewannis Princesses of Tusayan*. Her own confidence in her success and immediate popularity was certainly as naïve as her expression of it was frank but in explaining her reasons for the hope that was in her, she showed a reasonable formulation; so, she may be the next craze. She outlined the plot for me and narrated her abstracts and triumphs this far, as she and her husband drove back with us to Mr. Keam's [trading post]. After supper, a letter home and a luxurious bath were in order, and an early goodnight as we were to make an early start in the morning.

FR: We reached the Keams Canyon buildings at 10 o'clock where I found that the superintendent Mr. Charles Burton was at Washington and Mr. Rausch, the Reservation mechanic, was in charge.[13] I had met Mr. Rausch before and was fortunately able to obtain his consent to explore ruins on the Moki [Hopi] reservation with the proviso that I secure a permit from Washington as soon as possible. It being understood that I am working in the interests of an accredited public institution.

Now let me explain the circumstances that led me to undertake to reach the Blue Canyon. When at Keams Canyon two years ago I learned from Mr. William Williams whose father once kept an Indian trading store at the Blue Canyon that there was a very large ruin in that region that was in very good state of preservation. It was not an ordinary pueblo but "a big city." As Mr. Williams had seen the ruins and is a man of established veracity I became interested in the story and during the past winter have been corresponding with Mr. Hubbell regarding the whereabouts of the place. I wrote to Mr. Williams also but received no reply. Mr. Hubbell thought that the ruins must be those known to the Navajos as Kin-tiel that are on the north slope of the low peak called Zilt-sah-jini.[14] The Navajos now say, however, that Kin-tiel is a small ruin that shows the outlines of one building, long and narrow, with walls standing to height of a few inches.

In conversation with Dr. Fewkes at New York last week I again heard of this large ruin which Dr. Fewkes states was known to the Mokis [Hopi] who said their people, the "fruit clan," built the pueblo.[15]

Again, when I told Mr. Rausch that I had come to dig on the Moki [Hopi] Reservation he asked me would I now not explore one of the large ruins that had not been examined such, for example, as Mr. Needham had seen when he was taking the census this spring. He had ridden along for two miles and a half and seen ruins. He has seen a ruin two miles and a half in length in the Blue Canyon. Mr. Keam had also heard of a large ruin in that region and showed me a large olla that had been brought down from there by the Navajos. The Navajos who are supposed to know the country thoroughly say there is no large ruin within fifty miles of Blue Canyon. On the other hand, Mr. Williams (who passed part of his boyhood in the Canyon), Mr. Needham, Mr. Rausch, Dr. Fewkes, and Mr. Keam (though the last from hearsay evidence) declare that the ruin exists. I feel justified in making considerable effort to find this ruin for it is possible that the Navajos do not wish me to reach it as they obtain articles for sale from such ruins and may wish to keep white men away from this the largest in the country.

Sunday, the Fifteenth of July

We rode until about ten this morning in the direction of Hano, a Moki pueblo where resided an Indian youth who was supposed to have information useful to us concerning the ruins. While some miles away we halted as the village lay too far to the east to be on our direct route, and the horses taken for water while the men went for consultation, leaving Nosifor to get dinner and me to ornament the drawing room. I passed the hours in alternately perusing the Spanish grammar I had discovered in my husband's coat pocket and which was officiating as a small but well selected circulating library, and in grinning at the Mokis [Hopis] who passed by. There was a family party or two, the women always on burros, the men sometimes walking; children held in maternal arms or sticking out behind according to age.

The Moki [Hopi] is a milder and more refined type than the Navajo; neither so aggressive in his own interests nor so impartial in regard to your affairs. In feature they are broader, greater and more stolid perhaps than their neighbors. They stopped and surveyed us with a mingling of amazement and amusement; one old grandpa coming up to shake hands with me; and then went their way. We traveled toward the north all afternoon and camped dry for the night.

FR: Sunday. Started this morning for a spring 25 miles north of here called To-ga-hal-ta-se. The Moki [Hopi] boy, Percy (recommended by Dr. Fewkes), not having come to Keams Canyon on account of a dance at Hano the preceding day, I went out to a point about 4 miles from the First Mesa and left the wagon stand with its load while I pushed on upon Sliver's pony and while the boys rode the team to water at the Mesa. The Mokis [Hopi] could give no information about the large ruin and little about the road to the To-ga-hol-ta-se spring. We followed an obscure trail to the northward and camped at 7 o'clock. Sliver has searched in vain for a trace of the spring where there are Navajos who presumably can give us information about the ruins. A dry camp tonight.

Monday, the Sixteenth of July

A few hours ride this morning brought us to Togoholtazze spring. Frank and I went on ahead to find it and came into the Rip Van Winkle Dell from above;

by dint of some clamoring we descended far enough to discover a group of the [Navajo] inhabitants, enjoying a morning session in the glowing sunlight, though there was shade enough in the vicinity. It was evident the wagon could not come this way, so we went back, taking a little tramp of a mile or two to reach the lower entrance and found our family then ahead of us, only a few steps from our first landing. We brought up at the back door of a rather pretentious hogan, having the garden enclosed by a stone wall, shaded with cedars and furnished with some real chairs, though the natives preferred squatting on the ground. Our worthy host, Bishapper (or a word to that effect) seemed amiably disposed and listened with interested and inspiring grunts to Sliver's graphic tale of the wanderings of his Aeneas. He had an alert, intelligent old face and seemed quite a patriarch in embryo. After dinner, Frank went off on an exploring jaunt, the boys were set to work on a ruin nearby, and the others remained.[16] I was left with the Spanish grammar and the pistol for company; both were a consolation; the one active, the other potential so that I sought no opportunities for its use.

In the late afternoon our quarters became instantly alive. Our own party gathered in, and also a delegation of Navajo women and children with their ponies and some provisions. A few braves were not wanting to complete the household and its camp were set up forthwith. By means of liberal distribution of stick candy among the youngsters I secured a snap shot of the most cunning thereof though his own expression was not so happy during the operation as before and after.

Meanwhile supper was in process. A fire was built in the angle of a stone wall farthest from the house, meat cooked (our cook had secured a piece of thin mutton for our supper, by the way) and bread baked. There seemed to be a rotation in office in this performance among the several women clustered about. Nor was it done with just the efficiency of the New England housewife. Curled up comfortably in the sand, leaning back lazily against the stone wall, reaching round the baby in her arms, the dusky cook tossed and patted the dough into shape with a leisure and aplomb which her fairer sister would regard more appropriate to the drawing room than the kitchen. However, they all managed to dine on the installment plan before dark, and what more was necessary? Naught remained to do but roll up in blankets and enjoy the taking of "Nature's sweet restorer."[17]

FR: Monday. We reached the spring this morning at 9 o'clock. There are three small springs within a few hundred yards of each other that would altogether perhaps fill a two-inch pipe but they are not enclosed or cared for properly and the many sheep, goats, and horses belonging to the Navajo family that live at the spring are half famished for water.

The Navajo, Pel-a-si-shazzy, said there were four ruins in the neighborhood of Kin-tiel but had never heard of the large ruin. Two other Navajos came in from the north during the forenoon who declared there was no such ruin in the whole region. There is a small ruin on the rock above the spring at To-ga-hol-ta-se beside which skeletons and pottery have been uncovered from time to time by the wind. The Indians said there was some larger ruins ten miles northeast that from their report might be worth excavating.

Leaving the Mexicans [Pena and Garcia] to dig in the burial place I set off in the afternoon with Sliver to examine the ruins that were to be the "largest yet." They proved to be very small indeed and I had a ride of twenty miles [in] a very hot sun for nothing. Another "large ruin" was reported to exist to the eastward but it was "mucho lejos." The boys found nothing during their afternoon digging.[18]

Mr. Rausch told me that the Navajo teacher at the recently established school in the Blue Canyon has seen the large ruins that I am in search of and I shall now make a last effort to discover their whereabouts from him.[19] *As we are nearly out of feed for the horses and the team is getting tired out from dragging a heavy load over rough trails or no trails at all, I shall try to get the teacher to meet us on the road and perhaps save 25 miles of travel. To do this I shall send Sliver with a note to the school tomorrow and will undertake to guide the team myself to the White Cave Spring 12 miles south of the Canyon.*

Tuesday, the Seventeenth of July

Marching orders were given this morning, as the place was not interesting archaeologically, and so after breakfast (the old brave [Pel-a-si-shazzy] regaled himself of our bread and jam) we started due west for White Corn Spring, about 30 miles away. Once in the afternoon water was found, excellent but only enough for horses. It was eight in the evening when we reached the place in the supposed vicinity of the spring when the wagon road ended. Frank had gone on to investigate and reported trails leading presumably to water. The Mexicans [Garcia and Pena] started for it with the horses but darkness overtook them, and they returned nearly two hours later with the news that no water had been found.

FR: Tuesday: Came as near the Spring [White Corn Spring] today as the wagon could be taken and sent the boys with the horses to find it in the gathering dusk at 8 o'clock. They spent an hour and a half in a vain attempt to find water. The horses have been without water since morning and have hauled 12 hours in a burning sun. We have no good water for our own use. What we have is tainted with sheep dung. Canned peaches and very hard dry bread for supper.

Wednesday, the Eighteenth of July

I was awakened this morning by the cool touch of my husband's hand upon my forehead and his announcement that they were all going away, and I would be left alone: Sliver to Blue Canyon to find the mythical man with information; himself and Nosifor to look for water; and Erminio to recover the strayed members of the family [mules and horses]. For Bob, considering this country too much of a desert for himself, had deserted it during the night and made tracks for home and "agua" (water).

The spring was found about a mile up the ravine in a place characteristically unreachable and picturesque and *mirabile dictu*, free from Navajos. Erminio returned about noon with his dispirited horses and Sliver came at night with the report that he found no one at home but two women and they, of course, didn't know anything. We hadn't accomplished much at this place, except as Frank said, to distribute fruit cans around, and I had my first lesson on the typewriter.

FR: Wednesday, July 18: Owing to extreme thirst the horses broke away last night and two were not to be found this morning until Erminio had followed them 10 miles on the back trail. Sliver went on to Blue Canyon this morning on one of the mules so we must remain here another night. Nosifor found the spring this morning within a mile of our camp and we need have had no difficulty if we had reached this point a few minutes earlier last evening.

Sliver made his appearance this morning shortly after 8 o'clock: he had not reached the Blue Canyon yesterday but had wandered off to the northward an unknown distance but from his jaded appearance and the condition of his horse it must have been very far. I had told him to go to a point only about 35 miles distant from the To-go-hol-ta-se spring. He received directions from the Indians at his starting point and from others whom he found on the way. He is an unusually intelligent Navajo belonging to a tribe that is believed to be thoroughly familiar with every foot of this sparsely settled region, yet he failed to find the Blue Canyon school and camped for the night without finding his way to this point as he had been directed to do. He camped without food or water. His predicament seems worthy of mention if only as a warning to whites unacquainted with the country. Sent Sliver to Blue Canyon—36 miles, round trip—to inquire about route.

Thursday, the Nineteenth of July

My first horseback ride today. It was necessary that Sliver's failure at Blue Canyon be retraced, so taking him with us, Frank and I set out to be our own messenger boys. I felt privileged to be given the yellow pony, but soon found the little beast to be afflicted with a severe case of that tired feeling, accompanied by an aggravating unresponsiveness. It required a dollar's worth of pounding to incite five cents worth of speed and when secured it was of the churn-dasher variety that threw your internal paraphernalia into a state of confusion worse confounded, that is by being a novice and abundantly green. The distance was less than twenty miles and we reached our destination before noon, but I have known mornings to go more quickly. The first view of the [Blue] canyon is wünderschöne, and impresses you even though you are occupied in your own weariness of the flesh.

You see vistas and colors, and unnamable shades of colors, in which predominate the blue that gives the name.

Following the winding descent, you come upon the typical long, low adobe house. This is the school, closed now of course but left in charge of an Indian, the man we were after, who had the grace to be at home this time. Not that his presence was of any particular value for he didn't "savvy" any more than the rest, after all; but we had learned that much and that was something. Fortunately, they had closed the school with the back door open, so we went in like three little Golden Hairs [Goldilocks] and helped ourselves to table, chairs, and best of all, a bed with springs in it covered with a sheepskin. This I took possession of and had a glorious loaf. No other bears [were there]; nobody but a nice old cat who snoozed in company, and a Navajo mother with her cherub whom I insisted come in as they passed by. Conversation seemed to languish, however, and they cut their call short.

Later in the afternoon I went with Frank to see the "spring" and found to my delight and surprise a stream of running water! The first for too many days. It was clear, and had a bubbling little spring right in the middle of it where I wanted to bring my dolls and play; but I had to continue my equestrian exercise instead. We started at five and rode till eight, meeting Mr. Keam on the way, who was much astonished to find us in this neighborhood, but gave us some more directions as to a route. We camped in a little cedar grove. The continuous formalities of conventional living are here reduced to a minimum. You drink coffee and eat biscuits and bacon; take off your hat and shoes; roll up in your blanket with a saddle-pillow; and that is all.

FR: July 19, Thursday. Sliver found yesterday that the Navajo who lives at the Blue Canyon school was not at home and no one else could give him the information we need. Owing to his imperfect English Sliver could give no satisfactory account of what he learned or failed to learn so I went myself today as the teams are in bad condition from lack of rest and sufficient feed and should not be given unnecessary work.

I found that the Indian had returned and though he was the man who had accompanied Mr. Needham [conducting the U.S. Census survey] when the latter saw the mythical large ruins he now declares that they were small ones after all! Took Sliver along today as interpreter. We returned as far as a spring that is a short distance off the road about 6 miles above the White Cave Spring but as we had water enough in the canteen for supper we did not go to the spring.

Friday, the Twentieth of July

A ride of three hours brought us to camp in time for a seven o'clock breakfast and an hour later we were on the march again; this time in wagons; bound forth toward Moki [Hopi]-land. We camped near a spring for dinner, which is worthy of mention because it seldom happens. Moreover, we reached water that night. Wepo Spring, where some old Moki [Hopi] houses are situated and one or two occupied habitations. To add to the liquid extravagance a shower came up and we were moistened inside and out.

FR: July 20, Friday. Started for camp this morning at 5 o'clock and reached it at 6:30 AM. After breakfast we turned back on the Keams Canyon road with the intention of going to a ruin that a Moki [Hopi] named Tom Polacca had asserted to be very large and near his house on the northern part of the First Mesa.[20] *We camped for the night at Wepo Spring on the west side of the First Mesa.*

Saturday, the Twenty-First of July

On the hill hard by dwells a Moki [Hopi] of wealth and social prestige, Señor Tom Palaki.[21] It had been declared to us that information of the kind we wanted was lodged in his cranium, to be forthcoming on demand. That, in fact, was why we were there. He was interviewed this morning and seemed to live up to his recommendations. My husband says that we have tested the relative merit of the Navajo and Mokis [Hopis] as liars and are uncertain as to which to award the palm. But it seems to me that a man who can lie fluently and unfailingly in three languages concerning one fact, ought to have his abilities recognized and be known as Capital Liar, the Second to None. (Discoveries made since have led to the conclusion that Tom may have been trying to tell the truth; here we have done him an injustice. We apologize.)

We moved in accordance to his [Polacca's] directions until about ten o'clock when we came upon a parting of the ways where we did not know which part to take. A Mexican was sent out in each direction, but returned in two hours or so with the now familiar report of "Nada" (nothing). So, after dinner, Sliver was sent back to Wepo with instructions to bring Tom back with him as guide. Tom couldn't come on account of a dance, but he sent more directions, in line of which we moved on, until a good camping ground was found.

FR: July 21, Saturday: I visited Tom Polacca this morning but was unable to get him to accompany us to the ruin he claimed to have found. However, he told me in very fair English where the ruin was, intimating that it was actually in sight from the elevated site of his house. He had sent his son after us for the distance of a day's ride when we went to To-go-hol-tas-se so I was the more inclined to believe that he was telling the truth when he described the magnitude and value of these ruins. After giving me the directions, he walked a mile to tell Sliver, in Navajo, which he speaks quite fluently, about the best way to go. While at the wagon he took occasion to give the Mexicans [Garcia and Pena] advice about the way in their own language—which I hesitate to call Spanish—in which Polacca seemed to be quite fluent. I mention these details because he seems to me to be worthy of particular notice as a man who can lie in three languages as successfully as he did is not often met on the road even in Arizona. We went to the place pointed out by Polacca, some ten miles from the Wepo Spring but found nothing. I sent Sliver back to bring Polacca at all hazards. He returned with the word that Polacca was preparing for a dance the next day and could not possibly come but he, Sliver, obtained further information about the ruin that brought us a few miles further on our road before camping for the night.

Sunday, the Twenty-Second of July

Leaving me to play with the typewriter this morning, and the Mexicans to play with each other, Frank and Sliver went hunting. Not very sanctimonious employment for the Sabbath, but effectual, as the wanderers returned before noon with instructions to start the procession at once, as a "casa" had been found. Not the "grande," of which we had heard so much, but large enough to begin work on. We dined on the way and reached our new home in time to get our household set up before supper.

Our 9 x 9 tent is a marvel of comfort and cozy furnishing. It contains a bed, table, five trunks and chairs (i.e., things to sit on). Besides being general store and provisions room. It faces the rising sun and looks down a small valley; the hill holding the ruin bounding us on the north, and another well-endowed with shade trees, on the south; the tent is between two trees, one of which is fitted up as the bathroom, the other as drawing room. Material comforts are, therefore, abundant, except the trifling one of water which must be hauled five miles or so. It comes from a hole in an arroyo, is of a rich, tan shade, and has a soft, warm effect, as to taste. But taste is the minor, sight the major sense in this country.

From the hill-top the view is one to make you forget your troubles; vast rock cliff and mountain defined plains, with the clear outline of the San Francisco Mountains to the west; and no sign of human life anywhere, except a couple of abandoned winter hogans not far away. For our red brethren [the Navajo], be it understood, are in line with *swelldom*, in having differentiated abodes for the different seasons. These winter domiciles are beehive shape, made of logs, and plastered with earth, about forty feet in circumference, and having one opening, a low doorway. Their summer cottages are not much more than semi-circular enclosures, thatched with green branches. In these the women weave their gay and useful blankets, sometimes sitting alone, but more often in gossipy groups, all idle but one, while "the young folks roll on the sandy hogan floor." And they certainly look "merry" if not especially "bright."

FR: July 22, Sunday: Set off with Sliver on horseback this morning to look at the ruin [Hoyapi] which proves to be one of those described by Mindeleff and located in the Oraibi Wash. It is a medium-sized ruin with no water near it. I went back and brought up the team which arrived at 3 o'clock, giving time to pitch camp—the first time in two weeks that the tent has been put up.

Monday, the Twenty-Third of July

As befitted a proper housewife, on a Monday morning, I began my domestic career by doing the family washing. Having put out a whole tree full of clothes, as white as sand and water would make them; I took the Spanish grammar and a nap out under one of my old cedars. What an opportunity to indulge in delicious *dolce far niente*! To be sure the men are shoveling industriously over on the other hill and Sliver is pounding away towards Keams Canyon whither he has been sent with a number of letters, but as for me, my small avocations are just urgent enough to give a zest to dreaming while they wait. It is hard to decide which is the best part of the day, from morn to eve. The morning air and sunshine are like new wine; they give you an indescribable buoyancy and exhilaration. And even when the sun-god rides high and his *panoply* glitters fiercely, there is an unfailing wandering little breeze abroad, like a frolicsome fairy, from "green fields and running brooks" and cool grottos and bringing their freshness with it.[22] Sometimes to be sure, it waxes more sportive and carries off all our possessions that are not nailed down, substituting for them a deluge of sand, but that's only one of its little ways. And as the heat is not so hot, nor the dirt so dirty here as elsewhere, we can forgive it. And if compensation were needed it comes with the sunset; ever marvelous sowing a moderation of clouds and colors each evening; sometimes fantastic, sometimes simply clear, and always fascinating, touched with that wondrous glow.

FR: July 23, Monday: A day's digging about the ruin shows that it will not be an easy task to find the cemetery and that the whole pueblo is not large enough to warrant our excavating very extensively. This being the case I shall send Sliver to Keams Canyon tomorrow to carry a letter to Mr. Williams, who is said to be at Winslow, asking him the whereabouts of the large ruin. We will continue our work here in the meantime.

Tuesday, the Twenty-Fourth of July

[No entry by Theresa.]

FR: July 24, Tuesday: Rising at 5 o'clock each morning we have begun work at 6:30 and, with a two-hour nooning, have continued until 6 in the evening. We have not yet found a trace of a human bone nor an unbroken vessel of pottery. We spent one day in tracing the walls of the side buildings and of the main pueblo. The total length of the ruin is about 400 feet and the breadth is about 200. I have been making a rough plan of the whole measuring with the tape and getting angles roughly with the packet compass. Sliver returned from the post office at Keams Canyon late Thursday evening.

Wednesday, the Twenty-Fifth of July

We've had an agreeable change in diet since becoming domesticated. "Frijoles" (beans) are our portion now and fresh mutton. Sliver made successful negotiations with the Navajo, and we are now living on the fat of the lamb—as well as the more delectable portions. Besides, we have rice and fresh biscuits; that is, they were fresh once, just as every woman has had a youth, presumably sometime! But nothing ever molds or mildews or rots in this country; just dries up and blows away. That fate is the common fate of all. And then, we, the Russells, have some private luxuries that perhaps savor of exclusive aristocracy, and certainly smack of good taste! Notably a half dozen cunning little jars of jam (peach, blackberry, and such); bouillon capsules, meat extracts (which were not, however, what they were put up to be!); and, grape-nuts and shredded wheat biscuits, taken with hot water flavored with condensed cream. The hot water we consider our greatest privilege, for by means of it we can drink two cups of coffee without owing too great an apology to our stomachs for swamping them in the strong beverage indispensable to Mexican cookery; not to mention the English breakfast tea, which we take for supper; made in our cute little aluminum pot. We have a whole set of this material, besides a pair of china cups and saucers!

[FR: No entry for July 25.]

Thursday, the Twenty-Sixth of July

The event of today was Sliver's return with the mail. My share was only The Anamosa Journal and Eureka, but as they contained accounts of the "Russell-Peet Nuptials" they were perused with some interest.[23] The statement that the bridal couple were to spend the summer in Arizona where they would "enjoy their honeymoon and incidentally study ancient Indian life" was more fitting than they knew. The "vacation" is a success whether the "avocation" proves such or not.

[FR: No entry for July 26.]

Friday, the Twenty-Seventh of July

Another equestrian excursion occupied the day. Our Hermes [Sliver] had heard of a ruin some thirty-five miles east of our camp, for which we sallied forth about eight this morning. We had an early dinner in typical rock-and-cedar surroundings, getting some water from our neighbors for ourselves but none for the horses. In the afternoon we passed through the largest corn fields I have seen in this territory. To observe the Indian raising corn would be novel if not instructive to the Iowa farmer. The traveler will come upon a cornfield perhaps once in a day's journey; an irregular patch of most any size, enclosed if at all by disreputable fences of cedar branches or posts stuck together without nails. Sometimes some barbed wire is used. Our Red Brother never plows his corn but he must not on that account let the corn be neglected. Far from it, he waters it by ditching; places a little shade over each individual plant in its infancy; hangs out scarecrows, so like himself that no wonder the raven is deceived; and then builds himself a little shelter nearby where he can sit and watch it grow. Talk about assiduous devotion!

We reached the inevitable goal—a spring—about five o'clock, and never did water taste so good! Though in fact, it was alkaline, and not good at all. But enjoyment is only comparative and dependent on conditions. For instance, one would not in the abstract cite it as an instance of blissful comfort to stretch oneself at full length in a heap of sand and hang one's head over the root of a tree, but this position of repose appealed to me as ideal joy, especially when supplemented by the sound and sight of Sliver getting supper. What is more, we had a good wash later on! Frank and I, descending into the spring (which is deeper than most, enclosed by rough palings and provided with a trough, so that the stock are not paddling about in it as is usually the case) found it deserted. Rejoicing in the solitude we appropriated one of the horse pails and washed face and hands to our hearts content. Towels, of course, not down on the list.

FR: July 27, Friday: Left the Mexicans to work alone in search of the cemetery and set off this morning with Sliver to visit a ruin said to be "mucho lejos" to the eastward. After a rather trying day's ride we camped for the night at a small alkaline spring about 35 miles from our starting point. The spring is like so many others in the Navajo country—fenced in and used to its fullest capacity for watering sheep, goats, and horses belonging to the Indians. The compass indicates that Keam's store which can be seen (i.e., the mesa above it) from the mesa above the spring is directly south of us.

Saturday, the Twenty-Eighth of July

We had planned to see the light and be gone early this morning; but the White Rat balked such ambitious schemes by turning up missing when Sliver went after the horses. He could not break the bonds, but had probably consumed the night in hobbling away to parts unknown. So, we had to take up the role of loafers and scenery observers until half-past twelve when the culprit was ridden home and poor old Bill on whose patient back the brunt seems to fall, led alongside.

The ruin was to the west of us, so we took it in on our way home. It retaliated by taking us in, for it was even smaller than the one we were delving in already.

We attribute its failure to be any good to the fact that it would have been too charming a locality in which to place our camp. The spring is situated in the angle formed by two lines of cliffs, running north and west, the square this enclosed was all wrinkled up into ridges, hills and ravines all roughened with rocks and stumpy growth, on this north wall, crowning it like a feudal castle was the ruin; an ideal spot, and approved by everything except the facts. To the east across a valley, some two or three miles wide, extended the Black Mesa, itself an object that holds the gaze irresistibly, especially in the evening light; and to the south stretched the valley in a long, fascinating vista.

But we turned our backs, perforce, on it all, and went west once more. We camped for the night at the same place where we had dined the day before, the horses having been promised water this time. But a search of over an hour proved fruitless and the poor beasts had had the exercise for their pains.

FR: Saturday, July 28: "The little white rat," or mule that Sliver rides is not to be found this morning and the Indian is off in search of it. Sliver returned shortly after 12 with the mule which had traveled several miles during the night though securely hobbled.

The ruin which we came to see and which the Navajos reported to be very large indeed stands within about half a mile of the spring on the summit of the mesa in a situation very much resembling the Moki [Hopi] pueblos of the First Mesa though I was again disappointed in finding it only a small ruin. Traces of a narrow wall remain that was built to fill a crevice in the rock on which the stone buildings stood. Also, the outlines of the walls of two or three small houses that stood adjoining each other on the barren surface of the rock. Numerous fragments of pottery showed prolonged occupation, the pieces were in some cases of large size and diligent search would doubtless reveal pieces of sufficient size to enable one to make out the designs. For the most part they are of the ordinary "black and white" ware though a few pieces of neatly decorated red ware were seen.

Camped for the night half way back to camp where Sliver promised to find water for the horses but after a two-hour's search returned to report that the pool had been exhausted by the horses of the Navajos. We obtained a canteenful of water for our own use from a Navajo family that had a small patch of corn nearby.

Sunday, the Twenty-Ninth of July

A three-hour ride brought the weary wanderers home in time for a good rest and bath before dinner. Both were acceptable, but the latter a sacred Sabbath duty, for candor compels me to record that my ablutions had been nil since the ones last mentioned, two days ago! Clearly it was a case where cleanliness should come before godliness. But the scrubbing with a fresh toilette throughout solved my conscience sufficiently to allow me to enjoy our Sunday dinner, which was only preliminary enjoyment for our afternoon under the trees. I say trees advisedly, for though you can only get under one at a time owing to their isolated proportions, it is necessary to shift your location at intervals to avoid solar impertinence; for the shade of a cedar is like the affections of a flirt, intermittent and migratory. As recent equestrian performance had left me in a condition to take my meals from the mantelpiece (providing we had possessed one) they were not accomplished with that "softness and sweet attractive grace" which I should have inherited from Mother Eve.[24] Instead I illustrated the evolutionary rather than the theological theory, by reaching the erect posture by a series of slow jolts. But let us be progressive if not in actual navigation, then in exemplifying the most up-to-date thesis.

FR: July 29: Reached camp at 10 o'clock today and found that the men had done some digging during my absence but without result. Rested the remainder of the day for the first Sunday since leaving Ganado.

Monday, the Thirtieth of July

The Frau "was in the kitchen, washing out the clothes" this morning but her doings since haven't been worth recording.[25] My husband suggested that I might shorten the time apart on this record and make it quite as accurate as writing for the first day "Nada" (nothing) and filling in the succeeding days—"Ditto, ditto, ditto, ditto, ditto, ditto—Damn!" But this profane pessimism of his was amid his more discouraging unrevealed efforts to find that mythical, elusive, baffling "casa grande" which leads us on like an unholy specter—not to my diversions and pastimes—so it really ought not to be chronicled in this journal. Craving clerical pardon, however, we'll allow it to stand as an epitome of one's psychical condition under such circumstances.

FR: July 30. Kept the men at work today on the ruin and spent most of my own time digging. Found nothing. The cemetery seems to have been on the northeast side of the pueblo where a few crumbling fragments of a human skeleton indicate the location of a rifled grave, the potsherds are also very numerous thereabouts. The area covered by the pits sunk by those who anticipated us is not large and the cemetery seems to have been a small one.

Tuesday, the Thirty-First of July

July has taken its leave and gone. During its days we've been "'opeful and 'appy." But we hope August to bring us something more tangible.

FR: July 31. Owing to the condition of the teams I have thought it best to hire a Navajo pony for Nosifor and to send him and Sliver with a Navajo from this locality as a guide to look at a ruin known as Kin-tiel that lies some 20 miles to the northward of this point. I remain here to move camp if a letter comes during the three days that the men are to be gone. Besides visiting Kin-tiel the men are to go on to the Blue Canyon to see if there is water there in case we go through it with the outfit. I have learned to place no dependence upon a Navajo report which is to the effect that there is no water there. This seems very improbable as it is one of the largest canyons in the neighborhood and the map shows the presence of at least one spring on a branch of the canyon extending toward the northward.

August

Wednesday, the First of August

A tramp of ten or twelve miles occupied the morning for Frank and myself. Nosifor, with Sliver and another Navajo, all our Indian ponies, were sent to explore Kin-Tiel and the north and eastern part of Blue Canyon, yesterday morning. So, leaving Erminio on guard we went to investigate a ruin reported to be near our water supply. After climbing a hill or two our way lay over lowlands until we came upon an outlook even more wild and picturesque than our present location. The pueblo itself proved to be as large as the one we are working on, and the sample of pottery displayed is much more abundant and various.

In the evening we were surprised by the return of our scouts, whom we had expected to be gone three days. Their findings, according to their report, were all "chicito," so that hope is ended for the present.

Thursday, the Second of August

"The letter that we looked for" from Mr. Williams, not having come, we pulled up stakes this morning and moved to the place visited yesterday. The transition was made and a new house all furnished before dinner. In the afternoon we looked over our new ground. The pueblo was built on a rocky elevation, round in outline, crowned by boulders, the topmost of which is all of one hundred feet from the base of the mound. From this point you get a view worth climbing for. To the north the outlook is domestic in the foreground, the little white tents nestled cozily among the few trees in the vicinity, and nothing more interesting reaches the view until the eye rests upon the delicate, exquisite coloring and irregular shades of mountains bounding the horizon. On the south you face a valley where the corn fields shine with vivid green amidst the neutral tints of sand and sage brush surrounding. This valley stretches in an entrancing vista toward the south, with its cliffs standing grand on either side, and the terraced ends of a mesa just showing at the upper end. Westward the view meets a chaos of rock cliffs and chasms lying in rough disorder over the plain. The rocks near at hand bear testimony to the dwellers of long ago in the drawings, which adorn the smooth surfaces of the largest among them. These boulders are huddled together (if one may use that term in reference to anything so high) in such delightful disorder that one's fancy flits to enchanted halls as one clambers around about, beneath and above and within. For in a room-like enclosure, which was once probably a shrine, are seen the best carvings, circular and geometric designs, birds, cloud symbols and other fantasies. It was their art gallery and speaks with no less significant eloquence because it is crude and simple in expression.

Friday, the Third of August

The passing of the flocks is heralded hereabouts by a most peculiar little patter, the many hoofs in the sand; it suggests the rustling of leaves in trees, real trees, such as grow "on the banks of the Wabash, far away."[26] In the procession the goats are always in the lead, with a promiscuous mix-up of kids and lambs following, and the white, wooly, sheep bringing up a dignified rear. Such a crusade passed through our front lawn this morning; all but one. He was forcibly detained and contributed a fine fry to our dinner.

Saturday, the Fourth of August

Our household suffered a subtraction this morning and we number two less. Sliver felt moved to return to Ganado, principally on account of his pony, which has been slowly succumbing of late and evidently is in need of a hay and grain treatment. The other invalid was Nosifor, whose back-(bone) had given out. He loafed all yesterday until noon and in the evening announced his intention to leave us. He may have been disappointed at the cheerful resignation with which his employer received the news, but as a matter of fact his departure was not so melancholy an event as he perhaps fancied. At all events Frank declared at night that his colleague did as much work alone today as the two of them together had ever accomplished in their best day. Erminio the awkward hasn't a lazy bone in his body; Nosifor, the debonair hasn't any other kind. It was interesting though, that pathetic way of "wiping hypothetical sweat" from his brow and we'll miss a few little tricks like that, but will try and bear up, nevertheless.

Frank sent the train of mules home with him, so our outfit is lessened in every way. In every way except for the "finds" that are accumulating to such an extent that they threaten to turn us out of house and home. The men were fortunate enough to discover the cemetery first thing; and several skeletons have been exhumed, together with a few ollas (pottery), mostly in pieces; and a hat full of small trinkets; beads, turquoise, copper, lead and silver ore, arrowheads and flint knives beside some curiosities unaccounted for. This was all very interesting, and I was glad to be allowed to help, to sift dirt for small valuables, and clean up the vertebrae and things; these were my chief duties. Meantime I learned some things; one being that these Indians were not buried in a straight horizontal position, several feet under the ground, but curled up, perhaps on the side, perhaps in a sitting position, and near the surface. Consequently, the bones are found "all of a heap" and the excavations comparatively shallow, round or square holes, very unlike my conception of a grave.

Sunday, the Fifth of August

The cold wave came our way yesterday afternoon, so I wore my jacket for the first time this summer; it brought showers during the night and settled down for a steady pour this morning. While I read and loafed, Frank packed and catalogued his new acquaintances. We no longer use empty boxes as chairs at meal time, but disrespectfully sit on the bones of the departed. Skulls grin at me from odd corners, and there is a skeleton, not in our closet, but under our table. In the afternoon we played about the ruin, the one upon the little butte. Collecting bits of pottery becomes a fascinating employment. They are strewn thick as sea-shells along the southeastern side enticing one by their bright colors and curious designs. Two schemes seem to prevail; black and white, and reds in all shades, terra cotta, dark crimson, maroon and curious pinks. Sometimes you find a combination of black and red; still more rarely, white and red. The patterns are normally geometrical, but sometimes quite elaborate.

The sun had a new game tonight; it had subcommittees at work in the four quarters so that the entire horizon was "one continuous performance."

"Isn't it gorgeous!" I exclaimed.

"Yes," responded my fastidious, unsentimental husband, "and the gorge goes all the way around!"

Monday, the Sixth of August

The weather behaved herself her prettiest today after her frowns and tears; and our work has been rewarded by the discovery of the best skeletons yet, four in all, but not interred with the desirable abundance of treasures. A black cooking-jar, much shattered and a small bowl were found. The family seems small with only three members, but quite as harmonious and happy as before.

Tuesday, the Seventh of August

Cemetery number two was excavated today and yielded up half a dozen skeletons more or less fragmentary (chiefly more) and twice that number of ollas, large and small. Some bones of the coyote were also found, but the descendants of that tuneful creature do not seem so ubiquitous here as other where. In our last camp we were frequently serenaded, the soloist taking his stand in neighborly proximity and rendering a chorus that would make a chamber concert (or symphony orchestra) seem tame. The hardest thing to believe about this animal, on auditory evidence, is that there is only one of him. He is an accomplished ventriloquist. His favorite tune began with a series of short sharp yelps, succeeded by a plaintive wailing like a lost child, he sings this with more variations than Home Sweet Home ever dared to have. The coyote is not the only vociferous creature in the desert; second to him come the raven with his occasional hoarse croak. My husband says that sound is not reassuring when you have crawled under the shadow of a rock at noon, well-nigh overcome with the heat after hours of pedaling over the rocks and sand; and water twenty miles away, providing you're on the right road; and if on the wrong one—the black vision must have secured in every *Calaeno* with its evil prophecies.[27] That is a glimpse of real hardship, beside which our present outing seems conducted on lines of effete and enervating luxury.

I have observed only one other bird voice; a shrill plaintive note uttered monotonously in one key. It belonged to a plain gray specimen whose name I do not know. The prairie dog speech strangely resembles the chirp of a bird, and the little fellow looks at you with a bright-eyed bird—like curiosity as he sits erect and motionless on his haunches. The other denizens of the desert (the rabbit, the rattlesnake, the lizard and the ant) are silent members. An ant-hill in this region is not a small village, capable of being covered by a tin cup, but a veritable Matterhorn which a wash tub would scarcely encircle and built of shining, hard white pebbles which makes quite a showing as a big highway full of diligent dark liveried laborers.

While Frank and I were bringing in the wood for Erminio this evening (the wood-pile is about a quarter of a mile from the house), I saw some flowers in bloom; a white blossom something like that of the strawberry on a species of sage brush; a yellow flower on a lower plant, and one bearing a tuft of scarlet, very effective in its gray environment.

Wednesday, the Eighth of August

My husband apologized this morning for not having made up our rolling bed before breakfast. His excuse was that he became so absorbed in reading the morning tablecloth while engaged in setting the table, that he grew oblivious of other duties. In our professional labors today, we encountered a baby-farm as we came home at the close of day; bringing in the bones, they were not burdensome, as they included the minute remains of little Jimmie, little Willie, and littlest Tommy and were quickly done up in small packages, together with a couple others ferreted out in the morning. The accompanying pottery was also mostly small fry.

We had a couple of guests this morning, one at a time, and two last night in company. Frank put the latter on record in the Kodak. From the former we learned that the Moki [Hopi] Snake Dance is not to occur for fourteen days yet we had heard that it was to be earlier this year.

Thursday, the Ninth of August

This was our lucky day. A number of skeletons were found, though none in as good condition as those of Tuesday, with a liberal garnish of ollas; include a cooking pot, a very large jar, and a beauty of a red one, and that unbroken. This spasm of success, however, exhausted itself by noon. In the afternoon, after spending some time in packing and labeling, I continued my search for the much-distributed olla on whose track I had been for two or three days. Gluing with flour paste not proving satisfactory, I acted on Frank's suggestion to plant it in a bed of wet sand. This worked very well. I find that my 18 or so fragments fitted together forming what would be a lovely bowl if I could find a half-dozen more pieces. It is half globular in shape with capacity of perhaps a gallon, color, terra-cotta with rather elaborate design in dark brown.

This noon I read the last chapter of the book Frank brought along as our summer library, and which I had been reading aloud in our leisure moments. Its conclusion leaves me in a more interrogatory frame of mind than at any time during its perusal. What does "unleavened bread" signify? Did the heroine continue on her totally self-satisfied career to the end of time? Was her hopeless self-esteem never illuminated by a ray of introspective reason? And will Mrs. Robert Grant please write a sequel and let us know all about it?[28] The Spanish grammar I finished some time ago, though I do not claim to have transfigured its contents totally to my cranium, or the tip of my tongue.

Friday, the Tenth of August

Erminio was appointed mail-carrier this morning, and rode away to Keams [Canyon], taking a letter to Mazie from me (the first one to any outside the family) and some business letters sent by Frank which we hope will bring speedy returns. This departure left the Russell family as completely alone as their ancestors were in the garden of Eden. No loafing, however, permitted in the desert of Arizona, so these descendants of the denizens of Paradise took up "de trowel and de spade" and began the search for the ancestors of their red brethren. Efforts were futile at first, and the attempt was about to be given up and a move made to another place (this was near the first excavations made early in the week) when a tiny little bone came to light. This was a token to persevere, and perseverance was rewarded by the discovery in a short time of a skeleton in very good condition, with three large pieces of pottery, a cooking pot, a water-jar and a meal-bowl; all complete; though of course in fragments. The entire contents of the grave lay in so effective a position that it was thought just to photograph them in place. This means a vast deal of puttering work, getting the remains properly uncovered and in shape; and all that, together with the fussing necessary to put the camera and apparatus in best position consumed the forenoon; but the find was too good for us to begrudge the time. A Navajo came to bring back our horses (Erminio had taken one of the ponies for his trip) found us interesting until the picture taker came into view; then he silently but swiftly hove out.

It must also be recorded that on Thursday, I cooked my first meal since becoming Señora. The frijoles and carved beef were warmed up and the coffee made without a more serious mishap than a slight loss of temper, occasioned by the impertinence of the beans, to fall off the fire and spill over the sand as soon as my back was turned and the insolence of the coffee-pot lid to fall into the pot and carefully to be fished up with facility; but then, when one has such a large stock as Nosifor always had, a little less now and then can be afforded, without diminishing the supply.

Full moon tonight; full as he can stand up before the sun went down. The weird light intensified the vast desolation of the place, relieved only by a faint, intermittent, but cheerful twinkle down near the arroyo, declaring the habitation of a Navajo, the only human evidence in sight.

Saturday, the Eleventh of August

Returns were small this morning and a good share of the afternoon was spent in looking for Bill, who, contrary to expectation, had disappeared and in watching Bob, that he did not go and do likewise. When the Navajo, who had furnished Erminio a pony, came along he was engaged to secure Bob (which required a lasso) and to find Bill. He did both and at moonrise the other wanderers, Erminio and Sliver, returned. They had forgotten to bring our mail, but as they reported favorably of Awatovi, eight miles from Keam's, we decided to make for it immediately. We did not mind so much about the letters.

Sunday, the Twelfth of August

Stakes pulled up and an early start made this morning. We had a pleasant morning ride and shady camp for dinner; but the afternoon traveling was rough and sandy. While Frank scouted around on the pony for the mail, I walked a bit to spare my nerves as well as equine muscles on the hard pulls. After some three miles of pedestrianism I met the equestrian [Frank] at a very good halting place, the residence of Tom Palaka, Esq. I had seen it from afar, conspicuous on the side hill, with a background of sand dunes and a setting of corn and melon patches. The house is of adobe with two windows in front and a round peep-hole between where the door ought to be. But this part of the house, facing the descending sun was deserted, and the family were found around the shady side. Here also were small farm implements, grindstone, etc., and a couple of iron bedsteads with springs. Here they bring their blankets and plop at night.

I was warmly welcomed by Mr. and Mrs. Palaka, the former inviting me to "come in and have a chair." He speaks more or less in four languages. He is one of the aristocrats of Moki [Hopi], a landed proprietor and [it is] good to look at his short square figure clothed in white, a suit of two pieces, and his heavy black hair falling smoothly and in an even line to his neck. His wife, of more nondescript form and costume, could not "speak my talk" but we beamed amiably upon each other and the motherly dame signified her sympathy by pointing over the road I had walked, shaking her head and sighing with an expression of dolefulness. Her commiseration was quite cheering, though not deserved for I hadn't thought of reaching the "point of exhaustion" yet. And a drink of clean water (out of a two-quart pail) was a sufficient restorative. I would to take a snap of the youngsters, especially the youngest who mused persuasively, a genuine "frown study" by the bed post until his pessimistic meditation (there seemed to be no other cause) welled up into a wail and he had to flee to the maternal lap for consolation.

On our departure our host gave us an armful of roasting ears [of corn] from his garden, and sent his boy, a bright youth of about sixteen who has been to school and speaks some English, on with us to show us the way. Small tips were given, of course, for these favors but they seemed to be offered in a true spirit of hospitality. Mrs. Palaka showed some interest in my costume feeling my sleeve, pointing at the scarlet blossoms I had picked on the way and fondling my hair (which I wear braided down my back and tied up with a ribbon, having lost all my hair pins but one which I am saving as a curiosity), exclaiming at each turn "Lolornai, Lolornai." My husband says that being interpreted means "good to look at" but how do I know but what that is merely a polite fabrication on his part!

Keams [Canyon] was too far to reach that night so we camped by the roadside and slept under the mountains.

Monday, the Thirteenth of August

By the time we had finished our breakfast this morning there was no Mexican and no *caballas* (horses) in sight, and we had the pleasure of waiting indefinitely for their appearance (for it looked as though Bob and Bill had played hooky again) or start on ahead—and on foot. The wagon road lay around the southern point of the mesa on our left but there was a short cut over the right of it and this we determined to take. So, leaving Sliver in charge we sallied forth about six o'clock. The distance was supposed to be about four miles and probably was not really more than eight, but so large a portion of it was either up-hill or down-hill, on nice soft sand, on no trail at all, that it was ten o'clock before the weary Russells saw the welcome sight of a white man's settlement. While Frank attended to his mail and business, I read my two letters from home, had a nice visit with Mrs. Allen, absorbed a quart of water, externally and internally applied, and loafed luxuriously on her bed till dinner-time. Mr. Keam invited us to dinner with his family though he himself was just on the point of departing when we arrived. Mr. Thompson proved an entertaining host until our own time came to go. The eight miles between Keams and Awatovi was covered before sunset, but the men had to go back so far for wood and water that we ate supper by the light of the moon and Frank's ruby lamp.

Tuesday, the Fourteenth of August

Before we left the wagon Sunday morning we noticed an Indian hanging around our camp fire, but so frequent a spectacle occasioned no remark. We learned from Erminio later that he was a Moki [Hopi] in the employ of Mr. Owen, sent over to size up our outfit, and that later Mr. Owen himself had called. He is Mr. Dorsey's assistant working for the [Field] Columbian Museum, Chicago, and was intending to move to the Oraibi Wash when he found we had preceded him there. We were suspicious that he would precede us here, in consequence, and were much relieved to find ourselves the first arrivals last night. Relief was followed by amusement when we saw his white caravan, stuck on the sand ridge north of us. He is quite welcome to his situation for although the old cemetery is there it has been worked to death by Dr. Fewkes, Mr. Keam, and others, leaving a small harvest for this gleaner. Not that we would rejoice over the misfortunes of a rival, but since his code of ethics does not allow him to intrude onto another man's preserve (for he knew we were coming here), our religion allows a little fun at his failure. But we were neighbors, and Harvard fired the first salute by making a morning call upon Chicago. We found him at home, alone, and disposed to be nervous at first, and ingratiatingly communicative second and thereafter. He spent an hour or more with us in the afternoon and enlightened us to his past history, future prospects and his wife's pedigree. We invited him to supper and he said he would come if he did not start for the Flute Dance at Mishongnovi anon; as he did not show up we supposed him gone, and consoled ourselves by having pickles for supper, just the same.

Our new camp is located near by the old church, built by the Spanish priests in the seventeenth century and destroyed in the last year thereof by the Mokis

[Hopis]. The bits of wall still standing are quite an ornament to our lawn, and I found them useful, as well, to serve as clothes-lines, with stones for pins. The ruins of the pueblo extend for 1/8 of a mile to the west, bordering on a precipitous cliff that descends into the valley on the south. Across this arroyo-scarred bottom one sees the opposite mesa in jagged, perpendicular lines, the nearest buttes being some five miles away, the outer points two or more. With the wünderschöne light and shadows upon them they look like fairy-land castles.

But the cemetery proved disappointing. Not from lack of skeletons; they could be spaded up by the score; but from their decayed and useless condition. It seems a pity to see such good material utterly wasted, just as is the beautiful but broken pottery strewn around so extravagantly. This is the place to find the famous cream-colored ware. We have secured several specimens, some of them unique and all fine and pretty.

Wednesday, the Fifteenth of August

After a short horseback excursion this morning. Frank and Sliver return with news of a ruin 2 ½ miles from here [Kawaika-a]. During this absence I entertained a visitor, an aged and withered dame, who wandered into the tent; sat down and watched with intent my mending and writing, said she was "sleepy" and put her head on my table for a nap. [Later she] pried about outside and inadvertently got into a bag of bones, much to Erminio's amusement. Helping herself to the water pail and wash basin, she drank a cup of coffee while I took her picture, and finally wandered down to the diggings with me to see what our man Friday was doing. When I took up my knife and went to work on the bones she watched me with amused interest a few minutes and then ambled off. I supposed she had had enough, but behold here she comes back, armed with a spade which she proceeded to use for my benefit. She would uncover the bones and point them out to me, but on no account touch one herself, but finally in her zeal she did pick some up with her own fingers and throw them in my cup. Erminio explained that she must not break the bones up with the spade so she moseyed back to headquarters and got the firestick with which she punched industriously. Erminio followed her and she talked to him like a grandmother and all together we had quite a social occasion.

The afternoon was spent in collecting ollas, mostly in pieces, in the old graveyard, and in photographing the ruins.

Thursday, the Sixteenth of August

Noon today found us moved and established in new quarters, two and a half miles from Awatovi [at Kawaika-a]. After the outfit was started on its way, Frank and I lingered behind with the Kodak to get some snap-shots of the pictographs in the cliffs below the pueblo. An extensive art gallery was found but when the roll of film was filled, the photographers could do no more so we climbed out of the pre-historic halls and stairways and followed the wagon track. The outlook from this place is much the same as from the other, but the camp situation is improved by the presence of trees, the largest and most flourishing we have had. The pueblo was a large one and the cemetery on the side hills has been a rich mine of pottery and bones, but now well-nigh exhausted. The remnants here are the largest we have seen, halves and quarters of ollas abounding; a sight to make your mouth water at their beauty and your eyes to be similarly affected at their lost and ruined condition. As it was we picked up some ten dollars' worth of fragments, and the men cast about for a new graveyard, if, perchance they might discover one. Erminio was offered un peso (a dollar) if he should find it but so far has not been successful.

We were shown a new design in sunsets this evening, gold in the west and purple in the east, with a farewell light on the mountains for one radiant moment.

Friday, the Seventeenth of August

A day of downpour. The men worked between showers during the morning, while I did some typewriter practicing, to the apparent entertainment of an old brave who peered in curiously at the strange performance. In the afternoon Frank and Sliver took their horses and went to "buscar" (look) around the cemetery a bit.[29] I spent time in patching up some ollas, the pieces of which had been left in a heap under a tree in our front yard, by a party of Navajo, probably, who had rejected them as no good. Frank collected enough scraps to make a very pretty one, quite complete, last night, and today I put three more in shape so that the design at least could be seen.

The hunters returning reported five ruins. Three small and two large ones. The first of the large ones had been worked even more thoroughly than this one, not even potshards and bones being left, but the second about seven miles on seemed hopeful; it was situated near Jeddito Spring. So, from Awatovi to Jeddito there are seven ruins, four of which are good size, lying along the mesa in a NE direction; the Moki names are . . . [text blank, but the sites were Awatovi, Kawaika-a, Chakpahu, Pink Arrow, Nesuftanga, Kokopngyama, Lululongturque].

Saturday, the Eighteenth of August

The search for the undefiled, undiscovered cemetery having been unrewarded, stakes were pulled this morning and our house built upon the banks of the hill just above Jeddito. The pueblo lies along the crest of the hill, with the cemetery on the slope. The place may be identified by the presence of cottonwoods, a clump of them, on the hillside north of the burial place. In the shade thereof looked a likely place for internment, but our shoveling revealed nothing. The bones found further south were disappointing, too near the surface and [in] too poor a soil for preservation. Some pottery was found mostly of the black and white order; none of the yellow ware, characteristic of the neighboring pueblos. Flint flakes and chalcedony cover the ground like shells on the sea-shore; a lot of such dainty and unusual coloring it is a constant temptation to fill your pockets as you stroll along.

My husband came by way of Keam's [trading post] on pony and reached the place just after our arrival; his pockets full of mail, soon taken possession of. The letters were so convenient to help pass away the time while waiting for dinner. My share consisted of three home letters, one of July eight having traveled quite extensively around the territory (that's the fashion out here!); some prints of Hotart's taken in the last day of June; the home papers and some forwarded mail. Acknowledgements of announcements from Gertrude Howell and Mary Tilstrom, announcements of Ed Lornase's marriage—how those youngsters do pair off!—and a letter from a Kappa sister, Georgiana Cummings, who writes because she liked my remarks in the past Key and hopes to meet me at Radcliffe next year. No more Radcliffe for me, thank you, though I will be glad to welcome the child to my Cambridge home, and hope our sisterhood may lead to friendship.

Frank's communications were not too cheerful; one of them at least, for Professor Putnam enclosed a letter from the Indian Department of the Navajo saying it "could not consistently" grant the representative of Harvard's University permission to excavate on the Moki [Hopi] reservation. This [word illegible] but mysterious virtue of consistency must have been developed since the desired papers were issued to the man from Chicago! However, there is small regret in leaving a place that yields small returns.

Sunday, the Nineteenth of August

"Nothing to do but work" today and dig we did all of us, even to Sliver, though our spades and trowels, turned up nothing of value, except half-a-dozen ollas and things; not as bad in themselves if there had only been more of them. Photography of the place completed "the day's work."

Monday, the Twentieth of August

As Mr. Burton, Indian Agent was expected home Saturday, we expected our day of grace would be short, and since the Moki [Hopi] Snake Dance was to take place at Shungopavi on Second Mesa, it was deemed advisable to take the whole outfit to the middle mesa. At [this] point we would be 20 miles on our way to the Colorado Chiquito where we decided to spend the rest of the summer.

We reached Keams [Canyon] before noon and enjoyed his hospitality again for dinner, together with his other guest Mr. Ohrman [Vroman], photographer, and Dr. [no name], a friend of his, out for his health. They were on their way from the dance at Oraibi, which took place yesterday, to Holbrook, nearest R.R. station. After lightening our load nearly 300 pounds by storing everything but the necessities of life we drove on to the First Mesa. On the way we met more parties returning from Oraibi, people from Keams [Canyon] and a *Chicago Post* man. In the settlement at the foot of the mesa we found Miss Abbott, the field matron, who invited us to spend the night at her house. We spent a social evening with her and another guest, Mr. [Edward] Curtis, photographer from we didn't know where.[30]

Tuesday, the Twenty-First of August

The mesas of the Mokis [Hopi] are three, First, Second (or Middle), and Third; lying parallel with each other and to the north and south. Their pueblos are seven, as follows: on the first, Walpi, Sichomovi and Hano; on the second, Mishongnovi, Shipaulovi and Shungopavi; on the third, Oraibi, of about 1000 inhabitants, as many as all the others together.

Their famous annual ceremony, the Snake Dance was held this year at Oraibi on Sunday, Shungopavi on Tuesday and Shipaulovi on Thursday. The time fell just right for us to attend the second of the trio. The program opens with a foot race at sunrise, but being only so far as the First Mesa we did not see that part of the performance. Instead we spent the morning more profitably and pleasantly in a visit to the three pueblos, lying just above our camp, and all occupying a space less than a half a mile in length, each with a camera (according to our size). We made a short tour through the quaint and foreign-looking villages, which with their narrow alleys, their balconies and flat-roofs, filled with droopy idle gossipers, their front doors festooned with rows of dried corn and garrisoned by the ubiquitous burro assisted by coops of noisy chickens, make the visitor feel much more as though he were wandering in the old world than treading on American soil. Each village is really one dwelling, with the populous street on each side, these flanked perhaps by smaller sheds and the like which form a sort of parapet; for the mesa is narrow and its descent sheer. Many accidents are said to occur from falling and the mothers watch their little ones closely. Hano is the first pueblo and here a different language is spoken from that of any other place; they are of different stock. Sichomovi is the smallest, but here I snapped some of my best shots. I found both the young and the very old very susceptible to stick candy. In one hand I carried the Kodak and in the other the holder full of the delectable bribe; as the one filled, the other emptied, until my cartridge was filled up. Then I ceased playing Lady Bountiful.

Walpi is situated on the end of the mesa, with not much room to spare. Here my husband saw the Snake Dance two years ago riding 700 miles on his bicycle for that ceremony.

Owing to the arroyo that beset our path it was later than we expected when we reached the Middle Mesa. We dined on the way and pulled in at the place of residence of Mr. [text blank]. We found them about to start and we were informed to hurry. I started on foot and was well up on the trail, a distance of a mile or two, when I was commanded to halt and wait for the burros. My husband was elevated on one and an Indian on the other, the latter dismounting when they came up, and indicating that I was to take his place. It took the two of us, however, I to ride and the Navajo to impel the lazy little beast. By dint of much lashing both with whip and tongue, seasoned with frequent kicks we managed to keep moving, our progress being more picturesque, if not quite expeditious, as my preceding pedestrianism. As an experience just to add by one general versatility some twenty minutes of burro isn't bad to take, but I could not conscientiously commend it to the ambitious equestrian.

By and by we came to the place where everybody got off and walked or climbed, up Nature's precipitous stairway to the top of the mesa. On the way was a cunning little spring in a sequestered cave of rock. I had a good drink there from out of my husband's hat; passing that way on the return we were just in time to see a graceful Moki [Hopi] slipping out from our water pitcher which he had just used as his bath-room. He was attired in brown skin, and completing his scrub by washing his face, making his mouth as a wash bowl. Its capacity was remarkable. No Chinaman, squirting water over shirts in his laundry could hold a candle to him.

Up in the village we found quite a number of pale-faced visitors. Miss Collins and Miss [text blank], missionary and field matron, took care of me and presented me to some of their Moki [Hopi] friends. In fact we were upstairs enjoying the hospitality of an Albino when the ceremony below began.[31] We flew down the steps with our slices of pale pink melon in our hands (for Indians never allow their fruit to ripen if they can manage to eat it all green), ran across the court in the rear of the first half of the procession and calmly watched and feasted on the other side. At the upper end of the court (or street) about [text blank] feet wide stood the altar, a large box or something, draped and banked with branches of cottonwood. In front of this the dance took place.

All I had read and heard about this event was a preparation for it, but not it. Nothing can substitute the actual sight. In attempting to describe it I derive consolation from the experience of Jerome at Oberammergau.[32] The Passion Play had been told of so often that there was nothing left to say; and besides any attempt to put such a thing in black and white is futile and inadequate, but fortunately, after all, nobody ever pays any attention to what you say so it doesn't matter much how you put it, you can't do very much harm. However, I will record as best I can, the thing as I saw it.

At the opposite end of the court, the entrance, are the kivas, or sacred rooms, underground, reached by ladder, and jealously guarded. Sometimes the pushing photographer manages to crawl in but he is never welcome and often put out as unceremoniously as he came in. Here the priests dress and perform the preliminary rites; and from this point the procession starts on its solemn march to the farther end of the court. There, country men (most of them) watch the scene from the upper balconies, windows and flat roofs, thus, leaving the plaza quite free for visitors. And, as they were not numerous, it gave all an excellent opportunity to use eye-cameras and note-books. In fact, the spectators seemed as busy and active as the performers. My husband kindly took charge of our Kodak, leaving me free to look. I looked and I saw first the Antelope priests, fourteen in number, ranked according to age, from the gray-headed grandfather to the six-year-old cupid, with his bow and arrow bigger than himself. The priesthood is a hereditary aristocracy and the youngsters seem "to the manner born"; the dress and decorations were uniform. The lower part of the face is black; arm, and body ornamented with painted lines in black and white; colored shirt and waist scarf, said to be woven expertly for this occasion; feathered head and moccasined feet. Each man carried a rattle in his right hand, which he clicked unceasingly.

Directly in front of the altar was a hole in the ground, covered with a branch; over this passed the line of march. Each man stamping the ground with his right foot and shaking some sacred meal out of his rattle-box. The line formed into a circle and marched around three times, continuing the stamping performance, until the regular rhythmic thud had keyed your senses up to an expectant pitch. That wasn't the object, however. It was to call the attention of the spirits in the underworld to the ceremony, which is merely a prayer for rain, uttered with as much devout faith as ever a New England Pastor felt his beseeching for showers of aqueous blessing. Then the Antelopes ranged themselves side by side in a line between the altar and the board, facing the street, up which were advancing the Snake priests, of equal number and in same order, but more elaborately arrayed. In addition to the black and white paint there were literal dashes of paint all over the body, and all over the kilt. In the back hung a fox skin around the right leg, just underneath the knee was fastened a turtle-shell which rattled effectively with every step. Each man carried a rattle. After the circle march, like the others, they form in a line opposite and facing them, join in the chant, accompanied by swaying of the body, arm and leg movements and that suggestive rattle.

Presently one of them seems to crawl under the altar, reappearing with a bunch of snakes. And the next thing you saw was the circle of snake priests, only this time they were marching two by two, the one inside holding a snake in his mouth and his companion with his left arm around the neck of the snake bearer, teased the reptile with a feather held in his right hand and kept its tongue from playing too near its bearer's face and neck. Behind the two comes a third, alone and empty handed, but presently finds an occupation.

Around go the trios with their peculiar dancing step while the line of Antelopes chant monotonously, rising now and then into shrill cries and broken by abrupt, breathless pauses, during which the dancers halt and stand with one foot upraised until the chorus is taken up again and its march renewed simultaneously. Then you see a snake crawling on the ground, dropped from some dancer's mouth but his freedom is not for long, for the empty-handed member picks him up and carries him in his hand. This dropping and recapturing of snakes goes on for some time, while more are brought out of the altar box, until one man may have quite an armful of pets. The boys seemed even more fearless than the elder ones, and it was observed that the smallest member had collected the most snakes. The women assisted in this part of the performance by throwing out handfuls of sacred meal from bowls they held. They all advance a little way down the street and form in a circle, outlined by a sprinkle of sacred meal. Into the ring go the snakes, all them in a promiscuous heap, the dancers in after them and there is a swift game of grab. With as many snakes as he could get each man rushes out and away to set the reptiles free that they may go and tell the gods about the rain prayer. Those who got no snakes (there were three of them) had then to march around three times and stamp on the board as in the beginning. After this lonesome sort of booby-prize they marched away. The others fell in line and the whole procession passed back to the kiva.

That was all except for an after-show near the kivas, which anyone may witness who has stomach enough. Each and every priest had taken a strong emetic; and for the next few days there is a free-for-all feast. We lingered while chatting with other visitors; a party from Chicago traveling overland from the Grand Canyon for health and amusement; and some local celebrities.

Frank had the honor to receive a communication from Mr. Burton, requesting him to call and show his official permission to excavate on the reservation, but as we were already leaving it was deemed sufficient to send the agent a statement of the fact. It was exasperating to see how unmitigated a fool a man can make of himself, but after all, the maneuvers of our friend Mr. Owen, who wanted to be courteous and conciliatory all round, was alone worth the price of admission.

Wednesday, the Twenty-Second of August

Just plain plodding all day; and that over trackless sand, for the road from the Second Mesa to Burro Spring [to the southwest on the Oraibi Wash] kept itself coyly out of sight until we were within a mile or two of the latter place. Here we found a Moki [Hopi] house, with one lone man but plenty of water, wood, and corn for our poor old caballos. Frank had walked nearly the whole distance to spare the beasts, and I had tramped most of the forenoon and a few miles in the evening. The Moki [Hopi] asked us if we were Mormons; he also commented that my peridot [birthstone] was "lolorivas."

Thursday, the Twenty-Third of August

Another plain plod, but over a very good road, bringing us to Mr. Enderly's store about sunset.[33] Our Moki [Hopi] host of last night was sulky because we hadn't invited him to eat supper with us; so he had to be pacified the whole morning by a bid to breakfast (which he accepted and did full justice to) after which he accepted a knife, fork and spoon, a can of apricots and one of peaches, in return for his hospitality, besides which Erminio made him a present of Chola and her five puppies, who having arrived in the night, were much too youthful to set out upon their pedestrian peregrinations.

The store was about as dreary as a looking [illegible word] and its proprietor as laconic as an individual as one ever meets even in Arizona. But under my husband's blandishments he soon warms up and proves quite agreeable. His establishment consists of himself and a couple of Japanese servants. I was shown into the parlor about eight feet square furnished in Navajo blankets (about thirty of them), but after a few moments of solitary stuffiness I took to the woods. Yes, there were actually some cottonwood trees about.

I never want to see another such sight as our jaded old plugs were when they finally pulled in. They were utterly played out; especially Bill; last night it was Bob. Supper was cooked in the little basement kitchen, and we camped in the lot nearby.

Friday, the Twenty-Fourth of August

If in need of an exhilarating tonic, allow me to prescribe for you Mr. Enderly's buckskin pony and a stretch of twenty miles over the plains from his store, down the side of the mesa into the valley and on to the Colorado Chicito. Any morbidness or melancholy nuisances that may be moldering around in your brain will sail away into the clouds like a witch on a broomstick and you'll be convinced that life is worth living, for the rest of that day, anyhow. You'll also be ready to do full justice to the good dinner you'll get at Mr. McAdams' store, the site of your morning's ride.

Our poor old Bill was plainly played out this morning and too sick to budge an inch. So, getting a pony from the Navajo for Erminio and two from Mr. Enderly for ourselves, we left the outfit to recuperate if possible while we did a bit of reconnoitering. The view in the Colorado Valley is different from anything we had seen so far. Behind us the many tinted mesa. Before us the fringe of cottonwoods marking our destination, with the mountains looming up in the background and all around us the vastness of the lava-strewn plain. Here I had my first view of the demon of the desert, a mirage. We were not perishing from thirst and so were able to appreciate the beauty and interest of the enticing looking sight but how it must seem to the enchanted traveler.

We crossed the river at the mission station, which looked very inviting as we rode up, with its new building and white tents clustered under the trees, and a woman in a blue dress sitting sewing on the porch. But it looked less inviting as we rode on, having been directed laconically on to the store by the woman in blue who did not find us as interesting to look at as the shirt she was mending. We learned at the store—some three miles down the river [at Leupp, south of Sunrise]—that she was the wife of one of the missionaries, Mr. Ray, and was somewhat unbalanced; she has lost nine children and has one left. Mr. Ray was loafing about the store when we reached it, an old fatty, illiterate, but communicative enough for the whole family. He had been adrift for years until the Lord called him to the Navajo vineyard, where he is associated with his brother-in-law, Mr. Johnson.[34]

We did not reach the store until about two-thirty pm and our Mexican, who had lost us on the way, didn't show up for an hour or two after that. So not much more was done except to lay plans for the next day.

Saturday, the Twenty-Fifth of August

Frank, Mr. McAdams and Erminio were off this morning to "buscar" (hunt) around the neighborhood, leaving me to amuse myself at the Ticuday (store).[35] Mrs. McAdams is visiting her mother at Los Angeles so I had only Mr. [name blank], Mr. McAdam's nephew and clerk, for company, besides a shelf-full of books I found in the little 6 x 12 sitting room (which we also used as a sleeping room, bringing in our own blankets. Our host offered us his own bedroom but we didn't want to turn him out of house and home.) So, I took Conan Doyle, Kipling, Jerome K. Jerome, and some odd magazines down under the trees by the river bank and we spent a very delightful forenoon together.

About the middle of the afternoon my young host began to get dinner, expecting the wayfarers to be home by the time it was ready. Meanwhile I sat on one of the little wooden benches that serve as sitting room chairs and cultivated his acquaintance while he made bread and boiled potatoes. I found him a bit slow and shy, but amiable and responsive, and we had a very good time.

We dined all by ourselves, for our wanderers did not return till evening, and reported that they had dined at Mr. Diamond's, who has a large cattle ranch about ten miles west of the river. They had not found what they wanted, however; there are some ruins near Mr. Diamond's, but they would like to work them out for themselves, for the pottery. Frank had made Mr. McAdams the proposition that they work "on share," that is, together, and if they found anything, he to take the ollas and leave us the bones; but of course, neither of them would want to poach on another man's preserve. The Chicago outfit had been all through this country, and Mr. Williams with him, but we hope to find something they missed.

Sunday, the Twenty-Sixth of August

My husband's birthday. The naughty boy did not tell me of it till night, but it shall have first mention in the record. I knew it was about this time for it occurred during his visit (the first day of it, in fact) to Anamosa last summer, but I was foolish enough to forget the exact date. But hereby I have it in black and white. It was not a very satisfactory birthday, for he was away all day, with Mr. [name blank, nephew] this time, for Mr. McAdams being unaccustomed to riding was laid up from yesterday's trip. Erminio was sent back to Enderly's with his ponies and a horse of Mr. McAdams to take Bill's place in case he was no more.[36]

My day was spent much like yesterday, except that I had a different host. Mr. McAdams is a very interesting man, of athletic build, and a reserved, almost short, manner, but genuinely kind-hearted and of great common sense, so that when he does speak he says something. He has also been in the North; spent a few months at Cape N. H. [in the Arctic region] so that he and my husband had something in common and could compare notes.

This morning a free circus passed through our front yard and crossed the river, a procession consisting of four wagons with what looked like so many families, men, women, children, but I was informed it was only one, a Mormon and his wives, going to Utah.

Monday, the Twenty-Seventh of August

Frank and Mr. McAdams took another ride this morning, but were back by noon. Afternoon my boy took his shovel and me out for a little stroll. I took a nap on a nice clean sand bank while he dug up some suspicious looking spots and then we started home again. In the evening we sat out in front of the store where it was cool and our host told us Indian stories; one was an instance of how he was offered a Navajo wife, and another a story of a young squaw with two children who had been deserted by her husband and forced by her family to marry a man she didn't like. The next day her first husband returned, but because she had spent one night with the new husband he would have none of her. Her grief was something pitiful to see. In the midst of his narratives we saw our Mexican returning and—delectable vision—other horses, old Bill ambling peacefully alongside and seeming quite restored and in his right mind. Thanks, be!

Tuesday, the Twenty-Eighth of August

We became migratory again this morning. I had made myself quite at home at the little tienda on the banks of the Rio, even to the point of washing the dishes and cleaning up the kitchen so that I felt quite domesticated again. The two Señors went ahead on horseback, and by noon had come upon some ruins that looked promising. We had dinner, dug a little but found nothing; photographed the walls, and moved on. But I must not omit the mention of the fine musk-melon we had for dinner (and another that was "saved up") a Mr. McAdams treat. Frank invested in a watermelon which we ate then, and ordered the Navajo to leave the others in our wagon when he met us. He did it all right, though we were somewhat surprised to have fruit thrust upon us until we understood that "il Americano" had paid for it.

Along in the afternoon we met Mr. McAdams returning, and he told us we would find our stopping place just a little way on. Having had some experience with "little ways" in Arizona, I did not note the fact that we were traveling miles onward until sunset was fairly on us. Then I clambered out and ran on ahead to look for el Señor. But the plain was deserted as though no mortal had ever been near it. Just as old Sol sank out of sight I told Erminio to stop and come back with me to the tracks—foot prints I had been following but had lost. We found them finally and traced them into the river and were then as lost as ever. The boy went back to the wagon and I followed slowly and was surprised to find him turned around and coming back. When I asked why (as I had told him we would camp there) he pointed to the campfire gleaming away up the river and explained it was Señor Russell. So off we started, I, trudging on ahead in my impatience, for it was now dark and that fire might be five miles away. In fact, it was about four, as I learned later, for after running on a mile or so until both wagons and fire were out of sight and I was about giving up the lonely hunt, [when] I met my husband, hunting us. It seems he was at the crossing, about half-mile from the road and the other side of the river. He supposed, of course, our driver would know where to turn off and was surprised as well as exasperated to see him plod right by and on, in spite of all kinds of signals made to attract his attention. So, we had traveled those weary miles and late supper, all for nothing. "What fools these mortals be!"[37]

Wednesday, the Twenty-Ninth of August

We pulled straight across the [Little Colorado] river this morning from our camp and turned the horses loose. The mule Mr. McAdams had let us take was not equal to the emergency when we got stuck in the mud, so old Bill was put in the harness for ten minutes to help us over. He is having a vacation these days, and getting a much-needed rest. Frank then took the mule to go after his saddle where he left it last night and to explore the region; Erminio set out on foot to buscar, after I got back from climbing the hill nearby, and I took care of camp.

The family were reunited at noon, which I took the opportunity to do my long-neglected washing; and in the afternoon the boy was sent on the mule to look up the [word blank] ruins, while Frank and I kept house and made biscuits for supper. The wind was blowing such a gale we had to make the fire in the shelter of a bank down the river. This was mildly exciting but somewhat inconvenient to have the kitchen seventeen furlongs from the dining room when you are your own cook, but we got plenty of fresh air and exercise if not much supper. Those biscuits ought to be sent to the Museum! They would be received as specimens of ancient Indian stone housewares, and would be much more valuable as a curiosity than as article of diet. But my chivalrous husband never breathed a syllable about the biscuits his mother used to make, and more than that, he generously gave Erminio the impression that he himself was the author of those iniquities, when in reality I was responsible for the whole thing. If any wife has a story to beat that, bring it on!

Thursday, the Thirtieth of August

The ruins Erminio saw were large but had been all worked out; so, we started down the river this morning, intending to work at some small casas (houses) Frank had seen. At a short distance after our first halt (where we took nothing but pictures), a mile or so above the crossing, we saw some ruins [Homolovi] on the mesas along the river on both sides. Frank and I crossed the [Little Colorado] river while the boy [Sliver] climbed up on the west side. Our hopes were raised by the sight of eight different casas, the walls still standing enough to show the outlines, and stone stuck suggestively in the ground nearby. When I came upon Frank, after photographing the walls on the next hill, he was working away at what looked like a walled-in grave, and had already unearthed an olla. But that was all and that only a fragment there by accident. The "grave" was nothing but a "cache" where they kept their corn. However, there were plenty of sand dunes—fine for toboggan slides!—and perhaps here they left their dead. So, we dug away all the afternoon, a weary and thankless task, for the bones refused to turn up.

Friday, the Thirty-First of August

Eight more casas [Homolovi II] on the other side of the river; so large a settlement must have some "muerta" [human remains]. I think myself they all blew away. Anyway, the wind made such a howling maniac of itself the men could not work: The dust was intolerable. So, we sat down and held a family council. Our Mexican [Erminio] grew confidential and told on Nosifor. How he and not the Indian [Sliver] had lied to us about the road at Slohali [name unclear], and how they had slept half a day on the Blue Canyon trip [see July 18 entry]. What knaves these mortals be! So, our little manikin is largely responsible for our serious disappointment.

September

Saturday, the First of September

In the third month, on the first day of the month, we set our face homeward. We carried little away with us from the Colorado Chiquito except some enlightenment concerning the geographical and archaeological condition of that district, a small collection of disappointed expectations, and a number of pictographs caught by the Kodak, besides some larger views of the future. One important find had been made: the kivas are in front of each casa indicated by a circular depression in the ground. One of these Frank began to excavate yesterday and we remained to finish clearing out the corner of it, while Erminio took the wagon down to the crossing, a ride below. Then we cut across and met him on the other side. The kiva showed very good workmanship, the wall being very even more regular and smooth than those of the houses, while in the sides disclosed were two little cupboards, square and very neat, but alas as empty as that of old Mother Hubbard; and we wanted a bone worse than any little dog ever did!

If we had had more time and a good team we should probably have gone on further instead of turning back; for there were ruins west of us in the mountains. But we knew not where and had no guide. [There were] ruins south of us on the [Red] Mesa above the canyon, but inaccessible by wagon and [there was] an uncertain water supply. [They] could only be worked in the winter. [There were] besides ruins near Mr. Diamond's [ranch], but they wanted those [to dig the ruins themselves], and ruins near Mr. Schulz, already tagged by the Chicago outfit.[38] Moreover, our Mexican [Erminio] told us of a ruin twelve miles from Ganado which he knew contained *wesos* [*sic*]. If we decided to [we could] spend the rest of the time on that and go on to Canyon de Chelly.

Frank had a plan for our return trip which he thought would save us a day or a day and [a] half. Instead of going around by the stores about sixty miles south, [then] east, then north again, he thought to cut straight across the plains due east along the Nebito [Dennebito] Wash to Burro Spring. This road branched off seven miles [west] from McAdams' [store at Sunrise Springs] and we had his mule. No Indian could be found to take it back for us, so my husband started with the animal well packed with the tent, a sack of flour, bag of beans, and half a dozen cans of fruit which we wished to barter (á la Mormon [*sic*]) for our friend's good offices and for the sake of lightening our load.

So, we turned off to the right while he went on, giving him the prospect of a twenty-five-mile tramp before overtaking our camp at night. But on this night of all others it must needs rain and wet-blanket our plans. Erminio and I traveled until sunset, I walked a good deal of the way along the arroyo in the hope of finding water as a result of the recent rain, but it was as dry as though it had never heard of H_2O. We were about to halt, anyway, for darkness was hard upon us and thunder muttering, when I discovered the treasure shining in the bottom of the wash. I called to the driver to come and see if it were not "aqua." "Oh, no," he replied in the disdain of surprise knowledge, "no aqua, no nada aqui."[39] He jumped off, however, and came to the bank. His first exclamation, "Pridras" changed to the more hopeful one, "Quien sabe?" as he ran down the bank, and the next thing was "Oh mucha aqua" "in accent of joyful surprise." This heartened him up wonderfully, for with aqua, the horses "no vamos" in the night and "no cansados" in the morning.

But supper was barely ready when the storm was upon us. I told him [Erminio] to build a fire on the little hill nearby for the wanderer's beacon light; and ate my tortilla and drank my teas while leaning out the wagon to watch for attempts at kindling a blaze. He had to leave it, however, to pull in the wagon cover and make it snug and dry inside. Then he took the remains of his soaked supper and crawled inside to eat it. We lighted our little candles and smiled grimly at each other over the situation till the deluge let up a little, when I asked him to try the fire again. He was more hopeful this time for the flames shot up brightly only to be smothered soon by another downpour. So, there was nothing to do but lie down in the blankets and listen to the rain between naps. And no fervent revivalist ever inquired "Where is my wandering boy tonight?" more anxiously than I did. For he must be out somewhere in the storm, with not even a coat to keep him dry. And on our ninth anniversary, too! What a celebration!

Sunday, the Second of September

When I peeked out at daylight this morning I saw a gray world, but no rain, and Erminio's bed on a hillock nearby looking like a drenched chrysalis. That was all I saw. But presently a familiar hortatory ejaculation to old Bob clinched the whistler's identity, and next came the boy himself, driving up the horses as cheerfully as though he had been to breakfast. He hadn't, however, and that was the first thing he inquired for. Whereupon the household hustled. I did not deserve my lord's commendation of "What, up and dressed already?" as I had not been undressed and the Mexican [Erminio] had jumped out of his chrysalis with a wild-eyed expression at the unexpected matins.

We journeyed on all day, over trackless plains made heavy and bad by the rains. A stretch of clay bottom, almost the only escape from sand in the whole territory, which would have been like a paved highway in dry weather, was made so sticky our poor horses could barely pull through. During the morning Frank tried to get a little sleep to make up for his loss of last night. It seems he came within two miles of us, and if the night had been clear or if our beacon lights had been set on a high hill he would have reached us easily. As it was, having no guide or clue of any kind, and fearful of passing by us in the darkness, he had made his bed in the sand until morning. He built a fire and warmed up a sand bank, wherein he crawled but it took so much time hustling out for wood to keep the fire going (he burned half a cord of sagebrush during the night) that there wasn't much left by which to keep dry and enjoy it. But if the elements think they can fool with him any then they have stuck the wrong man.

This morning while trying to recuperate a little our driver added insult to injury by selecting the roughest, bumpiest, and most horrible piece of country and driving around in a circle. So that when Frank awoke to look after things, he found the wagon headed due south for the river. To get lost with the red mesa looming up before him, plain and constant, for a guide and landmark was a preposterous piece of foolishness. It lost much time and horse strength, both precious at this stage of the game. Consequently, we weren't much of anywhere by night, and pretty much played out inside.

Monday, the Third of September

Frank and I walked onto the [red] mesa [Painted Desert] this morning with the Kodak intending to climb it and get a view and perchance stumble on a ruin or so. As we approached the red wall that had been staring us in the face [for] so long, [we] began to make out corners, contours and turrets, lines and profiles of wonderful and surprising beauty. The echo was something worth traveling miles to hear. A shout would be answered four, five, even six distant times, each one more distant and fainter than the last. One fancied he was around Die Walkurie. Our climb to the top was rewarded by a view of true Arizonian fascination. Plains that teach one the meaning of vastness, bounded far, far away by mountain peaks and mesas that show what is meant by beauty of lines and color. Our mesa was of a deep rich red, with narrow strata of white at wide and rather regular intervals, so that you looked at high buildings of many stories, overtopping Chicago's sky-scrapers, or perhaps some grand cathedral. Frank says the real thing in Europe is not so grand, but with the organ pipes outside; it was all simply wünderschöne.

But the view included no wagon; so, finding a place to descend we walked back a mile or two and found the outfit stranded in the desert in front of the sand hill that led up to the point of the mesa toward which we had been set as our goal and beyond which lay the path that led north of the spring. The poor old animals were utterly played out; Bob especially was the image of incarnate despair. It is hard to tell with that old sinner how much is "can't" and how much is "won't" but it was certainly a hopeless looking sight. It was noon by this time and fortunately there was a good pool of some water and some green grass freshened up by the rains nearby. So the harnesses were pulled off, the patient ponies told to "go to grass," and we had dinner followed by a council of war. As a result, Frank walked over to Enderly's [Red Lake] store (ten miles) to see if he could get a team there and returned in the gloaming on foot and whistling with the news that at noon there had been four teams at the tienda, but when he reached there, none. Three of them were on their way to the store at Oraibi and it was thought we might get one of those.

Tuesday, the Fourth of September

This morning early Frank dispatched Erminio in search of caballo [horses]. He was to get a pony of the Indians and ride to Oraibi 20 miles with a note to young Mr. Scholy, son of the owner of the store, asking for one of his teams. We occupied the day playing with the scenery and echoes, and making frying pan bread for dinner.

Wednesday, the Fifth of September

Adam and Eve had Paradise all to themselves again today. And what with fetching wood and water, driving the horses to fresh ponds and pastures, new palavering with Navajo guests, reading of the Spanish prisoner, and cooking frijoles it came to pass that the Red Mesa did very well as a XIX century garden of Eden.[40] (N.B. This isn't the variety of garden where you gather fresh strawberries and green cucumbers from morn till dewy eve.) And it began to seem quite like home, sweet home.

Thursday, the Sixth of September

Ditto [from the previous day] until about the middle of the afternoon, when, having cleaned house and packed things snug, the "inmates" sat down in the library for a season of waiting for something to turn up. Nothing did, however, except a Navajo, who rode up on one pony and led another. Dismounting, he came up to the wagon, gave a commiserating grunt at sighting the castaways, and then leaning on the front-end gate proceeded to stare at everything in sight after the manner of his tribe. Frank remarked that he had good looking horses, and I was for striking a bargain with him but my husband thought best to let him alone and returned to his Spanish. Whereupon our Sphinx-like visitor fished a note out of his pocket and handed it over. It proved to be from Mr. Scholy, dated at the Navajo corn-field, and saying that this man would take us to Keam's [trading post] for ten dollars.[41] He was directed to hitch in quick, while I shipped out for our horses, grazing about a mile away. It seemed good to be on the move again, and to reach a settlement where there were people, if only Indians. We came to the corn fields about sunset and found our Mexican [Erminio] there with a letter from Mr. Scholy explaining why he could not let us have one of his own teams.

Friday, the Seventh of September

Having reached that luxury of Arizona, a real live road, we made a respectable day's journey with the Indian's mules and camped under the shadow of Middle Mesa. I secured several snapshots of the hogan and it inhabitants in the morning, winning favor by a bribe of green ribbon and pink satin collar! In the evening Brother Vahee called upon us giving us another dose of apology and confidential explanations of "just how it was." But he sold us some corn. We could get none of the Mokis [Hopi] so we forgave him.

Saturday, the Eighth of September

From the Second Mesa to Keam's trading post. In order to gain time Frank turned into a pedestrian soon after dinner, about nine miles from the canyon. I did not venture to go with him as he walks four miles an hour, but I slipped out when he did and trotted along behind all by myself and came in about an hour later, just in time to help a little with the cataloguing and packing before supper. In the evening there was a fine bunch of mail to devour: three letters from home, one from Mac and one from Susie. My husband received the lion's share, of course, but among the letters was a lot of bad news. His father and mother were at the point of death; no particulars so we do not know just what to expect.

Sunday, the Ninth of September

We expected to get off this morning but packing takes time, and though we began before breakfast we were barely through when the dinner bell rang. That McKinley pie of Jimmies' was worth staying for, though. Our collection filled seven coffin boxes and one smaller one, and was left to be shipped out from Keam's trading post. Here we met Mr. and Mrs. Gates, the Arkansas people [currently living in Pasadena, California], traveling for health and pleasure. Mr. Gates confided to Frank his own fondness for archaeological work and his intention to make a collection for some university in case he could not get a permit to do it for himself. Of course, we pricked up our ears at that and are in hopes to enlist his interest in our Harvard.[42]

Monday, the Tenth of September

By noon today our old Bill and Bob, who were put in the harness yesterday afternoon after a week's vacation, played out again. They could have pulled us through if they had had feed, but there was none at Keam's and the little Mr. Gates kindly spared us was finished for dinner. And Ganado [Hubbell's trading post] was twenty-two miles away. A Navajo who had dropped in informally to take dinner with us, agreed to furnish us a team of mules, providing he could find the one which had strayed. While he went off to "buscar" we drove on. Soon a bright idea came to Erminio. He went back to the Indian's house to bring, if bringable, [words missing] while we drove on to the spring, three or four miles down the road.

There are two ruins near this spring [Steamboat Springs], which we stopped to reexamine, until the Mexican [Erminio] came, but without mules, [for they] "could not be found." It was then about four o'clock. The horses were unhitched, Bill saddled and bridled, and the driver set forth to reach Ganado that night, while we camped and explored a little. We were first opposite "Steamboat Canyon," a high rock, much resembling a battleship. On the side of this is one ruin and "Arrita la mesa" is nearby, the other. Pottery abounds and that of fine quality and superior workmanship. The place certainly looks hopeful.

Tuesday, the Eleventh of September

We have hunted all day, but the earth refuses to yield up her bones. In the afternoon I took a note to Mr. Gates, who was to come along today or tomorrow, that the spring was about a mile up the cañada to the left, and we were about a mile up the main road. Would they please come and camp with us? When I returned our Navajo friend of yesterday was in conference with my husband. He said there is "nada aqui" but "mucho wesos" at a ruin nearby. He agreed to come in the morning and take Frank to the place. Before leaving he asked for the little glass jam-jar (empty) that we had thrown out on the ground. He a chief of wealth and distribution, for his apparel was rich, much silver and turquoise and he had been to Washington.[43] But an Indian will take anything; old Sliver carefully carried home my abandoned gloves, belt and collar, and Frank's worthless umbrella. Our Red Mesa man picked up the old brown skirt I had hung over the little ruined wall where we camped to add to the scarecrow force.

Wednesday, the Twelfth of September

When Erminio returned last night with four mules and a package of mail he also brought a note from Mr. Hubbell, saying that he and his family were about to start for Albuquerque—where they will spend the winter—and that if we came right in we could all go to the R. R. together. This was a disappointment, as it meant giving up prospects that were just beginning to brighten, but "ours not to reason why" in this case. We started about eleven—most of the morning we spent in chasing up runaway mules—and reached Ganado in time for a good bath and change of toilet before supper.

Thursday, the Thirteenth of September

We spent the day at Ganado, repacking our trunks, settling accounts, investing in some Navajo work—one blanket and five spoons—visiting and having a little breathing spell before moving on again. This silversmithing by the Indians is rather a new departure and though crude, quite interesting. The daughters of the house of Hubbell have each a leather belt set with silver disks, valued at $20.00. Señorita Adele gave me a pretty little bracelet "to remember her by," but I should never forget Ganado, even without a tangible reminder. Señorita Barbara was home this time, but Lorenzo, Jr. had gone back to his school in Indiana. It must also be recorded that on this day I wore my white gown, the first time it was unfolded all summer. Truly feminine frills and furnishings are at a discount in Arizona.

Friday, the Fourteenth of September

The Gates outfit arrived late last night and were camped on our front lawn when we arose this morning. They were going on to Canyon de Chelly and Mr. Hubbell offered us a conveyance if we wished to go. It was a great temptation, but as they would want to take more time than the four days we could spare, and as we were all ready to start for Gallup, we finally decided to go on and leave that excursion for some of those sweet days, by and by. Frank left his camera with Mr. Gates, so we hope to see the canyon by photographic proxy.

As it was 10:00 AM we were off, our four little mules on such a brisk trot that the iron chains of the harness jingled like sleigh-bells. But they had need to, for it was a long day's journey to Fort Defiance and the team, having had no food or water at noon, began to play out before their labors were over. On they trudged, however, urged forward by Erminio's frantic and agonized cries to "Gee up!" accompanied by a lively flourish of his old cowhide lash, until [we saw] from the crest of a little hill where the old Indian fort is located.

We were coming this way, though a few miles farther, on the invitation of Frank's friend, Mr. [George] Manning, a gentleman from Virginia, who with his wife had entertained the lone wheelman in their party at the Snake Dance two years ago.[44] They have the store and P.O. at the fort, and a very cozy little house, besides. It seemed luxurious to us to be shown in a room where there was a piano, a pack of cards and a box of bonbons, to say nothing of cozy curtains and cushions. A number of friends dropped in in the evening and the social chat with some music by our hostess, made us feel that we at least had our face set toward civilization again. But yes, the excellent supper was cooked and served by a Navajo.

Friday, the Fifteenth of September

[No entry by Theresa.]

Saturday, the Sixteenth of September

When you have to hustle out and dress to board a train at 3:00 AM, you sympathize with Jerome who "had no idea there were such times in the morning."[45] You don't have a very vivid idea of it either and once established in your seat as you doze off again, until daylight when you begin to pass the Indian pueblos, and the women and girls come running down to the train with pottery and fruit for sale. When you have By and By you reach Albuquerque and get off for breakfast, and then you are ready to sit up and take notice. All day the train whipped by Indian and Mexican villages, where a glimpse of a gay blanket or huge bunch of crimson chili against the gray adobe, gives the somber-hued landscape a vivid flash of color.

Monday, the Seventeenth of September

We awoke in another country this morning; mountain and mesa, dark skins and pueblos had vanished and in their place were the cornfields and homesteads of Kansas. After a good breakfast—our last meal at a Harvey House—we settled down for the day, tho' we couldn't settle together, for coming from the sleeper to the day coach we found the latter nearly filled. Nor could my husband "settle" for long at a time, for at every stop he made a desperate effort to discover the C. M. and H. P. folder.[46] One ingenious agent owned up that "he [had] never seen one in his life" but most of them were "first out." We had the hour between five and six in Kansas City and sent the telegram [to her family in Martelle] then; paying day rates in order to insure promptness.

Tuesday, the Eighteenth of September

When we awoke this morning, we were pulling into Cedar Rapids, so there was a great scramble to get dressed before we reached Marion where there was a twenty-minute stop and we were to get breakfast. From Marion it is only half an hour to Martelle where I expected to see my family. As the train slowed, we chased up the length of two chair cars and eagerly scanned the crowd at the depot. But we saw no familiar faces. The place looked as strange as though we were 1000 miles from home, instead of 10. There was a moment's halt, and the train steamed on, while we walked back again. It was a miserable, dirty rainy morning, too, which afforded small objective relief for the disappointment. We had no note paper with us, so I scribbled a note on some telegram blanks, which was mailed at Savannah.

It was touch and go at Chicago, no time for lunch and no chance to get any until the dinner was put on after six o'clock. But when it finally came, spiteful old Fate upset my little insides so that I merely took my seat at the table, and then suddenly vanished, and the place knew no me no more!

Wednesday, the Nineteenth of September

From Chicago we came on the Grand Trunk through Canada, reaching Toronto for breakfast. They gave us an hour to get it in and we found a nice place. I ordered my husband's prescription of cantaloupe and milk toast, and felt like a new woman after swallowing it. We reached Montreal for supper, where they were even more generous and gave us two hours.

Thursday, the Twentieth of September

Our train pulled into the North Station at 8:10 this morning and after a breakfast in town we took a car for Cambridge. We didn't hear any organ grinder playing *Home, Sweet Home,* as we went up Mr. Milner's steps, but that was because none of that musical fraternity realized what a great event was taking place. Nor is a little dose of domestication hard to take, after all. Still I fancy [that] a nine-month accumulation of juicy steaks and fresh fruits, of daily newspaper and gowns en traine, of gossip and theater, of trolley cars and Harvard Square will not be sufficient to tarnish the haunting memory and majestic influence of sand and sagebrush, tortillas and frijoles, of camp and caballos, of Sliver and Erminio, of the agua that was always "very lejoy," [*sic*] and of smiling skies, so that by next June the organ grinder may play "Someday I'll Wander Back Again."[47]

Appendix B. Collections

Table numbers refer to the corresponding chapter.

TABLE I.1. Frank Russell 1898 Photographs in NAA MS 4086

Community	Photographic subjects
Jicarilla Apache	**Archaeological Sites**: Cliff dwelling no. 3; outlook from Cliff dwelling no. 2, taken to show position of rock carvings **Portraits**: Unidentified Jicarilla men (2); two men in partial Native dress, one man with bow and arrow standing outside a tipi; portrait of unidentified man holding gun with girl; Gunsi Vigil, interpreter, taken in July 1898; Juan Vigil, "one of the few Apache who habitually wears trousers"; Kul-twi, Vascendo; another Vigil family member; So-tlin, the elder medicine woman; Grover Cleveland during San Antonio festival race, taken September 15; Reuben Quintana as runner awaiting start of San Antonio festival race, September 15 **Ethnographic**: Jicarilla houses; brush shelters and lodge poles; San Antonio camp; branding cattle at Vigil's camp **San Antonio Festival at Dulce**: No-ye and guard; racetrack; runners on march to begin a race; in-line dance before engaging in race (3); views of race from Dulce to Boulder Lake on the reservation, September 15; bread being thrown at end of race; crowd throwing food at end of race; unidentified Pueblo people visiting during festival (21) **Sarah B. Moore Portrait Negatives**: Unnamed men standing outside wood-frame house (4); Garcia and his brother-in-law in partial Native attire standing outside a wood-frame house; Jose de la Crus in Native attire on horse with his wife (wife died in March 1896); Treuclio holding gun and knife with wife in Native dress with blanket; John Lee and John Tomas in Native attire outside wood-frame house; Trucha and wife in Native attire outside wood-frame house; Lee Case in Native attire outside wood-frame house (3); group of young women wearing blankets standing outside in the snow; unidentified girl and infant outside wood-frame house; unnamed woman processing hide with child outside wood-frame house; unnamed women in Native attire standing in front of blanket (3)

Navajo Reservation	Archaeological Sites: Pueblo Colorado, near Hubbell Trading Post, Ganado (2)
Hopi	**Portraits**: Unidentified man; portraits of unidentified individual children at Oraibi (8) **Village Scenes**: View of entire unidentified village; street scene; chimney made of jars, bean patch, fields; mesa east of Oraibi, view from the plain east of Oraibi; view of Sichomovi from the south; view of First Mesa focusing on Walpi from the east
Jemez	**Portraits**: Group from Jemez and goods they had traded from the Jicarilla Apache, taken on Jicarilla Apache Reservation
Nambe	**Village Scenes**: View from the west, northwestern angle of the principal plaza, Nambe church; kiva
Sandia	**Village Scenes**: Views from south showing adobe houses and oven (2)
Santo Domingo	**Village Scenes**: View from east; views of children running away from Frank and his camera (2); views of plaza in the village; street (2); fences and field to north
Tesuque	**Village Scenes**: Plaza facing west showing the only two-story building in the village; beehive ovens in plaza and on rooftop, ladders, drying racks, trough and house

Note: Number in parentheses indicates number of photographs of similar subjects.

TABLE 1.2. Jicarilla Apache Artifacts Collected by Frank Russell in 1898, Peabody Museum Accession 98-15-10

Object Type	Specimens	Native Names	Catalogue Nos.
Baskets	Cylindrical utility basket jars with side handles (2 large, 1 medium, 1 small, 1 oblong)	In'-sai-i-zis	51914–20
	Oval coiled utility basket, fishing creel style with lid	Klu-ge-bi-in-sa-i-zis	51921
	Coiled basket tray (2 large, 2 medium, 1 small)	I-se-i-nas-ka-i	51922, 51924–28
	Coiled basket bowl		51923, 51929, 51931
	Twined wicker utility basket		51933
Ceramics	Micaceous jar with flared rim; pitchers	Koc-klic	51934–35.1
Clothing	Men: Pair of plain cloth leggings with side ties, beaded and fringed leggings; pair of old boot-style moccasins; beaded moccasins, various sizes	Is'-kle, Ke-ewt-tsun'-das-lai-in; It-zi-i-ta-ke	51909–13
Containers	Rawhide cylindrical case to hold *cerema*	Pe-sis-ta-a	51893
	Beaded rawhide paint stick case	Tsa-wi-sia	51903
	Long triangular beaded rawhide bags with fringe and metal cone jinglers (2); painted plain leather pouch (3)	Jatl'-wi-zis; Tcig-wi-zis; Kles-tso	51900–01, 51905
	Badger skin tobacco bag with red cloth ties		51908
Horse equipment	Braided rawhide horse whip; halter	Ot-tzis-ti	51895, 51907

Musical instruments	Beaded wooden flute; engraved lead pipe flute		51896–97
Ornaments	Beaded hair ties (2 pairs)	Kla-tas-la-yin	51898–99
Peyote, religious equipment	Fan with mirror in handle; bundle of deer hoofs strung on leather	Pe-a-ti-yoti-in-in; Pin-ke-e-gatl	51892, 51904
Pipes	Carved ceramic pipe	Na-tas-tsep-se-hi	51906
Raw materials	Yucca root (3)		51936–37
Tools	Grooved stone axes (2)		51937
	Arrow shaft straighteners and polishers (2)		51938
Weapons	Arrows with iron points (6); painted arrows with iron points and feathers (6)	K'a-k'as-tun, Ilt-tci-nia-na-ndla-ya, Ta-nac-gwo-ja	51888–91
	Sinew backed bow, painted blue; oak recurved bow		51886, 51887
	Stone-headed wooden club, beaded	Hati-i-ancin	51894
Non Jicarilla-Apache			
Hopi	Portions of wicker basket from cliff ruin		51940

Note: Linguistic information provided by Russell in original catalogues housed at the Peabody Museum. Blank cells indicate he did not provide any information.

TABLE 3.1. Identified Major Archaeological Sites the Russells Visited and Collections Obtained for Peabody Museum, 1900

Site	Dates	Human Remains	Objects collected according to Russell catalogue
Has-tin-t-sal	July [illegible]1	Field notes or collection record: none	No items listed
Tehugkihu (Fire House)	July [illegible]3	Field notes or collection record: none	No items listed, only photographs taken; "not worth excavating"
To-ga-hol-ta-se rock shelter	July [illegible]6	Field notes or collection record: none	No items listed
Hoyapi (7-Mile Ruin)	July [illegible]2–[illegible]6	Field notes or collection record: none	No items listed
Kwaituki, ruin 1	August [illegible]–3	Field notes or collection record: none	No items listed
Kwaituki, ruin 2	August [illegible]–6	**Russell osteology catalogue**: adult skeletons Nos. 114, 122, 134, 147, 150, 152, 173, 182, 198, 207, 216, 221 **PMAE inventory**: partial remains of skeletons Nos. 179, 204 **Field notes or collection record**: Adult skeleton No. 24 and "family of 3"	**Stone tools**: 2 abrading stones, bone awl **Ceramics**: perforated pottery sherd ornament **Associated burial materials**: (A) stone and shell beads, bone discoidal bead, projectile point, bone tube, chipped blade fragment; (B) black cooking jar with No. 24
Kwaituki, ruin 2 (undesignated location different from previous entry)	August 4–6	**Russell osteology catalogue**: adult skeletons Nos. 22, 28, 29, 31, 86 **PMAE inventory**: partial remains of skeletons Nos. 25, 35 **Field notes or collection record**: no information	Not listed on object inventory as separate category

Kwaituki, ruin 2, east cemetery	August 7–12	**Russell osteology catalogue**: several skeletons (includes Nos. 76, 79) **PMAE inventory**: partial remains of skeleton No. 47 **Field notes or collection record**: no information	No items listed
Kwaituki, ruin 2, southeast cemetery	August 7–12	**Russell osteology catalogue**: portions of adult skeletons Nos. 49, 55, 56, 57, 58, 60, 71, 80 **PMAE inventory**: o**Field notes or collection records**: adult skeletons Nos. 60, 76, 71, 49, 80, 86; 3 infant skeletons	**Ceramics**: bowl, jar, sherds **Associated burial materials**: (A) 2 bowls, jar, 2 sherds, box of seeds, ceramic jar, ceramic bowl fragment, complete ceramic bowl; (B) sherds, bowl; (C) jar; (D) cup, sherds; (E) sherd; (F) sherds; (G) with skeleton excavated on August 10: 3 cooking pots, water jar, meal bowl (photographed in place and published in *Out West*); (H) with babies: miniature pottery, unbroken red jar, coyote bone
Awatovi (no area specified)	August 14	Field notes or collection records: none	**Ceramics**: ladle handle, 4 rim sherds, ceramic bowl, ceramic 2 disks **Bone tools**: 2 bones
Awatovi, ruin 1, near old church	August 14	Field notes or collection records: none	**Tools**: 2 arrow points, carved stone, 4 awls, 8 small stone hammers, 3 mauls **Ceramics**: 4 cream-colored sherds, portion of large vessels showing meander design, 3 ceramic ladles **Misc.**: toy olla, 2 toy redware vessels

(*continued*)

TABLE 3.1. (*continued*)

Site	Dates	Human Remains	Objects collected according to Russell catalogue
Awatovi, outside ruin 1	August 14	Field notes or collection records: none	Cut bone
Awatovi, ruin 1, surface of cemetery	August 14	Field notes or collection records: none	Shell, crystal, olla
Kawaika-a (Mishiptonga, Kawaiokuh) [referred to as Awatovi, ruin 2]	August 14–15	**Russell osteology catalogue**: postcrania of at least two individuals, including skeleton No. 149 **PMAE Inventory**: none **Field notes or collection record**: 12 adult skeletons; portions of 6 skeletons; 2 juvenile skeletons; portions of 2 juvenile skeletons; jaw pieces; skull fragment; dog skull	**Stone tools**: 5 hammers, grooved hammer, pendant, stone bead, stone cylinder, knife, rubbing stone, hammer, polishing stone, 3 flint knives, flint flakes **Ceramics**: 4 small mortuary vessels, ladle, perforated pottery, corrugated cooking pot, 2 bowls, pottery fragments, ladle handle, piece of perforated pottery, piece of worked pottery, pottery disks **Bone tools**: bone cylinder **Raw materials**: crystal, crystal, 4 pieces of minerals **Associated burial goods**: (A) piece of copper ore, cut stone, and 8 turquoise beads; (B) knife, shell and turquoise bead found with one jaw, portion of polychrome ceramic bowl, portion of ceramic ladle, small clay vessel, copper bell, 15 arrows, and knife point with an adult skeleton; (C) black-on-white pottery vessel,

			beads, cup, and bowl; (D) knife and awl; (E) 2 stone hammers; broken vessels; (F) ladle, bowl, 2 small olla, flint knife, flint flakes; (G) broken ladles (2), polishing stone; (H) cup; (I) cup; (J) broken bowl, broken cup, small bowl; (K) bowl, bowl fragments found with juvenile skeleton; (L) grooved hammer; (M) cup, broken cup, worked bone, polishing stone; (M) cooking pot, bowl, portion of bowl, corn; (N) vase, broken bowl found with portions of a skeleton
Kawaika-a, east cemetery	August 14–15	Field notes or collection records: 2 adult skeletons; juvenile skeleton	**Associated burial goods**: 2 corrugated and decorated vessels **Stone tools**: 2 rubbing stones
Kawaika-a, house	August 14–15	Field notes or collection records: adult skeleton	No items listed
Kawaika-a, southeast cemetery	August 16	Field notes or collection records: 3 adult skeletons; 5 juvenile skeletons; portion of skeleton	**Associated burial goods**: (A) cup, ladle, corrugated vessel, flint, perforated stone and ornaments; (B) large olla, large bowl, 3 cups, olla with seeds, vase, matting; (C) miscellaneous animal bones, corrugated vessel, small vessel, red bowl; (D) bowl, pottery figurine, disk, and gorget; (E) animal head; unassociated cup

(continued)

TABLE 3.1. (*continued*)

Site	Dates	Human Remains	Objects collected according to Russell catalogue
Chakpahu (Bat House) [referred to as Awatovi, ruin 3]	August 17	**Russell osteological catalogue**: portions of 2 skeletons (Nos. 156, 162); skeletal portions (Nos. 92, 102, 103, 133, 141) **PMAE inventory**: no remaining skeletons **Field notes or collection records**: portions of skeletons more than 5 bones	**Ceramics**: 3 ladles, 2 bowls, 2 vessels, cup, 32 sherds, clay figurine, portions of 6 broken bowls, broken cup, 2 whole broken bowls, 4 bowls, cup, small ladle, bird vase, portion of a ladle, number of pottery disks, small olla **Stone tools**: 4 stone hammers, grooved hammers, 3 smoothing stones, gypsum crystal, 4 abrading stones, 8 flakes, flint flakes, obsidian flakes, ladle handle, stone object, fossil shell, pottery bird's head, 2 ornaments **Raw materials**: copper ore, piece of worked pottery, fragment of burnt pottery **Misc.**: 9 bone awls, 5 worked bones
Pink Arrow (referred to as Awatovi, ruin 4)	August 17–18	**Field notes or collection records**: 2 portions of skulls; 11 femerae; 3 humeri; radius; ulna; 6 tibia	**Ceramics**: 4 bowls, cup, 4 broken bowls, bowl fragment, 3 ladle handles, pottery disks **Stone tools**: stone hammer (largest size), flint flakes, obsidian, 3 grooved hammers, 6 hammers, 2 smoothing stones **Misc.**: bone awl, wooden object, 2 small ornaments, bird's head
Nesuftanga (referred to as Awatovi, ruin 5)	August 1[illegible]	**Russell osteological catalogue**: 2 skeletons (Nos. 156 and 162) **PMAE inventory**: none **Field notes or collection records**: 2 portions of skeletons	**Ceramics**: 3 bowls, 2 cups, fragment of thick pottery, ladle, 3 bowl fragments, portion of ceramic ladle, portion of clay figurine **Bone tools**: 5 bone awls, 4 pieces of worked bone, bone tubes

			Stone tools: flint flakes, smoothing stone, 2 rubbing stones
Kookopngyama (referred to as Horn House and Awatovi, ruin 6)	August 18–19	**Russell osteological catalogue**: 9 adult skeletons (includes Nos. 93–97) **PMAE inventory**: partial cranial remains of 2 individuals and fragmentary post cranial remains **Field notes or collection record**: humerus, ulna, 3 femerae	**Ceramics**: Jeddito black-on-yellow jar, 10 partial bowls, sherds, toy objects **Stone tools**: 2 ground hammerstones, rubbing stone
Homolovi, Little Colorado River	August 30–September 1	**Field notes or collection record**: none	Olla with corn
Steamboat Rock Canyon ruins	September 10	**Field notes or collection record**: none	Fragment of pottery, shell "highly valued by Hopi"
Nebito Canyon		**Field notes or collection record**: none	Round objects of pottery, pottery disks, pitted hammer, hammer

Note 1: Compiled from Peabody Museum object collection cards, accession papers 00-23-10 and Russell specimen catalogue lists (for objects 76144–388). Associated burial goods have been grouped by skeletal assemblage, but we have not been able to link all to a specific set of human remains. The letters in column 4, following associated burial goods, refer a set of grave goods. These are separated by a semi-colon at the end of each grouping.

Note 2: The different data sources for the human remains do not tally. Russell's numbering system does not make sense because we do not have his concordance or field inventory. Thus, we do not know definitively what Russell collected or what sets of bones arrived at the Peabody Museum. To add to the confusion, Russell also numbered the "Awatovi" sites differently in field notes and catalogues; we have chosen the site names that are most consistent with the field logs and reports. The human remains that were in the Peabody Museum osteological collections in 1990 are listed in column 3 under PMAE inventory; the catalogue given to the PMAE in 1900 but no longer there is listed under Russell osteology catalogue. The original catalogue has not survived but references have been compiled from other archival sources, including correspondence. The PMAE inventory also lists fragmentary remains of three individuals, including No. 48 from an unidentified Pueblo ruin, house.

TABLE 3.2. Frank Russell's 4 x 5 Photographic Negatives, Summer of 1900, Peabody Museum of Archaeology and Ethnology

Class one: Walls of Ruins	Fire House near Keams Canyon; Awatovi (4): church from north, plastered walls, straw adobe (2); Mishiptonga-plastered wall; Little Colorado River near Black Falls (16), including doorway, lava beds, a sweathouse, and the skeleton of a pony
Class two: Pictographs	Kwaituki (2), Awatovi (10), Little Colorado River valley (19)
Class three: Arizona Physiography	Kwaituki looking southwest down the Oraibi Wash (2); Kwaituki looking east toward the Ziltahjini Mountains; Little Colorado River, butte behind ruins; Red Mesa (4); Thiohale, spring in sand hill; Tehugkihu (Fire House); spring in rock cliff
Class four: Arizona Indian Portraits: Navajos	Women in Chinle Valley (2); Pel-a-si-shazzy family at Togoholtazze Spring, taken on July 16 (2); man near Kwaituki; men at Awatovi (2); man at Red Mesa; Navajo family at Navajo hogan located in Oraibi Wash (one with characteristic posture) (4); men near Ganado on the road to Keam's Canyon
Class four: Arizona Indian Portraits: Hopi	First Mesa (7) people at Hano, Sichomovi, flowers at altar at the Gap 5; Shipaulovi on Second Mesa of Snake Dance (5), includes Kisi, Antelope, and Snake priests
Class five: Miscellaneous	**Places**: Start of trip at Ganado, first camp in the Oraibi, second camp at Kwaituki, spring near Oraibi; Mishiptonga, cemetery showing dust; store and house at Keam's Canyon; Hubbell Trading Post: store (2), herd of sheep and goats **Participants**: Nosifor, Sliver, and a neighboring Navajo; Nosifor and Erminio near Oraibi; Erminio Pena; Sliver; Hubbell and family (4)

Note: Number of photographs of specific locations in parentheses.

TABLE 3.3. Russell's Large Format Photographs, Summer of 1900, Peabody Museum of Archaeology and Ethnology

Unnamed ruin 20 miles north of Oraibi, possibly Kwaituki	Landscapes toward north, east, south, and west (4)
Kwaituki	Landscapes toward north, east, and south (3); excavated grave (taken by Theresa on August 10)
Awatovi	Landscapes toward north, west, and east (3); church from north, facing buttes to the south, 15–35 miles in distance, largest cemetery, rooms at southwest corner recently cleared out (2); lower cemetery, one photo showing vandalism (2); from within rooms looking west (2); pictographs (2)
Kookopngyama (Horn House)	Landscape toward north and east (2)
Kawaika-a (Mishiptonga)	Landscapes toward north, south, and east (3)
Hopi villages	Hano from the north; Sichomovi from the north (2); Walpi from the north (3); dance rock
Little Colorado Black Falls	Landscapes (5)
Steamboat Rock Canyon	Spring with sixteenth-century Spanish inscription; landscape from the south with ruin at base; from the west taken on September 10 (2)
Miscellaneous	Baskincha, Indian store of George McAdams; Navajo weaver painting owned by J. L. Hubbell (2), Correggio painting owned by J. L. Hubbell

Note: Number of photographs of specific locations in parentheses.

TABLE 3.4. List of Canyon de Chelly Photographs Taken by Peter Gates with Frank Russell's Camera, September 1900, Peabody Museum of Archaeology and Ethnology

Cat. no.	Description
1	Casa Blanca ruins
2	Canyon del Muerto, Navajo dance, terrace right in middle ground
3	Canyon del Muerto, vicinity of dance
4	Cliff ruins in Canyon de Chelly near junction with del Muerto
5	Sheep and goats going to night corral near dance terrace
6	Looking up Canyon de Chelly, Casa Blanca at right middle
7	Ruins of circular kiva at base of Casa Blanca cliff
8	Casa Blanca ruins
9	Looking down Canyon de Chelly from Casa Blanca
10	Navajo wall and "Ah-way-elk si-si" Valley near mouth of the canyon
11	Looking up Canyon de Chelly near del Muerto, pictograph caves left middle
12	Canyon de Chelly, looking toward mouth of del Muerto, last gap
13	Navajo ranch near junction of two canyons
14	Eastern wall of Canyon de Chelly, about 2.5 miles from entrance
15	Navajo dance amphitheater, Canyon del Muerto
16	Canyon del Muerto, about 7 miles from Canyon de Chelly junction
17	Navajo cornfield and peach orchard
18	Canyon del Muerto Navajo cornfield, same as 17
19	Canyon del Muerto Navajo cornfield, same as 17
20	Western cliff of Canyon del Muerto
21	Ruins at base of cliff and stains on wall of Canyon del Muerto
22	Canyon del Muerto, 7 miles from de Chelly
23	Block of sandstone, Canyon del Muerto

TABLE 5.1. Akimel O'odham Artifacts Collected by Frank Russell for the Smithsonian Institution Using the Secretary's Reserve Fund (Accessions 39990 and 39991), 1902

Object Type	Catalogue Numbers
Agricultural (11); food gathering tools (2)	217972–78, 217992–93, 218013, 218039–40, 218133
Baskets: bowls (43), trinket baskets (2), cache basket and lid; head-ring (3)	217876–917, 218026–27, 218041, 218029-31
Basket-making materials (7)	217989, 218084–85
Beads: from graves (3 sets); beads; shell beads and stone pendant	218086, 218099–102, 218104–5
Calendar sticks (4)	218111, 218130, 218134–35
Carrying frame and pole	218033
Clothing: woman's blouse, headband, girdle, sandals	217926, 217927, 217932
Cooking utensils: wooden tray, ladles (2), spoons (2), pestles (2), mortars (2), parching pan, sieves (2), gourd containers (2)	218004–12, 218022, 218036–38, 217979-80
Cradle	218003
Fetishes and amulets (3)	218077–79
Fire-making equipment (2)	218034–35
Food, salt, seeds (35)	217948–64, 218112–29
Games: gambling (9), footballs (5), cards (40), darts (2), woman's stick and ball (5), dish (2), stones (2)	218042–45, 218047–51, 218093–94, 218131–32
Hairbrushes (2); human hair (3)	217933, 217934, 217946–47, 218032
Horse equipment: spur	218091
House sections and furniture: door, sleeping mat	218001–2
Hunting equipment: traps and cages	218014, 218040
Jewelry: glass bead necklace	217931
Masks (3)	218090–92
Medicine	218087
Musical instruments: flutes (3), rattle (7)	218053–55, 218065–71
Pottery: bowl (4); canteen, cooking pot, cup, dish (2); ollas (2); vase (3); fragments (17)	218015–21, 218023–25, 218028, 218089–90, 218095–96

(*continued*)

TABLE 5.1. (*continued*)

Object Type	Catalogue Numbers
Pottery-making materials (5)	217986–90
Religious paraphernalia (22)	218056–64, 218072–76
Rope, rope-making tools (7)	217966–71
Runner's head ornament	217930
Shrine and altar materials (22)	218097–98, 218103
Stones: tubes and rings (3), carving	218106–9
Tattooing materials, dyes, face painting materials (10), face painting drawing	217935, 217936–45
Toys: doll (2), slingshot	218046, 218052, 218092
War headdress	217928
Weapons (29): cartridge belt, arrows, quivers, bows	217994–8000, 218088
Weaving raw materials and tools (4)	217983–85, 218110

Note: number of artifacts in a category in parenthesis

Abbreviations

AAA	American Anthropological Association
AAAS	American Association for the Advancement of Science
AMNH	American Museum of Natural History
APS	American Philosophical Society
BAE	Bureau of American Ethnology
BAEIC	Bureau of American Ethnology Incoming Correspondence, 1888–1906
BAEOC	Bureau of American Ethnology Outgoing Correspondence, 1888–1906
BP	Franz Boas Papers
CR	Committee Report, charges against Frank M. Barnett. Records of the BAE. Additional Administrative Files: Records relating to the investigation of the BAE, 1903.
GLO	General Land Office
GPO	Government Printing Office
HUA	Harvard University Archives
NA	National Archives
NAA	National Anthropological Archives, Smithsonian Institution
NMNH	National Museum of Natural History
OIA	Office of Indian Affairs, predecessor to the Bureau of Indian Affairs
PMA	Frank Russell Correspondence. Archives of the Peabody Museum of Archaeology and Ethnology, Harvard University, Cambridge, MA.
PP	Frederic Putnam Papers
SIA	Smithsonian Institution Archives
SUA	Stanford University Archives
TRP	Frances Theresa Russell Papers, Call number SC0166. Special Collections Department, Stanford University Library, Stanford University.
USGS	United States Geological Survey
USNM	United States National Museum

Notes

Introduction

Citations to published works, correspondence, journal entries, and field reports by Frank Russell are credited simply to "Russell," while citations to works by Theresa are credited to "F. T. Russell" or "T. Russell" as appropriate.

1. "The World This Weekend: Sir Max Mallowan" (Christie interview with Max Mallowan, BBC archives, 1947, http://www.bbc.co.uk/archive/agatha_christie/12508.shtml, accessed November 9, 2017); exhibition brochure for *Agatha Christie Archaeology*, Trustees of the British Museum; Christie 1936, 1985; Mallowan 1947.
2. The travel narratives audience consisted of people curious about unexplored lands (Gordon 2010; Troelstra 2017). Tourism was equated with elevated social status, wealth, and expendable time. Scientific travel narratives were so popular and lucrative that almost all authors published them. The genre permitted authors to express their thoughts about a wide variety of topics. See Davis 2008, Lister 2000, Lister and Lister 1968 for other examples. In a 1983 interview, Rosamond Spicer told Nancy Parezo there were two kinds of anthropological wives. The first wanted to be waited on and complained bitterly. They tended not to participate in field seasons after the first couple of years. Others eagerly became part of the research team. Madeline Kidder worked with her husband, Alfred, at Pecos while overseeing the field laboratory, camp, and commissary. She did not write accounts of her travels but told many a good story at annual Pecos conferences.
3. Parezo 1993c:343–48, 352–54.
4. Morris 1931, 1933. Earl Morris wrote popular accounts about Mexico. Unable to obtain a permit due to gender prohibitions, Dr. Lucy Wilson had to have her husband obtain one to excavate Otowi in the 1910s. Isabel Kelly, Francis Watkins, and Eva Horner dug the Tecolote Ruin in 1929 under a permit for the School of American Research (C. Fowler and Parezo 2019).
5. Stevenson's maps, site sketches, and watercolors were archived under James Stevenson in the USGS record group, NA. Wives' participation was rarely acknowledged in official publications, nor were data collectors, assistants, and Indigenous participants. This helped make archaeology appear to be what men accomplished singularly and played into American myths about fieldwork professions being too dangerous for women (Papanek 1973:862). Few women wrote natural history

expedition narratives. Elizabeth Chabot Agassiz helped compose her husband's accounts (Agassiz and Agassiz 1868), and Mary Churchill Baird assisted her husband, Smithsonian secretary Spencer Baird, by transcribing, editing, and translating as well as drawing illustrations. Linguist Charlotte Murchison, the wife of famous British geologist Charles Lyell, sketched and classified specimens on their frequent trips through Europe in the 1830s and 1840s. They even had a geological honeymoon in 1832 that set the pattern for their scientific partnership (P. Adams 1988; for other examples, see Calderon 1843; Harper 2001; Lindsay 1998; Maddox 2017:57–58).

6. Haury 1983:83. Marion was a watercolor painter. She accompanied Cosmos to Arizona, New Mexico, Colorado, and southern Utah, "and assisted him in his studies of the cliff ruins and the old Indian village ruins in those regions" (Putnam County Courier 1933).
7. D. Fowler and Parezo 2012. An archaeologist searching for documentary information will be frustrated with Theresa's account as well as her writing style. She conveyed minimal factual information and rarely named all the tested or excavated sites. We have been able to glean some of these identifications from her journal, reading reports of subsequent archaeological work in the region and calling on our colleagues for assistance. This information has been placed in endnotes to aid readers seeking additional information.
8. Theresa's ethnic humor seems harsh and insensitive from a contemporary standpoint. Be forewarned: some of the adjectives she used, no travel author would use today. In addition, Theresa tended not to name individuals, transforming individuals into essentialized archetypes or stereotyped caricatures. We assume that this was intentional.
9. See Gero 1985; Gero and Root 1990; and Lutz and Collins 1993 for assessments of gendered writing of anthropology.
10. Chapters 2 and 3 and the *Out West* magazine chapters can be read in tandem with Theresa's 1900 field journal (appendix A). This will allow readers to see how Theresa remembered her experiences and transformed her daily thoughts in the field into a popular narrative.
11. Lewis 2016:1–8. So many tuberculosis sufferers came to Arizona and New Mexico that by the early twentieth century, both territories were health meccas. As the number of sanatoria increased, concomitant death rates from tuberculosis rose.
12. Theresa created a space for husband and wife archaeological teams by demonstrating women's capabilities. She was unique in recognizing the contributions of all participants—the scientist, Native assistants, Indigenous residents, traders, settlers met during the travels, and animals.
13. We transcribed these materials several years ago. They served as the basis for our first article documenting the Russells (D. Fowler and Parezo 2012). More recently, we annotated them to understand Theresa's literary and philosophical allusions.

Readers can compare what Theresa wrote for herself with what she published. See Sanjek 1990 for the nature of field notes and the standardization of anthropological research and data to ensure reliability and replicability.

14. Babcock and Parezo 1988; D. Fowler 2010; Leckie and Parezo 2008; Parezo 1993a, 1993c.
15. C. Fowler and Parezo 2019. This has included a systematic lack of recognition for ideas and work studied by both sociologists and psychologists since the 1960s. We have seen how other spouses, who had uncredited responsibility for accomplishing the domestic aspects of fieldwork, enabling a husband to concentrate on data collection, were data collectors themselves and participated in many aspects of anthropological work.
16. "Narrative styles" refers to how anthropology was written and presented to scientific, scholarly, and popular audiences. We query how rhetoric was used, as well as what information was deemed necessary to advance arguments for specific audiences. See especially D. Fowler 2010.
17. D. Fowler 2010; Parezo 1987; Snead 2001.
18. D. Fowler and Parezo 2018.
19. F. Russell to McGee, October 17, 1901, BAEIC; Bandelier 1892; Lange and Riley 1996; Parmenter 1966; Reid and Whittlesey 1997. Frank was familiar with the work of these archaeologists and most admired the Mindeleff brothers and Fewkes.

Chapter 1

1. Chamberlain 1904:208. Cushing was anthropology's young maverick, working on linguistic, archaeological, and ethnographic topics. He was a long-term BAE employee and the first to conduct intensive ethnography. He was excellent at writing both scholarly and popular experiential accounts. His magazine serial, later published as a book, *My Adventures in Zuñi* (Cushing 1970), made him recognized as a scientific explorer in both the United States and Europe. Unlike Russell, Cushing was able to acquire significant philanthropic patronage (J. Green 1990; Pandey 1972; Parezo 1985).
2. There are inconsistencies about Frank's siblings. A family Bible listed five siblings: James Russell, born May 23, 1844, in Iowa; Mary Ellen Russell, born April 23, 1847, in Illinois; Sarah Josephine Russell, born November 24, 1851, in Ohio; Flora Eugenie Russell, born March 25, 1853, in Ohio; and Carleton Russell, born August 10, 1855, in Wisconsin. Frank's mother stated her mother was Rachel Sprague, who married Samuel Morrill ("The Spragues of Malden, MA," posted January 6, 2016, Ancestry.com). It appears their ancestors migrated from England.
3. Nutting 1903; Roland Russell, "The Russell Family Story" (post by larainejy on Ancestry.com, accessed October 8, 2018). The Russells bought a 12-bedroom house in Fort Dodge to rent rooms to male students. In 1896 Frank's parents moved to Eagle Lake, Texas, to alleviate their rheumatism. The 1900 Galveston storm

destroyed their home and killed his father. Frank's mother returned to Iowa to live with her sister. This information contradicted Theresa's journal, which implied Frank's parents lived in Iowa. It explained, however, the letter that saddened Frank and why his parents had not attended his wedding ("Fort Dodge, Iowa," https://en.wikipedia.org/wiki/Fort_Dodge,_Iowa, accessed January 18, 2018; "Census of Population and Housing," Census.gov, accessed January 18, 2018).

4. Russell's Harvard graduate school application, 1895, noted in Roffler 2006:393, note 1. Gilmore City was a farming community near Fort Dodge founded in 1884 and incorporated in 1887. It had a population of 687 in 1900 (Johnson 1980:173). Today the town calls itself Iowa's limestone capital.
5. Nelson 2012; Steeples and Whitten 1998. The depression continued while Russell was in college.
6. Frank enrolled with only $10 in his pocket. Nutting 1903; F. Wilson 1903.
7. Nutting 1903. Nutting was a marine biologist, credited with describing 124 species. He produced beautiful monographs, illustrated by Frank. Nutting always gave public lectures after returning from each expedition and ensured Russell did the same.
8. Graduation Programme, University of Iowa, 1892, TRP, SUA.
9. F. Russell 1898b:iii–iv.
10. F. Russell 1899b:2.
11. F. Russell to Mr. von Jagermann, April 14, 1896, HUA. By "first man," Russell meant first Caucasian. He was not referring to American Indians, including those whose ancestors had long lived in the area.
12. Iowa City Press Citizen 1894a:5; Quad-City Times 1899:2.
13. Nutting 1895:45–46.
14. This unreflexive dedication to taxonomic preservation was a dominant impetus for Frank's work in the American Southwest when he and Theresa collected precontact human remains to place in an eastern museum for safekeeping and analysis.
15. F. Russell 1898b:157.
16. Iowa City Press Citizen 1894b:4.
17. Russell "was fortunate enough to wipe out of existence a monster walrus that yielded the largest tusk ever brought out of the land of perpetual ice" (Iowa City Press Citizen 1903:3). Russell also collected meteorological data for the U.S. Weather Bureau (Hodge 1903:738).
18. Articles were but one activity needed to build reputations. The best-selling book cemented the explorer as an adventurer overcoming dramatic and dangerous situations. Powell took his series for *Scribner's Monthly* and transformed it into *Explorations of the Colorado River of the West*, a book in print for more than 150 years. It helped him raise support for further explorations, including the federally sponsored Geographical and Geological Surveys between 1869 and 1879. In

1879 Powell founded the BAE, which he directed until his death in 1902 (D. Fowler 2010; D. Fowler and Fowler 1971). For more on the anthropologist as explorer, see Clifford 1988; Clifford and Marcus 1986; Crick 1995; Gordon 2010; Stocking 1992.

19. Estherville Daily News 1895:2; Powell 1875b, 1875c; F. Russell 1895; Rogers et al. 1896; Schrimper n.d.

20. F. Russell 1895, 1896a, 1896b, 1896c, 1898b; Roland Russell, "The Russell Family Story" (post by larainejy on Ancestry.com, accessed October 8, 2015). "Like most youth, Frank was seldom at home very long at a time after finishing high school." He was a devout man but not a "church worker." He loved to argue and debate philosophy, "just for the sake of clashing wits." He loved to speculate about ideas. "An impractical theorist and strong individualist," he was not particularly good at making money, was shy but had a keen sense of humor. "He did what he aimed to do and was loved, admired and respected by all who knew him." Russell gave a lecture for the Boston Society of Natural History titled "An Account of a Naturalist's Voyage Down the Mackenzie" on March 17, 1897 (American Naturalist 1897:361).

21. Putnam quoted in Hinsley 1985:55; see also Dexter 1965, 1966a, 1966b; Tozzer 1936:127.

22. Hinsley 1992; Swanton 1944:2.

23. Dorsey 1894, 1896:93–95; Hinsley and Wilcox 2016; Putnam 1903b:197; Stocking and Montague 1979:5. According to Swanton, Putnam only gave a couple of lectures on archaeology and left educational duties to others. Russell was the "real teacher and mentor at Harvard," someone who knew the rigors of fieldwork. "He was dedicated to his craft, extremely focused, with a personality to endure and overcome life's trials" (Swanton 1944:9–10).

24. We can speculate Putnam had doubts about the quality of an education earned at a midwestern state college (Putnam 1896:239, 1899:272).

25. Mark 1980:19.

26. Browman 2013:40–42; Fabian 2010; Putnam 1889:38, 1896:239–40; Studley 1884. See D. Cook 2006:47 for a history of the Peabody Museum's osteological collections. Studley took a job at a hospital when Putnam would not raise her pay. This was like the situation Russell faced in 1901 and 1902. Putnam had a history of paying his female and male staff wages so low they could barely live. Simultaneously, he demanded dedication and hard work, following his own uncompromising work ethic (Desanti 2012:73; Hinsley 1985:68). This was not a problem for those who had inherited wealth. For those without affluent families, it meant living in poverty.

27. F. Russell, anthropometry lecture notes, n.d., TRP, SUA. Frank repeated these assignments in 1898. Somatology became associated with race and was used to distinguish social units and establish their relationships in evolutionary hierarchical arrangements, with "Caucasians" at the top (D. Fowler and Parezo 2018). It was used to posit theories about physical and mental evolution and the environmental conditions that affected cultural development. It had two specialties: craniometry

and osteometry. Large numbers of skeletons were needed for analyses, so collecting human remains in the late nineteenth century was an archaeological priority (Spencer 1992; Topinard 1881). For a critical analysis on somatology's statistic weakness, see Gould 1996.

28. Blumenbach 1865; Boas 1891, 1893; Browman 2002b:509–10; Browman and Williams 2013:202; Galton 1891; Garson 1885; Hartwell 1893.
29. Evening Times 1896:4.
30. D. Cook 2006; F. Russell and Huxley 1899. Unlike Columbia, Harvard did not require that students publish their dissertations before the degree was awarded (Russell 1898h).
31. Fabian 2010; Russell, anthropology lecture notes. TRP, SUA; D. Fowler and Parezo 2018. Russell was blind to the effects of colonialism that skewed results (D. Thomas 2000:110).
32. Hinsley 1974.
33. Lewis 2016:2.
34. Chamberlain 1894; Darnell 1970; MacCurdy 1899.
35. Putnam 1890. In 1898 Cyrus Thomas was critical of European craniology. "The results so far obtained, except in cases of artificial pressure, are too unsatisfactory to justify its use except in broad generalizations, and then only as cumulative evidence" (C. Thomas 1898:10).
36. Meltzer and Dunnell 1992; Moorehead 1910; Willey and Sabloff 1974. If Russell's health had stabilized, he would have continued to study physical diversity (F. Russell 1898c, 1898g, 1899a, 1899c, 1899f, 1899e). The Trenton gravel pits were critical in debates about human occupation in North America during the PaleoIndian period. Putnam held that historical Native Americans were descendants. Holmes and Hrdlička argued the Americas were occupied after the Ice Age; they were quite nasty in their denunciation of any archaeologist who disagreed (Hinsley 1985; Meltzer 1985, 2015). Russell's support of Putnam would not have helped him obtain employment at the USNM.
37. Putnam encouraged students to become adept at Chautauqua-style lectures, given at the Lowell Institute. Russell presented lectures on his Arctic travels to raise money for the Peabody Museum (Browman 2002b:510; Dexter 1966a, 1966b; Putnam 1900). Frank was involved with managing journals as professional service, solidifying his growing reputation. At the time of his death, he had been an associate editor of the *American Naturalist* for several years.
38. F. Russell 1902a:2; American Naturalist 1904:895. He worked closely with McGee and McCurdy on curricular issues (McGee 1899a:759; McGee to Boas, December 27, 1899, BP, APS).
39. D. Fowler 2010:104–16; Hinsley 1981; D. Miller 2007; Parezo 1993c.
40. F. Russell to McGee, February 15, 1898, BAEIC. The period 1899–1904 was one of restructuring anthropological societies. Russell worked with the American

Folklore Society, while Boas tackled the American Ethnological Society. Others refined AAAS's Section H and established the AAA (McGee to Boas, January 9, 1900, BP, APS). Russell needed to attend the January 16, 1900, Philadelphia meeting in order to speak with Powell, Holmes, and McGee.

41. List of Manuscripts purchased by the BAE under the direction of W J McGee, Exhibit F, Box 1: Final Report, Folder 1: CR. Throughout the 1890s, McGee paid Boas $110 for vocabulary cards and $500 per year for articles and book-length manuscripts (McGee to Boas, January 25, 1899, BP, APS).

42. Eiselt 2012.

43. F. Russell to McGee, August 31, 1898, BAEIC; Matthews 1887, 1895.

44. F. Russell to McGee, November 19, 1898, BAEIC.

45. Hodge 1907:631–632; MS 1902a, NAA. Russell sketched a medicine lodge, described the Feast of San Antonio, and recorded a curing ceremony (Russell 1898a, 1898d, 1898e).

46. Stanley Coulter, a well-known Purdue University biologist, produced pamphlets to help people study nature. Sarah Moore was a Methodist missionary, whom the Indian Service agent felt was "doing good work here, holding weekly religious services and encouraging morality in every way possible" (Walpole 1898:210). See F. Russell 1898, 1900b.

47. Mason 1875; see also Parezo 1986, 1987. Today the Smithsonian Institution is composed of a series of museums, the national zoo, research agencies, and public programs. The Smithsonian museums include the National Museum of the American Indian and the National Museum of Natural History, which both concentrate on anthropology and contain collections of material culture from many societies. In 1900 these separate museums did not exist; anthropology and its disciplinary collections were a division of the United States National Museum. American history was a subdivision of anthropology. The Bureau of American Ethnology was a separate research organization that reported to the Secretary of the Smithsonian for oversight purposes.

48. To view photos of the artifacts Russell collected, visit the Peabody Museum Collections Online website https://pmem.unix.fas.harvard.edu:8443/peabody/ and search for Russell. No Jicarilla Apache items were accessioned into the federal (USNM) collections under Russell's name in 1898 and therefore we can tell that neither McGee nor Mason gave Russell funds to collect. In 1899 the Jicarilla Apache community earned about $7,000 from the manufacture of bows, arrows, and beadwork (Walpole 1899:255). Examples would have been available for Russell to purchase.

49. The Jicarilla Apache agent, also superintendent of the Rio Grande Pueblos, lived in Santa Fe. The Office of Indian Affairs (OIA) was part of the Department of the Interior. The agency's name was changed to the Bureau of Indian Affairs in 1947. We refer to the OIA as the Indian Service, as it was commonly known, throughout the manuscript.

50. F. Russell to McGee, November 19, 1898, BAEIC.
51. It is likely Frank felt he had limited time to live, given the tuberculosis death rate. He made no mention of his illness in any correspondence, however.
52. Swanton 1944; Parezo 1986, 1987. Researchers came, asked questions, took photographs, bought or took artifacts, and did not return, while assuming the research subjects were not interested in or would forget their traditions (Warren 1999).
53. F. Russell to McGee, November 19, 1898, BAEIC. The exception was one or two individuals who had worked with missionaries and adjusted their schedules to meet Frank's research needs in return for financial compensation.
54. Russell aimed for a population sample sufficient to establish the range of variation. This intellectually moved him from a concern for worldwide racial classification of specimens—where one "typical" individual stood for an entire ethnic group or race—to an analysis based on ethnic and regional characteristics.
55. Dupertuis and Tanner 1950. The combined information served as a proxy for an individual. Photographs had additional value; they provided ethnographic evidence of clothing. Such data could be used to grasp intracommunity variation as well as cultural norms.
56. Banta and Hinsley 1986; Edwards 1992; Pink 2001.
57. Every anthropologist who worked before digital cameras has shots that are a black negative (Fleming and Luskey 1986; D. Fowler 1972a, 1972b; Isaac 2005; Morrisey and Parezo 2005).
58. F. Russell to McGee, November 19, 1898, November 25, 1898, BAEIC. Russell sent a list of photo captions to Mason for exhibits (F. Russell to Mason, April 20, 1900, Box 6, Folder 75, Manuscripts and Pamphlet File, Records of Division of Ethnology, NMNH, NAA). Russell also sent McGee 85 photographs of the Jicarilla Apache, Hopi, Nambe, Sandia, Santo Domingo, and Tesuque. None matched the quality of John Hillers' photos (D. Fowler 1989).
59. F. Russell to McGee, August 31, 1989, BAEIC.
60. F. Russell to Putnam, September 2, 1898, September 22, 1898, HUG 1717.2, PP, HUA; F. Russell to McGee, August 31, 1898, BAEIC. Frank seems to have left no ethnographic field notes.
61. T. Russell, journal, August 7, 1900, SUA.
62. F. Russell to McGee, November 25, November 26, 1898, BAEIC. Russell did not publish an article on his journey or compose a "what I did this summer" notice for *The American Naturalist*, *Science*, or the *American Anthropologist*.
63. Russell served as vice president for the Boston branch of the American Folklore Society in 1898–99 (Journal of American Folk-lore 1898, 1900; Russell 1898a).
64. Exhibit F, list of manuscripts purchased, CR, NAA. Numerous vouchers, agreements, and letters about manuscripts in the Boas Papers, APS, show this was a long-standing practice. Since all manuscripts were published in BAE, USMN, and Smithsonian Institution annual reports, they could be considered

government-contracted work. The problem arose when McGee used the *American Anthropologist* and the *Journal of American Folk-lore* as outlets without approval.

65. Putnam presented "The Pueblos of Colorado and New Mexico," which described the Hyde Expedition research to the Boston chapter of the American Folklore Society on December 5, 1899 (Journal of American Folk-lore 1900:150). We found no records that Russell presented any lectures. He did write book reviews relating to folklore (F. Russell 1898f, 1898g, 1899b, 1899d).
66. NAA 4748. Russell's data were used by Edward Wilson, listed under the latter's name when deposited in the NAA. Russell's *Explorations in the North* was reviewed by Hrdlička, who found it "not too technical," with "many interesting incidents of hunt and travel . . . interspersed with valuable ethnological and zoological data" (Hrdlička 1899:514; see also Iowa City Press Citizen 1900:4).
67. F. Russell to McGee, February 15, 1900, BAEIC; Evening Star 1900:16.
68. J. H. Gore, director, International Congresses, Columbia University to Russell, March 23, 1900, TRP; F. Russell 1900e, 1900c, 1900d, 1900f. Hrdlička worked diligently to ensure observational replicability (Stojanowski and Euber 2011). Frank continued to strive to eliminate researcher error in physical measurements until the end of his life (F. Russell 1902b, 1903d).
69. Accession 00–23, basic catalogue card, Peabody Museum.
70. Hoxie 1984; Thompson 2000.
71. The Peet family was originally from Connecticut, and Gideon Peet fought at Valley Forge. Emma's obituary described her as "a low voiced, sweet tempered, pleasant mannered lady" (Anamosa Journal 1913:7; 1917; Anamosa Eureka 1917). Theresa was interested in history and civic causes, patterning herself after her paternal aunt, Theresa Vernette Peet, a founding member of the DAR chapter and Chautauqua Club. Aunt Theresa was highly educated and ensured that her son, Arthur, attended the State University of Iowa and earned an MD from the Chicago Homeopathic College (Anamosa Eureka 1896; 1903a:4).
72. Information on Martelle from City-Data.com ("Martell, Iowa," http://www.city-data.com/city/Martelle-Iowa.html, accessed January 18, 2018). Cedar Rapids had an ethnic composition similar to Anamosa.
73. Johnson 1980:172. Iowa did not pass compulsory education legislation until 1902, the last state outside the former Confederacy to do so. High schools became widespread in Iowa only after 1914 (Engelhardt 1987; Rasdal 2012).
74. Albert had a cheery disposition, and "to meet him was to turn the dark clouds inside out and show only the silver lining" (Anamosa Eureka 1887:3, 1896, 1917:1).
75. Binheim 1928; Sewanee Review 1930.
76. Daily Citizen (1893a:4, 1893b:3).
77. Daily Citizen (1892:2, 1893c:3, Iowa Citizen 1898).
78. Iowa City Daily Republican (1895b:4, 1895a:4).

79. Iowa City Daily Republican 1895c:4.
80. From this sum, teachers were expected to live, clothe, and feed themselves, as well as attend teachers' meetings and institutes; purchase books, supplies, and maps; and hire a janitor. Women earned less than most unskilled rural laborers and had no paid sick leave. Teachers had to rely on their families for room and board in order to survive (Johnson 1980:173, 183).
81. Howells 1978; McCord 1958. Between 1883 and 1894, the Society for the Collegiate Instruction of Women issued certificates (Gough 1931:339). Women were not allowed to attend Harvard classes until much later (see Parezo 1993c). Harvard faculty members were paid an additional salary to lecture to women. There is no indication that Frank taught at Radcliffe.
82. James was a highly influential philosopher, the founder of pragmatism, functionalism, and radical empiricism. Considered the "father of American psychology," he wrote the basic (1,200-page) textbook. He was interested in theology, epistemology, rationality, the role of geniuses in social change, and the nature of meaning. He developed theories about truth, emotion, free will, instincts, beliefs, and the self (James 1890, 1892, 1897, 1978; see also Cooper 2002; Gough 1931:173; Graduation Programme 1892 Radcliffe College 1916).
83. Anamosa Eureka 1900:5.

Chapter 2

1. Anamosa Eureka 1900:5.
2. We do not know why none of Frank's siblings attended the ceremony. "Just before leaving, the bride was surprised by the Francis Shaw chapter of DAR who mustered in force at the station and expressed their good wishes by presenting Mrs. Russell, a member of the chapter, with a very valuable and artistic DAR pin and badge" (Anamosa Eureka 1900:5). The group included two members of the Charles M. Hubbell family, Lena and her sister Rena, distantly related to the Arizona Hubbells; William and John Lorenzo's father was Captain James "Santiago" Lawrence Hubbell (Ancestry.com, accessed May 16, 2018).
3. Bolton 1916.
4. Fewkes 1896a; V. Mindeleff 1891; Powell 1875a, 1875b, 1875c; Webster 1883.
5. Fewkes 1898a, 1900, 1919; see also D. Fowler 2010:165–66.
6. D. Fowler and Wilcox 1999.
7. C. Thomas 1898:4.
8. Powell 1890:64, see also Powell 1883. Putnam had searched for evidence since analyzing Wheeler expedition data (Putnam et al. 1879).
9. Fabian 2010; Parezo 2006; Redman 2016.
10. Few tools were available to establish chronological controls at the time but would dominate Southwestern archaeology from the 1910s to the 1950s. Scholars had used ceramics as potential cultural and temporary indicators since the 1850s, but

formal seriation techniques were developed later (Cushing 1886, 1890; Holmes 1886a; Fowler 2010:289–310).

11. M. Graves 1998; Thomas 1898; Willey and Sabloff 1993.
12. W. Holmes 1886a; D. Fowler 2010:95; Wade and McChesney 1980.
13. Victor and Cosmos Mindeleff grew up in Washington, D.C., and attended the Emerson Institute College Preparatory School. They joined the BAE in 1881 to conduct studies of Pueblo architecture, surveying and mapping contemporary villages and sites in order to make scale models to be shown at world fairs (D. Fowler 2005, 2010; Hinsley 1983; Judd 1967; D. Smith 1948).
14. Cordell 1984:50. Frank did not have the tools to create a controlled internal site history.
15. Craniology was a separate subdiscipline from anthropometry and therefore skulls were separated from the other body bones and treated separately. Frank will follow this distinction, as seen in table 3.1 in appendix B.
16. D. Fowler 2010; Hinsley 1981; C. Mindeleff 1900; V. Mindeleff 1891. The bill establishing the Bureau of Ethnology (BAE) was U.S. Statute 20:397, March 3, 1879. The initial appropriation was $20,000, soon raised to $40,000. The name of the agency was changed to the Bureau of American Ethnology later. Sites were recorded in relation to landscape features.
17. Mary Tileston Hemenway wanted to establish an archaeological museum in Salem, Massachusetts. The Hemenway Southwestern Archaeological Expedition included Cushing's wife and sister-in-law, Hodge, journalist Sylvester Baxter, Bandelier, and two physicians, Frederik ten Kate and Jacob Wortman, who were to study the human remains.
18. Not every archaeological surveyor collected pottery fragments or human remains, so Frank thought revisiting sites had some potential. See W. Holmes 1886a, 1886b; Fewkes 1893, 1896a, 1896b, 1896c, 1896d, 1898a, 1898b; C. Mindeleff 1900; V. Mindeleff 1891, as well as the annual USGS reports. There were underexplored areas Cyrus Thomas (1898:215) felt could contain large above-ground pueblos.
19. Obtaining local knowledge was constituted a snowball survey, where the researcher sought key respondents conversant on a topic. Systematic walking by a small group of archaeologists over a small area of land searching for any human occupation was a future method.
20. It would be almost 100 years before the passage of the Native American Graves Protection and Repatriation Act (PL 101-601) would proscribe changes in many practices (Daehkne and Lonetree 2010). Repatriation today covers the human remains and associated burial artifacts the Russells removed from Hopi and Navajo lands.
21. Boas quoted in both Bieder 1986:66 and Riding In 2002:306; see also Fabian 2010. Many scholars have studied individuals who collected skeletons to study human origins and variability (Auerbach 2010; Platt 2011; Quigley 2001; Redman 2016;

Spencer 1981, 1992). See Harrison 2012 for an analysis of military trophies used by scientists. At this time, anthropologists were not using skeletal remains to study diet, gender, migration patterns, epidemics, reactions to climate change, social stratification, or violence (Harrod and Martin 2014; Kohler et al. 2004; Neitzel 2000; Palkovich 2012; Stodder 2008), nor did they include Native American perspectives (Ferguson 1996; Kintigh 2007; Mitchell and Brunson-Hadley 2004).

22. This presented a procedural problem for Frank. He had to be circumspect about the purpose of his archaeological survey even though it was obvious what he was doing.
23. T. Russell, journal, August 4, 1900.
24. Hrdlička 1902. Czech physical anthropologist Ales Hrdlička immigrated to the United States in 1881. He suffered from tuberculosis in his youth but earned a degree in homeopathic medicine. He practiced at a hospital for the insane, researching body measurements of 1,000 individuals grouped according to sex and form of insanity. In 1896 he studied with Leonce Manouvrier, Charles-Joseph Bouchard, and Paul Brouardel, and then researched normal individuals categorized by race. He searched for a permanent job in physical anthropology at the same time as Russell. In the spring of 1903, he was hired as the USNM's first physical anthropology curator and worked with the U.S. Army Medical Museum collections (Hrdlička 1900; Redman 2016; Schultz 1945). There is no paper record that Russell approached Holmes about this position with the USNM. We do not know why.
25. Putnam to Washington Matthews, August 3, 1900, Folder M, Box 11, HUG 1717.2.1, PP, HUA.
26. Hrdlička to Putnam, September 28, 1899, Box 10, Folder H-I, HUG 1717.2.1, PP, HUA. That Putnam had engaged Hrdlička as the anthropometrist for the Chaco Canyon project with the Hyde Expedition may explain why he did not offer Frank a position or suggest he visit in 1898.
27. Parezo 1987; see also D. Fowler 2010:104–16; M. Graves 1998; Hutchinson 2009.
28. Few controlled for where a feature or object was in a site. This does not mean that digging was haphazard (Cordell and McBrinn 2012:61–70; D. Fowler 2005:1–15). Putnam first articulated his techniques during a lecture at Johns Hopkins University on December 15, 1885, "On the Methods of Archaeological Research in America" (Putnam 1886).
29. Browman (2002a:250) noted this is the first instance of stratigraphic excavation techniques taught at an American university. The researcher also produced a topographic map.
30. Table 2.1 was constructed from a review of the collections' records at the Peabody Museum.
31. They did not dig in units, proceeding slowing in layers and recording what was found. If no skeletal remains or intact artifacts were found, they poked in another area.

32. F. Russell, monthly report, May 30, 1901, NAA. Frank made no notations in a log book that we have found of where his holes in each site were located. He did take the time to plot his exploratory holes in his initial site sketches.
33. F. Russell 1902a:5. Unfortunately, Theresa never discussed what they recorded or other methodological issues. The same was true for the collection of ethnographic information.
34. Much has been written about the gender myths of archaeology and how social views of women, their proper behavior, and lack of skills to be leaders kept women out of the profession (Cordell 1993; Gero 1985; Parezo 1993b).

Chapter 3

1. The monk named Father John in Theresa's text was a pseudonym (Franciscan Fathers 1910).
2. Theresa neglected to say that they paid for the breakfast as part of their supplies. Thus, Hubbell's legendary hospitality was not all-inclusive (J. Smith 1930). People called him *Don* as a sign of respect. Hubbell and his occasional partner, C. N. Cotton, dominated the Navajo weaving industry market for many years (Blue 2000; Cottam 2014, 2015; McNitt 1962:200). Burbank was supported by his uncle Edward E. Ayer (Burbank, Royce, and Taylor 1944).
3. See T. Russell, journal, July 5, 1900. Frank also knew not to show the powerful Hubbell his annoyance.
4. At the end of a researcher's trip, Hubbell facilitated packing and shipping collections by rail to eastern and midwestern institutions.
5. The bill and receipt for supplies purchased on July 26, August 11, 13, and 20 totaled $18. Peabody Museum Accession 00-23-10. Frank bought measuring tape, photographic equipment, film and developing materials ($25), and a compass for $9.75 from the Harvard Co-operative Society on June 16, for which he was reimbursed by the Peabody Museum. Writing books to record information cost $3.75. Russell used the equipment the museum had purchased for him in 1897 and 1898, as well as museum compasses, pantographs, and steel tape in 1900.
6. T. Russell, journal, July 9, 1900. Theresa learned that water was precious. While redonning her civilized clothing, she remarked that a bathtub full of water meant a return to personal comfort.
7. V. Mindeleff 1891:42, 32.
8. There are some site plans in the Peabody Museum collections but no labels (Peabody Museum Accession 00-23-10.100494.1.1).
9. Black Mesa is a large upland area in the heart of the Navajo Nation and includes much of the Hopi Reservation. Called Dziłíjiin ("Mountain that Appears Black") by the Navajo, it is 75 miles by 50 miles, composed of broad valleys, steep canyons, dramatic mesas, and buttes. It is drained by five Little Colorado River tributaries: Moenkopi, Dennebito, Oraibi, Wepo, and Polaca (Linford 2000:38). The

area was not systematically surveyed for sites until the late 1960s–1970s (Adler 1996).

10. F. Russell to Putnam, August 8, 1900, Box 11, Folder 1891–1900 Q-R, HUG 1717.2.1, PP, HUA.
11. D. Fowler 2010:166–68.
12. T. Russell, journal, July 7, 1900; Mount et al. 1993.
13. T. Russell, journal, July 9, 1900.
14. They were near Cornfields Chapter House (T. Russell, journal, July 10, 1900).
15. V. Mindeleff 1891:57–58.
16. Bourke 1884:82–85; L. Graves 1998; McNitt 1962; Wade and McChesney 1980. Keam gave the government land for their agency and school from his land claim in 1886. He amassed ethnographic and archaeological materials as part of a thriving ethnic art business. Between 1880 and 1900, he collected and sold more than 8,000 prehistoric, historic, and contemporary ceramic vessels and thousands of other Hopi artifacts to the Smithsonian Institution, German museums, and the Hemenway Southwestern Archaeological Expedition, which went to Harvard University.
17. T. Russell, journal, July 14 and 15, 1900.
18. It is possible these were early discussions of Betatakin, Inscription House, and Kiet Seel in the Tsegi Canyon system. The Wetherill brothers had dug Kiet Siel in 1897, with collections going to the AMNH. Betatakin was first recorded in 1909 by Bryon Cummings, who "cleaned it out." His collection is housed at the Natural History Museum of Utah (D. Fowler 2010:194, 256–60; see also Anderson 1969).
19. Theresa called this Wild Horse Spring, but it may be a well on the Moencopi Wash, near the Blue Canyon entrance. White Cave Spring was theoretically southeast of the wash on the northern part of Third Mesa, directly north of Oraibi.
20. Both Russells were frustrated when Natives did not stop their lives to accommodate them. This can be seen in the accusations Theresa leveled against Polacca, who would not guide them because he had duties for a "dance." She probably never understood that a "dance" was a religious ritual and each Hopi had obligations to fulfill.
21. NA 837 was occupied between AD 1250 and 1400 (V. Mindeleff 1891:54–55)
22. T. Russell, journal, July 27, 1900.
23. Theresa's July 28 journal entry provided a description of a site Frank thought occupied for a long period, based on sherd numbers. We have not been able to identify it.
24. NA 489 was occupied between AD 1250 and 1300 (V. Mindeleff 1891:56–57).
25. F. Russell to Putnam, August 18, 1900, Box 11, Folder 1891–1900 Q-R, HUG 1717.2.1, PP, HUA. A zooarchaeologist at the museum identified the materials as a dog (Catalogue No. 76185, collected on August 14 or 15 at Kwaituki, ruin 2).
26. T. Russell, journal, August 4, 1900.

27. Peter Goddard Gates collected contemporary, historic, and precontact Native art. Born in Iowa, he was a timber magnate, concentrating on Arkansas forests. An early supporter of the California Institute of Technology and Occidental College, he was a cultural preservationist and noted amateur photographer. Gates offered to underwrite the USNM field season if he could participate, splitting the artifacts obtained. Their journey was arduous; five wagons transported water to their dry camps over 800 miles. Eighteen sites were excavated and over 5,000 items collected. Hough conducted ethnographic and linguistic interviews with Western Apache, Navajo, and Hopi individuals, while Gates and his wife, Gertrude, continued to Canyon de Chelly in September (Hough 1903:358; Klyver 1989; Pavesic 1999; Williams 1992).
28. *Awatubi*, "singing house," was named for its Christian bell tower, ASM J:7:1 (Bandelier 1892; Fewkes 1896b, 1898a:592–631, 1904:18; Hough 1903:333; V. Mindeleff 1891:49). For a history of the site, see Davis 2008:5–10; Lomatuway'ma, Lomatuway'ma, and Namingha 1993; Stephen 1936.
29. T. Russell, journal, August 14, 1900, Peabody Museum Accession 2004.29.317.
30. A native of Granville, Ohio, George A. Dorsey was a Harvard graduate. An ethnographer, forensic anthropologist, and theoretician, he was fiercely territorial and ambitious, wanting to ensure the Field Museum was America's preeminent anthropological institution. He especially wanted to demonstrate he was a better institution builder than Putnam, Boas, or Holmes. Charles Owen, a graduate of Dennison College and Harvard University, had a BA in anthropology and trained as a civil engineer. He worked under Fewkes on the Hemenway Expedition and on the Field Museum's Ayer and McCormick expeditions on the Hopi Reservation and in the Little Colorado region. In 1900 he was appointed assistant curator of archaeology. Jesse A. Burt was a museum preparator, not a trained archaeologist. Almazan and Coleman 2003a, 2003b:4.
31. Permit No. 1900-1412, dated February 23, 1900. A lifelong Republican, Binger Hermann held many positions that went to loyal party members. He was a Congressman from Oregon from 1885 to 1893. He served as GLO commissioner under presidents McKinley and Roosevelt before returning to Congress in 1903. In 1904 and again in 1907, he was accused by Secretary of the Interior Hitchcock of land fraud but the jury acquitted him. From this history, we can imagine the permit to Dorsey would have been a political favor.
32. Voth correspondence file, 1897–1915, Folder 1, Henry Voth Papers, Dept. of Anthropology records, FM; Dorsey 1901:220–21. Owen spent approximately $2,100 (Dorsey to McCormick, December 20, 1900, FM) and worked from early May to September 1900 (Field Museum Accession Nos. 708 and 709). Owen visited old Shungopavi, old Mishongovi, Chukubi, Awatobi, Jeddito, Kissel, Burned Corn House, Kishuba, and the third ruin on the east side of Oraibi Wash. In 1901 he excavated at Payupki, Bettsocovi, and old Walpi (Accession Nos. 769, 780, and

834, FM; Owen field notebooks). Burton sided with the Field Museum: "Burton has been very good to you people in the museum. He told me just lately that the Indians used to come to him when Owen was excavating at the Second Mesa and that he quieted them" (Voth to Dorsey, February 8, 1901, Voth correspondence file, 1897–1915, Folder 1, Dept. of Anthropology records, FM). In his *Science* article, Dorsey thus effectively claimed supremacy and wrote Russell out of the record for 1900 research in the area.

33. T. Russell, journal, August 14, 1900; Owens field notebooks, Stanley McCormick Southwest Expedition Folder, 1899–1904, FM.

34. Quoted in Snead 2001:53; Russell to Putnam, August 3 and 13, 1900, HUG 1717.2.1, PP, HUA; Stanley McCormick Southwest Expedition Folder, 1899–1904, FM; Putnam to Commissioner of Indian Affairs, July 24, 1900, RG 75, Box 1812, NA. After 1904 the permits to excavate on federal land were placed under the jurisdiction of the Smithsonian Institution as a contract from the Department of the Interior (see Thompson 2000).

35. Hoxie 1984; McCormick to Sec. of Interior, January 27, 1900, Owen-McCormick Southwest Expedition, Folder 1899–1904, FM. Ethan A. Hitchcock was a Republican stalwart businessman from Missouri who had been appointed Ambassador to Russia before serving as Secretary of Interior under presidents McKinley and Roosevelt. Known for his dedication to conservation of natural resources and establishing the U.S. Reclamation Service, he also reorganized the Office of Indian Affairs and tried to prosecute land frauds (see Hoxie 1984).

36. The issue had ramifications for all Harvard researchers. Washington Matthews had contacted Putnam about looting. In response, Putnam noted the government was now energetically trying to prevent looting, "but by doing so it is also preventing scientific work." Referring specially to Russell, he stated, "I assured the commissioner that no vandalism would be permitted, but certain explorations would be carried on where it would do no harm to the walls." Putnam stated his own work was hampered. He asked Matthews to intercede with his Department of the Interior friends to "secure for me the right to make such exploration as I wish on public land, it would help me very much, and you may be very sure that I should not do any looting nor tearing down of walls." Putnam to Matthews, August 3, 1900, Folder M, Box 11, HUG 1717.2.1, PP, HUA; Putnam to Commissioner of Indian Affairs, July 24, 1900, RG 75, IIE3/6/7/6, Box 1812, NA; A. C. Tonner to Putnam, July 31, 1900, HUG 1717.2.1, PP, HUA.

37. While Dorsey and the Field Museum won in 1900, Harvard University performed the most extensive excavations at the Awatovi sites later. In the 1930s, they excavated at least 1,300 rooms and 3 Spanish-era churches, and collected more than 11,700 stone and bone artifacts, 8,500 ceramic specimens, and 1 million pottery sherds. In 1900 Russell created the type collection used for comparative purposes (Montgomery, Smith, and Brew 1949; W. Smith 2006).

38. Kawaika-a, Kawaiokuh, Kawaikuh, ASM J:7:2, NA 100, Peabody Museum Accession 2004.29.116; V. Mindeleff 1891:52; Hough 1903:288.
39. Bat House, NA 1039; Hough 1903:350; V. Mindeleff 1891:52.
40. ASM J:4:1; T. Russell, journal, August 17, 1900.
41. Nesuftangu (Nesheptanga), NA1048 and Kookopngyama (Kokopnyama, Horn House, Cottonwood Ruin), AZ J:8:5; V. Mindeleff 1891:50–51; Hough 1903:288, 333; Bernardine 2016.
42. Hough 1900. Figure 16.4 visualizes this problem of Euro-Americans inappropriately and disrespectfully intruding on ritual space. Our thanks to Stewart Koyiyumptewa of the Hopi Preservation Office, who gave us special and much-appreciated permission to reproduce this photograph of religious significance in order to make this point.
43. T. Russell, Journal, August 29, 1900.
44. T. Russell, Journal, September 1, 1900.
45. T. Russell, Journal, September 2, 1900.
46. Good photographs showed context and captured what could *not* be collected. Few of Frank's photographs have been preserved. He took many 4 × 5 negatives, including those in the Stanford University Special Collections. Tables 3.2 and 3.3 list how Frank categorized photos. Frank unfortunately did not distinguish between the photos he and Theresa took. Note Theresa's two depictions of the Pel-a-si-shazzy family at Togoholtazze Springs on July 13, 1900. She began to photograph Frank excavating sites. Frank took the larger, 6½ × 8½ negatives of sites and Hopi village architecture. Theresa tended to take photos of people and petroglyphs.
47. T. Russell, Journal, September 9, 1900.
48. Hubbell bill and accounts received statement from Russell, Peabody Museum Accession 00-23-10. On June 6, Russell remitted $25, and this left $160 for outstanding bills. He placed $75 on account as credit and kept $80 in an account at the trading post to cover wages (Hubbell receipt, July 9, 1900, Peabody Museum Accession 00-23-10).
49. There is no reprisal of Theresa's youthful play with the Hubbell women.

Chapter 4

1. Desanti 2012:120–21; Swanton 1944:21–22.
2. Evening Times 1900:5; program, twelfth annual meeting of the American Folk-lore Society (Journal of American Folk-lore 1901). In the same session, Dorsey discussed the Field Museum's summer activities without referring to the contretemps with Russell. Boas and Russell discussed the necessity for a uniform system for measuring skulls following his paper "A Catalogue of Crania and Skeletons" (Baltimore Sun 1900:7; F. Russell 1901b, 1901c, 1901d). At the December 1900 meeting, Frank presented an illustrated lecture on southwestern Native Americans as well as a theoretical paper (Journal of American Folk-lore 1901:52).

3. F. Russell 1902a:2. The word *men* is used intentionally here, for no women held academic positions in anthropology (Parezo 1993c).
4. The USNM anthropology staff in 1902 consisted of Otis T. Mason, Walter Hough, Paul Haupt, Cyrus Adler, Immanuel M. Casanowicz, and William Henry Holmes. BAE personnel included John Wesley Powell, W J McGee, Frank Russell, Frederick W. Hodge, Matilda Coxe Stevenson, and Jesse Walter Fewkes (American Southwest), Albert Gatschet (Nova Scotia), J. N. B. Hewitt (Iroquois in New York State and Ontario), James Mooney (Plains and Cherokee), and John Swanton (Northwest Coast) (Powell 1902, 1904a).
5. McGee to Boas, January 25, 1899, BP, APS.
6. McGee searched for the "most primitive" North Americans during the 1890s (Fontana 2000; McGee 1895, 1899b). Overextended, he sought money to forward the BAE agenda, performed the ailing Powell's administrative work, founded the American Anthropological Association, and ensured its journal, *American Anthropologist*, was published (Parezo and Fowler 2007).
7. John Swanton received his BA (1896) and MA (1897) from Harvard and was Frank's classmate and student. Like Theresa, he studied philosophy with James and Santayana. Despite his PhD, Swanton had to take a civil service exam to prove he met federal literacy requirements. He took the test in Washington, D.C., using the BAE's library. McGee used Russell's test as a model (Steward 1960).
8. McGee to F. Russell, January 3, 1901, Box 1: Final Report, Folder 1: CR, NAA.
9. McGee to F. Russell, January 4, 1901, BAEOC and CR, NAA. McGee sent a check for two weeks' salary ($62.50) on January 31, 1901.
10. McGee to F. Russell, January 9, 1901, BAEOC, NAA.
11. Snead 2001:43.
12. F. Russell to Charles Eliot, January 26, 1901, Eliot Papers, HUA.
13. Powell 1904a:xiii; F. Russell to Eliot, February 3, 1902, Eliot Papers, HUA.
14. Putnam 1903b:7–8. Henry M. Huxley was Frank's former student of somatology. He taught Russell's Anthropology 2: Somatology course while still working on his MA, which he received in 1902. His thesis was on Syrian populations (Browman and Williams 2013:299). He and Frank co-authored two papers, of which we have located one (F. Russell and Huxley 1899). Huxley left anthropology and gave his and Russell's research data to George Pepper, who apparently did not use it. It is in the Pepper Papers at Tulane University.
15. News of Russell's change in employment spread quickly. Dorsey wrote to Henry R. Voth that "Russell has resigned his position at Harvard and has accepted a permanent one in the Bureau of American Ethnology and is now in Tucson where he will begin archaeological investigations working in the north" (Dorsey to Voth, April 3, 1901, Henry Voth Papers, Dept. of Anthropology, FM).
16. Fewkes 1896a, 1896d, 1898a, 1904; C. Mindeleff 1896a, 1896b, 1897, 1900.

17. Simms visited Isleta and Laguna, where he obtained Hopi ritual attire Dorsey needed to complete an exhibit (Simms to Dorsey, January 10, 1901, Dept. of Anthropology correspondence files, Simms folder, FM).
18. Simms remained at the Field Museum for his entire career, eventually becoming director. He was not very good at field research, for things always went wrong, but was noted for his creativity in public education programs (Simms to Dorsey, January 10, 14, 15, 17, 22, 25, 26, 28, and 30, 1901; February 2, 6, 7, 10, 19, and 20, 1901; March 2 and 9, 1901, Dept. of Anthropology correspondence files, Simms folder, FM; Parezo and Fowler 2007).
19. McGee 1904a:xiii, 1904b:xvii; Accession 32434, Department of Anthropology, NMNH; Walcott 1900:72; F. Russell to McGee, May 30, 1901, BAEIC, NAA. We have no account of their route from the Colorado Plateau to Tucson.
20. Berger was a respected Tucson resident (F. Russell, monthly report, May 4, 1901, NAA).
21. Most likely AZ BB:2:83 (ASM site files). F. Russell, monthly report, May 30, 1901, p. 3, NAA.
22. Information in this section is from F. Russell, monthly report, May 30, 1901, NAA, unless otherwise noted. For information on place-names, we relied on Granger 1960. Pima, Arizona, was located on Highway 70, between Globe and Safford, about six miles north of Thatcher.
23. F. Russell, monthly report, May 30, 1901, pp. 3–4, NAA. David Wilcox, personal communication, 2015, felt Russell considered this an agricultural area. The stone pots were used to encourage agave; the linear borders and graded gardens would have been for corn.
24. Fort Thomas is on Highway 70, about ten miles northwest of Pima. Bandelier (1892:409) visited sites nearby but they do not appear to be the same ones visited by Russell. The ones he saw were like Pueblo Viego.
25. AZ CC:2:64 (ASM); Fewkes 1904:170–71.
26. Buena Vista, AZ CC:2:3 (ASM), is the largest site in the Pueblo Viejo valley, located a short distance north of San Jose village. Bandelier (1892:406) mentioned the site but did not visit it or Solomonville. Fewkes and Hough mentioned several nearby ruins, including house clusters, or *rancherias*, that Russell did not mention. Fewkes published a map in his 1897 report (Fewkes 1904:171–72). David Wilcox, personal communication, 2015 noted that Russell was using Cushing's term of *sun temple* to refer to what Haury (1937) in his Snaketown report called *ball courts*.
27. F. Russell, monthly report, May 30, 1901, November 7, 1901, NAA. Russell probably unearthed the skulls near Fort Bowie or at Apache Pass, where Chiricahua Apaches had fought the U.S. Army.
28. F. Russell to Powell, May 4, 1901, BAEIC, NAA.

29. F. Russell, monthly report, May 4, 1901, NAA. Scholars who had worked with McGee and the federal budgeting process knew to be skeptical. McGee had originally promised Boas $1,800 to support linguistic research. On May 22, 1901, he reported the amount was now, hopefully, $1,200. He had proposed to appoint Boas philologist and "the employment of expert field assistants precisely in accordance with the terms of our conference." Boas had to take reimbursement on trust: "I am confident you will have the formal guaranty of the acceptance of your plan before your departure" (McGee to Boas, May 22, 1901, BP, APS).
30. See Sauer and Brand 1931 for a description of this area.
31. F. Russell, monthly report, May 30, 1901, NAA. Frank does not mention Theresa in his reports. His field notes have not been located so we cannot identify sites.
32. F. Russell to J. Julius Lund, May 16, 1901, BAEIC, NAA.
33. McGee wrote Boas in frustration; he was trying to hire William Jones and H. H. St. Clair, at the rate of $100 per month, but the U.S. Civil Service Commission would not allow him to do so. "My arrangement with the Smithsonian Institution is now void for the Civil Service Commission finds my recommendation inconsistent with regulations" (McGee to Boas, June 11, 1902, BP, APS).
34. McGee to F. Russell, May 27, 1901, BAEOC, NAA.
35. F. Russell to Powell, June 30, 1901, BAEIC, NAA.
36. F. Russell to McGee, June 30, 1901, BAEIC; McGee to F. Russell, June 13, 1901, BAEOC, NAA.
37. McGee to F. Russell, May 27, 1901, BAEOC, NAA.
38. Richard Rathbun to Powell, July 9, 1901, BAEIC, NAA.
39. Richard Rathbun to McGee, July 24, 1901, BAEIC, NAA.
40. F. Russell, monthly reports, May and June 1901, p. 1, NAA. Frank searched unsuccessfully for a breathing appliance. With his lung problems, he could ill afford to trench in the dust. There was soon help at Casa Grande, for in September 1901, Frank Pinkley was appointed custodian. The site was designated as a national monument in 1906 (National Park Service 2011).
41. F. Russell, monthly report, June 1901, p. 2, NAA.
42. F. Russell to McGee, June 30, 1901, BAEIC, NAA.
43. Bandelier 1892. AR 03-R-02-225 has a compound and platform. As noted above, our thanks to David Wilcox for identifying this site at Wheatfields.
44. Sketches and plans of cliff dwelling near Tonto Creek, AZ U:8:47 and 48 attached to F. Russell, monthly report, June, 1901, BAEIC, NAA. The culture of the inhabitants is designated Salado. Numerous reports have been written on the extensive archaeological work at these sites (Caywood 1962). In 1937 these sites were designated Tonto Cliff Dwellings National Monument.
45. Cline Terrace complex (AR 03-12-06-132) was excavated by Arizona State University in the 1990s as part of the Roosevelt Platform Mound Study (Digital Archae-

ological Record site, https://core.tdar.org/project/394033/roosevelt-platform-mound-study-cline-terrace-complex-cline-mesa-sites, accessed July 13, 2017). Our thanks to David Wilcox for identifying this site (personal communication, 2015).

46. F. Russell, monthly report, June 1901, p. 4, NAA. David Wilcox (personal communication, 2015) identified this as the Park Creek Platform Mound (AZ 03-12-06-1044), which had approximately 50 rooms, in the Tonto Forest site system (Wilcox, Robertson, and Wood 2001). Russell referred to the Salt River as the Salado following popular usage at the time. Its longest tributary is the Verde River. We thank John Welsh, personal communication, 2019, for identifying Mt. Greenback as Greenback Peak, located about four miles northeast of Greenback Valley.

47. F. Russell, monthly report, June 1901, p. 5, NAA. Russell was referring to Tonto Natural Bridge north of Payson. Russell never identified the Western writer; dozens of writers used Arizona as the setting for their novels. One possibility is Karl May, a German author whose works had an Apache protagonist, Winnetou (see McVeigh 2007).

48. F. Russell, monthly report, June 1901, pp. 5–6, NAA. David Wilcox, personal communication, 2015, thought these were cavates visited by Cosmos Mindeleff (1896a:210–12). Russell did not visit sites in Fossil Creek or nearby tributaries.

49. F. Russell, monthly report, June 1901, pp. 5–7, NAA. Montezuma Castle was declared a national monument in 1906, based partly on Russell's and Mindeleff's reports (Joshua Miller 1897, 1899a, 1899b). In 1888 William Black bought Montezuma Well for two horses. A friend of Joshua Miller, Arizona Antiquarian Association president, he intended to homestead Montezuma Castle but was prevented in 1904 by the GLO's freeze on land claims containing archaeological sites (Protas 2002).

50. Harold Colton and the Museum of Northern Arizona later studied these sites (Colton 1946; Colton and Colton 1931).

51. We have not located information on Eugene Powell. Red Lake Trading Post was established by George McAdams in 1854 and acquired by the Babbitt brothers in 1891. We assume Powell was a Babbitt Brothers employee. The post was on U.S. 160 (old Navajo Route 1), 20 miles northeast of Tuba City, and served as the Western Navajo Agency headquarters.

52. F. Russell, monthly report, June 1901, pp. 8–9, NAA; Dorsey 1900.

53. Thanks to David Wilcox, personal communication, 2015, for suggesting Inscription House. Russell's notes are too cryptic to be certain, however.

54. F. Russell, monthly report, September 1901, p. 1, NAA. John Wetherill first visited Kiet Seel in 1895. Brother Richard wrote to B. Talbot Hyde about selling their collection: "We dug from one burial mound 400 pieces of pottery—very fine . . . this is by all odds the finest collection of pottery I have ever seen" (D. Fowler 2010:194). Inscription House and Betatakin were first recorded in 1909 by Byron Cummings, University of Utah, guided by John Wetherill (Dean 1969; H. Rothman 1991).

55. F. Russell, monthly report, September 1901, pp. 1–2, NAA. We are unsure of the modern name for the Blue Mountains. In 1896 and 1897, T. Mitchell Prudden published popular articles describing "the elder brothers of the Cliff Dwellers," which Russell would have read (Prudden 1897).
56. Jackson 1875, 1876; W. Holmes 1876. It was a trial-by-fire undertaking and sounds remarkably like the Russells' experience conducting a grand reconnaissance.
57. Courier 1901; Science 1901a:349, 1901b:352–53.
58. Denver Post 1901.
59. Denver Post 1901. McGee made national news. According to the Missouri Sharp Shooter (1901), the Courier-Journal (1901), the Indianapolis News (1901), and the Chicago Tribune (1901), he stated Adam and Eve never existed. "George Dorsey, who occupied a front seat at all gatherings of anthropologists, being the curator of the anthropology section of the Field Museum at Chicago, defended Adam and Eve, and gave exhaustive data to make his argument. He was ably seconded by Prof. Frank Russell, of Harvard, but the rest of the members went over to McGee, and it was soon apparent that the latter had won the day" (Evening Times Republican 1901). There may have been some leg-pulling on both sides.
60. Weekly Gazette 1901. McClurg arranged the trip specifically for AAAS members who would best appreciate the value of Cliff Dwellings. The trip was underwritten by the D&RG railroad (D. Fowler 2010:306–9; Nusbaum 1980:65).
61. F. Russell, monthly report, October 1901, NAA. Under Hodge's direction, the BAE worked with Hewett and the School of American Archaeology on several projects in the 1910s (D. Fowler 2010:272).
62. Victor Mindeleff (1891) published photographs documenting vandalism and looting. These have been used as a baseline for site stewards to determine the effects of visitation, natural weathering, and the collapse of rock cliffs onto sites.
63. F. Russell, monthly report, September 1901, p. 2, NAA. See Snead 2001 for more about the Hyde Exploring Company and Chaco Canyon.
64. D. Fowler 2003, 2005.
65. Richard Wetherill had been digging at Pueblo Bonito since 1896. In 1901 he filed a homestead claim on land that included Pueblo Bonito, Pueblo Del Arroyo, and Chetro Ketl. The GLO sent S. J. Holsinger to systematically survey for geological, geographical, and cultural features. He concluded that protection was needed for more than just the large sites and recommended creating a national park (National Park Service n.d.; Lister and Lister 1984).
66. Frank probably saw several ruins Bandelier recorded in the 1880s.
67. F. Russell to McGee, October 17, 1901, BAEIC; F. Russell, monthly report, October 1901, p. 2, NAA. Nantack Ridge contained evidence of Ancestral, Mogollon, and Hohokam cultures. The University of Arizona held a field school there for many years (Haury 1989; Thompson 2005).
68. Probably AZ W:11:12 (ASM). F. Russell to McGee, October 17, 1901, BAEIC, NAA.

69. F. Russell to Charles Eliot, February 3, 1902, PMA.
70. F. Russell to McGee, October 12, 1901; F. Russell, monthly report, October 1901, p. 4, NAA.

Chapter 5

1. So many lungers came to Tucson that by 1910 about one-quarter of new residents came for the promise of a climate cure. Consequently, tuberculosis became one of the leading causes of death (Gilbert and Ellis 2011; Hart 2012; Lewis 2016; S. Rothman 1994).
2. F. Russell, monthly report, December 1901, p. 1, NAA.
3. McGee estimated that Congress would approve the BAE's budget by August 15 (McGee to Boas, February 27, 1902, BP, APS; Powell 1904b: xviii–xxxi). He neglected to tell Russell.
4. McGee to F. Russell, October 18, 1901, Box 1: Final Report, Folder 1: CR, NAA. See Parezo and Fowler 2007:125–28 for how Sonoran Desert people fit into McGee's evolutionary model.
5. In 1939 the Pima and Maricopa tribes changed their official name to the Gila River Indian Community, following the adoption of a formal constitution under the Indian Reorganization Act.
6. State University of Iowa president George MacLean asked Russell to be its official representative at President McKinley's inauguration. Russell initially said yes but had to decline when his illness flared (MacLean to F. Russell, October 12, 1900, TRP, SUA). The other AAAS delegates were George Dorsey, George C. MacCurdy, Frederick Starr, and Stewart Culin (McGee to Boas, January 21, 1902, BP, APS). Frank could write books reviews while in the West (F. Russell 1901a, 1901d, 1902b).
7. McGee 1904b, 2000. Lewis was born in the Tohono O'odham village of Vainam Kug in the 1860s. He died in the Akimel O'odham village of Blackwater in the 1920s. Lewis wanted to record O'odham culture, history, and language (Fontana 1959). He became an outstanding ethnographer and folklorist, publishing independently after Russell's death. Donald Bahr and Ruth Underhill used his materials in their work.
8. McGee to F. Russell, April 15, 1902, Box 1: Final Report, Folder 1: CR, NAA.
9. Chemist Robert Forbes was dean of the College of Agriculture at the University of Arizona.
10. McGee to F. Russell, October 18, 1901, Box 1: Final Report, Folder 1: CR, NAA. In July, McGee hired Tucson lawyer Charles Blenman to oversee Lewis's defense and paid a $100 bond.
11. McGee to Lewis, July 16, 1901, August 15, 1901, October 2, 1901, BAEOC.
12. McGee to F. Russell, October 25, 1901, Box 1: Final Report, Folder 1: CR, NAA. McGee basically used federal funds for Lewis's debt. This was one of the reasons he would lose his position.

13. Lewis to McGee, November 2, 1901, BAEIC. For Antonio Azul, see Hackenberg 1974. Lewis told McGee about Tohono O'odham activities (Roffler 2006:385).
14. F. Russell, monthly report, November 1901, NAA; M. Cook 1976. See F. Russell 1908:17–18 for a complete list of Akimel O'odham consultants and interpreters. Russell earned $62.50 every two weeks.
15. F. Russell 1908:17; F. Russell, monthly report, January 22, 1902, NAA. Residents granted Lewis and Russell access to more than 200 Akimel O'odham households.
16. F. Russell 1908:17–18. Russell took several photographs of Sikachu for his anthropometric body study. She also demonstrated artifact use. Unfortunately, he only called her "a Pima woman," transforming her into an anonymous archetype.
17. F. Russell to McGee, January 22, 1902, BAEIC; Russell, Pima calendar sticks, Folder 3271; Pima glossary, MS 2507, NAA; Roffler 2006:374. Many authors have dealt with these issues (e.g., DeJong 2003, 2014; Rea 1997; Shaw 1974; J. Wilson 1999).
18. Roffler 2006:386.
19. Fontana 1975:x. Frank was interested in reconstructing Akimel O'odham life before it was transformed by Spanish, Mexican, and Euro-American colonialism. He strove to learn how cultural information about traditions was transmitted and memory activated. Material culture showed how abstract designs were transformed into symbols to retain history and aid in storytelling.
20. F. Russell, monthly report, December 1901, p. 1, NAA. David Wilcox (personal communication, 2015) noted that no Hohokam platform mounds were round. Only Mesa Grande had as large a mound, not the sites in the Tonto Valley. Pueblo Grande is now a Phoenix municipal park and a national historic landmark (Hinsley and Wilcox 1995; F. Russell 1908:24; Cushing 1995).
21. F. Russell, monthly report, March 1902, p. 1, NAA.
22. Russell was the first to use the term *Hohokam* to refer to the Salt and Gila River Valleys' ancestral inhabitants. An Akimel O'odham word, *Hohokam* means "that which has perished" or "the Finished Ones." Russell identified a plainware pottery associated with these ancestral peoples and sent an example to Holmes at the USNM.
23. F. Russell, monthly report, January 1902, NAA; F. Russell to McGee, March [illegible], 1902, BAEIC; McGee to F. Russell, January 4, 1902, January 31, 1902, Box 1: Final Report, Folder 1: CR, NAA.
24. Each year the secretary used part of his $5,000 reserve from the BAE appropriation for collections (McGee to F. Russell, February 4, 1902, BAEOC). The funds arrived so late in the season that Frank was able to collect little (Evening Star 1902). Some of Fewkes's artifacts were archaeological, excavated by a young Akimel O'odham man from a cave (Fewkes 1904:188).
25. F. Russell 1908:17–18.
26. F. Russell to Holmes, March 22, 1902, April 7, 1902, USNM correspondence files, NAA.

27. F. Russell, monthly report, February 1902, p. 2, NAA; Powell 1904a: xli.
28. McGee to Holmes, February 4, 1902; Mason to McGee, March 16, 1901, BAEIC; Accessions 39990 and 39991, NMNH; F. Russell, monthly report, March 1902, NAA; Collections Records, Dept. of Anthropology, NMNH; Mason 1904; see also Parezo 1987. In March, Frank had the opportunity to purchase a Western Apache basket collection for $67.75. Mason and McGee thought it an excellent addition to the USNM collections and Holmes convinced Langley to release funds (Holmes to Samuel Langley, April 18, 1902, USNM, letters sent, 1902–5, NAA; Accession 267595, NMNH).
29. F. Russell 1902a:4; Dorsey to Boas, June 16, 1902, BP, APS; McGee to F. Russell, January 21, 1902, BAEOC. Devaluing travelogues was a distancing position designed to establish a professional boundary. Frank's technique did not mean he did not use travelogues' rhetorical tools: literary illusions, and the witty language that made the reader part of a group of educated individuals (F. Russell 1902a:1). It meant science was a higher and more reliable form of knowledge, no matter how dry or unreadable than any written rendering of observations by nonprofessionals.
30. F. Russell to Eliot, February 3, 1902, HUA. Frank was referring to the 1901 surveys.
31. F. Russell to McGee, February 26, 1902, BAEIC.
32. F. Russell to McGee, May 30, 1902, BAEIC.
33. McGee to Boas, April 23, 1901, text 83667, May 7, 1902, BP, APS. The new director, Holmes, had no funds for Russell; all southwestern monies were obligated to Stevenson and Fewkes (W. Holmes 1907:xii–xii). Surprisingly, there was no discussion of paying Russell for a summary report on his archaeological activities for the *American Naturalist*.
34. F. Russell 1908:18.
35. F. Russell, monthly report, July 1902, p. 2, NAA. Frank bought wheels and chains, a typewriter, and a mimeograph machine for Hubbell (F. Russell to J. L. Hubbell, June 24, July 8, August 11, 1902, Hubbell Papers, Special Collections, University of Arizona Library).
36. F. Russell, monthly report, July 1902, p. 2, NAA. We are not sure of this site, but it was possibly AS K:8:235. Cienega Ruin was south of St. Michael's, not Fort Defiance. The second ruin was possibly Kinleechee (AS K:3:1) (David Wilcox, personal communication, 2015).
37. F. Russell to McGee, May 8, 1902, BAEIC. Jones was the first Native American to earn a PhD in anthropology (1904). He was hired as an assistant curator in the Field Museum but was killed by an Igorot on a collecting trip to the Philippines in 1909 (Hinsley 1996; Jones 1904;).
38. Lewis to F. Russell, September 15, 1902, BAEIC.
39. W. Holmes 1907:xx.
40. Stevenson, 1903 testimony, p. 366, Box 1: Final Report, Folder 1: CR, NAA.

41. F. Russell to Eliot, February 3, 1902, April 24, 1903, Papers of the President, HUA.
42. F. Russell 1903b, 1903c. Russell also worked on pedagogy papers, which were not included in the BAE bargain for compensation (F. Russell 1903a, 1903c). Unfortunately, this is still a pattern for funding agencies. They paid for artifacts and some collecting expenses but not for the inventory, cataloguing, and care in the museum. As a result, collection management was underfunded, as was turning raw data, that is, the artifacts, into usable data.
43. F. Russell to McGee, March 15, 1903, BAEIC.
44. His pride wounded, McGee resigned to become director of anthropology exhibits at the St. Louis World's Fair (Parezo and Fowler 2007; Hinsley 1981:254–55; Cyrus Adler investigation committee report 1903:40–42 NAA). Boas considered the proceedings a witch hunt to provide reasons to fire McGee.
45. T. Russell to Holmes, January 6, 1905, BAEIC.
46. Harvard Crimson 1903. We do not know why they did not live with Theresa's family.
47. By the end of World War II, Chloride was a ghost town. Today, 150 people reside there ("Chloride, Arizona," Western Mining History, https://westernmininghistory.com/towns/arizona/chloride/, accessed August 18, 2018; Chronic 1983:86; Dunning and Peplow 1959).
48. F. Russell to J. L. Hubbell, April 12, 1902, June 24, 1902, Hubbell Papers, Special Collections, University of Arizona.
49. F. Russell 1903b, 1903c.
50. F. Russell to Holmes, July 23, 1903, BAEIC.
51. F. Russell 1901c, 1902a, 1902b, 1903a, 1903d.
52. Mohave County Miner 1903; Des Moines Register 1903; MacCurdy 1903; Anonymous 1903.
53. Putnam 1903a:1. Putnam decided to write his obituary of Russell for the State University of Iowa alumnus journal rather than a professional outlet. As such, it was a more personal assessment of the man Putnam called his student, friend, and companion, a man he sincerely admired.
54. Journal of American Folklore [illegible]; see also Hodge 1903; Powell 1903a.
55. Iowa City Daily Republican 1903:1.
56. Smith quoted in F. Wilson 1903:20.
57. Pepper 1904:449. Interestingly, we have found no obituary written by McGee. He did add a small statement to Putnam's that said, "Frank Russell was a worthy son of his State and an honor to those sciences to which he was devoted. . . . His latest work was his best, and he was on the eve of his greatest achievements when cut off in his prime. Science suffers a grievous loss, and I mourn an honored friend" (quoted in Putnam 1903a:4). Fewkes similarly wrote, "It was my good fortune to have known his sterling character and to have followed his scientific career. No one could have known him without being impressed with his high ideals of what

Anthropology should be, and his great devotion to those ideas" (quoted in Putnam 1903a:4).

58. Quoted in Putnam 1903a:4.

Chapter 6

1. Anamosa Eureka 1903b:5.
2. Fontana 1975:xiii–xv; F. Russell 1908:19; 1909. Frank never acknowledged Theresa's participation in data collection, analysis, or writing, reflecting the conceit that the credentialed individual or research team head was the sole intellectual author. It was expected that a wife would help her husband with his occupation and needed no thanks.
3. T. Russell to Holmes, December 3, 1903, BAEIC; Hodge 1907–10.
4. F. Russell to McGee, May 30, 1901, BAEOC; McGee 1904a:xiii; McGee quoted in Powell 1904a; Fewkes 1904; Hough 1907.
5. Spencer 1981; Krugman 1976.
6. Russell 1909.
7. Grace married a man named Clark. Theresa's parents were transhumant, spending summers in Montana and winters in Southern California. Her mother died in Glendale, California, on July 21, 1913; her father in 1917 of influenza and a heart attack (Anamosa Eureka 1917:1).
8. James to Harold Höffding, January 28, 1906, April 25, 1906; James Diary, February 16, 1906, William James Papers, MS AM 1091–2.9, Houghton Library, Harvard University; Jordan 1906:507; Stanford Daily 1936. James suffered from gout and Theresa often accompanied him to meetings with other scholars in the area, in addition to her teaching duties.
9. Jordan 1906:507.
10. There were likely rumors that Theresa was more than James's protégée. We have found no evidence of this, but it was an unfortunate assumption of sexual politics in academia at the time.
11. Quoted in Bingham 1955:55–56. Lummis had attended Harvard University, edited the *Harvard Crimson*, and served as city editor of the *Los Angeles Times*. Following a stroke in 1887, he recuperated in New Mexico and wrote about Puebloan and Hispanic cultures. Biographers have noted that the unconventional and flamboyant man was attracted to young women and tried to either encourage or manipulate them (D. Gordon 1972:50). We have no indication Lummis pursued Theresa as a sexual partner, as he had other young women striving for professional status; at the time he was having an affair with Gertrude Redit (Snead 2019). We would expect Theresa would never entertain such an advance. We had hoped to find out how much Lummis paid her but were unsuccessful. There are no letters between them in Lummis's correspondence files at the Southwest Museum Braun Library, now part of the Autry National Center of the American West (NIMSY

MAi.i.3835), only four letters from Frank written in January 1903. The Lummis Papers held no *Out West* files.

12. Lummis thought women intelligent and powerful allies in promoting social reform and human rights. He wanted articles that described Western Indians in their natural settings and how Euro-Americans interacted with them. The institutional affiliation at the end of the articles is evidence that Theresa had a more permanent status at Stanford by the third installment.

Chapter 7

1. F. Russell 1902a:6. Frank was speaking of himself. The new territory was the Southwest and the old research territory the Arctic. Happiness had multiple meanings, due to Frank's illness. For Theresa, travel was an exhilarating undertaking, but it also created discontent. When at home, one yearned to return to the field. When in the field, one yearned to be home, if only for the physical comforts. While excavating one site, an archaeologist always sought the next site, anticipating the new information it held.
2. Gender norms limited the ways a woman could claim to be an explorer heroine. A "proper," self-effacing woman would not picture herself hanging from a cliff as Powell and Stevenson had both been depicted to show them overcoming the dangers of the wilderness. Instead, women used personal characteristics, like wit, that did not involve brute strength or surviving near starvation. Theresa also used male permission. She has Frank humorously chide her about clothing conventions—such as always wearing a corset, white gloves, and unfashionable hats without wide brims—or applying cold cream to ensure pale skin. Theresa used redonning a fashionable frock to mark the end of her journey and her return to civilization. Women wrote in journals such as *Appleton's Journal,* and less often in *National Geographic Magazine, Popular Science, The American Naturalist, Science,* or *The American Journal of Science* (see Lutz and Collins 1993).
3. *Foreign land* is used to mean a locale unfamiliar to the author, or occasionally some place revisited but seen through a new perspective.
4. Monger 2012:252. We consider their journey a rigorous trial-by-fire experience, with mutual affection reigning. No dewy-eyed young bride or groom was presented in Frank's or Theresa's field journals. There was certainly little privacy on the journey, and typical of their social class, the Russells did not speak of sexual intimacy. Visiting cemeteries and catacombs was a popular activity for Americans visiting Europe. Many travelogues contained descriptions of death as a moral and historical lesson (Gordon 2010; Melton 2002:42; Speake 2003). Theresa's account differed in that she did not associate places of death with disease or cruel political entities. If she desired to teach people about Ancestral Pueblo burial custom, there was little actual information in her texts. Similarly, she evidenced no concern for the topics dominating colonial settler migration narratives, what it was like to be

on a one-way journey from an increasingly distant home. Another major feature of her writing was temporary work in a strange place outside her comfort zone and learning to find pleasure in experiences Frank obviously enjoyed.

5. This type of narrative provided confidence to women who wanted to become archaeologists. We learned from watching people who viewed Parezo's exhibit *Daughters of the Desert* in the 1980s that women would see the stories, look to a friend, and state, "If she could do this, so can I." Such life journeys were powerful, enabling testimonials.
6. In his presidential lecture Frank explained how anthropology worked its magic on those who embraced its central message and made their lives richer. Theresa now had "the power of observation and of correct inference, important requisites for success in this workaday life" (F. Russell 1902a:4). But her thought process was still compartmentalized: "The theological student, however liberal, views but one side; the art student sees little more than the influence of religion upon painting or architecture or music; the sociologist deals primarily with Caucasian culture; the anthropologist alone investigates religion impartially in relation to other phases of thought" (F. Russell 1902a:3).

Chapter 8

Out West 24(1):39–49 (1906), based on F. and T. journal entries, July 3–5, 1900.

1. Kipling 1899.
2. "Beyond the veil" refers to the unknown state after death. The phrase was a figurative reference to the Jewish Temple's veil separating the tabernacle from the congregation.
3. The silver and golden cups are biblical references to Genesis 44.
4. "In Memoriam A. H. H." by Alfred Tennyson (1849) dealt with two companions walking through life until death sat in their path. The rest of stanza 22 reads, "Through four sweet years arose and fell / From flower to flower, from snow to snow." Later stanzas depict the speaker walking until she can rejoin the person she can no longer see.
5. Infinite silence defined an area without time or space, where God's wisdom is all-embracing and absolute, the ultimate reality. Theresa also referenced the spiritually refreshing quality of sleep for the regeneration of the mind and its ability to think.
6. The children's crusade against Jerusalem under Islamic governance in 1212 was a disaster and had no effect on political control. Many children were sold into slavery. Here Gallup is seen as a town that will never conquer the surrounding land.
7. Frank was referring to their bicycles. He originally intended he and Theresa would conduct their entire journey using them, as he had in 1898. Bicycling was considered an excellent way to restore health. Theresa was skeptical but game, at least for a few days. The next sequence describes both Theresa's and Frank's bikes quickly becoming crippled soon after they left Gallup.

8. "Jack and Jill" is a nursery rhyme where children climb a hill to fetch water and tumble down. In Virgil's *Aeneid*, Manes was the ghost of a deceased love one, whom Aeneas met in the underworld. All creatures and many inanimate objects had manes. Manes also referred to a ghost who protected loved ones or haunted the living who had injured them. In the Platonic sense, Theresa's bicycle was a tormenting demon that stood for her contention she could ride as well as Frank on uneven ground. Her scraped knees and elbows were a blood sacrifice to appease a Manes.
9. In Greek mythology, the Titans were the first children of Gaia (Mother Earth) and Uranus (Father Sky). They were overthrown by Zeus, Hades, Poseidon, Hestia, Hera, and Demeter.
10. St. Michael, Arizona is the name of the mission school. The route today goes north from Gallup past Gamerco, then west at Yah-Ta-Hey toward Window Rock.
11. In British and American literature, a long sleeve implied hiding something. In this case, Theresa hid her humor. Tortoise was a reference to *The Tortoise and the Hare* by Aesop, in which the speedster, in a race between unequals, finished last through hubris.
12. Hills of Enchantment was a magical place of great beauty in *One Thousand and One Nights,* Arabian folktales compiled during the Islamic Golden Age and translated into English in the eighteenth century as *Arabian Nights Tales.*

Chapter 9

Out West 24(2):139–47 (1906), journal, July 6, 1900.

1. Munk 1920:101, quoted in Cottam 2015.
2. In Theresa's accounts, Mexicans were laborers, distinguished from those of Hispanic descent, a distinction important for why it took New Mexico so long to gain statehood (Lears 1981:xv).
3. Stanza 14 in Robert Browning, "Rabbi Ben Ezra" (1864), about a man gathering his courage for battle. Theresa substituted *strange* for *brave* in the third line to show she was prepared for adventures in a very strange land, a land she would traverse with all male companions, which would require her to be courageous.
4. Lew Wallace wrote *Ben Hur* (1880) and other historical novels.
5. Antonio da Correggio (1498–1534) was a painter of the Parma school who developed foreshortening. He was known for his illusionist perspectives and considered the most impressive painter of his time. The country referred to in the final sentence was Spain.
6. Theresa uses a poetic concept for a transformation from a drab chrysalis into a colorful being. See Emily Dickinson's poem "From Cocoon Forth a Butterfly," which described metamorphosis as a change in clothing and appearance (Dickinson 1924). Butterfly allusions indicated happiness.

7. Many Catholic communities that followed the Vincentian tradition were referred to as Sisters of Charity. Begun in 1633 by Vincente de Paul and Louise de Marillac, the women took vows of poverty, raised money to help the poor, and established soup kitchens, community hospitals, schools, and orphanages. Elizabeth Ann Seton organized those in the United States.
8. The quotation continues Browning's "Rabbi Ben Ezra," stanza 16, which begins, "For note, when evening shuts, / A certain moment cuts," describing a magnificent sunset (Browning 1864).
9. A megatherium was an elephant-sized ground sloth from the Pliocene that lived in South America.
10. Theresa and Frank were not referencing any specific poem to our knowledge but playing with transcendence à la William James's nature of conscious form and Ralph Waldo Emerson.
11. Theresa is using a play on Colossians 2:21–23. Paul said, "Touch not; taste not; handle not," meaning all knowledge needed is available within Christ. The phrase served as the basis for asceticism and was used by Evangelicals to circumscribe the types of studies considered appropriate in schools.
12. The great common divisor was the largest positive integer that divided all numbers in a set without remainders. It referred to the idea that necessity was the common feature in all life. Theresa philosophically discussed the effects of extreme climates on life.
13. In Greek mythology, the Sirens were dangerous beings who lured sailors with enchanting songs, shipwrecking them on rocky coasts.
14. Wiggs is a character in *Mrs. Wiggs of the Cabbage Patch* (Rice 1901).

Chapter 10

Out West 24(3):201–7 (1906), T. Russell journal, July 9, 1900.

1. Theresa begins with the chorus to the folk song "Eureka," an upbeat yet ironic song sung by settlers migrating to Eureka Springs, Arkansas, from the East, only to find it was not their ideal Western locale. As a result they headed further West. This is how it felt to Theresa as they searched for possible sites. Theresa intentionally used a capital *W* to indicate she was in a new land and to ensure that her readers understood she was talking about a concept as well as a direction. A four-horse team pulled a Conestoga wagon (Cohen 2005:127).
2. Daniel, "God is my Judge" in Hebrew, was an Old Testament hero, held in captivity in Babylon. He served Nebuchadnezzar and his successors with dignity but stayed true to God, as witnessed by the tale of the lion's den. In Jewish theology, Shekinah referred to the glory of the divine presence as light found in a dwelling, denoting its feminine aspect.
3. *Melicano* in this and later articles was either a typographical error or an intentional play on *Mexicano*.

4. Philosophy IV was a course Frank and Theresa both took during their undergraduate studies in Iowa. Again, Theresa played intellectual and conceptualized games to keep them amused.
5. Theresa is referring to "My Double and How He Undid Me" by Edward Everett Hale, an *Atlantic Monthly* essay reprinted in Hale 1906.

Chapter 11

Out West 24(4):278–89 (1906), T. Russell journal, July 9–12, 1900.

1. The lack of an initial quote may have been a printing omission. Thesis, the mother of Achilles, was a sea nymph, a symbol of defense, who initiated desired action. Theresa wished for water and an intelligent route. Athena, the goddess of wisdom, courage, inspiration, and strategy, was a reiteration of this wish. The Pantheon and the Temple of Ivory referred to Athena's temple on the Acropolis in Athens.
2. Theresa was enamored with Robert Browning. Cisalpine referred to a camp on a mountain's south side. The referent mountains were the Alps as a region of Gaul, from Browning's poem "Sordello. (1840)."
3. The first American Arbor Day was held in 1872 in Nebraska. Arbor Day was a staple in the conservation movement with parades, picnics, and lots of speeches by 1900 ("The History of Arbor Day," Arbor Day Foundation, https://www.arborday.org/celebrate/history.cfm, accessed July 11, 2018).
4. Women's etiquette books, popular in the late nineteenth century, contained normative expectations for proper behavior by class, age, group affiliation, gender, and situation. They codified decorum, including when a "well-bred" woman should wear gloves.
5. The Hub was a designation coined by Oliver Wendell Holmes in *The Autocrat of the Breakfast Table*: "A jaunty looking person . . . said there was one more wise man's saying that he had heard; it was about our place—but he didn't know who said it. . . . 'Boston State House is the Hub of the Solar System'" (Holmes 1891:172).

6 "Hell with the fires burnt out" was a statement made by General Custer when speaking of South Dakota (Dohgan 2002:33).

7. "Fair Heart and Faint Lady" twists a phrase—a faint heart never won a fair lady—from *Adagia*, Greek and Latin proverbs published by Erasmus in 1500 (Phillips 1964). Beautiful but shy women will not fall in love with timid men. Theresa was Faint Lady and Frank Fair Heart.
8. Theresa was referring to football, a collegiate sport she had seen at Harvard.
9. *When Knighthood Was in Flower* is a 1901 Broadway play by Paul Kesler based on a novel by Charles Major (1898) about Mary Tudor, the younger sister of Henry VIII who had fallen in love with a commoner but was slated to marry the king of France. It was one of the best-selling novels in the United States.

10. Providentia was a Roman deity who foresaw the future. She helped an individual act appropriately, part of a cult that honored security, liberty, genius, peace, and justice.

Chapter 12

Out West 24(5):405–14 (1906), T. Russell journal, July 14, 1900.

1. Anthropology strove to combat ethnocentrism, but Theresa did not even consider that her stereotyped views held that other cultures were by definition inferior and that she felt her culture was inherently correct and natural. While female travelers tended to express sympathy with those observed (Harper 2001; Mills 1991; Morgan 1990, 1996), Theresa did not. She did become more cognizant of and reflexive about her cultural surroundings, but she always felt her own culture was superior.
2. Edward Noyes Wescott, *David Harum* (1897:9), dramatized in 1900. Another of this satirical humorist's famous sayings was "do unto the other feller the way he'd like to do unto you, and do it fast" ("Edward Noyes Westcott Quotes," http://www.azquotes.com/author/26954-Edward_Noyes_Westcott, accessed July 12, 2018).
3. L. Graves 1998:119. The Keams Canyon agency was founded in 1883; the boarding school was established in 1887 and is still functioning as an elementary school.
4. The image of women weaving or sewing and healing has symbolized togetherness since Greek times. Plato used the imagery in *The Republic* as a metaphor for the perfect political and social community. In Aristophanes' *Lysistrata,* the main character prepared the cloak of state. In William Blake's *The Four Zoas* (1893), weaving equated the act of knowledgeable speech (Blake 1893). Theresa had Mrs. Rausch sew a container for a useless substance but later found it to be what she needed (see Kruger 2002). Theresa saw this as a psychical archetype, Samuel Coleridge's phrase coined for his studies of the New Testament and Greek philosophy (see Barbeau 2008:77–110).
5. The quotation is from Henry Wadsworth Longfellow's poem "The Skeleton in Armor," first published in 1841 (Longfellow 1863:1l–12). It refers to being haunted unceasingly by a person.
6. Mrs. Rausch was referring to Fewkes or Hough. We have not located information about her.
7. Theresa is making a play on the words in act 4, scene 1, of William Shakespeare's *A Midsummer's Night Dream,* where Helena discusses how all men are equal.
8. Several references to listening are found in the Bible. For example, James 1:19: "Know this, my beloved brothers: let every person be quick to hear, slow to speak, slow to anger."
9. Named after President McKinley, who had been assassinated at the 1901 Pan-American Exposition, a McKinley pie was a sugar-butter tart seasoned with nutmeg, cinnamon, and allspice. It could be made easily with the dry ingredients, milk, and some butter.

10. The quotation is from Will Carleton's "Gone with a Handsome Man," stanza 20: "To appreciate heaven well, 'tis good for a man to have some fifteen minutes of hell" (Stokes Publishing Company 1906:11).
11. Theresa is making a play on Proverbs 17:1.
12. This quotation is an alteration of a saying by French mathematician Blaise Pascal found in *Pensées* (1958) that explains how a nonbeliever can come to embrace God.
13. The ten lost tribes of Israel were driven from Israel by the Neo-Assyrian Empire's conquest, ca. 720 BCE. Mormonism held that two groups (the ancestors of Native Americans and Polynesians) escaped and crossed the ocean. They would be restored by Zion built in North America, led by Joseph Smith and his followers in preparation for the Second Coming of Christ.
14. The quotation is from Hebrews 13:8, referring to unchangeability. It was a commonly used phrase of Mormon elders in their sermons (Woodruff 1895).

Chapter 13

Out West 24(6):544–48 (1906), T. Russell journal, July 16, 17, 18, and 19, 1900, and sections of earlier entries.

1. Cooper 1992; W. James 1890, 1897.
2. There are no photographs in this installment. Lummis saved the pages on which photographs could be printed for articles on the San Francisco earthquake.
3. The opening quotation comes from lyrics to a Universalist hymn by Julia Abigail Carney, "Little drops of water, Little grains of sand, Make the mighty ocean, and the beauteous land," from *The Hymnal for Boys and Girls* No. 116, about nature's beauty and how deeds of kindness, love, and mercy by children bless nations. See Hymnary.Org (https://hymnary.org, accessed, January 4, 2016).
4. Belshazzar, the last king of the Babylonian empire, held a feast and the guests drank from Yahweh's temple's holy vessels. Daniel interpreted handwriting on a wall as foretelling Babylon's fall. Lord Byron, Robert Frost, and Emily Dickinson all wrote poems about the event.
5. Aeneas was a Trojan hero, son of Aphrodite and Anchises. In Virgil's *Aeneid*, he fled with compatriots, landed in Italy, and became the ancestor of Romulus and Remus, who founded Rome.
6. The "core of the self" referenced James's spiritual self, an individual's stable, permanent center, the basis of *I* or pure ego. The self's subjective aspect included personality, core values, morals, religious aspiration, and conscience. Understanding the spiritual self required introspection, asking moral questions without the influence of objective thought (W. James 1890: chapter 10). The Jungian concept referred to an archetypal form of the unconscious, the basis of personal subjectivities (Alcaro, Carta, and Panksepp 2017). Writers used the concept to refer to the psyche's separate parts, which were fundamental and consistent throughout a person's life.

7. The Navajo women were making fry bread, a flat unleavened dough fried in lard.
8. Theresa is making a word play on the Lord's Prayer, recorded in the gospels of Matthew and Luke.
9. To sally forth was to leave a safe place in a confident manner to undertake a difficult task.
10. The child of Poseidon and Medusa, Pegasus was an immortal winged horse, which drew Zeus through the sky as he released thunderbolts. Pegasus was also capable of creating water streams and helped Bellerophon slay monsters, including the Chimera.
11. "Deep-sighted old Scot" is a reference to John Clerk, Lord Eldin, a lame judge noted for his pithy wisdom (Gray 1915).
12. "Little Goldenhair" is a reference to "Goldilocks and the Three Bears," first recorded and published by Robert Southe in 1837. As in "Snow White and the Three Dwarfs," the heroine entered a house, tasted food, and fell asleep (Opie and Opie 1992).
13. The expedition headed southeast to Kwaituki, where they remained for nine days.
14. Wepo Spring was north of Antelope Mesa, Wepo Village, on the mesa top. The dodo was an extinct Mauritian bird and a character in Lewis Carroll's *Alice's Adventures in Wonderland*, a symbol for exotic lands in British literature. In Genesis 2:18–13, Adam named the animals before Eve was created. Twain stated in "Extracts from Adam's Diary" that Adam said, "I get no chance to name anything myself. The new creature names everything that comes along before I get a chance to protest." Eve named beings because they looked like the names. "There is the dodo, for instance, says she. The moment one looks at it one sees at a glance that it 'looks like a dodo'" (Twain 1897:5).
15. The ship of the desert was a camel, adapted to survive arid habitats. The phrase was an image in legends about vessels lost in the California desert. Joaquin Miller, in his poem "The Ship in the Desert," referred to a Spanish galleon full of treasure (Miller 1875).

Chapter 14

Out West 25(1):27–36 (1906), T. Russell, journal, August 2–12, 1900.

1. W. James 1890:chapter 10; Cooper 1992:504.
2. Austin 2009; Reichard 1950. It was obvious that Theresa had not read Washington Matthews's (1887, 1895) ethnographies, which would have given her some Navajo concepts. In Diné philosophy, death and illness constitute disharmony (*hóchxó*), a world out of balance, not functioning as it should (*hózhó*). To keep hóchxó under the control of hózhó requires a great knowledge. To associate with the dead was to court disaster for everyone participating in the expedition and the Navajo community. It was likely that when they uncovered burials, Sliver prayed to counter the activity's effects. Frank dying of lung problems would have been considered

the outcome of his excavating and keeping human remains around him. Navajo *hatatli* and diagnosticians attributed Matthew's deafness to recording Navajo ritual and sandpaintings without being ritually prepared to be around intense power.

3. Kuklick 1987.
4. The quotation includes the first two lines from "A Camp" in *Travels with a Donkey in the Cevennes* by Robert Lewis Stevenson (1897), a humorous depiction of a stubborn traveling companion, Modestine the donkey. This was a theme broached in many of Theresa's journal entries, where Bill and Bob were the subject of her amusement and ire.
5. "A skeleton in the closet" was a colloquialism used to note an undisclosed fact about an irreproachable individual, which, if revealed, would lead to a loss of respect. Decomposition implied the individual had held a secret for so long it now smelled. The tent—with its insecure, porous walls—was reminiscent of the idea that a person living in a glass house should have no secrets. The phrase was used by Edgar Allan Poe in *The Black Cat* (1843) and William Thackeray in *The Newcomers: Memoirs of a Most Respectable Family* (1855). In 1830s England, it referred to body snatchers, who hid cadavers in chambers until they were sold (*Phrase Finder* n.d.).
6. *Dolce far niente* was an Italian phrase for pleasant relaxation in carefree idleness or sweetly doing nothing. It was also the title of a poem by Paul Hamilton Hayne (1882).
7. "The Shadow of the Heart" was a poem by Fiona Macleod, a pseudonym for poet and playwright Mrs. William Sharp (Macleod 1901). It later became a popular song lyric.
8. Ziltahjini Mesa (or Mount Ziltagini), is often referred as Black Mountain Peak. Little Black Spot Mountain was located fifteen miles southwest of Big Mountain on Black Mesa.
9. Theresa studied these philosophical topics with James at Radcliffe.
10. Mary Baker Eddy, founder of Christian Science, theorized that God was the only reality. Followers believed health was restored and character transformed by the heartfelt desire to experience God's love. Only prayer healed. Theresa lamented she had no liniment for her sore muscles. A bath would be a restorative reward when her prayers were answered.

Chapter 15

Out West 25(2):132–38 (1906), T. Russell, journal, August 14–18, 1900.

1. Stanza 10 from "The Rubaiyat of Omar Khayyam" dealt with potential conflict, possibly a hint about the problems between Frank and Owen and the peace between Theresa and the Navajo elder, or her desire to rest on a green piece of land, an oasis in the brown desert (Khayyám 1878).

2. Theresa includes a line from James Russell Lowell's "The Vision of Sir Launfal" (1848), used in schools to teach diction.
3. The quotation is from an unidentified poem by Lowell (see Hazen 1992:282).
4. A rag house was a building where rags were prepared for papermaking.
5. Theresa uses a play on Matthew 24:32–44, Revelation 16:15, and John 10:10. Thieves come silently in the night to steal property. Here the thief was a rival archaeologist stealing "their" human remains.
6. Mishongnovi is a Hopi village on Second Mesa.
7. The Wise Man in this case was James, who espoused these views in his theory of free will.
8. Russell paid the Navajo woman for each artifact and human remain she uncovered. We can guess that she received the same rate either Keams or Hubbell would have paid for artifacts.
9. Three Franciscan missions at Hopi (Oraibi, Awatobi/Aguatubi, and Shongopovi) were operated until the Pueblo Revolt of 1680. Hopi killed everyone in Awatovi in 1700 as a cleansing of evil. Theresa was clearly of the opinion that the missionaries were colonial martyrs. For nuanced perspectives about Awatovi and Native perspectives on forced proselytizing in colonial situations, see Brooks 2016; Sheridan et al. 2015.

Chapter 16

Out West 25(4):247–57 (1906), T. Russell journal, August 20–21, 1900, with earlier observations.

1. Putnam asked Edward E. Hale in early June 1900 to organize a party of alumni from Alpha Delta Phi fraternity that Russell could lead, thereby supplying him with money. Unfortunately, Hale informed Putnam that he could not generate enough interest (Hale to Putnam, June 9, 1900, Folder H-I, Box 10, HUG 1717.2.1, PP, HUA).
2. A tourist was a mindless herd animal who trampled inhabitants to experience that which they could never understand or appreciate. Travelers thought and journeyed rationally. In *Americans Abroad*, Henry James said tourists in Europe were ill-mannered and inappropriately dressed (1878:209). We think that Frank asked Theresa to observe specific aspects of the Hopi Snake Dances, but there is no indication in her journal of what observations he sought.
3. The quotation is from "The Sign in the Sky," a narrative poem by Henry Van Dyke (1896) about a wise man visiting the Nativity scene.
4. Polaki was Keam's former employee. Together they explored Antelope Mesa and the Jeddito Wash. Polaki was later a trader at First Mesa (McNitt 1962:190).
5. "Story-boy" is a reference to Mowgli in *The Jungle Book* (Kipling 1894).
6. The quotation is a play on Daniel 11:32: "*And such as do wickedly against the covenant shall he corrupt by flatteries;* but the people who know their God will be

strong, and do exploits. In this sense they will be also to console those who are scared or sad in times of great stress."

7. These are lines from a Baptist hymn based on George Klingle's "Recompense" (Sabbath Recorder 1914:578).
8. Passion plays were dramatic performances representing Jesus from the Last Supper to the Crucifixion, focusing on suffering, death, and resurrection.
9. Theresa equated Hopi individuals to tragic figures. Absalom rebelled against his father, David, and was murdered during the Battle of Ephraim's Wood (Samuel 2, 14:25). John Dryden wrote *Absalom and Achitophel* as a discourse on the politics of his time. Hecuba, the main character in Euripides's tragic plays *Hecuba* and *The Trojan Women*, was the queen of Troy, Priam's wife, and the mother of 19 children, including Nestor, the king of Pylos. She was depicted weaving as she plotted revenge for her children's murders. Nestor, chronicled in Homer's *Iliad* and *Odyssey*, was noted for his bravery, boastful advice, and speaking abilities.
10. Theresa is referring to Hopi female hair styles. Unmarried women wore their hair in buns at the side of the head. Once married, they wore braids.
11. James's essays on the nature of dreams were influenced by Freud's works (James 1892).

Chapter 17

Out West 25(4):341–47 (1906), T. Russell, journal, August 22–27, 1900.

1. The quotation about traveling in a desert is from *Between the Gates* by Benjamin F. Taylor (1878).
2. "Go West, young man, and grow up with the country" was a slogan written by John Soule in 1851. Horace Greely used it in a *New York Tribune* editorial in 1865 to symbolize American expansionism and encourage hard workers to migrate (Fuller 2004). Theresa used it to indicate her young man was now turning west to the country's unknown, like all good explorers and settlers, to integrate it into the nation.
3. Keams Canyon Trading Post was the official post office for the area.
4. Red Lake Trading Post was east of Newberry Mesa and State Route 2, west of Polacca Wash.
5. Theresa now referred to herself as Señora, designating a change in her status.
6. Rachel was a biblical personage in Genesis 29 used as a metaphor for tragic womanhood, someone dying in childhood, or a misunderstood person, unreasonably hated by her sister, Leah.
7. Brother Stauffer was a Mennonite missionary who served at Oraibi in 1900. He temporarily ran a hotel in Winslow, bankrupting it. Voth often complained that Stauffer was exceedingly lazy but proud, and his wife was depressed and a very nasty individual (Voth Diary, Voth Papers, Mennonite Archives, Bethel College).
8. "Señora" refers to Mrs. McAdams.

9. Star Plug was a raw pressed tobacco condensed with a binding sweetener into a brick. The user scraped it with a 10-cent cutter to smoke in a pipe. Star loose-leaf tobacco also came in pouches that sported a barbershop song, "Star, Star, you know the rest. Star Tobacco is the best."
10. "Center-rush" is a reference to football and rugby. The uncle was McAdams, owner of the Chinle Trading Post ("Looking Back," UITA Oral History Project, http://library.nau.edu/speccoll/exhibits/, accessed December 12, 2018).
11. Slat sunbonnets had a very wide brim, strengthened with cords of wooden slats, which extended from the neck over the head, to the other side. They were based on the biblical injunction that women should cover their heads and faces. Women could not look to the side without turning their heads but were well protected from the sun and wind.

Chapter 18

Out West 25 (5):425–31 (1906), T. Russell, journal, August 26–27, 1900.

1. The quotation is from Henry Wadsworth Longfellow, "Sandalphon" (Longfellow 1863; first published in *The Birds of Passage* [1858]), about how God told the angels to interact with humanity.
2. Theresa is referring to watermelon. *Ships That Pass in the Night* by Beatrice Harraden (1893) was a best-selling love story set in a tuberculosis sanatorium. Uncle Remus, a freeman who passed on wisdom via folktales, was the fictional narrator of African American folktales and songs collected by Joel Chandler Harris. He compiled seven Uncle Remus books, representing African American struggles on plantations. The most famous character was Br'er Rabbit, a trickster (Harris 1880).
3. "Store-man" refers to McAdams.
4. A gunnysack is an inexpensive bag made of burlap used for shipping flour or potatoes.
5. Theresa is referring to Marley and the Ghost from Charles Dickens's novella *A Christmas Carol in Prose* (Dickens 1843). The phrase *sea of silence* was used to refer to the liberation of silence in prayer and contemplation. Based on Luke 5:4, Ezekiel 16:4, and Second Kings 2:19–21, silence was both a skill and an act likened to when fishermen let down their nets. Prayerfulness cleansed the soul (see Laird 2011:10). The Dead Sea, the world's saltiest ocean, continued Theresa's idea of salt as a cleansing symbol in a place of desolation where one did not hear nature.
6. Theresa is making a word play on "Theirs not to make reply. Theirs not to reason why. Theirs but to do and die" from "The Charge of the Light Brigade." The phrase denotes troops senselessly sent to death following stupid orders (Tennyson 1854). Not recognizing the true meaning of the poem, Protestant ministers used the quote to honor duty and faith. Theresa is also using word play on William Blake's 1794 book of prophesy, *The First Book of Urizen* (see Bentley 2003), where darkness is scary and dangerous. Theresa creates the feel of a melodrama or gothic

novel. Our thanks to Franci Washburn for this insight, personal communication, 2018.

7. Commonwealth Avenue was a major Boston thoroughfare that began at the Boston Public Garden. A waist referred to a calico dress composed of a shirt and a matching but separate skirt.
8. Sarah Maud Ruggles was a character in Kate Douglas Wiggin's children's book *The Birds' Christmas Carol.* The quotation is from chapter 5, "Some Other Birds Were Taught to Fly," which deals with belief and morality (Wiggin 1903).
9. The quotation is from Hamlet's soliloquy, "O, that this too, too solid flesh would melt. How weary, stale flat, and unprofitable seem to me all the uses of this world!" (Mabillard 2000).
10. "Where is My Wandering Boy Tonight" by Robert Lowry (1877) in which a mother laments a son who has left home (https://hymnary.org/text/where_is_my_wandering_boy, accessed June 12, 2018). Theresa was referring to her husband, who was her joy, that is, unconditional love. Propriety forbade Theresa and Erminio sharing the only dry sleeping space. She banished him to a cold, wet night, showing little sympathy for his comfort. Her desire to assure her readers her sexuality remained pure was critical for her presentation of self.
11. Theresa is referring to the jubilant chorus of Handel's "Messiah" (1741). Frank's joke was about resurrection.
12. Tennyson's "St. Simeon Stylites" is about hope, redemption, and rebirth (Kramer 1909).
13. "The Lay of the Last Minstrel" was a long narrative poem written by Walter Scott (1805).
14. Theresa is referring to Richard Wagner's opera *The Valkyrie,* the second work in The Ring of the Niberlung cycle, based on Norse Volsunga Saga. The Valkyrie was a group of women who decided soldiers' fates in battle. The opera was first performed in New York in 1877.

Chapter 19

Out West 25(6):[illegible]–17 (1906), no specific journal dates.

1. T. Russell, journal, September 14, 1900.
2. The article begins with two lines from "Good Bye!," a song by George Whyte-Melville and F. Paolo Tosti (1881) ("Good Bye!," https://www.youtube.com/watch?v=D9h7m6dvO_c, accessed June 14, 2018).
3. The quotation is the last line of Edwin Arnold's 1879 narrative poem *The Light of Asia* (Parrinder 2005:315), about Prince Siddhartha's life as he became The Buddha. It was a free adaptation of the Lalitavistra, which discussed how suffering, mindfulness, and actions help one gain enlightenment. When Theresa studied world religions, she was drawn to Buddhist philosophy. A cloud-wraith was a ghost or a shadow with an insubstantial form.

4. We have not found the source of the illusion of time and the afterlife and how one should make the best of this life. Theresa may have been referring to a psychology concept about knowledge and the separation of consciousness from the rest of life, later elaborated by Erwin Schrodinger.
5. *The Bohemian Girl* is an 1843 opera by Michael William Balfe, libretto by Alfred Bunn, based on Cervantes's *La Gitanilla* (The Little Gypsy Girl). Theresa was referring to the well-known aria "I Dreamt I Dwelt in Marble Halls," in which Arline described childhood memories. *The Bohemian Girl* was often mentioned in the works of James Joyce, Booth Tarkington, and Willa Cather.
6. We have not found this quote's source. It appears to be a play on a tale of woe, which occurred frequently in Shakespeare's plays (for example, *Romeo and Juliet*, *Hamlet*). "The Strawberry Roan" was a poem and traditional ballad about an outlaw horse that could not be ridden. The idea became associated with Wild West show performances (Holder 2011). Frank was referring to the frequent occurrence of having to round up horses searching for water.
7. Poem 64 by Catullus contains a reference to the whirlwind of fate. It was a lamentation on the shameful confusion of familial and social relationships that turned a deity away from mankind (Debrohum 1999). Pink tea was made with salt, milk, and baking soda. Sand dervishes were a Sufi Muslim order known for their poverty and austerity, who deserted the self's illusions to reach God. Theresa equated southwest and Middle Eastern hospitality rules that held strangers could expect to be fed. The Russells discussed how to meet such obligations but save enough food to last the season.
8. Theresa and Frank used James's philosophy and Spencerian ideas about adaptation and survival of the fittest through adaptation and learning. "Work out your own salvation with fear and trembling, for it is God who works in you, both to will and to work for his good pleasure" is from Philippians 2:12–13, spoken by Paul. Frank secularized the idea for natural selection. Note that Theresa does not have Frank utter the second half of the quotation.
9. To strike a chord meant one had caused people—or, in this case, a place—to approve of something or agree with it, symbolizing Theresa's harmony with the environment.
10. This discussion about hiding depression and its nature, based on Theresa's studies with James, touches on smiling depression, which was likened to wearing a mask.

Chapter 20

1. Theresa probably did not see these topics as appropriate for a travelogue. They became apparent only when viewed against Frank's life and career.
2. For readers of *National Geographic Magazine*, "the Other" has always referred to aesthetically riveting exotic cultures whose members lived nonindustrialized lives in intimate contact with nature (Holly 2016; Lutz and Collins 1993).

3. High Culture is distinct from the anthropological concept of culture as a way of life held by a society or group of people. It encompasses those parts of a culture held by a social elite that deal with aesthetic value, including art and literature. It can also refer to behavior practices and norms that are felt to have philosophical, historical, or literary value as well as education that cultivates intellectual pursuits. High culture in this instance is contrasted with middlebrow culture held by the middle class or low culture, mass culture, or folk traditions associated with the masses or general population.
4. See Lőnneberg 1981 for information on the Digger stereotype.
5. F. Russell 1902a:8–9.
6. F. Russell 1902a:8–9.
7. Miscommunication and the translation problems were at the heart of Theresa's frustrations. She blamed Hopi and Navajo men for failing to understand English. This was a common stance among tourists, who expected Indigenous peoples to know English but not for the visitors to take the time and effort to communicate in Native languages. It was especially common where the people who represented colonial power felt Native peoples should learn the language of political control as a result of conquest. Theresa drew an erroneous deduction that Navajos, Hopis, and Mexicans were "stupid" because they did not understand English. However, she had misgivings about her conclusion and made a few half-hearted attempts to learn Spanish, Arizona's lingua franca. It never occurred to her that as an anthropological researcher she had linguistic obligations, nor did she recognize the mental agility of people code-switching among two or three languages. Theresa had begun to learn this lesson by the end of the 1900 trip; she had responsibilities to communicate. She vowed to learn Spanish before they returned. We have no indication if she did and it does not appear that she ever learned more than a few words of O'odham. She would have been capable since she spoke and read German and French.
8. Theresa disagreed with John Swanton, who had met Navajo in Chaco Canyon in 1896 and recorded in his journal, "The Navajos are a pretty decent set of red skins living principally by means of their herds of sheep and goats and the famous Navajo blankets made by the women" (Swanton 1944:17). Theresa was not convinced about their industriousness or morality and provided her readers with her evidence.
9. Twain 1869:v. Theresa's publications most closely mirrored Jerome K. Jerome's humorous travelogues, where the writer used self-depreciation to poke fun at the British leisured class during an enhanced journey. The British humorist is most noted for his travel satire *Three Men in a Boat* (1889), a book based on his honeymoon on the Thames River, but where he transformed his wife into two longtime friends to create comic situations he could entwine with a regional history and a

satire of idleness. *Three Men in a Boat* sold more than one million copies. Theresa carried it on her journey.

10. Theresa increasingly applied James's assumptions, logic, and conclusions as the chapters progressed. Essential philosophical debates increased as her journey reached its physical end. This allowed Theresa to make the point that she could teach philosophy and psychology. It was almost as if she had moved from naïveté in the first chapter to wisdom in the later chapters. Theresa's allusions were not common knowledge. Contemporary readers will not easily recognize many references since cultural erudition has changed. We spent what felt sometimes like endless hours deciphering Theresa's texts in order to understand her allusions, symbols, and metaphors.
11. F. T. Russell 1920:x; Anamosa Eureka 1936:1.
12. The one historical summary of the Stanford English Department discussed only the male professors, focusing on department chairs. Conspicuously absent was more than cursory information about the female professors and instructors seen in the publication's photographs: Theresa had been an instructor since 1906, and with Margery Bailey was "one of only a few women to have a significant place in the department in the years before the second war" (Carnochan 2002:8). The article did document how women started at lower ranks and took years longer to be promoted than their male colleagues. We assume, based on our work with women anthropologists in the American Southwest, that they also received lower wages, although we have not looked into the issue.
13. F. T. Russell 1920:viii.
14. Brooklyn Daily Eagle 1920:4; Word and Way 1920; San Francisco Chronicle 1920; Argus Leader 1920; E. B. F. 1922.
15. U.S. passport and visa applications for Theresa Peet Russell (widow), January 6, 1906, September 1922, March 31, 1925, roll 2095, NA; F. T. Russell 1921, 1923a, 1923b, 1924a, 1924b, 1925, 1927a, 1933b, 1933c; W. S. K. 1927; Greene 1928; Hartford Courant 1927; J. H. H. 1933; Oakland Tribune 1935.
16. F. T. Russell 1923a, 1928a, 1928c, 1928b, 1930a, 1930b, 1932a, 1932b.
17. Quad-City Times 1933.
18. F. T. Russell 1927b, 1933a. Some lectures became publications: "Charles Lamb, 1775–1834" (1934) was presented at the Modern Languages Association; "A Centenary Study of Leslie Stephen" at the Philological Association of the Pacific Coast and Modern Languages Association (1932); and "Utopian Esthetics" and "Beauty and Art in Utopian Literature" at the American Philological Association (1929). Theresa visited Great Falls and talked to the Lions Club about social criticism used by American playwrights as a means of social reform (Great Falls Tribune 1933). The *Brooklyn Daily Eagle* published Theresa's untitled quote on August 8, 1921, p. 17: "If a dilemma would be content to wear only one horn, innocent adventurers

into the field of debate and argument would be less generously beset by the beast of embarrassing alternatives." Book Table 1920; Who's Who 1976; Burke and Howe 1972; S. Wallace 1951.

19. F. T. Russell and Yvors 1934; Butcher 2000.
20. F. T. Russell 1929, 1930c, 1932d; Gessler 1933:26.
21. F. T. Russell 1930d. Theresa served on university committees that dealt with female students and their ability to pursue intellectual lives. She was the faculty advisor for the English Club during the 1920s and served as a judge for Stanford's annual poetry competition.
22. F. T. Russell 1932c.
23. F. T. Russell 1932c:314–15.
24. F. T. Russell 1933c.
25. Times-Republican 1920. Beyond brief hints, Theresa's life remains obscure. During 1906–8 she kept a "Book of Incidents," recording random thoughts and experiences. The most notable was what it was like to be in Palo Alto during the 1906 earthquake (Hartwig 1910).
26. Anamosa Eureka 1936:1.

Frank's and Theresa's Final Worlds

1. Russell 1902a:6–7.
2. T. Russell, "Untitled Poem," *Out West* 24 (4):310 (1906).

Documentary Sources

1. Six other photographs of the villages are housed at the Peabody Museum of Archaeology and Ethnology.
2. Our thanks to the University of Colorado–Boulder library for loaning volumes 24 and 25 of *Out West*. For readers who want to see copies of all the published illustrations, *Out West* has been digitized by the HathiTrust as public domain documents, but the photographs are very grainy.

Appendix A

1. The Fred Harvey Company owned the Harvey House restaurants, hotels, and souvenir and art shops located at railroad stations in the western United States. In 1900 there were 45 restaurants and 20 dining cars in 12 states (Henderson 1969; Poling-Kempes 1989).
2. The Page Hotel was located at 101 S. Second Street, only two blocks from the train station.
3. Russell 1900a. C. N. Cotton was a Navajo trader instrumental in developing the textile market. He owned the Round Rock and Chinle trading posts and had an exclusive license to sell Arbuckle's coffee and Pendleton blankets in New Mexico and Arizona (McNitt 1962:222).

4. Theresa was referring to Frank's 1898 bicycle trip. It is unclear how much they used bicycles in 1900.
5. The Haystacks, Tséta' Ch'ééch'í (Breeze Blow Out from Between the Rocks), are 100-feet-high sandstone features. The location memorialized one of the first stops on the 1864 Long Walk (Young and Morgan 1987:73; Linford 2000:86). The second reference is to St. Michael's, Arizona.
6. Hamlin Garland wrote about the Hopi, Zuni, and Navajo in *The Book of the American Indian* (1923). An aeolian was a harp-shaped wooden box with sounding board used by Aeolus, the god of wind. Aeolian referred to an upright pneumonic organ.
7. *Squaw* is now considered a derogatory word. In 1900, however, it was common and referred to older women who worked. We expect that if Theresa were writing today, she would use *woman* in her text, but we can never be sure (see Parezo and Jones 2009).
8. Suleiman I, sultan of the Ottoman Empire from 1520 to 1566, ruled an estimated 25 million people. He was a distinguished poet, goldsmith, and governmental and social reformer, always depicted in European portraits dressed in opulent clothing.
9. Apollo daily drove his chariot to ensure the Earth received light. His daily farewell, a colorful sunset, was a good omen. He was the god of music, poetry, healing, prophecy, and truth.
10. Shakespeare's *Macbeth*, act 2, scene 2: "Sleep that knits up the raveled sleeve of care. The death of each day's life, sore labor's bath, Balm of hurt minds, great nature's second course, Chief nourisher in life's feast." Fleshpots of Egypt (Exodus xvi:3) designated envious bodily comforts. The Israelites relinquished civilization's comforts to search for the Promised Land. The phrase symbolized Theresa's travails and envy of those who had bathwater.
11. Chinle, "Water Outlet," the mouth of Canyon de Chelly (Linford 2000:67–68).
12. "Toy-houses" is a reference to one-room structures Frank was not interested in (Adams and Duff 2004).
13. Charles E. Burton became Hopi superintendent in 1899. The Hopi disliked him; he had no interest in learning Hopi culture and brutally demanded that people acculturate. By 1900 Burton had a reputation for attacking anthropologists, arguing they supported primitivism (Bailey 1961:19). Russell assumed Burton would make him leave the reservation under military escort.
14. Zilt-sah-jini probably refers to Big Mountain or Little Spot Mountain (Linford 2000:35). Hubbell had owned the Big Mountain Trading Post so was familiar with the area. We have not located any of this correspondence in the Hubbell Papers, Special Collections, University of Arizona, or in Frank Russell's papers at any institution. Jonathan Williams opened Blue Canyon Trading Post in 1882. It was very isolated; freight took three days from Winslow. Williams had two sons, Ben and Bill, whom he often left at the post while prospecting (McNitt 1962:269–70).

15. There is no "fruit" clan, which Frank realized.
16. We have been unable to identify this ruin.
17. "Tired nature's . . . balmy sleep" is from English poet Edward Young's *Night Thoughts*, written between 1742 and 1745 (Young 1853).
18. Frank is referring to unidentified ruins on their route to Black Mountain.
19. The school and subagency were established in 1890 near Williams's trading post. When Williams left, the store was incorporated into the school (McNitt 1962:274).
20. Frank is referring to Kwaituki or Qöótsaptu-veta (NA1699), both visited by V. Mindeleff (1891).
21. Tom Polacca (Pavatea/Pavatewa) was born in Hano but forcibly taken to Keams Canyon Boarding School at age six. He herded sheep for Keam for about 15 years and started to trade in the 1890s. He established his store at the base of First Mesa in 1896. One popular writer called him "the merchant prince of the Hopi" (M. W. M. Smith 1938:4). He married a Hano woman, Quang, and they had six children.
22. The poem "Green Fields and Running Brooks" is by James Whitcomb Riley (1900).
23. The *Anamosa Eureka* published an article about the event, including a list of guests, which named Theresa's but not Frank's relatives (Anamosa Eureka 1900).
24. Theresa includes a John Milton quote from Mary Wollstonecraft's "Modern Ideal of Womanhood" (1796), in which Wollstonecraft argues that Milton's assessment of women's natures is a rationalization for men's tyranny. Theresa agreed that women were not frail or created for the pleasure of men who demand blind obedience.
25. An unidentified song lyric, nursery rhyme, or other German text.
26. "On the Banks of the Wabash, Far Away" was a best-selling song composed by Paul Bresser in 1897. The lyrics were a reminder of happy childhoods in rural areas.
27. In Greek mythology, the prophet Celaeno was considered the darkest Harpy and a demonic nemesis of wrongdoing who is indifferent to human suffering. She was also referred to as a Pleiades, one of the seven sisters, or an Amazon killed by Heracles during his ninth labor ("Celaeno," http://mythworld.wikia.com/wiki/Celaeno, accessed March 20, 2018).
28. Historian Amy Gordon Gait Grant was the wife of novelist Robert Grant, an overseer of Harvard University. In 1900 he published the novel *Unleavened Bread.* Theresa may be referring to this novel she read on the trip. The story is about a businessman's selfish wife, who forces her way into elite society. It was adapted as a play for Broadway in 1901. Theresa had to wait four years for Grant's next novel, *The Undercurrent* (1904).
29. Theresa is referring to the southeast cemetery at Kawaika-a.
30. A collector of Native American art, amateur archaeologist, and documentary photographer, Adam C. Vroman made nine southwestern trips, often accompa-

nying Lummis. In 1897 and 1899, he participated in the BAE summer field season, accompanying Hodge to Acoma (Webb and Weinstein 1973). Portrait photographer Edward S. Curtis produced the 20-volume *The North American Indians*, a project that published more than 1,500 photographs (Curtis 1907–30).

31. Mabel Collins worked in the Toreva mission with Miss Watkins (Voth diary, 1901, Henry Voth Papers, Mennonite Archives, Bethel College). Hrdlička visited Hopi albinos (three men and eight women) in March 1900. The Hopi called these honored individuals *ko-lo-ko-cha-te*. The individual the Russells visited was one of the following: Naqualashtiwa (man, age 30) or Shakwentiva (man, age 33), both of Mishongovi; Sivenka (woman, age 28) of Shipaulovi; or Lominimka (woman, age 35) of Shungopovi (Hrdlička 1908:195–96).
32. Jerome described the Oberammergau festival in *Three Men on the Bummel* (1898). The play has been performed since 1634 to thank God for saving the community from bubonic plague.
33. We have discovered no information about Mr. Enderly. He may have been an employee and not the owner. We think this was the trading post at Red Lake.
34. Mr. Ray was a Mennonite missionary.
35. J. Higgins McAdams ran the Sunrise Springs Trading Post, 15 miles southwest of Ganado (McNitt 1962:273). His relative, George McAdams, built a post at Red Lake on Tokesjhay Wash in 1881. He sold this post in 1888 and became a partner of the Babbitt brothers. McAdams returned to Red Lake when the Babbitts recouped a debt. McAdams returned to the store, staying until the early 1900s (Babbitt 1986:3; McNitt 1962:265–66).
36. McAdams's nephew referred to here was Hubert Richardson (McNitt 1962:273–74).
37. Shakespeare, *A Midsummer Night's Dream*, act 3, scene 2: "Lord, what fools these mortals be!" (spoken by Puck).
38. In December 1899, Jesse Burt explored Homolovi, then moved west and visited ruins for 75 miles along the Little Colorado River (Dorsey 1901:220). In May 1900, Dorsey sent him again to the Little Colorado. He went as far as Black Falls.
39. As has been obvious in several places, Theresa often misspelled Spanish words. For instance, here *agua* is spelled *aqua*.
40. Arthur Train's *The Spanish Prisoner* was the story of a con man who claimed to be imprisoned in Spain under false pretenses. He asked the mark to give him money to secure his release, promising the victim would be rewarded (Train 1910). It was the foundational story for contemporary money transfer or advance-fee frauds.
41. Scholy is also one of McAdams's nephews and has his own trading post at Oraibi (McNitt 1962:204).
42. Theresa interacted with Gertrude Lewis Gates, discussing health rather than archaeology. Lummis (1968:120) found her a woman of the "highest refinement and spotless character . . . noted for thoroughness, understanding and common

sense." She was interested in the Pueblo people, Indian education, and proselytizing. She and her husband were both members of the Sequoya League and the Arroyo scene (Pavesic 1999).

43. Theresa is referring to wealthy headman and singer Hoskinini (Handing Out War or Angry One), who lived west of Navajo Mountain. He and his band had resisted U.S. Army attempts to relocate to Fort Sumner in the 1860s and had been successful in repelling subsequent white incursions. In 1900 he lived near Oljetoh (Moonlight) Wash in Monument Valley (Indigenous Voices of the Colorado Plateau, Northern Arizona University).
44. George Manning's brother had a store in Gallup, New Mexico.
45. The quotation from Jerome's *Diary of a Pilgrimage and Six Essays* (1891:135) refers to rising at 2:30 a.m. to catch a train.
46. We have found no reference to this folder.
47. "Someday I'll Wander Back Again" is a traditional song written in 1870 by W. F. Shaw. Lyrics addressed returning to a childhood home from which one had wandered.

References

Adams, E. Charles, and Andrew L. Duff, eds. 2005. *The Protohistoric Pueblo World, A. D. 1275–1600*. University of Arizona Press, Tucson.

Adams, Percy F., ed. 1988. *Travel Literature through the Ages: An Anthology*. Garland and Speake, New York.

Adler, Michael, ed. 1996. *The Prehistoric Pueblo World, A. D. 1150–1350*. University of Arizona Press, Tucson.

Agassiz, Louis, and Elizabeth Agassiz. 1868. *A Journey in Brazil*. Ticknor and Fields, Boston.

Alcaro, Antonio, Stefano Carta, and Jaak Panksepp. 2017. The Affective Core of the Self: A Neuro-Archetypical Perspective on the Foundations of Human and Animal Subjectivity. In *Frontiers in Psychology* September 1. https://doi.org/10.3389/fpsyg.2017.01424, accessed December 1, 2019.

Almazan, Tristan, and Sarah Coleman. 2003a. George Amos Dorsey: A Curator and His Comrades. In *Curators, Collections and Contexts: Anthropology at the Field Museum, 1893–2002*, edited by Stephen E. Nash and Gary M. Feinman, pp. 87–98. Fieldiana: Anthropology n.s., No. 36. Field Museum of Natural History, Chicago.

Almazan, Tristan, and Sarah Coleman. 2003b. Stanley McCormick Funded Expeditions and Purchases, 1899–1901, 1911, 1913. Finding Aide. Field Museum Archives, Chicago.

American Naturalist. 1897. Proceedings of Scientific Societies. *American Naturalist* 31(364):361–65.

American Naturalist. 1904. Quarterly Record of Gifts, Appointments, Retirements and Deaths. *American Naturalist* 37 (444):893–95.

Anamosa Eureka. 1887. Married. *Anamosa Eureka* June 2:3. Anamosa, Iowa.

Anamosa Eureka. 1896. Obituary: Cordelia Wilcox Peet. *Anamosa Eureka* April 23:4. Anamosa, Iowa.

Anamosa Eureka. 1900. A Life Journey Together. *Anamosa Eureka* July 5:5. Anamosa, Iowa.

Anamosa Eureka. 1903a. Another Sudden Summons. Mrs. Charles T. Myrick Passed Away on Friday After a Very Brief Illness. *Anamosa Eureka* March 19:4. Anamosa, Iowa.

Anamosa Eureka. 1903b. Death of Dr. Frank Russell. *Anamosa Eureka* November 12:5. Anamosa, Iowa.

Anamosa Eureka. 1917. Death of A. C. Peet. *Anamosa Eureka* December 22:1. Anamosa, Iowa.

Anamosa Eureka. 1936. Mrs. Russell Dies Feb. 15. *Anamosa Eureka* February 27:1. Anamosa, Iowa.

Anamosa Journal. 1913. Mrs. A. C. Peet. *Anamosa Journal* July 31:7. Anamosa, Iowa.

Anamosa Journal. 1917. A. C. Peet. *Anamosa Journal* November 22:1. Anamosa, Iowa.

Anderson, Keith M. 1969. Tsegi Phase Technology. PhD dissertation, Department of Anthropology, University of Washington, Seattle.

Anonymous. 1903. Iowa Loses Noted Scientist. Frank Russell, Scholar and Explorer, Does Research While in Arizona. No paper name November 10:np. TRP.

Argus Leader. 1920. Literary Criticism. *Argus Leader* August 16:6. Sioux Falls, S.Dak.

Arnold, Edwin. 1879. *The Light of Asia: The Great Renunciation*. Roberts Brothers, Boston.

Auerbach, Benjamin M. 2010. *Human Variation in the Americas: The Integration of Archaeology and Biological Anthropology*. Occasional Paper No. 38. Center for Archaeological Investigations, Carbondale, Ill.

Austin, Raymond H. 2009. *Navajo Courts and Navajo Common Law: A Tradition of Tribal Self-Governance*. University of Minnesota Press, Minneapolis.

Babbitt, James E. 1986. Trading Posts Along the Little Colorado River. *Plateau* 57(3):2–9.

Babcock, Barbara A., and Nancy J. Parezo. 1988. *Daughters of the Desert: Women Anthropologists and the Native American Southwest, 1880–1980: An Illustrated Catalogue*. University of New Mexico Press, Albuquerque.

Bailey, Lynn R. 1961. Thomas Varner Keam: Tusayan Trader. *Arizoniana* 2(4):15–19.

Baltimore Sun. 1900. Find New Bacilli. Scientists Announce Important Discoveries. *Baltimore Sun* December 28:7. Baltimore, Md.

Bandelier, Adolph F. 1892. *Final Report of Investigations Among the Indians of the Southwestern United States*. Volume 2. Papers of the Archaeological Institute of America, American Series vol. 4. John Wilson and Son, Cambridge, Mass.

Banta, Melissa, and Curtis Hinsley. 1986. *From Site to Sight: Anthropology, Photography, and the Power of Imagery*. Peabody Museum Press, Cambridge, Mass.

Barbeau, Jeffrey W. 2008. *Coleridge, the Bible and Religion: Nineteenth-Century Major Lives and Letters*. Palgrave Macmillan, New York.

Bentley, G. E., Jr. 2003. *The Stranger from Paradise*. Yale University Press, New Haven, Conn.

Bernardine, Wesley. 2016. *Hopi Oral Tradition and the Archaeology of Identity*. University of Arizona Press, Tucson.

Bieder, Robert. 1986. *Science Encounters the Indian, 1820–1880*. University of Oklahoma Press, Norman.

Bingham, Edwin R. 1955. *Charles F. Lummis: Editor of the Southwest*. Huntington Library, San Marino, Calif.

Binheim, Max. 1928. Russell, Theresa Frances. In *U.S. Women of the West, 1928*, p. 80. Publishers Press, Los Angeles.

Blue, Martha. 2000. *Indian Trader: The Life and Times of J. L. Hubbell.* Kiva Publications, Walnut Creek, Calif.

Blumenbach, Johann F. 1865. *The Anthropological Treatises of Johann Friederich Blumenbach.* Translated by T. Bendyshe. Longman, Green, London.

Boas, Franz. 1891 Physical Characteristics of the Indians of the North Pacific Coast. *American Anthropologist* 4(1, o.s.):25–32.

Boas, Franz. 1893. The Theory of Anthropometrical Statistics. Papers read September 16, 1893, Before the International Statistical Institute at Chicago Quarterly Publications of the American Statistic Association, Boston.

Bolton, Herbert E., ed. 1916 *Spanish Exploration in the Southwest.* Charles Scribner's Sons, New York.

Book Table. 1920. Review of *Satire in the Victorian Novel,* by Theresa Russell. Book Table. *Journal of Education* 91(17, April 22):470.

Bourke, John G. 1884. *The Snake-Dance of the Moquis of Arizona.* Sampson, Low, Marston, Searle and Rivington, London.

Brooklyn Daily Eagle. 1920. The Place of Satire in Nineteenth Century Novels. *Brooklyn Daily Eagle* July 31:4. Brooklyn, N.Y.

Brooks, James F. 2016. *Mesa of Shadows: A History of the Awatovi Massacre.* W. W. Norton, New York.

Browman, David L. 2002a. Origins of Americanist Stratigraphic Excavation: The Peabody Museum Method and the Chicago Method. In *New Perspectives on the Origins of American Archaeology,* edited by David L. Browman and Stephen Williams, pp. 242–64. University of Alabama Press, Tuscaloosa.

Browman, David L. 2002b. The Peabody Museum, Frederic W. Putnam and the Rise of U.S. Anthropology, 1866–1903. *American Anthropologist* 104(2):508–19.

Browman, David L. 2013. *Cultural Negotiations: The Role of Women in the Founding of Americanist Archaeology.* University of Nebraska Press, Lincoln.

Browman, David L., and Stephen Williams, eds. 2013. *Anthropology at Harvard: A Biographical History, 1790–1940.* Peabody Museum Press, Cambridge, Mass.

Browning, Robert. 1840. Sordello. Edward Moxton, Ltd., London.

Browning, Robert. 1864. Rabbi Ben Ezra. In *Dramatis Personae.* Ticknor and Fields, London Poetry Foundation website. https://www.poetryfoundation, accessed June 12, 2018.

Burbank, E. A., Earnest Royce, and Frank J. Taylor. 1944. *Burbank among the Indians.* Caxton Publishers, Caldwell, Idaho.

Burke, W. J., and Will D. Howe. 1972. *American Authors and Books: 1640 to the Present Day.* 3rd rev. ed. Crown, New York.

Butcher, Bernard. 2000. Was It Murder? *Stanford Magazine* (January–February): n.p. https://stanfordmag.org/contents/was-it-murder.

Calderon de la Barca, Fannie. 1843. *Life in Mexico during a Residence of Two Years in That Country.* Chapman and Hall, London.

Carnochan, W. B. 2002. English at Stanford 1891–2000: A Brief History. *Sandstone & Tone* 26(1):2–15.

Caywood, Louis R. 1962. *Archaeological Studies at Tonto National Monument, Arizona.* Technical Series, vol. 2. Southwestern Monuments Association, Globe, Ariz.

Chamberlain, Alexander F. 1894. Anthropology in Universities and Colleges. *Pedagogical Seminary* 3:48–60.

Chamberlain, Alexander F. 1904. In Memoriam: Frank Russell. *Journal of American Folk-lore* 17(66):208–9.

Chicago Tribune. 1901. Do This Man and Woman Exist? *Chicago Tribune* August 31:5.

Christie, Agatha. 1936. *Murder in Mesopotamia.* Dodd, Mead and Co., New York.

Christie, Agatha. 1985. *Come Tell Me How You Live.* Bantam Books, New York [orig. pub. 1946].

Chronic, Halka. 1983. *Roadside Geology of Arizona.* Mountain Press, Missoula, Mont.

Clifford, James. 1988. *The Predicament of Culture: Twentieth-Century Ethnography, Literature and Art.* Harvard University Press, Cambridge, Mass.

Clifford, James, and George E. Marcus, eds. 1986. *Writing Culture: The Poetics and Politics of Ethnography.* University of California Press, Berkeley.

Cohen, Norm. 2005. *Folk Music: A Regional Exploration.* Greenwood Guides to American Roots Music. Greenwood Press, Westport, Conn.

Colton, Harold. 1946. "Fool's Names like Fool's Faces" (petroglyphs). *Plateau* 19(1):1–8.

Colton, Mary Ferrell R., and Harold S. Colton. 1931. Petroglyphs, the Record of a Great Adventure. *American Anthropologist* 33(1):32–37.

Cook, Della C. 2006. The Old Physical Anthropology and the New World: A Look at the Accomplishments of an Antiquated Paradigm. In *Bioarchaeology: The Contextual Analysis of Human Remains,* edited by Jane E. Buikstra and Lane A. Beck, pp. 27–72. Routledge, London.

Cook, Minnie. 1976. *Apostle to the Pima Indians: The Story of Charles H. Cook, the First Missionary to the Pimas.* Omega Books, London.

Cooper, Wesley E. 1992. William James's Theory of the Self. *The Monist* 75(4):504–20.

Cooper, Wesley E. 2002. *The Unity of William James's Thought.* Vanderbilt University Press, Nashville.

Cordell, Linda S. 1984. *Prehistory of the Southwest.* Academic Press, Orlando.

Cordell, Linda S. 1993. Women Archaeologists in the Southwest. In *Hidden Scholars: Women Anthropologists and the Native American Southwest,* edited by Nancy J. Parezo, pp. 202–20. University of New Mexico Press, Albuquerque.

Cordell, Linda S., and Maxine E. McBrinn. 2012. *Archaeology of the Southwest.* 3rd. ed. Left Coast Press, Walnut Creek, Calif.

Cottam, Erica. 2014. The Legend of Don Lorenzo: John Lorenzo Hubbell and the Sense of Place in Navajo Country. PhD dissertation, School of Historical, Philosophical and Religious Studies, Arizona State University, Tempe.

Cottam, Erica. 2015. *Hubbell Trading Post: Trade, Tourism, and the Navajo Southwest.* University of Oklahoma Press, Norman.

Courier. 1901. Brainy Men to Meet. *The Courier* August 6:4. Waterloo, Iowa.

Courier-Journal. 1901. Exeunt Adam and Eve. The *Courier-Journal* September 1:14. Nashville, Tenn.

Crick, Malcolm. 1995. The Anthropologist as Tourist: An Identity in Question. In *International Tourism: Identity and Change,* edited by Marie-Françoise Lanfant, John B. Allcock, and Edward M. Bruner, pp. 205–23. Sage, London.

Curtis, Edward S. 1907–30. *The North American Indians; Being a Series of Volumes Picturing and Describing the Indians of the United States, and Canada.* 20 vols. Vols. 1–5, Harvard University Press, Cambridge, Mass.; Vols. 6–20, Plimpton Press, Norwich, Conn.

Cushing, Frank Hamilton. 1886. A Study of Pueblo Pottery as Illustrative of Zuni Culture Growth. In *Fourth Annual Report of the Bureau of Ethnology for 1882–1883,* pp. 473–522. GPO, Washington, D.C.

Cushing, Frank Hamilton. 1890. Preliminary Notes on the Origin, Working Hypothesis, and Primary Researches of the Hemenway Southwestern Archaeological Expedition. In *Congrés international des americanistes, Compte-rendu, Berlin, 1888,* pp. 151–94. Nendeln, Liechtenstein.

Cushing, Frank Hamilton. 1970. *My Adventures in Zuñi.* American West, Palo Alto, Calif.

Cushing, Frank Hamilton. 1995. Itinerary of Reconnaissance to Casa Grande Ruins, Dec. 31, 1887 to Jan. 4, 1888. *Journal of the Southwest* 37(4):590–604.

Daehkne, Jon, and Amy Lonetree. 2010. Repatriation in the United States: The Current State of NAGPRA. In *Handbook of Postcolonial Archaeology,* edited by Jane Lydon and Uzma Z. Rizvi, pp. 245–55. Left Coast Press, Walnut Creek, Calif.

Daily Citizen. 1892. Won by the Ladies. *Daily Citizen* December 17:2. Iowa City, Iowa.

Daily Citizen. 1893a. Covered with Glory. *Daily Citizen* April 23:4. Iowa City, Iowa.

Daily Citizen. 1893b. Phi Delta Theta Party. *Daily Citizen* February 12:4. Iowa City, Iowa.

Daily Citizen. 1893c. St. Valentine Reigned Supreme. *Daily Citizen* February 15:3. Iowa City, Iowa.

Darnell, Regna. 1970. The Emergence of Academic Anthropology at the University of Pennsylvania. *Journal of the History of Behavioral Science* 6(1):80–92.

Davis, Hester A. 2008. *Remembering Awatovi: The Story of an Archaeological Expedition in Northern Arizona, 1935–1939.* Peabody Museum Monographs No. 10. Peabody Museum Press, Cambridge, Mass.

Dean, Jeffrey S. 1969. *Chronological Analysis of Tsegi Phase Sites in Northeastern Arizona.* Dissertation. Later published as Papers of the Laboratory of Tree Ring Research 3. University of Arizona, Tucson.

Debrohum, Jeri Blair. 1999. Ariadne and the Whirlwind of Fate: Figures of Confusion in Catullus 64.149–157. *Classical Philology* 94(4):419–30.

Dehgan, Bahman, ed. 2002. *America in Quotations*. McFarland, Jefferson, N.C.

DeJong, David H. 2003. A Scheme to Rob Them of Their Land: Water, Allotment, and the Economic Integration of the Pima Reservation, 1902–1921. *Journal of Arizona History* 44(2):99–132.

DeJong, David H. 2014. "Down the Gila": A. J. Chandler's Desert Land Scheme and the Gila River Indian Reservation, 1891–1911. *American Indian Culture and Research Journal* 38(3):1–24.

Denver Post. 1901. Cliff Dwellers Were Southerners. Dr. Frank Russell of Harvard Says, "They Were Not from Asia." *Denver Post* No month or day, no page. In scrapbook, Peabody Museum, Cambridge, Mass.

Desanti, Brady J. 2012. Arriving at a Common Ground: John Reed Swanton and American Anthropology. PhD dissertation, Department of History, University of Kansas, Lawrence.

Des Moines Register. 1903. Iowa Loses Noted Scientist. Frank Russell, Scholar and Explorer, Dies While in Arizona. *Des Moines Register* November 11:3.

Dexter, Ralph W. 1965. Contributions of Frederic Ward Putnam to Ohio Archaeology. *Ohio Journal of Science* 65(3):110–17.

Dexter, Ralph W. 1966a. Frederic Ward Putnam and the Development of Museums of Natural History and Anthropology in the United States. *Curator* 9(2):151–55.

Dexter, Ralph W. 1966b. Putnam's Problems Popularizing Anthropology. *American Scientist* 54(3):315–32.

Dickens, Charles. 1843. *A Christmas Carol in Prose, Being a Ghost Story of Christmas*. Chapman and Hall, London.

Dickinson, Emily. 1924. *The Complete Poems of Emily Dickinson*. Little, Brown, Boston.

Dorsey, George A. 1894. The Study of Anthropology in American Colleges. *The Archaeologist* 2:368–73.

Dorsey, George A. 1896. The History of the Study of Anthropology at Harvard. *Denison Quarterly* 4(2):77–97.

Dorsey, George A. 1899. The Department of Anthropology of the Field Columbian Museum: A Review of Six Years. *American Anthropologist* 1(n.s., 1):247–65.

Dorsey, George A. 1901. The Stanley McCormick Hopi Expedition. *Science* 13(319, February 8):219–22.

Dunning, Charles H., and Edward H. Peplow Jr. 1959. *Rocks to Riches: The Story of American Mining*. Southwest Publishing, Phoenix.

Dupertuis, C. W., and J. M. Tanner. 1950. The Pose of the Subject for Photogrammetric Anthropometry, with Especial Reference to Somatotyping. *American Journal of Physical Anthropology* 89(10):27–42.

E. B. F. 1922. Review of T. Russell's *Satire in the Victorian Novel*. *Sewanee Review* 30(1):117–19.

Edwards, Elizabeth. 1992. Introduction. In *Anthropology and Photography: 1860–1920*, edited by Elizabeth Edwards, pp. 3–17. Yale University Press in association with the Royal Anthropological Institute, New Haven, Conn., and London.

Eiselt, B. Sunday. 2012. *Becoming White Clay: A History and Archaeology of Jicarilla Apache Enclavement*. University of Utah Press, Salt Lake City.

Engelhardt, Carroll. 1987. Compulsory Education in Iowa, 1872–1919. *Annals of Iowa* 49(1):58–76.

Estherville Daily News. 1895. Literary Notices. *Estherville Daily News* June 6:2. Estherville, Iowa.

Evening Star. 1900. In the Frozen North. Dr. Frank Russell's Explorations around the Arctic Circle. *Evening Star* February 3:16. Washington, D.C.

Evening Star. 1902. Collection of Curios Obtained by Dr. Frank Russell of U.S. Bureau of Ethnology. *Evening Star* July 10:10. Washington, D.C.

Evening Times. 1896. Will Study the Eskimos. *Evening Times* February 20:4. Washington, D.C.

Evening Times. 1900. Scientists in Session. The American Society of Naturalists Meets in Baltimore. *Evening Times* December 27:5. Washington, D.C.

Evening Times Republican. 1901. No Adam nor Eve. Science Association at Denver Denies They Ever Existed. *Evening Times Republican* August 30:1. Marshalltown, Iowa.

Fabian, Ann. 2010. *The Skull Collectors: Race, Science, and America's Unburied Dead*. University of Chicago Press, Chicago.

Ferguson, T. J. 1996. Native Americans and the Practice of Anthropology. *Annual Review of Anthropology* 25:63–79.

Fewkes, Jesse Walter. 1893. A-wa'-to-bi: An Archaeological Verification of a Túsayan Legend. *American Anthropologist* 6(4):363–75.

Fewkes, Jesse Walter. 1896a. The Prehistoric Culture of Tusayan. *American Anthropologist* 9(4, o.s.):151–73.

Fewkes, Jesse Walter. 1896b. Preliminary Account of an Expedition to the Cliff Villages of the Red Rock Country, and the Tusayan Ruins of Sikyatki and Awatobi, Arizona in 1895. *Annual Report of the Smithsonian Institution for 1895*, pp. 557–88. GPO, Washington, D.C.

Fewkes, Jesse Walter. 1896c. Preliminary Account of Archaeological Field Work in Arizona in 1896. *Smithsonian Annual Report for 1896*, pp. 602–23. GPO, Washington, D.C.

Fewkes, Jesse Walter. 1896d. Two Ruins Recently Discovered in the Red Rock Country, Arizona. *American Anthropologist* 9(o.s., 8):263–83.

Fewkes, Jesse Walter. 1898a. Archaeological Expedition into Arizona in 1895. In *Seventeenth Annual Report of the Bureau of American Ethnology for the Years 1895–1896*, pp. 519–42. GPO, Washington, D.C.

Fewkes, Jesse Walter. 1898b. Preliminary Account of an Expedition to the Pueblo Ruins near Winslow, Arizona, in 1896. In *Annual Report of the Smithsonian Institution for 1896*, pp. 517–39. GPO, Washington, D.C.

Fewkes, Jesse Walter. 1900. Tusayan Migration Traditions. In *Nineteenth Annual Report of the Bureau of American Ethnology for 1898*, Part 2, pp. 927–1011. GPO, Washington, D.C.

Fewkes, Jesse Walter. 1904. Two Summers' Work in Pueblo Ruins. In *Twenty-Second Annual Report of the Bureau of American Ethnology for the Years 1900–1901*, Part 1, pp. 1–196. GPO, Washington, D.C.

Fewkes, Jesse Walter. 1919. Designs on Prehistoric Hopi Pottery. In *Thirty-Third Annual Report of the Bureau of American Ethnology for 1911–1912*, pp. 207–84. GPO, Washington, D.C.

Fleming, Paula R., and Janet Luskey. 1986. *The North American Indians in Early Photographs*. Phaidon Press, London.

Fontana, Bernard L. 1975. Introduction to the Re-edition: The Pima Indians of Frank Russell and of Today. In *The Pima Indians*, by Frank Russell, pp. ix–xv. University of Arizona Press, Tucson.

Fontana, Bernard L. 2000. Introduction and Annotations. In *Trails to Tiburón: The 1894 and 1895 Field Diaries of W J McGee* by W J McGee, translated by Hazel McFeely Fontana, pp. xi–xxx. University of Arizona Press, Tucson.

Fontana, Bernard L., ed. 1959. Jose Lewis Brennan's Account of Papago "Customs and Other References." *Ethnohistory* 6(3):226–37.

Fowler, Catherine S., and Nancy J. Parezo. 2019. They Also Dug: Women Archaeologists in the Southwest. *El Palacio* 124(1):50–55.

Fowler, Don D. 1972a. *In a Sacred Manner We Live: Photographs of the North American Indians by Edward S. Curtis*. Barre Publishers, Barre, Mass.

Fowler, Don D. 1972b. *"Photographed All the Best Scenery": Jack Hiller's Diary of the Powell Expedition, 1871–1875*. University of Utah Press, Salt Lake City.

Fowler, Don D. 1989. *The Western Photography of John K. Hillers: Myself in the Water*. Smithsonian Institution Press, Washington, D.C.

Fowler, Don D. 2003. E. L. Hewett, J. F. Zimmerman, and the Beginnings of Anthropology at the University of New Mexico, 1927–1946. *Journal of Anthropological Research* 59(3):305–27.

Fowler, Don D. 2005. The Formative Years: Southwest Archaeology: 1890–1910. In *Southwestern Archaeology in the Twentieth Century*, edited by Linda Cordell and Don D. Fowler, pp. 16–26. University of Utah Press, Salt Lake City.

Fowler, Don D. 2010. *A Laboratory for Anthropology: Science and Romanticism in the American Southwest, 1846 to 1930*. University of Utah Press, Salt Lake City.

Fowler, Don D., and Catherine S. Fowler. 1971. *Anthropology of the Numa: John Wesley Powell's Manuscripts on the Numic Peoples of Western North America, 1868–1880*. Smithsonian Contributions to Anthropology No. 14. Smithsonian Institution, Washington, D.C.

Fowler, Don D., and Nancy J. Parezo. 2012. "The Trail of an Archaeological Wedding Journey"—and Beyond, Frank and Theresa Russell in the Southwest, 1898–1903.

In *Glen Canyon, Legislative Struggles, and Contract Archaeology: Papers in Honor of Carol J. Condie*, edited by Emily J. Brown, Carol J. Condie, and Helen K. Crotty, 57–69. Papers of the Archaeological Society of New Mexico No. 38. Archaeological Society of New Mexico, Albuquerque.

Fowler, Don D., and Nancy J. Parezo. 2018. Nomenclature and Numbers: Ethnologists and Anthropologists Seeking to Become Scientists, 1840–1930. *Journal of Anthropological Research* 74(3):388–411.

Fowler, Don D., and David R. Wilcox. 1999. From Thomas Jefferson to the Pecos Conference: Changing Anthropological Agendas in the North American Southwest. In *Surveying the Record: North American Scientific Explorations to 1930*, edited by E. C. Carter II, pp. 197–223. American Philosophical Society Memoirs 231. American Philosophical Society, Philadelphia.

Franciscan Fathers. 1910. *An Ethnological Dictionary of the Navaho Language*. The Franciscan Fathers, Navajo Indian Mission, St. Michaels, Ariz.

Fuller, Thomas. 2004. "Go West, Young Man." An Elusive Slogan. *Indiana Magazine of History* 100:231–43.

Galton, Francis. 1891. Useful Anthropometry. *Proceedings of the American Association for Advancement of Physical Education* 6:51–57.

Garland, Hamlin. 1923. *The Book of the American Indian*. Harper and Bros., New York.

Garson, J. G. 1885. The Frankfort Craniometric Agreement, with Critical Remarks Thereon. *Journal of the Anthropological Institute of Great Britain and Ireland* 12(1): 64–83.

Gero, Joan M. 1985. Socio-Politics of Archaeology and the Woman-at-Home Ideology. *American Antiquity* 50(2):342–50.

Gero, Joan M., and Delores Root. 1990. Public Presentations and Private Concerns: Archaeology in the Pages of the National Geographic. In *The Politics of the Past*, edited by Peter Gathercole and David Lowenthal, pp. 19–36. Unwin Hyman, London.

Gessler, Clifford. 1933. Tour of Utopia Is Conducted by Stanford Prof. *Honolulu Star-Bulletin* February 18:26.

Gilbert, Geoffrey N., and Catherine H. Ellis. 2011. "What Will You Do to Save a Consumptive Brother?": Freemasonry, the Oracle Sanatorium and the Anti-Tuberculosis Movement in the Southwest. *Journal of Arizona History* 52(3):213–44.

Gordon, Dudley. 1972. *Charles Lummis: Crusader in Corduroy*. Cultural Assets Press, Los Angeles.

Gordon, Robert. 2010. *Going Abroad: Traveling Like an Anthropologist*. Paradigm, Boulder, Colo.

Gough, Priscilla, ed. 1931. *Radcliffe College Alumnae Directory*. Radcliffe College, Cambridge.

Gould, Stephen Jay. 1996. *The Mismeasure of Man*. W. W. Norton, New York.

Graduation Programme. 1892. Class of 1892, State University of Iowa. Held in TRP.

Granger, Byrd H. 1960. *Arizona Place Names*. University of Arizona Press, Tucson.

Grant, Robert. 1900. *Unleavened Bread.* Charles Scribner's Sons, New York.

Grant, Robert. 1904. *The Undercurrent.* Charles Scribner's Sons, New York.

Graves, Laura. 1998. *Thomas Varker Keam, Indian Trader.* University of Oklahoma Press, Norman.

Graves, Michael W. 1998. The History of Method and Theory in the Study of Prehistoric Puebloan Pottery Styles in the American Southwest. *Journal of Archaeological Method and Theory* 5(4):309–43.

Gray, W. Forbes. 1915. *Some Old Scot Judges: Anecdotes and Impressions.* E. P. Dutton, New York.

Great Falls Tribune. 1933. Mrs. Russell Is Guest of Falls Lions. Professor of English at Stanford University Tells of Books and Plays. *Great Falls Tribune* March 22:7. Great Falls, Mont.

Green, Jesse, compiler and editor. 1990. *Cushing at Zuni: The Correspondence and Journals of Frank Hamilton Cushing, 1879–1884.* University of New Mexico Press, Albuquerque.

Greene, H. E. 1928. Review of *One Word More on Browning,* by Frances Theresa Russell. *Modern Language Notes* 43(8):550–51.

J. H. H. 1933. "Two Poets, A Dog and a Boy" by Frances Theresa Russell. *Minneapolis Star* August 24:14.

Hackenberg, Robert A. 1974. *Aboriginal Land Use and Occupancy of the Pima-Maricopa Indians.* Testimony and Report for the Indian Land Claims Cases. Garland, New York.

Hale, Edward Everett. 1906. *The World's Wit and Humor: An Encyclopedia of the Classic Wit and Humor of All Ages and Nations in 15 Volumes.* Vols. I–V, America. Review of Reviews Co., New York.

Harper, Lila Marz. 2001. *Solitary Travelers: Nineteenth-Century Women's Travel Narratives and the Scientific Vocation.* Associated University Presses, London.

Harraden, Beatrice. 1893. *Ships That Pass in the Night.* G. P. Putnam's Sons, New York.

Harris, Joel Chandler. 1881 *Uncle Remus, His Songs and Sayings.* D. Appleton, New York.

Harrison, Simon. 2012. *Dark Trophies: Hunting and the Enemy Body in Modern War.* Berghahn Books, New York.

Harrod, Ryan P., and Debra L. Martin. 2014. *Bioarchaeology of Climate Change and Violence: Ethical Considerations.* Springer Science and Business Media, Berlin.

Hart, Thomas A. 2012. When Lungers Came to Tucson: Seeking Recovering and Discovering Tuberculosis as a Social Disease. University of Arizona Campus Repository. http://hdl.handle.net/10150/243890, accessed November 18, 2017.

Hartford Courant. 1927. One Word More on Browning. *Hartford Courant* July 17:50.

Hartwell, Edward Mussey. 1893. A Preliminary Report on Anthropometry in the United States. *Publications of the American Statistical Association* 3(24):554–68.

Hartwig, Daniel. 2010. Guide to the Frances Theresa and Frank B. Russell Papers. Stanford University Libraries, Department of Special Collections and University

Archives. http://pdf.oac.cdlib.org/pdf/stanford/uarc/sc0166.pdf, accessed January 18, 2018.

Harvard Crimson. 1903. Dr. Russell Resigns. *Harvard Crimson* May 30:np. http://www.thecrimson.com/article/1903/5/30/dr-russell-resigns-pdr-frank-russell/, accessed November 1, 2017.

Haury, Emil W. 1937. A Pre-Spanish Rubber Ball Court from Arizona. *American Antiquity* 2(4):287–88.

Haury, Emil W. 1983. Madeleine Appleton Kidder, 1891–1981. *American Antiquity* 48(1):83–84.

Haury, Emil W. 1989. *Point of Pines, Arizona: A History of the University of Arizona Archaeological Field School.* Anthropological Papers of the University of Arizona No. 50. University of Arizona Press, Tucson.

Hayne, Paul Hamilton. 1882. *Poems of Paul Hamilton Hayne.* D. Lothrop, Boston.

Hazen, Edith, ed. 1992. *The Columbia Granger's Dictionary of Poetry Quotations.* Columbia University Press, New York.

Henderson, James D. 1969. *Meals by Fred Harvey.* Texas Christian University Press, Fort Worth.

Hinsley, Curtis M. 1974. Amateurs and Professionals in Washington Anthropology, 1879 to 1903. In *American Anthropology: The Early Years,* edited by John V. Murra, pp. 36–68. West Publishing, St. Paul.

Hinsley, Curtis M. 1981. *The Smithsonian and the American Indian: Making a Moral Anthropology in Victorian America.* Smithsonian Institution Press, Washington, D.C.

Hinsley, Curtis M. 1983. Ethnographic Charisma and Scientific Routine: Cushing and Fewkes in the American Southwest, 1879–1893. In *Observers Observed: Essays on Ethnographic Fieldwork,* edited by George W. Stocking Jr., pp. 53–69. University of Wisconsin Press, Madison.

Hinsley, Curtis M. 1985. From Shell Heaps to Stelae: Early Anthropology at the Peabody Museum. In *Objects and Others: Essays on Museums and Material Culture,* edited by George Stocking Jr., pp. 49–74. University of Wisconsin Press, Madison.

Hinsley, Curtis M. 1992. The Museum Origins of Harvard Anthropology, 1866–1915. In *Science at Harvard University: Historical Perspectives,* edited by Clark A. Elliott and Margaret W. Rossiter, pp. 121–47. Lehigh University Press, Bethlehem, Pa.

Hinsley, Curtis M. 1996. Jones, William (Megasiawa: Black Eagle). In *Encyclopedia of North American Indians,* edited by Frederick E. Hoxie, pp. 308–9. Houghton Mifflin, Boston.

Hinsley, Curtis M., and David R. Wilcox, eds. 1995. A Hemenway Portfolio: Voices and Views from the Hemenway Archaeological Expedition, 1886–1889. *Journal of the Southwest* 37(4):519–744.

Hinsley, Curtis M., and David R. Wilcox, eds. 2016. *Coming of Age in Chicago: The 1893 World's Fair and the Coalescence of American Anthropology.* University of Nebraska Press, Lincoln.

Hodge, Frederick W. 1903. Frank Russell. *American Anthropologist* 5(n.s., 4):737–38.

Hodge, Frederick W. 1907. Jicarilla Apache. In *Handbook of American Indians North of Mexico*, vol. 1, edited by Frederick Webb Hodge, pp. 632–33. Bureau of American Ethnology No. 30. GPO, Washington, D.C.

Hodge, Frederick W., ed. 1907–10. *Handbook of Indians North of Mexico*. 2 vols. Bureau of American Ethnology No. 30. GPO, Washington, D.C.

Holder, Mick. 2011. The True Origins of "The Strawberry Roan." *Globe Miami Times* May 11:n.p. Globe, Ariz.

Holly, Donald H., Jr. 2016. In Search of My Original Affluent Self and Other Tropes in Travel Writing on Hunters and Gatherers. *Journeys* 17(1):96–112.

Holmes, Oliver Wendell. 1891. *The Autocrat of the Breakfast Table*. Houghton, Mifflin, Boston.

Holmes, William Henry. 1876. A Note on the Ancient Remains of Southwestern Colorado Examined during the Summer of 1875. *Bulletin of the Geological and Geographic Survey of the Territories* 2(1):3–24, GPO, Washington, D.C.

Holmes, William Henry. 1886a. Origin and Development of Form and Ornament in Ceramic Art. In *Fourth Annual Report of the Bureau of American Ethnology for 1882–1883*, pp. 443–71. GPO, Washington, D.C.

Holmes, William Henry. 1886b. Pottery of the Ancient Pueblos. In *Fourth Annual Report of the Bureau of Ethnology for 1882–1883*, pp. 257–360. GPO, Washington, D.C.

Holmes, William Henry. 1907. Report of the Director. In *Twenty-Fourth Annual Report of the Bureau of American Ethnology to the Secretary of the Smithsonian for 1902–1903*, pp. ix–xl. GPO, Washington, D.C.

Hough, Walter. 1900. *The Moki Snake Dance*. Passenger Department, Santa Fe Railroad, Chicago.

Hough, Walter. 1903. Archaeological Field Work in Northeastern Arizona: The Museum-Gates Expedition of 1901. In *Annual Report of the United States National Museum for 1901*, pp. 279–358. GPO, Washington, D.C.

Hough, Walter. 1907. *Antiquities of the Upper Gila and Salt River Valleys in Arizona and New Mexico*. Bureau of American Ethnology Bulletin No. 35. GPO, Washington, D.C.

Howells, Dorothy Elias. 1978. *A Century to Celebrate Radcliffe College, 1878–1979*. Radcliffe College Press, Cambridge, Mass.

Hoxie, Frederick E. 1984. *A Final Promise: The Campaign to Assimilate the Indians, 1880–1920*. University of Nebraska Press, Lincoln.

Hrdlička, Aleš. 1899. Review of "Exploration of the Far North." *American Naturalist* 33(390):514.

Hrdlička, Aleš. 1900. Physical and Physiological Observation on the Navaho. *American Anthropologist* 2(n.s., 3):339–45.

Hrdlička, Aleš. 1902. Anthropological Work in the Southwestern United States and Mexico. *Journal of the American Museum of Natural History* 2:68–72.

Hrdlička, Aleš. 1908. *Physiological and Medical Observations Among the Indians of the Southwestern United States and Northern Mexico.* Bureau of American Ethnology Bulletin No. 34. GPO, Washington, D.C.

Hutchinson, Elizabeth. 2009. *The Indian Craze: Primitivism, Modernism, and Transculturation in American Art, 1890–1915.* Duke University Press, Durham, N.C.

Indianapolis News. 1901. Just a Fairy Tale. *Indianapolis News* August 30:1.

Iowa Citizen. 1894. On Good Footing. The Y.M.C.A. Is in a Prosperous Condition. *Iowa Citizen* September 28:3. Iowa City, Iowa.

Iowa City Daily Republican. 1895a. Class Day. On the Campus. *Iowa City Daily Republican* June 10:4. Iowa City, Iowa.

Iowa City Daily Republican. 1895b. Happy Alumni. *Iowa City Daily Republican* June 12:4.

Iowa City Daily Republican. 1895c. Local News. *Iowa City Daily Republican* June 14:4.

Iowa City Daily Republican. 1903. Dies in the West. Frank Russell, the Arctic Explorer Passes Away at Kingman, Arizona. *Iowa City Daily Republican* November 9:1.

Iowa City Press Citizen. 1894a. Not a Paradise. Frank Russell, in a Private Letter to a Fellow-Student Describes the Country and Some of the Things to Be Seen in the Northern Regions. *Iowa City Press Citizen* February 9:5. Iowa, City, Iowa.

Iowa City Press Citizen. 1894b. Russell Returns. *Iowa City Press Citizen* November 3:4.

Iowa City Press Citizen. 1900. Lecture by Frank Russell. *Iowa City Press Citizen* January 27:4.

Iowa City Press Citizen. 1903. A Brave Man's Memory Honored. University Pays Tribute to Frank Russell. *Iowa City Press Citizen* November 18:3.

Isaac, Gwyneira. 2005. Re-Observation and the Recognition of Change: The Photographs of Matilda Coxe Stevenson (1879–1915). *Journal of the Southwest* 47(3): 411–55.

Jackson, William Henry. 1875. Ancient Ruins in Southwestern Colorado. *Bulletin of the Geological and Geographical Survey of the Territories* 2(1):17–30, GPO, Washington, D.C.

Jackson, William Henry. 1876. A Notice of Ancient Ruins in Arizona and Utah Lying about the Rio San Juan. *Bulletin of the Geological and Geographical Survey of the Territories* 2 (2):25–45, GPO, Washington, D.C.

James, Henry. 1878. Americans Abroad. *The Nation* (26, October 3):208–9.

James, William. 1890. *The Principles of Psychology.* 2 vols. Henry Holt, New York.

James, William. 1892. *Psychology: Briefer Course.* Henry Holt, New York.

James, William. 1897. *The Will to Believe, and Other Essays in Popular Philosophy.* Longmans, Green, London.

James, William. 1978. *Essays in Philosophy.* Harvard University Press, Cambridge, Mass.

Jerome, Jerome K. 1889. *Three Men in a Boat (To Say Nothing of the Dog).* J. W. Arrowsmith, London.

Jerome, Jerome K. 1891. *Diary of a Pilgrimage and Six Essays.* Three and Sixpenny Series. J. W. Arrowsmith, London.

Jerome, Jerome K. 1900. *Three Men on the Bummel.* J. W. Arrowsmith, London.

Johnson, Keach. 1980. Elementary and Secondary Education in Iowa, 1890–1900: A Time of Awakening. *Annals of Iowa* 45(3):171–95.

Jones, William. 1904. Some Principles of Algonquian Word-Formation. *American Anthropologist* 6(n.s., 3):369–407.

Jordan, David Starr. 1906. The Earthquake at Stanford University. *Out West* 26(6):507–13.

Journal of American Folk-lore. 1898. Local Meetings and Other Notices. *Journal of American Folk-lore* 11(41):164–66.

Journal of American Folk-lore. 1900. Local Meetings and Other Notices. *Journal of American Folk-lore* 12(49):149–53.

Journal of American Folk-lore. 1901. Twelfth Annual Meeting of the American Folklore Society. *Journal of American Folk-lore* 14(52):52–55.

Journal of American Folk-lore. 1904. Annual Meeting of the American Folklore Society. *Journal of American Folk-lore* 17(64):80–82.

Judd, Neil M. 1967. *The Bureau of American Ethnology: A Partial History*. University of Oklahoma Press, Norman.

Khayyám, Omar. 1878. *The Rubáiyám, the Astronomer-Poet of Persian*. Translated by Edward Fitzgerald. 1st American ed. Houghton, Osgood, Boston.

Kintigh, Keith W. 2007. Repatriation as a Force of Change in Southwestern Archaeology. In *Opening Archaeology: Repatriation's Impact on Contemporary Research and Practice*, edited by Thomas W. Killion, pp. 195–207. School of American Research Press, Santa Fe.

Kipling, Rudyard. 1894. *The Jungle Book*. Macmillan, New York.

Kipling, Rudyard. 1899. *Departmental Ditties and Barrack Room Ballads*. Macmillan, New York.

Klyver, Craig. 1989. Adam Clark Vroman and the 1901 Museum-Gates Expedition. *The Masterkey* 63(January):8–11.

Kohler, Timothy A., Scott G. Ortman, Katie E. Grundtisch, Carly M. Fitzpatrick, and Sarah M. Cole. 2004. The Better Angels of Their Nature: Declining Violence through Time Among Prehispanic Farmers of the Pueblo Southwest. *American Antiquity* 79(3):444–64.

Kramer, Harold Morton. 1900. *The Chrysalis*. Lothrop, Lee and Shepard, Boston.

Kruger, Kathryn S. 2002. *Weaving the Word: The Metaphorics of Weaving and Female Textual Production*. Susquehanna University Press, Selinsgrove, Pa.

Krugman, Wilton M. 1976. Fifty Years of Physical Anthropology: The Men, the Material, the Concepts, the Methods. *Annual Review of Anthropology* 5:1–14.

Kuklick, Bruce. 1987. Introduction to William James's *Pragmatism*. In William James: *Writings, 1902–1910*, edited by Bruce Kuklick, p. 479. Library of America, New York.

Laird, Martin. 2011. *A Sunlit Absence: Silence, Awareness and Contemplation*. Oxford University Press, Oxford.

Lange, Charles H., and Carroll L. Riley. 1996. *Bandelier: The Life and Adventures of Adolph Bandelier*. University of Utah Press, Salt Lake City.

Lears, J. J. Jackson. 1981. *No Place of Grace: Antimodernism and the Transformation of American Culture, 1880–1920*. Pantheon, New York.

Leckie, Shirley A., and Nancy J. Parezo, eds. 2008. *Their Own Frontier: Women Intellectuals Re-visioning the American West*. University of Nebraska Press, Lincoln.

Lewis, Nancy Owen. 2016. *Chasing the Cure in New Mexico: Tuberculosis and the Quest for Health*. University of New Mexico Press, Albuquerque.

Lindsay, Debra. 1998. Intimate Inmates: Wives, Households, and Science in Nineteenth Century America. *Isis* 89:631–52.

Linford, Laurence D. 2000. *Navajo Places: History, Legends, Landscape*. University of Utah Press, Salt Lake City.

Lister, Florence C. 2002. *Behind Painted Walls: Incidents in Southwestern Archaeology*. University of New Mexico Press, Albuquerque.

Lister, Florence C., and Robert H. Lister. 1968. *Earl Morris & Southwestern Archaeology*. University of New Mexico Press, Albuquerque.

Lister, Robert H., and Florence C. Lister. 1984. *Chaco Canyon: Archaeology and Archaeologists*. University of New Mexico Press, Albuquerque.

Lomatuway'ma, Michael, Lorena Lomatuway'ma, and Sidney Namingha Jr. 1993. *Hopi Ruin Legends*. Edited by Ekkehart Malotki. University of Nebraska Press, Lincoln.

Longfellow, Henry W. 1863. *The Complete Poetical Works of Henry Wadsworth Longfellow*. Edited by Horace E. Scudder. Cambridge Edition of the Poets. Houghton Mifflin, Boston.

Lőnneberg, Allan. 1981. The Digger Indian Stereotype in California. *Journal of California and Great Basin Anthropology* 3(2):215–23.

Lowell, James Russell. 1848. *The Vision of Sir Launfal*. George Nichols, Boston.

Lummis, Charles F. 1968. *Bullying the Moqui*. Prescott College Press, Prescott, Ariz.

Lutz, Catherine A., and Jane L. Collins. 1993. *Reading National Geographic*. University of Chicago Press, Chicago.

Mabillard, Amanda. 2000. Hamlet Soliloquy Glossary. In *Shakespeare Online*. http://shakespeare-online.com/plays/hamlet/soliloquies/flat.html, accessed June 12, 2018.

MacCurdy, George C. 1899. The Extent of Instruction in Anthropology in Europe and the United States. *Science* 10:910–17.

MacCurdy, George C. 1903. Anthropology at the Washington Meeting. *American Anthropologist* 5(n.s., 1):118–25.

Macleod, Fiona. 1901. *Poems and Dramas of "Fiona Macleod."* Duffield, New York.

Maddox, Brenda. 2017. *Reading the Rocks: How Victorian Geologists Discovered the Secret of Life*. Bloomsbury, New York.

Major, Charles. 1898. *When Knighthood Was in Flower: The Love Story of Charles Brandon and Mary Tudor, the King's Sister*. Bowen-Merrill, New York.

Mallowan, Agatha Christie. 1947. *Come Tell Me How You Live*. Bantam, New York.

Mark, Joan. 1980. *Four Anthropologists: An American Science in Its Early Years*. Science History Publications, New York.

Mason, Otis T. 1875. *Ethnological Directions Relative to The Indian Tribes of the United States Prepared Under the Direction of Indian Bureau.* Smithsonian Institution. GPO, Washington, D.C.

Mason, Otis T. 1904. *American Indian Baskets.* Doubleday, New York.

Matthews, Washington. 1887. The Mountain Chant: A Navajo Ceremony. In *Fifth Annual Report of the Bureau of Ethnology, 1883–84*, pp. 379–467. GPO, Washington, D.C.

Matthews, Washington. 1895. Mythological Paintings of the Navajos. *Anthropological Society of Washington Transactions* 3:139–40.

McCord, David. 1958. *An Acre for Education: Being Notes on the History of Radcliffe College.* Radcliffe College Press, Cambridge, Mass.

McGee, W J. 1895. The Beginning of Agriculture. *American Anthropologist* 8(o.s., 4): 350–57.

McGee, W J. 1899a. Anthropology at Columbus. *American Anthropologist* 1 (n.s., 4): 759–63.

McGee, W J. 1899b. The Trend of Human Progress. *American Anthropologist* 1(n.s., 3):401–47.

McGee, W J. [for John Wesley Powell]. 1904a. Report of the Director. In *22nd Annual Report of the Bureau of American Ethnology to the Secretary of the Smithsonian, for 1900–1901*, pp. ix–xliv. GPO, Washington, D.C.

McGee, W J. [for John Wesley Powell]. 1904b. Report of the Director. In *23rd Annual Report of the Bureau of American Ethnology to the Secretary of the Smithsonian, for 1901–1902*, pp. ix–xxxviii. GPO, Washington, D.C.

McGee, W J. 2000. *Trails to Tiburón: The 1894 and 1895 Field Diaries of W J McGee.* Transcribed by Hazel McFeely Fontana; annotated and with an introduction by Bernard L. Fontana. University of Arizona Press, Tucson.

McNitt, Frank. 1962. *The Indian Traders.* University of Oklahoma Press, Norman.

McVeigh, Stephen. 2007. *The American Western.* Edinburgh University Press, Edinburgh.

Melton, Jeffrey. 2002. *Mark Twain, Travel Books, and Tourism: The Tide of a Great Popular Movement.* University of Alabama Press, Tuscaloosa.

Meltzer, David J. 1985. North American Archaeology and Archaeologists, 1879–1934. *American Antiquity* 50(2):249–60.

Meltzer, David J. 2015. *The Great Paleolithic War: How Science Forged an Understanding of America's Ice Age Past.* University of Chicago Press, Chicago.

Meltzer, David J., and Robert O. Dunnell. 1992. Introduction. In *The Archaeology of William Henry Holmes*, edited by David J. Meltzer and Robert O. Dunnell, pp. vii–l. Smithsonian Institution Press, Washington, D.C.

Miller, Darlis. 2007. *Matilda Coxe Stevenson, Pioneering Anthropologist.* University of Oklahoma Press, Norman.

Miller, Joaquin. 1875. *The Ship in the Desert.* Robert Brothers, Boston.

Miller, Joshua. 1897. The Montezuma Caste Repair Expedition. *Antiquarian* 1 (September):225–28.

Miller, Joshua. 1899a. Montezuma's Castle. *Arizona Graphic* 1 (December 9):6.

Miller, Joshua. 1899b. Montezuma's Well. *Arizona Graphic* 1 (December 16):1–2.

Mills, Sara. 1991. *Discourses of Difference: An Analysis of Women's Travel Writing and Colonialism.* Routledge, London.

Mindeleff, Cosmos. 1896a. Aboriginal Remains in Verde Valley, Arizona. In *Thirteenth Annual Report of the Bureau of American Ethnology for the Years 1891–1892*, pp. 185–261. GPO, Washington, D.C.

Mindeleff, Cosmos. 1896b. Casa Grande Ruin. *Thirteenth Annual Report of the Bureau of American Ethnology for the Years 1891–1892*, pp. 289–319. GPO, Washington, D.C.

Mindeleff, Cosmos. 1897. The Repair of Casa Grande Ruin, Arizona, in 1891. In *Fifteenth Annual Report of the Bureau of American Ethnology for the Years 1893–1894*, pp. 321–48. GPO, Washington, D.C.

Mindeleff, Cosmos. 1900. Localization of Tusayan Clans. In *Nineteenth Annual Report of the Bureau of American Ethnology for the Years 1897–1898*, Part 2, pp. 635–53. GPO, Washington, D.C.

Mindeleff, Victor. 1891. A Study of Pueblo Architecture in Tusayan and Cibola. In *Eighth Annual Report of the Bureau of American Ethnology for the Years 1886–1887*, pp. 3–228. GPO, Washington, D.C.

Missouri Sharp Shooter. 1901. West and South. *Missouri Sharp Shooter* September 6:2. Rolla, Mo.

Mitchell, Douglas R., and Judy L. Brunson-Hadley, eds. 2004. *Ancient Burial Practices in the American Southwest: Archaeology, Physical Anthropology and Native American Perspectives.* University of New Mexico, Albuquerque.

Mohave County Miner. 1903. Death of a Harvard Professor. *Mohave Count Miner* November 7:3. Mineral Park, Ariz.

Monger, George P., ed. 2013. *Marriage Customs of the World: An Encyclopedia of Dating Customs and Wedding Traditions.* 2nd ed. ABC-CLIO, Santa Barbara, Calif.

Montgomery, Ross G., Watson Smith, and John Otis Brew. 1949. *Franciscan Awatovi.* Reports of the Awatovi Expedition 3. Papers of the Peabody Museum of American Archaeology and Ethnology 36. Peabody Museum, Cambridge, Mass.

Moorehead, Warren K. 1910. *The Stone Age in North America.* Houghton Mifflin, Boston.

Morgan, Susan. 1990. Women, Wisdom and Southeast Asia. In *Victorian Sages and Cultural Discourse: Renegotiating Gender and Power*, edited by Thaïs F. Morgan, pp. 207–24. Rutgers University Press, New Brunswick, N.J.

Morgan, Susan. 1996. *Place Matters: Gendered Geography in Victorian Women's Travel Books about Southeast Asia.* Rutgers University Press, New Brunswick, N.J.

Morris, Ann Axtel. 1931. *Digging in Yucatan: Archaeological Expeditions in 1924 Mexico.* Doubleday, Doran, Garden City, N.Y.

Morris, Ann Axtell. 1933. *Digging in the Southwest.* Doubleday, Doran, Garden City, N.Y.

Morrisey, Katherine G., and Nancy J. Parezo. 2005. Scientific Photography? Cameras and 1930s Southwestern Archaeology. In *Picturing Arizona: The Photographic Record of the 1930s*, edited by Katherine G. Morrisey and Kirsten Jensen, pp. 144–68. University of Arizona Press, Tucson.

Mount, James E., Stanley J. Olsen, John W. Olsen, George A. Teague, and B. Dean Treadwell. 1993. *Wide Reed Ruin: Hubbell Trading Post National Historical Site.* Southwest Cultural Resources Center, Professional Papers No. 51. National Park Service, n.p.

Munk, Joseph A. 1920. *Southwest Sketches.* G. P. Putnam's Sons, New York.

National Park Service. 2011. Frank "Boss" Pinkley (1881–1940). In *National Park Service: First Seventy-Five Years. Biographical Vignette.* https://www.nps/gov/parkshistory online, accessed November 16, 2017.

National Park Service. n.d. A Brief History of Chaco Culture National Historical Park. https://www.nps.gov/chcu/planyourvisit/upload/Brief-History.pdf, accessed November 16, 2017.

Neitzel, Jill E. 2000. Gender Hierarchies: A Comparative Analysis of Mortuary Data. In *Women and Men in the Prehispanic Southwest: Labor, Power and Prestige*, edited by Patricia L. Crown, pp. 137–68. School of American Research Press, Santa Fe.

Nelson, Scott Reynolds. 2012. *A Nation of Deadbeats.* Alfred Knopf, New York.

Nusbaum, Rosemary. 1980. *Tierra Dulce: Reminiscences from the Jesse Nusbaum Papers.* Sunstone Press, Santa Fe.

Nutting, C. C. 1895. Geography and Travels. *American Naturalist* 29(337):45–48.

Nutting, C. C. 1903. Frank Russell. *Iowa Alumnus* December 15:n.p. Iowa City, Iowa.

Oakland Tribune. 1935. The Little Theater. *Oakland Tribune* March 8:25. Oakland, Calif.

Opie, Iona, and Peter Opie. 1992. *The Classic Fairy Tale.* Oxford University Press, Oxford.

Palkovich, Ann M. 2012. Reading a Life: A Fourteenth-Century Ancestral Puebloan Woman. In *The Bioachaeology of Individuals*, edited by Ann L. W. Stodder and Ann M. Palkovich, pp. 242–54. University Press of Florida, Gainesville.

Pandey, Triloki Nath. 1972. Anthropologists at Zuni. *Proceedings of the American Philosophical Society* 116(4):321–37.

Papanek, Hanna. 1973. Men, Women, and Work: Reflections on the Two-Person Career. *American Journal of Sociology* 78(4):852–72.

Parezo, Nancy J. 1985. Cushing as Part of the Team: The Collecting Activities of the Smithsonian Institution at Zuni. *American Ethnologist* 12(4):763–74.

Parezo, Nancy J. 1986. Now Is the Time to Collect. *The Masterkey* 59(4):11–18.

Parezo, Nancy J. 1987. The Formation of Ethnographic Collections: The Smithsonian Institution in the American Southwest. In *Advances in Archaeological Method and Theory*, edited by Michael Schiffer, pp. 1–16. Academic Press, Orlando.

Parezo, Nancy J. 1993a. Conclusion: The Beginning of the Quest. In *Hidden Scholars: Women Anthropologists and the Native American Southwest*, edited by Nancy J. Parezo, pp. 334–68. University of New Mexico Press, Albuquerque.

Parezo, Nancy J. 1993b. Matilda Coxe Stevenson: Pioneer Ethnologist. In *Hidden Scholars: Women Anthropologists and the Native American Southwest*, edited by Nancy J. Parezo, pp. 38–62. University of New Mexico Press, Albuquerque.

Parezo, Nancy J. 2006. Collecting Diné Culture in the 1880s: Two Army Physicians and Their Ethnographic Approaches. *Museum Anthropology* 20(2):95–117.

Parezo, Nancy J., and Don D. Fowler. 2007. *Anthropology Goes to the Fair: The 1904 Louisiana Purchase Exposition*. University of Nebraska Press, Lincoln.

Parezo, Nancy J., and Angelina Jones. 2009. What's in a Name? The 1940s–1950s "Squaw Dress." *American Indian Quarterly* 33(3):373–404.

Parezo, Nancy J., ed. 1993c. *Hidden Scholars: Women Anthropologists and the Native American Southwest*. University of New Mexico Press, Albuquerque.

Parmenter, Ross. 1966. *Explorer, Linguist, Descriptive Bibliography of Alphonse Louis Pinart*. Frederick Webb Hodge Anniversary Publication No. 9. Southwest Museum, Los Angeles.

Parrinder, Geoffrey. 2005. *The Routledge Dictionary of Religious and Spiritual Quotations*. Routledge, London.

Pascal, Blaise. 1958. *Pensées*. With an Introduction by T. S. Eliot. E. P. Dutton and Co., New York.

Pavesic, Max G. 1999. Reflections on the United States National-Museum-Gates Expeditions to the American Southwest, 1901 and 1905. *Journal of California and Great Basin Anthropology* 21(1):136–45.

Pepper, George H. 1904. Section H-Anthropology. *Science* 19(n.s., 4181):449–53.

Phillips, Margaret Mann. 1964. *The Adages of Erasmus*. Cambridge University Press, Cambridge, Mass.

Phrase Finder. n.d. A Skeleton in the Closet. In *Phrase Finder*. https://www.phrases.org.uk/meanings/skeleton-in-the-closet.html, accessed December 18, 2018.

Pink, Sarah. 2001. *Doing Visual Ethnography: Images, Media and Representation in Research*. Sage, London.

Platt, Tony. 2011. *Grave Matters: Excavating California's Buried Past*. Heyday, Berkeley, Calif.

Poe, Edgar Allan. 1843. The Black Cat. *United States Saturday Post* August 19:1.

Poling-Kempes, Lesley. 1989. *The Harvey Girls: Women Who Opened the West*. Paragon House, New York.

Powell, John Wesley. 1875a. The Ancient Province of Tusayan. *Scribner's Monthly* 11:193–213.

Powell, John Wesley. 1875b. The Canons of the Colorado. *Scribner's Monthly* 9:293–310, 523–37.

Powell, John Wesley. 1875c. An Overland Trip to Grand Canyon. *Scribner's Monthly* 10:659–98.

Powell, John Wesley. 1883. On the Limitations to the Use of Some Anthropologic Data. *Smithsonian Miscellaneous Collections* 25(502):113–36.

Powell, John Wesley. 1890. Problems of American Archaeology. *The Forum* 8:638–52.

Powell, John Wesley. 1902. Report of the Director. In *Twenty-First Annual Report of the Bureau of American Ethnology for 1899–1900*, pp. x–xlv. GPO, Washington, D.C.

Powell, John Wesley. 1904a. Report of the Director. In *Twenty-Second Annual Report of the Bureau of American Ethnology for 1900–1901*, Part 1, pp. ix–xliii. GPO, Washington, D.C.

Powell, John Wesley. 1904b. Report of the Director. In *Twenty-Third Annual Report of the Bureau of American Ethnology for 1901–1902*, pp. ix–xlv. GPO, Washington, D.C.

Protas, Josh. 2002. *A Past Preserved in Stone: A History of Montezuma Castle National Monument*. Western National Parks Association, Tucson.

Prudden, T. Mitchell. 1897. An Elder Brother of the Cliff Dweller. *Harper's New Monthly Magazine* 95(September):62–66.

Putnam, Frederic W. 1886. On the Methods of Archaeological Research in America. First presented 1885. *Johns Hopkins University Circular* 5(40):n.p.

Putnam, Frederic W. 1889. Report of the Curator. Twenty-Second Annual Report. *Annual Reports of the Peabody Museum of American Anthropology and Ethnology* 4(2):31–52.

Putnam, Frederic W. 1890. Prehistoric Remains in the Ohio Valley. *Century Magazine* 39:698–703.

Putnam, Frederic W. 1896. Report of the Curator. *Annual Reports of the Peabody Museum of American Anthropology and Ethnology* 11(3):239–49.

Putnam, Frederic W. 1899. Report of the Curator. In *Thirty-Third Annual Report of the Peabody Museum of American Anthropology and Ethnology for 1897–1898*, pp. 266–75. Harvard University, Cambridge, Mass.

Putnam, Frederic W. 1900. The Pueblos of Colorado and New Mexico. *Journal of American Folk-lore* 13(48):150.

Putnam, Frederic W. 1903a. Frank Russell. *Iowa Alumnus* December 15:1–4. Iowa City, Iowa.

Putnam, Frederic W. 1903b. Report of the Curator. In *Thirty-Sixth Report of the Peabody Museum of American Archaeology and Ethnology, Harvard University, 1901–1902*. Harvard University, Cambridge, Mass.

Putnam, Frederic Ward, et al. 1879. *Archaeology Report of the U.S. Geological Survey West of the 100th Meridian* 7:1–497. GPO, Washington, D.C.

Putnam Country Courier. 1933. Mrs. Mindeleff Dies Here on Saturday. *Putnam Country Courier* April 14:1. Cold Spring, N.Y.

Quad-City Times. 1899. An Iowa Explorer. Frank Russell and His University Collecting Tour. *Quad-City Times* April 30:2. Davenport, Iowa.

Quad-City Times. 1933. Ladies in Washington. *Quad-City Times* April 12:12. Davenport, Iowa.

Quigley, Christine. 2001. *Skulls and Skeletons: Human Bone Collections and Accumulations*. McFarland, Jefferson, N.C.

Radcliffe College. 1916. Registry of College Students. Radcliffe College, Cambridge, Mass.

Rasdal, Dave. 2012. 50 Years After Closing, Martelle High Still "Lives." *The Gazette* June 4:6. Cedar Rapids, Iowa.

Rea, Amadeo M. 1997. *At the Desert's Green Edge: An Ethnobotany of the Gila River Pima*. University of Arizona Press, Tucson.

Redman, Samuel J. 2016. *Bone Rooms: From Scientific Racism to Human Prehistory in Museums*. Harvard University Press, Cambridge, Mass.

Reichard, Gladys A. 1950. *Navajo Religion: A Study of Symbolism*. Bollingen Series No. 18. Pantheon, New York.

Reid, J. Jefferson, and Stephanie M. Whittlesey. 1997. *The Archaeology of Ancient Arizona*. University of Arizona Press, Tucson.

Rice, Alice Hagen. 1901. *Mrs. Wiggs of the Cabbage Patch*. Hodder and Stoughton, London.

Ridgway, Robert. 1887. *A Manual of North American Birds*. J. B. Lippincott, Philadelphia.

Riding In, James. 2002. Our Dead Are Never Forgotten: American Indian Struggles for Burial Rights and Protections. In *"They Made Us Many Promises": The American Indian Experience, 1524 to the Present*, edited by P. Weeks, pp. 291–323. Harlan Davidson, Wheeling, Iowa.

Riley, James Whitcomb. 1900. *Green Fields and Running Brooks*. Charles Scribner's Sons, New York.

Roffler, Joshua. 2006. Frank Russell at Gila River: Constructing an Ethnographic Description. *The Kiva* 71(4):373–95.

Rogers, Archibald, Brige Harrison, W. S. Rainsford, Harry C. Hale, Frederic Ireland, Frank Russell, and George Bird Grinnell. 1896. *Hunting*. The Out of Door Library. Charles Scribner's Sons, New York.

Rothman, Hal. 1991. *Navajo National Monument: A Place and Its People*. New Mexico Professional Papers No. 40. Southwestern Cultural Resources Center, Santa Fe.

Rothman, Sheila M. 1994. *Living in the Shadow of Death: Tuberculosis and the Social Experience of Illness in American History*. Basic Books, New York.

Russell, Frances Theresa. 1920. *Satire on the Victorian Novel*. Macmillan, New York.

Russell, Frances Theresa. 1921. A Poet's Portrayal of Emotion. *Psychological Review* 28(3):222–38.

Russell, Frances Theresa. 1923a. Browning's Account with Tragedy. *Sewanee Review* 31(1):86–99.

Russell, Frances Theresa. 1923b. In a Pungent Poet. *University of California Chronicle* n.d.:n.p. TRP.

Russell, Frances Theresa. 1924a. Gold and Alloy. *Studies in Philology* 21(3):467–79.

Russell, Frances Theresa. 1924b. The Pessimism of Robert Browning. *Sewanee Review* 32(1):69–77.

Russell, Frances Theresa. 1925. The Browning Stock Company. *English Journal* 14 (3): 175–82.

Russell, Frances Theresa. 1927a. *One More Word on Browning*. Stanford University Press, Stanford, Calif.

Russell, Frances Theresa. 1927b. Review of *The Outlook for American Prose*, by Joseph Beach. *American Speech* 2(6):290–92.

Russell, Frances Theresa. 1928a. Apropos of a Birthday: A Conversation with Henrik Ibsen. *Sewanee Review* 36(1):76–85.

Russell, Frances Theresa. 1928b. Laurel for George Meredith. *South Atlantic Quarterly* 27:367–75.

Russell, Frances Theresa. 1928c. The Young Mr. Lewis. *University of California Chronicle* 30(January):417–27.

Russell, Frances Theresa. 1929. Utopian Esthetics. *Transactions and Proceedings of the American Philological Association* 60(January):xvi.

Russell, Frances Theresa. 1930a. *Complicated Bernard Shaw*. Stanford University Press, Stanford, Calif.

Russell, Frances Theresa. 1930b. The Growing Up of Sinclair Lewis. *University of California Chronicle* July: n.p.

Russell, Frances Theresa. 1930c. Ironic John Galsworthy. *University of California Chronicle* February: n.p.

Russell, Frances Theresa. 1930d. Our Victorian Greeks: A Diagnosis of the College Fraternity. *Sewanee Review* 38(1, January–March):71–80.

Russell, Frances Theresa. 1932a. Edith Wharton's Use of Imagery. *English Journal* 21(6): 452–61.

Russell, Frances Theresa. 1932b. Melodramatic Mrs. Wharton. *Sewanee Review* 40(4): 425–37.

Russell, Frances Theresa. 1932c. Indians as They Are. *English Journal* 21(4):314–16.

Russell, Frances Theresa. 1932d. *Touring Utopia: The Realm of Constructive Humanism*. Dial Press, New York.

Russell, Frances Theresa. 1933a. Review of *Sketches in Criticism*, by Van Wyck Brooks. *English Journal* 22(7):607–8.

Russell, Frances Theresa. 1933b. The Romanticism of Irving Babbitt. *South Atlantic Quarterly* 32:399–411.

Russell, Frances Theresa. 1933c. *Two Poets, a Dog, and a Boy*. Stanford University Press, Stanford, Calif.

Russell, Frances Theresa. 1934. Charles Lamb, 1775–1834; Read by Title. *Proceedings of the Modern Languages Association* 49(Supplement 1934):134.

Russell, Frances Theresa, and David Yvors. 1934. *The Case of David Lamson*. Privately printed.

Russell, Frank. 1895. A Naturalist's Voyage Down the Mackenzie. *Midland Monthly* 3(6, June):522–31; 4(1, July):3–11.

Russell, Frank. 1896a. Hunting Musk-Ox with the Dog Ribs. In *Hunting*, by Archibald Rogers, Brige Harrison, W. S. Rainsford, Harry C. Hale, Frederic Ireland, Frank Russell, and George Bird Grinnell, pp. 301–27. Charles Scribner's Sons, New York.

Russell, Frank. 1896b. Hunting Musk-Ox with the Dog Ribs. In *Big Game Shooting*, by Archibald Rogers, Brige Harrison, W. S. Rainsford, Harry C. Hale, Frederic Ireland, Frank Russell, and George Bird Grinnell, pp. 301–27. Kegan Paul, Trench Trubner, London.

Russell, Frank. 1896c. Musk-Ox Hunting with the Dog Ribs. *Scribner's Magazine* 19(2, February):235–45.

Russell, Frank. 1898a. An Apache Medicine Dance. *American Anthropologist* 11(o.s., 4):367–72.

Russell, Frank. 1898b. *Explorations in the Far North.* University of Iowa Press, Ames.

Russell, Frank. 1898c. Gauging Cranial Capacity with Water. *American Anthropologist* 11(2):52–53.

Russell, Frank. 1898d. The Jicarilla Apache and Vocabulary with Juan and Reuben Quintana. Manuscript 1302a. NAA.

Russell, Frank. 1898e. Myths of the Jicarilla Apache. *Journal of American Folk-lore* 11(43): 253–72.

Russell, Frank. 1898f. Review of *The Import of the Totem*, by Alice Fletcher. *American Naturalist* 32(373):54–55.

Russell, Frank. 1898g. Review of *The Mounds of Louisiana*, by George E. Beyer. *American Naturalist* 32(380):587.

Russell, Frank. 1898h. A Study of a Collection of Eskimo Crania from Labrador, with Observations on the Prevailing System of Craniometry. PhD dissertation, Department of Anthropology, Harvard University, Cambridge, Mass.

Russell, Frank. 1899a. Human Remains from the Trenton Gravels. *American Naturalist* 33(386):143–55.

Russell, Frank. 1899b. Review of *Culture der Usprung der Akrikanischen Kulturen*, by L. Frobenius. *American Naturalist* 33(387):255–56.

Russell, Frank. 1899c. Review of *Man Past and Present*, by A. H. Keane. *American Naturalist* 33(393):738–40.

Russell, Frank. 1899d. Review of *Mythology of the Bella Coola Indians*, by Franz Boas. *American Naturalist* 33(390):516–17.

Russell, Frank. 1899e. Review of *The Races of Europe*, by W. Z. Ripley. *American Naturalist* 33(394):827–31.

Russell, Frank. 1899f. Review of *West African Studies*, by Mary Kingsley. *American Naturalist* 33(390):514–16.

Russell, Frank. 1900a. Anthropology at the New York Meeting of the American Association. *Science* 12(294, August 17):265–69.

Russell, Frank. 1900b. Athabascan Myths. *Journal of American Folk-lore* 13(48):11–18.

Russell, Frank. 1900c. A New Instrument for Measuring Torsion. *American Naturalist* 35(412):299–300.

Russell, Frank. 1900d. Physical Structure of the Labrador Eskimos and the New England Indians. *Scientific American* 49(Supplement 1254):106–7.

Russell, Frank. 1900e. The Races of Man. *American Naturalist* 34(402):521–22.

Russell, Frank. 1900f. Studies in Cranial Variation. *American Naturalist* 34(405):737–45.

Russell, Frank. 1901a. Anthropology at Baltimore. *Science* 13(317, January 25):139–12.

Russell, Frank. 1901b. Laboratory Outlines for Use in an Introductory Course in Somatology. *American Anthropologist* 3(n.s., 1):28–50.

Russell, Frank. 1901c. A New Instrument for Measuring Torsion. *American Naturalist* 35(412):299–300.

Russell, Frank. 1901d. Review of *The Seri Indians*, by W J McGee. *American Naturalist* 35(418):853–54.

Russell, Frank. 1902a. Know, Then, Thyself. *Journal of American Folk-lore* 15(56):1–13.

Russell, Frank. 1902b. Review of *Schadel und Skeletteile aus Peking*, by K. A. Haberer. *American Anthropologist* 4(n.s., 4):760–62.

Russell, Frank. 1903a. Anthropology in American High Schools and After. *Education* 23(May):530–37.

Russell, Frank. 1903b. Pima Annals. *American Anthropologist* 5(1):76–80.

Russell, Frank. 1903c. A Pima Constitution with Notes by Frank Russell. *Journal of American Folk-lore* 16(63):222–28.

Russell, Frank. 1903d. Review of *A Manual for Physical Measurements*, by William Hastings. *American Anthropologist* 5(n.s., 1):133.

Russell, Frank. 1908. The Pima Indians. In *Twenty-Sixth Annual Report of the Bureau of American Ethnology for 1904–1905*, pp. 3–389 [reissued 1975, University of Arizona Press, Tucson].

Russell, Frank. 1909. Pima Myths. *Out West* 30(5):485–95; (6):571–82; 31(1):643–44; (3):828–34; (4):890–95.

Russell, Frank, and Henry M. Huxley. 1899. A Comparative Study of the Physical Structure of the Labrador Eskimos and the New England Indians. *Proceedings of the American Association for the Advancement of Science* 48:265–70

Russell, Theresa. 1906. In Pursuit of a Graveyard: Being the Trail of an Archaeological Wedding Journey. *Out West* 24(1):39–49; (2):139–47; (3):201–07; (4):278–89, 310; (5):405–14; (6)544–48; 25(1):27–36; (2)132–38; (3):247–57; (4):341–47; (5):425–31; (6): 511–17.

Sabbath Recorder. 1914. Words of Pastor Shaw. *Sabbath Recorder* 76(19):578–79.

San Francisco Chronicle. 1920. Satire in Victorian Fiction. *San Francisco Chronicle* April 18:2. San Francisco, Calif.

Sanjek, Roger, ed. 1990. *Fieldnotes. The Making of Anthropology.* Cornell University Press, Ithaca, N.Y.

Sauer, Carl, and Brand, Donald. 1931. Prehistoric Settlements of Sonora with Special Reference to Cerros de Trincheras. *University of California Publications in Geography* 5(3):67–148.

Schrimper, George D. n.d. He Searched the Arctic Wilds. Single page newspaper clipping without attribution, TRP.

Schultz, Adolph H. 1945. *Biographical Memoir of Aleš Hrdlička, 1869–1943*. Biographical Memoirs No. 23. National Academy of Sciences, Washington, D.C.

Science. 1901a. The American Association for the Advancement of Science: Proceedings of the Denver Meeting. *Science* 14(349, September 6):345–48.

Science. 1901b. Proceedings of the Fiftieth Annual Meeting of the American Association for the Advancement of Science. *Science* 14(349, September 6):348–57.

Scott, Walter. 1805. *The Lay of the Last Minstrel*. Longman, Hurst, Rees and Orme, Edinburgh.

Sewanee Review. 1930. Concerning the Contributors: Frances Theresa Russell. *Sewanee Review* 38(1):ii.

Shaw, Anna Moore. 1974. *A Pima Past*. University of Arizona Press, Tucson.

Sheridan, Thomas E., Stewart B. Koyiyumptewa, Anton Daughters, Dale S. Brenneman, T. J. Ferguson, Leigh Kuwanwisiwma, and Lee Wayne Lomayestewa, eds. 2015. *Moquis and Kasiilam: Hopis, Spaniards, and the Trauma of History*. University of Arizona Press, Tucson.

Smith, Delos. 1948. Obituary of Victor Mindeleff (1841–1948). *Journal of the American Institute of Architects* 9:219–20.

Smith, Joseph E. 1930. Greatest Patron of Navajo Artistry in Rug Weaving Dies. *Denver Post*, November 30:n.p.

Smith, Watson. 2006. *Kiva Mural Decorations at Awatovi and Kawaika-a*. Papers of the Peabody Museum of American Archaeology and Ethnology No. 37. Peabody Museum, Cambridge, Mass.

Smith, Mrs. White Mountain. 1938. Tom Pavatea, Hopi Trader. *Desert Magazine* 1(February 4):3–5.

Snead, James E. 2001. *Ruins and Rivals: The Making of Southwest Archaeology*. University of Arizona Press, Tucson.

Snead, James E. 2019. Hunting Miss Deuel: Confronting Sexual Politics in the Archives of Anthropology. Unpublished draft paper.

Speake, Jennifer. 2003. *Literature of Travel and Exploration: An Encyclopedia*. Fitzroy Dearborn, New York.

Spencer, Frank. 1981. The Rise of Academic Physical Anthropology in the United States (1880–1980): A Historical Overview. *American Journal of Physical Anthropology* 56:353–64.

Spencer, Frank. 1992. Some Notes on the Attempt to Apply Photography to Anthropometry during the Second Half of the Nineteenth Century. In *Anthropology &*

Photography, 1860–1920, edited by Elizabeth Edwards, pp. 99–107. Yale University Press, New Haven, Conn.

Stanford Daily. 1936. Mrs. Russell Dies After Long Illness. *Stanford Daily* February 18:n.p. Stanford, Calif.

Steeples, Douglas, and David O. Whitten. 1998. *Democracy in Desperation: The Depression of 1893*. Greenwood, Westport, Conn.

Stephen, Alexander M. 1936. *Hopi Journal of Alexander M. Stephen*. 2 vols. Edited by Elsie C. Parsons. Columbia University Contributions to Anthropology No. 23. Columbia University Press, New York.

Stevenson, Robert Louis. 1897. *Travels with a Donkey in the Cevennes*. Charles Scribner's Sons, New York.

Steward, Julian H. 1960. *John Reed Swanton, 1873–1958*. Biographical Memoir No. 34. National Academy of Sciences, Washington, D.C.

Stocking, George W., Jr. 1992. *The Ethnographer's Magic and Other Essays in the History of Anthropology*. University of Wisconsin Press, Madison.

Stocking, George W., Jr., and Susan P. Montague. 1979. Interview and Department Focus: George Stocking on Fay-Cooper Cole. *Journal of Anthropology* 1(2):1–17.

Stodder, Ann L. W. 2008. *Reanalysis and Reinterpretation in Southwestern Bioarchaeology*. Anthropological Research Papers No. 59. Arizona State University, Tempe.

Stojanowski, Christopher M., and Julie K. Euber. 2011. Comparability of Hrdlička's *Catalog of Crania Data Based on Measurement Landmark Definition*. *American Journal of Physical Anthropology* 143(1):143–49.

Stokes Publishing Company. 1906. *Stokes' Encyclopedia of Familiar Quotations: Containing Five Thousand Selections from Six Hundred Authors*. Compiled by Elford Eveleigh Treffry. Frederick A. Stokes, New York.

Studley, Cordelia A. 1884. Notes upon Human Remains from the Caves of Coahuila, Mexico. *Reports of the Peabody Museum of American Archaeology and Ethnology* 3:233–59.

Swanton, John R. 1944. Notes Regarding My Adventures in Anthropology and with Anthropologists. MS 4651, NAA.

Taylor, Benjamin F. 1878. *Between the Gates*. S. C. G. Riggs, Chicago.

Tennyson, Alfred. 1849. "In Memoriam A. H. H." Edward Moxon, London. Reprinted in *The Literary Network*. www.online-literature.com/tennyson/718, accessed August 22, 2018.

Tennyson, Alfred. 1854. The Charge of the Light Brigade at the Battle of Balaclava during the Crimean War. *The Examiner* December 9:5. London.

Thackeray, William. 1855. *The Newcomers: Memoirs of a Most Respectable Family*. Bradbury and Evans, London.

Thomas, Cyrus. 1898. *Introduction to the Study of North American Archaeology*. Robert Clarke, Cincinnati.

Thomas, David Hurst. 2000. *Skull Wars: Kennewick Man, Archaeology, and the Battle for Native American Identity*. Basic Books, New York.

Thompson, Raymond H. 2000. An Old and Reliable Authority: An Act for the Preservation of American Antiquities. *Journal of the Southwest* 42(2):191–379.

Thompson, Raymond H. 2005. Anthropology at the University of Arizona, 1893–2005. *Journal of the Southwest* 47(3):327–74.

Times-Republican. 1920. Gala Week at S.U.I. *Times-Republican* June 10:3. Marshalltown, Iowa.

Topinard, Paul. 1881. Observations upon the Methods and Processes of Anthropometry. *Journal of the Anthropological Institute* 10(2):212–24.

Tozzer, Alfred M. 1936. *Frederic Ward Putnam, 1839–1915*. Biographical Memoirs 16. National Academy of Sciences, Washington, D.C.

Train, Arthur. 1910. The Spanish Prisoner. *Cosmopolitan* 48(4):465–74 [orig. pub. 1898].

Troelstra, Anne S. 2017. *A Bibliography of Natural History Travel Narratives*. KNNV Publishing, Amsterdam.

Twain, Mark. 1869. *The Innocents Abroad*. American Publishing, Hartford, Conn.

Twain, Mark. 1897. Following the Equator. *Extracts from Adam's Dairy, Translated from the Original MS*. Reprinted 1904. Harper and Brothers, New York.

Van Dyke, Henry. 1896. *The Poems of Henry Van Dyke*. Harper and Brothers, New York.

Wade, Edwin L., and Lea McChesney. 1980. *America's Great Lost Expedition: The Thomas Keam Collection of Hopi Pottery from the Second Hemenway Expedition, 1890–1894*. Heard Museum, Phoenix.

Walcott, Charles H. 1900. *Report of the U.S. National Museum for the Year ending June 30, 1898*. GPO, Washington, D.C.

Wallace, Lew. 1880. *Ben Hur: A Tale of the Christ*. Harper and Brothers, New York.

Wallace, Stewart. 1951. *A Dictionary of North American Authors Deceased Before 1950*. Ryerson Press, Toronto.

Walpole, N. S. 1898. Reports of Agencies of New Mexico. In *Annual Reports of the Department of the Interior for the Fiscal Year Ended June 30, 1898*, pp. 210–11. 55th Congress, Indian Affairs. Third Session, House of Representatives Document No. 5. GPO, Washington, D.C.

Walpole, N. S. 1899. Reports of Agencies of New Mexico. In *Annual Reports of the Department of the Interior for the Fiscal Year Ended June 30, 1899*, Part 1, pp. 243–55. GPO, Washington, D.C.

Warren, Louis S. 1999. Vanishing Point: Images of Indians and Ideas of American History. *Ethnohistory* 46(2):361–77.

Webb, William, and Robert A. Weinstein. 1973. *Dwellers at the Source: Southwestern Indian Photographs of A. C. Vroman, 1895–1904*. Grossman, Los Angeles.

Webster, A. L. 1883. Map of the Province of Tusayan. Surveyed by A. L. Webster. In *United States Geological Survey, Third Annual Report*, Map 1. GPO, Washington, D.C.

Weekly Gazette. 1901. Enthusiastic Annual Meeting of the Colorado Cliff Dwellers Association. *Weekly Gazette* August 21:5. Colorado Springs, Colo.

Wescott, Edward Noyes. 1897. *David Harum: A Story of an American Life.* D. Appleton, New York.

Who's Who. 1976. *Who Was Who Among North American Authors, 1921–1939.* Compiled from *Who's Who Among North American Authors,* vols. 1–7, 1921–39. Gale Research, Detroit.

Wiggin, Kate Douglas. 1888. *The Birds' Christmas Carol.* Houghton and Mifflin, Boston.

Wilcox, David R., Gerald Robertson Jr., and J. Scott Wood. 2001. Organized for War: The Parry Mesa Settlement System and Its Central Arizona Neighbors. In *Deadly Landscapes: Case Studies in Prehistoric Southwestern Warfare,* edited by Glen R. Rice and Steven A. LeBlanc, pp. 141–94. University of Utah Press, Salt Lake City.

Willey, Gordon R., and Jeremy A. Sabloff. 1974. *A History of American Archaeology.* W. H. Freeman, San Francisco.

Williams, Robert A., Jr. 1992. *The American Indian in Western Legal Thought: The Discourses of Conquest.* Oxford University Press, New York.

Wilson, Frank R. 1903. Science Has Lost an Unusual Man in the Death of Frank Russell. *Des Moines Register* November 15:20.

Wilson, John P. 1999. Peoples of the Middle Gila: A Documentary History of the Pimas and Maricopas, 1500–1945. Manuscript on file at the Gila River Indian Community's Cultural Resource Management Program Office, Sacaton, Ariz.

Wollstonecraft, Mary. 1796. *The Vindication of the Rights of Women: With Strictures on Political and Moral Subjects.* T. Fisher Unwin, London.

Woodruff, President Wilford. 1895. The Power of Evil. Discourse Delivered at the Grand Conference of the Church in the Tabernacle, Salt Lake City, Utah, April 7, 1895. *Deseret Weekly* 1(19): 577–79.

Word and Way. 1920. Satire in the Victorian Novel. *Word and Way* May 20:16. Kansas City, Mo.

W. S. K. 1927. Browning Passes. *Sewanee Review* 35(4):502–5.

Young, Edward. 1853. *Night Thoughts.* James Nichol, London.

Young, Robert W., and William Morgan. 1987. *The Navajo Language: A Grammar and Colloquial Dictionary.* University of New Mexico Press, Albuquerque.

Index

About the Authors

Theresa Russell (1873–1936) was a noted scholar of satire in British Victorian novels and American utopianism, especially well known for her many analyses of Robert and Elizabeth Barret Browning. One of the first female professors of English and philosophy at Stanford University, she wrote five well-received books and dozens of articles, in addition to teaching and mentoring thousands of students.

Nancy J. Parezo is professor emerita, American Indian studies, University of Arizona. In addition to teaching at the institution for almost 40 years, she was curator of ethnology at the Arizona State Museum and loaned executive to the Arizona Board of Regents. She also participated for 10 years in the Smithsonian Summer Institute in Museum Anthropology. The author of more than 265 books and articles, she is currently working through the nine large, four-drawer file cabinets that are full of data for more histories of anthropologies and museums as well as studies of collecting behavior, women in science, and Euro-American stereotyping of Native Americans. Her next project documents Mennonite missionary Henry Voth's collecting and ethnographic activities among the Hopi and Cheyenne.

Don D. Fowler is Mamie Kleberg Distinguished Professor of Anthropology and Historic Preservation, Emeritus, at the University of Nevada, Reno (UNR), where he taught anthropology and historic preservation for 40 years. In 2019 the Don Frazier-Don Fowler Endowed Chair in Great Basin Archaeology was established at UNR in his honor. His PhD is from the University of Pittsburgh. He was a postdoctoral fellow in anthropology at the Smithsonian Institution from 1967 to 1968 and a research associate in anthropology at the Smithsonian Institution from 1970 to 2004. A past president of the Society for American Archaeology, he received the society's Lifetime Achievement Award in 2003, and the Byron Cummings Award from the Arizona Archaeological & Historical Society in 1998, among other honors. He is the author or co-author of dozens of papers and reports on Southwestern and Great Basin archaeology and cultural resources management, and, with co-author and great friend, Nancy Parezo, publications on the history of European and American archaeology and ethnology.